THE ROUTLEDGE HANDBC EARLY CHRISTIAN ART

Combining coverage of the major media of early Christian art and a selection of key themes and issues, this volume of contributions by a galaxy of experts is a treasure-trove for the study of its specific subject and also for wider historical work on early Christianity. Those new to the visual culture of early Christianity will find this a competent guide, and students and scholars of early Christian art also will find here a resource to consult on many matters.

Larry Hurtado, University of Edinburgh, UK

The Routledge Handbook of Early Christian Art surveys a broad spectrum of Christian art produced from the late second through the sixth centuries. The first part of the book opens with a general survey of the subject and then presents fifteen essays that discuss specific media of visual art—catacomb paintings, sculpture, mosaics, gold glass, gems, reliquaries, ceramics, icons, ivories, textiles, silver, and illuminated manuscripts. Each is written by a noted expert in the field. The second part of the book takes up themes relevant to the study of early Christian art. These seven chapters consider the ritual practices in decorated spaces, the emergence of images of Christ's Passion and miracles, the functions of Christian secular portraits, the exemplary mosaics of Ravenna, the early modern history of Christian art and archaeology studies, and further reflection on this field called "early Christian art." Each of the volume's chapters includes photographs of many of the objects discussed, plus bibliographic notes and recommendations for further reading.

The result is an invaluable introduction to and appraisal of the art that developed out of the spread of Christianity through the late antique world. Undergraduate and graduate students of late classical, early Christian, and Byzantine culture, religion, or art will find it an accessible and insightful orientation to the field. Additionally, professional academics, archivists, and curators working in these areas will also find it valuable as a resource for their own research, as well as a textbook or reference work for their students.

Robin M. Jensen is the Patrick O'Brien Professor of Theology at the University of Notre Dame, USA, and a member of the faculty of Medieval Institute and the Department of Art, Art

History, and Design. Her published work explores the intersection of early Christian iconography, ecclesial architecture, ritual practices, and theological discourse.

Mark D. Ellison is an associate professor in the Department of Ancient Scripture at Brigham Young University, USA. He received a PhD and MA from Vanderbilt University, USA, in Early Christianity and Early Christian Art, and an MA from the University of South Florida, USA, in Religious Studies (Biblical Archaeology).

THE ROUTLEDGE HANDBOOK OF EARLY CHRISTIAN ART

Edited by Robin M. Jensen and Mark D. Ellison

LONDON AND NEW YORK

First published 2018 by Routledge

2 Park Square, Milton Park, Abingdon, Oxon, OX14 4RN
605 Third Avenue, New York, NY 10017

Routledge is an imprint of the Taylor & Francis Group, an informa business

First issued in paperback 2020

British Library Cataloguing-in-Publication Data
A catalogue record for this book is available from the British Library

Library of Congress Cataloging-in-Publication Data
Names: Jensen, Robin Margaret, 1952- editor.
Title: The Routledge handbook of early Christian art / edited by Robin M. Jensen and Mark D. Ellison.
Description: First [edition]. | New York : Routledge, 2018. | Includes bibliographical references and index.
Identifiers: LCCN 2017043217 | ISBN 9781138857223 (hardback : alk. paper) | ISBN 9781315718835 (ebook) | ISBN 9781317514176 (epub) | ISBN 9781317514169 (mobi/kindle)
Subjects: LCSH: Christian art and symbolism—History.
Classification: LCC N7832 .R68 2018 | DDC 704.9/482—dc23
LC record available at https://lccn.loc.gov/2017043217

ISBN: 978-1-138-85722-3 (hbk)
ISBN: 978-0-367-73439-8 (pbk)

Typeset in Bembo
by Swales & Willis Ltd, Exeter, Devon, UK

CONTENTS

FIGURES

TABLES

CONTRIBUTORS

Jennifer L. Ball is Associate Professor at The City University of New York, USA, specializing in art of the Byzantine, Western Medieval and Islamic worlds, especially focusing on portraits, dress and textiles. Her several publications on the subject include *Byzantine Dress: Representations of Eighth- to Twelfth-Century Secular Dress in Painting* (2005).

Niamh Bhalla has been an Associate Lecturer at The Courtauld Institute of Art in London, UK, since 2011, teaching courses on the transformation of art in Late Antiquity and the body in western art of the Middle Ages. She is also a visiting lecturer on the MA program *Byzantium and it Rivals*. Her research focuses on using contemporary theory to open up fresh insights into how classical, byzantine and medieval images were experienced. She explores themes such as space, memory, the body and gender in relation to the experience of visual imagery. Niamh has considerable teaching experience at both undergraduate and postgraduate level and she is also the research assistant and project coordinator for the Getty-supported project, *Crossing Frontiers: Christians and Muslims and their art in Eastern Anatolia and the Caucasus* at the Courtauld Institute.

Robert Couzin, AB (1967), AM (1968) University of Chicago; BCL (1972) McGill University Faculty of Law. After practicing law for several decades, he turned to art history: MA (2008), PhD (2013) University of Toronto. Second career publications include *The* Traditio Legis: *Anatomy of an Image* (2015), *The Handedness of Historiated Spiral Columns* (2017), and *Uncircumcision in Early Christian Art* (forthcoming, 2018).

Jutta Dresken-Weiland, PhD 1990 in Classical Archaeology; travel scholarship of the German Archaeological Institute 1991–1992; from 1990–1996 at the German Archaeological Institute in Rome. Post-doctoral degree in "Christian Archaeology and History of Byzantine Art" in 2002 at the Georg August-Universität Göttingen, Germany, since 2009 außerplanmäßige Professorin (adjunct professor) there. Since 2015 she has been responsible for the sector archaeology at the publishing house Schnell & Steiner in Regensburg, Germany.

Mark D. Ellison is an Associate Professor in the Department of Ancient Scripture at Brigham Young University, USA. He received a PhD and MA from Vanderbilt University, USA, in Early

Christianity and Early Christian Art, and an MA from the University of South Florida, USA, in Religious Studies (Biblical Archaeology). As part of his research on intersections of early Christian texts, artifacts, iconography, and practices, his dissertation *Visualizing Christian Marriage in the Roman World* (2017) examined the portraiture of married Christians in third- and fourth-century visual art.

Felicity Harley-McGowan is an historian of art whose research centres on the origins and development of Christian iconography within the visual culture of Roman Late Antiquity. She currently teaches at Yale University, USA, and is a Research Associate in Yale's Institute of Sacred Music.

John J. Herrmann, Jr. is Curator of Classical Art, Emeritus, Museum of Fine Arts, Boston. He has excavated in Italy, collaborated with scientists in the study of marble, published on ceramics of all kinds, and co-authored *Pottery, Pavements, and Paradise* with Annewies van den Hoek (2013).

Annewies van den Hoek taught at Harvard University, USA, and is now retired. She wrote a monograph on Clement of Alexandria and Philo (1988), a Greek text edition of Clement's *Stromateis* IV (2001), and co-authored with John Herrmann: *Pottery, Pavements, and Paradise* (2013).

Heidi J. Hornik is Professor of Renaissance and Baroque Art History at Baylor University. Author of *Michele Tosini and the Ghirlandaio Workshop in Cinquecento Florence*, she also co-authored a three-volume interdisciplinary work on art and theology with Mikael C. Parsons, *Illuminating Luke*. Their recent project, *Acts of the Apostles Through the Centuries*, appeared in the Blackwell Bible Commentaries. Hornik's newest project, *The Art of Christian Reflection*, was completed while a visiting scholar at Harvard University.

Janet Huskinson has been a Visiting Fellow in Classical Studies at the Open University, UK, since her retirement from the post of Reader there. Her main research has been in private art of the western Roman empire during the third and fourth centuries, especially in subjects such as decorating marble sarcophagi, conventional and Christian.

Lee M. Jefferson is the NEH Associate Professor of Religion at Centre College, USA. He has authored *Christ the Miracle Worker in Early Christian Art* (2014), and co-edited *The Art of Empire: Christian Art in Its Imperial Context* (2015).

Robin M. Jensen is the Patrick O'Brien Professor of Theology at the University of Notre Dame, USA, and a member of the faculty of Medieval Institute and the Department of Art, Art History, and Design. Her published work explores the intersection of early Christian iconography, ecclesial architecture, ritual practices, and theological discourse.

Guntram Koch is an expert in Classical and Christian Archaeology. He was Professor of Christian Archaeology and Byzantine Art History in the Faculty of Theology at the University of Marburg, Germany (retired, 2006). Previously he was a professor at the University of Göttingen, Germany. He has authored numerous essays and monographs, including *Früchristliche Sarkophage* (*Early Christian Sarcophagi* [2000]).

Ruth Leader-Newby is an independent scholar who is a recognized authority on late antique silver. She has published widely on the subject, including her 2004 book *Silver and Society in Late Antiquity.*

Sean V. Leatherbury is Assistant Professor of Ancient Art & Culture at Bowling Green State University, USA. His research focuses on late antique art, particularly on mosaics in the eastern Mediterranean, word-image relations, and the material culture of votive dedication.

Katherine Marsengill received her PhD from Princeton University. She is the author of *Portrait and Icon: Between Reality and Spirituality in Byzantine Art* (2013) and has published articles on icons, spiritualized portraiture, early Christian attitudes about sculpture, and the Christian imperial cult.

Deborah Mauskopf Deliyannis is Associate Professor of History at Indiana University. Her research focuses on the intersections of bishops, historiography, and church-building. She is the author of *Ravenna in Late Antiquity* (2010), and a co-author of *Fifty Early Medieval Things* (2018).

Michael Peppard is Associate Professor of Theology at Fordham University in New York, USA. His most recent book is *The World's Oldest Church: Bible, Art, and Ritual at Dura-Europos, Syria* (2016).

Jeffrey Spier is Senior Curator of Antiquities at the J. Paul Getty Museum in Los Angeles, USA. He has published widely on Greek, Roman, and Byzantine jewelry and other luxury objects, as well as on ancient magical amulets.

Rina Talgam is Associate Professor of Art History at the Hebrew University of Jerusalem, Israel. She researches the art of the Middle East from the Hellenistic period to the beginning of the Abbasid period and is author *of Mosaics of Faith: Floors of Pagans, Jews, Samaritans, Christians, and Muslims in the Holy Land* (2014).

Erik Thunø is Professor of Medieval Art in the Department of Art History at Rutgers, The State University of New Jersey, USA. His books and articles focus on a variety of topics ranging from reliquaries, monumental decorations in fresco and mosaic, icons and altar decorations in places such as Italy, Greece, and the South Caucasus region.

Dorothy Verkerk is an Associate Professor of Art History at the University of North Carolina at Chapel Hill, USA, and is the Whitton Fellow (2016) at the Institute for Arts and Humanities. She has published on early Christian manuscripts, sarcophagi and the Irish high crosses.

Susan Walker is Honorary Curator and former Keeper of Antiquities at the Ashmolean Museum, and Emerita Fellow of Wolfson College, University of Oxford, both in the UK. She recently completed *Saints and Salvation: Charles Wilshere's Collection of Gold-Glass, Sarcophagi and Inscriptions from Rome and Southern Italy*, written with Sean Leatherbury and David Rini.

Norbert Zimmermann is Scientific Director at the German Archaeological Institute at Rome, Italy. He has studied Christian Archaeology, Art History, and Italian Philology at Bonn,

Rome, and Munich. From 1998 to 2014 he was researcher at the Institute for the Study of Ancient Culture, Austrian Academy of Sciences, and is a member of the Austrian excavation team at Ephesus. His main field of interest is the cultural changes between antiquity and the Middle Ages. His research focuses on wall paintings, residential architecture, and sepulchral art. He has published, among other things, the monograph *Werkstattgruppen römischer Katakombenmalerei* (2002), and conducted the Austrian sciences fund (FWF) START-project on the Domitilla catacomb in Rome.

FOREWORD

In recent decades, students of early Christianity have become more and more interested in incorporating the study of visual art into their research, teaching, and writing. Material culture has come to be appreciated as a rich resource for a better understanding of lived religion in all times and places, and no less so for the complex and diverse practice of Christianity in the Greco-Roman world. At the same time, both art historians and historians of religion in Late Antiquity now recognize that Christianity emerged within pre-existing cultures with established artistic forms, iconographic prototypes, and manufacturing techniques that it drew upon, adapted, and transformed as it gradually developed its own distinctive iconographic vocabulary. Thus, recent debates over questions of cultural continuity and change among Christians, Jews, and traditional polytheists are relevant to any discussion of these objects. Similarly, scholars in recent years have come to reassess the so-called anti-classical styles of early Christian artworks, granting them their own aesthetic value while reevaluating the gradual return of mythological figures and classical styles at the end of the fourth century.

However, while the academic study of early Christianity has become more attuned to the value of including non-documentary evidence, the training of scholars in the field has remained focused predominately on the analysis of surviving texts, particularly texts that tend to be associated more with the development of Christian dogma, discipline, and ecclesiology than with the nature of the wider community's lived experience of the faith. The desire of many of these same scholars to expand their investigation into material manifestations of early Christian belief and practice created a need for a handbook to the basic corpus of early Christian artifacts—one that would offer introductions to the variety of objects, the manner of their fabrication, issues of style, and basic visual content, along with overarching essays on fundamental problems regarding influences, contexts, and categorization. In addition to matters touching upon formal art historical analysis, such a handbook also needed to attend to the theological, liturgical, and exegetical significance of these objects, thus not losing sight of their place in the formation and transmission of beliefs, values, and religious identity. Beyond the provision of a basic overview of the primary material, this work also includes helpful lists of resources for further study.

This book attempts to meet these needs. Part I opens with a general survey of the subject and then presents fifteen essays, each of which considers one traditionally identified category of early Christian art. The first of these chapters discusses the earliest acknowledged examples of Christian painting in the Roman catacombs, and the chapters continue through sarcophagus reliefs, freestanding sculpture, mosaics, gold glasses, ceramics, engraved gems, panel paintings, ivories, textiles, silver, and illuminated manuscripts. As these essays demonstrate, early Christian art was produced for burial, ecclesiastical, and domestic contexts, and while rightly considered a subset of late antique Roman art, possesses a distinctive character and purpose. Part II takes up themes relevant to the study of early Christian art. These chapters consider the ritual practices in decorated spaces, the emergence of images of Christ's passion and miracles, the functions of Christian secular portraits, and the exemplary mosaics of Ravenna. The first of two concluding essays discusses the early modern history of Christian art and archaeology studies, while the second invites further reflection on this field of study, and correctly problematizes the book's titular terminology of "early," "Christian," and "art."

The editors are first of all grateful to all the authors who agreed to contribute their expertise and effort to produce this volume. They are the heart of this project and we are fortunate to count them all as colleagues. We also wish to thank our editors at Taylor and Francis, Elizabeth Risch and Amy Davis-Poynter, who were both supportive and patient with the time and trouble involved in compiling both essays and images. We are likewise grateful to all those who assisted us with acquiring the illustrations, the photographers (and authors) who generously supplied them, the staff of Art Resource, and the rights and reproductions departments of museums around the world. We also acknowledge the financial and moral support of the University of Notre Dame, Vanderbilt University, and Brigham Young University. Finally, we would like to thank Robert McFadden for his proofreading and correction of style after the essays were initially edited for publication, and Jennifer McDaniel, Suzy Bills, McCall Kelson, and Scarlett Lindsay for their help preparing the index.

Robin M. Jensen and Mark D. Ellison

1
INTRODUCTION
Early Christian art

Robin M. Jensen

Historians generally agree that first- and second-century Christians left behind few material artifacts that historians could recognize as specifically theirs. Adherents to this new faith evidently began to decorate their tombs, places of worship, and even small domestic objects with iconography that reflected their distinct religious identity only in the late second or early third century. Scholars have offered various explanations for this seemingly late emergence of Christian pictorial art. Some suggest that Christians did not possess the numbers, social status, or economic resources to commission objects that depicted scenes from their own sacred stories or reflected their particular beliefs about God, salvation, or the afterlife.[1] Others, arguing for some degree of common culture as well as a more fluid set of religious identities in Late Antiquity, argue that Christian art may be a misnomer when historians too hastily try to distinguish among artifacts probably produced in common workshops for various religious groups.[2] Thus, they see more continuity than discontinuity in the material record. Recently, one scholar even proposed that the supposed absence of Christian art in the first centuries is resolved by regarding Christian art as Jewish art.[3]

An older, but still circulating, argument argues that Christians regarded the pictorial arts and divine images of their polytheistic neighbors as idols and, faithfully obedient to the prohibition of graven images in the Mosaic Law, avoided making or possessing any of their own.[4] Historians have now largely repudiated this by demonstrating that while ancient Christians may have disapproved of images or statues of the Greco-Roman gods (and the honors bestowed upon them), they did not reject representational art as such.[5] Moreover, the little surviving documentary evidence for critique of images takes aim primarily at practices rather than at objects, denouncing only idolatrous reverence for created things of nature or human craft, while presuming that Christians might properly make and own images. For example, Clement of Alexandria, one of the most severe critics of such misplaced veneration around the turn of the third century, nevertheless made concrete suggestions for what Christians should engrave on their signet rings:

> And let our seals be either a dove, or a fish, or a ship scudding before the wind, or a musical lyre, which Polycrates used, or a ship's anchor, which Seleucus got engraved as a device; and if there be one fishing, he will remember the apostle, and the children drawn out of the water. For we are not to delineate the faces of idols, we who are prohibited to cleave to them; nor a sword, nor a bow, following as we do, peace; nor drinking-cups, being temperate.[6]

Clement's suggestions of images deemed appropriate for Christian seals suggests that, in fact, Christians did wish to differentiate themselves from their non-Christian neighbors, to some extent through the images they chose to decorate items they used in their daily life. Consequently, scholars are able to classify certain motifs as Christian, whether or not they were made for or used exclusively by self-identified members of that group. Notably, many rings or gems have survived that display such designs (Figure 9.4).[7] Hence, much early Christian art usually is demarcated by its subject matter—in other words that it bears what could be regarded as typically Christian symbols or biblical narrative scenes (both Old and New Testament). However, because other religious groups might have used similar iconographic conventions and Jews might also have chosen to represent certain biblical subjects, the setting or context of these objects can be decisive, as well as their overall composition and practical function. Consequently, historians have urged that clearly defined classifications can be dangerous. What looks like a Good Shepherd to one set of eyes could be regarded as a representation of Hermes as the ram bearer to another. An image of Sol Invictus, Apollo, or Orpheus could be adapted to a Christian iconographic purpose in order to relay the idea of Christ as bringer of light into the world or a tamer of souls, without necessarily verging on religious syncretism.[8] This is especially vivid in a late third- or early fourth-century mosaic of Christ in the guise of the sun god found in the Vatican necropolis (Figure 6.1).

Corresponding to Christian apologists who elucidated the faith for their learned audiences by reference to accepted philosophical ideals or who drew upon the stories of the gods for the sake of comparison in words, artisans likewise used the pictorial vocabulary of their surrounding culture, especially when relaying an aspect of their Savior or tenet of faith that had resonance with pre-Christian myths.[9] This is not a case of syncretism so much as the effective deployment of images for communicating meaning in visual rather than verbal language. Yet, the language is not necessarily precise, insofar as it could convey different messages to different viewers, depending on attitude, expectations, socialization, or experience. This may be its most characteristic and—depending on one's point of view—its most valuable quality.

Moreover the materials, manufacturing techniques, and even style of works classified as Christian are often quite similar to those presumed to be Jewish or polytheist objects. Motifs like the personified four seasons evidently were inoffensive enough to be acceptable for a variety of religiously identified patrons (Figure 1.1). The fact that artisans were trained similarly, and that workshops followed prevailing fashions and used the same types of tools, meant they presumably catered to different kinds of clients, most likely customizing pre-made objects as needed.[10] For this reason, many art historians choose to describe early Christian art as a sub-category of Roman art.[11]

Yet, while early Christian iconography often bears some similarities to non-Christian art of the same place and period, distinctions between them are not altogether absent. Early Christian wall paintings were executed in a sketchy, impressionistic style and were framed with colored borders similar to—although not usually as carefully executed as—those produced for contemporary Roman tombs and domestic interiors (Figures 2.4, 2.7, 2.9–11). Friezes carved on fourth-century stone coffins (sarcophagi) tend to display an almost random assortment of biblical characters, overlapping and often crowded onto a single panel rather than the more carefully composed reliefs of their non-Christian counterparts (Figures 3.3, 19.3, 19.7).[12] Moreover, an evolution of motifs or narrative themes can be discerned. In general, Christian art proceeds from being primarily symbolic, to illustrating biblical narratives, to presenting certain dogmatic developments, and finally to embracing iconic, or portrait, types as it proceeds from domestic and funereal settings to monumental, ecclesial spaces. These distinctions in content or even style

Figure 1.1 Seasons sarcophagus with menorah, fragment, last quarter of the third century. Origin unknown. Now in the Museo Nazionale Romano, Inv. no. 67611. Photo: Robin M. Jensen.

do not presuppose the existence of workshops catering exclusively to Christian clients, but they do suggest an attention to particular religious identity.

Based on stylistic analysis, it appears that a limited number of commercial workshops were the source of much early Christian art. These workshops most likely catered to private individuals and we have no evidence that either artisans or their clients were supervised by ecclesiastical officials or underwritten by church funds. Presumably patrons chose the décor of their burial places from among a stock repertoire of figures that artisans presented as samples. Many of the final programs included dedications to deceased spouses or reflections on the domestic life (and anticipated future reunion) of married Christians (Figures 20.1, 20.4, 20.10).[13] The evidence for episcopal management of Christian cemeteries may have meant a certain degree of official oversight of their decoration, but it seems as likely that content and quality were entirely personal choices based on financial means and personal preferences. While surviving literary sources indicate scattered critique of certain types of pictorial subjects, no evidence supports the claim that church authorities actively regulated or censured the content or style of the iconography.[14]

Most of the earliest extant examples of Christian visual art have come from funerary settings. They embellished the walls of the chambers of Christian catacombs (*cubicula* and *arcosolia*) and the fronts and sides of sarcophagi, as well as less pretentious illuminated epitaphs (Figure 1.2).[15] These paintings and carvings survived largely because they were underground and so not as easily lost to neglect, deliberate destruction, renovation, or natural erosion. Even the gems, lamps, gold glasses, ceramic ware, or other small objects that add to the collection of artifacts were commonly found in burial contexts. In addition to that, the largest percentage of surviving evidence was found in the West, particularly in and around Rome. Unfortunately, very little that can be dated prior to the fifth or sixth century has been discovered in the eastern part of the Roman Empire. One outstanding, significant exception to both the funerary

Figure 1.2 Burial epitaph of Victoria, a consecrated virgin, early fourth century. Find spot unknown. Now in the Museo Nazionale di Roma. Photo: Robin M. Jensen.

context and Western provenance of early Christian art is the Christian building discovered in Syria at the site of Dura-Europos, whose cycle of wall paintings has no exact parallel in either subject matter or style elsewhere.[16] The fourth-century pavement from Hinton St Mary, with its presumed portrait of Christ (Figure 7.1) or the impressively detailed mosaic floor of a fourth-century basilica in Aquileia (Figure 1.3) are also important examples of early church decoration.

Early Christian symbols

The oldest surviving material evidence largely corroborates Clement of Alexandria's list of appropriate iconography on Christian signet rings. Figures of doves, fish, boats, and anchors were popular signs, not only for inscribed gems but were also commonly found on early wall paintings, funerary epitaphs, sarcophagi, gilded drinking vessels and bowls, pottery lamps, and ceramic dishware (Figures 8.9, 17.3).[17] Reminiscent of favorite Roman decorative motifs, early Christian tombs also displayed popular pastoral, harvesting, and maritime themes (Figure 6.2). Walls and vaults of burial chambers were adorned with painted garlands, vases of flowers, grapevines, bowls of fruit, brimming fountains, sheep and rams, doves, quail, and peacocks (Figure 1.4). Whether they had particular religious significance is difficult to know for certain but, like their appearance in Roman art, they may have been generic allusions to a safe passage to a blissful afterlife or a paradisiacal garden.[18] Of course grapevines and vintaging scenes could have an eucharistic reference and shepherds with their sheep allude to the Christian flock, but such subjects might simply evoke the beauties of the earthly world and nature's abundance. Whereas a dove could represent the Holy Spirit, it frequently appeared with an olive branch near the legend "*in pace*," so it more likely symbolizes the hope for peaceful rest until the final resurrection.

While maritime scenes were popular subjects for Roman funerary art, the fish and fishermen may have had specific Christian resonance. The fish by itself could symbolize Christ, especially when joined by an acrostic based on the letters of the Greek word *ichthys* (fish), which fill out

Figure 1.3 Jonah and the Big Fish, Basilica of Aquileia mid-fourth century. Photo: Wikimedia Creative Commons.

the title *Iēsous Christos Theou Huios Sotēr* (Jesus Christ, Son of God, Savior). Fish also could represent the followers of Christ, hooked by the anchor of faith (Figure 1.5).[19] Because fish also appear frequently in New Testament narratives—the calling of the disciples from their nets to become fishers of men, the miracle of the multiplication of loaves and fish, or the miraculous catch of fish at the end of John's Gospel—fishing scenes or platters of fish may refer to particular biblical stories.

Added to these relatively generic floral and bucolic themes were regularly recurring human figures: the praying figure (*orant*), the shepherd, and the seated reader. The *orant* was frequently (but not always) depicted as a standing female with outstretched arms, upturned eyes, a long tunic, and a veiled head (Figures 1.6, 1.7, 19.6). Her (or his) posture replicates the traditional ancient prayer stance and gestures. In some instances the figure appears to be a portrait of the deceased buried nearby, but could also personify the soul, or perhaps the virtue of piety (*pietas*). The shepherd, usually shown as a beardless youth, wears a short tunic and boots and carries a sheep over his shoulders and may be intended to represent the biblical "Good Shepherd"

Figure 1.4 Detail, vase with birds, from the Catacomb of Praetextatus. From Joseph Wilpert, *Die Malereien der Katakomben Roms* (Freiburg: Herder, 1903), pl. 50.

Figure 1.5 Epitaph of Licinia Amias, Rome, late third century, found in the vicinity of the Vatican Necropolis. Now in the Museo Nazionale Romano-Terme di Diocleziano, Inv. number 67646. Photo: Robin M. Jensen.

(cf. Psalm 23; John 10.1–9). The shepherd is also among the rare examples of early statues in the round (Figures 5.5–6).[20] In some instances, the shepherd appears more than once (Figure 3.2) and occasionally in an expanded pastoral setting where putti are shown milking or harvesting. Because the figure of a shepherd carrying a ram over his shoulders has an ancient pre-Christian precedent in a depiction of Hermes, the gods' messenger and caretaking guide to the underworld, this motif could have conveyed different meanings to various viewers.

The shepherd and the *orant* frequently appear with a third figure: a seated reader garbed as a philosopher (Figure 1.7). Like the *orant* and the shepherd, this figure appeared in non-Christian funerary settings, often assumed to allude to the intellectual accomplishments of the deceased. So too, in Christian contexts, it might depict the deceased as a learned man or could have more generally alluded to Christian teaching as true philosophy. Together this trio may have been intended to personify piety, philanthropy, and love of wisdom—virtues that were not uniquely Christian—or perhaps the theological virtues of faith, hope, and charity (cf. 1 Corinthians 13.13).

Figure 1.6 *Orant* (portrait of the deceased woman) from Catacomb of the Giordani. From Joseph Wilpert, *Die Malereien der Katakomben Roms* (Freiburg: Herder, 1903), pl. 174b.

Figure 1.7 Sarcophagus from the Basilica of Sta Maria Antiqua, Rome, late third century. Photo: Robin M. Jensen.

An image that frequently turns up both in Christian catacomb paintings and on sarcophagus reliefs depicts five or seven diners sitting at a horseshoe-shaped table sharing a meal of bread, wine, and fish (Figure 19.6). Scholars have variously interpreted these as images of the Last Supper, the miracle of the multiplication of loaves and fish, eucharists, or agape meals.[21] Yet, as almost identical versions appear frequently in non-Christian contexts, the composition cannot depict exclusively Christian rituals or refer to any single biblical narrative. Most likely, the motif alludes to funeral meals shared by the deceased's family and friends at the tomb, and perhaps represents the wish for a happy repast in the next world. In a Christian context, the scene could evoke the celestial banquet promised by Jesus at the Last Supper (cf. Mark 14.25 and parallels), and thus bear an eschatological significance. In some examples the diners are served by female figures who bear the names Irene (peace) and Agape (love/charity), probably a further indication of the meal's meaning. In any case, like all of these early images, they could bear multiple connotations and mean different things to different viewers.[22]

Biblical subjects

Throughout the third century biblical narrative scenes gradually joined the symbolic motifs described above.[23] Initially, a select repertoire of characters and stories from the Hebrew Scriptures significantly outnumbered those from the New Testament. Among these early subjects were depictions of Adam and Eve (shown flanking the tree with the forbidden fruit), Noah in his ark, Abraham offering his son Isaac for sacrifice, Moses striking the rock in the wilderness, Daniel in the lions' den, the three Hebrew Youths in the fiery furnace, Jonah being swallowed and then spit up by the sea creature, and Susanna with the elders. Though no two images are completely identical, the scenes are so similar as to be easily identified as standard types. For example, Adam and Eve stand to either side of the tree that bears the forbidden fruit. They usually are shown with their hands covering their genitals and with their eyes cast down. Noah is ordinarily portrayed as an *orant*, standing in a small boxlike ark, its lid rising behind him (Figure 19.5). Daniel, also an *orant*, is represented as a heroic nude flanked by two lions (Figure 1.8).

This early preference for Hebrew Scripture subjects has caused some commentators to suggest the influence of Jewish visual art on these early Christian paintings, even to posit the existence of an illustrated Septuagint as a kind of missing link.[24] In addition to the problem that no such model exists, surviving examples of Jewish art show little in common, either stylistically or in subject matter, with Christian catacomb paintings. Nevertheless, even if such models could be identified, it is more reasonable to conclude that the popularity of these stories reflects their prominent place in Christian exegesis, catechesis, prayer, and preaching. For example, scholars have suggested that prayers offered for the souls of the dead were given as assurance of God's faithful deliverance from death and danger.[25]

Figure 1.8 Ceiling fresco, Catacomb of Peter and Marcellinus, Rome, late third or early fourth century. Center: Daniel and lions; surrounding: Noah in the ark and scenes from the Jonah cycle. From Joseph Wilpert, *Die Malereien der Katakomben Roms* (Freiburg: Herder, 1903), pl. 104.

More generally, however, these images were not mere illustrations of favorite Bible stories. Christians maintained the importance of Hebrew Scriptures as part of their own story of salvation and saw these biblical characters as types that pointed to the future coming of Christ and the establishment of the church and its sacraments. In other words, they perceived prophetic meaning in these images and maintained continuity between Hebrew Scriptures and their New Testament narratives. For example, Abraham's obedience to God's command that he offer his son Isaac as a sacrifice was interpreted already in the New Testament as a sign of Abraham's faith (Heb 11.8–11). Isaac—the innocent but willing victim—subsequently became a type of Christ (1.9).[26] The story of Jonah, one of the most popular motifs for funerary art (and a rare sequential cycle), was edited down to depict only the episodes in which Jonah was tossed overboard, swallowed by a large fish, and then spit out onto dry land where he rested under a gourd vine (Figures 1.3, 1.8, 3.2, 11.2). According to the Gospels, Jesus refers to the "sign of Jonah" as a prediction of the Son of Man's three days in the heart of the earth, just as Jonah was for three days in the belly of the fish (Matt 12.40; cf. Luke 11.29).[27] Daniel was imprisoned in the lions' den and presumed dead, only to be found the next morning alive in his ostensible tomb (Dan 6.19; Figure 11.14). Early Christian exegetes understood these stories as types of Christ's sacrificial death and resurrection, as well as indications of God's deliverance of his faithful people from danger and death, or even allusions to Christian sacraments. The rescue of Noah from the flood prefigured Christian baptism (1 Pet 3.20), as did Moses' striking of the rock from which a spring of water emerged to slake the wandering Israelites' thirst.

These themes, which appeared on tomb walls as well as on small personal objects, also evidently found their way into worship spaces. The wall paintings found in the Christian building at Dura-Europos also demonstrate the linking of biblical narratives with baptismal interpretation. They include depictions of Jesus healing the paralytic (19.1), Jesus walking on the water, and possibly the Samaritan woman at the well. In this instance, the decoration of the space has an immediate resonance with the activities taking place within it and allows what one commentator has called a "ritual-centered visuality" that attends to the ways imagery, environment, and events interact in the expression of meaning and purpose.[28]

By the late third and early fourth centuries, New Testament Gospel scenes began to appear alongside these Hebrew Scripture narratives. One of the earliest was the portrayal of John the Baptist baptizing a small, nude Jesus (Figures 1.7, 19.2, 19.6). More scenes from Jesus's ministry gradually appeared on tomb walls and sarcophagus reliefs, especially representations of Jesus healing the paralytic, the woman with the issue of blood, and the man born blind (Figure 19.5). Other popular compositions included the adoration of the magi, and Jesus raising Lazarus, meeting the Samaritan woman at the well, multiplying the loaves and fish, and changing water to wine (Figures 2.2–4, 19.3, 19.6, 19.8). Depictions of Jesus performing miracles such as raising Lazarus generally show him wielding a staff, a possible reference to the authority of Moses or the priestly-assigned power of Aaron (Figures 19.7, 19.10).[29]

Additional Old Testament subjects appeared in the fourth century, including some still unique depictions of stories from the Joseph cycle found in the Via Latina catacomb. Besides these stories, this catacomb, which also had wall paintings depicting pagan gods, contained representations of Abraham entertaining his three angelic guests and of Moses and the Israelites crossing the Red Sea—representations that also began to be carved on sarcophagus reliefs. Other previously unknown images that appeared on sarcophagi included depictions of the Trinity creating Adam and Eve, Cain and Abel presenting their sacrifices to God, Elijah's ascent to heaven, Jesus entering Jerusalem mounted on a donkey (Figure 19.4), and Jesus (in the guise of Ezekiel) raising the dead.

The book of Acts inspired an image of Peter's arrest, which was frequently juxtaposed with an image of the saint striking a rock to baptize his Roman jailers, an image that has a surviving textual parallel in a later apocryphal source, the *Acts of Peter*. Clearly based on an earlier representation of Moses striking the rock, this iconographic transformation indicates the important role of Peter as a "new Moses" or the rock on which Jesus would found his church (cf. Matthew 16.18). At the same time, allusions to Peter's denial are also evident in the appearance of a rooster, often near his feet (Figure 19.3). During this period of innovation in iconography, compositions often became more complex, and the quality of technique, workmanship, and materials improved. One famous example, the Junius Bassus sarcophagus, shows extraordinary skill and sophistication, combining biblical narrative scenes like the fall of Adam and Eve, Abraham's offering of Isaac, Daniel, and Jesus entering Jerusalem, with an early depiction of the Jesus before Pilate, the martyrdoms of Peter and Paul, and the ascended and enthroned Christ giving the law to these same two—Rome's traditional founding apostles (Figure 18.5).

Given its ubiquity in later Christian art, depictions of Christ's crucifixion are notably absent from Christian art prior to the early fifth century, and then still rare until the sixth century and later. A small group of early gems engraved with crucifixion images has been hypothetically dated as early as the late third or early fourth century, but beyond those are only two fifth-century examples, one a small panel of the carved wooden doors of Rome's basilica of Santa Sabina (dated to *ca.* 420) that depicts Christ between the two thieves, and the other one of the sides of a small ivory box or reliquary casket that shows Christ with the Virgin and Beloved Disciple (Figures 18.9–10). None of these examples shows Christ as suffering, but rather as open-eyed and alive upon his cross.[30]

Dogmatic and imperial motifs

By the mid-fourth century, the biblical narrative scenes of Old Testament characters and Jesus' miracles were joined by more dogmatically oriented and imperially influenced subjects. Some of this evolution may reflect the contemporary debates over the nature of the Trinity or the person and work of Christ, but the increasing prosperity and security of the Church during the fourth century must have contributed as well. Images of Jesus as a teacher surrounded by his apostles show up in catacomb paintings (Figure 2.8), sarcophagus reliefs (Figure 20.10), and even later fourth-century mosaic programs (Figure 1.9). Portraits of Christ, the apostles, and other saints also began to appear with more regularity, often as devotional images without specific narrative contexts (Figures 8.11–12, 12.10).[31] Their tombs became sites for pilgrimage, their physical remains became objects of veneration, often inserted into elaborately decorated containers made from precious metals or studded with gems (Figures 10.1, 10.6, 10.9).[32]

Many of these new types of compositions began to appear soon after Emperor Constantine I's rise to power, the so-called Peace of the Church, and the imperial patronage of the Christian faith, which included the construction of major basilicas and shrines in Rome, Palestine, and Constantinople. While lay clients were probably the primary clients of workshops that produced funerary art, the development of new motifs seem to reflect the rising prestige of the Christian religion following the emperor's conversion to the faith. At the same time, iconographic themes and artistic styles from the imperial court influenced the decoration of the new church buildings, which displayed lavish mosaic decoration on walls and apses, as well as carved capitals, and embellished liturgical objects made from precious metals and ivory, much of this construction underwritten by the imperial family (Figures 13.3–4).[33]

Figure 1.9 Mosaic from the Sant'Aquilino chapel, Milan, fourth century. Photo: Mark D. Ellison.

For example, among the many gifts that Constantine donated to his first Roman basilica—now known as Saint John Lateran but originally called simply the Constantinian Basilica—was a hammered silver *fastigium* (a pediment supported by columns) that displayed a life-size seated image of Christ accompanied by silver statues of the twelve apostles and four spear-carrying angels. In addition to these impressive (and heavy) silver figures, the pediment supported gold and silver lamps and wreaths. The emperor furnished that basilica's baptistery with a statue of a lamb in solid gold, almost life-sized silver representations of Christ and John the Baptist, and seven silver stags.[34] Other objects of gold and silver, from candle stands to altars, exhibit an appreciation for fine craft, a love of luxury, and a desire to give precious donations to the church, sometimes inscribed as personal memorial gifts (Figures 15.3–4). By the end of the fourth century luxury objects of ivory and silver began to be made for private individuals, and these often showed a combination of Christian and mythological motifs—an indication that the ancient gods and their stories had not been completely eclipsed as subjects for visual art (Figure 15.6).

Along with objects of ivory, silver, and gold, were probably less costly and certainly less enduring textiles that included items of clothing as well as sanctuary curtains and altar cloths, mainly made from wool, linen, and silk. Because of their fragility, they mostly survive in fragments and come predominately from dry climates such as Egypt. These woven objects displayed colorful images of biblical characters, saints, and crosses, as well as less animals, flowers, and geometric patterns.[35] One of the most impressive examples is a tapestry icon of the Virgin and Child now in the Cleveland Museum of Art (Figure 14.8). Along with these personal objects are small souvenirs, purchased by pilgrims to the holy sites, especially in Palestine, Syria, and Egypt. Often clay or pewter ampullae that were designed to contain blessed oil or perhaps consecrated soil, they were stamped with the figures of saints or biblical scenes to remind travelers of the places they visited along their journeys (Figures 10.8, 11.15).

Many of these compositions represented Jesus as the new lawgiver, assuming the role of Moses, conveying a scroll to the holy apostles, Peter and Paul (Figures 4.6, 18.5, 20.10).[36] He also appears as the enthroned heavenly sovereign (Figure 6.5). Scholars often have described this change of emphasis—from Jesus as healer or miracle worker to Jesus as enthroned king—as the adaption of imperial iconography. However, now depicted as thickly bearded rather than youthful, seated on a jeweled throne rather than a folding curule chair, and garbed in resplendent gold and purple robes rather than simple tunic and *pallium*, Christ appears more like a cosmic king of kings than a rival for the earthly emperor.[37] Even as the references to the passion began to make their appearance in visual art, the cross was first displayed without the body, as a symbol of his overcoming death. As it is surmounted by a wreath and christogram, an image modeled after the emperor's own emblem of military conquest, it bears allusions to imperial triumph while being adapted to convey the assurance of divine victory (Figure 18.6).[38]

The emperor's example inspired a church building boom across the Roman world. As elite and wealthy Romans joined the faith, they often redirected their wealth from sponsoring civic projects to generously endowing ecclesiastical foundations. These structures were adorned with magnificent mosaics on floors and walls, and furnished with elegantly crafted objects. The official function of these structures meant that their design and decoration were most likely supervised by church officials rather than lay or even imperial sponsors, some of whom would have underwritten the projects from their own funds.

The application of colored small tesserae to church walls and vaults was a technical innovation during this period.[39] The image placed in the apse replaced the cult statue (or imperial portrait) that would have been there in pre-Christian basilicas and became a focus for the liturgy (Figure 6.4).[40] One of the oldest surviving examples, in Rome's church of Santa Pudenziana, depicts Christ enthroned among his apostles and before the cityscape of the New Jerusalem (Rev 21.2). A gemmed cross rises from the site of Golgotha and in the sky above are the four living creatures described in the Book of Revelation (Rev 4.6–8). Two female figures, probably personifications of the churches of the Jews and the Gentiles, offer crowns to Peter and Paul (Figure 6.5).

Throughout the fifth and sixth centuries the decorative programs of churches became more and more elaborate and iconographically innovative. The mosaics that decorated the church of Santa Maria Maggiore (built by Sixtus III, *c.* 435) depicted a cycle of subjects from Genesis and Exodus in the nave (Figure 6.7), as well as previously unknown scenes from Christ's nativity narratives, including the magi before Herod and the massacre of the innocents on the triumphal arch (Figure 1.10). By contrast, the original arch program for San Paolo Fuori le Mura, created about the same time, displayed another scene from the Book of Revelation. On the uppermost register a bust of Christ adorned with the radiate nimbus of the sun god hovered among the four beasts of Paradise and above the twenty-four elders of Revelation bearing crowns to cast before him (cf. Revelation 4.1–11). The mosaics of Ravenna are among the most magnificent of all. Their stunning pictorial compositions are often surrounded by geometric and floral designs and exemplify the ways that liturgy is illuminated by the decoration of its environment (Figures 21.5–10). Furthermore, as the Ravenna mosaics represent the transitions from Roman to Gothic to early Byzantine culture and theology, they provide an unsurpassed and extremely precious visual archive.[41]

Paulinus of Nola, an aristocratic early-fifth-century bishop who built churches on his ancestral lands between Rome and Naples, described the apse mosaics he commissioned. For his church at Nola, Paulinus evidently commissioned a representation of the Holy Trinity. A poem that he composed describes the iconography as depicting Christ in the form of a lamb standing on a rock from which four rivers flowed, the Father as a voice thundering from above (almost certainly depicted as a hand from heaven), and a dove for the Holy Spirit. The image also included a cross within a wreath, which was itself surrounded by a circle of twelve doves

Figure 1.10 Triumphal arch, Basilica of Santa Maria Maggiore, Rome, *ca.* 432. Photo: Robin M. Jensen.

to represent the apostles. The central image was a cross within a wreath. The other, at Fundi, depicted the final judgment. Christ was depicted as a lamb beneath a bloody cross. Above him hovered the Holy Spirit in the form of a dove, and the hand of God descended to offer a crown. The Christ-lamb was busy separating sheep from goats, with the assistance of the Good Shepherd, who herded off the goats and welcomed the lambs into a bucolic paradise.[42]

Around this same time, the shift from a book roll to a codex allowed the production of illustrated Bibles, which provided a different context for scripture-based images. The oldest surviving example of these, the Quedlinburg Itala, dates to the early fifth century and consists of five leaves from the books of Samuel and Kings. The style of these manuscript illuminations starkly contrasts with that of the catacomb paintings. Richly detailed and finely painted, some made from purple-dyed parchment, a complete manuscript may have had dozens of illustrations, many presented in sequenced cycles (Figures 16.1, 16.5–6, 18.11).[43]

Conclusion

Although scholars disagree on the reasons for the seeming absence of Christian art prior to the early third century, it is clear that no later than that, those who became adherents to the new religion were beginning to decorate their homes, bodies, tombs, and places of worship with iconography that reflected their religious identity and can still be identified as distinctively Christian insofar as they depicted biblical narratives or referred to central dogmatic or theological ideas. Although much of the surviving remains were found in burial contexts, they include objects like lamps, rings, or gold glasses that would have been made for domestic use or personal adornment. Eventually, these private or personal objects were joined by monumental works of art, liturgical furnishings of precious materials, and illuminated sacred books that were commissioned by members of the imperial family or other elite individuals and almost certainly approved by church authorities. Although one cannot know how any object was used or much less perceived by ancient owners or viewers, it can be assumed that they were intended to express both individual and communal identity and religious commitments, while also stimulating devotion, prompting prayer, and enhancing corporate worship.

Notes

1 Jeffrey Spier, "The Earliest Christian Art: From Personal Salvation to Imperial Power," in *Picturing the Bible: The Earliest Christian Art*, ed. Jeffrey Spier (New Haven, CT: Yale University Press, 2007), 1; also Paul Corby Finney, *The Invisible God* (Oxford: Oxford University Press, 1994), 110.
2 Jaś Elsner, "Archaeologies and Agendas: Reflections on Late Ancient Jewish Art and Early Christian Art," *Journal of Roman Studies* 93 (2003): 114–15; and Leonard Rutgers, *The Jews in Late Ancient Rome: Evidence of Cultural Interaction in the Roman Diaspora* (Leiden: Brill, 2000), 75–6 and 92–3. See Robert Couzin's chapter in this volume for further discussion of this problem.
3 Markus Vinzent, "Earliest 'Christian' Art is Jewish Art, in *Jewish Art in Its Late Antique Context*, ed. Uzi Leibner and Catherine Hezser (Tübingen: Mohr Siebeck, 2016), 263–77.
4 Earlier scholars include Gerhard Ladner, "The Concept of the Image of the Greek Fathers and the Byzantine Iconoclastic Controversy," *Dumbarton Oaks Papers* 7 (1953): 5, and Ernst Kitzinger, "The Cult of Images before Iconoclasm," *Dumbarton Oaks Papers* 8 (1954): 85.
5 Among these are Mary Charles Murray, "Art and the Early Church," *Journal of Theological Studies* 32 (1977): 303–45; Finney, *Invisible God*, 3–14; Robin M. Jensen, *Face to Face: Portraits of the Divine in Early Christianity* (Minneapolis, MN: Fortress Press, 2004), 4–9.
6 Clement of Alexandria, *Christ the Teacher* 3.11, trans. ANF vol. 2, 285–6; see Paul Corby Finney, "Images on Finger Rings and Early Christian Art," *Dumbarton Oaks Papers* 4 (1987): 181–6; James A. Francis, "Clement of Alexandria on Signet Rings: Reading an Image at the Dawn of Christian Art," *Classical Philology* 98 (2003): 179–83.
7 See the chapter by Jeffrey Spier in this volume.
8 On the parallels between Christ and figures like Hermes, Orpheus, and Sol, see Robin M. Jensen, *Understanding Early Christian Art* (London: Routledge, 2000), 41–4 (with bibliography). On other Christian adaptations of mythological figures and types see Mary Charles Murray, *Rebirth and Afterlife: A Study of the Transmutation of Some Pagan Imagery in Early Christian Art* (Oxford: BAR International Series, 1981); and Marion Lawrence, "Three Pagan Themes in Christian Art," in *De Artibus Opuscula* Vol. 40. ed., M. Meiss (New York, NY: New York University Press, 1961): 323–34.
9 See, for example, Justin Martyr *1 Apol.* 21ff.
10 See the chapter by Jutta Dresken-Weiland in this volume.
11 For example, see Jaś Elsner's introduction to *Art and the Roman Viewer* (Cambridge: Cambridge University Press, 1995), 1–14.
12 On this stylistic approach see Robin M. Jensen, "Compiling Narratives: The Visual Strategies of Early Christian Art," *Journal of Early Christian Studies* 23 (2015): 1–26.
13 See the chapter by Mark D. Ellison in this volume.
14 See the somewhat different point of view in Roald Dijkstra, *The Apostles in Early Christian Art and Poetry* (Leiden: Brill, 2016), 32–3.
15 See the chapters by Norbert Zimmerman, Jutta Dresken-Weiland, and Gutram Koch in this volume.
16 See the chapter by Michael Peppard in this volume.
17 See the chapters by Susan Walker and John J. Herrmann, Jr. and Annewies van den Hoek in this volume.
18 On these motifs see the work of Paul Zanker and Björn Ewald, *Living with Myths: The Imagery of Roman Sarcophagi* (Oxford: Oxford University Press, 2012). 28–9, 127–9.
19 On this acrostic see Tertullian *On Baptism* 1; *Sibylline Oracles* 8.217–250; and Optatus of Milevis *Against Parmenian* 3.2.1.
20 See the chapter by Heidi J. Hornik in this volume.
21 For example see André Grabar, *Early Christian Art* (New York, NY: Odyssey Press, 1968), 8–9; Robert Milburn, *Early Christian Art and Architecture* (Berkeley, CA: University of California Press, 1988), 25; and Graydon Snyder, *Ante Pacem: Archeological Evidence of Church Life before Constantine* (Macon, GA: Mercer University Press, 2003), 124–6.
22 For more discussion on this subject, see Robin M. Jensen, "Dining in Heaven," *Bible Review* 14.5 (1998): 24–36.
23 See the chapter by Norbert Zimmerman in this volume.

24 Articulated by Kurt Weizmann in "The Illustration of the Septuagint," in *Studies in Classical and Byzantine Illumination* ed. H. Kessler (Chicago, IL: University of Chicago Press, 1971), 45–75; and reiterated in Kurt Weitzmann and Herbert Kessler, *The Frescoes of the Dura Synagogue and Christian Art* (Washington, DC: Dumbarton Oaks Press, 1990).
25 This theory summarized (with bibliography) by Catherine Brown Tkacz, in *The Key to the Brescia Casket: Typology and the Early Christian Imagination* (Paris: University of Notre Dame Press, 2002), 109–37.
26 On the image of Isaac as a type of Christ in both early Christian art and literature see Robin M. Jensen, "Isaac's Sacrifice in Jewish and Christian Tradition: Image and Text," *Biblical Interpretation* 2 (1994), 85–110.
27 A summary of the typological application of Jonah can be found in Everett Ferguson, "Jonah in Early Christian Art: Death, Resurrection, and Immortality," in *Text, Image, and Christians in the Graeco-Roman World*, eds A. Niang and C. Osiek (Eugene, OR: Pickwick Publications, 2012), 342–53.
28 Jaś Elsner, *Roman Eyes: Visuality and Subjectivity in Art and Text* (Princeton, NJ: Princeton University Press, 2007), 24–5. On the baptismal significance of these scenes see Michael Peppard, *The World's Oldest Church: Bible, Art, and Ritual at Dura Europos, Syria* (New Haven, CT: Yale University Press, 2016).
29 See the chapter by Lee M. Jefferson in this volume.
30 See the chapter by Felicity Harley-McGowan in this volume.
31 See the chapter by Katherine Marsengill in this volume.
32 See the chapter by Erik Thunø in this volume.
33 See the chapters by Niamh Bhalla and Ruth Leader-Newby in this volume.
34 *Liber Pontificalis* 34. 9–13.
35 See the chapter by Jennifer L. Ball in this volume.
36 On this motif see Robert Couzin, *The Traditio Legis: Anatomy of an Image* (Oxford: Archaeopress, 2015).
37 This is a central thesis of Thomas Mathews, *The Clash of Gods: A Reinterpretation of Early Christian Art* (Princeton, NJ: Princeton University Press, 1993).
38 See the chapter by Felicity Harley-McGowan in this volume. Also see Robin M. Jensen, "The Emperor Cult and Christian Iconography," in *Rome and Religion: A Cross-Disciplinary Dialogue on the Imperial Cult*, eds J. Brodd and J. Reed (Atlanta, GA: SBL Publications, 2011), 153–71.
39 See the chapters by Sean Leatherbury and Rina Talgam in this volume.
40 On the development of apse iconography see Christa Ihm, *Die Programme der christlichen Apsismalerei vom vierten Jahrhundert bis zur mitte des achten Jahrhunderts* (Wiesbaden: Franz Steiner, 1960); Beat Brenk, *The Apse, the Image and the Icon* (Wiesbaden: Ludwig Reichert, 2010); and Erik Thunø, *The Apse Mosaic in Early Medieval Rome* (Cambridge: Cambridge University Press, 2015).
41 See the chapter by Deborah Mauskopf Deliyannis in this volume.
42 Paulinus of Nola *Epistle* 32.10, 17.
43 See the chapter by Dorothy Verkerk in this volume.

Further reading

Selected, broad, and English-language introductions to the study of early Christian art or scholarly studies on the general subject of the emergence of Christian art and its relationship to Greco-Roman art and iconography include the following general works, some of them edited collections of essays by important scholars. More focused studies on different media or thematic questions are included at the ends of the rest of the chapters in this volume.

Belting, Hans. *Likeness and Presence: A History of the Image before the Era of Art*, trans. Edmund Jephcott. Chicago, IL: University of Chicago Press, 1994.

Charles Murray, Mary. *Rebirth and Afterlife: A Study of the Transmutation of Some Pagan Imagery in Early Christian Art.* Oxford: BAR International Series, 1981.

Elsner, Jaś. *Imperial Rome and Christian Triumph.* Oxford: Oxford University Press, 1998.

Finney, Paul Corby. *The Invisible God.* Oxford: Oxford University Press, 1994.

Grabar, André. *Christian Iconography: A Study of its Origins.* Princeton, NJ: Princeton University Press, 1968.

Jefferson, Lee M. and Jensen, Robin M., eds. *The Art of Empire: Christian Art in its Imperial Context.* Minneapolis, MN: Fortress Press, 2015.

Jensen, Robin M. *Understanding Early Christian Art.* London: Routledge, 2000.

Koch, Guntram. *Early Christian Art and Architecture.* London: SCM Press, 1996.

Lazaridou, Anastasia, ed. *Transition to Christianity: Art of Late Antiquity, 3rd–7th Century AD.* New York, NY: The Onassis Foundation, 2011.

Lowden, John. *Early Christian and Byzantine Art*. London: Phaidon, 1997.
Matthews, Thomas F. *The Clash of Gods: A Reinterpretation of Early Christian Art*, revised edition. Princeton, NJ: Princeton University Press, 1993.
Milburn, Robert. *Early Christian Art and Architecture*. Berkeley, CA: University of California Press, 1988.
Nicolai, Vincenzo Fiocchi, Bisconti, Fabrizio and Mazzoleni, Danilo, eds. *The Christian Catacombs of Rome: History, Decoration, Inscriptions*, second edition, trans. C. C. Stella and L-A Touchette. Regensburg: Schnell & Steiner, 2002.
Snyder, Graydon. *Ante Pacem: Archaeological Evidence of Church Life before Constantine*, revised edition. Macon, GA: Mercer University Press, 2003.
Spier, Jeffrey, ed. *Picturing the Bible: The Earliest Christian Art*. New Haven, CT: Yale University Press, 2007.
Tronzo, William. *The Via Latina Catacomb: Imitation and Discontinuity in Fourth-Century Roman Painting*. University Park, PA: Pennsylvania State University Press, 1986.
Weitzmann, Kurt, ed. *The Age of Spirituality*. New York, NY: Metropolitan Museum of Art, 1979.

PART I

Media

2

CATACOMB PAINTING AND THE RISE OF CHRISTIAN ICONOGRAPHY IN FUNERARY ART

Norbert Zimmermann

For more than a hundred years, from the late first to the late second century CE, the Christian religion, then only one of many oriental resurrection cults in the Roman Empire, left no material traces, and the Christians produced no identifiable artifacts nor developed a distinctive iconography or art. This changed from the early third century onwards, when members of the Christian community of Rome started to imitate the behavior of their surrounding society, expressing their religious hopes and beliefs through images, and so inventing the first stages of a Christian, mostly biblical, iconography. This emergence of Christian art is best documented for us in the Roman catacombs—the extensive subterranean parts of Christian collective cemeteries, dug along the consular roads outside the city walls. The catacombs were used for burials from *ca.* 200 CE until the early fifth century, when Christianity had become the official religion. The Roman catacomb paintings gain particular importance because of the loss of nearly all other Christian paintings that may have existed at the same time outside the catacombs. As the only surviving evidence, the funerary paintings at graves preserve the first images of western Christian iconography.

Tracing the development of catacomb painting, one follows the first stages of development in Christian art. This art is usually of a quite modest quality, and in most cases it is an individual expression of self-representation and hope for an eternal life of a private owner/commissioner. The care for the deceased was a duty of the family, and every painted monument reflects a single, private order and not an official, public statement of the church. Only very few examples, usually in topographical contact with a tomb of a venerated martyr, show better quality and a richer decoration, and eventually also an ecclesiastical and therefore somewhat official commissioner.

Today we know up to 70 catacombs or hypogea outside the Roman city walls,[1] and in total a grid of more than 150 kilometers of catacomb galleries extended under the earth, with certainly hundreds of thousands of buried persons. In the catacombs only the subterranean parts of the cemeteries are preserved, and they without doubt contained mostly the tombs of the poorer part of the society. The majority of the burials remained anonymous, without any kind of decoration or inscription.[2] About 400 painted units are known to us today, either in entire rooms (cubicula) or in single graves (arcosolia or loculi) in the galleries. The paintings therefore form a relatively small group of monuments; statistically, every year during the 200 years of catacomb use, only two paintings were created.[3] In comparison with the thousands of Christian sarcophagi from

Rome, it is clear how unusual it was to order a painting within the context of a catacomb burial. Catacomb research has been able to identify most of the iconographic scenes, and to reconstruct their chronology at least in general lines.[4] However, without evidence that could support an absolute dating, the paintings often remain ordered only by more or less uncertain stylistic arguments.

The introduction of images at graves

Experimentation and the first biblical scenes

Until the end of the second century, it is practically impossible to distinguish between Christian and pagan burials. But, from that time on, the Christian communities began to create their own cemeteries, as is best documented in both written and archaeological sources for the catacomb of Callixtus (San Callisto), on the via Appia, where the bishop Zephyrinus (198–217) sent the deacon Callixtus as supervisor of the *coemeterium*. Callixtus's name was later given to the cemetery, and he later became the bishop himself. This oldest region of the Callixtus catacomb (so-called Area I) not only had a cubiculum that collected the burials of the third-century bishops (today known as "Crypt of the Popes"), but also contained a line of six private family cubicula with wall paintings, the so-called "Chapels of the Sacraments," A1–A6. It is in these small, cubic rooms with rectangular loculi-openings on all three main walls that we find the earliest attempt to depict biblical stories in images (Figure 2.1). Around the grave openings, on the ceiling, and left and right of the entrance door appear selected stories of the Old and New Testament. They were set among traditional decorations like flowers, birds, or masks on a white ground and usually without any background painting.

The most interesting aspect is that the S Callixtus scenes themselves document the creative moment of formation, showing on the one hand some iconographic innovations that became from then on the standard form of certain biblical scenes, while revealing on the other hand that some images had less success, and later found a different standardized form.[5] Moreover, a few additional scenes had no success at all, and were later eliminated. For example, one of the most meaningful scenes at the tombs, the rising of Lazarus, was painted here in a cubiculum (A5) in a quite literary way, with Jesus holding his right hand elevated, calling Lazarus out of his tomb, and Lazarus obeying him directly, stepping out of the grave architecture (Figure 2.2). Later versions of this story usually depict Lazarus in the way the deceased were brought into their tombs beneath the painting, wrapped in linen strips, and not striding out but immobile, appearing within the tomb aedicula (Figure 2.3). Jesus touches Lazarus's front with a *virga*, a staff representing his supernatural power, to indicate even more clearly the salvific action.[6]

Another example of an iconographic form that did not endure is a scene of Abraham's offering of his son Isaac (again room A2, Figure 2.1), with both father and son praying to God with upraised arms. In all later versions, Abraham holds a knife uplifted for the offering, and is prevented by the hand of God. In the neighboring room A5, however, the scene of Moses striking the rock with the water appearing is shown already in the same iconography that would last essentially unchanged until the end of catacomb painting. Finally, and curiously, in room A2 an enigmatic scene with a man holding his hand over perhaps a loaf of bread on a table, and a woman beside him preaching as an orant (with raised, extended arms) has often been interpreted as a eucharistic meal. It remains completely unique and did not find its way

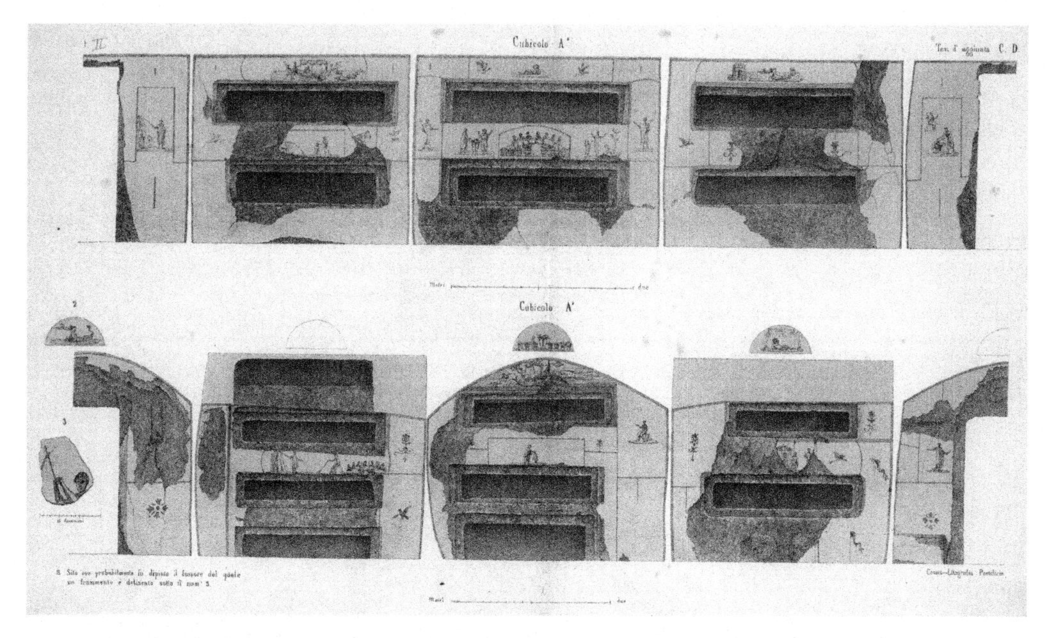

Figure 2.1 Chapel of the Sacrament A3, wall spool, from Giovanni Battista de Rossi, *Roma Sotterranea Cristiana*, vol. II (Roma: Cromo-Litografia Pontificia, 1867).

into the broader Christian funerary repertory. This diversity of innovations for biblical scenes has rightly been characterized as the first moments of Christian art and as a laboratory of iconography.

The repertory of Christian scenes at the end of the third century

By the end of the third century, a relatively limited repertory of scenes had developed in catacomb paintings and had begun to appear also on Christian sarcophagi.

Incorporation of traditional motifs in a Christian perspective

Four traditional pagan motifs were incorporated into the Christian repertory of images: (1) the former bucolic shepherd, becoming now Jesus the Good Shepherd of John's parable; (2) Orpheus, the mythical singer who went to Hades and calmed the wild animals with his singing and playing, both aspects that gave reason to identify him with Christ; (3) the orant, the figure of a woman or man with hands raised in prayer personifying piety to men and gods, becoming a Christian *pietas* or prayer and often at the same time a representation of the deceased; and (4) the banquet scene, becoming both a *refrigerium* (funerary meal) for or with the bereaved and symbolizing therefore an eternal meal.

Figure 2.2 Chapel of the Sacrament A5, entrance wall, raising of Lazarus, from Joseph Wilpert, *Die Malereien der Katakomben Roms* (Freiburg: Herder, 1903)

Figure 2.3 Raising of Lazerus, Domitilla catacomb, arcosol 73, from Joseph Wilpert, *Die Malereien der Katakomben Roms* (Freiburg: Herder, 1903), pl. 192 (part.).

Scenes from the Old and New Testament

In addition to the appropriation of existing images, completely new iconographies were invented for what may be called the "new myths," or the Christian—usually biblical—stories: a group of over twenty biblical scenes, illustrating intense moments of salvation, healing, or revelation.[7]

We find quite regularly about eleven scenes from the entire Old Testament, given here in order of their statistical occurrence: Moses striking the rock (Exod 17:1–6, Num 20:1–11); Jonah's story (Jonah 1–4); Daniel between the lions (Dan 14); Noah in the ark (Gen 7–8); Adam and Eve (Gen 3); Abraham offering Isaac (Gen 22:1–18); the three Hebrews in the fire (Dan 3); Job (Job 2:7–8); Moses removing his sandals (Exod 3); Moses receiving the law (Exod 24); Susanna with the elders (Dan 13); and finally Balaam pointing to the star (Num 24:17). A similar number of at least twelve scenes from the New Testament were often requested, listed again in order of the frequency with which they occur: the raising of Lazarus (John 11:1–24); the multiplication of bread (Matt 15:32–39); the healing of the paralytic (Figure 2.4) (John 5; Matt 9:5; Mark 2,9; Luke 5:23); a baptism (Matt 3:13–17; Mark 1:1–9; Luke 3:21); the healing of a blind person (Luke 18:35–43; Mark 10:46–52; John 9:1–7); Jesus with the Samaritan woman at the well (John 4); the transformation of water to wine (John 2), which often appears in conjunction with the multiplication of the bread; the healing of the bleeding woman (Matt 9:18–22; Mark 5:25–34; Luke 8:43–48); and finally the less frequent scenes of the annunciation (Luke 1), the healing of the demoniac (Matt 8:28–34; Mark 5:1–20; Luke 8:26–40), the healing

Figure 2.4 Miracle of the paralytic, Domitilla (detail from Figure 2.9), from Joseph Wilpert, *Die Malereien der Katakomben Roms* (Freiburg: Herder, 1903), pl. 239.

of the leper (Matt 8:1–4; Mark 1:40–45), and a very few instances of the parable of the wise virgins (Matt 25).

Generally, one can summarize that nearly all these newly created scenes were carefully selected from the entire biblical text (both Old and New Testament) and show a common semantic line: They all illustrate moments of dense salvific history, reporting stories of salvation from danger to life, like Daniel between the lions, the three Hebrews in the fire, or Moses striking the rock for water. Some tell miracles of healings of an illness, like the paralytic or the blind, or they relate miracles of immediate salvation from death, like Lazarus. Finally, they also document moments of a direct contact between God and men during a salvific act, speech, or lesson, such as Moses who receives the law at Mount Sinai, or the Samaritan woman at the well who is told by Jesus himself about the meaning of the holy water. The criteria of selection seems quite clear, as the plot of each story is usually, with only a very few exceptions, directly salvific and therefore meaningful in the funerary context.

However, the images do not try to tell the biblical story as a narration, but they concentrate the attention directly on the salvific content. The narration is always reduced to one emblematic moment and is restricted to the most important persons, normally only one or two. For example, in the image of Daniel the lions are usually shown as docile, primarily as attributes to identify the scene. The image of Noah does not show the punishment of men in the flood, but concentrates exclusively on the moment when Noah receives the branch announcing the end of the flood. In the New Testament scenes, Jesus is often present in person (Figures 2.1, 2.2), but he can also be absent, as in the miracle of the paralytic (Figure 2.4). If he is present, he can talk or act with his hand or, more often, with his *virga*, the non-biblical attribute of his divine power.

Generally, other figures are limited to the main protagonists, and one can assume that for the creators and viewers of these images, textual literacy was not as important as a general familiarity with the biblical narratives. Sometimes no attention was paid to specifying which miracle among several in the synoptic texts was intended, as, for example, the healing of a blind person. One can imagine that not only literary sources but also oral traditions served as the bases for the images.

Because the images possess a static character, concentrating on the most important part of the story in order for it to be readable, art historians have commonly classified them as symbolic.[8] That is true even for scenes of the prophet Jonah, the only subject that is illustrated, from its first appearance, in a cycle of first three and later even four scenes. While the text of his story focuses on the inhabitants of Nineveh and their sinful behavior, the images of the cycle accent a secondary aspect of the story. Jonah is thrown in the mouth of the fish (represented as a sea dragon, called *ketos* in Greek literary sources), and after three days disgorged, to finally rest, saved from the sea monster, lying under a pergola like the sleeping Endymion. In this case, it becomes clear that the motivation for illustrating this story with this particular iconography was only partly based on the biblical narrative. Rather, the painted cycle follows the same common salvific line, displaying an early Christian typology between Jonah and the anticipated future salvation from death and the following rest, in the pattern of Christ's own rising after three days (like Jonah was delivered from the sea monster after three days; Matt 12:40).

Embodying of the funerary portrait

Imbedded in this clear repertory of mostly biblical scenes, at the very end of the third century, a further new, most important image, widespread in the traditional art, was added to this meaningful content: the portrait of the deceased.[9] Even though it appears relatively late, it soon became the statistically most represented single motif of catacomb art,[10] appearing in different forms and places around the graves. The portraits may be classified in six sometimes overlapping categories: (1) orants, surely the most popular image, sometimes stand as a group without distinction between bereaved and deceased; (2) busts in medallions or frames; (3) standing or sitting persons holding *codici* or *rotuli* (books or scrolls); (4) persons representing their professions; (5) members of agape or *refrigeria* meals; and (6) persons in scenic moments, for example showing the deceased already resting in a paradisiacal place like a garden (Figure 2.5), or as part of a biblical scene. Two emblematic examples are the scene of Susanna between the elders, where Susanna becomes a portrait of the deceased woman, evidently in praise of her virtue, and the Samaritan woman beside Christ at the well, possibly to identify the deceased as a person in close contact with Christ.

The portraits are not intended to depict the exact likenesses of the pictured persons—in fact the modern concept of portraying an individual in his or her natural physiognomy is far from these images. Only very few portraits seem to give a concrete idea of what the persons really looked like. More often they offer, instead of a natural aspect, a "typical" view, presenting a vision of a young/old man/woman, characterized as a member of a certain social class, a rich family, an educated person dressed in precious clothing and with a certain haircut. Inscriptions sometimes help to identify the individual deceased (Figure 2.6). These portraits send messages of the status of the depicted in society and identify membership in a group or class in life or hopefully in the afterlife. Some of them become proper prayers when the deceased is shown making eye contact with Christ, bringing personally the wish for salvation before his face. A good example is in arcosolium 70 of the Domitilla catacomb: Christ appears

Figure 2.5 Wall of the "Cubiculum of the 5 Saints," Callixtus catacomb, from Joseph Wilpert, *Die Malereien der Katakomben Roms* (Freiburg: Herder, 1903), pl. 111.

Figure 2.6 The deceased Elio-(dora), in a cubiculum of catacombs of Sts Peter and Marcellinus, from Joseph Wilpert, *Die Malereien der Katakomben Roms* (Freiburg: Herder, 1903), pl. 43,2.

Figure 2.7 Christ as the Good Shepherd with the deceased as orants in the flock, from Joseph Wilpert, *Die Malereien der Katakomben Roms* (Freiburg: Herder, 1903), pl. 190.

as the Good Shepherd, and the deceased as part of his flock, a female orant at his right side looking directly at him, as if praying personally for her salvation (Figure 2.7).[11] However, in the majority of portraits the individual depicted looks straight ahead out of the image, as if to make eye contact with the viewer. And this seems to be their function in most cases: to communicate directly with the viewer in the moments of cultic commemoration and contemplation.[12] At least two times a year the family held a meal and visited the tomb, during the *rosalia* (feast of roses), the commemoration day for the deceased, and the day of passing away, regarded by Christians as the deceased's birthday to the eternal life. It is interesting in this context to observe the nearly complete lack of any indications of personal sorrow, one of the regular themes of traditional Roman funerary art. At least in the imagery, Christians concentrated faithfully on the hope for salvation.

Effects of the "Constantinian turn" on architecture and imagery

The historical process usually called the "Constantinian turn," meaning the changes following Constantine's victory against Maxentius on the Milvian Bridge (312 CE) and the recognition of the Christian religion as *religio licta* in east and west as arranged between Constantine and Licinius at Milan (313 CE), initiated the general process of the Christianization of the Roman empire. In Rome, the persecutions had ended under Maxentius, but Constantine's orientation on Christ and his subsequent long reign caused a rapidly growing number of Christians in all social classes, including the rich and members of the court. For the church now everything changed drastically: its members turned in less than ten years from public enemies to imperial friends, supported and promoted in many ways by the emperor. If we look, for example, at the basilicas and their decoration, we see the clear imprint of the imperial court. From that moment on, we can really talk about an official, ecclesiastical art and architecture.

This process of Christianization is clearly visible also in the catacombs. There is an enormous topographical extension in fourth-century areas, reflecting the growing number of members. Additionally, one sees a proper monumentalization of the dimension and architectural forms of *cubicula* and their paintings. The chambers became larger and their architecture became more impressive, with groined vaults resting on columns and important burials being emphasized by *acrosolia*. These new structures offered new spaces for images in the arches of *arcosolia* and in their lunettes—spaces that were used to distinguish and differ layers of content and to specify pictorial hierarchies. However, despite the fact that there were now often larger spaces available for decoration, there was not usually a larger total number of scenes.

A new image of Christ

While in the third century more scenes from the Old Testament were depicted, at the time of Constantine the attention gave slightly more focus to the New Testament. At the same time, beside the figure of Jesus represented as a young philosopher in the biblical scenes, a new image of a long-haired and bearded Christ was developed for non-biblical scenes. Adopting the model of a Father God, Christ appeared now with all honors of imperial iconography, such as the nimbus, the throne, the *suppedaneum* (a little footrest), and the imperial purple as the color for his mantle or *chlamys*. From at least the late Constantinian time or the mid-fourth century on, this image in the form of a bust or full figure takes the central positions, usually getting the highest attention (Figure 2.8). This new image did not completely replace the older images, and Christ as Orpheus or the Good Shepherd also appear here and there, always in central positions.

Private, personal representation also usually takes an important position in the inner topography of the grave monuments, *arcosolia* or *cubicula*. The painters invented different ways to connect private portraits with scenes of biblical salvation, and often the funerary portrait and the image of Christ show a kind of concurrence for the most attractive position in terms of visibility and topographical hierarchy in a painted context.

Figure 2.8 Christ on his throne with his 12 apostles around; the so-called "Apostles council" of the crypt of mensores at Domitilla, from Joseph Wilpert, *Die Malereien der Katakomben Roms* (Freiburg: Herder, 1903), pl. 193.

More traces of imperial iconography

Some further images show their clear dependence on the imperial art. With eighteen images, the adoration of the magi (Matt 2) is depicted quite often (Figure 2.9, upper right). Normally centralized with two or four symmetrical magi, but also with Mary holding Jesus on her knees on one side and three magi arriving with their gifts from the other, the scene represents the moment of adoration itself. It seems doubtful that this scene emerged before the time of peace; it very much reflects imperial images with barbarians in adoration before the emperor. Therefore it should be dated from the time of Constantine onwards.

Another new image is Christ enthroned (and in one case standing) between the two most important Roman martyrs, Peter and Paul. Both appear in white clothing often with red stripes, like Christ's senators of his heavenly court, in gestures of veneration. Finally, we find Jesus teaching, surrounded by his apostles, clearly influenced this time by images of the seven philosophers of Greece. This scene with Christ in the middle and his disciples seated to his left and right, identified as a gathering of the apostles, is also not an illustration of a biblical event, but rather a theme that transcends time and can clearly be traced back to theological reflection.[13] The scene occupies a semi-circular pictorial space. It is therefore quite possible that the gathering of apostles first arose as an apse image in the emerging space of Christian worship—the church building in the form of a long basilica with an apse at the far end.

Monumental structures reached their high point in the middle of the fourth century. Cubicula were occasionally built as ovals or as four-, six-, or eight-cornered rooms, sometimes

Figure 2.9 Arcosolium 77 in the Catacomb of Domitilla, from Joseph Wilpert, *Die Malereien der Katakomben Roms* (Freiburg: Herder, 1903), pl. 239.

with columns in the corners and quasi-entablatures or domes (Figure 2.10). Imitations of marble in the base areas and geometric ornamentation on the surfaces of arches and vaults were popular painted forms of decoration.

Private hypogea and co-existing traditional and Christian iconography

A group of private *hypogea* from the mid-fourth century with articulated architecture and relatively high-quality wall paintings shows a very interesting co-existence of the Christian and the traditional Roman imagery. The most famous is the via Latina catacomb (Ipogeo of via Dino Compagni), a little, private *hypogeum*. Its galleries and rooms are nearly completely painted with an extraordinary selection of both unusual Christian scenes and traditional heroes and deities. In one room, Old and New Testament images including scenes of the exodus from Egypt appear on all the walls as a salvific narrative frieze, while close by, in another room, paintings portray Hercules, Athena, Ceres, and Proserpina. The large number of unique scenes has led to the supposition that the painters had a specific external model for their images, such as an illustrated Bible manuscript. In the fourth century, at least two generations of a family or an association buried their members here. The scenes were not ordered to show Christian and traditional figures, such as Christ and Athena, together in the same tomb, mixing completely both worlds. Rather, it appears that the *hypogeum* served members of an educated family with different approaches to the afterlife. The surprise with which modern interpreters have responded to this co-existence of Christian and traditional images, and the problems it has posed, reveal more about the modern concept of "struggle of religions" than about the late antique society these paintings document.[14]

Figure 2.10 Cubiculum of Orpheus, from Joseph Wilpert, *Die Malereien der Katakomben Roms* (Freiburg: Herder, 1903), pl. 229.

In addition to multiple religious values, stylistically similar *hypogea* from the mid-fourth century express in different ways the multiple expectations and hopes for the afterlife. While the *hypogeum* of Trebius Justus[15] is limited to various kinds of representative images commissioned by the mourning parents with the intent of creating a visual memorial for their deceased son showing his wealth and his education, at the little private Vibia catacomb a priest of the god Sabazius depicted his wife on her way to paradise in narrative scenes in an *arcosolium*.[16] Vibia is first abducted by Pluto and brought into the underworld on a chariot, in the pictorial tradition of the abduction of Proserpina. In the underworld, Hermes leads the deceased before the judge's throne and, after a positive verdict, an *angelus bonus* (good angel) introduces her into paradise where she participates in the feast of the blessed. In the same spirit, in the Jewish catacomb of villa Torlonia, some paintings connect Jewish religious objects (menorah, Torah shrine, shofar, lulav) with cosmic symbols (sun and moon) to form an apocalyptic dimension.[17] Together with the Christian paintings in the catacombs, these images document a common quest to express a more or less clear hope of a religiously or philosophically based afterlife.

Damasus, the reliquary cult, and the church as commissioner

As mentioned, with the construction and decoration of Christian churches, Roman catacomb painting from the middle of the fourth century onwards generally became less innovative but more reflexive: the monumental art outside the catacombs, mainly in the huge Roman basilicas, began to serve as examples for the subterranean images. Instead of the former biblical scenes, theologically motivated images now quite often appeared, such as Christ between his twelve apostles, certainly generated for apses or similar spaces. The experience of cultic rooms with images but without graves also profoundly changed the character of the decoration of the tombs: instead of little *cubicula* with images surrounding the tombs, we find more and more the architecture of little chapels, still with the same imagery of scenes, but now ordered into lateral friezes.

The promoter of this important step and of the final flourishing of catacomb painting was Pope Damasus (366–384). He patronized the ritual veneration of persecution-era martyrs and systematically ensured that their tombs were furnished with their own stairways, light wells, and monumental presentation, with marble inscriptions and architecture.[18] Since Christian theology holds that only martyrs stand already in the presence of Christ without having to wait for the final judgment, only they could be direct advocates for the deceased who were forced to await that final judgment. Accordingly, martyr theology was echoed strongly in the images.

At least two cases of Damasian sanctuaries conserve parts of their painted decoration: the chapel for SS Felix and Adauctus, at Comodilla,[19] and the sanctuary of SS Nereus and Achilleus, at Domitilla.[20] They are particularly important because they document for the first time not private but official, ecclesiastical commissioners (that is, bishop Damasus) decorating a cultic space. The stairways and the entrance to the saints' tombs were decorated by crosses or christograms that served as a guiding system for visitors to find their way through the catacomb, and the saints themselves appeared in paintings, gesturing in veneration of Christ, in apsidal-like images over the entrances or over the graves. Every martyr's tomb in the catacombs known to Damasus was adorned and enlarged in a similar manner, with impressive architecture, a marble inscription with a poem, and a proper painting. Channeling and structuring the veneration of the numerous Roman martyrs strengthened the position of the Roman bishop, and Damasus without doubt influenced the emerging supremacy of the papacy as it developed.

On one hand, the promotion of the martyrs as patrons for the deceased and their intercessors to God advanced martyr veneration and led people to choose a saint as their personal patron, as best documented in the post-damasian *arcosolium* of Veneranda at Domitilla. The wealthy matron Veneranda is introduced into the garden of paradise by her personal patron Petronilla, a legendary daughter of Peter (Figure 2.11). On the other hand, the former intimacy between the individual and Jesus became a more distant relationship.

From an art historical point of view, the Damasus-era images depict relatively large persons with big heads and limbs. These figures appear against a dark, often red or blue, surface rather than the white backgrounds used formerly.

The end of catacomb painting

The loss of the need of the subterranean space

Disregarding a few early medieval paintings in context with martyr sanctuaries,[21] catacomb painting came to an end in the early fifth century, with the end of the use of catacombs as cemeteries. The Roman population shrank drastically, and open-air spaces (*sub divo*), especially in and nearby the huge cemetery basilicas, could satisfy the demand for tombs.[22]

The so-called last painting in the catacombs is the ceiling of a monumental cubiculum close to the graves of SS Marcellinus and Peter in the homonymous catacomb (Figure 2.12). It shows all the characteristics of a late painting: Christ with nimbus and dressed in purple is sitting on his

Figure 2.11 Arcosolium of Veneranda in the Catacombs of Domitilla, from Joseph Wilpert, *Die Malereien der Katakomben Roms* (Freiburg: Herder, 1903), pl. 213.

throne in the upper register, between Peter and Paul. Scattered flowers around them indicate the place as an eternal, paradisiacal space. In the lower register, Christ is repeated in the center as a lamb standing on a hill with four springs, the paradisiacal rivers. On the left and right side, four martyrs of the catacomb, Marcellinus and Peter and Tiburtius and Gorgonius, approach the lamb, venerating with elevated arms both lamb and Christ on the throne. The image has left the direct contact with the graves that fill the wall beneath the ceiling, and no individual representation reaches Christ's sphere. Instead, the prayers are conveyed by his saints, and expressed in their gesture. The image evidently had its origin in an apse, maybe in an above-ground basilica. Fortunately, at the same time the last catacomb paintings appear in the early fifth century, the open-air (*sub divo*) monumental tradition began.

The end of the unity of tomb and cult

To summarize, catacomb painting as private sepulchral art had two main subjects: the self-representation of the deceased and the illustration and expression of his or her hope for salvation and a Christian afterlife. All single paintings are unique and individual and are the result of a single contact between a private client or applicant and the executor, who may be called an artist or rather a craftsman. The images were part of the private funerary cult, as is best attested in the individual portraits that face the family visitors in most cases directly and break the real existing

Figure 2.12 Ceiling painting in the catacombs of Sts Peter and Marcellinus, from Joseph Wilpert, *Die Malereien der Katakomben Roms* (Freiburg: Herder, 1903), pl. 252.

border between commemorated deceased and commemorating bereaved. The catacomb tomb became, through the display of its figurative illustration, a stage of cultic action, as best shown in the *refrigeria* images at SS Marcellino e Pietro, where the scenery is displayed three dimensionally around the visiting member of the family, re-unifying the family and anticipating the unity hopefully reached in an eternal future.[23]

The private funerary ritual at the graves was suppressed only at the very end of the fourth century, with the intervention attested by S Ambrose in Milan and S Augustine in North Africa. Although some continued to practice the traditional rituals, families were instructed to celebrate a eucharistic meal in the church instead of drinking and feasting in the cemeteries. To separate the place of the burial and the place of the cultic performance made the communicative portrait at the tomb useless, and this is one more reason why with the end of the catacombs came also the end of funeral portraits.[24] To celebrate a mass instead of holding a meal at the tomb truly brought an ancient tradition to an end, and the former family duty was now taken over by the church. One effect was that women who had before held an important role in the cultic event were now replaced by the clergy. In a certain way, this is one of the tesserae that describes the end of antiquity.

Notes

1 Philippe Pergola, *Le catacombe romane: Storia e topografia* (Roma: NIS-Nuova Italia Editrice, 1997); Vincenzo Fiocchi Nicolai, *Strutture funerarie ed edifici di culto paleocristiani di Roma dal IV al VI secolo* (Vatican City: Istituto Grafico Editoriale Romano, 2001).
2 Donatella Nuzzo, *Tipologia sepolcrale delle catacombe romane: I cimiteri ipogei delle vie Ostiense, Ardeatina e Appia* (Oxford: Archaeopress, 2000).
3 Norbert Zimmermann, *Werkstattgruppen römischer Katakombenmalerei* (Münster: Aschendorff, 2002).
4 Fabrizio Bisconti, ed., *Temi di iconografia paleocristiana* (Vatican City: Pontificio Istituto di Archeologia Cristiana, 2000).
5 Fabrizio Bisconti, "L1–L2, A1–A6, X–Y, C–E. Relitti iconografici e nuovi tracciati figurativi alle origini della pittura catacombale romana," *Rivista di Archeologia Cristiana* 85 (2009): 7–53.
6 Vasiliki Tsamakda, "Eine ungewöhnliche Darstellung der Heilung des Paralytikers in der Domitilla-Katakombe: Zur Verwendung des Wunderstabes in der frühchristllichen Kunst," *Mitteilungen zur Christlichen Archäologie* 15 (2009): 25–46.
7 Norbert Zimmermann, "The Healing Christ in Early Christian Funeral Art: The Example of the Frescoes at Domitilla Catacomb/Rome," in *Miracles Revisited: New Testament Miracle Stories and their Concepts of Reality*, eds Stefan Alkier and Annette Weissenrieder (Berlin: De Gruyter, 2013), 251–274.
8 Zimmermann, "The Healing Christ in Early Christian Funeral Art," 253–255.
9 Norbert Zimmermann, "Verstorbene im Bild: Zur Intention römischer Katakombenmalerei," *Jahrbuch für Antike und Christentum* 50 (2007): 154–179.
10 Ibid.
11 Zimmermann, *Werkstattgruppen römischer Katakombenmalerei*, 146, Abb. 93.
12 Norbert Zimmermann, "Am Ende einer Gattung. Spätantike Verstorbenen-Porträts in christlichen Grabkontext," in *Privatporträt: Das Bildnis privater Personen zwischen Antike und Mittelalter, Akten der Tagung* 14.–16.02.2013 Wien, ÖAW (forthcoming).
13 Joseph Wilpert, *Die Malereien der Katakomben Roms* (Freiburg: Herder, 1903), pl. 148.2.
14 Zimmermann, *Werkstattgruppen römischer Katakombenmalerei.*
15 Rossella Rea, *L'ipogeo di Trebio Giusto sulla via Latina: Scavi e restauri* (Vatican City: Pontificio Istituto di Archeologia Cristiana, 2004).
16 Wilpert, *Die Malereien der Katakomben Roms*, pls 132–133.
17 Leonard V. Rutgers, *The Jews in Late Ancient Rome: Evidence of Cultural Interaction in the Roman Diaspora* (Leiden: Brill, 1995).
18 *Saecularia Damasiana: atti del Convegno Internaz. per il XVI Centenario della Morte di Papa Damaso I* (Città del Vaticano, 1986).
19 Albrecht Weiland, "'Conposuit tumulum sanctorum limina adorans.' Die Ausgestaltung des Grabes der hl. Felix und Adauctus durch Papst Damasus in der Commodillakatakombe in Rom," in *Historiam picture refert: Miscellanea in onore di Padre A. Recio Veganzoges O.F.M.*, (Vatican City, Pontificio Istituto di Archeologia Cristiana, 1994), 625–645; Johannes G. Deckers, Gabriele Mietke and Albrecht Weiland, Die *Katakombe "Commodilla": Repertorium der Malereien* (Vatican City: Pontificio Istituto di Archeologia Cristiana, 1994), 49.
20 Later adopted as the semi-underground Church of S Petronilla; Norbert Zimmermann, "Rilettua di pitture a Domitilla. Tracce del santuario damasiano dei SS. Nereo e Achilleo?" in *Scavi e scoperte recenti nelle chiese di Roma. Atti della giornata tematica dei Seminari di Archeologia Cristiana (Roma – 13 marzo 2008)*, eds Hugo Brandenburg and Federico Guidobaldi (Vatican City: Pontificio Istituto di Archeologia Cristiana, 2012), 189–212.
21 Raffaele Farioli, *Pitture di epoca tarda nelle catacombe romane* (Ravenna: Edizione Dante, 1963); John Osborne, *The Roman Catacombs in the Middle Ages* (London: British School at Rome, 1985).
22 Fiocchi Nicolai, *Strutture funerarie ed edifici di culto paleocristiani di Roma*, 49–62.
23 Norbert Zimmermann, "Zur Deutung spätantiker Mahlszenen: Totenmahl im Bild," in *Rituale: Identitätsstiftende Handlungskomplexe*, eds Georg Danek and Irmtraud Hellerschmid (Wien: Verlag der Österreichischen Akademie der Wissenschaften, 2012), 171–185.
24 Norbert Zimmermann and Vasiliki Tsamakda, eds, *Die Domitilla-Katakombe: Repertorium der Malerei* (forthcoming).

Further reading

The best introduction to the topic of the catacombs and the different approaches through the long history of research is still offered by Fiocchi Nicolai, Bisconti and Mazzoleni (1999), and Pergola (1997). Complex information on every single catacomb, with a comment on the ancient sources and a complete bibliography, is given in the *LTUR, Suburbium*. For the beginning of the catacombs, see Fiocchi Nicolai (2001), and Fiocchi Nicolai and Guyon (2006). All catacomb paintings are listed in the catalogue of iconography and topography by Nestori (1993); the biggest collection of images of the paintings is still Wilpert (1903). Three repertories for the catacombs of Marcellino e Pietro, Anapo, and Commodilla already exist: Deckers et al. (1987), Deckers et al. (1991), and Deckers et al. (1994). The repertory on Domitilla is in preparation (Zimmermann and Tsamakda in preparation). The via Latina catacomb is completely published by Ferrua (1991). The complex question of the dating of catacomb painting is discussed in De Bruyne (1969), Kollwitz (1969), Reekmans (1973), Deckers (1992), Guyon (1994), and Zimmermann (2002). Bisconti (2000) gives a comprehensive introduction into the iconography of Christian scenes; the results of recent restorations are published in Bisconti (2011) and Mazzei (2010). A scientific guideline to understand the content and meaning of the Christian imagery is given by Engemann (1997). Monographs on this topic are published in the series *Monumenti di Antichita Cristiana*, *Roma Sotterranea Cristiana*, *Studi di Antichita Cristiana*, and *Sussidi allo studio delle Antichita Cristiane*, published by the Pontificio Istituto di Archeologia Cristiana. A specialized journal is the PIAC's *Rivista di Archeologia Cristiana,* publishing current research results, studies, and reviews related to catacomb research, and also the reports of the Pontificia Commissione di Archeologia Sacra, which manages the catacombs. Additionally, PCAS manages the archive of catacomb excavations as well as a photo archive, which contains many unpublished photographs (in part online: www.archeologiasacra.net/pcas-web/).

Bisconti, Fabrizio. *Le pitture delle catacombe romane: Restauri e interpretazioni*. Todi: Tau, 2011.

__________, ed. *Temi di iconografia paleocristiana*. Vatican City: Pontificio Istituto di Archeologia Cristiana, 2000.

De Bruyne, Lucien. "La peinture cemeterial constantinienne." In *Akten des Internationalen Kongresses für Christliche Archaologie 7, Trier 5–11 September 1965*, 159–214.Vatican City: Pontificio Istituto di Archeologia Cristiana, 1969.

Deckers, Johannes G., Gabriele Mietke and Albrecht Weiland. *Die Katakombe "Anonima di via Anapo": Repertorium der Malereien*. Vatican City: Pontificio Istituto di Archeologia Cristiana, 1991.

——————. *Die Katakombe "Commodilla": Repertorium der Malereien*. Vatican City: Pontificio Istituto di Archeologia Cristiana, 1994.

Deckers, Johannes G., Hans Reinhard Seeliger and Gabriele Mietke. *Die Katakombe "Santi Marcellino e Pietro": Repertorium der Malereien*. Vatican City: Pontificio Istituto di Archeologia Cristiana, 1987.

Deckers, Johannes G. "Wie genau ist eine Katakombe zu datieren? Das Beispiel Ss. Marcellino e Pietro." In *Memoria sanctorum venerantes: Miscellanea in onore di Mons. V. Saxer*, 217–238. Vatican City: Pontificio Istituto di Archeologia Cristiana, 1992.

Engemann, Josef. *Deutung und Bedeutung frühchristlicher Bildwerke*. Darmstadt: Wissenschaftliche Buchgesellschaft, 1997.

Ferrua, Antonio. *The Unknown Catacomb: A Unique Discovery of Early Christian Art*. Florence: Nardini, 1991.

Fiocchi Nicolai, Vincenzo. *Strutture funerarie ed edifici di culto paleocristiani di Roma dal IV al VI secolo*. Vatican City: Istituto Grafico Editoriale Romano, 2001.

Fiocchi Nicolai, Vincenzo, Fabrizio Bisconti and Danilo Mazzoleni. *The Christian Catacombs of Rome*. Regensburg: Schnell und Steiner, 1999.

Fiocchi Nicolai, Vincenzo, and Jean Guyon. "Relire Styger: Les origines de l'Area I du cimitiere de Calliste et la Crypte des Papes." In *Origini delle catacombe romane: Atti della giornata tematica dei Seminari di Archeologia Cristiana*, eds Vincenzo Fiocchi Nicolai and Jean Guyon, 121–161. Vatican City: Pontificio Istituto di Archeologia Cristiana, 2006.

Guyon, Jean. "Peut-on vraiment dater une catacombe? Retour sur le cimitiere 'Aux deux Lauriers,' ou catacombe des saints Marcellin-et-Pierre sur la via Labicana a Rome." In *Bild und Formensprache der spatantiken Kunst: Festschr. H.Brandenburg*, ed. Martina Jordan-Ruwe, 89–103. Muster: Archaologisches Seminar, 1994.

Kollwitz, Johannes. "Die Malerei der konstantinischen Zeit." In *Akten des Internationalen Kongresses fur Christliche Archaologie 7, Trier 5–11 September 1965*, 29–158. Vatican City: Pontificio Istituto di Archeologia Cristiana, 1969.

Mazzei, Barbara, ed. *Il cubicolo degli apostoli nelle catacombe romane di Santa Tecla: Cronaca di una scoperta*. Vatican City: Pontificia Commissione di Archeologia Sacra, 2010.

Nestori, Aldo. *Repertorio topografico delle pitture delle catacombe romane*, 2nd edition. Vatican City: Pontificio Istituto di Archeologia Cristiana, 1993.

Osborne, John. *The Roman Catacombs in the Middle Ages*. London: British School at Rome, 1985.

Pergola, Philippe. *Le catacombe romane: Storia e topografia*. Roma: NIS – Nuova Italia Editrice, 1997.

Reekmans, Louis. "La chronologie de la peinture paleochretienne: Notes et reflexions." *Rivista di Archeologia Cristiana* 49 (1973): 271–291.

Wilpert, Joseph. *Die Malereien der Katakomben Roms*. Freiburg: Herder, 1903.

Zimmermann, Norbert. "The Healing Christ in Early Christian Funeral Art: The Example of the Frescoes at Domitilla Catacomb/Rome." In *Miracles Revisited: New Testament Miracle Stories and their Concepts of Reality*, eds Stefan Alkier and Annette Weissenrieder, 251–74. Berlin: De Gruyter, 2013.

———. *Werkstattgruppen römischer Katakombenmalerei*. Münster: Aschendorff, 2002.

Zimmermann, Norbert and Vasiliki Tsamakda, eds, *Die Domitilla – Katakombe: Repertorium der Malerei* [forthcoming].

3
CHRISTIAN SARCOPHAGI FROM ROME

Jutta Dresken-Weiland

Because they are so numerous, Christian sarcophagi from Rome are the most important group of objects for the creation and invention of a Christian iconography. Although the production of Christian sarcophagi started only towards the end of the third century, later than catacomb painting, the many surviving examples give a good impression of the development of early Christian imagery. More than 2,000 sarcophagi or fragments are preserved; their original number must have been many times higher.[1] They are momentous testimonies for the Christianization of everyday life, which begins in the realm of the sepulchre. The role of laymen as the inventors of a peculiar and innovative iconography has to be stressed.

The production of early Christian sarcophagi

Early Christian sarcophagi were produced in the same way as pagan exemplars.[2] Most sarcophagi were produced on commission. This was different for children's sarcophagi, where half-finished and finished examples are known. The inscriptions of two Constantinian child sarcophagi mention that the child was buried three days after it had passed away, an interval in which it is not possible to produce a figural sarcophagus *ex novo*.[3] The nine-year-old Domitius Marinianus Florentius was buried in a half-finished sarcophagus that shows standardized elements, among them erotes (putti). The central image of the young deceased in a military costume was probably worked out on commission of his parents, because children are normally represented in "civilian" clothes.[4] The sarcophagus of the five-year-old Aurelius, *eques romanus*, is a Constantinian frieze sarcophagus; here one may assume it was already finished to a large extent and only "individualized" by a portrait on the lid.[5]

Most probably, the early Christian sarcophagi of the city of Rome were produced in numerous small workshops, a sort of bazaar industry.[6] Evidence in favor of this includes the surprisingly vast production in the Constantinian period, and the diversity and variety of individual pieces in relation to craftsmanship and elaborateness.[7] No two sarcophagi are identical. This variety in style continues throughout the fourth century until the end of production of sarcophagi in the city of Rome. Painted sarcophagi are preserved only rarely; a painted sarcophagus with bucolic images, dated about 300 CE and preserved in the Museo Pio Cristiano, is very sophisticated and adapted for the semi-darkness of a burial chamber.[8]

Figure 3.1 Fragment of an unfinished columnar sarcophagus, Rome, Catacomb of Marcellino e Pietro, second part of the fourth century (Rep. II 129). Photo: Archive Jutta Dresken-Weiland.

Due to their production, there are three distinctive features of late Roman and early Christian sarcophagi.

1. Use of unfinished relief: Beyond unfinished busts of the deceased, known from pagan sarcophagi, early Christian sarcophagi differ from earlier pagan production by using relief that is not completed or completely worked out (Figure 3.1). This phenomenon was not new and occurred a few times during the late third century, becoming frequent in the fourth century. It certainly was not financially motivated, since a sarcophagus was expensive due to the costs of the marble and transportation. In comparison to these costs the expense for the relief was much lower. Since non-finished reliefs adorn even the arch of Constantine, this phenomenon must have been aesthetically and socially accepted. It can be found throughout the fourth century.
2. The traditional production of sarcophagi is from a marble block, but in Late Antiquity a sarcophagus could also be assembled from several pieces or slabs of marble. These are skillfully put together and sealed with lead.[9] This method can also be observed on pagan, "neutral," and undecorated late Roman sarcophagi,[10] and has systematically been examined only for the city of Arles so far.[11] It seems likely that there was not enough marble for the production of sarcophagi, so the material at hand had to be used in an optimal way; maybe the popularity of marble sarcophagi in the fourth century contributed to the shortage of material. The reuse of architectural elements for sarcophagi can be observed already in the imperial period.[12]
3. Less-skilled workmanship is evident, even in pieces of high quality. For example, the figure of Paul on the upper zone of the sarcophagus of Junius Bassus, second scene from the left, is not standing steadily on his feet but slanting and nearly toppling over (see Figure 18.5).[13] On the city-gate sarcophagus of Milan the artisans obviously had difficulties fitting the

> twelve apostles in the space available on the front and back: On the front, the outermost figures are extremely slender, on the back they seem to glide from their seats.[14] No other sarcophagus of the late fourth century exhibits such a mass of figures and is so lavishly worked out on all four sides; the sculpting emphasizes the abundance of elegant details over the completion of a harmonic whole.

Roman sarcophagi were exported into the regions of modern Italy, France, and Spain from Constantinian times until the end of Roman sarcophagus production in general. In Dalmatia, only examples from the later fourth and the end of the fourth century are preserved;[15] the few sarcophagi findings in Algeria and Tunisia date from the fourth century.[16] From the East of the Roman Empire we do not have any Christian sarcophagi produced in the city of Rome.

Buyers and commissioners

The price of sarcophagi was high, and it is clear that they were a luxury good and only accessible for a well-to-do clientele.[17] Their inscriptions inform us about the names and social rank of the buyers and mark an important change: Among the early Christian sarcophagi buyers, members of the upper class can be found more often than in pagan sarcophagi in the second and third centuries. Obviously marble sarcophagi were favored by people ennobled by Constantine; as social climbers, they were intensely interested in a traditional form of sepulcher updated with Christian images.[18]

The buyers were laymen; clerics never chose marble sarcophagi with Christian reliefs for burial until the end of the fourth century. The sarcophagus of bishop Concordius of Arles, (late fourth century) is the first known example.[19] But it was, as the iconography shows, originally produced for a couple, and must have been handed over for the bishop's interment.[20] A lid fragment[21] of a . . . *pus episcopus* cannot be dated more precisely than fourth–fifth century; nothing can be said about the chest and its possible decoration.[22] For these reasons, it is clear that the iconography of these sarcophagi was invented and created by laymen.[23]

Dating, sarcophagus types, and chronology

The beginning of the production of Christian sarcophagi in the late third century can be dated by comparison with contemporary pagan sarcophagi and with dated monuments. Before this, Christians chose the same images as their pagan contemporaries. Some pagan sarcophagi are provided with a Christian inscription. The first known example is the sarcophagus of Prosenes.[24] At first, Christian images were limited to a few themes.[25] Christian images probably first appeared on the lids, whereas the chests, more difficult to produce, kept traditional images.[26] While the choice of Christian themes generally implies a positive attitude towards Christianity, the use of pagan or neutral images does not necessarily indicate a pagan buyer.[27] The relatively late appearance of Christian images on Roman sarcophagi may be explained by their highly traditional and conservative character. It took until the end of the third century, when Christianity was sufficiently widespread among a well-to-do group, before the wish arose for an adequate iconography, peculiar to this group (Figure 3.2).

The historic reliefs of the arch of Constantine (312–315), whose workshops were also active in the production of sarcophagi, are of particular importance. They mark the beginning of the most intensive period of sarcophagus production in the first third of the fourth century. Sarcophagi dated by their inscriptions are rare, see, for instance, the frieze sarcophagus of Marcia Romania Celsa in Arles who died after 328 (Figure 3.3);[28] or the columnar sarcophagus of

Figure 3.2 Frieze sarcophagus with Jonah scenes (Rep. II 7), *ca.* 300 AD, Ny Carlsberg Glyptotek, Copenhagen. Photo: Ole Haupt, with kind permission of the Ny Carlsberg Glyptotek.

Figure 3.3 Frieze sarcophagus of Marcia Romania Celsa, after 338 (Rep. III 37), Arles, Musée de l'Arles Antique. Photo: Thomas Bersy. With kind permission of the Musée départemental Arles Antique.

Junius Bassus, who passed away when serving as *praefectus urbis* in 359.[29] The city-gate sarcophagi in Tolentino and Ancona were commissioned by high-ranking officials, whose inscriptions confirm the production of this prestigious group in the 380s.[30] Another sarcophagus probably belonged to Sextus Petronius Probus,[31] rich and notorious, whose death shortly after 390 gives a *terminus post quem* or *ad quem*.

The great number of sarcophagi and fragments makes it possible to establish a dense relative chronology. Due to the activities of numerous workshops, the difference in quality, and the crudity of many objects, a cautious and approximate dating within a quarter or third of a century is adequate. Stylistic changes take place and can be described. The rectangular, compact and robust figures of the Constantinian age change at the end of the fourth century into elongated, discarnate and abstract figures, wearing clothing having ornamental lines. When describing the style of a sarcophagus for the purpose of establishing its date, several criteria should be considered: design/composition of the bodies, shapes, configuration of head and hair, proportions of body and garment, handling of the surfaces, proportions of figure, and the relationship of the figures to the background of the relief.

Frieze sarcophagi appear at the beginning of Christian sarcophagus production and are the most frequently used type. Very few sarcophagi, among them the famous the sarcophagus of S Maria Antiqua,[32] *ca.* 290 CE, combine Christian scenes with traditional bucolic elements[33] or with maritime landscapes.[34] Obviously, the buyers were not much interested in them, but opted for the frieze sarcophagus with a sequence of scenes from the Old and New Testament and the Apocrypha.

Strigillated sarcophagi, already a very frequent form in pagan sarcophagi, remain popular. They could be produced more quickly and by less specialized workmen, as only the central and the two lateral panels were decorated with figures (Figure 3.4; see also Figures 20.1 and 20.4). The production of columnar[35] and tree sarcophagi starts in the second third of the fourth century; the latter are a creation of early Christian art. The creation of these sarcophagus types coincides with the creation of private mausolea as annexes of cemeterial basilicas, where a series of them have been excavated.[36]

In the last third of the fourth century, new sarcophagus types are invented: the "stars and crowns" type, the Bethesda-type, and the city-gate sarcophagus. The "stars and crowns" sarcophagi[37] show the twelve apostles in front of a neutral background, with apocalyptic clouds and stars in its upper part. These and the hand of God, giving crowns to the apostles, indicate a situation at the end of time, when the apostles are recompensed for their deeds. In the middle of the front, the tropaion points to Christ's victory over death, his resurrection and his time-transcending sovereignty, in which the apostles take part and to which they render homage.

The Bethesda sarcophagi[38] show several healing scenes from the New Testament and therein hark back to the Constantinian frieze sarcophagi, where these scenes were popular (Figure 3.5). They may be interpreted as hope in afterlife.[39]

A single theme decorates the front of the sarcophagi with the passage of the Red Sea.[40] At the right end of the front, the Israelites have already traversed the Red Sea, while at the left half of the front the Pharaoh with his chariot and his soldiers are sinking and drowning in the flood (Figure 3.6). In the theological literature, this story is interpreted as a reference to baptism and the overcoming of death.[41]

Table 3.1 Sarcophagus types of the fourth century and their dating.

Sarcophagus type	*Dating*
Frieze sarcophagi	Entire fourth century, most examples from the first third.
Strigillated sarcophagi	Entire fourth century
Columnar sarcophagi	Second third of the fourth century to the end of the fourth century.
Tree sarcophagi	Second third to later fourth century.
"Stars and crowns" sarcophagi	Last third of the fourth century.
Bethesda sarcophagi	Last third of the fourth century.
Sarcophagi with the passage of the Red Sea	Last third of the fourth century.
City-gate sarcophagi	Last third of the fourth century.
Sarcophagi with symbols	End of the fourth/fifth century.

Figure 3.4 Fragment of a strigillated sarcophagus with Jesus between apostles in the center, end of the fourth century (Rep. II 114), Germany, private collection. Photo: Jutta Dresken-Weiland, with kind permission of the owners.

Figure 3.5 Bethesda sarcophagus, detail, healing scenes and Christ with Zachaeus, end of the fourth century (Rep. II 145), Ischia, Museo Diocesano. Photo: Jutta Dresken-Weiland, with kind permission of the Museo Diocesano.

Figure 3.6 Red Sea sarcophagus, Church of St Trophime, Arles. Photo: Mark D. Ellison.

The denomination "city-gate sarcophagi" refers to the architectural elements that are used in high relief and as a background decoration (see Figure 20.5). H. von Schoenebeck has argued against interpreting this decoration as a reference to the heavenly Jerusalem.[42] As this small and prestigious group of sarcophagi uses the "city gates" in different manners and dimensions, it is probable that they were meant as a decorative element or a sumptuous background and do not have any deeper sense.

Themes of Christian sarcophagi

Late third and first third of the fourth century

On Christian sarcophagi, the orans and the (good) shepherd are two important themes taken and reinterpreted from the earlier pagan art. Orans figures very often occupy the center of the front; they may be understood as a symbol of the soul of the deceased. As the Latin word *anima* (soul) is female, the female orans is used for women and for men. There is no difference in meaning between orans figures with ideal features, with portrait heads, contemporary hairstyles, fashionable clothing, or jewelry. Their frequency harks back to the wish of the commissioners to represent themselves in the context of images that express the hope for afterlife. Interestingly, the orans figure with raised hands is more numerous than the figures of the deceased with a scroll in their hands: The orans refers to the praying soul of the deceased who wants to represent his positive fate in the other world. Of particular interest is the figure of the orans or the deceased accompanied by two male figures (Figure 3.7). When these men perform gestures of escort and protection, these may refer to different aspects: (a) To the interim state, where the soul of the dead is protected; (b) to the escorting of the soul on its voyage after death; (c) to the arrival of the dead before Christ, maybe in the moment of judgment.[43]

The shepherd is one of the most complex and chameleonic figures of early Christianity. When it appears without Christian themes or inscriptions and without iconographic particularities, it continues the pagan tradition of the *vita felix*, the idea of a blissful afterlife. Together with the orans or figures of the dead, it expresses a personal hope of life after death; when these

Figure 3.7 Orans with apostles from the center of a strigillated sarcophagus, Barcelona, Museo d'Arquelogía di Catalunya. Photo: Jutta Dresken-Weiland, with permission of the museum.

Table 3.2 Most frequent biblical themes of Christian sarcophagi.

Frequent scenes from the Old and New Testaments and the Apocrypha on sarcophagi	*Number*	*Frequency of occurrence*
Jonah scenes	171	Late third century, first third of fourth century
Multiplication of the loaves	143	Fourth century
Healing of the blind	129	First third of fourth century
Birth of Christ/adoration of the magi	114	Fourth century
Resurrection of Lazarus	101	First third of fourth century
Peter striking water from the rocks	98	First third of fourth century
Sacrifice of Abraham	94	Fourth century
Peter with his guards	90	First third of fourth century
Christ, Peter and the cock	86	Fourth century
Daniel in the lion's den	80	Fourth century

Figure 3.8 Fragment of a sarcophagus lid with the image of a family, first third of the fourth century (Rep. I 896, Schaffer Inv. A 0004), Rome, Campo Santo Teutonico. Photo: Archive Jutta Dresken-Weiland, with kind permission of the rector of the Erzbruderschaft zur Schmerzhaften Muttergottes der Deutschen und Flamen am Campo Santo Teutonico.

are represented together with Christian scenes, this hope is a Christian one. Christ as the Good Shepherd can be recognized on some sarcophagi mainly of the later fourth century.[44]

From the late third century, images of the deceased appear in various forms and contexts on Christian sarcophagi (Figure 3.8).[45] Singular is a sarcophagus lid in New York presenting an allegory of the Last Judgment, dated about 300 CE.[46]

Among the most frequent scenes, images from the New Testament are dominant on sarcophagi. This preference of Jesus's life and deeds is distinctive to sarcophagi, as scenes from the Old Testament are generally more frequent in early Christian art. Most of the images are Christian inventions *de novo*.[47] The sequence of the scenes does not follow any rule, nor should they be addressed as "images of salvation" taken from the *commendatio animae*.[48] More simply, the choice of many images is motivated by a theological interpretation as an indication of afterlife. So Jonah is a sign of the hope of resurrection and life after death (Figure 3.2), as is Daniel and the sacrifice of Abraham.[49]

The multiplication of the loaves (Figures 3.3, 3.9) was interpreted as a symbol of the eucharist and eternal life very early on. Interestingly, both the multiplication of the loaves and the multiplication of the loaves and fishes are represented. The miracle can be operated by the imposition of the hand and by touching the food with a rod, the *virga*. Both procedures cannot be distinguished in their meaning. The transformation of water into wine at the wedding in Cana is frequently represented with the multiplication of the loaves, but does not develop a separate meaning.

The importance of the multiplication of the loaves is underlined by the fact that this image replaces the so-called sigma meal, which shows people reclining around a semicircular table. This image, very popular on sarcophagus lids of the later third century, disappears about 300 from Christian sarcophagi, probably substituted by the multiplication of the loaves. In the catacombs, where different social groups are active, the sigma meals continue to be represented.[50]

Figure 3.9 Fragment of a frieze sarcophagus with the multiplication of the loaves and fishes, first third of the fourth century. Cerveteri, Scuola materna Maria SS del Carmelo. Photo: Archive Jutta Dresken-Weiland.

A special eucharistic interpretation of the multiplication of the loaves and fishes can probably be read on the so-called "eucharistic sarcophagus" in Arles, a columnar sarcophagus of the second third of the fourth century.[51] It depicts only the multiplication with the apostles, Abraham, and Daniel as spectators, and thus gives a particular emphasis to this theme.[52]

The resurrection of Lazarus was a popular image on sarcophagi as the most direct expression of the hope for afterlife. The healing of the blind is not only the most popular of Christ's healing miracles in the New Testament, but also frequently mentioned in sermons and connected to the hope of resurrection.[53] The *virga*, or wand-like staff that is the frequent attribute of Christ when healing men or executing miracles, was not used in reference to healing in pagan iconography, but it is a genuine Christian invention.[54]

Not all frequently used themes refer to hope of afterlife. In theological texts, the birth of Christ (the nativity and the adoration) is interpreted as a soteriological event, which is the reason for the future overcoming of death. The fall of Adam and Eve has many theological interpretations with different facets, which means that the image was not used to express ideas on afterlife. The pleasure of those who produced these images to tell a spectacular story and the behavior of a couple in a moment of crisis is apparent.

The scenes "Peter walking between two soldiers" and "Peter striking water from the rocks in his prison" (Figure 3.3) refer to stories about St Peter, which were so common and famous in fourth-century Rome that nobody bothered to write them down. They are known only in outline from the later Apocrypha: Peter converts the soldiers who have arrested him and baptizes them in his cell. The scene with Christ, Peter, and the cock is another favored theme on sarcophagi, but refers to New Testament texts. This choice of Peter scenes is extraordinary and probably to be explained by the intensive veneration of Peter by the upper class, motivated by their self-conception and the self-image. Feeling themselves as the elite of Rome, they put the image of a leading figure on their marble coffins; they chose the image of the man who was venerated as the founder of the Roman community and as the successor of Christ. In St Peter's basilica, the most distinguished church in fourth-century Rome with the greatest number of sarcophagus burials, Peter is especially frequent in the images on sarcophagi. Probably persons buried in a sarcophagus depicting scenes with Peter expected from him as the prince of the apostles some help in the afterlife, and thus expressed their hope of well-being and his protection.[55] Interestingly, soldiers appear in these images, and thus reflect the contemporary reality: In fact, soldiers assumed a multitude of administrative tasks after the reorganization of the public administration in the third century and were, according to these functions, present in everyday life. Their clothing with a short tunic and a cloth cap shows their contemporary dress. The prevalence for Peter-scenes is peculiar to the Christian sarcophagi and cannot be found in this intensity in any other group of objects. It suggests that this iconography was created by a theologically educated elite.

Themes on sarcophagi since the second third of the fourth century

As indicated in Table 3.2, some themes disappear whereas others continue to be represented. There may be different reasons for this. On the one hand, the interest in images may shift for reasons we cannot fully explain from a distance of more than 1,500 years. In the second third of the fourth century, the appearance of columnar sarcophagi, which offer less space for images than the frieze sarcophagi, resulted in fewer represented themes. On the other hand, it has long been noted that in the course of time Christ the miracle worker was replaced by Christ the sovereign. The first examples of this concept are the sarcophagi with a representation of the enthroned Christ, venerated by apostles and the deceased who enshroud their faces. The oldest example, a frieze sarcophagus in Florence, belongs to the first decade of the fourth century;[56] two other pieces in Rome and Arles to the later first third of the fourth century.[57]

As to the miracle scenes, the interest shifts from the resurrection of Lazarus, only rarely represented after the first third of the fourth century, to Christ's resurrection. It appears in a fairly abstract form, a tropaion with sleeping soldiers underneath, which occupies the center of a sarcophagus front (see Figure 18.6). Tropaion and soldiers point to the resurrected Christ, who has vanquished death and whose sign of triumph is the christogram in the laurel wreath.[58] Christ or the angel with the women at the tomb is represented only rarely.[59]

Themes on sarcophagi in the last third of the fourth century

The scene *dominus legem dat* ("The Lord gives the law") is not mentioned in the New Testament. It shows Christ standing on the mountain of paradise between Peter and Paul. He raises his right hand and holds the end of a scroll in his left; the other end of the scroll is held by Peter, who carries a cross bar. This scene is often called unfoundedly *traditio legis* ("handing over of the law") because, according to the rules of ancient iconography, Christ does not hand over anything here. When handing something over, Christ (or the emperor) is portrayed sitting. On the contrary, the standing position and raised hand characterize Jesus as speaking; in imperial iconography, both elements are known from the *adlocutio*, which can be seen on the reliefs of the arch of Constantine.[60] The addendum *dominus legem dat* on a few monuments[61] should be used as its ancient name. Other meaningful components of this image are the apocalyptic elements, i.e., the mountain of paradise with its four rivers, the apostles as lambs, the lamb of God, the palms, and the Phoenix.[62] They show that the image of Christ proclaiming his message is not only a historical yet time-transcending event, but also the epiphany of the resurrected Christ at the end of time. There are different temporal levels: Christ is at the same time the historical, the future, and the present sovereign. Beyond any doubt, Peter receiving the scroll is of particular importance to the scene. Peter's cross indicates his martyrdom, the scroll his missionary work and priority. His priority falls into line with his significance on earlier Constantinian sarcophagi, but is here transformed in a new image and a new context.

The theme of the *dominus legem dat* is most frequently represented on sarcophagi from the last third of the fourth century; in other monuments, it is not documented before the middle of the fourth century.[63] As the theme appears earlier in other monuments, it cannot have been invented for sarcophagi. The most appealing hypothesis is that this iconography was invented for the apse of Old St Peter. In contrast to the widely accepted date about 350, the attribution of the apse inscription to the age of Constantine makes it possible to think of an earlier date for apse decoration.[64]

For other images characteristic of the late fourth century see Table 3.1 above and the respective commentary. As a singular image, the first known representation of the crucifixion of Jesus Christ in a Christian context has been reconstructed on a fragment of a frieze sarcophagus dating from the end of the fourth century.[65]

The location of early Christian sarcophagi

Like their pagan predecessors, Christian sarcophagi were placed in tomb buildings. Due to the fact that fewer tomb buildings were erected after the third century, only a few examples are known from such contexts.[66]

Both pagan and Christian sarcophagi could be placed outside of buildings, namely in caverns dug in the earth or in tuff, or built with bricks. Frequently, these sarcophagi were additionally protected by brickwork. A location of sarcophagi above-ground, on a pedestal or a stone platform, or in a prestigious manner near the street, is documented for only a few pieces. Inscriptions that claim the payment of a fine in the case of an unauthorized inhumation may indicate the above-ground location of a sarcophagus.[67]

Christian sarcophagi were also deposited in the new burial spaces in catacombs and in churches. Due to their dimensions, sarcophagi could be positioned only in niches near the catacombs' entrance. Alternatively, they could be placed in burial chambers situated near an entrance or a lightwell, through which the sarcophagus could be let down. The majority of the sarcophagi found in the catacombs date from the first third of the fourth century, which was also a period of intensive expansion of the catacombs. Predominant are sarcophagi with non-Christian images,[68] which illustrate the acceptance of these themes by Christian commissioners and the early origins of the catacombs. A peculiarity of the catacombs are special areas reserved for the interment of children, who were buried outside their family contexts. Such an area is known for the Praetextatus catacomb, where a chamber unites children of the noble *gentes* Insteia, Postumia, and Annia, interred in sarcophagi with inscriptions.[69] In one room of the catacomb of Novatian there were three children's sarcophagi and a fourth sarcophagus whose owner is unknown.[70] In Ponticello near S Paolo fuori le mura, three children's sarcophagi, dated to about 300, were found probably in a subterranean tomb. The sarcophagi show pagan and neutral scenes that were prevalent at this time.[71] In the catacomb of Domitilla, a third-century cubiculum with niches for the location of children's sarcophagi has been interpreted as a special burial room for children.[72] This phenomenon deserves further research.

Most Christian sarcophagi were placed in the early Christian cemetery churches, in the connecting or nearby constructed mausolea, and in the surrounding cemeteries, where they were interred very often with supplementary brickwork with concrete above them. The use of brickwork even in churches shows how much people cared to avoid the reuse of a sarcophagus, and that even a church was not necessarily a safe place to wait for resurrection. Areas of privileged burials were the apses.[73] The most sumptuous sarcophagi were found in mausolea, which were generally constructed as family graves.[74] Burials within cemetery basilicas could take place while the basilicas were still under construction.[75]

Although some sarcophagi may have been displayed openly in churches, most of them were not visible at all after the funeral, where they must have expressed the rank of the dead and the prestige of his or her family. The images were apparently directed to the deceased and were, like the inscriptions, to express his or her hope in afterlife and for community with God.

The end of sarcophagus production in the city of Rome and its reasons

The sarcophagus production in the city of Rome is assumed to have ended at the beginning of the fifth century; it is not possible to give a more exact date. The traditional opinion attributing the end of sarcophagus production to the conquest of Rome is obsolete, because the economic consequences were less serious than supposed by earlier research. The hesitant start of sarcophagus production in southwestern Gaul may indicate that at least a few sarcophagi were produced in Rome at the beginning of the fifth century. It is possible that at this time sarcophagi with "symbolic" representations with a cross in the center of the front[76] were produced because they were still exported (Figure 3.10).[77]

Probably changes in burial customs caused the end of sarcophagus production. In the course of the fourth century, burial in churches became more and more popular. In order to offer burial space, many deceased had to find their place under the pavement in graves. The grave inscription became, as the increasing number of dated tomb slabs in the course of the fourth century shows, the monuments that commemorated the deceased. From the middle of the

Figure 3.10 Sarcophagus decorated with a cross in a wreath, end of the fourth century (Rep. I 859, Schaffer Inv. A 0018), Rome, Campo Santo Teutonico. Photo: Archive Jutta Dresken-Weiland, with kind permission of the rector of the Erzbruderschaft zur Schmerzhaften Muttergottes der Deutschen und Flamen am Campo Santo Teutonico.

fourth century, metric epitaphs gain some popularity; they make use of the language of Virgil and express an interest in education and culture of well-to-do classes and aristocracy.[78] This applies to Gaul, where the importance of epigraphic grave monuments is underlined by their great quantity in the fifth and sixth centuries. Most purchasers belonged to the upper class and metrical epitaphs were so important to them that they had texts composed even for family members who had died long ago.[79]

For the city of Rome, the end of sarcophagus production with figural representations, a leitmotif of Roman art since the second century, marks an important break and a step towards the Middle Ages.

Notes

1 For example, see, with caution, the calculations by Robert Couzin, "The Christian Sarcophagus Population of Rome," *Journal of Roman Archaeology* 27 (2014): 275–303.
2 Guntram Koch, *Frühchristliche Sarkophage* (München: C. H. Beck, 2000), 72–75.
3 ICUR VII, 20373, 20422.
4 Friedrich Wilhelm Deichmann, Giuseppe Bovini and Hugo Brandenburg, *Repertorium der christlich-antiken Sarkophage, Bd 1 Rom und Ostia* (Wiesbaden: Franz Steiner, 1967), 663; Manuela Studer-Karlen, *Verstorbenendarstellungen auf frühchristlichen Sarkophagen* (Turnhout: Brepols, 2012), 47f. figs 40–41.
5 Deichmann, *Repertorium* I, 662; Jutta Dresken-Weiland, *Sarkophagbestattungen des 4.–6. Jahrhunderts im Westen des römischen Reiches* (Rome: Herder, 2003), 57, 358f.; see also *ibid.* 91 with further examples of inscriptions that indicate the days of death and burial.
6 Couzin, "Christian Sarcophagus Population," 279.
7 Jutta Dresken-Weiland, "Pagane Mythen auf Sarkophagen des dritten nachchristlichen Jahrhunderts," in *Griechische Mythologie und frühes Christentum*, ed. Raban von Haehling (Darmstadt: Wissenschaftliche Buchgesellschaft, 2005), 106–131.
8 Paolo Liverani, "Osservazioni sulla policromia e la doratura in età tardoantica," in *Il colore nel medioevo: Arte, simbolo, tecnica*, Atti delle giornate di studio, Lucca 22–23–24 settembre 2007 (Lucca: Istituto Storico Lucchese, 2009), 10–13, figs 1–8.11.
9 See, e.g., Jutta Dresken-Weiland, *Repertorium der christlich-antiken Sarkophage, Band II: Italien mit einem Nachtrag Rom und Ostia, Dalmatien, Museen der Welt* (Mainz am Rhein: Verlag Philipp von Zabern, 1998), 20 pl. 9, pl. 10.6; 102; Deichmann, *Repertorium* I, 240, 241, 681, 694, 696, 781; see also the sarcophagi from the basilica of Pope Marcus: V. Fiocchi Nicolai, "La nuova basilica circiforme della via Ardeatina," *Rendiconti Pontificia Accademia Romana di Archeologia* 58 (1995–1996): 111.
10 Dresken-Weiland, *Sarkophagbestattungen des 4.–6. Jahrhunderts*, 325 nr. A 85; 330 nr. A 89, nr. A 90; Bernard Andreae, *Die römischen Jagdsarkophage* (Berlin: Mann, 1980), 158, nr. 78, taf. 53,1.
11 V. Gaggadis-Robin, "Usage du marbre et techniques de fabrication des sarcophages d'Arles," in *Marbres et autres roches dans la Méditerranée antique: études interdisciplinaires. Actes du VIIIe colloque international de l'Association for the Study of Marble and other Stones used in Antiquity (ASMOSIA)*, ed. Phillippe Jockey (Paris: Maisonneuve and Larose, 2011), 663–675. For a few Roman examples see J. J. Hermann Jr., "Late Roman Sarcophagi in Central Italy made from Scavenged Blocks," in *Interdisciplinary Studies on Ancient Stone. Proceedings of the IX Association for the Study of Marbles and Other Stones in Antiquity (ASMOSIA) Conference*, eds A. Guttiérrez Garcia-M., P. Lapuente Mercadal and I. Roda de Llanza (Tarragona: Institut Català d'Arqueologia Clàssica, 2012), 93–103.
12 Stine Birk, "Carving Sarcophagi: Roman Sculptural Workshops and their Organization," in *Ateliers and Artisans in Roman Art and Archaeology*, eds Troels Myrup Kristensen, Birte Poulsen and Stine Birk (Portsmouth: *Journal of Roman Archaeology*, 2012), 13–37.
13 Deichmann, *Repertorium* I, no. 680.
14 Dresken-Weiland, *Repertorium* II, no. 150, pl. 60–61.
15 Dresken-Weiland, *Repertorium* II, nos. 146, 153, 219.
16 Brigitte Christern-Briesenick, *Repertorium der christlich-antiken Sarkophage, Band III: Frankreich, Algerien, Tunesien* (Mainz am Rhein: Verlag Philipp von Zabern, 2003), nos 436, 437, 593, 594, 642, 644.
17 Couzin, "Christian Sarcophagus Population," 275–284.
18 Dresken-Weiland, *Sarkophagbestattungen des 4.–6. Jahrhunderts*, 33f., 42f., 46f.

19 Christern-Briesenick, *Repertorium* III, no. 65.
20 Jutta Dresken-Weiland, Andreas Angerstorfer and Andreas Merkt, *Himmel, Paradies, Schalom: Tod und Jenseits in christlichen und jüdischen Grabinschriften der Antike* (Regensburg: Schnell and Steiner, 2012), 172–174 no. III 1.
21 Deichmann, *Repertorium* I, no. 141.
22 Dresken-Weiland, *Sarkophagbestattungen des 4.–6. Jahrhunderts*, 122, 381 nr. E 41; Jutta Dresken-Weiland, "Sarcophages épiscopaux dans l'antiquité tardive et le haut Moyen Âge," in *L'èvêque, l'image et la mort: Identité et mémoire au Moyen Âge*, eds N. Bock, I. Foletti and M. Tommasi (Rome: Viella, 2014), 37–51.
23 See Jutta Dresken-Weiland, "Zur Entstehung der frühchristlichen Kunst," *Das Münster* 65 (2014): 244–250.
24 Anne Kolb and Joachim Fugmann, *Tod in Rom: Grabinschriften als Spiegel römischen Lebens* (Mainz: von Zabern, 2008), 106–110 nr. 25; sarcophagi with Christian inscriptions are compiled in Dresken-Weiland, *Sarkophagbestattungen des 4.–6. Jahrhunderts*, 216–238.
25 See the table in Jutta Dresken-Weiland, "Bilder im Grab und ihre Bedeutung im Kontext der Christianisierung der frühchristlichen Welt," *Antiquité tardive* 19 (2011): 66, tab. 2.
26 Dresken-Weiland, "Bilder im Grab und ihre Bedeutung," 67.
27 Jutta Dresken-Weiland, "Due sarcofagi sconosciuti e la storia delle sepolture a San Pietro," *Atti del XVI congresso internazionale di archeologia cristiana* (Vatican City 2016), 915–922.
28 Christern-Briesenick, *Repertorium* III, 37, fig. 3.
29 Deichmann, *Repertorium* I, no. 680.
30 Dresken-Weiland, *Repertorium* II, no. 148 (Tolentino), no. 149 (Ancona).
31 Deichmann, *Repertorium* I, no. 678.
32 Deichmann, *Repertorium* I, no. 747.
33 Dresken-Weiland, *Repertorium* II, nos 241, 243.
34 Deichmann, *Repertorium* I, no. 35; Dresken-Weiland, *Repertorium* II, no. 7, fig. 2.
35 Jutta Dresken-Weiland, "Zwei Fragmente eines Säulensarkophags in Bonn und Berlin," *Jahrbuch für Antike und Christentum* 39 (1996): 165–169.
36 Dresken-Weiland, *Sarkophagbestattungen des 4.–6. Jahrhunderts*, 46f.
37 Koch, *Früchristliche Sarkophage*, 315f.
38 Koch, *Frühchristliche Sarkophage*, 314f.; Rep. II 31 and 32 belong to the same sarcophagus.
39 Jutta Dresken-Weiland, *Bild, Grab, und Wort: Untersuchungen zu Jenseitsvorstellungen von Christen des 3. und 4. Jahrhunderts* (Regensburg: Schnell and Steiner, 2010), 247–266; idem, translated by Jutta Dresken-Weiland as *Immagine e parola: Sulle origini dell'iconografia cristiana* (Rome: Libreria Editrice Vaticana, 2012), 196–209.
40 Koch, *Früchristliche Sarkophage*, 313f .
41 Robin M. Jensen, *Baptismal Imagery in Early Christianity: Ritual, Visual, and Theological Dimensions* (Grand Rapids, MI: Baker Academic, 2012), 20–23.
42 Hanns Ulrich von Schoenebeck, *Der Mailänder Sarkophag und seine Nachfolge* (Città del Vaticano, Rome: Pontificio istituto di archeologia cristiana, 1935), 4–10; see Rev 21:10–22:5.
43 Dresken-Weiland, *Bild, Grab, und Wort*, 51–58; Dresken-Weiland, *Immagine e parola*, 45–50.
44 E.g., Deichmann, *Repertorium* I, nos. 30, 829; Dresken-Weiland, *Repertorium* II, nos. 113, 148.
45 Studer-Karlen, *Verstorbenendarstellungen auf frühchristlichen Sarkophagen*.
46 Dresken-Weiland, *Repertorium* II, 162.
47 Robin M. Jensen, "Compiling Narratives: The Visual Strategies of Early Christian Visual Art," *Journal of Early Christian Studies* 23, no. 1 (Spr. 2015): 1–26.
48 This view was persuasively refuted by Paul Styger, *Die altchristliche Grabekunst, Ein Versuch der einheitlichen Auslegung* (Munich: J. Kösel and F. Pustet, 1927).
49 Dresken-Weiland, *Bild, Grab, und Wort*, 96–119, 233–247; Dresken-Weiland, *Immagine e parola*, 93–108, 187–196.
50 Dresken-Weiland *Bild, Grab, und Wort*, 162–213; Dresken-Weiland, *Immagine e parola*, 139–174.
51 Christern-Briesenick, *Repertorium* III, no. 61.
52 Dresken-Weiland *Bild, Grab, und Wort*, 167; Dresken-Weiland, *Immagine e parola*, 143.
53 Dresken-Weiland *Bild, Grab, und Wort*, Dresken-Weiland, *Immagine e parola*, 196–200.
54 V. Tsamakda, "Eine ungewöhnliche Darstellung der Heilung des Paralytikers in der Domitilla-Katakombe," *Mitteilungen zur Christlichen Archäologie* 15 (2009): 42f.
55 Dresken-Weiland, *Bild, Grab, und Wort*, 144–146; Dresken-Weiland, *Immagine e parola*, 125–127.
56 Dresken-Weiland, *Repertorium* II, no. 10.

57 Deichmann, *Repertorium* I, no. 241; Christern-Briesenick, *Repertorium* III, no. 32.
58 Dresken-Weiland, *Bild, Grab, und Wort*, 229–232; Dresken-Weiland, *Immagine e parola*, 183–186.
59 Deichmann, *Repertorium* I, no. 933; Dresken-Weiland, *Repertorium* III, no. 20.
60 Achim Arbeiter, *Das Mausoleum der Constantina in Rom*, Spätantike Zentralbauten in Rom und Latium 4 (Mainz:Von Zabern, 2007), 134, 146, pl. 114.
61 Arbeiter, *Das Mausoleum der Constantina in Rom*, 134, 142, 145.
62 Arbeiter, *Das Mausoleum der Constantina in Rom*, 125.
63 Arbeiter, *Das Mausoleum der Constantina in Rom*, 145f; see also G. Pelizzari, "Dominus legem dat. Le origini cristiane tra legge e leggi: La documentazione iconografica," *Lex et religio: XL incontro di studiosi dell'antichità cristiana* (Rome: Institutum Patristicum Augustinianum, 2012), 729–769.
64 P. Liverani, "Old St. Peter's and the emperor Constans: A debate with G. W. Bowersuck," *Journal of Roman Archaeology* 28 (2015) 494–496.
65 Jutta Dresken-Weiland, "A New Iconography in the Face of Death? A Sarcophagus Fragment with a Possible Crucifixion Scene in the Museo Pio Cristiano," in *The Face of the Dead and the Early Christian World*, ed. Ivan Foletti (Rome:Viella, 2013), 133–148.
66 E.g., Dresken-Weiland, *Sarkophagbestattungen des 4.–6. Jahrhunderts*, 295, no. A 2; 312, no. A 60; 325, no. A 81, 327, no. A 86; 339, no. A 110.
67 Dresken-Weiland, *Sarkophagbestattungen des 4.–6. Jahrhunderts*, 103–107.
68 Dresken-Weiland, *Sarkophagbestattungen des 4.–6. Jahrhunderts*, 107–112.
69 Lucrezia Spera, *Il complesso di Pretestato sulla via Appia: Storia topografica e moumentale di un insediamento funerario paleocristiano nel suburbio di Roma* (Rome:Vatican City, 2004), 129–131.
70 Dresken-Weiland, *Sarkophagbestattungen des 4.–6. Jahrhunderts*, 112, 176, 358f., nr. D 2.
71 Dresken-Weiland, *Sarkophagbestattungen des 4.–6. Jahrhunderts*, 325, nr. A 82.
72 L. Pani Ermini, "L'ipogeo dei Flavi in Domitilla," *Rivista di archeologia cristiana* 48 (1972): 254.
73 Dresken-Weiland, *Sarkophagbestattungen des 4.–6. Jahrhunderts*, 122; 123–125 for St Peter and S Sebastiano.
74 Dresken-Weiland, *Sarkophagbestattungen des 4.–6. Jahrhunderts*, 118–121, 125–131, 131–144, see, as an illustrative example, the mausoleum of the "Lot sarcophagus," ibid., 386 no. E 59.
75 Dresken-Weiland, "Due sarcofagi sconosciuti e la storia delle sepolture a San Pietro."
76 See Deichmann, *Repertorium* I, nos. 243, 687, 758, 859; Dresken-Weiland, *Repertorium* II, nos. 115, 160; Christern-Briesenick, *Repertorium* III, nos. 202, 276, 306, fig. 10.
77 Dresken-Weiland, *Repertorium* II, no. 160 in Catania, and three pieces in Gaul, Christern-Briesenick, *Repertorium* III, nos. 202, 276, 306.
78 Dresken-Weiland, *Himmel, Paradies, Schalom*, 80.
79 Dresken-Weiland, *Himmel, Paradies, Schalom*, 186.

Further reading

For the sarcophagi in the Museo Pio Cristiano, it is important to consult Gennaccari (1996), who, on the basis of an analysis of the account books, describes the extent of the complements and the revisions of these pieces.

Christern-Briesenick, Brigitte. *Repertorium der christlich-antiken Sarkophage, dritter Band: Frankreich, Algerien, Tunesien.* Mainz am Rhein: Verlag Philipp von Zabern, 2003.

Couzin, Robert. "The Christian Sarcophagus Population of Rome." *Journal of Roman Archaeology* 27 (2014): 275–303.

Deichmann Friedrich Wilhelm, Giuseppe Bovini and Hugo Brandenburg. *Repertorium der christlich-antiken Sarkophage, Bd 1 Rom und Ostia.* Wiesbaden: Franz Steiner, 1967.

Dresken-Weiland, Jutta. *Bild, Grab, und Wort: Untersuchungen zu Jenseitsvorstellungen von Christen des 3. und 4. Jahrhunderts.* Regensburg: Schnell and Steiner, 2010.

__________. "Bilder im Grab und ihre Bedeutung im Kontext der Christianisierung der frühchristlichen Welt," *Antiquité tardive* 19 (2011): 79–94.

__________. "Due sarcofagi sconosciuti e la storia delle sepolture a San Pietro," in *Atti del XVI congresso internazionale di archeologia* cristiana, 915–922. Rome 2013; Vatican City 2016.

__________. *Immagine e parola: Sulle origini dell'iconografia cristiana* (Italian translation of *Bild, Grab und Wort*). Città del Vaticano: Libreria Editrice Vaticana, 2012.

__________. *Repertorium der christlich-antiken Sarkophage, zweiter Band: Italien mit einem Nachtrag Rom und Ostia, Dalmatien, Museen der Welt.* Mainz am Rhein: Verlag Philipp von Zabern, 1998.

__________."Sarcophages épiscopaux dans l'antiquité tardive et le haut Moyen Âge," in *L'èvêque, l'image et la mort: Identité et mémoire au Moyen Âge*, eds Nicolas Bock, Ivan Foletti and Michele Tomasi, 37–51. Roma: Viella, 2014.

__________. *Sarkophagbestattungen des 4.–6. Jhs. im Westen des Römischen Reiches.* Rome: Herder, 2003.

Dresken-Weiland, Jutta, Andreas Angerstorfer and Andreas Merkt. *Himmel, Paradies, Schalom: Tod und Jenseits in christlichen und jüdischen Grabinschriften der Antike.* Regensburg: Schnell and Steiner, 2012.

Gennaccari, Cristina. "Museo Pio Cristiano: Documenti inediti di rilavorazioni e restauri settecenteschi sui sarcofagi paleocristiani," *Bollettino: Monumenti, Musei e gallerie pontificie* 16 (1996): 153–284.

Jensen, Robin Margaret. *Baptismal Imagery in Early Christianity: Ritual, Visual, and Theological Dimensions.* Grand Rapids, MI: Baker Academic, 2012.

__________, "Compiling Narratives: The Visual Strategies of Early Christian Visual Art." *Journal of Early Christian Studies* 23.1 (2015): 1–26.

Schumacher, Walter Nikolaus. "Dominus legem dat," *Römische Quartalschrift* 54 (1959): 1–39.

Studer-Karlen, Manuela. *Verstorbenendarstellungen auf frühchristlichen Sarkophagen.* Turnhout: Brepols, 2012.

4
EARLY CHRISTIAN SARCOPHAGI OUTSIDE OF ROME

Guntram Koch

Three main centers of sarcophagus production existed in Roman imperial times, namely Rome, Athens, and Dokimeion (Phrygia, Asia Minor).[1] In early Christian times Rome remained a center; numerous sarcophagi with Christian themes were produced there. However, in Athens and Dokimeion the production came to an end completely about 250–260 CE because of the political and economic situation.[2] Sarcophagi with Christian themes were never produced in either of those places.

When Constantine the Great became absolute monarch of the whole Roman Empire in the year 324 CE, he transferred the seat of government to the east. Byzantium was appointed as new capital and inaugurated in 330 CE as "New Rome" or "Second Rome," although it soon acquired the name "Konstantinoupolis," (Constantinople or city of Constantine, today Istanbul). Constantinople became the second center of production of sarcophagi in the empire. After the death of emperor Theodosius I in 395 CE the empire was divided between his two sons. Arcadius became emperor of the east (395–408, ruling from Constantinople), Honorius of the west. Honorius soon realized that Rome was not safe enough, and therefore preferred to reside, initially, in Milan (Mediolanum) and subsequently transferred the seat of government to Ravenna in 402 (or 408). A rather small number of sarcophagi with Christian themes is preserved in Ravenna, most of them made from Proconnesian marble. It is an open problem whether these pieces were produced in Ravenna, which would make that city the third center of production, or were for the most part imported fully executed from Constantinople, as seems more likely.

In addition to these centers, sarcophagi have been carved in many of the provinces of the Roman Empire in local workshops, but in totally different numbers and with various representations. Some pieces are spread over Italy, outside of Rome. A very large number is preserved in Gallia (France), extremely few in Germania and Belgica (Germany). A considerable number have survived in two of the three provinces of Hispania (Spain, Portugal), that is in Tarraconensis and Baetica, as well as a few pieces in the western part of North Africa.

Sarcophagi decorated only with crosses were produced in the provinces of the Balkans, Asia Minor and Syria; in these areas not even one surviving example contains figural Christian themes. Alexandria is a special case for this was the source of porphyry sarcophagi, which were destined for the emperors and their families and exported above all to Rome and to Constantinople.

The sarcophagi in Constantinople

Constantinople was inaugurated as the new capital of the Roman Empire in 330. There are no known sarcophagi with Christian themes from the first decades after this date; rather they emerge in the later fourth century, about 370–380 CE. Only one small fragment survives, made of marble, with wine scrolls and a putto gathering grapes. Although this theme is not distinctively Christian, it could have been used by Christians (about 350).[3] It is unclear whether sarcophagi were used by high-standing persons of the imperial administration, by rich landowners, or by merchants. In contrast to Constantinople, a large number of excellently carved pieces with figural scenes from the years between 330 and 380–390 survives in Rome. Thus, it is unknown how, as one example, the eastern "colleagues" of Junius Bassus, *praefectus urbi* (d. 359), were buried. Also in contrast to Rome, the few existing examples preserved in Constantinople are mostly in fragments (*ca.* 160, including the exported pieces; in addition *ca.* 20–25 examples brought to Ravenna), although whether they were destroyed or their overall numbers were rather small is not known. Among these fragments are examples of figural (frieze and columnar sarcophagi) and decorative ("symbolic") sarcophagi. In terms of quality they show substantial differences; there are few outstanding works (from marble) and a larger number of examples with modest workmanship (of limestone, with one exception of marble). Byzantium /Constantinople had no sarcophagus production tradition of its own; the sculptors seem to have immigrated from Rome or from the provinces, including from elsewhere in Asia Minor.[4]

There are several evident differences between sarcophagi from Rome and Constantinople. In Rome a sarcophagus usually is a chest with a lid. Although chests with lids were used in Constantinople as well, more frequently the container for the deceased was constructed of bricks or stones with mortar, and only the front side was a marble or limestone slab carved with figural reliefs. Thus the containers are not "real" sarcophagi, but "pseudo-sarcophagi." Sometimes these "pseudo-sarcophagi" even have acroteria.

While Rome produced frieze, architectural (columnar), and strigillated sarcophagi, strigil decoration was extremely rare in the eastern empire during the second and third century and not used at all for Christian sarcophagi. Frieze and architectural sarcophagi were known in Constantinople, but with some peculiarities, including columns or pilasters bordering the edges of the friezes. Thus the sarcophagi belong to the "Torre-Nova-Group," examples of which are totally unknown in pagan Rome or Athens.[5] These were initially produced in the third quarter of the second century only in Dokimeion (the third center of production). It is unknown why workshops in Constantinople adopted this kind of decoration for sarcophagi in the late fourth and early fifth century, after a gap of about 220 years.

Another kind of decoration was popular in Asia Minor, above all in the provinces of Bithynia and Pisidia, as well as in Thessaloniki in the second and third century.[6] The sides lack projecting borders at the lower and upper edges; instead they were surrounded by profiled frames. They appear somewhat like wooden chests, and therefore have been called "chest-sarcophagi." This kind of decoration is totally unknown in the West and in Athens, and it is typical for Asia Minor and the East. One may ask why sculptors reintroduced this century-old decoration as well in the late fourth century.

In Rome sarcophagi had, as a rule, figural decoration on at least the front side. Some examples from the late fourth and early fifth century have a cross in the middle field flanked by panels of strigils. But in Constantinople many sarcophagi are decorated just with crosses, including large and excellently carved examples. The sarcophagi of the emperors and their families have—with one exception—only crosses.

Sarcophagi in Constantinople and Rome feature approximately the same selection of biblical themes, but with differences. Scenes from the Old Testament, which were used in Rome above all in pre-Constantinian and Constantinian times, were popular in Constantinople in the late fourth and early fifth centuries. In Rome the front panels were filled with several biblical scenes, and the figures were packed closely together. But many sarcophagi in Constantinople represent only one theme, with few persons, while large parts of the background are left empty. These distinct differences enable art historians to identify even fragments as belonging to a Constantinopolitan or a Roman sarcophagus. But we do not have any hint to explain these differences.

Another problem concerns the difference between the excellent quality of marble sarcophagi in Constantinople and the roughly cut limestone pieces for which we do not find any parallel at Rome. For instance, the person who ordered the grave building near Silivri Kapı in Constantinople must have been extremely rich, but the building's limestone "pseudo-sarcophagi" with figural decorations are of a crude, low quality.[7] Comparable pieces cannot be found in Rome. Yet the marble slab with a cross, used for the sarcophagus of the owner of the grave-building, seems to be quite well executed.[8] An explanation for this situation may be that all sculptors in Constantinople who were well trained to carve marble were required to work at the large religious and secular buildings, and only in few cases did they have the time to produce a sarcophagus for a private person.

A masterwork of east-Roman sculpture is the "prince-sarcophagus" (370–380 CE), which has reliefs on all four sides and belongs to the category "chest-sarcophagi" (Figure 4.1).[9] In its time it stands alone. Marble frieze, columnar and "Torre-Nova-sarcophagi" of good quality are represented by several fragments and the slabs in Venice and Barletta, which can be dated to the decades around 400 CE. Among the fragments of limestone have been parts of sarcophagi or "pseudo-sarcophagi" with friezes (Figure 4.2), including, apparently, some double-register

Figure 4.1 "Prince-sarcophagus," 370–380 CE. Istanbul Archaeological Museum. Photo: G. Koch.

frieze sarcophagi. Other pieces feature both figural and architectural decoration (e.g., the slabs from Taşkasap and Amberliköy) (Figure 4.3).[10] These are executed rather roughly, and therefore they can be dated only approximately to the end of the fourth and the first half of the fifth century. The slabs from the tomb near the Silivri Kapı must have been carved shortly after 415 CE.[11]

Figure 4.2 Fragment of a limestone pseudo-sarcophagus with Christ entering Jerusalem, Istanbul Archaeological Museum. Photo: G. Koch.

Figure 4.3 Limestone pseudo-sarcophagus with architectural decoration and miracles of Christ, Istanbul Archaeological Museum. Photo: G. Koch.

The decorative sarcophagi—as well as the figural ones—seem to begin in the late fourth century. One of the earliest examples is made from Proconnesian marble and belongs, like the "prince-sarcophagus," to the "chest-sarcophagi."[12] In its proportions, the shape of the roof-like lid, and the acroteria, it is very similar to examples of the late second or early third century. Besides this one there exist various other decorative sarcophagi from the fifth, sixth, and early seventh centuries. The latest pieces are very low and narrow, have simple crosses as decoration, and show inside the outline of a human body with head and shoulders.[13]

In a few cases sarcophagi produced in workshops of Constantinople were exported, but only pieces made of Proconnesian marble, not those rather rough examples of limestone. They have been found, for example, in north-western and northern Asia Minor, on the island of Naxos, in Nikopolis (western Greece), in Doclea (Doljani, Montenegro) and in Massilia (Marseille).[14] Some fragments from Bithynia (north-western Turkey), and pieces in Venice, Barletta, and Trani also seem to come from Constantinople. But presumably they were not imported in the early Christian era, but in medieval times, perhaps during the Crusades of 1204 or later.[15]

In some cities in the west—Milan (Mediolanum), Marseille (Massilia), Arles (Arelate), Las Vegas de Pueblanueva (near Toledo, Spain; now in Madrid) and Ecija (southern Spain)—there are figured sarcophagi that do not have any connection with the production of Rome or with the local tradition, but show some influences from Constantinople.[16] One might add a limestone fragment, perhaps from a sarcophagus, carved in Roman Syria apparently in imitation of a sarcophagus imported from Constantinople.[17] These pieces enrich our knowledge about the production of early Christian sarcophagi in Constantinople.

Sarcophagi of the emperors and their families

A special category of sarcophagi in Constantinople are those made of colored stone and destined presumably for members of the imperial family.[18] They have only crosses as decoration (Figure 4.4). The varieties of stone used include the greenish sprinkled *marmor Thessalicum*

Figure 4.4 Porphyry sarcophagus with christogram, possibly meant for the imperial family. Istanbul Archaeological Museum. Photo: G. Koch.

(from Thessaly, Greece; "verde antico"); a reddish sprinkled stone (perhaps "puddinga di Hereke"); another reddish stone (origin not yet clarified); a black granite (from Egypt); a stone which looks like alabaster; and another type which has not yet been identified.

Most of the emperors and their wives were buried in sarcophagi in an annex of the Church of the Holy Apostles in Constantinople. Medieval sources describe the material of each sarcophagus, but it is not possible to ascribe any of the preserved pieces to a certain emperor, with two exceptions. The exceptionally large chest made of the unidentified stone may have been created for Justinian (d. 565),[19] and the example made of alabaster for Herakleios (d. 641).[20] These, however, are only presumptions. The porphyry sarcophagi, which certainly were used only for the emperors and their families, presumably were produced in Alexandria (see below).

Early Christian sarcophagi from Constantinople decorated with crosses and other ornaments were very famous still in medieval times.[21] They were represented in wall-mosaics and paintings (for example, in Constantinople and Greece), in reliefs of stone or ivory, in Bible illustrations, or in other materials. In these illustrations the sarcophagi contain various decorations. It is not known whether there was still a relatively large number of these 500–900-year-old sarcophagi visible for medieval artists to see, or if there were drawings of the sarcophagi that artists used as patterns.

The sarcophagi in Ravenna

About 35 sarcophagi with Christian decoration survive at Ravenna, dating to the period after the emperor moved his residence there from Milan in 402 (or 408?). The local production of pagan sarcophagi had ended about 260–270 CE.[22] It is clear that there was no production of sarcophagi in Ravenna in the fourth century. There are a few imports from Rome, and in some cases older local sarcophagi were recut and reused.[23] The Christian sarcophagi of the fifth century show totally new shapes and representations that do not have any connections with the styles produced in Rome or the few Christian pieces from northern Italy, nor the much older pagan examples in Ravenna or other regions in northern Italy (Figure 4.5).[24] Presumably most of the examples were imported from Constantinople fully executed, and thus they are precious works of the capital. The series began in the early fifth century with some "Torre-Nova-sarcophagi." Few figures appear in the reliefs. The back sides depict symbolic figures (lambs, stags, pigeons, or peacocks) beside a christogram. This kind of decoration spread a little bit later to the small sides and even to the front panels. A few examples of columnar sarcophagi date perhaps to a little later than the "Torre-Nova-sarcophagi," but still in the early fifth century. No figural sarcophagi date to after the middle of the firth century; thereafter only decorative ones are preserved—a pattern that corresponds exactly with Constantinople.

The later examples are much simpler. The animals seem to be carved with poor skill; there is much empty space between them. Columnar sarcophagi from this period depict only animals, crosses, and trees. These modest pieces can be dated perhaps to the rule of the Ostrogoths, thus after 493. It is uncertain whether they were imported from Constantinople or locally produced. On the few later examples of the sixth century, after the reconquest of Ravenna by the Byzantines in 540, the representations are even more simplified. The relief is totally flat, and the pieces are obviously local works. The last products were carved in the seventh century.

Figure 4.5 Marble columnar sarcophagus with Christ between St Peter, Paul, and two other apostles. Ravenna, San Francesco. Photo: G. Koch.

The sarcophagi in the provinces of the Roman Empire

There are very few sarcophagi preserved from pre-Constantinian times. They include examples in Velletri and Naples (Italy), Berlin (exported from the area of Rome), Aire-sur-l'Adour (southern France), London (origin not known),[25] and maybe Belgrade (Serbia) and Trier (Germany).[26] Two sarcophagi in Ikonion (Konya, Turkey) stand in the local pagan tradition (dating to 200 and the mid-third century), but their inscriptions indicate that they were used by Christians.[27] A few lead sarcophagi from the province of Syria (from Sidon, today southern Lebanon) may have been produced in the pre-Constantinian period.[28]

Constantinian and post-Constantinian period

Italy (outside of Rome)

A larger number of sarcophagi exported from Rome are preserved from the north to the south of Italy and over the islands of Sardinia and Sicily.[29] Additionally some local works followed prototypes from the city of Rome; the same is the case with the pagan sarcophagi of the second and third centuries.[30] A chest in Milan is presumably a local work, which copies an original from Constantinople.[31]

Gallia (France)[32]

In the Constantinian and post-Constantinian period, the provinces of Gallia remained under the influence of Rome, as they had in the second and third centuries. In this region some imports of originals from Rome and one from Constantinople are preserved,[33] in addition to numerous local works, which follow patterns of sarcophagi from Rome. One sarcophagus in Marseille and one in Arles are possibly copies of pieces from Constantinople.[34] Altogether about 580 Gallic sarcophagi are preserved, many times only in fragments. This is the largest number of sarcophagi after Rome (which has about 1,200 examples).

A considerable number of the Gallic pieces (about 250) differ from the sarcophagi in Arles, Marseille, Narbonne and other sites in Gallia Narbonensis. These examples were produced in Aquitania (south-western France) in local workshops, made with local marble (from the Pyrenees) and constitute a totally separate group. A striking characteristic of this group is the preference for variety—no two pieces have the same decoration (early fifth to early sixth centuries).[35]

Germania-Belgica (Rhine-Mosel region; Germany)[36]

Most of the sarcophagi of the Germania-Belgica region that may originate from early Christian times do not have any decoration. Only in Trier are there two examples with figural scenes. One of them, which shows Noah with his family in the ark, is totally unique in early Christian art (early fourth century).[37]

Spanish peninsula[38]

Some sarcophagi imported from Rome are preserved in the Spanish peninsula,[39] but a larger number seem to be local works, which copy examples from Rome. One example from Pueblanueva and another in Ecija are obviously imitating prototypes from Constantinople.[40] In the first half of the fifth century, several strigillated sarcophagi were imported from Carthage to Tarragona (Tarraco) and from Aquitania to northern Spain, at a time when sarcophagi from the city of Rome were no longer available.[41] In addition there are a few late pieces produced by local workshops (e.g., a piece from the Bureba in north-western Spain),[42] that contain images not found on any other sarcophagi.

Western North Africa[43]

There are relatively few finds preserved in North Africa. Some follow the style of Roman frieze sarcophagi. A small group of strigillated sarcophagi were produced in Carthage (or another city of that region?), presumably in the first half of the fifth century, using local limestone and marble imported from Proconnesus.[44] Some pieces of this group were exported to Tarragona (Tarraco).[45] An outstanding example is the marble frieze sarcophagus found in Leptis Minor (Lamta, Tunisia), which is well preserved with its lid (*ca.* 400); it must have been carved in a local workshop by sculptors who were excellently trained and probably came from Rome after production there came to an end, *ca.* 400–410 (Figure 4.6).[46] They must have produced a large number of sarcophagi, and it is a pity that only one example has survived.

Provinces of the Balkans[47]

Very few early Christian sarcophagi are preserved in the whole of the Balkans and the islands of the Aegean. This region produced a variety of sarcophagi in the second and third centuries, and in some regions such as Thessaloniki it was a rather rich production, but everywhere it

Figure 4.6 Marble frieze sarcophagus found in Leptis Minor (Lamta, Tunesia), *ca.* 400 CE. Photo: G. Koch.

came to an end soon after the middle of the third century.[48] Sarcophagi from early Christian times, beside a few particular pieces, include only the very modest pieces decorated with crosses, which were carved from local limestone on the island of Brattia (Brač, near Split) and exported in some cases even to eastern Italy.[49] An outstanding work is the "Good Shepherd sarcophagus" found in Salona, the capital of the province Dalmatia (early fourth century).[50] The images are not Christian, but the piece obviously was ordered by a wealthy Christian and used in his grave precinct in the Christian cemetery of Manastirine (Salona).

Asia Minor

Sculptors in Asia Minor produced a very large number of sarcophagi in the second and third centuries, and many local workshops and production centers can be identified.[51] The tradition came to an end soon after the middle of the third century. Very few sarcophagi in this region date to early Christian times.[52] This stands in contrast to the churches that were built in very large numbers in many regions of Asia Minor during the fifth and sixth centuries, and which were supplied with rich furnishing, floor mosaics and wall-paintings or wall-mosaics.[53] Evidently well-to-do people did not spend much money for their grave buildings and sarcophagi, but donated to churches and their furnishings. The few preserved sarcophagi are nearly all decorative ones (Figures 4.7 and 4.8). Exceptions are a few imports from Constantinople[54] and two columnar sarcophagi in Adrassos (Balabolu, "Rough Cilicia," now destroyed) with several figures; these two pieces may have been carved about 400, but they do not have Christian themes.[55]

Syria, Palaestina, and Arabia

In these regions the situation is comparable with Asia Minor.[56] In Syria a relatively large number of sarcophagi survive from the second and third centuries. One can even recognize local peculiarities typical of some of the towns (e.g., Tyrus, Sidon, Berytus [Beirut] or Tripolis).[57] Very few

Figure 4.7 Limestone sarcophagus, necropolis at Arykanda (Turkey). Photo: G. Koch.

Figure 4.8 Marble sarcophagus from Amorion, Afyon Museum, dated 591–592 CE. Photo: G. Koch.

sarcophagi survive from early Christian times, and only pieces decorated with crosses, predominantly from Syria, with exceptions from Palaestina (Israel, Palestine) and Arabia (Jordan). They are mostly disparate, idiosyncratic pieces (Figures 4.9 and 4.10).[58]

Figure 4.9 Limestone sarcophagus (now destroyed), El Bara (north-western Syria). Photo: G. Koch.

Figure 4.10 Volcanic stone sarcophagus, Qanawat (southern Syria), "Serail" (or "Saray"). Photo: G. Koch.

An unusual example in Emesa (Homs) was a half-finished marble garland sarcophagus from Proconnesus from the late second century;[59] in Emesa, probably about 432, it was totally reworked and crosses were added, to receive the bones of Mar Elian (Saint Ioulianos), a local saint of Emesa (Figure 4.11). In Kanatha (Qanawat, southern Syria) two examples made from

Figure 4.11 Marble sarcophagus of Mar Elian, reworked from a Proconnesian half-finished garland sarcophagus, dated 432 CE, Homs, church Mar Elian (St Iulianos). Photo: G. Koch.

basalt are decorated a little bit more. One piece is a pagan example, which was reused in early Christian times; the other one was produced in a local workshop for a Christian customer. A unique fragment with architectural and figural decoration is mentioned above.[60] If it was really part of a pseudo-sarcophagus, one can argue that it was not the only one produced in Syria, but that there must have been many comparable examples that are now lost. Also in early Christian times some lead sarcophagi were produced in the provinces Syria and Palaestina.[61]

Aegyptus (Egypt)

Almost nothing is known about early Christian sarcophagi in Egypt.[62] A group of painted wooden examples from early Christian times is not yet published. Some sarcophagi were modest works made of clay. It was presumably in Alexandria where the porphyry sarcophagi were carved, which are now found in Rome, Constantinople, and a few other sites.[63] Few of these contain figural decoration. The huge battle sarcophagus from the mausoleum of Helena, the mother of Constantine, in Rome (Tor Pignattara), perhaps originally was destined for emperor Constantine the Great (d. 337), and was given to Helena when he moved to the east.[64] The comparably large porphyry sarcophagus with Erotes gathering grapes stood in the mausoleum of Constantina (d. 357), the daughter of Constantine.[65] A fragment in Istanbul also shows Erotes gathering grapes.[66] Later, plain porphyry sarcophagi were used for the funerals of some of the emperors. These pieces are huge in size, feature profiles at the lower and upper border, and in several cases contain crosses in the gables of the roof-like lids.[67] There have been several attempts to assign some of these pieces to a certain emperor or another, but certain identifications seem to be impossible.[68] To provide only one example, there are some hints that the only porphyry sarcophagus preserved with rounded small sides might have been destined for the emperor Iulianus (Julian "the apostate," d. 363), but this is not at all certain.[69] Written sources mention that the sarcophagus of emperor Constantine was decorated with gilded bronze ornaments.[70] A porphyry sarcophagus in the atrium of St Eirene in Constantinople has on its lid numerous drilled holes in which bars of gilded bronze might have been fitted, but it remains uncertain whether this piece really was destined for Constantine.[71]

Notes

1 G. Koch and H. Sichtermann, *Römische Sarkophage*, Handbuch der Archäologie (München: Beck, 1982), 35–275 (Rome), 366–475 (Athens), 497–509 (Dokimeion).
2 Koch and Sichtermann, *Römische Sarkophage*, 457–460.
3 J. G. Deckers and G. Koch, eds, *Repertorium der christlich-antiken Sarkophage*, Bd. 5, Konstantinopel und das östliche Mittelmeer (forthcoming), no. 2.
4 Koch and Sichtermann, *Römische Sarkophage*, 345 f. pl. 367, 369–371; G. Koch, *Türkiye'deki Roma Imperatorluk Dönemi Lahitleri: Sarkophage der Römischen Kaiserzeit in der Türkei* (Antalya: Suna-Inan Kiraç akdeniz medeniyetleri arastirma enstitüsü, 2010), 56 f. 112, fig. 31.
5 For the "Torre-Nova-Group" see Koch and Sichtermann, *Römische Sarkophage*, 500 f.
6 Koch and Sichtermann, *Römische Sarkophage*, 350–352, 509–514 fig. 19, 544 f., fig. 23 pl. 380–381, 384–388, 526; Koch, *Türkiye'deki Roma Imperatorluk Dönemi Lahitleri*, 57 f., 63 f., 113, fig. 34, 119, fig. 51–52.
7 Deckers and Koch, *Repertorium* 5, nos 22, 31, 35, 71.
8 Deckers and Koch, *Repertorium* 5, no. 143.
9 G. Koch, *Frühchristliche Sarkophage*, Handbuch der Archäologie (München: Beck, 2000), 399–445, pl. 111–113; Deckers and Koch, *Repertorium* 5, no. 88.
10 Koch, *Frühchristliche Sarkophage*, s. Register 645, pl. 117–119; Deckers and Koch, *Repertorium* 5, nos 68–70.
11 See n. 7.
12 Koch, *Frühchristliche Sarkophage*, s. Register 645, pl. 120; Deckers and Koch, *Repertorium* 5, no. 92. Presumably it dates to the end of the fourth century, perhaps reworked from an older example.
13 Koch, *Frühchristliche Sarkophage*, 414, fig. 51.
14 Koch, *Frühchristliche Sarkophage*, 436–443; Deckers and Koch, *Repertorium* 5, nos. 147. 149–151, 154, 161, 163, 164, 171.
15 Deckers and Koch, *Repertorium* 5, nos. 167, 168, 169.
16 Koch, *Frühchristliche Sarkophage*, s. Register 641, pl. 159 (Arles); 643 pl. 187 (Ecija); 647 pl. 186 (Madrid); 648, pl. 134 (Milan); 648 (Marseille).
17 Private collection: Koch, *Frühchristliche Sarkophage*, 409 with n. 66; 573; Deckers and Koch, *Repertorium* 5.
18 Koch, *Frühchristliche Sarkophage*, 420–432 pl. 122, 123, 125 (with a list of the pieces); Deckers and Koch, *Repertorium* 5, nos. 66, 67, 94, 95, 97, 103–105, 118, 123, 132–134.
19 Koch, *Frühchristliche Sarkophage*, 426 no. 12; s. Register 646; Deckers and Koch, *Repertorium* 5, no. 134.
20 Koch, *Frühchristliche Sarkophage*, 426, no. 14; 431, fig. 54; s. Register 646; Deckers and Koch, *Repertorium* 5, no. 94.
21 Koch, *Frühchristliche Sarkophage*, 600–609, esp. 608 f.
22 Koch and Sichtermann, *Römische Sarkophage*, 283–287.
23 Koch, *Frühchristliche Sarkophage*, 379 with n. 4.
24 Johannes Kollwitz and Helga Herdejürgen, *Die ravennatischen Sarkophage*, Die antiken Sarkophagreliefs 8.2 (Berlin: Mann, 1979); Jutta Dresken-Weiland, *Repertorium der christlich-antiken Sarkophage, Band II: Italien mit einem Nachtrag Rom und Ostia, Dalmatien, Museen der Welt* (Mainz: Verlag Philipp von Zabern, 1998), 118–125 nos 376–409 pl. 108–114; Koch, *Frühchristliche Sarkophage*, 379–398 pl. 91–107; Deckers and Koch, *Repertorium* 5 (with proposals to distinguish imports from local works and for the chronology).
25 Dresken-Weiland, *Repertorium* II, 2 no. 6 pl. 2, 5; 84 f. no. 241–243 pl. 80, 1–2; 81, 1–3; Koch, *Frühchristliche Sarkophage*, s. Register 639 (Aire-sur-l'Adour), 641 (Berlin), 647 (London), 649 (Naples), 663 (Velletri) pl. 129–132, 135; Brigitte Christern-Briesenick, *Repertorium der christlich-antiken Sarkophage, Band III: Frankreich, Algerien, Tunesien* (Mainz: Verlag Philipp von Zabern, 2003), 6–8 no. 18 pl. 4, 5, 1–4.
26 Dresken-Weiland, *Repertorium* II, 130 f. no. 419 pl. 118 (Belgrade); no 420 pl. 119, 1 (Trier); Koch, *Frühchristliche Sarkophage*, s. Register 660 pl. 180 (Belgrade); 13, 549 pl. 194 (Trier).
27 Deckers and Koch, *Repertorium* 5, s.v. Konya.

28 Koch, *Frühchristliche Sarkophage*, 580–584 fig. 87; Deckers and Koch, *Repertorium* 5.
29 Koch, *Frühchristliche Sarkophage*, 368–371.
30 Dresken-Weiland, *Repertorium* II, 83–99 no. 241–296 pl. 80–93; Koch, *Frühchristliche Sarkophage*, 444–465 pl. 126–134.
31 See n. 16.
32 Koch, *Frühchristliche Sarkophage*, 466–514 pl. 135–176; Christern-Briesenick, *Repertorium* III, 1–273, nr. 1–592 pl. 1–141; see review: G. Koch, *Göttinger Gelehrte Anzeigen* 256 (2004): 179–199.
33 Koch, *Frühchristliche Sarkophage*, 371–376, 472–474; Constantinople: Deckers and Koch, *Repertorium* 5, no. 161.
34 See n. 16.
35 Koch, *Frühchristliche Sarkophage*, 501–514 pl. 165–176; Christern-Briesenick, *Repertorium* III (2003), e.g., pl. 45–50, 63 f. 105, 2–3; 106, 125–135.
36 Dresken-Weiland, *Repertorium* II, 130 f. nos 420–421 pl. 119, 1–2; Koch, *Frühchristliche Sarkophage*, 514–519, pl. 179–180.
37 See n. 26.
38 Koch, *Frühchristliche Sarkophage*, 519–535 pl. 177–188, 190, 191.
39 Koch, *Frühchristliche Sarkophage*, 376–378, 521–527.
40 See n. 16.
41 Koch, *Frühchristliche Sarkophage*, 527–529 pl. 190–191.
42 Koch, *Frühchristliche Sarkophage*, 530–533, fig. 75, 2–3, pl. 188.
43 Koch, *Frühchristliche Sarkophage*, 535–548 pl. 189–192; Christern-Briesenick, *Repertorium* III, 274–298 nos 593–650 pl. 142–156.
44 Koch, *Frühchristliche Sarkophage*, 527 f. pl. 190–192; Christern-Briesenick, *Repertorium* III, 288–293, 297 f., nos 627–638, 648–649, pl. 149, 2–8; 150, 151, 1–2.
45 See n. 41.
46 Koch, *Frühchristliche Sarkophage*, s. Register 647; Christern-Briesenick, *Repertorium* III, 293–295, no. 642, pl. 152–153; G. Koch, "Zum Sarkophag in Leptis Minor (Lamta): Ist er Import aus Rom oder eine lokale Arbeit?" *Sarkophag Studien* 6 (2012): 141–148.
47 Dresken-Weiland, *Repertorium* II, 105–117, nos 279–375, pl. 97–107; Koch, *Frühchristliche Sarkophage*, 544–557, pl. 193–195.
48 Koch and Sichtermann, *Römische Sarkophage*, 314–365 pl. 344–405; G. Koch, "Some Considerations on the Sarcophagi of Roman Imperial Times in the Provinces of the Balkans, especially Moesia Inferior", in *Cult and Votive Monuments in the Roman Provinces*, ed. C.-G. Alexandrescu (Cluj-Napoca: Mega, 2015), 359–373.
49 Koch, *Frühchristliche Sarkophage*, 550–554, pl. 204.
50 Koch and Sichtermann, *Römische Sarkophage*, s. Register 665, pl. 351; Dresken-Weiland, *Repertorium* II, 105 f., no. 297, pl. 97; Koch, *Frühchristliche Sarkophage*, 550, 552, fig. 80; s. Register 659.
51 Koch and Sichtermann, *Römische Sarkophage*, 476–557 pl. 480–550; Koch, *Frühchristliche Sarkophage*.
52 Koch, *Frühchristliche Sarkophage*, 558–571; Deckers and Koch, *Repertorium* 5.
53 E.g., G. Koch, *Erken Hiristiyan Sanati. Giriş. Türkiye'deki erken hiristiyanlik dönemi önemli merkezler ile birlikte* (Istanbul: Arkeoloji ve Sanat Yayınları, 2007), 206–319.
54 Deckers and Koch, *Repertorium* 5, nos 147, 148 (?), 149–151, 154.
55 Koch and Sichtermann, *Römische Sarkophage*, 552 f.; Koch, *Frühchristliche Sarkophage*, s. Register 539 pl. 202–203; Deckers and Koch, *Repertorium* 5.
56 Koch, *Frühchristliche Sarkophage*, 571–584; Deckers and Koch, *Repertorium* 5.
57 Koch and Sichtermann, *Römische Sarkophage*, 560–576, pl. 561–582.
58 All included in Deckers and Koch, *Repertorium* 5.
59 Koch, *Frühchristliche Sarkophage*, s. Register 645 pl. 208; G. Koch, "Zu einem frühchristlichen Sarkophag in Emesa – Homs," *Études et Travaux* 25 (2012): 132–148; Deckers and Koch, *Repertorium* 5.
60 See n. 17.
61 Koch, *Frühchristliche Sarkophage*, 580–584, fig. 87, pl. 219; Deckers and Koch, *Repertorium* 5.
62 Koch, *Frühchristliche Sarkophage*, 584–590.
63 Koch, *Frühchristliche Sarkophage*, 420–429, 584–590; Neslihan Asutay-Effenberger and Arne Effenberger, *Die Porphyrsarkophage der oströmischen Kaiser: Versuch einer Bestandserfassung, Zeitbestimmung und Zuordnung* (Wiesbaden: Reichert, 2006); see important review: R. Amedick, review of *Die Porphyrsarkophage der oströmischen Kaiser: Versuch einer Bestandserfassung, Zeitbestimmung und Zuordnung*, by Neslihan Asutay-Effenberger and Arne Effenberger, *Byzantinische Zeitschrift* 100 (2008): 823–826.

64 Koch and Sichtermann, *Römische Sarkophage*, 578, pl. 599; Koch, *Frühchristliche Sarkophage*, s. Register 663, pl. 213.
65 Koch and Sichtermann, *Römische Sarkophage*, 578 pl. 598; Koch, *Frühchristliche Sarkophage*, s. Register 663, pl. 212.
66 Koch, *Frühchristliche Sarkophage*, 423, no. 1; s. Register 645, pl. 210; Deckers and Koch, *Repertorium* 5, no. 1.
67 Koch, *Frühchristliche Sarkophage*, 423 f., nos 2–10, pl. 211; Deckers and Koch, *Repertorium* 5, nos 100–102, 111, 116, 130, 131, 145.
68 Koch, *Frühchristliche Sarkophage*, 427–429; see also the review by R. Amedick above, n. 63.
69 Koch, *Frühchristliche Sarkophage*, 424 no. 10; 428 f. fig. 52, 2; s. Register 645; Rep.V (in print) no. 11.
70 Koch, *Frühchristliche Sarkophage*, 429.
71 Koch, *Frühchristliche Sarkophage*, s. Register 646 pl. 211; Asutay-Effenberger and Effenberger, *Die Porphyrsarkophage*, 18, no. 6; s. Register 173, figs 7–9; Deckers and Koch, *Repertorium* 5, no. 130.

Further reading

The following sources include mostly works that came out after Koch, *Frühchristliche Sarkophage* (2000), or could not be considered there.

Constantinople

G. Koch, *Frühchristliche Sarkophage*. München: C. H. Beck, 2000, 399–443, pl. 108–125.
J. Deckers and G. Koch, *Repertorium der christlich-antiken Sarkophage Bd. 5: Konstantinopel und das östliche Mittelmeer*. Forthcoming.

Ravenna

J. Deckers and G. Koch, *Repertorium* V, forthcoming.
G. Koch, *Frühchristliche Sarkophage*, 379–398, pl. 95–107.
J. Kollwitz and H. Herdejürgen, *Die ravennatischen Sarkophage*, Die antiken Sarkophagreliefs 8.2 (Berlin: Mann, 1979).
E. M. Schoolman, "Reassessing the Sarcophagi of Ravenna," *Dumbarton Oaks Papers* 67 (2013): 49–74.

Italy (outside of Rome)

J. Dresken-Weiland, *Repertorium der christlich-antiken Sarkophage, Band II: Italien mit einem Nachtrag Rom und Ostia, Dalmatien, Museen der Welt*. Mainz am Rhein: Verlag Philipp von Zabern, 1998.
G. Koch, *Frühchristliche Sarkophage*, 444–465, pl. 126–134.
G. Koch, "Review of Dresken-Weiland, *Repertorium* II," *Göttinger Gelehrte Anzeigen* 252 (2000): 39–58.

Gallia

B. Christern-Briesenick, *Repertorium der christlich-antiken Sarkophage, Band III: Frankreich, Algerien, Tunesien*. Mainz am Rhein: Verlag Philipp von Zabern, 2003.
G. Koch, *Frühchristliche Sarkophage*, 466–514, pl. 135–176.
G. Koch, "Review of Christern-Briesenick, *Repertorium* III," *Göttinger Gelehrte Anzeigen* 256 (2004): 179–199.
G. Koch, "Zu einigen kaiserzeitlichen Sarkophagen in Arles: Sind sie Importe aus Rom, Athen und Kleinasien oder lokale Arbeiten?" *Sarkophag Studien* 6 (2012): 95–110.
G. Koch, "Zu einigen frühchristlichen Sarkophagen in Gallien: Sind sie Importe aus Rom oder lokale Arbeiten?" *Sarkophag Studien* 6 (2012): 111–124.

Germania - Belgica

G. Koch, *Frühchristliche Sarkophage*, 514–518, pl. 179–180.
W. Weber, "Der Holzsarg des Trierer Bischofs Paulinus († 358) – ein einzigartiger spätantiker Befund," in *Bau und Schrift. Studien zur Archäologie und Literatur des antiken Christentums für Hans Reinhard Seelinger*, eds Tinatin Khidesheli, Nestor Kavvadas and Hans Reinhard Seeliger, 39–51. Münster: Aschendorff, 2015.

Hispania

N. Büchsenschütz, *Repertorium der christlich-antiken Sarkophage Bd. 4: Iberische Halbinsel und Marokko*, forthcoming.
X. Dupré Raventos, "Il mausoleo di Centcelles e l'alveus in porfido nel Monastero di Santes Creus," in: *Centcelles: El monumento tardoromano: iconografía y arquitectura*, ed. J. Arce, 83–96. Rome: L'Erma di Bretschneider, 2002.
G. Koch, *Frühchristliche Sarkophage*, 519–535, pl. 177, 178, 181–192.
I. Rodà, "Los sarcófagos cristianos de Barcino y su material," *Sarkophag Studien* 2 (2002): 179–186.
I. Rodà, "El sarcófago de la casta Susana dentro del conjunto cristiano de Gerona," *Sarkophag-Studien* 3 (Mainz 2007): 205–213.
I. Rodà de Llanza, "Los sarcófagos cristianos importados de Cartago en Tarraco: Un inventario," in *Iconographie funéraire romaine et societé: Corpus antique, approches nouvelles?*, eds M. Galinier and F. Baratte, 193–202. Perpignan: Presses universitaires de Perpignan, 2013.
S. Vidal Álvarez, "La escultura hispánica figurada de la Antigüedad Tardía (siglos IV–VII)," *Corpvs Signorvm Romani, España* 2 (2005).

Western North Africa

B. Christern-Briesenick, *Repertorium* III, 274–298, nos. 593–650, pl. 142–156; reviewed: G. Koch, *Göttinger Gelehrte Anzeigen* 256 (2004): 179–199.
G. Koch, *Frühchristliche Sarkophage*, 535–543, pl. 189–192.
G. Koch, "Zum Sarkophag in Leptis Minor (Lamta): Ist er Import aus Rom oder eine lokale Arbeit?", in *Sarkophag Studien* 6 (2012) 141–148.
A. Ovadiah, "Symbolism in Jewish and Christian Works of Art in Late Antiquity," *Δελτίον ΧΑΕ 20* (1998): 55–63, esp. 62, fig. 11.
I. Rodà de Llanza, "Los sarcófagos cristianos importados de Cartago en Tarraco," in *Iconographie funéraire romaine et societé: Corpus antique, approches nouvelles?*, eds M. Galinier and F. Baratte, 193–202. Perpignan: Presses universitaires de Perpignan, 2013.

Provinces of the Balkans, islands of the Aegeis

I. I. Bolanakis, "Palaiochristianikes sarkophagoi tes Dodekanesou," in *Miltos Garidis (1926–1996). Aphieroma I*, eds A. Paliouras and A. Stauropoulu, 99–122. Ioannina 2003.
N. Cambi, "Sarcofagi con la croce nel centro della cassa," in *Sarkophag Studien* 2 (Mainz 2002): 47–56.
N. Cambi, "I sarcofagi della tarda antiquità in Istria e Dalmazia," in *Sarcofagi tardoantichi, paleocristiani e altomedievali. Monumenti di Antichità Cristiana*, eds F. Bisconti and H. Brandenburg, 75–96. Pontificio Istituto di Archeologia Cristiana 18, Città del Vaticano 2004.
G. Koch, *Frühchristliche Sarkophage*, 544–557. pl. 193–195.

Asia Minor

S. Durugönül *et al.*, "Adrassos'da (Isauria) Paganizm ve Hiristiyanlik Arasinda Bir Lahit," *Adalya* 16 (2013): 261–284.
G. Koch, *Frühchristliche Sarkophage*, 558–571, pl. 196–203, 220, 221.

Roman Syria and Palaestina

J. Deckers and G. Koch, *Repertorium* V.
G. Koch, *Frühchristliche Sarkophage*, 571–584, pl. 205–209, 222.
G. Koch, "Zu einem frühchristlichen Sarkophag in Emesa – Homs," *Études et Travaux* 25 (2012): 132–148.
L. Y. Rahmani, *A Catalogue of Roman and Byzantine Lead Coffins from Israel*. Jerusalem: Israel Antiquities Authority, 1999.

Alexandria

N. Asutay-Effenberger and A. Effenberger, *Die Porphyrsarkophage der oströmischen Kaiser*, reviewed: R. Amedick, *Byzantinische Zeitschrift* 100 (2007): 823–826.
G. Koch, *Frühchristliche Sarkophage*, 584–590, pl. 210–213.
E. Marin, "La tomba di Diocleziano," *Rendiconti* 78 (2005–2006): 499–526.
K. Parlasca, "Anthropoide Tonsärge für Christen: Ein Beitrag zur 'protokoptischen' Archäologie," in *Et in Arcadia Ego: Studia Memoriae Professoris Thomae Mikocki Dicata*, ed. V. Dobrowolski, 241–249. Warsaw: Uniwersytet Warszawski, 2013.

Afterlife

Koch, *Frühchristliche Sarkophage*, 600–609, esp. 608 f.
E. Jastrzebowska, "Der Sarkophag des Jaroslav in Kiev," *Sarkophag Studien* 2 (2002): 129–135.
T. Pazaras, "Die frühchristliche Tradition in der mittelalterlichen Sarkophagkunst und in gleichzeitigen Sarkophagdarstellungen," *Sarkophag Studien* 2 (2002): 167–178.

5
FREESTANDING SCULPTURE

Heidi J. Hornik

The worshipping of objects was never authorized by either Jews or early Christians. In fact, their scriptures strictly forbade it. It was once thought that Christianity was founded in the eastern Mediterranean as a mystical cult that was an offshoot of Hebraic teachings in the Old Testament and that Christians had embraced literally the second commandment: "You shall not make for yourself an idol in the form of anything in heaven above or on the earth beneath or in the waters below. You shall not bow down to them or worship them; for I, the Lord your God, am a jealous God" (Exod 20:4–5).[1] However, both Jews and Christians depicted images in mosaics on floors and walls.[2] They were neither aniconic nor iconophobic.[3] Relief sculpture is found on numerous marble sarcophagi (see Chapters 3–4) and ivory diptychs (see Chapter 13).[4] We also have a limited, but important, number of early Christian sculpted marble objects in the round and in relief.

The focus of this chapter is on select freestanding extant objects from the period *c.* 200 to 400 CE that are distinctly Christian in theme. These sculptures were not worshipped but were viewed during prayer and contemplation and utilized to comprehend the biblical narratives. Visual imagery was found in catacombs and burial places as the earliest church was virtually invisible to outsiders.[5] "The signs and symbols that early Christians chose were illative and mediated, not direct and unmediated," notes Paul Corby Finney.[6] The meaning of the fish, that its Greek letters spelled out Christ, God's son and Savior, was known to insiders, and the artisans borrowed heavily from Greek imagery.[7] The objects were not direct references to spiritual reality or spiritual truth but indirect ones, and the viewer was to look beyond the objects to the stories and reality that lay behind them.[8]

Jonah and the Good Shepherd

Early Christian art depicts narrative scenes from the Bible that are intentionally memorable. Whether it is the idea that Jonah can be swallowed by a big fish, survive within its belly or be cast out and live to tell about it, Jonah's tale is not easily forgotten. Beginning in the third century images of Jonah appeared on Christian sarcophagi and in the catacomb paintings. Joining these third-century images of Jonah in funerary art is the Jonah Marbles, a group of sculptures usually dated to the second half of the third century CE.[9] There are four symbolic sculptures depicting selected events in the book of Jonah: *Jonah Swallowed* (Figure 5.1); *Jonah Praying to God*

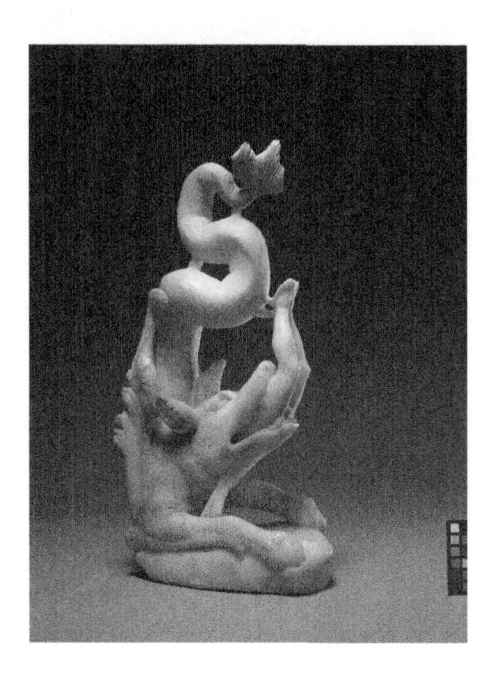

Figure 5.1 Marble sculpture of *Jonah Swallowed*, Cleveland Museum of Art, 280–290. Late Roman, Asia Minor, early Christian, 3rd century. Marble; overall: 50.3 × 15.5 × 26.9 cm (19 13/16 × 6 1/16 × 10 9/16 in). The Cleveland Museum of Art, John L. Severance Fund 1965.237.

Figure 5.2 Marble sculpture of *Jonah Praying*, Cleveland Museum of Art, 280–290. Late Roman, Asia Minor, early Christian, 3rd century. Marble; overall: 47.5 × 14.8 × 20.3 cm (18 11/16 × 5 13/16 × 7 15/16 in). The Cleveland Museum of Art, John L. Severance Fund 1965.240.

Figure 5.3 Marble sculpture of *Jonah Cast Up*, Cleveland Museum of Art, *c.* 280–290. Late Roman, Asia Minor, early Christian, 3rd century. Marble; overall: 41.5 × 36 × 18.5 cm (16 5/16 × 14 1/8 × 7 1/4 in). The Cleveland Museum of Art, John L. Severance Fund 1965.238.

Figure 5.4 Marble sculpture of *Jonah under the Gourd Vine*, Cleveland Museum of Art, 280–290. Late Roman, Asia Minor, early Christian period, 3rd century. Marble; overall: 32.3 × 46.3 × 18 cm (12 11/16 × 18 3/16 × 7 1/16 in). The Cleveland Museum of Art, John L. Severance Fund 1965.239.

Figure 5.5 Marble sculpture of the *Good Shepherd*, Cleveland Museum of Art, 280–290. Late Roman, Asia Minor, early Christian, 3rd century. Marble; overall: 49.5 × 26 × 16.2 cm (19 7/16 × 10 3/16 × 6 3/8 in). The Cleveland Museum of Art, John L. Severance Fund 1965.241.

(Figure 5.2); *Jonah Cast Up* (Figure 5.3); *Jonah under the Gourd Vine* (Figure 5.4). In addition to these four, a well-preserved *Good Shepherd* (Figure 5.5) sculpture completes the group.

These five works were acquired, along with three pairs of male and female bust portraits, by the Cleveland Museum of Art in 1965.[10] The eleven sculptures (ranging in height from 13 to 20 1/2 inches, or 33 to 52 cm) were carved from blocks of the same "white-grained, well-crystallized marble and are thought to have come from the same source in the Eastern Mediterranean."[11] Recent analysis, according to the museum, identifies the Roman Imperial quarries at Docimium in Ancient Phrygia (now Central Turkey) as the source for the marble.[12]

These quarries supplied the Roman Empire with high-quality marble in the form of unfinished blocks that were used for sculpture, paving, and veneer. The location where they were originally found remains unknown. The entire group may have been unearthed together from a large pithos, or jar.[13]

The high quality of the material and artisanship suggests that a wealthy Christian patron may have commissioned all of the sculptures and displayed the portrait busts inside the home.[14] As freestanding sculptures, the Jonah marbles are rare. The figures were probably meant to be seen from three sides, in niches, though some might have been displayed in the round.[15] Scholars debate the function of the Jonah Marbles, but recent studies argue that the group may have originally formed a domestic fountain group.[16] There are documented examples of marble sculptures in fountains, domestic and public, between 200 and 400 CE.[17] Eusebius also writes a description of "fountains in the midst of the market place graced with figures of the Good Shepherd . . . and Daniel in the Lion's Den," in his biography of Constantine.[18] In the case of both the Jonah and Daniel narratives, Christians took Jewish scripture and gave them a Christological focus. The water theme of the Jonah Marbles would have been quite appropriate to a fountain setting in a domestic garden. The gardens in this period were places where family would take meals and congregate. Fleigel also believes that the gardens were the focal point for piety in a variety of forms, so it is not difficult to imagine the Jonah Marbles in such a context.[19]

Abraham Heschel, the great Jewish scholar, pointed out that Hebrew prophets were both *foretellers* and *forthtellers*, that is, their prophetic ministry included both a predictive aspect of telling what God would do in the future (foretelling) as well as a social aspect where the prophet exposed the injustices of society (forthtelling).[20] Jonah was a reluctant prophet of God who initially rejected God's command to be foreteller and forthteller to the residents of Nineveh His disobedience led him to spend three days in the belly of a whale before he finally, though still only half-heartedly, agreed to deliver God's message to the foreigners of Nineveh.

Early Christians interpreted Old Testament prophecies and events as announcing and prefiguring the ministry of Jesus or the church. Their interpretation of the book of Jonah was inspired by Jesus' mysterious rebuke of some religious leaders demanding a prophetic sign: "You know how to interpret the appearance of the sky," Jesus warned them, "but you cannot interpret the signs of the times. An evil and adulterous generation asks for a sign, but no sign will be given to it except the sign of Jonah" (Matt 16:4). In another passage, Jesus elaborates this typology by identifying his own ministry as the fulfillment of the sign of Jonah: "For just as Jonah was three days and three nights in the belly of the sea monster [Jonah 2:1], so for three days and three nights the Son of Man will be in the heart of the earth. The people of Nineveh will rise up at the judgment with this generation and condemn it, because they repented at the proclamation of Jonah, and see, something greater than Jonah is here!" (Matt 12:40–41; cf. Luke 11:29–32).

The Christological interpretation of the Jonah story was continued in the patristic period. From the late second century forward, Christian writers extended the Jonah–Christ typology, pointing to Jonah not only as a foreshadowing of Christ's death and resurrection, but also as an assurance of the resurrection of all believers.[21] For example, around 180 CE, Irenaeus of Lyons wrote regarding Jonah's deliverance from the "great fish":

> [This was done] that man, receiving an unhoped-for salvation from God, might rise from the dead, and glorify God, and repeat that word which was uttered in prophecy by Jonah: I cried by reason of my affliction to the Lord my God, and He heard me out of the belly of hell [Jonah 2:2]; and that he might always continue glorifying God, and giving thanks without ceasing, for that salvation which he has derived from Him.[22]

Since belief in resurrection was central to Christian faith (1 Cor 15:12–19), this may partially explain why Jonah was "far and away the most popular story from the Old Testament in pre-Constantinian Christian art."[23]

In a letter to Deogratias in 409 CE, Augustine expounded further upon the Jesus/Jonah typology:

> As to the question, What was prefigured by the sea monster restoring alive on the third day the prophet whom it swallowed? Why is this asked of us, when Christ Himself has given the answer . . . As, therefore, Jonah passed from the ship to the belly of the whale, so Christ passed from the cross to the sepulchre, or into the abyss of death. And as Jonah suffered this for the sake of those who were endangered by the storm, so Christ suffered for the sake of those who are tossed on the waves of this world. And as the command was given at first that the word of God should be preached to the Ninevites by Jonah, but the preaching of Jonah did not come to them until after the whale had vomited him forth, so prophetic teaching was addressed early to the Gentiles, but did not actually come to the Gentiles until after the resurrection of Christ from the grave.[24]

And how do we explain the inclusion of the Christ figure as the Good Shepherd? One source for *The Good Shepherd* (Figure 5.5) may be the Greek *Hermes Criophorus* figure; often Hermes was shown bringing an offering to the altar, and, by the third century CE, he represented the ram bearer with its connotations of philanthropy and loving care. Its adoption by Christians would probably have passed unnoticed by pagan neighbors.[25] Another possible pagan source is Orpheus who himself is depicted as a Good Shepherd in catacomb paintings and statuettes from the third century.[26] The wild beasts that he soothes with his lyre are replaced by sheep and doves. Various reasons are given why and how Orpheus became a "purified pagan type" and a prototype for Christ as Good Shepherd.[27]

A gospel reference to Christ as "the good shepherd" appears in John (10:11–16) but the sculpture more closely echoes the passage in Luke (15:4–7), with its detail of a sheep borne upon the shoulders of a rescuing shepherd:

> Which one of you, having a hundred sheep and losing one of them, does not leave the ninety-nine in the wilderness and go after the one that is lost until he finds it? When he has found it, he lays it on his shoulders and rejoices. And when he comes home, he calls together his friends and neighbors, saying to them, 'Rejoice with me, for I have found my sheep that was lost.' Just so, I tell you, there will be more joy in heaven over one sinner who repents than over ninety-nine righteous persons who need no repentance.

The Cleveland sculpture (Figure 5.5) is one of the best preserved of the some twenty-six extant marbles depicting *The Good Shepherd*. The figure is a "type" sharing common compositional traits such as a youthful, beardless shepherd with a sheep draped over the shoulders. He wears a low-waisted tunic and holds the sheep with his left hand. His right hand grasps a crook, and he stands in a *contrapposto* position with one weight-bearing leg straight and the other bent naturally as the weight shifts. The artist surely knew of this fifth-century BCE stance made known by the Greek sculptor Polykleitos as copies were plentiful throughout the ancient world. Three small sheep and a tree trunk are visible at the base of the sculpture. The unique qualities of this work include the use of a drill to add contrast of light and dark in the hair. This is a technical element shared by all the Jonah marbles in Cleveland.

The image of God as a shepherd watching over the flock of covenant people is a popular and powerful image in the Jewish Scriptures (Gen 48:15; Ps. 23, 79, 80, 100; Isa 40:11; Jer 50:7; Ezek 34:31). The image is transferred to Jesus in early Christian writings, and is adopted as a description/title for church leadership.[28] A visual representation of Christ as the Good Shepherd bore rich meaning for the early Christians during times of persecution because it could symbolize a leader who would sacrifice his life for his flock, or Christ's salvific care for the soul in the afterlife;[29] yet, as an already popular image among non-Christians as well, it did not draw attention to the persecuted believers. Later, after the peace brought by Emperor Constantine in 306 CE, the Good Shepherd became the most popular symbol of Jesus Christ.

A youthful and beardless Christ appears in the Cleveland *Good Shepherd* (Figure 5.5) discussed above and also in the Vatican *Good Shepherd* (Figure 5.6). These two are the most frequently discussed and illustrated in the scholarship probably because of their excellent state of preservation. Although the provenance of the Vatican *Good Shepherd* is unknown, it also can be dated to the mid-fourth century. Unlike the Cleveland *Good Shepherd*, this figure wears a sleeveless tunic, or *exomis*, with cross-body purse draped over his right shoulder.[30] He stabilizes the sheep on his back with both hands to create a sense of balance and ease to the figure. The bulk of the weight is effortlessly supported by his right leg while the left bends gently in a slight *contrapposto* stance. The head is turned to his left. Robert Milburn states that the pupil of the eye is slightly off center in order to emphasize the reflective upward glance that is found in sarcophagi dating from the middle of the fourth century.[31] The striations of the *exomis* are defined yet delicate. The sheep's curls are echoed in the hair of the shepherd to contribute to a regal portrayal when compared with the clumsy and bulky drapery of the Cleveland shepherd (Figure 5.5). The Good Shepherd figures may have appeared in the center of fountains as discussed above. Another possibility is that they may have been thought useful in protecting homes from misfortune.[32]

Jonah Swallowed (Figure 5.1) and *Jonah Cast Up* (Figure 5.3) are particularly dramatic representations in marble. The artist sculpts a *ketos*, or Greek sea monster, that is part land animal and part fish.[33] Its hybridity adds to its repulsiveness. The Early Christian artist likely borrowed from the *ketea* found in Greek and Roman sculptures, wall paintings, relief sculpture, and mosaics, but found a new narrative in which the sea monster could function. The "large fish" (Jonah 1:17) is terrifying with such a monstrous body, recoiling back upon itself with its tail high above its head. This strong vertical representation, combined with the circularity of the two forms, helps us to identify the two figures as one.

Jonah within the belly of the fish is a far more difficult subject to depict. In *Jonah Praying* (Figure 5.2), the sculptor chose to show the sole figure of Jonah in the gesture of an orant, with arms outstretched and palms up, as he prays to God for deliverance. The bearded Jonah wears the same tunic as in the marble showing him under the gourd vine. The *contrapposto* stance, as seen in the *Good Shepherd* marble (Figure 5.5), invokes a figure at rest. These two pieces and *Jonah under the Gourd Vine* (Figure 5.4) convey a sense of relaxation, meditation, and prayer in contrast to the scenes with the fish that are heightened in drama and action. This alternation of action and calm reflects the biblical story and creates a narrative flow among the five marbles.

Jonah Cast Up (Figure 5.3) continues the drama of the story and repeats the bizarre form of the fish. The bearded Jonah emerges from the mouth with arms extended and a strong upper body visible. The fish can be clearly seen as the same form as in *Jonah Swallowed*. It possesses the head of a dog, wings of a bird, and the paws of a lion. The tail of the fish wraps up and

Figure 5.6 Marble sculpture of the *Good Shepherd*, Vatican Museums, first half of fourth century. Museo Pio Cristiano, Vatican Museums, Vatican State. Scala/Art Resource, NY.

over itself and almost touches the right hand of Jonah. This composition is more horizontally oriented than the vertical *Jonah Swallowed* marble (Figure 5.1). The two figures are united much like the mythological character, the centaur. The centaur has the upper body of a man and the lower body of a horse. The forceful regurgitation of Jonah indicates the power of God as Jonah is expelled from the insides of this sea monster. The force is not that of Jonah alone but rather Jonah's prayers answered by God's involvement in his situation.

In *Jonah under the Gourd Vine* (Figure 5.4), the prophet reclines and relaxes. He raises his right arm over his head. The body position recalls river god types known throughout the Greek and Roman world. Endymion, the shepherd boy in Greek mythology who slept eternally underneath a tree, may be an inspiration for this depiction of Jonah. Endymion symbolized repose, peace, and well-being; here Jonah has received peace and rests in the calm after the events of the story. Beneath a creeping gourd, Jonah contemplates the miracle of his salvation. Viewers might have seen this posture as an allusion to resurrection to a blissful state, reclining in the shade of a fertile gourd vine.

In these Jonah marbles we glimpse Christian life before its official acceptance in the Roman Empire. When, during the third and early fourth centuries, Christians were threatened by persecution and death, they found hope in the "sign of Jonah" that promised life would follow death.

The parallels between the three-day period of Jonah in the fish and Jesus in the tomb allowed these believers to understand the prophecy of Jonah in a new way, as pointing toward the resurrected Christ who is the shepherd and savior of those who believe in him.

After Christianity became an accepted religion in the Empire by the Edict of Milan in 313, artists also portrayed Christ using imperial imagery, with royal attributes such as a halo, purple robe, and throne. This type becomes known as Christos Pantocrator. A separation occurred between Jonah and Christ in the visual art and theology of Christianity. As Christ became more regal, the popularity of Jonah's story decreased significantly. Perhaps the concerns of the Christians expanded from uncertainty about their own death, which had been a very real issue during the early centuries, to the eternal kingdom of God after resurrection. The symbol of Jonah was not less important to this next generation of Christians, but Christ's triumphant rule over the secular powers became more prevalent.

Jesus brought God's prophetic message to the residents of Galilee and Judea. Unlike Jonah, Jesus was fully obedient to God's command; in the garden of Gethsemane he prayed, "Not my will but yours be done" (Luke 22:42), and this obedience led him to spend three days in the "belly of Death." Jesus' message of God's redeeming love, like Jonah's, was intended to be inclusive, inviting Jew and non-Jew alike to become people of God's kingdom (Matt 28:16–20).

Teaching figures

The marble known as *Christ Teaching* or *Cristo Docente* (Figure 5.7), whose provenance is unknown, is housed in the Museo Nazionale (Palazzo Massimo) in Rome. The youthful, beardless figure was originally known as the "seated poetess." It was initially dated to the second century based on stylistic characteristics.

The youth holds a scroll in the left hand and has effeminate, delicate features and curly hair. The soft lines and drapery contour, enveloping the body but revealing the knees beneath, all contribute to an early date. A sculptural representation of Christ as teacher without a beard in the second century is highly unlikely for a variety of reasons. The bearded philosopher is another figural type taken from Greek sources by early Christian sculptors.[34] Early interpreters may have resisted identifying this beardless Christ as a seated philosopher because beards were a typical feature of philosophers in antiquity, regardless of their particular philosophical associations. Lucian tells of the encounter between the Cynic philosopher, Demonax, and Favorinus, a eunuch philosopher. Favorinus asks Demonax which philosophical school he favors, and Demonax responds by asking how Favorinus knew he was a philosopher. When Favorinus answers he knows Demonax is a philosopher because he has a beard, Demonax chuckles at the notion that the beardless Favorinus can judge philosophers by their beards.[35]

The depiction of Christ as youthful, beardless, and curly-haired appears on many early Christian sarcophagi, including the Sarcophagus of Junius Bassus (see Figure 18.5) and the Passion-Sarcophagus in the Vatican (see Figure 18.6). These are both securely dated *c.* 360 CE and the *Christ Teaching* should be considered a contemporary work and share this dating. A youthful Christ may be a precedent to Jesus among the elders that is a popular theme across the history of Christian art. Drawing on Luke 2:41–52, the only canonical Gospel text that describes Jesus as a child, later artists used the scene to foreshadow Jesus's impending role as an adult as "Lord of the Temple."[36] Scholars now date the *Teaching Christ* to the third century, concluding that the "second century" style continues into the third century in aristocratic and religious circles.[37]

The bearded, philosopher type gets fully acculturated into Early Christian art by the late fourth century to the early fifth century, as seen in *St Peter with a Cross* (Figure 5.8) located in

Figure 5.7 Marble sculpture of *Christ Teaching*, Museo Nazionale (Palazzo Massimo), Rome, early Christian. Museo Nazionale Romano (Palazzo Massimo alle Terme), Rome. Scala/Ministero per i Beni e le Attività culturali/Art Resource, NY.

the State Museum, Berlin. It depicts Peter as the traditional Greek philosopher type. The bronze statuette is 3 11/16 inches (9.4 cm) in height and shares the same curly hair and soft drapery as the other figures discussed here. It was reportedly found in a catacomb in Rome and is dated from the late fourth to the early fifth century.[38] Peter is in a teaching pose, as is the seated Christ figure (Figure 5.7), with right hand raised in a speaking gesture. He carries a cross with its top shaped in the shape of the Greek *rho* from Christ's monogram.[39]

Another small bronze figure, also dating to the late fourth century, is the *Statuette of Saint Paul* in the Museo Archeologico Nazionale in Calgary, Sardinia. Paul, typically recognizable by his baldness and scroll, is a bearded, teaching figure. The apocryphal *Acts of Paul* 3.2 gives us a physical description of Paul that appears in repeated works of visual art beginning in the fourth century. The lower portion of Paul's legs have been broken in this depiction but it has a similar size to the *St Peter* (Figure 5.8) discussed above (3 11/16 in). The bronze was discovered in the excavations of the Christian cemetery at Cornus, Sardinia.[40] Its function is uncertain. It has been suggested that the figure may have been attached to the handle of a lamp.[41]

Figure 5.8 Bronze statuette of *St Peter with a Cross*, State Museum, Berlin, 4th–5th century CE. Bronze, 9.5 × 5 × 4.4 cm. bpk Bildagentur/Art Resource, NY.

Although there are still many unanswered questions regarding freestanding sculpture in the Early Christian period, one can examine figural types, study antique precedents, and reflect upon visual sources to formulate a fairly comprehensive understanding of the subjects, persons, and issues significant to the believers of the period.

Notes

I wish to thank my Baylor University colleagues, Dr Mikeal C. Parsons, Professor of Religion (New Testament and Early Christianity) and Dr Nathan T. Elkins, Associate Professor of Art History (Roman Art and Archeology), for their careful reading of this chapter and sharing their expertise with me.

1 James Snyder, Henry Luttikhuizen and Dorothy Verkerk, *Art of the Middle Ages*, 2nd ed., (Upper Saddle River, NJ: Prentice Hall, 2006), 3.
2 On Jewish art in antiquity, see E. R. Goodenough, *Jewish Symbols in the Greco-Roman Period*, 13 vols (New York, NY: Pantheon Books, 1953–1968); more recently, Rachel Hachlili, *Ancient Jewish Art and Archaeology in the Diaspora* (Leiden: Brill, 1998); idem, *Ancient Jewish Art and Archaeology in the Land of Israel* (Leiden: Brill, 1988).

3 Steven Bingham, *Early Christian Attitudes Towards Images* (Rollinsford, NH: Orthodox Research Institute, 2004), 1–2.
4 For this author's commentary on the Junius Bassus sarcophagus (Figure 18.5) and the Munich *Ascension* ivory diptych (Figure 23.1), see Heidi J. Hornik, "The Influence of the Junius Bassus Sarcophagus on Italian Renaissance Art," in *"Let the Reader Understand": Essays in Honor of Elizabeth Struthers Malbon*, ed. Edwin Broadhead (London: Bloomsbury Press, forthcoming 2018); Heidi J. Hornik and Mikeal C. Parsons, *The Acts of the Apostles Through the Centuries* (Oxford: Wiley Blackwell Bible Commentaries, 2016), 22–23.
5 William A. Dyrness, *Visual Faith. Art, Theology, and Worship in Dialogue* (Grand Rapids, MI: Baker Academic, 2001), 26.
6 Paul C. Finney, *The Invisible God: the Earliest Christians on Art* (Oxford: Oxford University Press, 1994), 291.
7 Finney, *The Invisible God*, 293.
8 Dyrness, *Visual Faith*, 27.
9 Earlier versions of the Jonah marbles discussion appeared in Heidi J. Hornik, "The Sign of Jonah?" in *Christian Reflection: A Series in Faith and Ethics*, V. 6, Prophetic Ethics (Waco, TX: The Center for Christian Ethics at Baylor University, 2003), 54–59; Heidi J. Hornik and Mikeal C. Parsons, "Art," in *The Blackwell Companion to the Bible and Culture*, ed. John Sawyer (Oxford: Blackwell Publishing, 2006), 299–322, 300–305.
10 Cleveland Museum of Art Object Files, reviewed April 5, 2017. Special thanks to Amanda Mikolic, Curatorial Assistant for Medieval Art, Cleveland Museum of Art, for allowing me to consult the museum's object files on all of the Jonah Marbles. The references included in this chapter are relevant and germane. They are a small representation of the voluminous scholarship published on the Jonah Marbles. For information related to the location of the marble, see the unpublished thesis by Donald A. McColl, *Early Christian Sculptures at Cleveland in Their Eastern Mediterranean Context* (Master's thesis, Oberlin College, 1991) and "Signs of the Times: The Cleveland Marbles, *Dumbarton Oaks Research Library and Collection*, accessed June 18, 2017, www.doaks.org/research/support-for-research/fellowships/reports/2006-2007/mccoll.
11 William D. Wixom, "Early Christian Sculptures at Cleveland," *The Bulletin of the Cleveland Museum of Art* (March, 1967): 67–88; Wolfgang Wischmeyer, "Die vorkonstantinische christliche Kunst in neuem Licht. Die Cleveland-Statuetten," *Vigiliae Christianae* 35.3 (1981): 253–287.
12 Cleveland Museum of Art Object Files, reviewed April 5, 2017.
13 Stephen N. Fliegel, *A Higher Contemplation. Sacred Meaning in the Christian Art of the Middle Ages* (Kent, OH: The Kent State University Press, 2012), 19.
14 Snyder *et al.*, *Art of the Middle Ages*, 5.
15 Wixom, "Early Christian Sculptures at Cleveland," 75.
16 Fliegel, *A Higher Contemplation*, 23, 191.
17 For more on this, see Brenda Longfellow, *Roman Imperialism and Civic Patronage: Form, Meaning, and Ideology in Monumental Fountain Complexes* (Cambridge and New York, NY: Cambridge University Press, 2011); Elisabeth Blair MacDougall and Wilhelmina F. Jashemski, eds, "Ancient Roman Gardens," *Dumbarton Oaks Colloquium on the History of Landscape Architecture, VII* (Washington, DC: Dumbarton Oaks, 1981); Elisabeth Blair MacDougall, ed., "Ancient Roman Villa Gardens," *Dumbarton Oaks Colloquium on the History of Landscape Architecture,* × (Washington, DC: Dumbarton Oaks, 1987).
18 Eusebius, *The Life of Constantine*, Book 3, XLIX, accessed April 27, 2017, https://sourcebooks.fordham.edu/basis/vita-constantine.asp.
19 Fliegel, *A Higher Contemplation*, 23.
20 Abraham J. Heschel, *The Prophets*, 2 vols (New York, NY: Harper & Row, 1962), I: xii.
21 See, e.g., Irenaeus, *Against Heresies* 3.20.1; 5.5.2; Tertullian, *On the resurrection of the flesh* 58; *Apostolic Constitutions* 5.7.12.
22 Irenaeus, *Against Heresies*, 3.20.1, trans. Ante-Nicene Fathers 1:450.
23 Everett Ferguson, "Jonah in Early Christian Art: Death, Resurrection, and Immortality," in *Text, Image, and Christians in the Graeco-Roman World: A Festschrift in Honor of David Lee Balch*, eds Aliou Cissé Niang and Carolyn Osiek (Eugene, OR: Pickwick, 2012), 342.
24 Augustine, *Epistle* 102, 34, accessed April 29, 2017, www.newadvent.org/fathers/1102102.htm.
25 Fliegel, *A Higher Contemplation*, 20.

26 See Janet Huskinson, "Some Pagan Mythological Figures and Their Significance in Early Christian Art," in *Papers in the British School at Rome*, V. 42 (1974): 68–97, esp. 69–73.
27 See also John Black Friedman, "Syncretism and Allegory in the Jerusalem Orpheus Mosaic," in *Traditio*, V. 23 (1967), pp. 1–13; *idem*, *Orpheus in the Middle Ages* (Cambridge, MA: Harvard University Press, 1970).
28 E.g., Matt 2:6, 26:31; John 10:1–16; Luke 15:3–7; Heb 13:20; Acts 20:28–29; 1 Pet 5:2–4; Clement of Alexandria *Stromata* 1.26.169; John Chrysostom *In Matthaeum*, Homily 77.6.
29 See Robin M. Jensen, *Understanding Early Christian Art* (London: Routledge, 2000), 39.
30 Robert Milburn, *Early Christian Art and Architecture* (Berkeley and Los Angeles, CA: University of California Press, 1988), 80.
31 Milburn, *Early Christian Art and Architecture*, 80–81, fig. 48. (The quotation by Milburn is on p. 80; the photo of the *Good Shepherd* statuette being discussed is fig. 48 on p. 81.)
32 Milburn, *Early Christian Art and Architecture*, 80.
33 John Boardman, "'Very Like a Whale' – Classical Sea Monsters," in *Monsters and Demons in the Ancient and Medieval Worlds*, eds Ann E. Farkas, Prudence O. Harper and Evelyn B. Harrison (Mainz am Rhein: Philipp von Zabern, 1987), 73–84.
34 See Paul Zanker, *The Mask of Socrates: The Image of the Intellectual in Antiquity* (Berkeley, CA: University of California Press, 1995).
35 Lucian, *Demonax* 13.
36 See Heidi J. Hornik and Mikeal C. Parsons, "Jesus Among the Doctors: A Visual Exegesis of Luke 2:41–52 in Select Italian Renaissance Paintings," book chapter in *Anatomies of the Gospels and Early Christianities* (New York, NY, and the Netherlands: Brill Academic Press, forthcoming 2018).
37 Robert Milburn, *Early Christian Art and Architecture*, 80.
38 Kurt Weitzmann, ed., *Age of Spirituality: Late Antique and Early Christian Art, Third to Seventh Century* (New York, NY: Metropolitan Museum of Art, 1979), 571–572.
39 Weitzmann, *Age of Spirituality*, 571–572.
40 Jeffrey Spier, ed., *Picturing the Bible. The Earliest Christian Art* (New Haven, CT, and London: Yale University Press and the Kimbell Museum of Art, 2007), 240, fig. 62.
41 Spier, *Picturing the Bible*, 240.

Further reading

An early study of the figure of Christ in sculpture is Friedrich Gerke, *Christus in der spätantiken Plastik* (Mainz: F. Kupferberg, 1948). William D. Wixom's lead article on the Cleveland marbles, "Early Christian Sculptures at Cleveland," *Bulletin of the Cleveland Museum of Art* 54.3 (1967): 65–88, was followed a decade later by Ernst Kitzinger's article "The Cleveland Marbles," which appeared in the Acts of the *Congrès international d'archéologie chrétienne* 9.1 (1978): 653–675, and later in *Art, Archaeology, and Architecture of Early Christianity*, edited by Paul Corby Finney (New York: Garland, 1993), 117–139. While Wixom had proposed that the sculptures may have come from a family mausoleum, Kitzinger argued against a funerary context. Some of the latest thinking on early Christian freestanding sculpture can be found in Katherine Marsengill's article, "The Christian Reception of Sculpture in Late Antiquity and the Historical Reception of Late Antique Christian Sculpture," *Journal of the Bible and its Reception* 1.1 (2014): 67–101. Marsengill nuances interpretation of the late antique transition from three-dimensional portraits to panel paintings, discusses the few freestanding sculptures of biblical subjects, cites textual evidence of now-lost early Christian statues, and presents an intriguing argument for identifying small bronze statuettes of Peter, Paul, and other saints as objects of veneration that late antique Christians placed in household shrines in continuation of ancient traditions of domestic ritual.

6

CHRISTIAN WALL MOSAICS AND THE CREATION OF SACRED SPACE

Sean V. Leatherbury

While the medium of mosaic, formed of small pieces, or tesserae, of stone, brick and sometimes glass, was employed extensively by the Romans to decorate the floors of elite private houses and public buildings, wall mosaics only began to be produced on a large scale beginning in the fourth century CE.[1] Roman artists had begun to explore the potential of walls as zones for figural mosaic by the first century CE, most famously in the houses of the cities of Pompeii and Herculaneum, as well as in baths and imperial dwellings, including the emperor Nero's notorious Golden House (*Domus Aurea*).[2] Other Roman buildings certainly bore wall mosaics, but the early story of the medium is difficult to reconstruct, as the walls of most Roman buildings have collapsed over the intervening centuries, eliminating our access to their decoration.

Once the emperor Constantine legalized the Christian religion in the early fourth century, the medium appears to have become more popular than it had been previously, perhaps driven by the construction of monumental basilicas in Rome, Constantinople, and elsewhere, sponsored by Constantine and his sons.[3] The emergence of wall mosaic as a major art form signaled the decline, though not the death, of *opus sectile* wall decoration, composed of marble pieces cut into shapes to create figural and floral or geometric motifs on the interior walls of buildings, as some of the last great extant works in the medium, such as the panels of the Basilica of Junius Bassus in Rome, date to the fourth century.[4] Though mosaic was by far the more popular art form chosen for the prestige churches and chapels of the empire, it also did not wholly replace Roman traditions of wall painting, which were adapted as a vehicle for Christian images in catacombs as well as churches. While painting and mosaic programs were related in terms of their style and imagery, mosaics had particular effects on, and meanings for, their viewers because of their materials, typically glass tesserae and, especially in the later fifth and sixth centuries, gold-glass tesserae.

Walls as spaces for images

A major reason for the rise of walls and ceilings as zones for decoration was the new need for an adorned interior space appropriate for the Christian liturgy. The rituals associated with Greco-Roman pagan traditions typically took place outside of the god's temple, in the surrounding sacred precinct (*temenos*) and next to the sacrificial altar.[5] The Christian liturgy, however, required participants to enter and remain inside the church to take part in rites. Because of this, the walls and ceilings of church interiors became essential spaces for the display of figural images. The majority of early Christian wall mosaics are found in the interiors of sacred buildings, but some also appeared on the façades of churches. Few traces of façade mosaics survive, though textual evidence indicates that major churches did occasionally feature mosaics on their exteriors, including the church of Hagios Polyeuktos, built in Constantinople by the noblewoman Anicia Juliana in the early sixth century, whose façade bore a mosaic of the baptism of Constantine.[6]

From their beginnings, the schemes of early Christian wall mosaics appear to have been indebted to cycles of images used for the decoration of the floors of buildings. A third- or early fourth-century mosaic that survives from the Mausoleum of the Julii, located underneath St Peter's Basilica in Rome, depicts a haloed figure riding into the sky in a chariot, a figure that may represent an early version of Christ whose iconography is derived from images of the Greco-Roman sun god Helios/Sol, often found in a similar format on pavement mosaics (Figure 6.1).[7] In Rome, the figure appears in a funerary context with other "Christian" scenes (e.g., Jonah and the sea creature or *ketos*), on a golden background, revealing artists actively adopting Roman imagery for use in new Christian contexts.[8]

The wall mosaic program of Santa Costanza in Rome is one of the earliest surviving programs to reveal the influence of schemes from floor mosaics. The rotunda, located outside of the city walls within the complex of the church of Sant'Agnese, was built in the mid-fourth

Figure 6.1 Mosaic with haloed chariot rider, perhaps Christ as Helios/Sol, ceiling of Mausoleum M (of the Julii) beneath St Peter's Basilica, Rome. Scala/Art Resource, New York.

century as a mausoleum for Constantine's daughter, Constantina. The vaulted ceiling of the circular passageway bears traces of later restorations, but preserves much of its original decorative scheme: putti harvesting grapes for winemaking, floral/vegetal motifs, and images of luxury objects (silver and gold vessels, crowns) strewn about on a white ground (Figure 6.2).[9] These panels most likely derive their formats, with their multiple perspectives, from those of floor mosaics, which require the viewer to walk around them in order to see the motifs head-on.[10] The artists who produced the mosaic panels created a lush environment for worship and for the remembrance of Constantina, mosaics that could be read as images of earthly wealth and privilege—the precious metal vessels, taken from the sphere of elite dining and bathing—as coded symbols of Christ and his self-proclaimed status as the "true vine" (John 15:1), or as allusions to salvation and the afterlife.

While the passageway vault derives its format and imagery from the repertory of floor mosaics, other spaces in Santa Costanza were decorated with different types of images. The dome over the central rotunda originally bore a complex program in which scenes from the Old and New Testaments were framed by large, elaborate plant candelabra, decorative motifs that emphasized the upward stretch of the dome towards its apex. The dome mosaics no longer survive, but the scheme is preserved in early modern watercolors that suggest that the biblical images were combined with classical motifs, including caryatids, a Nilotic scene with putti rowing boats, and extensive vegetal decoration.[11]

Images of Christ in two different aspects appear in the two smaller apse conches off the circular passageway: as a triumphant young man standing on a hill from which the four rivers of paradise flow, handing an unrolled scroll to the apostle Peter, with Paul appearing to his other side (Figure 6.3); and as an older bearded figure seated on the globe of the world, handing a

Figure 6.2 Mosaic with putti harvesting grapes for wine and floral/vegetal motifs, ceiling of Mausoleum of Santa Costanza, Rome. Sean V. Leatherbury.

Figure 6.3 Apse mosaic with a young Christ handing a scroll to Peter, with Paul appearing to his other side, Mausoleum of Santa Costanza, Rome. Sean V. Leatherbury.

scroll to an apostle.[12] Influenced by earlier images of Christ among his apostles in catacomb paintings and in other media such as gold-glass, the mosaicists created scenes that celebrate Christ's relationship with his most important disciples (the scene of Christ giving the law to Peter, the so-called *traditio legis*) and cast him as the central figure to whom viewers' prayers should be addressed.[13] These two types of images—biblical narrative scenes in the dome, and iconic images of Christ in the apses—reveal the range of functions that wall mosaics had in Christian interiors: narrative scenes could act as educational images for viewers, teaching or reminding the faithful of important episodes in the Bible,[14] and images of the most important figures in the heavenly hierarchy such as Christ could serve as channels for personal and communal devotion. Both types of more explicitly "Christian" scenes also had important aesthetic functions, as their glass and metallic tesserae highlights created a brilliant backdrop for worship, whose blue and green hues produce a garden-like setting that may have evoked a vision of paradise for the viewer.[15]

Development of popular images

As we have seen previously, the mosaics of Santa Costanza showcase fourth- and fifth-century artists exploring the use of different types of images in different spaces within the building. Over time, as the basilica became the primary architectural form for the church, the curved vault over the main apse, also called the apse conch, became the primary space for sacred images due to its location within the church interior, at the east end of the church over the main altar. As a cultic space—that is, a liturgical space, the setting for the celebration of the eucharist—the apse was a primary zone for the display of powerful images of Christ, the Virgin Mary, and the saints that may have been ill suited for other zones in the church, especially the floor.[16]

Like that of early Christian wall mosaics generally, the story of the development of apse imagery is also one with many gaps, heavily inflected by accidence of survival. In addition, virtually all extant wall mosaics are *in situ* in living, functioning churches, and have been restored many times over the intervening centuries, so their iconography and style must be considered with caution.[17] Art historians have tended to treat western and eastern apse mosaics as belonging to entirely separate traditions, as mosaics from churches in the western regions of the empire, especially Italy, tend to depict Christ interacting with saints and, occasionally, with the patron of the building, while the few extant apse mosaics from churches in the east (Greece, Egypt) often show Christ appearing in more miraculous contexts, often referred to as theophanies.[18] However, though eastern and western mosaics reveal different influences at work, the traditions intersected at different points as groups of mosaicists shared motifs with each other, traveled and saw mosaics firsthand, or perhaps as pattern-books circulated between groups of artists. This influence most often appears to have moved from east to west, as artists working in Italy began to include theophanic elements such as the four creatures (lion, ox, eagle, and winged man), symbols of the four evangelists but also of Christ's return at the end of time as described in the Book of Revelation.[19]

Unfortunately, one of the earliest western apse mosaics, the early or mid-fourth-century mosaic from the church of Old St Peter's in Rome, does not survive, as the church was replaced in the sixteenth century by the church at the heart of the Vatican complex today. However, drawings made of the apse during the Renaissance provide at least an idea of what the early Christian program may have been, though they reflect thirteenth-century restorations.[20] Strikingly, these drawings reveal an image not dissimilar to those in the small apses of Santa Costanza: Christ stands between the apostles Peter and Paul within a paradisiacal landscape setting, on a hill from which the four rivers of paradise flow, while below runs a band with twelve lambs (representing the apostles) processing out of the holy cities Bethlehem and Jerusalem towards a central lamb, the Lamb of God. The small apse mosaics of Santa Costanza, as well as those of other later apses in Rome and elsewhere, may have been influenced by the Old St Peter's mosaic, an influence that makes sense given the importance of its setting, in the largest new church built by Constantine and his sons in the old imperial capital.[21] Alternatively, the Santa Costanza mosaics may reflect a more complicated artistic development involving a larger set of ideas from the sphere of Christian funerary art.[22]

Whatever its source, this Christocentric program continued to loom large in the minds of mosaicists and their patrons in the city of Rome, as the sixth-century apse mosaics of Santi Cosma e Damiano in the old Roman Forum reveal. In this later mosaic, commissioned in 526–530 by Pope Felix IV, a golden-robed Christ floats in a fiery sky, but is still flanked by Peter and Paul, who introduce the titular saints Cosmas and Damian and the patron, Felix, to him; below the apse conch runs another band of lambs processing towards the Lamb of God (Figure 6.4).[23] These compositions emphasized Christ's status as heavenly ruler, though using visual cues, including costumes, slightly different from those used in representations of Roman emperors.[24] Similar compositions continued to be popular in Rome in the ninth century and beyond, allowing papal donors to connect themselves to their early Christian predecessors through wall mosaic commissions.[25]

In other fourth- and fifth-century churches in Italy, Christ appeared in a range of guises as artists experimented with different visual strategies. In the apse of the church of Santa Pudenziana in Rome, executed around 400, the image of Christ instructing his disciples, a popular one in fourth-century catacomb paintings, has been transported to an urban setting that may represent the heavenly kingdom of Jerusalem over which Christ will reign after the Second Coming (Figure 6.5).[26] Above his head hover the four creatures mentioned previously, as well as a

Figure 6.4 Apse mosaic with golden-robed Christ flanked by Peter and Paul, saints Cosmas and Damian, Pope Felix, St Theodorus, and processing lambs, church of Sts Cosmas and Damian, Rome. Scala/Art Resource, New York.

monumental jeweled cross that stands on the hill above Christ, perhaps a visual reference to the golden cross set up on the hill of Golgotha in Jerusalem by the emperor Theodosius, connecting the church to the holiest city in Christendom.

Other images of Christ instructing his disciples transplant this scene to alternate settings. In one of the late fourth- or early fifth-century apses of the chapel of Sant'Aquilino in Milan, Christ sits surrounded by his twelve apostles, who are arranged in a semicircle around him.[27] This arrangement emphasizes his relative importance within the composition, but instead of stressing his status as a heavenly ruler, as does the Santi Cosma e Damiano mosaic, it highlights his role as teacher, a role made clear by his gesture and by the presence of a basket filled with scrolls at his feet (*capsa*). The inclusion of a gold background transports the scene from a realistic setting to a heavenly one, encouraging viewers to see Christ as a simultaneously accessible and distant divine teacher.

In the period, Christ also appeared in more symbolic guises, as in the early fifth-century mosaic in the pilgrimage church of Nola, near Naples in Italy. The mosaic does not survive, but its iconography was described by the bishop who renovated the church, Paulinus: in the apse, the Trinity is represented by a central cross surrounded by a wreath, with Christ depicted as a lamb, the Holy Spirit as a dove, and the voice of God the Father, most likely invisible in the mosaic itself, is described as descending from above, perhaps represented as a downward-reaching hand.[28] While a more abstracted scheme, this mosaic reveals the influence of ideas present already in the mosaics of Old St Peter's and Santa Costanza, including the presence of the Lamb of God.

Though Christ featured prominently in church apses, especially in Rome, other figures in the heavenly hierarchy also made appearances. After the Council of Ephesus in 431, at which

Figure 6.5 Mosaic with enthroned Christ instructing his disciples before a cityscape, apse of Santa Pudenziana, Rome. Scala/Art Resource, New York.

the Virgin Mary was proclaimed the bearer of God (*Theotokos*), the Virgin began to appear more prominently in church mosaics. In the fifth-century mosaics of the church of Santa Maria Maggiore in Rome, dedicated to Mary herself, the Virgin may have appeared in the apse originally, though we cannot be sure; the current apse mosaic of the coronation of the Virgin by Christ, purportedly based on the early Christian original, was created by the artist Jacopo Torriti in the thirteenth century.[29] Whatever the original image in the apse, Mary does appear in the mosaics of the church's triumphal arch, the arch-shaped zone above the apse, where she is presented as an imperial figure, dressed in the costume of a Byzantine queen during the Annunciation. Viewers may have connected Mary's costume to the extra-biblical myth of her royal descent, as well as to her newly elevated theological status.

In the sixth century, the Virgin took pride of place in the apse of the church, in the churches of Kiti and Lythrankomi on Cyprus,[30] and in the Basilica of Eufrasius at Poreč (Figure 6.6).[31] In Poreč, she appears as she often does in sixth-century and later mosaics, dressed in a simple but richly colored purple robe, seated on a throne and holding the Christ-child in her lap. Rather than telling a specific story, as do the mosaics of the Annunciation and the Visitation on the side walls of the apse, the apse mosaic presents an iconic image of Christ and his mother surrounded by angels, saints, and donors, including the local bishop, Eufrasius. In the sixth century and afterwards, images of saints continue to grow in popularity in church interiors, exemplified by the seventh-century apse mosaic of the church of Sant'Agnese fuori le mura in Rome, in which St Agnes appears in the center against a golden ground, flanked only by two papal donors.[32]

Figure 6.6 Apse mosaic with the Virgin holding the Christ-child in her lap, Basilica of Eufrasius at Poreč. Cameraphoto Arte, Venice/Art Resource, New York.

Unfortunately, very few wall mosaics survive in churches in the eastern provinces of the empire. While these mosaics share many similarities with those in western churches, they tend to illustrate miraculous appearances ("theophanies") of Christ and other figures in the heavenly hierarchy more frequently. Extant mosaics from Greece, Cyprus, Egypt (Sinai), and Constantinople reveal the popularity of the gold ground, seen in the Poreč apse, which peaked in the sixth century.[33] A series of mosaics from Thessaloniki in Greece showcases different mystical appearances of Christ and the saints: the fifth-century vault mosaics of the church of Hagios Georgios (St George), a rotunda originally built by the emperor Galerius, depict a series of saints standing in front of monumental architectural façades on a heavenly gold ground,[34] while the late fifth- or sixth-century apse mosaic of Hosios David (St David) shows Christ appearing in a halo of light, surrounded by the four creatures and apostles, perhaps related to the apocalyptic imagery of the Book of Revelation.[35] By depicting visions of Christ and the saints, these mosaics construct a distance between the viewer and the figures depicted, encouraging worshippers to perceive a distance between the space of the physical church and the heavenly space of the images.[36]

While the apse was the key focal point in the church, images also adorned the walls of the nave and sanctuary. The lengthy expanses of the walls of the naves of churches in Rome, including Old St Peter's, were perfect zones for narrative cycles of images drawn from the Old and New Testaments.[37] While these paintings do not survive, an extensive program of mosaics decorates the nave walls of the church of Santa Maria Maggiore, depicting Old Testament scenes and featuring important biblical figures, most notably Moses, who was seen by early Christians as a precursor, or type, of Christ. Framed in separate panels, these mosaics include large numbers of figures that are difficult to make out from the nave: for example, a panel with Moses, Aaron, and Hur fighting against the Amalekites, a nomadic people who settled in the Negev Desert (Exodus 17), presents a busy scene in which Moses and his companion stand on a hilltop facing the massed Amalekite soldiers (Figure 6.7).[38] Impressionistically rendered, with alternating shades of white, blue, yellow, and orange tesserae used to differentiate parts of figures and create a sense of illusionism and motion, this panel is quite different from the sixth-century wall mosaics of churches in Ravenna, including the sanctuary wall mosaics of San Vitale, with its reduced cast of characters, in which an isolated Moses receives the law from the hand of God, while above the evangelist Luke holds an open copy of his Gospel (Figure 6.8).[39] In this panel,

Figure 6.7 Mosaic with Moses, Aaron, and Hur above the battle of the Israelites and Amalekites, nave wall, Santa Maria Maggiore, Rome. Nimatallah/Art Resource, New York.

which reveals a much greater focus on the mountainous landscape in which Moses and Luke appear, the scenes have broken out of their strict square-paneled organization, stretching over more of the wall, while the outlines and contour lines of the figures are emphasized, breaking Moses' body into different planes and foreshadowing the stylistic move towards increasing abstraction seen in the later sixth and seventh centuries.[40]

Seeing and reading wall mosaics

Tracing the changing images found in early Christian wall mosaics reveals evolving concepts of the nature of sacred images and spaces. However, Christian viewers did not view these works of art in isolation, but as part of the living fabric of the buildings to which they were attached. In the past decade, scholars have begun to consider the reception of mosaics as multifunctional artworks situated in sacred spaces. These new approaches give us additional insight into the

Figure 6.8 Mosaic with Luke the evangelist and Moses receiving the law, San Vitale, Ravenna. Sean V. Leatherbury.

different ways in which mosaics acted as powerful images within the context of early Christian religious life.

The relationship between mosaic images and the texts inscribed next to them was an important one. While images such as those that decorate the walls of Santa Maria Maggiore in Rome could act as "books for the illiterate,"[41] wall and apse mosaics were sometimes paired with inscribed texts that served to guide viewers' experiences and interpretations of these works of art. No surviving mosaic cycle is paired with inscriptions, often referred to as "titles" (*tituli*), but cycles of these typically short verse inscriptions are preserved through textual transmission.[42] What is most interesting about these "titles" is that they do not typically offer novel theological interpretations of the scenes, but instead turn static, two-dimensional mosaics into active works of art by emphasizing the actions and movements of key characters in the scene. Apse mosaic inscriptions do survive *in situ* in greater numbers, especially in Rome. These texts, frequently written in verse either below or above the apse conch, praise Christ, saints, and the patrons of the church, their golden letters explicating the connection between the material and spiritual realms that worshippers were encouraged to perceive in the glittering church interior.[43]

Wall mosaics also inspired lengthier verbal responses in the form of literary descriptions (*ekphraseis*). These descriptions, frequently performed out loud by the poet within the very church he purports to describe, are not particularly useful for the reconstruction of lost mosaic programs, but can tell us a great deal about the reception of early Christian works of art.[44] One of the most frequently described monuments in the period is Hagia Sophia, Justinian's great church in Constantinople, whose golden mosaics inspired sixth-century authors such as Procopius and Paul the Silentiary to compose lengthy *ekphraseis*.[45] These descriptions do not dwell on the details of the geometric patterns of the mosaics, which appear to have been non-figural in the period, but instead convey the wonder that viewers must have felt when entering the church for the first time. Perceived according to their brightness rather than their hue,[46] the mosaics encourage the eye to move around the building, embracing the shimmering golden tesserae that makes the church seem like a kind of heaven on earth, urging viewers to use the reflected light in the interior to contemplate the invisible light of the divine.[47]

The images and texts of wall mosaics not only reinforced each other, but also emphasized the ritual and lived dimensions of the mosaics. In particular, mosaics with images of donors were experienced by early Christian viewers very differently than they are by modern viewers today. While we may tend to use donor images to clarify the historical specifics of the church's construction, these images were in fact powerful visual arguments about the donor and his or her connection to the heavenly hierarchy and, by extension, his or her power and influence.[48] Donors often appeared in the apses of western churches, including the apse of the Basilica of Eufrasius at Poreč, and in eastern wall mosaics, as in the late sixth- or early seventh-century pier mosaics of the church of St Demetrios at Thessaloniki, where two donors who were still alive (as indicated by their square haloes) are embraced by Demetrios, emphasizing their intimacy with the saint (Figure 6.9).[49] The style of this panel is radically different from that of fifth- and sixth-century mosaics in Italy, and reveals changing aesthetic tastes in the period, most importantly an emphasis on spiritual bodies instead of physical ones: so Demetrios' tunic and cloak hang straight down from his shoulders, as if his body has lost all of its physical form.

In their arrangements and their details, mosaic images and texts worked to encourage specific mental and physical responses, allowing lay as well as clerical viewers to connect their own experiences to the actions of Christ and the saints. The poses of biblical figures or saints

Figure 6.9 Pier mosaic with St Demetrios flanked by donors, church of St Demetrios, Thessaloniki. Image in the public domain, courtesy of The Yorck Project, Wikimedia Commons.

in mosaics might encourage congregants to adopt similar poses: for example, worshippers in the sixth-century church of Sant'Apollinare in Classe, just outside of Ravenna, could adopt the same orant pose of prayer as St Apollinaris does in the apse, connecting their bodies to that of the saint.[50] Similarly, pilgrims to the Monastery of St Catherine on Mount Sinai could structure their experience in the church through its apse and triumphal arch mosaics, which lead viewers on a visual (and spiritual) ascent that parallels Moses' ascent up Mount Sinai itself, depicted on the triumphal arch, as well as the companion scene in the apse, the apostles witnessing the Transfiguration.[51] This connection between art and ritual actions in church is perhaps most clear in the context of baptisteries, whose walls and vaults often depict scenes related to the ritual of baptism. In the Neonian (Orthodox) Baptistery at Ravenna (Figure 6.10), the mosaic images and texts work together to structure the initiate's experience of the ritual: the golden texts on the lower zone of the walls describe certain parts of the ritual, connecting the initiate's experience to that of Christ's baptism in the River Jordan,[52] while the images in the dome above illustrate Christ's baptism, surrounded by a ring of processing apostles who award crowns to Christ and to the newly baptized initiate.[53]

Figure 6.10 Mosaic illustrating Christ's baptism encircled by processing apostles, dome of Neonian (Orthodox) Baptistery of Ravenna. Sean V. Leatherbury.

Making wall mosaics

Closely examining how early Christian patrons and viewers looked at wall mosaics—as beautiful and educational images, as guides for ritual action—is essential to understanding how they functioned within their spatial contexts. However, we must also consider how these works of art were made. Wall mosaics were produced in multiple stages, beginning with the preparation of the "ground" with two or three layers of lime plaster of increasing fineness.[54] Once the ground was prepared, an under-drawing (*sinopia*) was often made to guide mosaicists in setting the initial tesserae. Traces of surviving under-drawings give us a sense of artists at work revising their compositions. In the course of the restoration of the apse mosaic of the sixth-century church of Sant'Apollinare in Classe, outside of Ravenna, in the late 1940s and early 1970s, restorers found that the under-drawing beneath the mosaic differed from the final composition: instead of depicting a cross flanked by two figures, as in the underdrawing, the scene was reorganized to emphasize its vertical axis, placing the patron saint of the church, Apollinaris, immediately underneath the golden cross floating in the sky, highlighting his role as intercessor on the congregation's behalf.[55] Sometimes the plaster ground was painted more fully to emphasize tesserae colors: for example, gold tesserae were often set into a red-painted plaster ground to heighten their reddish gleam.[56] Once the under-drawing was made, multiple artists would work on the program at once from scaffolding set up inside the building.[57] Tesserae were set into their bedding carefully, taking into account their material properties: glass tesserae were often set in at an angle to maximize their reflective capabilities.[58]

The materials of wall mosaics changed dramatically in the later fourth and fifth centuries. While earlier fourth-century mosaics such as those of Santa Costanza were made primarily of stone tesserae, later fourth- and fifth-century mosaics feature increasing numbers of glass and gold and silver tesserae, creating the glittering effect for which early Byzantine mosaics are now famous.[59] Wall mosaics of glass and metallic tesserae were not new in the fourth century, but became much more common from the late fourth century onwards. The mosaics of the highest quality that survive from the fifth century, including those of the "Mausoleum" of Galla Placidia (actually a small chapel) and the Orthodox Baptistery in Ravenna, are made almost entirely of glass tesserae, with mother of pearl as the sole non-glass material used for small but significant details.[60]

Through their glazed materials, these programs testify to the great amounts of money spent on the decoration of these buildings by Placidia, noblewoman of the Theodosian house, and by the clergy in Ravenna. In the sixth century, mosaicists in Italy and the surrounding region appear to have begun to use other materials, such as stone and brick, more liberally, especially white marble (for faces and backgrounds) and pink limestone (for faces).[61] However, glass remained the main material for wall mosaics, with stone and other materials used to supplement glass, or to replace glass if the required shades were difficult to produce or acquire (especially opaque white) or perhaps if money was tight. For example, the mosaics of two of the side apses of the Basilica of Eufrasius in Poreč, both of which depict Christ and saints, are made almost entirely of stone tesserae, suggesting that mosaicists ran out of glass tesserae while producing the mosaics of the main apse and triumphal arch.[62] In the same period, mosaicists begin to reuse glass and stone tesserae to a much greater extent than they had previously, sometimes cutting tesserae down to the size required, or alternatively melting down older glass to create new tesserae.[63]

In the past two decades, archaeologists and art historians have begun to study the make-up of early Byzantine glass in more detail. Scholars have begun to test the glass tesserae with which wall mosaics were made in order to get a sense of their chemical composition, and have constructed a database of glass mosaics in recorded archaeological finds of loose glass tesserae and references in primary texts to wall mosaics. Both efforts have yielded important insights. The glass used to produce wall mosaics was of the soda-lime-silica variety common in the Roman period, produced in furnaces using large quantities of natron (mineral soda) and silica, derived from sand. The production of raw glass in the period was centered in the Levant (modern Syria, Lebanon and Israel/Palestine) and Egypt, close to readily available sources of raw materials.[64] After the raw glass was produced, glassworkers needed to add elements to the glass to make it opaque (often manganese, antimony or tin) and color it: for example, the addition of cobalt produced deeper shades of blue glass, while copper was used to create light blue or green glass.[65] It is unclear whether these secondary processes were performed near the sites at which raw glass production occurred, or if they were undertaken near the job sites, the buildings themselves, though finds of tesserae from locations such as Sagalassos in modern Turkey suggest that secondary glass workshops sometimes were located at sites not far from the buildings in which the mosaics were to be installed.[66]

The work of Liz James and her team has placed these scientific findings into an art historical and trans-Mediterranean context, supplementing extant *in situ* wall mosaics with fragmentary archaeological and textual evidence.[67] James' work, for example, has shown that while gold tesserae were expensive, the amount of gold foil necessary to produce them was extremely small, allowing even village churches to feature mosaics with golden backgrounds.[68] Wall mosaics decorated not just the most significant churches in the major cities of the empire, but also small and "apparently insignificant" churches in small cities and towns.[69] James' database, as well as recent archaeological reports and museum catalogues, has drawn attention to fragments of wall mosaics that survive from a number of sites in the eastern Mediterranean.

While technical studies of mosaics can provide important information about stages of production and restoration, we still know almost nothing about the names, identities, and organization of the mosaicists themselves. A reference in the Edict of Maximum Prices issued by the emperor Diocletian in 301 indicates that different types of mosaicists were paid at different rates for their work: *tessellarii* could earn up to 50 denarii per day, while *musearii* were paid up to 60. However, it remains unclear whether these two terms referred to wall mosaicists (*musearii*) and floor mosaicists (*tessellarii*) or to specialists in different types of figural or decorative work.[70] Scholars have proposed a variety of models for the organization of mosaicists, from workshops based in major cities of the empire (Rome, Constantinople, Alexandria) to itinerant teams of mosaicists that moved from site to site. It continues to be impossible to identify the origins of mosaicists that executed the major programs of churches in Rome, Ravenna, and Constantinople, just as it remains difficult to link the wall mosaics of early Islamic monuments such as the eighth-century mosaics of the Great Mosque in Damascus to specific groups of mosaicists, who perhaps traveled to Syria from Constantinople, Alexandria, or another location, and who may themselves have been Christian.[71]

Notes

1 Frank Sear, *Roman Wall and Vault Mosaics* (Heidelberg: F. H. Kerle, 1977); Liz James, "Successors of Rome? Byzantine Glass Mosaics," in *Neighbours and Successors of Rome: Traditions of Glass Production and Use in Europe and the Middle East in the Later First Millennium* AD, eds Daniel Keller, Jennifer Price and Caroline Jackson (Oxford: Oxbow, 2014), 128–136.

2 Sear, *Roman Wall and Vault Mosaics*, 90–92; Katherine M. D. Dunbabin, *Mosaics of the Greek and Roman World* (Cambridge: Cambridge University Press, 1999), 240–241.

3 Wall mosaics continued to be used in domestic and funerary contexts as well, as in the dome mosaics of the mausoleum at Centcelles in Spain, which feature a mix of scenes drawn from Christian and Roman iconographic traditions: see, e.g., Javier Arce, ed., *Centcelles. El monumento tardorromano: iconografía y arquitectura* (Rome: "L'Erma" di Bretschneider, 2002).

4 Giovanni Becatti, "Edificio con opus sectile fuori Porta Marina," in *Scavi di Ostia VI: La basilica di Giunio Bassio sull'Esquilino* (Rome: La Libreria dello Stato, 1969), 181–215. *Opus sectile* does feature in some Christian buildings into the sixth century, including the Basilica of Eufrasius in Poreč, on the coast of modern-day Croatia: see Ann Terry, "Opus Sectile in the Eufrasius Cathedral at Poreč," *Dumbarton Oaks Papers* 40 (1986): 147–164.

5 Some temples, including mithraea (temples to the god Mithras), did feature wall mosaics from the second century onwards: see Sear, *Roman Wall and Vault Mosaics*, cat. nos 112–118.

6 Christine Milner, "The Image of the Rightful Ruler: Anicia Juliana's Constantine Mosaic in the Church of Hagios Polyeuktos," in *New Constantines: The Rhythm of Imperial Renewal in Byzantium, 4th–13th Centuries. Papers from the Twenty-sixth Spring Symposium of Byzantine Studies, St Andrews, March 1992*, ed. P. Magdalino (Aldershot, UK: Ashgate Variorum, 1994), 73–82.

7 Dunbabin, *Mosaics of the Greek and Roman World*, 249–250.

8 Thomas F. Mathews, *The Clash of Gods: A Reinterpretation of Early Christian Art* (Princeton, NJ: Princeton University Press, 1993).

9 Henri Stern, "Les mosaïques de Sainte-Costance à Rome," *Dumbarton Oaks Papers* 12 (1958): 160–218; James, "Successors of Rome?"

10 Dunbabin, *Mosaics of the Greek and Roman World*, 248–249.

11 Allan Doig, *Liturgy and Architecture: From the Early Church to the Middle Ages*, (Aldershot, UK: Ashgate, 2008), 40–41.

12 The date of these two mosaics is debated, as both have been restored since their original installation in the late fourth or early fifth century: see David J. Stanley, "The Apse Mosaics at S. Costanza," *Römische Mitteilungen* 94 (1987): 29–42; Herbert Kessler, "Bright Gardens of Paradise," in *Picturing the Bible: The Earliest Christian Art*, ed. Jeffery Spier (Fort Worth, TX: Kimbell Art Museum, 2007), 115.

13 For opposing views on the development and meaning of this scene, see Walter N. Schumacher, "Dominus Legem Dat," *Römische Quartalschrift* 54 (1959): 1–39; Jean-Michel Spieser, *Autour de la Traditio Legis*

(Thessaloniki: Hypourgeion Politismou, Ephoreia Vyzantinōn Archaiotētōn, 2004); Robert Couzin, *The Traditio Legis: Anatomy of an Image* (Oxford: Archaeopress, 2015); Armin F. Bergmeier, "The *Traditio Legis* in Late Antiquity and Its Afterlives in the Middle Ages," *Gesta* 56. 1 (Spring 2017): 27–52.

14 Herbert Kessler, "Pictures as Scripture in Fifth-Century Churches," *Studia Artium Orientalis et Occidentalis* 2 (1985): 17–31.

15 Kessler, "Bright Gardens of Paradise."

16 Beat Brenk, *The Apse, The Image, and the Icon: An Historical Perspective of the Apse as a Space for Images* (Wiesbaden: Reichert, 2010).

17 For examples of restorations in Rome, see the diagrams in Guglielmo Matthiae, *Mosaici medioevali delle chiese di Roma*, 2 vols (Rome: Istituto Poligrafico dello Stato, 1967); recent examinations include Cetty Muscolino, Antonella Ranaldi and Claudia Tedeschi, *Il battistero Neoniano: uno sguardo attraverso il restauro* (Ravenna: Longo Angelo, 2011).

18 Christa Ihm, *Die Programme der christlichen Apsismalerei vom vierten Jahrhundert bis zur Mitte des achten Jahrhunderts* (Wiesbaden: Steiner, 1960); Christa Belting-Ihm, "Theophanic Images of Divine Majesty in Early Medieval Italian Church Decoration," in *Italian Church Decoration of the Middle Ages and Early Renaissance: Functions, Forms, and Regional Traditions*, ed. William Tronzo (Bologna: Nuova Alfa Ed, 1989), 43–59; Jean-Michel Spieser "The Representation of Christ in the Apses of Early Christian Churches," *Gesta* 37 (1998): 63–73.

19 Belting-Ihm, "Theophanic Images." On other theophanic imagery in sixth-century churches in Rome, see Armin F. Bergmeier, "Anleitung zum Sehen. Göttliche Visionen in den Apsismosaiken von SS. Cosma e Damiano, Sant'Apollinare in Classe und Hosios David," *Millenium, Jahrbuch zu Kultur und Geschichte des ersten Jahrtaustends nach Chr.* 11 (2014): 187–238.

20 Spieser, *Autour de la Traditio Legis*; Erik Thunø, *The Apse Mosaic in Early Medieval Rome: Time, Network, and Repetition* (Cambridge: Cambridge University Press, 2015), 31–32, 35–36.

21 Walter N. Schumacher, "Eine römische Apsiskomposition," *Römische Quartalschrift* 54 (1959): 137–202.

22 Spieser, *Autour de la Traditio Legis*, 67–69.

23 Ihm, *Die Programme der christlichen Apsismalerei*, 5–41, 137–138.

24 Mathews, *Clash of Gods*, whose work critiques that of André Grabar, *L'empereur dans l'art byzantin* (Paris: Les Belles Lettres, 1936).

25 Thunø, *Apse Mosaic.*

26 Ihm, *Die Programme der christlichen Apsismalerei*, 130–132, 153–155.

27 Ibid., 5–10, 158–159.

28 Dennis Trout, *Paulinus of Nola. Life, Letters, and Poems* (Berkeley and Los Angeles, CA: University of California Press, 1999); Tomas Lehmann, *Paulinus Nolanus und die Basilica Nova in Cimitile/Nola. Studien zu einem zentralen Denkmal der spätantik-frühchristlichen Architektur* (Wiesbaden: Reichert, 2004).

29 Beat Brenk, *Die frühchristlichen Mosaiken in S. Maria Maggiore zu Rom* (Wiesbaden: Steiner, 1975); Spieser, "Representation of Christ," 72 n. 19.

30 Spieser, "Representation of Christ," 70.

31 Ann Terry and Henry Maguire, *Dynamic Splendor: The Wall Mosaics in the Cathedral of Eufrasius at Poreč*, 2 vols (University Park, PA: Penn State University Press, 2007).

32 Thunø, *Apse Mosaic*, 24–27; on images of the saints generally, see Ann Marie Yasin, *Saints and Church Spaces in the Late Antique Mediterranean: Architecture, Cult, and Community* (New York, NY: Cambridge University Press, 2009).

33 On gold-ground mosaics, see Dominic Janes, *God and Gold in Late Antiquity* (Cambridge: Cambridge University Press, 1998), 105–139.

34 Laura Nasrallah, "Empire and Apocalypse in Thessaloniki: Interpreting the Early Christian Rotunda," *Journal of Early Christian Studies* 13 (2005): 465–508; Bente Killerich and Hjalmar Torp, *The Rotunda in Thessaloniki and Its Mosaics* (Athens: Kapon Editions, 2016).

35 Laura Nasrallah, "Early Christian Interpretation in Image and Word: Canon, Sacred Text, and the Mosaic of Moni Latomou," in *From Roman to Early Christian Thessalonikē: Studies in Religion and Archaeology*, eds Laura Nasrallah, Charalambos Bakirtzis and Steven J. Friesen (Cambridge, MA: Harvard Theological Studies, 2010), 361–396.

36 Spieser, "Representation of Christ," 70–71.

37 Jean-Michel Spieser, "Le décor figure des edifices ecclésiaux," *Antiquité Tardive* 19 (2011): 95–108.

38 Hans Peter L'Orange and Per Jonas Nordhagen, *Mosaics from Antiquity to the Middle Ages*, trans. A. E. Keep (London: Methuen, 1966), 64–65; Brenk, *Die frühchristlichen Mosaiken.*

39 Friedrich W. Deichmann, *Ravenna, Hauptstadt des spätantiken Abendlandes*, Vol. 1, *Geschichte und Monumente* (Wiesbaden: Steiner, 1969).

40 Otto Demus, *Byzantine Mosaic Decoration: Aspects of Monumental Art in Byzantium* (London: Routledge, 1948); Ernst Kitzinger, *Byzantine Art in the Making, Main Lines of Stylistic Development in Mediterranean Art, 3rd–7th Century* (Cambridge, MA: Harvard University Press, 1977).
41 Herbert Kessler, "Pictures as Scripture."
42 Arwed Arnulf, *Versus ad Picturas. Studien zur Titulusdichtung als Quellengattung der Kunstgeschichte von der Antike bis zum Hochmittelalter* (Munich: Deutscher Kunstverlag, 1997).
43 Thunø, *Apse Mosaic*; Sean V. Leatherbury, "Reading and Seeing Faith in Byzantium: The Sinai Formula as Verbal and Visual 'Text'," *Gesta* 55.2 (2016): 133–156.
44 Liz James and Ruth Webb, "'To Understand Ultimate Things and Enter Secret Places': Ekphrasis and Art in Byzantium," *Art History* 14 (1991): 1–17.
45 Nadine Schibille, *Hagia Sophia and the Byzantine Aesthetic Experience* (Farnham, UK: Ashgate, 2014); Bissera Pentcheva, *Hagia Sophia: Sound, Space, and Spirit in Byzantium* (State College, PA: Penn State University Press, 2017).
46 Liz James, *Light and Colour in Byzantine Art* (Oxford: Oxford University Press, 1996).
47 Schibille, *Hagia Sophia*; Kessler, "Bright Gardens of Paradise."
48 Jean-Pierre Caillet, "L'image du dédicant dans l'édifice cultuel (IVe–VIIe s.): aux origins de la visualisation d'un pouvoir de concession divine," *Antiquité Tardive* 19 (2011): 149–170.
49 Robin Cormack, "The Mosaic Decoration of St. Demetrios, Thessalonica: A Reexamination in Light of the Drawings of W. S. George," *The Annual of the British School at Athens* 64 (1962): 17–52.
50 Glenn Peers, *Sacred Shock: Framing Visual Experience in Byzantium* (University Park, PA: Penn State University Press, 2004), 27–34.
51 Jaś Elsner, "The Viewer and the Vision: The Case of the Sinai Apse," *Art History* 17 (1994): 81–102.
52 Robin M. Jensen, "Poetry of the Font: Inscriptions in Early Christian Baptisteries," *Acta ad archaeologiam et artium historiam pertinentia* 24, n.s. 10 (2011): 65–83.
53 Annabel Jane Wharton, "Ritual and Reconstructed Meaning: The Neonian Baptistery in Ravenna," *Art Bulletin* 69 (1987): 358–375.
54 L'Orange and Nordhagen, *Mosaics from Antiquity*, 56–57; Robin Cormack, "Wall-Paintings and Mosaics," in *The Oxford Handbook of Byzantine Studies*, eds Robin Cormack, John F. Haldon and Elizabeth Jeffries (Oxford: Oxford University Press, 2008), 385–396.
55 Deborah Mauskopf Deliyannis, *Ravenna in Late Antiquity* (Cambridge: Cambridge University Press, 2010), 269.
56 James, *Light and Colour.*
57 Claudia Tedeschi, "Mosaics and Materials: Mosaics from the 5th and 6th Centuries in Ravenna and Poreč," in *New Light on Old Glass: Recent Research on Byzantine Mosaics and Glass*, eds Christopher Entwhistle and Liz James (London: British Museum Press, 2013), 60–69.
58 James, *Light and Colour.*
59 James, "Successors of Rome?"
60 Tedeschi, "Mosaics and Materials."
61 Ibid.
62 Terry and Maguire, *Dynamic Splendor.*
63 James, "Successors of Rome?"
64 Liz James, "Byzantine Glass Mosaic Tesserae: Some Material Considerations," *Byzantine & Modern Greek Studies* 20 (2006): 29–47.
65 James, "Successors of Rome?" 133.
66 Nadine Schibille, Patrick Degryse, Markku Corremans and Christian Specht, "Chemical characterisation of glass mosaic tesserae from sixth-century Sagalassos (south-west Turkey): chronology and production techniques," *Journal of Archaeological Science* 39 (2012): 1480–1492.
67 Liz James's database is accessible at www.sussex.ac.uk/byzantine/mosaic/.
68 James, "Byzantine Glass Mosaic Tesserae;" Liz James, Emöke Soproni and Bente Bjørnholt, "Mosaics by Numbers: Some Preliminary Evidence from the Leverhulme Database," *New Light on Old Glass*, 310–328.
69 James, Soproni and Bjørnholt, "Mosaics by Numbers," 311.
70 Dunbabin, *Mosaics of the Greek and Roman World*, 275–276; James, "Successors of Rome?" 131.
71 Judith McKenzie, "Alexandria on the Barada: The Mosaics of the Great Mosque in Damascus," *New Light on Old Glass*, 291–309.

Further reading

One of the best general introductions to wall mosaics written in English remains Hans Peter L'Orange and Per Jonas Nordhagen, *Mosaics from Antiquity to the Middle Ages*, trans. A. E. Keep (London: Methuen, 1966). On the iconography of wall mosaics, see Herbert Kessler, "Bright Gardens of Paradise," in Jeffery Spier (ed.), *Picturing the Bible: The Earliest Christian Art* (Fort Worth, TX: Kimbell Art Museum, 2007), 11–39; and on specific issues of iconography, see Christa Belting-Ihm, "Theophanic Images of Divine Majesty in Early Medieval Italian Church Decoration," in William Tronzo (ed.), *Italian Church Decoration of the Middle Ages and Early Renaissance: Functions, Forms, and Regional Traditions* (Bologna: Nuova Alfa Ed, 1989), 43–59; Thomas F. Mathews, *The Clash of Gods: A Reinterpretation of Early Christian Art* (Princeton, NJ: Princeton University Press, 1993); and Jean-Michel Spieser, "The Representation of Christ in the Apses of Early Christian Churches," *Gesta* 37 (1998): 63–73. On the development of apse imagery, other useful works include Beat Brenk, *The Apse, The Image, and the Icon: An Historical Perspective of the Apse as a Space for Images* (Wiesbaden: Reichert, 2010); and Erik Thunø, *The Apse Mosaic in Early Medieval Rome: Time, Network, and Repetition* (Cambridge: Cambridge University Press, 2015). Scholars who productively consider the multivalent impact of wall mosaics upon early Christian viewers include Jaś Elsner, "The Viewer and the Vision: The Case of the Sinai Apse," *Art History* 17 (1994): 81–102; Annabel Jane Wharton, "Ritual and Reconstructed Meaning: The Neonian Baptistery in Ravenna," *Art Bulletin* 69 (1987): 358–375; and Nadine Schibille, *Hagia Sophia and the Byzantine Aesthetic Experience* (Farnham, UK: Ashgate, 2014). On the materials of wall mosaics, see Liz James "Byzantine Glass Mosaic Tesserae: Some Material Considerations," *Byzantine & Modern Greek Studies* 20 (2006): 29–47; and Liz James, "Successors of Rome? Byzantine Glass Mosaics," in Daniel Keller, Jennifer Price and Caroline Jackson (eds), *Neighbours and Successors of Rome: Traditions of Glass Production and Use in Europe and the Middle East in the Later First Millennium AD* (Oxford: Oxbow, 2014), 128–136. Two recent works will be vital for further study, Liz James' encyclopedic *Mosaics in the Medieval World* (Cambridge: Cambridge University Press, 2017), and Jutta Dresken-Weiland's *Mosaics of Ravenna: Image and Meaning* (Regensburg: Schnell & Steiner, 2017), the latter a translation of the German original published in 2015.

7

CHRISTIAN FLOOR MOSAICS

Modes of study and potential meanings

Rina Talgam

Mosaic floors are a modest artistic medium that does not bear comparison in its content with the wall mosaics that once adorned the important and wealthy churches of the Christian world. Given the restrictions that Christians imposed upon themselves with regard to what was worthy of depiction on areas where people would tread, the creators of the floor mosaics were obliged to adopt a more limited repertoire of motifs of a secular nature. Mosaic floors lack contents comparable with those located on wall decorations and even those presented on sarcophagi and Christian miniature art. The great importance of the floor mosaics stems, first and foremost, from their extant quantity and good preservation. While the ceilings and walls of ancient buildings have generally not survived, their debris, which covered the pavements, helped to preserve the latter. The number of Christian floor mosaics that have been discovered in churches and chapels in cities, towns, and villages, as well as in monasteries and in the sumptuous homes of the affluent, is extremely large. Mosaic art flourished especially within the Byzantine realm, but Christian floor mosaics also existed in the western regions of the Roman Empire. Christian use of mosaic floors continued without great change in areas that were later cut off from Byzantium at the time of the Muslim conquest. The discussion in this chapter will therefore also relate to Christian mosaics of the seventh and eighth centuries CE.

The floor mosaics of humble churches were generally made from stones obtained from the nearby surroundings and their installation was therefore simpler and cheaper. The floors of the luxurious churches, on the other hand, were decorated with colored pieces of marble—a common type of paving in the Roman period, mainly in public halls such as basilicas and bathhouses, although such floors are sometimes also found in private houses of the very wealthy. This method, which is known as opus sectile, called for the import of slabs of colored marble from afar. The upper parts of the walls in churches with opus sectile floors were often covered with glass mosaics portraying scenes featuring figures from the Holy Scriptures. In the more modest churches, murals replaced the glass mosaics, and there were churches in which only the apse was decorated with a mural or alternatively with an icon or cross.

The portrayal of a more limited repertoire of images on floor mosaics in churches raises the question of whether they counterbalance the meager preservation of the wall decorations. The answer to this question is positive. Mosaic floors provide much information that sheds light on significant processes in the fields of religion, culture, and society in Late Antiquity. This applies both to the floor mosaics in churches and to those that adorned secular buildings of Christian patrons. A discussion of mosaics' role, and what can be learned from them as historical documents about their period, necessarily distinguishes between those that adorn churches, chapels, and baptisteries, and those located in the private or public secular realm.

This short chapter will focus on the Christian mosaics adorning religious structures and offer a few brief comments about Christian mosaics incorporated in other areas. The mosaics that decorated the reception rooms in the homes of the wealthy and in public areas intended for secular affairs were made by the same artists who created the church mosaics. One can divide these mosaics into three categories that reflect various manners of response to the Classical heritage. Some patrons apparently saw no contradiction between their Christian religious identity and embracing the Classical heritage, as floors of the reception rooms in their homes were decorated with depictions from Greek mythology. Such depictions enabled people of means to give expression to their classical education (*paideia*). In most cases, this tolerance for mythological subjects should be regarded as an expression of Hellenism in Late Antiquity, which should be distinguished from religious syncretism. By contrast, other patrons adopted a more severe approach by giving preference to patterns with a neutral connotation over mythological depictions. The third group evidently blended themes from mythology with motifs originating in church mosaics or other Christian contexts. Striking examples of combining pagan mythology and significant Christian motifs are the Hinton St Mary mosaic (Figure 7.1) and the Frampton mosaic (both in Britain). Throughout the Roman world there is no example for the replacement of mythological depictions on mosaic floors in private dwellings by biblical scenes.

Figure 7.1 Mosaic at Hinton St Mary (Britain). Courtesy of the British Museum, London.

The sources of the early Christian mosaics

In order to understand the uniqueness of Christian floor mosaics one must compare them with their predecessors in the Roman Empire and to the mosaics of other communities, primarily those in synagogues. The earliest Christian mosaics presently known date from the end of the third century to the beginning of the fourth century CE. At the time when the first Christian mosaics were being produced, the tradition of Roman mosaics already had a long history. Roman floor mosaics were very common in the homes of the affluent, and less so in tombs and buildings of a public–civic character, such as bathhouses. Only very rarely are mosaics encountered in a pagan religious context. This practice changes in the fifth and sixth centuries. Floor mosaics continued to adorn wealthy homes, tombs, and civic buildings, but most of the mosaics decorated churches and synagogues, which raises the question of why floor mosaics became the preferred medium for decoration in Christian religious buildings and pushed aside other decorative fashions. The answer is that the change resulted from the transition in cultic buildings from extrovert architecture, in which believers generally remained outside the building, to introvert architecture that housed the community. As a result of this, attention shifted to the design of the interior from the exterior. However, another reason is the idolatrous association with sculpted, cultic images and their use for the decoration of temple pediments and niches, while two-dimensional painting and mosaic art had a more neutral connotation. The preference for painting over sculpture also found expression in Christian writings. The clearest expression of this is to be found in a letter written by Bishop Hypatius of Ephesos (in office

Figure 7.2 Mosaic floor of a Christian prayer hall at Kefar 'Othnay (in ancient Palestine). Courtesy of Y. Tepper and Israel Antiquities Authority.

from 531 to 538) to Julian of Artamytion, one of his suffragans.[1] This preference was possibly also influenced by the fact that the first Christian assembly halls, prior to the declaration of Christianity as the official faith of the Roman Empire, were in domiciles that were adapted to serve as spaces for religious gatherings. A well-preserved example has been discovered at Kefar 'Othnay (Figure 7.2) near Legio (in ancient Palestine).

Another question considers which elements of the Roman mosaic tradition were passed on to the new religious context. The answer to this lies in the compositional features and themes depicted in the Roman mosaics. Despite the geographic spread of Roman art, there are notable differences between the mosaic traditions of the Greek-speaking East and the Latin-speaking West. The late Roman mosaics in the East maintained the tradition of the Greek *emblema(ta)* mosaics and are characterized by pictorial panels whose number could range from one to fifteen. A spectator viewing the floor was obliged to stand outside a panel and to move from a point located opposite its center to a point located opposite the center of the neighboring panel. The themes depicted in these panels were generally drawn from Greek mythology, theater, and philosophy. By contrast, the mosaics that were created in the Roman West in the second and third centuries CE are characterized by their simulation of a carpet decorated with a geometric or floral network in which figures were incorporated. In other cases, the figures are depicted against a white background and are spread out over the surface of the floor carpet in an entirely free arrangement or in registers without a frame. The common motifs on this type of mosaic floor are hunting scenes; agricultural labors; the personification of the seasons of the year, the months, and also the Genius of the year or Aion; depictions derived from the amphitheater, and those of edible objects (xenia). Mythological scenes appear only occasionally.

North African mosaics enjoyed great popularity at the end of the third century/beginning of the fourth century CE, and influenced the compositions and repertoire of mosaics in Italy and the eastern provinces of the Roman world. In many Christian mosaics decorating churches from the end of the fourth century/beginning of the fifth century up to the eighth century CE, one can discern the adoption of compositional ideas and motifs from North Africa. These mosaics featured geometric networks populated initially by animals and later also by human images engaged in hunting, agriculture, herding sheep, and even with the portrayal of xenia (edible objects seen to represent hospitality). The figured panels that characterized the Roman mosaics in the East were regarded as unsuitable for churches by the Church clergy and the Christian congregations, not only on account of their mythological content but also because these compositions suited triclinia or rooms in which the seats were arranged along the walls.

Even the adoption of motifs drawn from nature was cautious and carried out gradually. Many of the fourth-century churches are aniconic (Figure 7.3), as shown by Kitzinger and Maguire.[2] In the few cases where figural motifs do appear within geometric or floral patterns, they are mainly fishes and birds. Texts written in the fourth century testify to the apprehension that certain animals would continue to be comprehended in their pagan significance, and that the adoration of the forces of nature, including the sun, the moon, the sky, the earth, and water would take the place of adoration of their creator. For most of the fourth century, aside from the reign of Julian the Apostate, Christianity enjoyed imperial support and eventually became the official religion of the Roman Empire, but the struggle against paganism did not end, and there was no place in church floors for images likely to be perceived as idolatrous. This began to change during the fifth century, particularly in its second half, as floor mosaics in churches began to lose their severe character (Figure 7.4), though some communities continued to create non-figured mosaics.

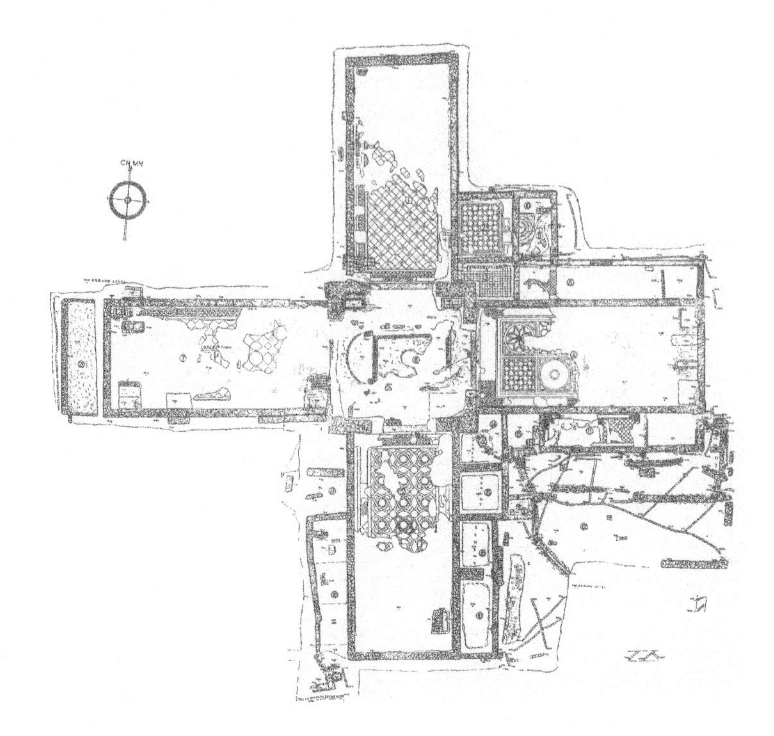

Figure 7.3 Plan of floor mosaics with non-figural geometric designs in a cruciform church, Kaoussie at Antioch. After D. Levi, *Antioch Mosaic Pavements*, Princeton, NJ: Princeton University Press, 1947, 283.

Figure 7.4 Mosaic with inhabited vine scrolls in a church at Aluma (in ancient Palestine). Courtesy of D. Varga.

Figure 7.4 (continued)

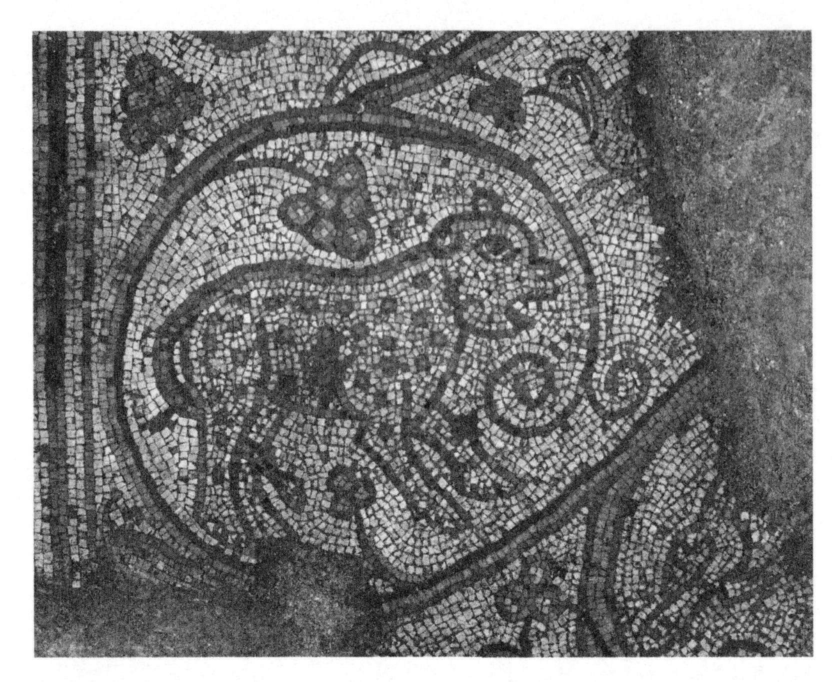

Figure 7.4 *(continued)*

In the Justinianic period, personifications of the seasons of the year, the months, the heavenly winds, the earth, the sea, the rivers of Paradise, and in one case even of Wisdom (Sophia) began to appear in the churches. Maguire sets an earlier date for this phenomenon and holds that these personifications started to appear in church mosaics as early as the second half of the fifth century, and the variety thereof increased in the sixth century.[3]

The personification of the sun is notable for its absence, appearing only once—in the yard of a monastery at Beth Shean (Scythopolis). Helios, who is featured in this mosaic, has been brought down from his chariot and is portrayed as a bust next to Selene, who equals him in size, at the center of the cycle of the months. Apart from this instance, the absence of the figure of Helios in Christian contexts stems from the tremendous importance of the cult of Sol Invictus in Roman polytheism up to the fourth century CE, and from his prominent appearance in the central panel in synagogues. In contrast to the use of personifications, depictions of figures from Greek and Roman mythology were regarded as unsuitable for the adornment of churches, and there was no change in this regard even in the time of Justinian.

The Christians' attitudes towards images depicted on floors

The Christians adopted a perception, common in the Roman world, that the attitude toward an image is what determines its status. The Romans distinguished between cultic images, honorific sculptures, and profane (decorative) images mainly by the attitude toward them. Ritual and liturgical procedures marked the difference between cultic and non-sacred. Hence, it would have been problematic for Christians with a Roman background to depict scenes from Scripture or other holy images in places that were meant to be trodden on.

The Jews, who sought to heighten the distinction between synagogues and churches, chose a solution opposite to that of Christians regarding the placement of images. Depictions drawn from the Old Testament and the portrayal of the utensils of the Tabernacle and the Temple, which in the third century appeared on synagogue walls, appeared in floor mosaics at the beginning of the fourth century. Treading on these images made possible their use for didactic purposes but neutralized their sacred dimension. Many Jews adopted this course up to the seventh century, when the severe interpretation of the Second Commandment was readopted and Jewish art reverted to aniconism, as it was during the Second Temple period. Jews also differed from Christians by depicting Helios at the center of the zodiac in some synagogues in the land of Israel. This image began to appear as early as the second half of the fourth century and its use continued up to the end of the sixth century.

Only on rare occasions do we find an exception to the Christian perception that considered floor mosaics an unfitting place for the depiction of human figures from the Scriptures, as can be seen at Aquileia, Mopsuestia (Misis in Cilicia), three times in Syria, in Beth Guvrin (Palestine), in a mosaic of unknown provenance in the Louvre and in a baptistery at Pitsound on the shores of the Black Sea. Each of these examples requires separate discussion, since no single explanation can account for them all.

The exact dating of the twin basilicas at Aquileia is a controversial issue. Some hold that the northern basilica was built as early as the time of the Constantinian Edict of Toleration of the Christians, while others accepts the date 313–319 for the entire complex.[4] The northern building contains a depiction of mammals and birds and lacks clear Christian motifs. The floor mosaic of the southern basilica is made of nine carpets of equal size featuring geometric patterns populated by a plethora of motifs taken from nature and personifications or portraits of local donors, and a panel in the eastern part of the nave features a seascape with fishing boats. Incorporated in this panel are three scenes from the story of Jonah: Jonah being thrown from the boat into the sea and swallowed by the jaws of a fish; Jonah being cast up on the shore from the jaws of the fish; and Jonah lying beneath a hut of twigs on which a Ricinus vine climbs. The Jonah cycle enjoyed great popularity in early Christian art and often appeared on sarcophagi and murals in catacombs. Some scholars are of the opinion that the Jonah cycle at Aquileia was added to the existing seascape later on, while others consider that it was made together with the other depictions. Those supporting the view that the Jonah cycle was part of the seascape from the outset hold that the depictions of Jonah took the place of mythological depictions that were sometimes incorporated in seascapes in the mosaics of North African villas and bathhouses.

The questions discussed in the research literature with regard to this mosaic are: Why was the Jonah cycle chosen to decorate a church floor? Was the significance of the subject equal to that of its appearances in a burial context? Was its appearance in the new context accompanied by other layers of liturgical and theological significance? And was the number of fishermen in the marine scene (twelve) intentional? In order to answer these questions, one must examine the Christian interpretations of the story of Jonah during the period preceding the laying of the mosaic, and contemporary sermons on boats, fishermen and fish by peoples from the close surroundings, such as Chromatius, bishop of Aquileia (388–407).[5] One must also ask whether the Book of Jonah was read as part of the liturgy and to what extent the community was acquainted with the text. Also worthy of elucidation is whether this mosaic was possibly in some way a reaction to the theological struggles and schisms that split the Christian world at that time.[6]

More than two centuries later the Jonah cycle reappeared on the floor of a Christian church in the area of Beth Guvrin in Palestine. The geographical distance and time gap oblige us not to infer an influence from the earlier depiction at Aquileia. There was also a change in the visual presentation, and Jonah, who appeared naked on the early Christian sarcophagi and at Aquileia, was now depicted clothed. The mosaic at Beth Guvrin raises the question of whether the depiction of a biblical figure reflects the influence of the widespread custom in Palestinian synagogues of featuring biblical scenes in the floor mosaics.

At Mopsuestia a mosaic dated to the fifth century was discovered in a building with an asymmetrical plan, including a nave flanked on one side by a single aisle and on the other side by two aisles. The western part of the nave is decorated with Noah's ark surrounded by animals (Figure 7.5). Surprisingly, this panel lacks human figures. The outer northern aisle was adorned with a series of nine (according to Budde) or eleven (according to Kitzinger) episodes from the life of Samson (Judges 14–16).[7] The scenes are unframed and above each of them is a citation from the appropriate verse from Septuagint. This mosaic gives rise to several questions. Why did the members of the community choose to depict so extensively episodes from the life of Samson? Does this general format bear a relationship to an illustrated scroll, and, if so, why are the scenes to be viewed from right to left? And can one learn of the extent of the community's literacy from the long text accompanying the decorations? In two recently excavated Galilean synagogues depictions from the life of Samson were discovered, and in one of them was found a portrayal of Noah's ark, which, like the one at Mopsuestia, lacks human figures and features

Figure 7.5 Floor mosaic with Noah's ark surrounded by animals, Mopsuestia (Turkey). Courtesy of the Center for Jewish Art, The Hebrew University of Jerusalem.

only animals. The thematic and iconographic similarity calls for a discussion of the contacts between the rival communities who shared a common religious text.

Three fifth-century mosaics from Syria, the best preserved one of which was found in the church at Huarte, depict Adam naming the animals. Adam is accorded the privileged location at the foot of the bema, on the axis to its entrance. He is seated clothed on a backless throne holding a book in his hands. Among the animals surrounding him are seen a phoenix and a gryphon. Maguire, who studied this group of mosaics, claims that the composition blends a liturgical and allegoric significance within a single image.[8] The mosaic portrays Adam's wisdom and glory, which before the fall saved him from the attacks of wild animals and which were to be restored to him by Christ. The depiction is located in a place that generally features pastoral images that represent the earthly Paradise, the entrance to which passes through the Church. Adam surrounded by animals is reminiscent of Orpheus and even more of David/Orpheus who appears on the floor mosaic of a synagogue in Gaza (Palestine). A fragmentary mosaic at the Louvre and a mosaic of a baptistery in the area of the Black Sea depict the three youths in the fiery furnace. This theme was one of the most popular Old Testament subjects in early Christian funerary art. The three youths in the furnace were considered prototypes of the early Christian martyrs, baptism and symbols of salvation.[9]

The imperial edict of 427 banning the depiction of crosses on floors is indicative of a growing Christian sensitivity to the motifs portrayed in floor mosaics. A survey of archaeological finds reveals that this edict was put into practice, but not in an absolute manner. Relatively few mosaics feature crosses or a Christogram, not including crosses incorporated in the opening and closing parts of dedicatory inscriptions. Most of the examples known to us are from the fifth century, but one is not always able to determine whether they preceded the edict of Theodosius II. Nevertheless, examples from the sixth century show that the edict did not lead to the disappearance of this phenomenon, but its scope was more limited numerically and the crosses in places intended for people to walk upon were generally of a rather modest size. The perception that the treading on visual images or the refraining therefrom reflected the degree of sacredness of the depicted images and perhaps made possible the continued portrayal of mythological scenes on floors in secular contexts.

Deciphering the significance attributed to churches' floor mosaics

None of the researchers has any doubt that the iconographic sources of most of the motifs depicted on floors of churches and chapels were secular and well known in Roman villas, but opinions are divided on the question of whether a significant change in meaning took place with their transfer from a secular context to a religious one, and whether one can attribute to them a Christian content and significance. Moreover, during the Byzantine period, many of the compositions and motifs were not exclusive to churches, but also appeared in synagogues and secular buildings. To what extent do depictions that resemble one another in form within the same geographical environment and in the same period also share a common significance?

In order to answer this question, one must clarify an even more basic issue: how should the significance of mosaic floors be explained? Anyone studying floor mosaics, like every art historian who seeks to comprehend the significance of a work of art in the historical, sociological, and cultural context in which it was created and functioned, is obliged to compare visual and textual media. Formalistic and comparative analysis of a work of art furnishes only partial information. One of the important questions confronting the art historian when attempting to interpret the significance of visual images is which of all the known texts from the period and area under study can be linked with the particular work of art and shed light on it.

The answer to this question calls for the clarification of the identities of those who had the authority to determine the content of the church decorations. Was this authority vested in the hands of the person who financed the work or are we dealing with other bearers of authority, such as the local priest or a more senior Church institution? Another question that needs to be asked is what was the role of the artists in the formation of the decorative scheme? Also, speaking generally, how was consensus reached with regard to what was permissible and what was forbidden for presentation in a religious context? If one assumes that floor mosaics in churches were an expression of the popular art of simple folk or, alternatively, of the wealthy but uneducated patrons, one limits the use of texts representing the intellectual elite of that time. On the other hand, if one assumes that the decoration indicates the involvement of the intellectual elite, one faces the question of whether there were mechanisms to provide viewers with tools for an educated viewing that would ensure the correct interpretation. Moreover, due to the interactive nature of the viewing experience, one should discuss not only the creator but also the viewer. Are we in possession of sources that enable us to know how the images on the floor were conceived by the community that entered the doors of the church? Did the extent of the viewer's education have an influence on the significance of a church's decorative scheme?

The first impression one gains when studying the floors in Christian religious buildings is that, although they were generally created by local workshops that made use of stones familiar to them from the immediate surroundings, one can detect a considerable measure of uniformity. Notwithstanding the broad geographic spread, a limited number of types appears again and again over a period of 350 years. This was popular art that showed a large measure of conformity. But in no case was there absolute copying of an earlier floor, and one can suppose that in many cases the innovations are nothing but variations of existing themes. The consistency in decorative schemes indicates the existence of a norm regarded as suitable for the decoration of church floors. More than in a private context, an encounter with the accepted had great importance. Despite the repetition, the process that we are witnessing over a long time span is not in the direction of degeneration but was dynamic and innovative. A notable feature was the desire to maintain the delicate balance between deviation from the accepted and the desire to go deeper and diversify.

The answer to the question whether this was art that was motivated from above by the Church or from below by the masses is probably that we are dealing with a combination of the two. The dedicatory inscriptions in most of the communal churches in cities, towns, and villages bear testimony to the close cooperation between the donors who were members of the community and the holders of office of various ranks in the Church establishment. The bishop is generally mentioned at the beginning of the inscription as a denotation of the time but also in order to express his benediction for the act of the erection or renovation of the church. He is often followed by the priest; the deacon is also mentioned, followed by the donors who were members of the community. From this we learn that in the consciousness of the people of that time the laying of a mosaic was regarded as an enterprise shared by the Church authorities and the members of the community. Nevertheless, there is a possibility that the measure of power held by the local bishops in private chapels of the aristocracy was much weaker. An indication that patrons of churches consulted with Church authorities is the reply of St Nilus of Sinai (early fifth century) to the Prefect Olympiodorus when the latter intended to decorate his church with animals and plants. To this proposal Nilus answered: "I say that it would be childish and infantile to distract the eyes of the faithful with the aforementioned (images)."[10] Evidence does not support a sharp distinction between the categories of low culture (those coming from the masses) and high culture (originating in the church establishment) as influences on floor mosaics in churches.

The spread of the fashion throughout the Christian world was facilitated, inter alia, by the mobility of people. There is no evidence supporting the conjecture about the existence of pattern books of a set type, indicating the centralization and control of the floor mosaic programs by governmental systems or by means of "creation centers" or "schools." However, artists could have been aided by sketchbooks that they created for the purpose of showing their repertoire to potential customers and as a guide for themselves. These pattern books could have been passed from father to son, assisting in the preservation and spread of artistic traditions. With regard to the floor mosaics in churches, one should employ the term "workshops" rather than "schools." In the field of mosaics there are local phenomena, compositions, and motifs characteristic of certain areas, but the use of the term "school" in this context is misleading. The level of complexity of the mosaics could change from place to place and there are also areas in which one can discern a clear development over time from simple compositions to ones more complex and much richer.

The floor mosaics were intended to adorn the building and transform it into one that was pleasing and attractive, but in many cases it is notable how the floor mosaics helped to clarify the symbolism of the church building, explain the liturgy, and intensify the religious experience. The interior of the church served as a space for liturgical performance incorporating the movement of the clergy conducting the ceremony, as well as the movement of the community itself. Within the space of the church there was a hierarchy, and the area of the bema closed off by a screen was regarded as more sanctified than the nave and could be entered only by priests. These hierarchical relations often also found expression in the mosaic floors, as one can see for example in the Chapel of Theotokos on Mount Nebo or the Church of the Lions at Umm al-Rasas (both in ancient Arabia, present-day Jordan).

Visual art exerted an enormous influence on ancient society at the time when literacy was the lot of the few. Anyone living in the realm of Roman culture was surrounded by visual images both in public and in private spaces, and it is thus not surprising that the Church authorities hastened to adopt art and architecture as a tool for the education of believers and a means of heightening religious experience. However, visual images are often ambiguous and their interpretation is dependent on the choice, associations, and personality of the viewer. This is the secret of art's charm but it can also be a source of its weakness as a didactic tool for conveying theological messages. In order to ensure the correct reading of the things that were observed, the Church establishment set up a supporting system that provided the broad public with the necessary information. These compositions belonged to various genres and they included sermons delivered on the occasion of the consecration of churches, ekphraseis (descriptions of works of art that reconstructed the experience of observation), and sermons meant to explain the liturgy and liturgical poetry. The importance attributed by the Church establishment to verbal means of directing the observers toward a proper understanding of architecture and visual representations is already notable in the opening remarks of the panegyric delivered by Eusebius, the bishop of Caesarea Maritima (in Palestine), at the time of the consecration of the new church building in Tyre.[11]

Although sermons, ekphraseis, and liturgical texts do not mention mosaic floors directly, they provide us with important keys for understanding the way in which the floor decorations were integrated into the general perception of the church. These texts, that were read to the broad public, reflect a multi-layered perception of the church by the people of the time: a communal institution, a cosmic temple, an earthly Paradise, and the successor to the Tabernacle and Solomon's Temple. And the area of the bema, where the church's altar was located, was regarded as heavenly Jerusalem. This is notable as early as the panegyric of Eusebius (315 CE), and a complex perception featuring additional layers of significance appears in the sermon delivered by John II, the bishop of Jerusalem, on the occasion of the consecration of the Church of Holy Zion (394 CE).[12] John presents the complex symbolism of the church in seven metaphors: the church is heaven of heavens, heavenly Jerusalem, Paradise, Noah's Ark, Mount Moriah, and the site of the Binding of Isaac; it symbolizes Jacob's ladder, the Tabernacle, Solomon's Temple and the Temple in the vision of Ezekiel, and the internal Tabernacle. Not all of these metaphors are reflected in floor mosaics of various churches. Some are more prominent and appear more frequently; some floors present only a single metaphor while others present a number of them simultaneously. Sermons and ekphraseis from the sixth century explain church architecture and decoration to the broad public.[13]

The inscriptions incorporated in floor mosaics are generally dedicatory ones. In many cases they provide information about the time of erection of the church, the reason for its construction, and its administrative organization. Only rarely do mosaic inscriptions shed light on their artistic elements. An example is the basilica at Paphos Chrysopolitissa on Cyprus, dated to the fourth century. Portrayed in this mosaic is a vine medallion laden with clusters of grapes, and above it is a citation from John 15:1: "I am the true vine." According to Maguire, this inscription was intended to draw a distinction between the vine in its Christian sense and that of the pagans, which was associated with Dionysos.[14] Another example is the inscription around the image of Thalassa, the personification of the sea, in the Church of the Apostles

Figure 7.6 Mosaic with the figure of Thalassa, the Church of the Apostles at Madaba (in ancient Arabia). After M. Piccirillo, The Mosaics of Jordan, Amman, 1993, with the kind permission of the Studium Biblicum Franciscanum in Jerusalem.

at Madaba (in ancient Arabia). The paraphrase of the Psalm 115:15 ("O Lord God who has made the heavens and the earth") was intended to make clear that the sea (Thalassa) depicted in the medallion was created by God who also made heaven and earth (Figure 7.6). A third example is the inscription in the northern transept of Basilica A at Nikopolis in Epirus. There are cases where the inscription on the floor relates to the significance of the entire building, as, for example, in Psalm 118:20: "This gate of the Lord, into which the righteous shall enter," which appears in several churches. For believers partaking in the liturgy, the church opens the gate to redemption. In John 10:7 Jesus likens himself to a gate.

There are inscriptions that shed light on the significance of the bema, such as one in the Church of Sergius at Umm al-Rasas, which cites Psalm 87:2: "The Lord has loved the gates of Zion more than all the tents of Jacob." The continuation of this Psalm relates to the city of God. Judaism ("the tents of Jacob"), including biblical Jerusalem, the earthly city in which blood sacrifices were offered, was banished in favor of the earthly church, "Israel in spirit," that serves as a gate to the divine and eternal heavenly city ("Zion"). The area bounded by a screen and intended for priests thus denotes the gate to the Heavenly Jerusalem in the Earthy Church. In addition, there are several mosaics featuring an illustration of a biblical passage from the end of days prophecies of Isaiah or Psalms. These illustrations do not include depictions of human beings and are not narrative biblical scenes in the full sense. Examples of this can be found in a few churches in Turkey, Corsica, and the Church of the Acropolis at Ma'in (in Jordan).

Floor mosaics as a tool for clarifying the symbolism of the church and intensifying the religious experience

The church as a microcosm

The most frequent metaphor reflected in church floor mosaics presented the church as a microcosm, by representation of plants, birds, beasts and sea creatures. As shown by Mircea Eliade, this is a universal idea in religious architecture in general.[15] The penetration of this idea into early Christian theology can be attributed to the influence of Philo and Flavius Josephus who gave an allegoric interpretation to the Tabernacle and its furnishings. Both of them regarded the Tabernacle as a simulation of the cosmos.[16] Similar ideas appear in the writings of Origen and later in those of Theodore of Mopsuestia (350–428) and Constantine of Antioch (sixth century).[17] The perception of the church as a microcosm appears in the hymn of the Edessa Cathedral, written in the time of Justinian. The depiction of the world in a church was intended to bridge the gap between two dichotomous approaches, termed by Smith as concepts of a "locative religion" (in which the worship of God takes place in an enclosed particular space) and a "utopian religious" orientation (in which the worship of God can take place anywhere).[18] This dualism finds expression in the words of Maximus the Confessor who, according to a recent study, was active in Palestine.[19]

Moreover, the depiction of the created world on the floors of churches reflects the power and sovereignty of God in the universe. From the sermon delivered by Cyril, the bishop of Jerusalem, to catechumens in the fourth century, we learn that the reference to the created world was part of the eucharist. Cited in the liturgy of St Basil are verses 5 and 6 of Psalms 146: "Happy is he . . . whose hope is in the Lord his God: which made heaven, and earth, the sea, and all that therein is."[20]

The church as a domus ecclesia *and a* domus dei

Beginning in the fifth century, the animals that were generally incorporated in the floral and geometrical carpets were joined by human figures engaged in agricultural activities and hunting, as well as images of donors. This was a natural development, since human figures were part of the repertoire of the North African mosaics that were the source of inspiration for many church mosaics. The incorporation of human figures engaged in activities of a rustic nature brought the depiction closer to the world of the community members and connected the everyday to the sanctified. The inclusion of donor portraits emphasized the character of the church as a communal institute. The donors appeared next to other images in the mosaic carpets decorating the nave and rarely in the aisles, but they were sometimes given a privileged position, such as in a separate panel at the foot of the presbytery or less often in the presbytery itself.

These depictions might also have been intended to harmonize the practice of constructing church buildings with the stance in the New Testament that downplayed the significance of the Jerusalem Temple and characterized the faith community itself as "the Temple of the living God" (2 Cor 6:16; cf. Acts 7:48–50; 1 Cor 3:9, 16). The perception that God is located everywhere at all times and that the adoration of which He is worthy is in the hearts of the believers and not in the place designated for this purpose encouraged the view that church buildings were not temples of the Divinity but places of assembly for believers. The community was hallowed, rather than the building in which its members assembled. This stance was also repeated by the Church Fathers. The idea that the physical structure of the church becomes an allegory of the spiritual church made up of the community of believers appears as early as Eusebius' panegyric delivered at the time of the consecration of the church in Tyre.[21]

Yet Eusebius also used Temple terminology to refer to the church building, as did some of the inscriptions incorporated into floor mosaics.[22] These testify that the Christians had an ambivalent attitude toward the church. The church was not only a *domus ecclesia* but also a *domus dei*. The following inscription appears at the center of the early church at Magen in ancient Palestine: "The holiest dwelling place of the Most High God is in the midst of her." A ten-line inscription in the early church of Bahan in Palestine includes the following citation from the Psalms: "Holiness befits thy house, O Lord, forever more" (Psalm 93:5). The presentation of other metaphors for the church are much less frequent.

The church as an earthly Paradise

In the writings of the church fathers, the church is compared with Paradise. The presentation of Paradise in a church was achieved in one of two ways: A portrayal of the four rivers of Paradise by means of the use of personifications, generally as part of a Christian topographic depiction, as can be seen, for example, in the central panel of the Church of St Paul at Umm el-Rasas, which features Ge, the personification of Earth, surrounded by personifications of the seasons of the year and the four rivers of Paradise. The other way of presenting Paradise in a church was by means of the depiction of fruit trees, sometimes shown next to the donors, or of the comradeship between predators and their prey. Fruit trees were an important part of the Christian image of earthly Paradise that was based on Genesis 2:8–9.

The placement of most of these depictions in the presbytery close to the altar indicates that they had another significance connected with the church liturgy. The depiction of Paradise denotes the redemption that is the legacy sought by believers who participate in the Communion that takes place there. Anyone who takes part in the church sacrament ensures his entry into a world that has been redeemed from the ancient sin. The crucifixion of Jesus, which according to a church tradition took place in the same place where the first man was created and buried, purified humanity from the original sin and opened the way for its redemption. The eucharist ceremony on the church altar restores the community of believers to the lost Paradise. The appearance of the rivers of Paradise close to the baptismal fonts is also of liturgical importance. The baptismal font takes the place of the "fountain of life" whose waters fed the rivers of Paradise. This Christian perception of the spring stemming from Paradise is based on what is said in Genesis 2:6 and 10.

The church as the successor of the Tabernacle and the Temple

The words of praise delivered by Eusebius, bishop of Caesarea in Palestine, to Paulinus, bishop of Tyre, during the consecration of the new church building revealed that, as early as the fourth century, the Christian basilica was symbolically regarded as the successor to the Temple of Solomon. The perception of the church as the successor of the Tabernacle and the Temple recurs in the fifth to sixth centuries in the words of praise uttered at church consecrations and in dedicatory inscriptions. Thus, for example, Choricius of Gaza ends his oration, which was probably delivered at the consecration of St Stephen's Church in that city, by comparing the church building with the Jewish Temple, saying that if the church in Gaza had competed against the world's most famous temple, it would undoubtedly have won.[23] And a hymn for the cathedral of Edessa (mid-sixth century) reads: "Bezalel it was who, instructed by Moses, erected the tabernacle to serve us as a model."[24] An arrogant statement by the church's patrons about it being superior to Solomon's Temple also appears in a dedicatory inscription in a church that was built by Anicia Juliana in Constantinople. Shortly thereafter, in a kontakion composed for the re-consecration of the Hagia Sophia Church in Constantinople in 562, the building project was compared with that of Solomon.[25]

During the fifth and sixth centuries we also see a visual expression of these perceptions in Christian floor mosaics. Generally, these depictions would be located close to the liturgical foci. In churches with a regular plan, depictions of this type would appear at the foot of the church's bema. In Syrian churches with a central bema for the reading of the Holy Scriptures (which preceded the eucharist ceremony), these depictions are located at the foot of the bema at the center of the nave. In the vicinity of the altar or bema appear a pair of bulls or sheep, an allusion to the blood sacrifices that were offered in the Temple in Jerusalem. Here we are dealing with a typological depiction, since such sacrifices were replaced by the eucharist ceremony that was carried out on the church's altar. In the Chapel of Theotokos on Mount Nebo (in ancient Arabia), between the two bulls appears a sketch that is a combination of the plan of the Temple in Jerusalem and a church building, as suggested by the apsidal end and the small structure located at the center, which can be understood as a ciborium above the church's altar. A citation from Psalm 51:19 was added to this depiction: "then bulls will be offered on thy altar."

The significance of special motifs

In addition to examining the ways floor mosaics related to the theological significance of church buildings, one should pay attention to the significance of a few of the motifs that were incorporated in mosaics. Various animals such as a fish (whole or halved), a ram (Figure 7.7), an eagle, a sheep, a bull, a peacock, a phoenix or a plant like the vine could have had a very important symbolic significance. Some of them were regarded as images symbolizing Jesus himself. However, as indicated by Henry Maguire, artistic motifs are not mere signposts and their meaning is not unequivocal.[26] One can often discern in them a number of layers of significance and intentional ambivalence.

Figure 7.7 Mosaic with a ram and other animals, the Church of St George at Khirbat al-Mukhayyat (ancient Arabia). Photo: G. Laron.

It is possible to determine the primary significance of a motif by examining its location in the entire composition and within the architectural space, its size, the sequence of motifs in which it is incorporated and the way in which they interrelate, and the elements that are integrated into the image itself and serve as pointers. Thus, for example, a ram depicted next to a tree to which he is tethered or stands in front of in a composition that creates the shape of a cross would allude to the ram in the story of the Binding of Isaac, which prefigures the crucifixion of Jesus. When such a depiction appears close to the church's altar it will also take on a liturgical significance. The portrayal of two rams flanking the altar or a sacred façade could refer to the two covenants and to the daily sacrifices offered in the Temple in Jerusalem, which were replaced by the eucharist ceremony.

Some floor mosaics reveal that by means of animal images and topographic elements it was possible to create compositions that were not inferior to the wall mosaics in their complexity and the importance of the message conveyed by them. A mosaic of this type is the one located at the foot of the central bema that was used for the reading of the Holy Scriptures in the church of Tayibat al-Imam in Syria (Figure 7.8). Another example is the bema mosaic in a church at Kiustendil (Bulgaria). Depicted in this mosaic is a kantharos from which a vine spreads and which is flanked by a pair of peacocks. Above it is the Hill of Golgotha as the source of the four rivers of Paradise, on top of which is a medallion containing the Greek letters alpha and omega. Below the kantharos appears a gate that is reminiscent of the church's screen. The entire depiction is surrounded by twelve sheep, like the number of the apostles. This composition includes elements also seen in wall mosaics. Fruit trees laden with fruit, which appear on many of the church floors in order to denote that the church is the earthly Paradise or to express the idea that the entrance to Paradise passes through the church, were also depicted on wall mosaics, as were Nilotic landscapes and birds. This we learn from Choricius' description of two of the churches of Gaza (in Palestine).[27] Despite the distinctive features of each of the media and what was forbidden and allowed to be depicted on floors, we note a measure of commonality and mutual influence.

Figure 7.8 The central bema's mosaic in the church of Tayibat al-Imam (in Syria). Courtesy of the Studium Biblicum Franciscanum in Jerusalem.

Notes

1 Paul J. Alexander, "Hypatius of Ephesus: A Note on Image Worship in the Sixth Century," *The Harvard Theological Review* 45 (1952): 177–184; Ernst Kitzinger, "Stylistic Developments in Pavement Mosaics in the Greek east from the Age of Constantine to the Age of Justinian," *La mosaïque Gréco-romaine: Paris, 29 août–3 septembre 1963* (Paris: Colloques internationaux du Centre national de la recherché scientifique, 1965), 341–352, esp. 343–344, reprinted in *idem, The Art of Byzantium and the Medieval West: Selected Studies* (Bloomington, IN: Indiana University Press: 1976), 64–68; Henry Maguire, "Christians, Pagans, and the Representation of Nature," *Rhetoric, Nature and Magic in Byzantine Art* (Aldershot: Ashgate, 1998), 131–160.

2 Maguire, "Christians, Pagans, and the Representation of Nature," 147–153.

3 Ibid., 143–144.

4 Luisa Bertacchi, "Nuovi mosaici figurati di Aquileia," *Aquileia Nostro* 34 (1963): 19–84; Giovanni Brusin and Paolo Zovatto, *Monumenti Paleocristiani di Aquileia e di Grado* (Udine: Deputazione di storia patria per il Friuli, 1957), 20–125; Katherine M. D. Dunbabin, *Mosaics of the Greek and Roman World* (Cambridge: Cambridge University Press 1999), 71–72.

5 Joseph Lemarié, "Symbolisme de la mer, du navire, du pêcheur et de la pêche chez Chromace d'Aquilée," *Antichita' Altoadriatiche* 34 (1989): 141–152.

6 Margo Stroumsa Uzan, "Jonas of Aquileia: A Gesture to Constantine the Great," in *Between Judaism and Christianity; Art Historical Essays in Honor of Elisheva (Elisabeth) Revel-Neher*, eds Katrin Kogman-Appel and Mati Meyer (Leiden: Brill, 2009), 55–71.

7 Ludwig Budde, *Antike Mosaiken in Kilikien*, Vol. 1 (Recklinghausen: Bongers, 1969); Ernst Kitzinger, "Observations on the Samson Floor at Mopsuestia," *Dumbarton Oaks Papers* 27 (1973): 133–144; Rainer Stichel, "Die Inschriften des Samson-Mosaiks in Mopsuestia und ihre Beziehung zum biblischen Text," *Byzantinische Zeitschrift* 71 (1978): 50–61; Michael Avi-Yonah, "Mosaics of Mopsuestia – Church or Synagogue?", in *Ancient Synagogues Revealed*, ed. Lee I. Levine (Jerusalem: Israel Exploration Society, 1981), 186–190.

8 Henry Maguire, "Adam and the Animals: Allegory and the Literal Sense in Early Christian Art," *Dumbarton Oaks Papers* 41 (1987): 363–373.

9 Robin M. Jensen, *Understanding Early Christian Art* (London: Routledge, 2000), 79–84.

10 Nilus of Sinai, *Epistulae*, 4.61, PG, LXXIX, cols 577–580; for Nilus of Sinai, see Cyril Mango, *The Art of the Byzantine Empire, 312–1453: Sources and Documents* (Toronto: University of Toronto Press, 1986), 33; Maguire, "Christians, Pagans, and the Representation of Nature," 148–149.

11 Eusebius, *Ecclesiastical History* X, 4, 37–68; for a comprehensive discussion of this text, see Christine Smith, "Christian Rhetoric in Eusebius' Panegyric at Tyre," *Vigiliae Christianae* 43 (1989): 226–247.

12 Michel Van Esbroeck, "Une homélie sur l'église attribuée à Jean de Jérusalem," *Le Muséon* 86 (1973): 283–304; *idem*, "Jean II de Jérusalem et les cultes de S. Étienne, de la Sainte Sion, et de la Croix," *Analecta Bollandiana* 102 (1984): 115–125.

13 For example, two ekphraseis by Choricius of Gaza of two churches in his city: St Stephen's Church and St Sergius' Church; Choricius of Gaza, *Laudatio Marciani* I, 17–76; II, 38–45. For Choricius, see Mango, *Art of the Byzantine Empire*, 57–60; A Syrian hymn for the Cathedral of Edessa (modern Urfa in Turkey); Mango 1986; André Grabar, "Le témoignage d'une hymne syriaque sur l'architecture de la cathédral d'Edesse au VI siècle et sur la symbolique de l' édifice chrétien," *Cahiers Archéologiques* (1947): 41–67; Kathleen McVey, "The Domed Church as Microcosm: Literary Roots of an Architectural Symbol", *Dumbarton Oaks Papers* 37 (1983): 91–121, reprinted in *Studies in Early Christianity: A Collection of Scholarly Essays*, Vol. 18, ed. Paul Corby Finney (New York, NY: Garland, 1993), 183–213; for Paulus Silentiarius' poetic description of St Sophia at Constantinople, see Mango, *Art of the Byzantine Empire*, 80–91.

14 Maguire, "Christians, Pagans, and the Representation of Nature," 148.

15 Mircea Eliade, *The Sacred and the Profane: The Nature of Religion* (New York, NY: Harcourt, Brace, and World, 1959), 20–65.

16 Philo, *The Life of Moses*, 2.74–76; *idem, Questions and Answers on Exodus*, 2.52; Flavius Josephus, *Jewish Antiquities*, 3.7, 7 (179–187).

17 Origen, *Homilies on Exodus* 9.4; Robert Devreesse, *Essai sur Théodore de Mopsueste*, Studi e Testi 141 (Vatican City: Biblioteca Apostolica Vaticana, 1948), 26, note 1; Wanda Wolska-Conus, *Topographie chrétienne* (Paris: Éditions du Cerf, 1968), 40–42.

18 Jonathan Z. Smith, *Map is not Territory* (Leiden: Brill, 1978), 83–128; 172–189.

19 Maximus the Confessor, *Selected Writings*, trans. G.C. Berthold (London: Paulist Press, 1985), 188–189.
20 Patrologiae cursus completes, Series Graeca (J.-P. Migne ed.) 31, col. 1635.
21 Eusebius, *Ecclesiastical History* 10. 4. 21–22, 63–65.
22 Eusebius, *Ecclesiastical History* 10. 4. 2–3, 45–46.
23 Choricius, *Laudatio Marciani*, II, 52. See in Mango, *Art of the Byzantine Empire*, 72.
24 Mango, *Art of the Byzantine Empire*, 57.
25 Andrew Palmer with an appendix by Lyn Rodley, "The Inauguration Anthem of Hagia Sophia in Edessa: A New Edition and Architectural Notes and a Comparison with Contemporary Constantinopolitan Kontakion," *Byzantine and Modern Greek Studies* 12 (1988): 140–144.
26 Henry Maguire, *Earth and Ocean; The Terrestrial World in Early Byzantine Art* (University Park, PA: The Pennsylvania State University Press, 1987), 1–15.
27 Choricius, *Laudatio Marciani* I, 35; see Mango, *Art of the Byzantine Empire*, 63; *idem, Laudatio Marciani* II, 34, 69.

Further reading

Alföldi-Rosenbaum, Elisabeth and John Ward-Perkins. *Justinianic Mosaic Pavements in Cyrenaican Churches.* Rome: Monografie di Archeologia Libica, 14, 1980.
Balty, Janine. *Mosaïques antiques du Proche-Orient: chronologie, iconographie, interpretation.* Paris: Centre de Recherches d'Histoire Ancienne 140, Annales Littéraires de l'Université de Besancon, 1995.
Bowersock, Glen W. *Mosaics as History; The Near East from Late Antiquity to Islam.* Cambridge, MA: Harvard University Press, 2006.
Burns, J. Patout and Jensen, Robin M. *Christianity in Roman Africa the Development of its Practices and Beliefs.* Grand Rapids, Michigan and Cambridge: William B. Eerdmans Publishing Company, 2014.
Donceel Voûte, Pauline. *Les pavements des églises byzantines de Syrie et du Liban: Décor, archéologie et liturgie.* Louvain: Université Catholique de Louvain, 1988.
Dunbabin, Katherine M.D. *Mosaics of the Greek and Roman World.* Cambridge: Cambridge University Press, 1999.
Kitzinger, Ernst. *Byzantine Art in the Making: Main Lines of Stylistic Development in Mediterranean Art, Third-Seventh Century.* Cambridge, MA: Harvard University Press, 1977.
Levi, Doro. *Antioch Mosaic Pavements.* Princeton, NJ: Princeton University Press, 1947.
Maguire, Henry. *Earth and Ocean; The Terrestrial World in Early Byzantine Art.* University Park, PA: The Pennsylvania State University Press, 1987.
Michaelides, Demetrios. *Cypriot Mosaics.* Nicosia: Department of Antiquities, 1987.
Piccirillo, Michele. *The Mosaics of Jordan.* Amman: American Center of Oriental Research Publications, 1993.
Spiro, Marie. *Critical Corpus of the Mosaic Pavements on the Greek Mainland, Vol. 1, 4th–6th centuries.* New York, NY: Garland, 1978.
Talgam, Rina. *Mosaics of Faith; Floors of Pagans, Jews, Samaritans, Christians, and Muslims in the Holy Land.* University Park, PA: The Pennsylvania State University Press, 2014.
Yasin, Ann Marie. *Saints and Church Spaces in the Late Antique Mediterranean; Architecture, Cult, and Community.* Cambridge: Cambridge University Press, 2009.

8

GOLD-GLASS IN LATE ANTIQUITY

Susan Walker

The history of gold-glass

Ancient gold-glass has survived as a grave-good or grave marker. It has been found in pagan and, during the fourth century CE, also in Christian and Jewish burials, principally located in the catacombs of Rome and in the suburban cemeteries of Cologne, Germany. In broken or intact state, ancient gold-glass vessels were given to the dead, while purpose-made medallions and broken, sawn or grozed (clipped) vessel bases were used as grave markers. In both usages, the combination of gold and glass would surely have been appreciated not only as a sign of material wealth but also for the luminescent glitter of these materials in a dark, subterranean environment.

Late antique gold-glass was a revival based in Rome of a craft developed over six hundred years earlier in the eastern Mediterranean. Glass plaques decorated with gold leaf featured among the lavish ornament of the funerary couches discovered in the fourth-century BCE tomb of Philip II at Aigai, Macedonia; gold motifs also adorned glass set into finger-rings from Macedonia.[1] Though lidded gold-glass vessels are known from the Acropolis at Athens, Greece,[2] the complex technique of making gold-glass vessels most likely developed in Ptolemaic Egypt. Two gold-glass objects were carried in the procession of Ptolemy II Philadelphus (284–247 BCE), described half a millennium later as ὑάλινα διάχρυσα (glass shot through with gold) by the writer Athenaeus.[3] Indeed, Egypt retained into Late Antiquity a tradition of making luxurious, colored glass.[4] By the third century BCE, gold-glass vessels were used in southern Italy: a pair of double-layered glass bowls, decorated in applied gold leaf with acanthus, lotus and rosette, was found in a grave at Canosa, Apulia.[5] Other glass vessels in this grave included a mosaic glass dish with gold leaf sandwiched amidst the canes of colored glass; with a cluster of other finds these are now known as the "Canosa Group."[6] But these are rare instances, with the use of gold in the later Hellenistic world typically taking the form of flowing bands set within coloured cast glass vessels.[7]

Gold-glass remained an exceptional product: a few, ill preserved, finds from France and Egypt are of early Roman imperial date.[8] However, gold-glass medallions, small drinking cups and plaques of exceptionally fine quality were made in Rome for individual use in the second and third centuries CE, and gold-glass platters and shallow bowls of more variable quality, probably intended for communal use, in the fourth century.[9] What prompted the revival in

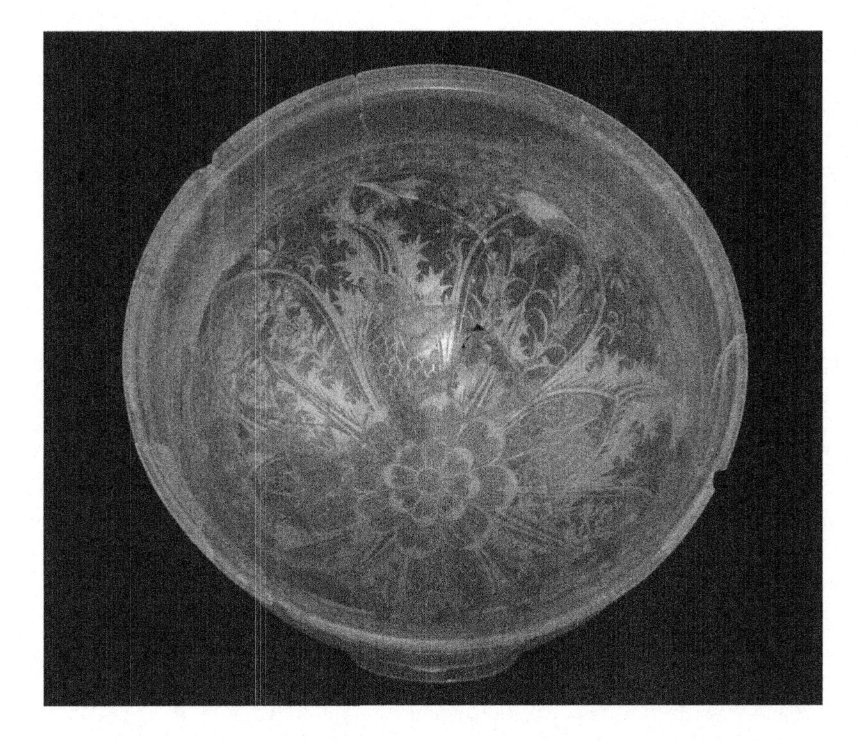

Figure 8.1 Gold-glass cup from a tomb at Canosa, south-east Italy, d. 19.3 cm. Hellenistic Greek, perhaps made in Alexandria, 250–225 BCE. British Museum 1871,0518.02 © Trustees of the British Museum/Art Resource, NY.

Rome remains unknown, as does the inspiration for later antique design, which seems closest to the pictorial Canosan bowls (Figure 8.1); it could have been part of the much wider interest in classical Greek culture that so permeated later Roman imperial society, and it could also be linked to the change in burial practice (itself poorly understood) from cremation to inhumation of the dead.

History of discovery and research

The surviving corpus of late antique gold-glass (nearly 500 pieces) was mostly found during seventeenth- to nineteenth-century CE exploration of the catacombs of Rome. The long-neglected ancient cemeteries and early Christian shrines were hollowed out from former quarries of volcanic tufa, deposits of which were located on the outskirts of the city. The catacombs of Rome were rediscovered by the Maltese scholar Antonio Bosio (1575/6–1629), whose guardian uncle represented the Knights of Malta at the Holy See. After Bosio's premature death, the publication of his pioneering account *Roma Sotterranea* (*Subterranean Rome*) was completed by Giovanni Severini, a follower of the sixteenth-century Saint Filippo Neri, who had spent ten years at prayer in the catacombs.[10]

In the early modern period care of the catacombs and the objects had not been so rigorously enforced and some pieces of gold-glass were sold or given to individual collectors in the course of the seventeenth and eighteenth centuries. However, the mid-nineteenth century saw a revival of interest in the cult of Filippo Neri and renewed interest in the catacombs. The first systematic archaeological exploration of the catacombs was undertaken by the brilliant archaeologist and epigraphist Giovanni Battista de Rossi (1822–1894), who modified Bosio's title for his own magisterial survey.[11] To control scientific exploration of the catacombs and the management of finds, de Rossi suggested to Pope Pius IX the formation of the *Pontificia Commissione di Archaeologia Sacra* (Pontifical Commission for the Archaeology of the Sacred), which was inaugurated in 1852. de Rossi became director of the Christian Museum that received the finds within the Vatican, and of the Pontifical Academy that managed research on early Christian art and archaeology. To this day the Pontifical authorities retain control of the Christian catacombs and the associated finds are mostly deposited in the Vatican Museums.[12] The Vatican Museums therefore hold the largest collection of ancient gold-glass in the world with 219 catalogued pieces.[13] Next in significance is the British Museum, with a gold-glass collection comprising fifty-five ancient pieces largely assembled in the mid-to-later nineteenth century from sales and gifts of private collections, most of which were first formed in Italy and Germany.[14] The German nineteenth-century collections included recent finds from Roman cemeteries in Cologne (see below).

A third large collection of thirty-six pieces is held in the Ashmolean Museum, Oxford; the history of this collection illustrates the close connection in the nineteenth century between contemporary religious movements and the growth of early Christian archaeology. The collection was purchased in Rome from 1864–1894 by the English antiquary Charles Wilshere (*ca.* 1814–1906), a passionate follower of the Oxford or Tractarian Movement, which sought to revive Catholicism in England, with a particular focus on the practices of the early Church. Wilshere's personal mission as a wealthy, highly educated collector was to acquaint the English with the art and archaeology of early Christian and contemporary Jewish Rome. To this end the finest pieces in his collection of ancient gold-glass were lent for some twenty-four years during Wilshere's lifetime to the South Kensington Museum (the predecessor of the Victoria and Albert Museum, London). The collection was subsequently bequeathed to Pusey House, the center of the Oxford Movement, with a view to educating young candidates for the priesthood and other students of Oxford University. The collection was purchased by the Ashmolean Museum in 2007.

Wilshere worked closely with de Rossi, who was revered in his lifetime and is still regarded as the founder of early Christian archaeology as a scholarly discipline. Wilshere corresponded with de Rossi for nearly thirty years and in 1893 returned a gold-glass to the Vatican in de Rossi's honour. De Rossi had long objected to the export of this glass from Rome, which uniquely depicts St Genesius, an actor who had fatally displeased Diocletian by publicly confessing to Christianity at a performance attended by the emperor. Genesius enjoyed a cult in nineteenth-century Rome; even today his relics are kept in the church of Santa Susanna.

The glass depicting Genesius[15] was one of twelve acquired by Wilshere from the sale in 1862 of the collection of antiquities assembled by Baron Alessio Recupero of Catania, Sicily. Recupero had bought the pieces about 1800 in an unauthorised sale of objects formerly curated by the Abbot Severini.[16] Less happily, Wilshere worked with the demanding Neapolitan Jesuit scholar Raffaello Garrucci, a rival to de Rossi who published several well-illustrated accounts of gold-glass.[17] Significant collections of ancient gold-glass are held in many other museums, including the Louvre, the Bibliothèque Nationale, and the Petit Palais, Paris; the Corning Museum of Glass, Corning, New York, and the Metropolitan Museum, New York; in Italy the Museo Bargello in Florence, the Museo di Castelvecchio in Verona and the Museo Civico, Pesaro hold important collections of gold-glass.

A corpus of gold-glass in the Vatican and other museums by the American scholar Charles Morey was published posthumously in 1959. Though poorly illustrated and occasionally confused, Morey's work has remained indispensable for the modern study of late Roman gold-glass and his catalogue still provides the basic reference numbers for individual pieces.[18] Much effort has been made in subsequent years to develop Morey's understanding of the gold-glass workshops, notably by the Italian scholar Lucia Faedo (1978) and the German Hans-Georg Nüsse (2008).[19] All three scholars compared style, pattern, and textual content within the gold leaf to suggest relationships between individual gold-glasses, and hence to identify workshops that were placed in a much debated chronological order. In recent years Claudia Lega of the Vatican Museums has analyzed the lettering style of the texts on gold-glass, relating the letter forms to the workshops proposed by Faedo and Nüsse.[20]

However, new methods of scientific analysis and imaging have opened up new paths to understanding the production of late antique gold-glass, allowing a focus on the chemistry of the glass in addition to art-historical and textual analysis of the gold leaf. In the last twenty years scientists have developed non-intrusive methods of analysis, notably XRF, in which the surface of the glass is bombarded with high energy X-rays, causing the emission from the glass of secondary or fluorescent X-rays, from which individual chemical elements may be identified, quantified, and compared. The XRF and other more intrusive analytical techniques have informed recent catalogues of gold-glass in the British Museum[21] and Oxford.[22]

Significantly, over a century ago, the author of a prescient German study of late antique gold-glass had recommended chemical analysis of the glass as potentially a more effective means of distinguishing workshops than studying the gold leaf.[23] In recent practice chemical analysis has delivered a framework for dating gold-glass in a broad chronological sequence of three bands, within which iconographical and textual observations can be made concerning workshops and response to pressure from the increasingly influential Church (see below). With regard to the role of the gold-leaf engraver in glass workshops, the results suggest that gold-leaf engravers specialized in decorating particular types of vessel. As with variation in quality, the function of a gold-glass object and the nature of the commission, individual or public, is likely to have determined the development of gold-glass workshops (Figure 8.2).

The burial context of gold-glass

The loss of original context and the subsequent incorporation of attractively gilded vessel fragments and medallions within church, state, and private collections naturally give rise to questions about the condition of gold-glass at the time of burial. Were gold-glass vessels deliberately broken in antiquity or, as some early drawings suggest, were they buried complete and only broken on or after removal from the tomb? Some gold-glass medallions were certainly cut after discovery.[24] However, some broken gold-glass vessel bases remain bedded within the mortar used to seal the individual grave or *loculus* within the catacomb.[25] Some of these vessel bases have been turned inwards so the gold-leaf decoration, always intended to be seen from the inside of the vessel, could be "read" by the deceased. Such an arrangement also meant that no jagged edges of glass threatened visitors to the narrow passages between the grave slots in the catacombs, and the broken walls of the vessels maintained a good grip on the mortar bedding. Indeed, most of the glasses facing out of the mortar were carefully trimmed in antiquity or purpose-made as medallions with smooth edges.

Surviving fragments set in the mortar to face outwards include smaller medallions with colored outer layers of glass. These were designed not as bases but to be set within vessel walls.[26] In the nineteenth and twentieth centuries complete glass vessels of this type were excavated in late antique graves in the cemeteries of Cologne (Figure 8.3). A clear glass plaque decorated in gold leaf but without a covering layer of glass was also found in a woman's grave (Figure 8.4); her Christian affiliation is evident from the biblical scenes of salvation radiating around the center of the plaque.

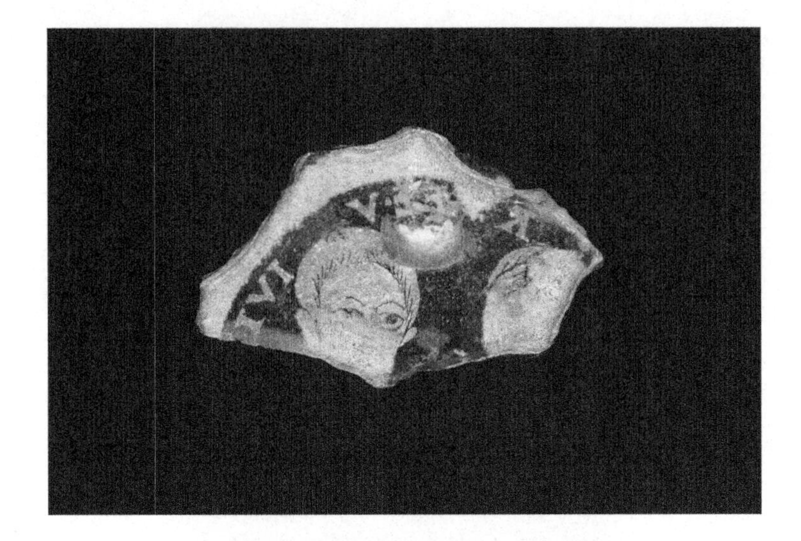

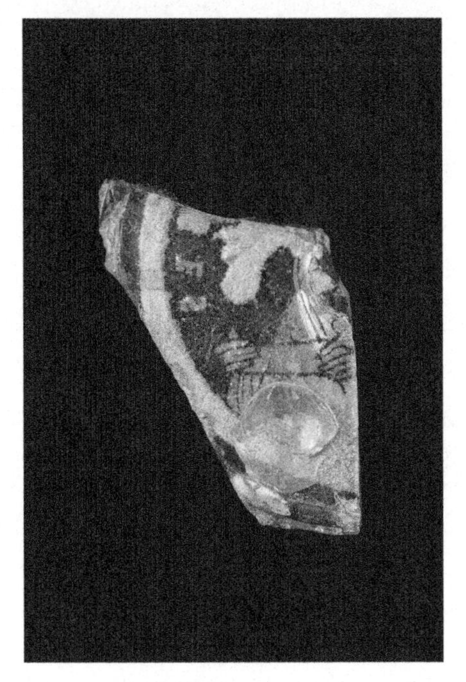

Figure 8.2 Part of a gold-glass portrait medallion and a small cup: the lettering of the gold leaf is by two different hands, but the same batch of glass was used to make, respectively, the outer and inner layers of the two vessels. Max. dimensions (above) w. 3.9 cm and (below) h. 5.0 cm. Late 4th century CE. Ashmolean Museum, Oxford, AN2007.24, 27.

Similarities in the gold-leaf decoration and technique of manufacture of the gold-glass from Cologne to finds from Rome suggest that the gold-glass vessels were imported from Italy to the river-port on the northern imperial frontier. The reason for their presence in fourth-century CE Cologne, itself a great centre of Roman glass manufacture, most likely reflects the proximity of Cologne to the imperial capital of Trier. However, other significant imperial centres in the

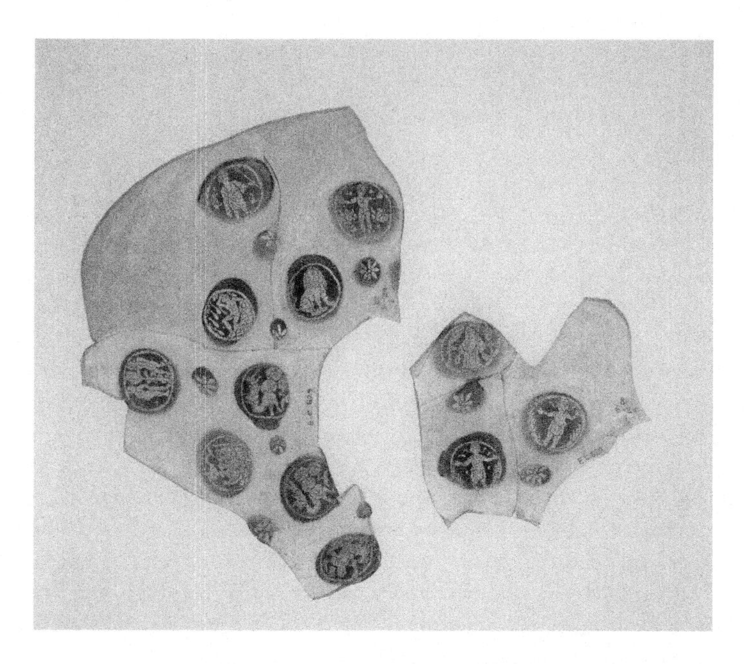

Figure 8.3 Part of a shallow bowl decorated with swirls of gold-glass medallions with colored outer layers, from the cemetery of St Severin, Cologne, Germany. Max. d. about 21 cm. British Museum PE 1881.6.24–1. Photo: © Trustees of the British Museum/Art Resource, NY.

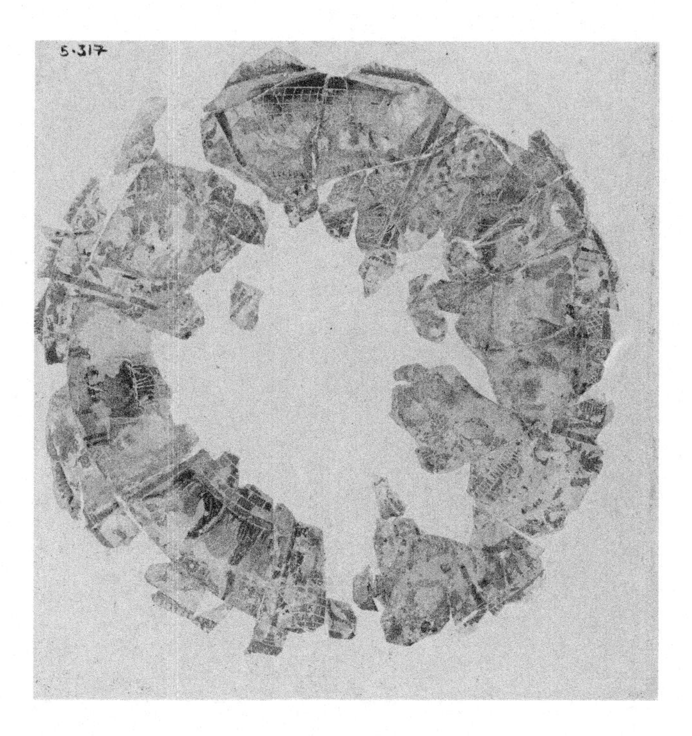

Figure 8.4 Watercolor painting of the remains of an unprotected gold-glass plaque excavated in 1866 in the cist grave of a woman, Ursulagartenstrasse, Cologne, d. about 19 cm. British Museum BEP S.317. Photo: © The Trustees of the British Museum.

Balkans have not produced quantities of gold-glass apparently imported from Rome, though isolated finds of gold-glass have been made within reach of the Rhine-Danube frontier and elsewhere in southern Europe.[27]

The social status of gold-glass

Much argument has arisen over the social status of gold-glass. Given by relatives and dependents of the deceased, gold-glass does not appear to have had the same cachet as, say, late antique silver tableware or ivory diptychs.[28] Artistic quality is very variable within the corpus: portraits apparently intended as grave-markers and made from the second to the fourth centuries CE are of an exceptional standard of craftsmanship, easily comparable with the finest painted mummy-portraits from Egypt or to portraits carved in marble. Powdered glass and gold leaf were brushed to great effect to create shading and a sense of three-dimensionality in these objects of modest scale (Figure 8.5). Though loss of archaeological context impedes recognition of the users of late Roman gold-glass, two portrait medallions remain in place in the catacomb of Pamphilus. This and many other catacombs in suburban Rome were developed on land that was in imperial ownership in the third century.[29] Many members of the wider imperial family of servants and courtiers were buried there, and it seems reasonable to suggest that the people portrayed in late second and third-century gold-glass medallions and drinking cups, which are only known from Rome, were members of that group of often wealthy freedmen who served the emperor and his family as musicians, scribes, bodyguards and so forth.

Figure 8.5 Gold-glass medallion of a mother with her children, about 250–300 CE, later mounted on the cross of St Desiderius. Museo di Santa Giulia, Brescia. Photo: Wikimedia Commons.

In contrast, many of the fourth-century Christian gold-glasses appear to have been mass-produced to a pedestrian standard rather than individually commissioned. Nonetheless, in terms of glass-making all gold-glass lies at the expensive end of the market (see further below).

Many scholars have taken the view that gold-glass vessels were commissioned or purchased for special events, from personal milestones such as weddings to gifts auguring good fortune for the New Year.[30] Nonetheless, the similarity of the iconography of the gold leaf to the decoration of contemporary sarcophagi and wall-paintings within the catacombs indicates that much was ordered specifically for funerary use. Whatever its purpose, gold-glass offers evidence of conspicuous consumption, being rarely used, perhaps only once at the funeral feast and then buried with the deceased, if not specifically commissioned to accompany the dead (Figure 8.4).

Within the surviving corpus of gold-glass, we can trace some evidence in the decoration of the gold leaf of response from glassmakers and their clients to complaints by prominent bishops of the early Christian church concerning the sumptuous nature of Roman funerals and the continued cult of the dead.[31] By the early fifth century CE, the church appeared to have won the arguments in favor of personal austerity:[32] no doubt the glassmakers also lost their market to the relocation of the capital to Ravenna in 402, the sack of Rome by Alaric in 410, and the consequent dispersal of many of the city's wealthier inhabitants. Gold-glass does not appear to have accompanied the dead in inner-city burials of the fifth century and later. Rare survivals of leather bands, perhaps made in the sixth century CE, include tiny gold-glass medallions within their decoration, the gold leaf adhering to richly colored glass.[33] By the time these were made (most likely in Egypt), the countryside around Rome had become unstable, the catacombs exposed to looting and ripe for abandonment.

Making gold-glass

Gold-glass is a term commonly applied to the bases of glass vessels and to glass medallions in which a layer of gold leaf, incised and cut with figures and/or text, is sandwiched between two layers of glass. The technique has inspired the alternative term "sandwich gold-glass", in German "Zwischengoldglas", distinguishing these vessels from other artefacts in which a layer of gold leaf was applied to an exterior surface with no covering glass layer. In sandwich gold-glass, one layer of clear glass served as the base to which the gold leaf was glued, cut, engraved and sometimes painted with coloured enamel. The gold leaf and its base were then fused to a second, covering layer of glass that formed the walls of the vessel, usually a shallow bowl. At the height of the late antique fashion for gold-glass in the middle years of the fourth century CE, smaller medallions were made in which the gold leaf was stuck to a protective layer forming the wall of a shallow bowl. As their gold-leaf decoration was cut in reverse, the small medallions offered no scope for text or embellishment with coloured enamel. Nonetheless, a sequence of medallions could deliver a narrative, and the careful arrangement of contrasting colours of glass produced attractive swirls of colour around the walls of the bowls (Figure 8.3, where the covering outer layers of glass were alternately coloured with blue-green copper and deep blue cobalt). It is likely that sandwich gold-glass vessels were designed for use by the living, even if only once, while unprotected gold-glass had no function other than to accompany the dead or embellish their graves (Figure 8.4).[34]

Although levels of artistry in preparing the gold leaf were variable throughout the late antique period of production of gold-glass, the manufacture of gold-glass vessels required considerable dexterity and the careful control of temperatures in multiple kilns. Recent experimental archaeology by Daniel Howells has clarified the likely process that baffled craftsmen and scholars for centuries.[35] Early written accounts, while illuminating, are not entirely helpful. Chapter 13 of the second book of the treatise of the twelfth-century German monk Theophilus, *De vitreis Scyphis, quos graecia uro at argento decorant* (*On glass goblets, which the [Byzantine] Greeks decorate with gold and silver*) describes how glassmakers worked with gold leaf,[36] as does the late fourteenth-century account by Cennino Cennini.[37] However, neither scholar described the making of sandwich gold-glass. Fortunately, a tenth-century writer, the Italian monk Eraclius, did describe the process in *De coloribus et artibus Romanorum* (*On the colours and arts of the Romans*), part 5, 187–188; this last account proved the formative influence on Howells' work.

As revived by Howells, the process for making glass vessels with sandwich gold leaf bases is as follows. A bubble of glass is gathered and blown, with a constriction (parison) formed with metal pincers between the blowpipe and the bubble. The bubble is then slowly cooled in an annealing oven, after which the pad can be separated from it, in the process creating a shallow, downturned foot-ring. The upper surface of the pad is painted with vegetable gum or animal glue and a very thin layer of gold leaf is brushed upon it. The design is cut into the gold leaf with a needle or stylus, using guidelines for lettering and/or grids for the composition. Additional details painted in coloured enamel may be added. Excess gold leaf is trimmed for recycling. The decorated base is slowly reheated in the annealing oven. It is then placed in a box on the floor while the much larger and hotter clear blown glass covering layer is lowered onto it. This process is especially tricky: some gold-glass vessel fragments show evidence of at least two covering layers, suggesting that the glassmaker was not always satisfied with the first attempt. The fused whole vessel is then removed from the blow-pipe and slowly cooled in the annealing oven. Any excess glass is later removed for recycling, leaving a shallow bowl.

To make the medallions decorating the walls of vessels, the inner layer of transparent glass of the entire bowl is first blown, detached from the blowpipe and cooled in the annealing oven. A grid of medallion locations is marked on it and the gold-leaf decoration applied. The decoration of each medallion is cut retrograde, inhibiting the use of text; no enamel paint can be added to it. The bowl is then slowly reheated, and small gathers of colored glass are applied with a rod to seal the medallions into position. In the finer medallions, decorated with brushed, powdered gold leaf and coloured glass, both layers of glass are blown in near-identical fashion, the gold-leaf decoration sealed and the edges clipped, beveled and ground smooth.

Primary and secondary production of Roman glass and the use of decolourants

Recent chemical analysis of late antique gold-glass bases and medallions set into the walls of vessels shows that all Roman glass used in the manufacturing process was decoloured. From prices given for glass in the Edict on Maximum Prices issued on behalf of the Emperor Diocletian in 301 CE, the consistent use of decolourants indicates that gold-glass invariably fell within the more expensive, "Alexandrian" category of glass, listed at twice the price (twenty-four *denarii* per pound) of "Judaean" glass (twelve–thirteen *denarii* per pound): a good account of the likely application of the Edict to late antique glass-working, with citations of the relevant section of the text of the edict in Greek and Latin and English translation, is given by Stern.[38] "Judaean" glass is understood to have been used in its natural state, the glass coloured a bluish green from deposits of iron within the sand used in the primary manufacturing process. To remove the iron, a chemical agent was required. As decolouring agents are known from stratigraphically dated glass to have changed over time, a relative chronology of Roman gold-glass may be constructed from recording the decolourants.[39] Roman glass is very consistent in character, allowing comparison across much of Europe and the Mediterranean region; the lack of variability is understood to be the result of large-scale manufacture in a two-stage process.[40] Primary glass was largely produced in kilns located within an arc ranging from northern Egypt to Syria. Here the sand was considered of suitable quality for glass-making, and there were plentiful natural deposits of natron for use as a flux. The sand in question was alluvia dumped by the Nile in its delta, whence it was blown by the prevailing winds onto the beaches of the south-east sector of the Mediterranean coast. Decolouring took place as part of the primary production process. Raw glass was produced in this region in enormous kilns (excavated examples are of very late antique date).[41] Glass was exported in its raw state to Europe, where secondary workshops of glassmakers melted down the lumps, blocks and slabs to make vessels and other products. Here there were plentiful resources of timber and metal, both commodities lacking in the area of primary production, which could be used respectively to fire kilns and make heavy-duty blowpipes of a weight to pick up large gobs of molten glass. Production was thus able to expand from perfume and oil flasks to bottles large enough to be used for transporting oil used for cooking and lighting, or wine.[42]

The use of decolourants and the development of gold-glass from the third to the fifth centuries CE

Gold-glasses of the second and third centuries CE were decoloured with antimony alone. Some small medallions forming the narrow bases of chalices were simply decorated in gold leaf with a text toasting the named honorand, with an injunction to "Drink! May you live!" written in Greek rendered in a Latin script, the style resembling modern stencilled lettering (Figure 8.6). That toast is often understood to have the implied Christian sense of "May you live [forever]!" though this sense cannot be verified without overtly Christian iconography, present in some later glasses (Figure 8.7). Some larger bases, apparently of straight-walled beakers, were elaborately decorated with similar texts rendered in trailed gilding. Both vessel types appear to have been used at feasts honouring the deceased before burial. The larger, shallow bowls typical of later gold-glass vessel production are not much seen at this period, though unprotected gold-leaf plaques for placement on the corpse were certainly made (Figure 8.4; the Christian narrative scenes indicate a fourth-century date for this piece). Some very high quality gold-leaf portraits were crafted of individuals or family groups (see above and Figure 8.5). These medallions appear to have been used as tomb markers and did not form the base of vessels.

In the fourth century CE, antimony was replaced as a decolourant with the more widely available and less toxic manganese. Gold-glass was then widely used to decorate the bases of shallow bowls that appear to have been used at funeral feasts. The bowls and dishes are of open form, more suited to food than to drink, a characteristic of late antique dining observed in other media.[43] Overtly Christian themes appeared, recounting stories from the Old and New Testaments of individuals such as Isaac, Jonah, Susannah and the paralytic healed by Christ, among others who had been saved by divine intervention (Figures 8.4 and 8.7).

Vignettes from these biblical stories of personal salvation were also popular subjects for the small medallions set in the walls of glass bowls (Figure 8.3). An engraved glass bowl found in a tomb in Podgoritza, Montenegro, and now in St Petersburg includes above the vignettes lines from the *commendatio animae*, or prayer for the commendation of the soul, one of the earliest surviving Christian prayers (Figure 8.8).

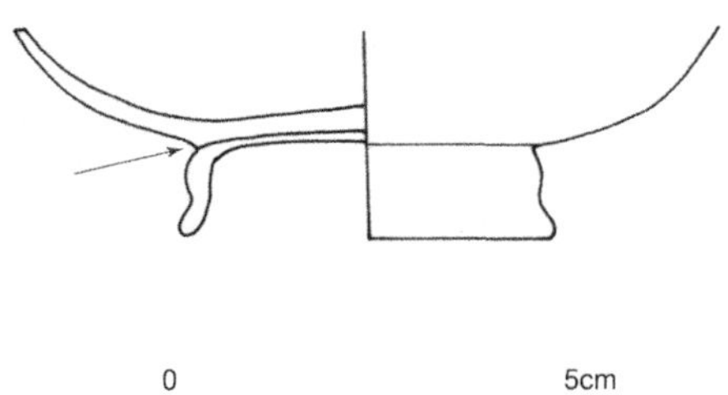

Figure 8.6 Backlit, detailed photograph taken from above of the base of an inscribed chalice enjoining Heraclides to drink and live (photo: Dana Norris), with a drawing of the fragmentary chalice by Yvonne Beadnell. Ashmolean Museum, Oxford, AN2007.38.

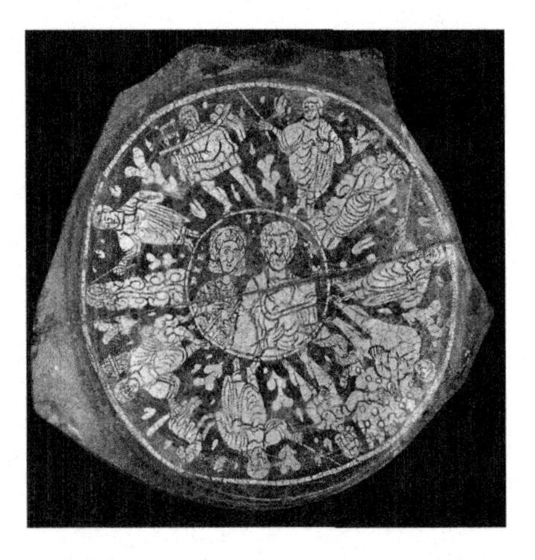

Figure 8.7 Gold-glass base of an oval dish: one of an unnamed couple in the central medallion is enjoined to drink and live; around them are vignettes of stories of personal salvation taken from the Old and New Testaments, d. 10.8 cm. Photo: David Gowers, Ashmolean Museum, Oxford, AN2007.13.

Figure 8.8 Engraved glass bowl from a 4th-century CE tomb in Podgoritza, Montenegro. Scenes of personal salvation taken from the Bible are accompanied by text from the prayer for the commendation of the soul, d. about 25 cm. Inv. No. W. 73, The State Hermitage Museum, St Petersburg. Photograph © The State Hermitage Museum, photo by Svetlana Suetova.

Similar biblical narratives of personal salvation appear painted on the walls of the catacombs, and carved on the personalized lids of marble sarcophagi; in a funerary context, these too surely evoke the prayer commending the soul of the deceased. Within the circular format of the bases of gold-glass vessels the vignettes sometimes surrounded portraits of an individual or a couple, one or both of whom might be toasted in the old fashion (Figure 8.7). It is striking that all such figures portrayed in gold-glass are sumptuously dressed in contemporary style (Figures 8.2, 8.5 and 8.7). However, these apparently wealthy individuals were the recipients rather than the commissioners of gold-glass, which cannot therefore be used as evidence for self-representation. Those who gave the glass vessels might be of considerably lower status.

In the mid-fourth century CE gold-glass reached its acme of popularity, and workshops in Rome expanded to produce a wider range of goods, including flat inlays and perfume jars. The inlay illustrated here (Figure 8.9) was cut down for reuse in a Christian context. Originally the engraver depicted a secular scene of fishing; in second use the Christian symbol of paired fish was retained.[44]

In the mid-fourth century CE Jewish clients commissioned gold-glass vessels of the same shape, using the same toasts and apparently the same workshops. However, the gold-leaf decoration, sometimes further embellished with enamel paint, was restricted to objects of Jewish liturgy in sacred settings (Figure 8.10).

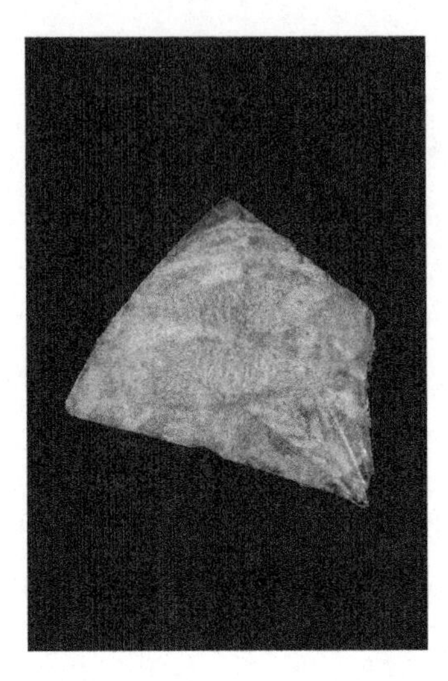

Figure 8.9 Gold-glass inlay with a secular scene of fishing, cut down for reuse in a Christian context, w. 5.5 cm. Photo taken from the clearer underside, so the lettering is reversed. Photo: David Gowers. Ashmolean Museum, Oxford, AN2007.23.

Figure 8.10 Bowl fragments with Menorah, Shofar, and Torah Ark, 300–500 CE. Rogers Fund, 1918. Photo from the underside: The Metropolitan Museum of Art, metmuseum.org.

As happened with Christian decoration of gold-glass, Jewish motifs complemented the decoration of contemporary funerary memorials in stone and the painted walls of catacombs in Rome. It is likely that the appearance of sacred symbols in Jewish funerary art at Rome

Figure 8.11 Segment of the base of a glass plate or shallow bowl: central medallion of Christ, surrounded by figures of Saint Peter, Saint Luke, and the martyred Pope Sixtus. The centres of the rosettes between the saints were picked out in green enamel paint. Max. l. 9.6 cm. Photo: David Gowers. Ashmolean Museum, Oxford, AN2007.10.

reflected growing awareness of Jerusalem in the city, following the legalisation of Christianity and the arrival in Rome of Christian relics from Jerusalem.

Records survive of senior Christian clerics railing against the continued practice of pagan funerary cults by Christian families.[45] The Christian Fathers urged the faithful to remember the martyrs rather than toasting their loved ones with wine served in inappropriate chalices, and to spend money on the living poor rather than wasting it on the funerals of the rich. Apparently in response, the decoration of some gold-glass moved from themes of personal salvation to celebrate the martyrs and saints of the Church. Though much glass of this sort was carelessly produced, some examples were of higher standard and decorated with added enamel paint. The illustrated fragment (Figure 8.11) was cut in half, a phenomenon also known in late antique undecorated glass. Perhaps its value had to be shared. The edges of this fragment were clipped at an unknown date.

Despite increasing interest in saints and martyrs, portraits of individuals continued to be commissioned until the end of the fourth century (Figure 8.2). Unlike private individuals, martyrs and saints were invariably labelled with their names, though it is not always clear whether unnamed miracle-workers should be identified as Old Testament prophets or as Christ (Figures 8.3 and 8.7). In the later fourth century, Christian figures became overwhelmingly dominant, with a clear focus on the rise to prominence of Peter and Paul as patron saints of Rome (Figure 8.12).

Though by this time much glass was recycled, with a mix of decolourants visible in the chemistry, it was still possible to commission gold-glass vessels of high quality (Figure 8.2). The prominence of Saints Peter and Paul and the sometimes outstanding quality of the latest gold-glass recall the outstanding craftsmanship of some marble sarcophagi of the age of Theodosius. These exceptional works show that individual commissions by wealthy patrons could still produce art of a high order even within a decade or two of the demise of the art of making gold-glass.

Figure 8.12 Clipped gold-glass base of a vessel: Saints Peter and Paul watch over medallion portraits of the martyred popes Julius and Sixtus, d. 10.5 cm. Photo taken from the more visible outer surface of the glass, with text reversed, by David Gowers. Ashmolean Museum, Oxford, AN2007.7.

Notes

1 Despina Ignatiadou, "Three cast-glass vessels from a Macedonian tomb in Pydna", in *Annales du 14e Congrès de l'Association internationale pour l'histoire du verre*, ed. Jennifer Price (Venice – Milan: Association internationale pour l'histoire du verre, 1998): 35–38; *idem*, "Glass and gold on Macedonian funerary couches". *Annales du 15e Congrés de l'Association internationale pour l'histoire du verre* (New York/Corning: Association internationale pour l'histoire du verre, 2001): 4–7.

2 E. Marianne Stern, "Ancient glass in Athenian temple treasures". *Journal of Glass Studies* 41 (1999): 19–50.

3 Athenaeus, *Deipnosophistae: The learned banqueters* V.30, 199; see Donald B. Harden, "The Canosa Group of Hellenistic glasses in the British Museum". *Journal of Glass Studies* 10 (1968): 41.

4 Marie-Dominique Nenna, "Verreries de luxe de l'antiquité tardive découvertes à Douch (oasis de Kharga, Égypte)". *Annales du 15 Congrès de l'A.H.I.V (New York 2001)* (Nottingham, 2003), 93–97.

5 See Harden, "The Canosa Group", fig. 1.

6 David F. Grose, *Early ancient glass: core-formed, rod-formed, and cast vessels and objects from the late Bronze Age to the early Roman Empire, 1600 BC to AD 50* (New York, NY: Hudson Hills and Toledo Museum of Art, 1989).

7 Andrew Oliver, "Late Hellenistic glass in the Metropolitan Museum". *Journal of Glass Studies* 9 (1967): 13–33.

8 Danièle Foy and Marie-Dominique Nenna, *Tout feu tout sable. Mille ans de verre antique dans le Midi de la France.* (Marseille, Aix-en-Provence: Musée d'histoire de Marseille, 2001); J.D. Cooney, *Glass. Catalogue of Egyptian antiquities in the British Museum* (London: The British Museum, 1976).

9 Charles R. Morey, *The gold-glass collection of the Vatican Library, with additional catalogues of other gold-glass collections* (Vatican City: Bibliotheca Apostolica Vaticana, 1959); Daniel T. Howells, edited by Chris Entwistle and Liz James, *A catalogue of the late antique gold glass in the British Museum* (London: British Museum Press, 2015).

10 Antonio Bosio, *Roma sotterrannea, opera postuma compita, disposta & accresciuta dal M.R.P.G. Severani, publ. dal commendatore F.C. Aldobrandino*, Rome, 1632.

11 Giovanni Battista de Rossi, *La Roma sotterranea cristiana*, Vols 1–3. Rome, 1864, 1867, 1877.

12 Vincenzo Fiocchi Nicolai, Fabrizio Bisconti, and Danilo Mazzoleni, *The Christian catacombs of Rome. History, decoration, inscriptions*, 3rd ed., trans. Cristina Carla Stella and Lori-Ann Touchette (Regensburg: Schnell and Steiner, 2009).

13 Morey, *Gold-glass collection.*
14 Howells, *A catalogue of the late antique gold glass*, 12–21.
15 Morey, *Gold-glass collection*, no. 79.
16 Susan Walker, ed. *Saints and Salvation: the Wilshere Collection of gold-glass, sarcophagi and inscriptions from Rome and Southern Italy. Ashmolean Museum, University of Oxford* (Oxford: Ashmolean Museum, 2017).
17 Raffaele Garrucci, *Vetri ornati di figure in oro trovati nei cimiteri dei cristiani primitivi di Roma*, Rome, 1858; *idem*, 'Un vetro cimiteriale', *La Civiltà cattolica* 13, serie 5.1 (1862): 691–703; *idem*, *Descrizione dei vetri ornati di figure in oro appartenenti al sig. Tommaso Capobianchi, negoziante d'antichità in Via del Babuino n. 152*, Rome, 1864; *idem*, *Vetri ornati di figure in oro, trovati nei cimiteri dei cristiani primitivi di Roma*, 2nd ed., Rome; and *idem*, *Storia della arte cristiana nei primi otto secoli della chiesa*, V. 3, *Pitture non cimiteriali*, Prato, 1870–1876.
18 Morey, *Gold-glass collection.*
19 Lucia Faedo, "Per una classificazione preliminare dei vetri dorati tardoromani". *Annuario della Scuola Normale di Pisa*, 8.3 (1978): 1025–1070; Hans-Georg Nüsse, "Römische Goldgläser – alte und neue Ansätze zu Werkstattfrage". *Prähistorische Zeitschrift* 83: 222–256.
20 Claudia Lega, "Il corredo epigrafico dei vetri dorati: novità e considerazioni". *Sylloge Epigraphica Barcinonensis (SEBarc)* 10 (2012): 263–286.
21 A. Meek, "Gold Glass in late antiquity: analysis of the British Museum's collection," in *A catalogue of the late antique gold glass in the British Museum*, by Daniel T. Howells, ed. Chris Entwistle and Liz James (London: British Museum Press, 2015), 121–130.
22 Walker, *Saints and Salvation.*
23 Hermann Vopel, *Die altchristlischen Goldgläser: ein Beitrag zur altchristlichen Kunst und Kulturgeschichte* (Freiburg: J.C.B. Mohr, 1899).
24 Howells, Entwistle and James, *A catalogue of the late antique gold glass*, 24–25.
25 Morey, *Gold-glass collection*: nos 11, 24, 42, 68, 103, 166, 170, 220–225, the last group still located in the Catacomb of Pamphilus.
26 Morey, *Gold-glass collection*: nos 166, 170.
27 See most recently Howells, Entwistle and James, *A catalogue of the late antique gold glass*, 153–162, Appendix A.
28 Alan Cameron, "Orfitus and Constantia: a note on Roman gold-glasses". *Journal of Roman Archaeology* 9 (1996): 295–301; Howells, Entwistle and James, *A catalogue of the late antique gold glass*, 52; Walker, *Saints and Salvation*, 84.
29 See n. 24 above and Barbara E. Borg, *Crisis and ambition: tombs and burial customs in third century CE Rome* (Oxford: Oxford University Press, 2013), 79.
30 Stephanie L. Smith, *Gold-glass vessels of the late Roman Empire: production, context, and function* (PhD diss., Rutgers, NJ: The State University of New Jersey, 2000).
31 Walker, *Saints and Salvation*, 78–79; Eric Rébillard, *The care of the dead in late antiquity*, trans. Elizabeth Trapnell Rawlings and Jeanine Routier-Pucci (Cornell, NY: Cornell University Press, 2009).
32 Peter L. Brown, *Through the eye of the needle: the fall of Rome and the making of Christianity in the West 350–550* (Princeton, NJ: Princeton University Press, 2012).
33 Morey, *Gold-glass collection*, no. 444, now in Vienna.
34 Ignatiadou, *Glass and gold.*; Walker, *Saints and Salvation*, 76–77.
35 Howells, Entwistle and James, *A catalogue of the late antique gold glass*, 43–52 with Appendix C.
36 *Theophilus, On diverse arts*, trans. John G. Hawthorne and C.S. Smith (Chicago, IL: University of Chicago Press, 1963).
37 C.J. Herringham, trans., *Il Libro dell'Arte o Trattato della Pittura: The book of the art of Cennino Cennini: a contemporary practical treatise on quattrocento painting translated from the Italian, with notes on Medieval art methods* (London: G. Allen & Unwin, 1899), Chapter 172, 154–156.
38 E. Marianne Stern, "Roman glass-blowing in a cultural context". *American Journal of Archaeology* 103 (1999): 441–484.
39 C. Jackson, "Making colourless glass in the Roman period," *Archaeometry* 47.4 (2005): 763–780.
40 I. Freestone, Y. Gorin-Rosen and M.J. Hughes, "Primary glass from Israel and the production of glass in late antiquity", in *La route du verre: ateliers primaires et secondaires du second millénaire avant J.-C. au moyen age*, ed. Marie-Dominique Nenna (Lyon: Maison de l'Orient et de la Méditerranée 2001), 65–84.
41 Freestone, Gorin-Rosen and Hughes, "Primary glass from Israel".

42 Stern, "Roman glass blowing".
43 Katharine Dunbabin, *The Roman banquet. Images of conviviality* (Cambridge: Cambridge University Press, 2003).
44 Walker, *Saints and Salvation*, 149–150, no.16.
45 Rébillard, *Care of the Dead*, 144–146.

Further reading

Auth, S. H. "Drink may you live! Roman motto glasses in the context of Roman life and death", in *Annales du 13e Congrès de l'Association Internationale pour l'Histoire du Verre, Pays Bas, 28 aout–1 septembre, 1995, 103–112*. Lochem: Association internationale pour l'histoire du verre, 1996.

Cameron, A. "Orfitus and Constantia: a note on Roman gold-glasses". *Journal of Roman Archaeology* 9 (1996), 295–301.

Cooney, J. D. *Glass. Catalogue of Egyptian antiquities in the British Museum*. London: British Museum Press, 1976.

Entwistle, C. and James, L. (eds). *New light on old glass: recent research on Byzantine mosaics and glass*. London: British Museum Research Publication 179, 2013.

Fülep, F. "Early Christian gold glasses in the Hungarian National Museum". *Acta Antiqua Adademiae Scientiarum Hungaricae* 16 (1968), 401–12.

Harden, D. B. "The Canosa Group of Hellenistic glasses in the British Museum". *Journal of Glass Studies* 10 (1968), 21–47.

Howells, D. T., Entwistle, C. and James, L. *A catalogue of the late antique gold glass in the British Museum*. London: British Museum Research Publication 198, 2015.

Lutraan, Katherine L. "Late Roman gold-glass: images and inscriptions". MA Thesis, McMaster University, 2006.

Meek, A. "Gold glass in Late Antiquity: scientific analysis of the British Museum's collection", in *New light on old glass*, (eds) Entwistle and James, 2013, 121–30.

Morey, Charles Rufus. *The gold-glass collection of the Vatican Library with additional catalogues of other gold-glass collections*, ed. Guy Ferrari. Vatican City: Biblioteca Apostolica Vaticana, 1959.

Smith, S. L. *Gold-glass vessels of the late Roman Empire: production, context, and function*. PhD diss., Rutgers, NJ: State University of New Jersey, 2000.

Stern, E. M. "Roman glass-blowing in a cultural context". *AJA* 103 (1999), 441–484.

Walker, Susan (ed.). *Saints and salvation. Charles Wilshere's collection of gold-glass, sarcophagi and inscriptions in the Ashmolean Museum, University of Oxford*. Oxford: Ashmolean Museum, 2018.

Walker, Susan. "The Wilshere Collection of late Roman gold-glass at the Ashmolean Museum, University of Oxford", in *Neighbours and successors of Rome: traditions of glass production and use in Europe and the Middle East in the later 1st millennium AD*, eds Daniel Keller, Jennifer Price and Caroline Jackson. Oxford: Oxbow, 2014, 68–72.

9

ENGRAVED GEMS AND AMULETS

Jeffrey Spier

The use of engraved gems as personal seals was a centuries-old tradition in the Roman Empire in the early decades of the third century, when examples with Christian inscriptions and imagery first appeared. These seals are identical in style, shape, and material to contemporary pagan examples and were likely made by the same gem engravers, but the distinctive iconography and explicit words and phrases allow for identification and provide a remarkable iconographical repertoire for a period when Christian imagery, especially in the eastern part of the empire, is poorly attested. The well-studied typology of Roman gems provides considerable confidence in dating the earliest Christian examples to the first half of the third century, although other distinctive workshops continued to produce gems with Christian imagery as personal seals or amulets throughout the third and fourth century and as late as *c.* 500. Although few gems have been found in archaeological contexts, the vast majority of surviving Christian gems are believed to have been found in the Greek-speaking eastern half of the Roman Empire, especially in Asia Minor and Syria.

Although literary and epigraphic evidence for the use of seals in the third century is minimal, the large number of surviving engraved gems makes clear that they were indeed considered a necessity for daily use. Gems and rings were used as marks of individual identification and to seal documents, packages, and everyday items in the household, as numerous surviving clay sealings, some affixed to folded papyri, attest. Typically set in rings or other types of jewelry, gems also served as personal decoration as well as an indication of an individual's social standing and religious beliefs. However, the great variety of images seen on pagan gems, ranging from deities to mythological scenes, animals, and inanimate objects, make the interpretation of the meaning of particular devices difficult. In contrast, gems with Christian imagery or inscriptions clearly announce the religious convictions of the owner.

It is evident that the early Christians did in fact need to use seals but were concerned about the images displayed on them. A famous passage written by Clement of Alexandria around AD 200 demonstrates the theological apprehensions about pictorial representation:

> And let our seals be either a dove, or a fish, or a ship running with a fair wind, or a musical lyre, which Polycrates used, or a ship's anchor, which Seleucus had engraved; and if the seal is a fisherman, it will recall the apostle, and the children drawn out of the water. For we are not to depict the faces of idols, we who are prohibited from attaching

> ourselves to them, nor a sword, nor a bow, since we follow peace, nor drinking cups, since we are temperate. Many of the licentious have their (homosexual) lovers engraved, or prostitutes, as if they wished to make it impossible ever to forget their erotic passions, by being continually reminded of their licentiousness.[1]

However morally didactic the passage may be, it does reflect an awareness of actual seal usage and is addressed to an audience familiar with this everyday concern.

The first Christian gems (third century)

No Christian gems dating as early as the time of Clement can be identified, probably because at that time traditional pagan devices were chosen in the manner Clement suggests, namely from a traditional stock of images, and these cannot now be identified as specifically Christian. The earliest gems with explicit Christian content date probably from the second quarter of the third century. Most are simply engraved on small oval or octagonal cornelians and jaspers, which were once set in rings made of gold, silver, bronze or iron. Few of the original rings survive, but those that do are of typical shapes datable to the first half of the third century. Many of these gems bear no image but only an inscription, nearly always in Greek, reading either IHCOY XPICTOY (Figure 9.1), IHCOY, or XPICTOY, "Jesus Christ" in the genitive, signifying that the owner was a "servant of Jesus Christ." Closely related to these gems, and perhaps from the same workshops, are those engraved with the *chi-rho* monogram signifying *Christos* (Figure 9.2), a symbol rarely found elsewhere before the fourth century. A second group of gems with a wider variety of shapes but of similar date, around the middle of the third century, bear the inscription IXΘYC (Figure 9.3). The word, meaning "fish" in Greek, also served as an acrostic for Ἰησοῦς Χριστός Θεοῦ υἱός σωτήρ, "Jesus Christ, son of God, savior," a formula attested as early as the late second century.[2] There is little evidence to suggest that these early Christian gems were aniconic for theological reasons. Pagan gems of similar shape and perhaps from the same workshops are often engraved only with personal names or simple acclamations

Figure 9.1 Red jasper engraved IHCOY XPICTOY in silver ring. Private collection.

Figure 9.2 Cornelian engraved with the *chi-rho* monogram. Private collection.

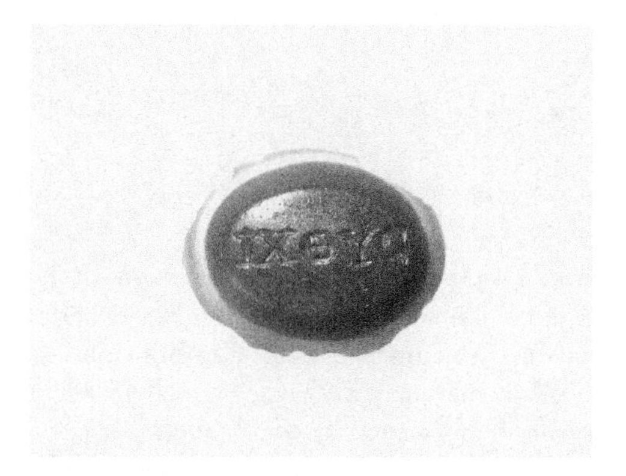

Figure 9.3 Banded agate engraved IXΘYC. Munich, Collection C.S.

(such as EYTYXI, "good luck"). Inscriptions were likely easier to engrave, and perhaps suitable images had not been considered worth having.

A contemporary group of gems of very similar shape and style, and perhaps deriving from related workshops in the eastern Mediterranean, are, however, engraved with a pictorial device: the emblem of a fish or a pair of fish flanking an anchor. The image ultimately derives from Hellenistic models but appears to have been reinterpreted as alluding to Jesus and adopted for Christian use. Clement's reference to the seal of Seleucus with the anchor as an acceptable image may have been remembered as well. Inscriptions are generally not found on these gems, but a few are inscribed with the name of Christ or the acrostic IXΘYC, thus demonstrating their Christian origin (Figure 9.4).

Aside from the fish and anchor, the most popular image on seals of the third and early fourth centuries was the Good Shepherd. The shepherd is nearly always shown standing frontally with a sheep carried over his shoulders, as is so often found in early catacomb painting in Rome and on a wide variety of other small objects of the later third and fourth centuries.[3] Christians would have viewed the image as a reference to Jesus, who explicitly calls himself the Good Shepherd (John 10:1–18) and also tells the parable of the shepherd searching for the lost sheep, which

Figure 9.4 Red jasper engraved with two fish, an anchor and XPICTOY. Munich, Collection C.S.

accords well with the image on the gems: "when he has found it, he lays it on his shoulders and rejoices" (Luke 15:5). Not all images of shepherds in Roman art of the third century need be Christian, as is evident from a number of sarcophagi primarily from Rome, but the gems do all have a consistency of style that suggests they are closely related in origin. That they were indeed made for Christians is demonstrated by the frequent appearance of subsidiary symbols with explicit religious significance, including the fish, the anchor, the *chi-rho* monogram, and occasionally the name Jesus or Christ. A very high percentage of the surviving gems, around a third, bear these additional symbols or inscriptions.

Gems with other Christian images are rare, but there are some notable examples. Several display Old Testament scenes, including Adam and Eve, Noah in the Ark, the Sacrifice of Isaac, Daniel in the Lion's Den, and a cycle of episodes from the story of Jonah. These stories are similarly popular in the catacomb paintings in Rome, on early sarcophagi, and on a variety of other small objects of the period. A few gems combine these episodes, sometimes with the Good Shepherd (Figure 9.5).

New Testament scenes are far rarer, but several gems can be dated on stylistic grounds to the late third or early fourth century, if not earlier. Examples include an unusual depiction of the baptism and a raising of Lazarus.[4] Most remarkable are three gems engraved with unconventional renderings of the Crucifixion, a scene rarely depicted in early Christian art before the sixth century. Two of these, both cornelians datable to the early fourth century, similarly show Jesus on the cross with arms outstretched flanked by the twelve apostles, a composition that does not accord with the Gospel accounts but may have theological connections to depictions on Roman sarcophagi of the fourth century.[5] The third gem is even more unusual and earlier in date, perhaps as early as the year 200.[6] The large bloodstone intaglio shows a naked, bearded Jesus tied to a cross with legs held apart (see Figure 18.1). The image is surrounded by a Greek inscription invoking "Jesus Christ, Son, Father" and also listing magic names of the sort found on amulets and papyri in Egypt in the second and third centuries (for which, see below, "Magic

Figure 9.5 Cornelian engraved with Good Shepherd and Daniel in a silver ring. Munich, Collection C.S.

amulets"). Whether the gem was created for a Christian or a pagan seeking to use the magical power of the image is unclear, but the gem provides what is probably the earliest surviving representation of the Crucifixion, one that in turn must follow now lost models.

The gems outlined here comprise the extent of the early Christian use of the medium of engraved seals, which were generally falling out of fashion over the course of the third century. The number of Christian gems is modest, with several hundred examples surviving, in contrast to the many thousands of pagan gems of the period, which is consistent with the small number of Christians in the pagan communities at the time. Stylistic similarities and find sites suggest the gems were used primarily in Asia Minor and the Syria–Palestine area, although gems have been discovered in Greece and the Balkans as well. Examples from Italy and North Africa are rare. The great majority of the gems were simply engraved with inscriptions naming Jesus Christ, the *chi-rho* monogram, the acrostic IXΘYC, the fish-and-anchor symbol, or the Good Shepherd. This body of material provides important evidence for the popularity of the acrostic and for the early use of the *chi-rho* monogram, at least in the eastern Mediterranean. Although Old and New Testament scenes are rare on these gems, enough survive to demonstrate the existence of a rich pictorial tradition not easily discerned elsewhere.

Magic amulets

Around the beginning of the second century, there developed in Egypt a fashion for the use of engraved gems as magical amulets. These objects, often of exotic materials not normally employed for personal seals and believed to have special powers—especially haematite (iron oxide) and lapis lazuli—displayed images of various deities and creatures drawn from the Hellenistic Egyptian magical tradition and were frequently inscribed with magical names and phrases. Literary sources and surviving papyri document the widespread use by magicians of magical books that contained spells (in the manner of recipes) to provide a wide range of services, for the most part medical cures, love charms, and general protection from harm. How the fashion for amulets moved from strips of papyri to engraved gems is unclear, but the relatively large number of surviving amulets (at least several thousand) attests to their popularity, as does their wide distribution. Although most have been found in Egypt and the Syria–Palestine region, amulets traveled throughout the Roman Empire. These amulets have been the subject of considerable study in recent years,[7] but they are largely beyond the scope of the present article because they rarely have Christian inscriptions or images; it seems that Christians were at first wary of these objects, about which the church fathers warned.[8] It is only over the course of the fourth and fifth centuries that the extensive magical tradition (both pagan and Jewish) became Christianized, with the name of Christ, the Virgin, saints, and angels substituted for pagan deities and demons. Many amulets made for Christians from this period also survive, especially from Egypt and Syria–Palestine, although they are typically engraved on metal rather than gemstones.[9]

Relatively few surviving magical gems of the third and fourth centuries display Christian words or images. There are rare instances of the pairing of the Good Shepherd with a pagan deity, such as Hekate or Harpokrates, as well as the use of magic words.[10] Very rarely (only three examples are recorded) gems are engraved with specifically Christian exorcistic texts of the sort better attested on papyri and metal lamellae; it is notable that although these texts are exorcisms, they contain no magic words or references to pagan deities and may be considered orthodox.[11] The bloodstone gem engraved with the representation of the Crucifixion discussed above (see Figure 18.1) is also related stylistically to the main body of magical amulets in vogue during the second and third centuries. The style of material, style of carving, and use of inscriptions, some words of which find parallels in magical papyri, suggest that an amulet maker versed in the Hellenistic Egyptian magical tradition created the work for a client in Egypt, perhaps a Christian, but the image and text remain unique. In the fifth and sixth centuries, amulets for the most part were written on metal pendants, lamellae that were rolled up and carried in amulet cases, and papyri, but there are some engraved stone amulets as well, including a group of crudely carved soft stone amulets with Christian images probably manufactured in Palestine.[12]

Later Christian gems, 300–600

The pervasive use of gems as personal seals declined quickly after the middle of the third century and nearly disappeared by the century's end, but there were some significant revivals. During the reign of Constantine (306–337) and his son Constantius II (337–361), a workshop probably located in the new capital of Constantinople, which was founded in 330, produced large and finely engraved gems in amethyst and sapphire with portraits of the emperor.[13] Although Christian images were rare, one sapphire survives engraved with the *chi-rho* monogram.[14] A small *chi-rho* or cross sometimes appears alongside portraits of aristocratic individuals on gems of the fourth and fifth centuries to denote their faith.[15]

Gems continued to be produced in imperial workshops in Constantinople throughout the fifth and into the sixth century, but surviving examples are rare. An exception is a group of engraved garnets and sapphires, some of exceptional quality, including a large facing portrait of Emperor Theodosius II (401–450) and some other portraits of contemporary aristocratic men.[16] Other, more modest, gems from the workshop typically bore personal monograms in Byzantine style, as well as suitably Christian images of doves, peacocks, eagles, dolphins, and crosses, along with Jesus and the Virgin (Figure 9.6). A number of these gems were set in rings and belt buckles of the type presented by the imperial court on official occasions.[17]

Figure 9.6 Garnet engraved with the Virgin as orans. Munich, Collection C.S.

Aside from the Constantinopolitan workshop that produced the garnets, there are few other identifiable workshops. One slightly later group of rock crystal gems were engraved primarily with scenes from the life of Jesus and set as pendants (Figure 9.7); they have been found in

Figure 9.7 Rock crystal engraved with Jesus healing the leper, set in a gold pendant. Munich, Collection C.S.

Figure 9.8 Cornelian engraved with Daniel in the lion's den. Munich, Collection C.S.

several hoards of gold jewelry of typical Byzantine manufacture datable to the later sixth century.[18] Another workshop, probably working in Syria–Palestine in the sixth century, appears to be influenced by the earlier tradition of magical gems in its use of haematite as a material and inscriptions, but notably no magical images or words are used. The images include Jesus, the Virgin, saints, and angels, and the inscriptions are typical invocations.[19]

There can be no doubt that gems were highly valued in Late Antiquity and indeed that rarer stones were increasingly sought. Sapphire and emerald (as well as pearls) were seen as an imperial prerogative as early as the third century, although aristocrats were allowed by the emperor to wear them as personal adornment.[20] From the time of Constantine the Great until the seventh century, the polychromatic use of gems, including sapphire, emerald, amethyst, cornelian, and rock crystal, was characteristic of the finest gold jewelry. Rarer stones, such as pink tourmaline, spinel, and yellow sapphire, began to appear in early Byzantine jewelry in the sixth century. Such gems were rarely engraved, however, and it is doubtful that they had theological significance in the manner of a gem engraved with a Christian image.

Ironically, it was within the Sasanian Empire (224–651), the hostile rival to the Byzantines, that the art of gem carving flourished. Enormous numbers of engraved gems in Sasanian style survive, including a small number with Christian and Jewish images and inscriptions. For the most part the imagery is not rich, the simple compositions of Daniel standing between lions (Figure 9.8) and the Sacrifice of Isaac being the most common types. A number of gems inscribed with Christian names and phrases in Persian and Syriac, as well as Jewish gems inscribed in Hebrew, provide rare evidence for the presence of those communities.[21]

Notes

1 Clement of Alexandria, *Paedagogus: Christ the Educator* 3.59.2–3.60.1. For further literature, see Jeffrey Spier, *Late Antique and Early Christian Gems*, 2nd ed. (Wiesbaden: Reichert, 2013), 15.

2 For further bibliography, see Spier, *Late Antique and Early Christian Gems*, 35, n. 21.
3 Ibid., 53–54.
4 Ibid., 72–73, nos 441–442.
5 Ibid., 73–74, nos 443–444; Felicity Harley, "The Crucifixion," in *Picturing the Bible: the Earliest Christian Art*, ed. Jeffrey Spier (New Haven: Yale University Press, 2007), 227–232; see also Harley-McGowan in this volume.
6 Spier, *Late Antique and Early Christian Gems*, 73, no. 444; Harley, *Picturing the Bible*, 228–229, no. 55.
7 Campbell Bonner, *Studies in Magical Amulets, Chiefly Graeco-Egyptian* (Ann Arbor: University of Michigan Press, 1950); Hanna Philipp, *Mira et Magica. Gemmen in Ägyptischen Museum der Staatlichen Museen Preussischer Kulturbesitz Berlin-Charlottenburg* (Mainz am Rhein: P. von Zabern, 1986); Simone Michel, *Die magischen Gemmen im Britischen Museum* (London: British Museum, 2001); *idem*, *Die Magischen Gemmen* (Berlin: Akademie Verlag, 2004); Attilio Mastrocinque, *Les intailles magiques du département des Monnaies, Médailles et Antiques* (Paris: Éditions de la Bibliothèque nationale de France, 2014).
8 Spier, *Late Antique and Early Christian Gems*, 81–86.
9 Ibid., 82, note 9 for further literature; for Jewish magic, see Gideon Bohak, *Ancient Jewish Magic: a History* (Cambridge: Cambridge University Press, 2008).
10 Spier, *Late Antique and Early Christian Gems*, 82–83.
11 Ibid., 84–85.
12 Ibid., 109–114.
13 Ibid., 18–20.
14 Ibid., 32, no. 140.
15 Ibid., 20–21, nos. 25–26.
16 Ibid., 25, nos. 76–80.
17 Ibid., 87–95.
18 Ibid., 115–126.
19 Ibid., 103–108.
20 For the use of precious gems, see Jeffery Spier, *Byzantium and the West: Jewelry in the First Millennium* (London: Paul Holberton, 2012), 17–25.
21 Spier, *Late Antique and Early Christian Gems*, 143–157 and 167–169.

Further reading

Early Christian gems

Spier, Jeffrey. *Byzantium and the West: Jewelry in the First Millennium*. London: Paul Holberton, 2012.
————. *Late Antique and Early Christian Gems*, 2nd ed. Wiesbaden: Reichert, 2013.
————. "Late Antique and Early Christian Gems. Some Unpublished Examples." In *"Gems of Heaven": Recent Research on Engraved Gemstones in Late Antiquity* c. *AD 200–600*, edited by Chris Entwistle and Noël Adams, 193–207. London: British Museum, 2011.
————, ed. *Picturing the Bible: the Earliest Christian Art*. New Haven and London: Yale University Press, 2007.

Magical amulets

Bohak, Gideon. *Ancient Jewish Magic: a History*. Cambridge: Cambridge University Press, 2008.
"Campbell Bonner Magical Database," accessed June 16, 2017 www2.szepmuveszeti.hu/talismans/.
Bonner, Campbell. *Studies in Magical Amulets, Chiefly Graeco-Egyptian*. Ann Arbor: University of Michigan Press, 1950.
Mastrocinque, Attilio. *Les intailles magiques du département des Monnaies, Médailles et Antiques*. Paris: Éditions de la Bibliothèque nationale de France, 2014.
Michel, Simone. *Die Magischen Gemmen*. Berlin: Akademie Verlag, 2004.
————. *Die magischen Gemmen im Britischen Museum*. London: British Museum, 2001.
Philipp, Hanna. *Mira et Magica. Gemmen in Ägyptischen Museum der Staatlichen Museen Preussischer Kulturbesitz Berlin-Charlottenburg*. Mainz am Rhein: P. von Zabern, 1986.

10

RELIQUARIES AND THE CULT OF RELICS IN LATE ANTIQUITY

Erik Thunø

In spite of their very distinct purpose—to shelter and embellish a relic—reliquaries from the early centuries of Christianity were made from a variety of materials, and their patrons and makers were not obliged to follow any specific form or size. They thereby differ from other objects with a well-defined function, such as censers, chalices, or book covers, in that they do not make up a coherently configured and easily distinguishable group. Dependent on the wealth of the individual patron and whether reliquaries were shaped as, for example, a casket, cylindrical box, sarcophagus, flask or cross, these containers could be made of stone, lead, terracotta, glass, wood, ivory, and of various precious metals like gold or silver, or combinations thereof. While hiding their relics from view, some reliquaries during this period were adorned with precious stones and with images or symbols while others were left completely aniconic.[1]

Reliquaries depend on the cult and circulation of relics. Although the earliest evidence of Christian relic veneration goes back to the middle of the second century, when the bones of St Polycarp, bishop of Smyrna, were deemed "more precious than precious stones, and finer than gold," a cult of martyrs and, by extension, of their relics had to wait until the middle of the third century when numerous witnesses of Christ died for their faith during the empire-wide persecutions of Christians.[2] Shortly thereafter, the legalization of Christianity in 313 gradually paved the way for a publicly sponsored cult of martyrs so that, by the end of the century and the beginning of the next, the areas of the dead outside the walls of late antique towns were given unprecedented priority through the building of monumental shrines and pilgrimage sites. The earliest reliquaries are from this period. Yet, the fact that they can be traced back to a wide variety of shrines and sites across the Christian world should not lead us to believe that the cult and circulation of relics during this period unfolded smoothly and with the same intensity everywhere. In fact, whereas the cult of relics was initiated in the East, it did not encounter the same degree of attention and diversity as in the Latin West. At the same time, very few Byzantine reliquaries have survived before Iconoclasm in the ninth century. The best way to glean an overall picture of the cult of relics and reliquaries is therefore to give priority to the West where the material and written evidence is quite substantial. A good starting point for this endeavor is Saint Ambrose who was bishop of Milan from 374–397.[3]

Ambrose of Milan and the San Nazaro reliquary

Among the earliest and best-known reliquaries is the silver casket found in 1578 under the main altar of the church of San Nazaro in Milan. The cube-shaped box (Figure 10.1) is believed to have contained relics of some of the apostles, possibly of John, Andrew, and Thomas, to whom the church was originally dedicated (*Basilica Apostolorum*) in 386 by Ambrose. Perhaps commissioned by the Milanese bishop himself for the occasion, the silver casket stands out for its figurative repoussé imagery that, in addition to the lid, which features an enthroned Christ surrounded by the twelve apostles, shows the Judgment of Daniel (front?), the Adoration of the Magi (back?) and the Judgment of Solomon and the Three Hebrews in the Fiery Furnace. Contrary to what one might expect, the images do not explicitly refer to any of the individual apostle martyrs represented inside by virtue of their scarce corporeal remains. Instead, the biblical scenes, which might seem randomly chosen at first, gather around the general theme of Christian salvation as foreshadowed during the Old Law and realized through the coming of Christ. The imagery's generic nature with respect to the relics they envelop is far from unusual for reliquaries of this period, which were dictated by neither any particular iconography nor type of imagery, whether narrative or iconic.[4]

The physical need for a precious reliquary, such as the one from San Nazaro, that contains *reliqua*, leftover bits of bodies of martyrs, is directly tied to two fundamental circumstances: 1) the leftover bits of the martyrs must carry some kind of value, and 2) to encase and embellish them, their bodies first needed to be dismembered for translation and circulation beyond their original resting places, the tombs, where, as the sixth-century bishop Gregory of Tours put it, "there should be no doubt that the saints are present."[5]

Value of relics

As far as we know, Victricius, bishop of Rouen and a friend of Ambrose of Milan, was the first to attempt a theological explanation of what had already been affirmed by several Christians: relics of saints had healing and intercessory faculties and were thus in possession of the *virtus*, the virtue or power, of the holy person from which they derived. In a sermon through which Victricius thanked Ambrose for sending him relics of saints, he also argued that the healing

Figure 10.1 Silver casket, San Nazaro, Milan. Late 4th century. Photo: Diocesan Museum of Milan.

power of relics "is no less in the parts than in the entirety."[6] In this way, the relic *of* a saint *was* the saint. Just as the bread and wine of the eucharist contained the real presence of God, so too did the relic contain the real presence of the saint. Furthermore, the division of relics contributed to making them objects of devotion in their own right. The late fourth-century Cappadocian Father Gregory of Nyssa said of them:

> Those who behold them embrace, as it were, the living body in full flower: they bring eye, mouth, ear, all the senses into play, and then, shedding tears of reverence and passion, they address to the martyr their prayers of intercession as though he were present.[7]

No wonder why Ambrose chose a casket of precious silver to authenticate the sacred importance of his newly acquired relics and, more specifically, a pictorial program that revolves around the power of God. Indeed, image and relic work in reciprocal ways that are meaningful to both the relic and its imagery: through their healing powers, the relics share in the divine heavenly power that, as visualized on the casket, had descended on earth through Christ. In this way, the imagery makes the tiny disembodied bits of bone significant, alive, and even more precious than the material silver that embellishes them. Since their healing power is no less significant "in the parts than in the entirety," it also follows that the relics *are* the apostles (the church of San Nazaro's dedicatees) who are simultaneously present on earth and in heaven. Conversely, the miracle-working relics inside the silver box are physical proof of the claim made by the imagery that God had finally come to be among men. Clearly, the relics alone cannot convey such complex theological contents. They need the reliquary, and its images, to mediate between them and their audiences.[8]

Dismemberment, translation and circulation of relics

In 386—the same year in which Ambrose installed the apostle relics in his reliquary—an imperial ruling, issued at Constantinople, had reaffirmed Roman tradition that bodies of the dead (including bodies of martyrs) were not to be moved, divided or marketed.[9] Ambrose of Milan was the first church leader in the Latin West to clearly ignore those stipulations. Since no apostle lay buried in Milan, the remains of any apostle inside the reliquary from San Nazaro had to be translated from their original resting place by the fourth-century bishop. In this way, Ambrose's actions were similar to (and inspired by) those of the earliest emperors residing in Constantinople. Clearly the latter's deeds had become known in the West because Paulinus, bishop of Nola south of Naples, wrote in the early fifth century that Emperor Constantine the Great "removed Andrew [the apostle] from the Greeks and Timothy [the apostle] from Asia; and so Constantinople now stands with twin towers, vying to match the hegemony of great Rome . . . for he counterbalanced Peter and Paul with a protection as great, since Constantinople gained the disciple of Paul and the brother of Peter."[10] In reality, this famous translation of the apostles took place, not under Constantine, but his son and successor, Constantius II, in 356–357, and also included the apostle Luke.[11]

The translation of the three bodies to the church of the Holy Apostles in Constantinople, a city without martyrs, serves as key evidence that the fragmentation and translation of relics—and hence of violation of the tombs of the martyrs—first began in the East. However, whereas not a single body is recorded to have been moved from its original resting place before 350, it became common practice by 400 in both East and West. Victricius defended the dissemination of relics on theological grounds by arguing that relics, whose healing power "is no less in the parts than in the entirety," should circulate as widely as possible in order to "distribute benefactions" and create faith, equality and unity among Christians.[12] Paulinus echoes that sentiment in saying that since the faith had not initially spread evenly throughout the entire world, many areas were without martyrs and therefore Christ had given authorization to "summon martyrs from their earlier homes and translate them to fresh lodgings on earth."[13] Yet, in the case of Constantius' translation of the apostles, Paulinus offers an additional and far more prosaic motivation, namely that of rivalry with the city of Rome which, to the jealousy of any Christian city, was loaded with Christian martyrs, not to mention the apostle princes. Indeed, the same is true for Ambrose's translation that conspicuously resembles that of Constantius, not only with regard to the type of relics translated, but also to the church that was built to shelter them. In terms of both its dedication and cross plan, Ambrose's church made obvious allusions to the Constantinopolitan church of the Holy Apostles.[14] In so doing, Ambrose made Milan compete with Constantinople, and additionally, just like the Byzantine emperors, he may have aimed, albeit indirectly, at rivaling Rome, the Eternal City.

Paulinus' account of Emperor Constantius' relic translation immediately follows his defense of Ambrose's most famous translation, which is not that of the three apostles to the *Basilica Apostolorum*, but of the local protomartyrs of Gervasius and Protasius. In a letter to his sister Marcellina, Ambrose wrote how, after having built the suburban Basilica Ambrosiana for himself, the people of Milan had requested: "Consecrate this as you did the Roman basilica [the *Basilica Apostolorum*]. I will, I said, if I find relics of martyrs."[15] And so he did: On June 17, 386, Ambrose went to the martyr shrine of Saints Felix and Nabor and unearthed the two protomartyrs' bodies which were "of wondrous stature . . . the bones were all intact and there was much blood."[16] After two days, he moved them into his new basilica and placed them under the altar, where his own sarcophagus was to have stood. Ambrose's pioneering effort lies not in the translation itself which, as we have seen, he had already undertaken a few months earlier at the *Basilica Apostolorum*. Instead the novelty was that this time he transferred some of the city's own martyrs, taking them out of a graveyard dotted with other martyr tombs and giving them a clear focus by linking them to the communal liturgy in a public church built by the bishop himself and in which he would frequently preside. This process has famously been rendered in metaphorical terms as an electrician's rewiring of an antiquated wiring system in order that more power pass through better insulated wires toward the bishop.[17]

In his letter to Marcellina, Ambrose also provided one of the earliest justifications for placing the martyr relics under the altar, a practice that soon became a commonality among both suburban and urban churches: "Let these triumphant victims be brought to the place where Christ is the victim. But he upon the altar, who suffered for all; they beneath the altar, who were redeemed by his passion."[18] The celebration of the eucharist thereby unites the martyrdom and triumph of the saints with the sacrifice and resurrection of Christ. Finally, Ambrose was also the first to name the local martyrs "patrons," thus alluding to their protective role of the community.[19] In this way, the new city patrons served both to build a new and stronger Christian identity for the city of Milan and, by linking the relics to the altar, to strengthen the bishop's role as mediator of the sacred.[20]

Rome and its early martyrs

Ambrose's interest in the martyrs of his city had also gained currency elsewhere, in particular in Rome, where Pope Damasus (366–384) only a few years earlier had begun to rediscover some of the numerous martyrs buried in the catacombs encircling the walls of the city. Hence, at no less than eighteen separate sites, Damasus renovated a series of tombs by providing them with more accessible settings. He also embellished them with monumental and beautifully carved metrical verse inscriptions, the so-called Damasian epigrams, which—just like a precious reliquary—served to enhance the value of the martyrs' bones often by reference to their earthly deeds and simultaneous presence in both the tomb and heaven (Figure 10.2).[21] In honor of the Roman martyrs Felicissimus and Agapitus, who were deacons under Pope Sixtus II (257–258) and beheaded during Emperor Valerian's Christian persecution in 258, Damasus wrote:

> Behold! This tomb, too, preserves the celestial limbs of saints whom suddenly the palace of heaven snatched up. These, at once comrades and attendants of the unconquered cross, imitating both the model and the faith of their holy bishop, won an aetherial home and the realms of the righteous. The singular glory of the Roman people rejoices in them because with Sixtus as their leader at the time they merited Christ's triumphs. For Felicissimus and Agapitus, the holy martyrs, Damasus the bishop made (this).[22]

Damasus' celebration of the martyrs in this fashion created nothing less than a milestone in the cult of martyrs in Rome and the Christian world in general. Certainly by the time Damasus was elected to the Holy See, a series of large funerary basilicas placed on top of or adjacent to the martyrs' graves (i.e., Sant'Agnese, San Lorenzo fuori le Mura and St Peter's) had already been constructed a few decades earlier and begun to change the city's suburban landscape. Yet, the sheer range and number of martyrs made known and promoted by the fourth-century bishop was unprecedented. By renovating and facilitating access to the martyrs' graves along the main roads leading into the *Urbs*, Damasus contributed substantially to the remapping of Rome's sacred landscape outside the walls and gave the popular and episcopal cult of martyrs' relics a significant boost. Thanks to Damasus, whom the *Book of Pontiffs* (Liber Pontificalis), compiled in the 530s and 540s, still remembered as the impresario of the Roman saints, Rome had become *the* city of martyrs by the end of the fourth century.[23]

The Damasian enterprise of taking the shrine to where the remains of martyrs lay buried rather than dislocating those remains to a new shrine, as exemplified by Bishop Ambrose, testifies to the acceptance of Roman law, which, as mentioned above, dictated that the tombs of the dead remain inviolable. Hence, when Emperor Justinian wrote to Pope Hormisdas in 519 to ask for relics of the apostles and of St Lawrence, as would have been the practice in the East, the pope rejected the request and replied that he had instead sent *sanctuaria*—not corporeal remains, but objects (presumably cloth) that had been in touch with the tombs of the apostles and thus absorbed some of their sanctity. In short, the Emperor had to content himself with what are also called "secondary relics" because they had only touched but were not part of the revered

Figure 10.2 Damasian epigram, 366–384, Sant'Agnese fuori le Mura, Rome. Photo: Erik Thunø.

body. The same happened a few years later, in 594, when Byzantine Empress Constantina, wife of Maurice, asked Pope Gregory for the head of St Paul, but received only sanctified cloth in return. This policy, which endured until the seventh century, kept the rest of Europe in poor supply of relics while Rome, on the other hand, remained a power house of untouched martyrs and, consequently, an international center of pious tourism.[24]

Seen in this perspective, Ambrose of Milan's attitude towards the martyrs was completely at odds with Damasus' law-obeying scheme. Are we, then, dealing with two different approaches of the late fourth century that can only be seen as in conflict with one another? Yes and no. Although often presented as clear opposites, each represents a different side of the same coin: the ambition to obtain episcopal control of the martyrs. Hence, whether or not the latter were left *in situ* or had been moved from elsewhere, they were the key elements in the new wiring system through which more power could flow directly to the bishop. Whereas Damasus was the first to realize this scheme by working within the law, Ambrose was the more innovative in applying the translation habits of the East that were at odds with ancient burial customs. In doing so, as testified by the silver casket from San Nazaro, he initiated a practice that, in turn, generated a need for reliquaries not only in Milan, but also elsewhere. Thus, Ambrose distributed relics on an unprecedented scale to other bishops in the West including Paulinus of Nola, Gaudentius of Brescia and Victricius of Rouen. We recall that Victricius' sermon, quoted above, was delivered in 396 on the occasion of the arrival of relics from Ambrose to the city of Rouen. From it, we gather that the arrival was a deliberately orchestrated celebration along the lines of the Roman emperor's *adventus* into a city, joyously welcomed by "all ages" and social hierarchies of the city.[25] A unique sixth-century eastern ivory plaque from Trier (Figure 10.3) that probably stems from a reliquary casket represents such an *adventus* of relics: two bishops seated in a carriage and holding the relics in a casket with a pitched lid arrive through the gate of a city, possibly Constantinople, in a procession led by the emperor and received by the empress standing in the doorway of the about-to-be-finished church (workmen are still busy on the roof) where the relics will be deposited. The ceremony unfolds before an architectural backdrop with personages of various ranks, some holding censers and singing in acclaim.[26]

Figure 10.3 Ivory plaque, 6th century, Rheinisches Landesmuseum, Trier. Photo: Wikimedia Commons.

Paulinus of Nola's *arcula* and other reliquaries

Paulinus of Nola also wrote about the relics that he had received from Ambrose and installed in the church in Fundi, just south of Naples:

> Under the lighted altar, a royal slab of purple marble covers the bones of holy men. Here God's grace sets before you the power of the apostles by the great pledges contained in this meagre dust. Here lie father Andrew, the gloriously famed Luke, and Nazarius, a martyr glorious for the blood he shed; here are Protasius and his peer Gervasius, whom God made known after long ages to His servant Ambrose. One simple casket (*arcula*) embraces here his holy band, and in its tiny bosom embraces names so great.[27]

We recognize from this that we have already encountered the martyrs inside Paulinus' altar; they overlap to a significant extent with those we have already encountered in Milan: St Andrew and Saints Gervasius and Protasius. Hence, to establish a special relationship with his recipients Ambrose wanted them to have relics of the same saints that he kept in Milan. To that end he had no qualms about dismembering his own saints because, as we still recall from his friend Victricius: the whole is in the part, and no matter how small, the saint is still present.

Paulinus' text provides early written evidence about the use of caskets as containers of relics and about their placement under the altar of the church. However, as far as the more precise appearance of his "simple casket" is concerned, the Latin term for it, *arcula*, still leaves us with a lot of leeway. Paulinus' reliquary could, for example, have been shaped according to a very popular design for the period's reliquaries: a small sarcophagus with either a flat, curved, or pitched lid and rendered in either stone or silver. As such, the design would serve as a sort of replacement tomb for the saint at the same time as evoking the relics inside as representing the martyrs with their full bodies. A sixth-century example of such a reliquary is at the Metropolitan Museum of New York. The pocket-size rectangular coffin is topped by a pitched lid with a hole for oil in the top center (Figure 10.4). It is decorated with Greek crosses on either side and originates, like most such reliquaries, in Southeastern Europe or Asia Minor.[28]

The casket could also have followed a decisively more luxurious, albeit quite exceptional, type: the ivory box with carved images. A deluxe example from late fourth or early fifth-century Rome or Milan is the famous Brescia casket decorated on all sides with scenes from both the Old and New Testament and with a number of bust portraits of the apostles. Because of its relatively large size (Figure 10.5) and profusion of elaborate imagery, some have challenged the casket's original function as a reliquary, that is, made to be hidden from view inside an altar. If not, maybe it served as a container for the transfer of relics during such translation ceremonies as shown on the Trier ivory, where the two bishops on the cart are holding a casket. Yet, the fact that its shape, material, and figural representations made it suitable as a container for precious relics provides good reason to assume that the Brescia casket was already in the early Middle Ages used as a relic-container.[29]

Given that ivory was even more exceptional than gold as a material for reliquaries, it is more likely that Paulinus' casket was made of silver just like that of his fellow bishop Ambrose and a few others that have been found in churches in both the East and West. It could have been box-like, like Ambrose's, or oval-shaped like the well-known silver casket from Grado (Figure 10.6) from *ca.* 500 that was found in a stone coffin under the main altar in the northern Italian city's cathedral. Contrary to the Brescia and San Nazaro caskets, this one is not adorned with biblical narratives, but with engraved and embossed iconic imagery. The lid shows a large

Figure 10.4 Marble reliquary in the shape of a sarcophagus, 6th century. New York, Metropolitan Museum of Art, metmuseum.org. Accession no. 49.69.2a, b. Rogers Fund, 1949.

Figure 10.5 Ivory casket, late 4th/early 5th century, Brescia, Museo di Santa Giulia, San Salvatore. Photo: Wikimedia Commons.

crux gemmata (jeweled cross) atop the four rivers of paradise and flanked by two lambs. Its body has eight bust medallions of Christ, the apostle princes, and five other saints, including one woman. Unusual for reliquaries of this period, we know the names of each one of the portrayed saints (apart from Peter and Paul) through an inscription that runs around the body (the local saints of Cantius, Cantianus, Cantianilla, Quirinus and Latinus). There can be little doubt that the casket contained relics of the saints that it portrays. By identifying the relics—and contrary to the biblical representations of the above-mentioned caskets—the iconic imagery is directly related to the contents of the reliquary.

Another inscription reveals the names of its three secular patrons and the motivation behind their commissioning of the casket: "The dignified Lawrence, the esteemed John and Nicephorus have fulfilled their vow to the saints." The oval reliquary from Grado, in other words, was a gift offered to the saints inside the reliquary—an *ex voto*—upon their fulfillment of a wish that had been made to them by the patrons of the casket. The function of a reliquary as an *ex voto* to the saints, which is not unique to the Grado example, testifies to their intercessory power, and the role of artifacts in facilitating this sort of exchange between the faithful and the divine. In this way the reliquary aligns with liturgical objects such as patens, chalices, and censers that often carried similar kinds of inscriptions.[30]

If made of silver, Paulinus' casket could have been decorated with engraved or embossed representations of symbolic, narrative, or iconic character, or all of those combined. A preference for biblical scenes would have generated contents less specific to the relics of the saints inside but serving more overarching theological meanings. An iconic portrait imagery, by contrast, would have personalized the saints whose disembodied and unidentifiable body parts were contained inside. Even if made of silver, however, the reliquary from Fundi could have been left blank or just decorated with a cross as in the case of the stone sarcophagus from the Metropolitan Museum.

Figure 10.6 Silver casket, c. 500, Cathedral of St Eufemia, Grado. Photo: Galit Noga-Banai.

The history of the cult of relics and reliquaries during the first centuries of the Latin Church can, as we have now seen, be written through a small number of bishop impresarios, among whom Ambrose of Milan was the protagonist and ahead of his time. His fragmentation, translation, and incorporation of the bodies of the martyrs became a model for other bishops and gathered followers from Nola to Rouen and beyond. Indeed, the letters and poems mentioned above demonstrate a tight and authoritative network of episcopal friendships through which relics of saints traveled rapidly across large distances. Among the motivations that led Ambrose and his peers to change the relic policy of the West was, as we have seen, the ambition to strengthen the identity of the community and the role of the bishop within it. What prompted this development and the interest in relics to begin with was, more broadly speaking, a basic human need to make the divine—invisible and abstract—tangible in some form. Through their relics, the saints opened a channel of communication with God, a corridor between earth and heaven that made God present among the everyday lives of people. What made it possible for these late third- and early fourth-century bishops to implement their new approach, eventually changing the spiritual topography of the late antique world, was less an increasing demand from the new Christian masses than the growing material wealth of the Church. Only so could magnificent shrines, lavish processions, and reliquaries of ivory, silver and gold see the light of day.[31]

The poetics of relics

The material splendor that came to be associated with relics overlapped and interacted with a literary genre, the ekphrasis, that in Late Antique literature developed around the martyrs. By linking the bare bits of bones with an aesthetic dazzle through associations to art and evocative metaphors, ekphrasis appealed to the sensuous imaginations of both readers and listeners and, in turn, made the relics come alive as spiritual living objects in their own right. The Christian Latin poet Prudentius, in particular, excelled in making art, poetry and relics fuse into one whole. In his *Peristephanon*, a collection of hagiographic poems, Prudentius wrote about the church placed over the body of St Paul in Rome:

> the Ostian Road keeps the memorial church of Paul, where the river grazes the land on its left bank. The splendour of the place is princely, for our good emperor dedicated this seat and decorated its whole extent with great wealth. He laid plates on the beams so as to make all the light within golden like the sun's radiance at its rising, and supported the gold-panelled ceiling on pillars of Parian marble set out there in four rows. Then he covered the curves of the arches with splendid glass of different hues, like meadows that are bright with flowers in the spring.[32]

Such poetry exemplifies the late antique attitude about relics. As a forceful appeal to the reader's or listener's imaginative senses, this kind of hyper-real imagery contributed in no small part to the empowerment of relics and, of course, to the art that both contained and surrounded them. In particular, the frequent literary associations of the saints' resting places with light and brilliance, as generated by precious metals, sparkling colors and even jewels, do much to explain the increasingly frequent choice of silver and gold for reliquaries, and glittering apse mosaics as the backdrop of the altar where they were deposited. Through their material glitter the reliquary, as well as its church, would become both a receptacle and generator of light—the spiritual light of the living saints.[33]

The *loca sancta* of the Holy Land

Although the bodies of saints were initially the only source of relics, the rise of pilgrimage to places associated with the life of Christ provided additional holy matter to mediate between humans and God. This matter was not a body part but any kind of material—wood, pieces of cloth, oil, stone, or dirt—that one could claim to have been in direct contact with Christ's body or a relic, or to have derived from places (*loca sancta*) in the Holy Land associated with his life on earth as recorded by the Gospels. A sixth-century wooden box (Figure 10.7) from Syria or Palestine provides an example of the connection between relic and place. A sliding lid opens up to an interior of stones and small pieces of wood embedded in a layer of plaster in the shape of the cross. Labels on several of the stones indicate their place of origin: the Mount of Olives, Bethlehem, Sion, and the Anastasis. The lid's interior is painted with five scenes from the life of Christ: *The Nativity, Baptism of Christ, Crucifixion, the Women at the Tomb* and *the Ascension.* The stones and pieces of wood derive from places that are key to Christian salvation and are therefore imbued with the holy power of these particular sites. Just as the tiny piece of bone would represent the martyr saint in his entire body, so does each of these objects embody a *locus sanctus.* As on the reliquary of San Nazaro, image and relic stand in a meaningful relationship. On the one hand, the painted scenes link the *loca sancta* objects in the casket with the life and passion of Christ. The objects, on the other hand, serve as historical and topographical proof of the historical events and their sites. The casket is not just a pilgrim's souvenir box, but a Holy Land *en miniature* that continues to ensure its owner access to the sacred power of its historical places, on the journey and at home.[34]

(a)

Figure 10.7 Sancta Sanctorum wooden reliquary box, 6th century, Syria or Palestine, showing (a) the container, and (b) the lid. Photo: Vatican Museums.

(b)

Figure 10.7 (continued)

Constantine the Great, in the wake of 313, made Palestine, and Jerusalem in particular, a special destination for pilgrims that lasted until the Arab conquest of the Eastern Mediterranean in the seventh century. By sending his mother, Helena, to the Holy Land to dedicate his newly sponsored churches that marked the sites of Christ's birth (Bethlehem), death (Golgotha), and Ascension (Mount of Olives), Constantine initiated a process that transformed the places of Christ's life from being merely historical to being *loci sancti*. The Emperor's decision enabled pilgrims to see and touch the sites sanctified by Christ's former living presence. Again, we can turn to Paulinus of Nola for a description of this experience:

> No other sentiment draws men to Jerusalem but the desire to see and touch the places where Christ was physically present . . . So if the desire is a truly religious one to see the places in which Christ walked, suffered, rose again, and ascended into heaven, and if there is a blessing in taking and keeping a pinch of dust from these places or a mere mote from the wood of the Cross, just think how much greater and fuller is the grace of beholding an old man yet alive who is walking proof of divine Truth.[35]

During the following decades a sacred topography emerged around sites within and outside Jerusalem that was marked by events or commemorations of people from both the Old and New Testaments and, in turn, produced new types of relics and reliquaries. Prime among them, and different from the relics of place discussed above, was the relic of the True Cross. According to traditions dating back to the late fourth century, the cross on which Christ was crucified was discovered by Helena in *c.* 326 and installed in Constantine's basilica on Golgotha where pilgrims venerated it. The anonymous pilgrim from Piacenza in Italy, who visited Jerusalem around 570, wrote in his diary:

> In the courtyard of the basilica [at Golgotha] is a small room where they keep the wood of the Cross. We venerated it with a kiss . . . At the moment when the Cross is brought out of this small room for veneration . . . a star appears in the sky, and comes over the place where they lay the Cross. It stays overhead whilst they are venerating the Cross, and they offer oil to be blessed in little flasks. When the mouth of one of the little flasks touches the Wood of the Cross, the oil instantly bubbles over, and unless it is closed very quickly it all spills out.[36]

The little flasks containing such sanctified oil by direct contact with the Cross are the so-called *ampullae*. They were likely worn around the neck of pious pilgrims to ensure good health and protection during the journey and at home. Such *ampullae* could be made of lead or terracotta, even silver, and were widely used at different holy sites, including the burial places of martyrs, and contained substances such as oil or wax from the sites that were called *eulogiae* (blessings). Inscriptions on the *ampullae*, such as a sixth- or seventh-century example from the Cleveland Museum of Art, identifies the substance as "oil of the wood of life," and is decorated with images of the *Crucifixion* and *Ascension* (Figure 10.8). Similar to the wooden box from the Vatican Museums, such representations documented the sacred origin of the oil, whereas the miraculous oil would authorize the sanctity of the depicted sites.[37]

Figure 10.8 Tin-lead alloy pilgrim's ampulla with scenes of (a) the crucifixion and (b) the ascension, *c.* 600 CE. Cleveland Museum of Art.

(b)

Figure 10.8 (continued)

The True Cross

Real bits and pieces from the wooden instrument of Christ's Resurrection, and not just substances that had touched it, were put in circulation from very early on. Even before the legend of the True Cross was recorded towards the end of the fourth century, Cyril, bishop of Jerusalem, had commented that "already the whole world is filled with fragments of the wood of the Cross."[38] As with the bodies of the saints, such fragmentation did not diminish the power of the relics. Paulinus of Nola, who had acquired a piece of the wood from Jerusalem and decided to send it to his friend Severus for the consecration of his basilica, explained:

> Indeed this cross of inanimate wood has living power, and ever since its discovery it has lent its wood to the countless, almost daily, prayers of men. Yet it suffers no diminution; though daily divided, it seems to remain whole to those who lift it, and always entire to those who venerate it. Assuredly it draws this power of incorruptibility, this undiminishing integrity, from the Blood of that Flesh which endured death yet did not see corruption.[39]

Before sending his sliver of the holy wood away, Paulinus enclosed it in a "golden casing." He did so, he explained, as an imitation of Severus' faith that had been "tried in the fire" and equivalent to the "kingdom of God."[40] He moreover recommended that Severus either use it for his daily protection and healing, or bury it within the altar, although there it might not "be always accessible according to the need." In that case, Paulinus assured his friend, it would be sufficient if Severus' basilica were entrusted to the apostles and martyrs.[41]

Among the relics of the Holy Land, the True Cross was in a league of its own. Although a contact relic associated with a particular place (Golgotha), pieces of the Cross were first of all considered a relic of Christ himself who had left no corporeal remains. They were also different from relics of martyrs that, as we have seen, were associated with a particular city and community for which they served as patrons and protectors. Beginning with fourth-century bishop and Church historian Eusebius, the sign of the Cross, which appeared to Constantine in a vision and secured his victory over co-emperor Maxentius at the battle of the Milvian Bridge in 312, became the triumphant standard for the new Christian Empire. Significantly, it was Constantine's mother, as mentioned above, who shortly thereafter discovered the True Cross and made an imperial claim to it. And during the centuries that followed, it was less from Jerusalem than from Constantinople, to where large parts of the Cross had been transferred, that relics of the True Cross were distributed.[42]

In Rome, first the emperor, and then the popes, were equally keen on linking their rule with the standard-bearer of Christian truth and power. The sources reveal the early presence of relics of the True Cross in Rome; Constantine erected a basilica in the Sessorian Palace (Santa Croce in Gerusalemme) where he installed a golden, jewel-encrusted reliquary for the

Figure 10.9 Reliquary cross of Justin II (r 565–578) (Crux Vaticana). Byzantine (Constantinople), 6th century, with later additions, Treasury of S. Peter's. Photo:. Scala/Art Resource, New York.

True Cross. Pope Leo I (440–461) acknowledged receipt of a fragment of the True Cross from Jerusalem, which he highlighted as important material proof of the Incarnation. Pope Hilarus (461–468) deposited a relic of the True Cross in an oratory of the Holy Cross he commissioned adjacent to the Lateran baptistery. Likewise, Pope Symmachus (498–514) built an oratory at St Peter's for a fragment of the True Cross installed in a gold cross with jewels.[43] Finally, among the earliest surviving reliquaries of the True Cross is the Cross of Justin II (565–574) in the Treasury of St Peter's (Figure 10.9), which served as a diplomatic gift between two Christian powers: Rome and Constantinople. At the juncture of its arms, the silver gilt cross, which was restored in 2001, contains a capsule for the cross-shaped piece of the True Cross. An inscription surrounded by precious stones informs us that Emperor Justin, portrayed with his wife in medallions on the ends of the cross arms, gave this cross "to Rome."[44] Although we do not know of the particular circumstances of the gift, there can be little doubt that the sixth-century reliquary rendered as a victorious standard served as a powerful display of Byzantine imperial power vis-à-vis a papal Rome weakened by foreign invasion in the wake of the collapse of the Roman Empire in 476.

Notes

1 Joseph Braun, *Die Reliquiare des christlichen Kultes und ihre Entwicklung* (Freiburg im Breisgau, Herder, 1940), 83ff; Anja Kalinowski, *Frühchristliche Reliquiare im Kontext von Kultstrategien, Heilserwartung und sozialer Selbstdarstellung* (Wiesbaden, Reichert, 2011), 73ff; Holger Klein, "Materiality and the Sacred. Byzantine Reliquaries and the Rhetoric of Enshrinement," in *Saints and Sacred Matter. The Cult of Relics in Byzantium and Beyond*, eds Cynthia Hahn and Holger Klein (Washington, DC: Dumbarton Oaks Research Library and Collection, 2015), 231–253.

2 Eusebius of Caeserea, *Ecclesiastical History*, IV, 15, trans. Kirsopp Lake, Loeb Classical Library 153 (Cambridge, MA, and London: Harvard University Press, 1926, repr. 2001), 357; Derek Krueger, "The Religion of Relics in Late Antiquity and Byzantium," in *Treasures of Heaven. Saints, Relics, and Devotion in Medieval Europe*, exh. cat., eds Martina Bagnoli et al. (New Haven, CT, and London: Yale University Press, 2010), 5–19. For the pre-Christian origins of the cult of relics and reliquaries, see Jaś Elsner, "Relic, Icon, and Architecture. The Material Articulation of the Holy in East Christian Art," in *Saints and Sacred Matter*, eds Cynthia Hahn and Holger Klein, 13–41, 13–18 with bibliography.

3 Bernhard Kötting, *Der frühchristliche Reliquienkult und die Bestattung im Kirchengebäude* (Cologne and Opladen: Springer, 1965), 7–13; Nicole Herrmann-Mascard, *Les reliques des saints. Formation coutumière d'un droit* (Paris: Editions Klincksieck, 1975), 11–26; Peter Brown, *The Cult of the Saints. Its Rise and Function in Latin Christianity* (Chicago, IL: University of Chicago Press, 1981), 7–9; *idem*, "Relics and Social Status in the Age of Gregory of Tours," in *Society and the Holy in Late Antiquity* (Berkeley and Los Angeles, CA: University of California Press, 1982), 222–251; *The Cult of Saints in Late Antiquity and the Middle Ages: Essays on the Contribution of Peter Brown*, eds James Howard-Johnston and Paul Antony Hayward (Oxford: Oxford University Press, 1999); John Crook, *The Architectural Setting of the Cult of Saints in the Early Christian West, c. 300–1200* (Oxford: Oxford University Press, 2000), Chapters 1 and 2. On the cult of relics in Jewish culture, see Ra'anan Boustan, "Jewish Veneration of the 'Special Dead' in Late Antiquity and Beyond," in *Saints and Sacred Matter*, eds Cynthia Hahn and Holger Klein, 61–81.

4 Helmut Buschhausen, *Die spätrömischen Metallscrinia und frühchristlichen Reliquiare*, I. Teil (Vienna, Böhlau in Komm., 1971), 223–234; Ruth E. Leader-Newby, *Silver and Society in Late Antiquity* (Aldershot: Ashgate, 2004), 102–105; Galit Noga-Banai, *The Trophies of the Martyrs. An Art Historical Study of Early Christian Silver Reliquaries* (Oxford: Oxford University Press, 2008), 9ff, 155; Kalinowski, *Frühchristliche Reliquiare*, 155–166.

5 Gregory of Tours, *Liber de passione et virtutibus sancti Iuliani martyris*, 30; trans. Brown, *Cult of the Saints*, 109.

6 Victricius of Rouen, *Praising the Saints* (*de laude sanctorum*), trans. Gillian Clark, *Journal of Early Christian Studies*, 7, 3 (1999): 377–399, esp. p. 393, with introduction by Gillian Clark (365–376). See also Gillian Clark, "Translating relics: Victricius of Rouen and fourth-century debate," *Early Medieval Europe* 10 (2001): 161–176.

7 Gregory of Nyssa, *Encomium on Saint Theodore*, trans. Brown, *Cult of the Saints*, 11.
8 Erik Thunø, *Image and Relic. Mediating the Sacred in Early Medieval Rome* (Rome: L'Erma di Bretschneider, 2002); Cynthia Hahn, "What do Reliquaries do for Relics?", *Numen* 57 (2010): 284–316; *idem*, *Strange Beauty. Issues in the Making and Meaning of Reliquaries, 400–circa 1204* (University Park, PA: Penn State University Press, 2012), 8–10; Elsner, "Relic, Icon, and Architecture," 13–41.
9 *Codex Theodosianus* 9, 17, 17; in *Theodosiani. Libri XVI*, ed. Theodor Mommsen (Berlin, Berolini, apvd Weismannos, 1905), I, 2: 466. See also Kötting, *Reliquienkult*, 21.
10 Paulinus of Nola, *Poem 19*, in *The Poems of Paulinus of Nola*, trans. P. G. Walsh, Ancient Christian Writers 40 (New York, NY: Newman Press, 1975), 142–143. See also Noga-Banai, *Trophies of the Martyrs*, 121.
11 Cyril Mango, "Constantine's Mausoleum and the Translation of Relics," *Byzantinische Zeitschrift* 83 (1990): 51–61.
12 Victricius of Rouen, *Praising the Saints*, trans. Clark, 391.
13 Paulinus of Nola, *Poem 19*, trans. Walsh, 142.
14 Richard Krautheimer, *Three Christian Capitals. Topography and Politics* (Berkeley and Los Angeles, CA: University of California Press, 1983), 80.
15 Saint Ambrose, *Letter 22*, trans. Mary Melchior Beyenka, The Fathers of the Church 26 (Washington, DC: Catholic University of America, 1954), 376.
16 Ibid.
17 Brown, *Cult of the Saints*, 36–37.
18 Ambrose, *Letter* 22, trans. Melchior Beyenka, 380; Robin M. Jensen, "Saint's Relics and the Consecration of Church Buildings in Rome," *Studia Patristica*, 71 (2014): 153–169; Ann Marie Yasin, "Sacred Installations. The Material Conditions of Relic Collections in Late Antique Churches," in *Saints and Sacred Matter*, eds Cynthia Hahn and Holger Klein, 133–151, with bibliography.
19 Ambrose, *Letter* 22, trans. Melchior Beyenka, 380.
20 Ernst Dassmann, "Ambrosius und die Märtyrer," *Jahrbuch für Antike und Christentum* 18 (1975), 49–69; Neil McLynn, *Ambrose of Milan. Church and Court in a Christian Capital* (Berkeley and Los Angeles, CA: University of California Press, 1994), 209ff. See also Jean-Michel Spieser, "Ambrose's Foundations at Milan and the Question of Martyria," in *Urban and Religious Spaces in Late Antiquity and Early Byzantium* (Aldershot: Ashgate, 2001), VII, 1–12.
21 The epigrams, many of which exist only in very fragmentary condition, have been critically edited by Antonius Ferrua, *Epigrammata Damasiana. Recensuit et adnotavit* (Rome: Pontificio Istituto di Archeologia Cristiana, 1942), who counted almost sixty authentic examples in stone composed by Damasus himself or by clerics commissioned by this pope. For recent scholarship on the epigrams, see Steffen Diefenbach, *Römische Erinnerungsräume. Heiligenmemoria und kollektive Identitäten im Rom des 3. bis 5. Jahrhunderts n. Chr.* (Berlin: De Gruyter, 2007); Markus Löx, *Monumenta sanctorum. Rom und Mailand als Zentren des frühen Christentums: Märtyrerkult und Kirchenbau unter den Bischöfen Damasus und Ambrosius* (Wiesbaden: Reichert, 2013). For English translations of the epigrams and a recent discussion of them in their literary, archeological and topographical contexts, see Dennis Trout, *Damasus of Rome. The Epigraphic Poetry. Introduction, Texts, Translations, and Commentary* (Oxford: Oxford University Press, 2015).
22 Trout, *Damasus*, no. 25, 126–127.
23 *The Book of Pontiffs (Liber Pontificalis). The Ancient Biographies of the First Ninety Roman Bishops to AD 715*, trans. Raymond Davis (Liverpool: Liverpool University Press, 1989), 29; Trout, *Damasus*, 39–47.
24 John M. McCulloh, "From Antiquity to the Middle Ages: Continuity and Change in Papal Relic Policy From the 6th to the 8th Century," in *Pietas. Festschrift für Bernhard Kötting*, eds E. Dassmann and K. Frank (Münster, Aschendorf, 1980), 313–324.
25 Victricius of Rouen, *Praising the Saints*, trans. Clark, 378.
26 Hahn, *Strange Beauty*, 149–150; *Treasures of Heaven*, no. 14, p. 38.
27 Paulinus, *Letter* 32, 17, trans. Walsh, 150–151; Noga-Banai, *Trophies*, 1.
28 *Age of Spirituality. Late Antique and Early Christian Art, Third to Seventh Century*, exh. cat. (New York, NY: Metropolitan Museum of Art, 1979), no. 570, p. 632; Buschhausen, *Metallscrinia*, no. C. 59, pl. C23.
29 Hahn, *Strange Beauty*, 45–61, esp. 46ff; Kalinowski, *Reliquiare*, 168–174.
30 Noga-Banai, *Trophies*, 95–98; Kalinowski, *Reliquiare*, 29–30, 119–123.
31 Brown, *Cult of the Saints*, 39–49; *idem*, *Through the Eye of a Needle: Wealth, The Fall of Rome, and the Making of Christianity in the West, 350–550 AD* (Princeton, NJ: Princeton University Press, 2012).
32 Prudentius, *Liber Peristephanon*, XII, trans. H. J. Thomson, in *The Poems of Prudentius* (Cambridge, MA: Harvard University Press, 1953), 327.

33 Patricia Cox Miller, *The Corporeal Imagination. Signifying the Holy in Late Ancient Christianity* (Philadelphia, PA: University of Pennsylvania Press, 2009), 62–81; Thunø, *Apse Mosaic*, 50–51.
34 Charles Rufus Morey, "The Painted Panel from the Sancta Sanctorum," in *Festschrift zum sechzigsten Geburtstag von Paul Clemen* (Bonn, Fr. Cohen, 1926), 151–168; Bruno Reudenbach, "Reliquien von Orten. Ein frühchristliches Reliquiar als Gedächtnisort," in *Reliquiare im Mittelalter*, eds B. Reudenbach and G. Toussaint (Berlin: Akademie, 2005), 21–43; Derek Krueger, "Liturgical Time and Holy Land Reliquaries in Early Byzantium," in *Saints and Sacred Matter*, eds Cynthia Hahn and Holger Klein, 111–131.
35 Paulinus of Nola, *Letter 49, 14*, trans. Walsh, 273. On pilgrimage and *loca sancta*, see *The Blessings of Pilgrimage*, ed. Robert Ousterhout (Urbana and Chicago, IL: University of Illinois Press, 1990). Eusebius, *Life of Constantine* III, 25–47, intro., trans., and comm. by Averil Cameron and Stuart G. Hall (Oxford: Clarendon Press, 1999), 132–138. On the pilgrimage experience, see Georgia Frank, *The Memory of the Eyes. Pilgrims to Living Saints in Christian Late Antiquity* (Berkeley and Los Angeles, CA: University of California Press, 2000).
36 The Piacenza Pilgrim, *Travels from Piacenza*, 20, trans., John Wilkinson, *Jerusalem Pilgrims before the Crusades* (Warminster: Aris & Phillips, 1977), 83. On the discovery of the True Cross, see Jan Willem Drijvers, *Helena Augusta. The Mother of Constantine the Great and the Legend of her Finding of the True Cross* (Leiden: Brill, 1992).
37 *Treasures of Heaven*, no. 23, p. 43 and the article in that same volume by Holger Klein, "Sacred Things and Holy Bodies. Collecting Relics from Late Antiquity to the Early Renaissance," 55–67, 57. See also Gary Vikan, *Byzantine Pilgrimage Art* (Washington, DC: Dumbarton Oaks Byzantine Collection, 1982), esp. 20–27, 2nd ed 2010.
38 Cyril of Jerusalem, *Catacheses*, IV, 10; trans., Drijvers, *Helena Augusta*, 82; Anatole Frolow, *La Relique de la Vraie Croix. Recherches sur le development d'un culte* (Paris, Institut français d'Études byzantines, 1961), 155.
39 Paulinus of Nola, *Letter 31, 6*, trans. Walsh, 132–133.
40 Paulinus of Nola, *Letter 31, 2*, trans. Walsh, 126.
41 Paulinus of Nola, Letter *32, 8*, trans. Walsh, 142.
42 Frolow, *Relique*, 55–107; Holger A. Klein, *Byzanz, der Westen und das "wahre" Kreuz* (Wiesbaden: Reichert, 2004), 19–47.
43 Leo the Great, *Epistula*, 139, PL 14, 1106; *Book of Pontiffs*, 20–21; 39; 45; Frolow, *Relique*, 173–177 (nos 20, 23, 27); Sible de Blaauw, "Jerusalem in Rome and the Cult of the Cross," in *Pratum romanum, Richard Krautheimer zum 100. Geburtstag*, ed. R. Colella et al. (Wiesbaden: Reichert, 1997), 55–73.
44 Frolow, *Relique*, no. 34; 180–181; Anatole Frolow, *Les reliquaires de la Vraie Croix* (Paris, Institut français d'études byzantine, 1965), 187ff; Hahn, *Strange Beauty*, 73–74.

Further reading

Martina Bagnoli et al., *Treasures of Heaven. Saints, Relics, and Devotion in Medieval Europe*. Exhibition Catalogue. New Haven, CT, and London: Yale University Press, 2010.

Peter Brown, *The Cult of the Saints. Its Rise and Function in Latin Christianity*. Chicago, IL: University of Chicago Press, 1981.

John Crook, *The Architectural Setting of the Cult of Saints in the Early Christian West*, c. *300–1200*. Oxford: Oxford University Press, 2000.

Georgia Frank, *The Memory of the Eyes. Pilgrims to Living Saints in Christian Late Antiquity*. Berkeley and Los Angeles, CA: University of California Press, 2000.

Cynthia Hahn, *Strange Beauty. Issues in the Making and Meaning of Reliquaries, 400*–circa *1204*. University Park, PA: Penn State University Press, 2012.

Cynthia Hahn and Holger Klein, eds, *Saints and Sacred Matter. The Cult of Relics in Byzantium and Beyond*, Dumbarton Oaks Byzantine Symposia and Colloquia. Washington, DC: Dumbarton Oaks Research Library and Collection, 2015.

Nicole Herrmann-Mascard, *Les reliques des saints. Formation coutumière d'un droit*. Paris: Éditions Klincksieck, 1975.

James Howard-Johnston and Paul Antony Hayward, eds, *The Cult of Saints in Late Antiquity and the Middle Ages: Essays on the Contribution of Peter Brown*. Oxford: Oxford University Press, 1999.

Robin M. Jensen, "Saint's Relics and the Consecration of Church Buildings in Rome," *Studia Patristica*, 71 (2014): 153–169.

Anja Kalinowski, *Frühchristliche Reliquiare im Kontext von Kultstrategien, Heilserwartung und sozialer Selbstdarstellung*. Wiesbaden: Reichert, 2011.

Galit Noga-Banai, *The Trophies of the Martyrs. An Art Historical Study of Early Christian Silver Reliquaries*. Oxford: Oxford University Press, 2008.

Robert Ousterhout, ed., *The Blessings of Pilgrimage*. Urbana and Chicago, IL: University of Illinois Press, 1990.

Victricius of Rouen, *Praising the Saints (de laude sanctorum)*, trans. Gillian Clark, *Journal of Early Christian Studies*, 7, 3 (1999): 377–399, esp. 393, with introduction by Gillian Clark (365–376).

Erik Thunø, *Image and Relic. Mediating the Sacred in Early Medieval Rome*. Rome, L'Erma di Bretschneider, 2002.

Dennis Trout, *Damasus of Rome. The Epigraphic Poetry. Introduction, Texts, Translations, and Commentary*. Oxford: Oxford University Press, 2015.

Gary Vikan, *Byzantine Pilgrimage Art*. Washington, DC: Dumbarton Oaks Byzantine Collection, 1982 (new 2010 ed.).

11

CERAMICS IN THE EARLY CHRISTIAN WORLD

John J. Herrmann, Jr. and
Annewies van den Hoek

Pottery is a material of prime importance for the archaeology of the early Christian period. It can be broken, but its fragments are almost imperishable, and often their original form, date, and place of manufacture can be identified. Pottery is an abundant material on archaeological sites and can provide invaluable evidence for establishing their dates and cultural and economic orientation. This is particularly true in the early Christian period, when coinage becomes rare, and often ceramics (particularly fragments of fine tableware) are the main basis for establishing the chronology. Ceramic vessels provide evidence for the technology, the economy, the practices of daily life, and, of particular relevance here, the artistic culture of early Christianity. The imagery on early Christian pottery provides reflections of cultural currents on the popular level and at times reveals otherwise undocumented iconographic traditions. On occasion individual pieces rise to the level of minor artistic masterpieces.

Shipwrecks have produced the best-preserved ceramics, usually utilitarian amphorae. Well-preserved finer wares come primarily from burials, where ceramics were placed with the deceased to accompany them to the hereafter or as the apparatus of a last meal. Ceramic vessels could form part of a sacrifice and be buried with the victim.[1] Rich finds also come from dumps in abandoned wells or buildings[2] and even from caves used as refuges in times of danger.

Precursors: early Judeo-Christian influence

Long before the reign of Constantine (313–337) and the start of the Christian Roman Empire, the Judeo-Christian tradition had an influence, albeit a small one, on Roman ceramics. In the Severan period (193–235) the potter Florentius produced a fine lamp with the Good Shepherd flanked by Noah and Jonah (Figure 11.1).[3] The shepherd is surrounded by his flock, and Jonah regurgitated from the sea monster and reclining under the gourd vine appear on either side of him. The box-like ark of Noah surmounted by a bird appears above the sea monster, and busts of the sun and moon appear at the top. A shepherd with a lamb over his shoulders was an image that had appeared in non-Christian art, but the presence of the two biblical stories makes it clear that this lamp was intended for a Christian audience. In the same period several other central Italian potters produced a fair number of lamps showing the Good Shepherd alone, but in this case the intended audience is less sharply defined. Menorahs make their appearance as early as the first century and continued to be produced into the fifth century.[4] While they undoubtedly

Figure 11.1 Ceramic lamp with the Good Shepherd, Jonah, and Noah, by Florentius. Central Italian, 175–225. Skulpturensammlung und Museum für Byzantinische Kunst, Staatliche Museen zu Berlin (2354). Bildarchiv Preussischer Kulturbesitz; photographed by Juergen Liepe.

targeted the Jewish market, Christians apparently used them as well: menorah lamps have been excavated in tombs in Sardinia of the fifth century along with lamps with Christian monograms.[5]

Late Antiquity, the early Christian period

Pottery production in the fourth to seventh centuries is essentially a continuation of Roman tradition, with its separate regional branches. Biblical or specifically Christian imagery gradually expands to take a dominant position, but it is a slow and intermittent process. The pottery "industry" itself has a variegated history, with an interplay of failures, survivors, and newcomers throughout a turbulent period both militarily and economically. Its occasional ups and the many downs can often be keyed to the barbarian invasions from the mid-third to the late seventh century, but foreign conquest of a territory did not always lead to the end of pottery production in the Roman manner. The primary focus of attention here will be fine wares: that is, relatively thin-walled, smooth-surfaced, hard-fired clay for lighting, the dining table, or the tomb. Fine wares were traded around the late antique world and reflect areas of economic strength and commercial creativity. They also reflect the fashions of the upper classes by imitating tableware and tokens of status made of silver or ivory. Fine ceramics reveal both the emergence of biblical imagery and its prolonged coexistence with pagan and secular subject matter.

As in presentations of pottery from excavations, the ceramics of the early Christian world will be arranged in approximate order of their refinement: from vessels with the glossiest surface coatings, to the less shiny, to those without any coating at all. Fitted into this scheme will be different kinds of firing: oxidizing conditions (relatively high temperatures), which produced red ceramics, and reducing conditions (lower firing temperature), which produced gray or black ceramics. In general, only types of pottery with some artistic aspirations will be presented here.

Red slip ware/terra sigillata

Potters used a variety of techniques for elite tableware, but the most widespread and artistically important type or "ware" was *terra sigillata* or "red-gloss" or "red slip" pottery (Figures 11.2–11.6). The technique was descended from earlier Roman Imperial times. Vases were coated with slip (liquid clay) made of a highly purified version of the body clay. As in earlier High Imperial *terra sigillata*, the slip might become a lustrous dark red or red-orange when fired in an oxidizing environment, but usually early Christian *sigillata* was lighter in color, more orange or even

Figure 11.2 African red slip bowl (*patena*) with biblical subjects (Lazarus, Joseph and Potiphar's wife, Abraham and Isaac on the way to the sacrifice, Adam and Eve, and a Jonah cycle), 320–360 CE. Museum of Fine Arts, Boston, 2002.131. Museum purchase with funds donated in memory of Emily Townsend Vermeule.

Figure 11.3 African red slip bowl with barbarian attacked by a bear, 350–440 CE. Private collection.

brownish, and less red and shiny than in earlier centuries. Because of this technical shift, there is some ambiguity in the terminology for the early Christian wares, which are called "light *terra sigillata*" (*terra sigillata chiara, sigillée claire*) in continental Europe and "red slip ware" or "red gloss pottery" in England.

Figure 11.4 African red slip platter *(lanx)* with a goatherd and lion hunts, 350–440 CE. Private collection.

Figure 11.5 African red slip platter *(lanx)* with Peter and Paul flanking a cross; the story of Jonah on the rim, 350–440 CE. Benaki Museum, Athens, 12405, 124–6b, 12431.

Figure 11.6 African red slip plate with stamped figure of Christ, 500–550 CE. Oppidum Sainte-Propice, Velaux. Photo: Service patrimoine Velaux (France).

Early Christian red slip ware was separated into its different regional workshops, and its chronology was established primarily by John W. Hayes.[6] By far the most important centers for the production of *sigillata* were in Tunisia; they can be grouped into two divisions: the Roman province of Africa Proconsularis in the north, with its principal city of Carthage; and the province of Byzacena in central Tunisia, with important cities at Sbeitla (a UNESCO World Heritage site) and El Djem, with its giant and well-preserved amphitheater. The fine pottery from these regions, which has been named African Red Slip Ware (ARS) or *sigillata chiara africana* in Italian, was produced not in the great cities but at numerous small sites in the countryside from the first century onward.[7] Most of the production was dedicated to sturdy open forms (plates and bowls), which tended to have simple rims and minimal feet. Over 100 different vase forms were produced over the centuries, and fragments of them offer the principal means of dating late Roman excavations. In post-Constantinian times, patterns were often stamped into the vases with punches or with rollers ("rouletting"). In the fourth century ARS dominated the market in the western Mediterranean, and in the fifth century its hegemony extended into the Eastern Mediterranean. Exportation of ARS also reached territories north of the Alps.[8] From 350 to 550, figural decoration blossomed on ARS (Figures 11.2–11.5), and other pottery production centers could hardly begin to match its richness.

Two principal types of fabric were used for ARS. Africa Proconsularis in the north produced a heavier more orange-colored ware (the earlier type A and the later type D), and Byzacena in the center produced a redder and thinner-walled ware (type C). From the second quarter of the third century onward, the potters producing ARS type C cast figures in molds and applied them to wheel-turned jugs and bowls. Around the beginning of the early Christian period, production was reorganized. After about 320, ARS potters seem to have stopped producing closed forms (jugs and jars) and focused their attention on the more easily stacked and shipped open forms (dishes and plates). From about 300 CE onward, in an apparently cost-saving move, both northern and central Tunisian workshops stopped applying slip on the sides and bottoms of dishes.[9] After the first quarter of the fourth century, applied figures proliferated. During the span from about 330 to 440, production of plates, bowls, and occasionally plaques with figures in relief exploded in quantity and richness of subject matter (Figures 11.2–11.5).[10] Biblical subject matter was introduced alongside traditional mythological and secular subjects. Often the figures would be applied at random, but sometimes they could be assembled in coherent narrative compositions, a practice rarely seen since the early Imperial period.

As in earlier *terra sigillata*, non-Christian imagery continued to play a large role in ARS type C. Animals evoke the pleasures of country life and the excitement of hunts, whether in the amphitheater or in the wild (Figure 11.4). Fish and fishermen allude to the most highly prized food of antiquity. Grasshoppers and baskets of fruit continue still-life traditions known from Pompeian painting. Tales of mythological heroes are popular; the labors of Hercules are particular favorites, with sixteen different episodes represented. Orpheus' ability to charm animals also had considerable currency. Odysseus makes rare appearances tied to the mast of his boat. Divinities, both Olympian and Eastern, appear, but religious themes are usually treated in a light vein; Bacchus and his retinue of satyrs and maenads engage in happy revelry. Venus is less popular than playful Cupids. Demigods and benign sea monsters turn the sea into a mythological funland. Isis takes a concert cruise in a boatload of musicians. Mithras is something of an exception by appearing in key images of his cult: on one bowl he kills the bull and also drags it away.

Biblical subject matter gradually erodes the position of mythology. The Good Shepherd appears occasionally, but the main biblical themes are stories with happy endings, especially salvation scenes from the Hebrew Bible and some miracles from the New Testament (Figures 11.2 and 11.5).[11] Only three of Jesus' miracles appear on ARS (Lazarus, the healing of the paralytic and the healing of the woman with the issue of blood). Thecla's escape from the beasts of the amphitheater adds a salvation story from apocryphal Christian sources.[12] An allegory of a watchman in a tree house adds a theme from North African patristic writing.[13]

Gladiatorial combat was forbidden by Constantine and later emperors,[14] and the subject, which had been popular on earlier pottery, disappears from the repertory of ARS in the fourth century. Criminals or barbarian captives exposed to wild animals in the arena, however, continue to appear (Figure 11.3). The lions or bears often turn their heads aside, thereby seeming to betray ambivalence about performing their grisly roles as executioners, leading some scholars to hesitantly interpret such scenes as martyrdoms.[15] The interpretation seems unlikely since often enough the animals leap upon the unfortunate convict at the stake without turning their head, as they had in a multitude of earlier mosaics and ceramic vases and lamps.[16] Male victims are characterized as barbarians by long hair and beards (Figure 11.3). Biblical figures, on the contrary, spread their arms in prayer and escape harm from the beasts. In pottery as in other branches of early Christian art, martyrdoms seem to have been shunned as subject matter except at cult places dedicated to the martyrs.[17]

Some figure-decorated vases of central Tunisia were entirely mold-made. They take the form of platters (*lances* or "lanxes") (Figures 11.4. 11.5). In these outspoken imitations of silver platters of the very wealthy, scenes from mythology or epics frequently occupied the central field, and scenes of country life with tender goatherds and ferocious hunts (Figure 11.4) appear in ways that foreshadow major monuments of secular art, such as the mosaic of the Great Palace in Constantinople. Games or hunts in the arena appear and, like platters in precious materials, some of them may have been made to commemorate specific public entertainments.[18] Platters with Christian themes seem to be in the minority. Perhaps in keeping with the high-status pretentions of this genre, the "Christian" pieces usually limit the imagery of the central field to authoritative, dogmatic images: usually a pair of Apostles flanking either Christ or a cross (Figure 11.5).[19] The borders of the Christian pieces display Apostles, Jonah, or occasionally Lazarus in his tomb. A puzzling syncretistic image also appears: the Dioscuri occupy the central field of a platter and are accompanied by an inscription of veiled Christian content.[20] These ARS platters were valuable enough to merit preservation even when broken; an example in Carnuntum on the Danube (Austria) was repaired with bronze wire.[21]

By far the most important of the kilns producing figure-decorated ARS was an unremarkable site in the interior of central Tunisia now covered by farmland and olive orchards called Sidi Marzouk Tounsi. The kilns were probably attached to a villa owned by ambitious senatorial entrepreneurs.[22]

In the second quarter of the fifth century the rich figural culture of ARS type C suffered a notable setback, probably in connection with the Vandal conquest of Africa Proconsularis, which was completed in 439 with the fall of Carthage. Molded figures were no longer applied to dishes, although molded lamps with figures did to some extent continue the figural tradition. In spite of the disappearance of the elite line of production with figures in relief, the exportation of "smooth" ARS plates and bowls continued unabated.

Starting around 320 Tunisian potters introduced a technique for decorating smooth dishes: that is, without applied figures; decorative motifs were stamped on the interior of ARS of bowls and plates (Figure 11.6).[23] In a first phase, stamps were stylized palm branches, rosettes, fringed circles, hearts, and cloverleaf patterns. In the fifth century, roughly in correspondence with the Vandal conquest, stamped designs became more varied. Christian monograms and small animals began to be used abundantly, and on occasion tiny human figures appeared. In the first half of the sixth century stamped motifs became larger still, and the repertory expanded to jeweled crosses and large anthropomorphic figures. These figures tend to be uninhibited and innovative iconographically. They include Bacchus as well as saints. Christ holds the cross, trophy of his victory, and unexpectedly wears the sleeveless tunic or *colobium*, the garment in which he was crucified (Figure 11.6),[24] as in paintings of the later sixth through the eighth century.

Around the time of the Byzantine conquest of North Africa in 533, production at Sidi Marzouk Tounsi and other central Tunisian sites stopped.[25] Open forms in ARS, however, continued to pour out of kilns in northern Tunisia until the Arab conquest of Carthage in 698.

The ARS did not have a monopoly of the market of *terra sigillata* during the early Christian period. Some producers survived the military crises and reorganizations of Roman society during the second half of the third century.[26] A few producers in the western Mediterranean managed to preserve a share of their own regional markets through the fourth and into the fifth century by introducing new forms, which often imitated ARS: the hardy survivors included Spanish *sigillata*[27] and "shiny *sigillata*" (*sigillée luisante*) from Savoy in southeast Gaul.[28] In the eastern Mediterranean, the potteries at Sagalassos in southwest Asia Minor sustained their robust activity into the seventh century.[29] New pottery producers also emerged with imitations of ARS and, from the fifth century onward, these newcomers progressively eroded the dominance of ARS in their regions.[30] Phocaean Red Slip ware (Late Roman C) was produced at Phocaea near Izmir (Smyrna) on the Aegean coast of Turkey. This ware was decorated with stamps similar to those of ARS. Cypriot Red Slip ware (Late Roman D) and Egyptian Red Slip ware (ERS) were also competitors who on occasion made use of stamped ornaments, usually crosses or a meager floral ornament.

In the early Christian period potteries of Asia Minor occasionally produced red-slip ware with figures in relief. A small number of mold-made "pilgrim's flasks" or costrels in Sagalassos Red Slip ware are decorated with hunts or Bacchic themes, and from *ca.* 500 onwards biblical themes are occasionally worked in as well. The Christian subjects often seem to put a religious gloss on traditional activities; Daniel and the lions are mixed into a hunting scene, and the Adoration of the Magi includes a tiny bust of Bacchus, which probably alludes to the wine contained in the costrel.[31]

In northern Europe, important sources of *terra sigillata*/red slip pottery survived in the Argonne area in northeastern France, and throughout the fourth century they distributed their wares through northern Gaul, the Rhineland, and Britain.[32] The Argonne kilns produced a great variety of open forms (plates and bowls), whose exteriors were frequently decorated with bands of pattern impressed with a roller. Unlike ARS, Argonne kilns also produced attractive closed forms, including beakers and pitchers in a variety of traditional Roman shapes, which were often enlivened with linear decoration in white paint. Potters of Trier on the Moselle occasionally took casts of metal (presumably silver) bowls with rich figural decoration and reproduced them in red *terra sigillata*; a fine but isolated example shows Orpheus enchanting a multitude of animals.[33]

Gray wares: gray and black terra sigillata and fine gray burnished ware

Ceramics were also fired in a reducing atmosphere to turn them black, gray, or dark brown. Some were coarse cooking pots made with a large admixture of fine gravel, which kept them from cracking when used in kitchen fires. Other dark ceramics were fine tableware, whose glossy surfaces could suggest tarnished silver or pewter (Figures 11.7–11.8). As in red slip ware, their glossy coating was a purified version of the body clay and similar in color to it. Between about 350 and 500, gray *sigillata* was taken up in two separate areas with similar results. In central and especially southern Gaul it is called *sigillée grise*, or Narbonne *sigillata* (Figure 11.7).[34] The region centered on the city of Narbonne itself produced both red and gray versions, while the region centered on Marseille and Bordeaux produced almost exclusively gray wares. A similar fine gray pottery called Macedonian gray *terra sigillata* is found in northern Greece and FYROM (Figure 11.8). The ware was probably produced at Stobi.[35] A very similar and contemporary ware ("Thracian Gray Ware") appears in Thrace and Moesia (Bulgaria).[36] The repertory of shapes consisted of open forms, plus the occasional jar or jug.

These gray wares made considerable use of stamped decoration on the exterior of cups and bowls. Wheels were rolled over the exterior to give texture (rouletting) (Figure 11.7). Punches were used to stamp ornaments into the mold for the vase or the vase itself (Figures 11.7–11.8). Stamps were abstract ornaments or else palm branches, wreaths, discs, rosettes, and arches, which give a mildly celebrative effect. Human figures, which had been abundant on cups and bowls in earlier times, were eliminated, and animals were reduced to the occasional rabbit or deer. The popularity of fine gray ware in these various areas has been linked to the arrival and passage of the Visigoths.[37] Modest and dry as these stamped wares may seem, they could apparently hold considerable value for their owners; a gray Narbonne ware cup, made in Marseille and excavated in Florence was important enough to its owner to be worth restoring with lead bindings (Figure 11.7).[38]

North of the Alps fine black ceramics were a long-lived Celtic tradition. Black *terra nigra* was pre-Roman in origin, but it eventually took on Romanized shapes.[39] During the fourth century *terra nigra* vases along the northern frontiers are decorated with burnished linear decoration organized in bands of cross-hatching and undulating lines. Such vases can be tracked from

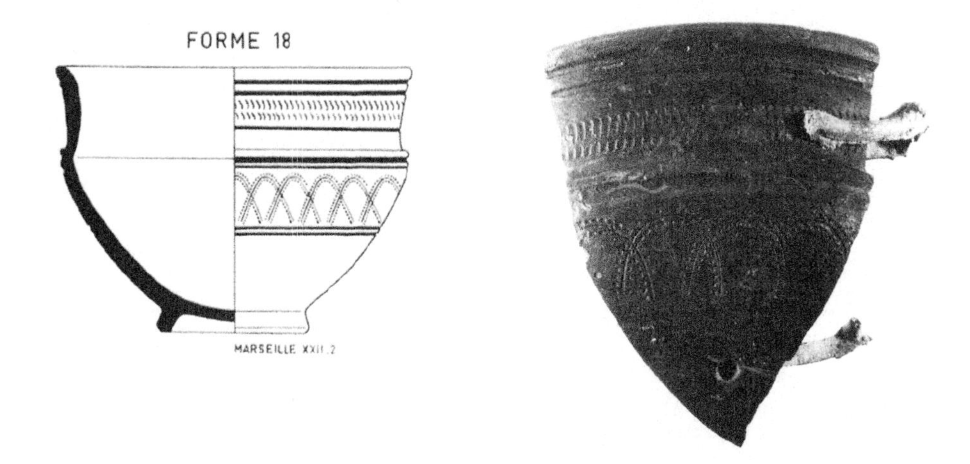

Figure 11.7 Narbonne *sigillata*, Rigoir, form 18, 5th–early 6th century. Left: Rigoir 1968; right: example repaired with lead. Florence, S Reparata excavations; photo: Soprintendenza alle Antichità d'Etruria, 22/43/1.

Figure 11.8 Macedonian gray *terra sigillata*, 4th–early 5th century. Museum of Byzantine Culture, Thessaloniki.

Britain through the Rhineland in the fourth century and along the Danube through the fifth. Production sites have been identified on both the Roman and the barbarian sides of the river, and some date after the Hunnic conquest *ca.* 420. These burnished black pots apparently reflect the movements of barbarians into Roman lands all along the northern frontier, first as settlers then as conquerors.

Lead-glazed ware

Technically outstanding is the fine pottery coated with a vitreous lead-based glaze. These green or brown lead glazed wares flourished along the Danube in the province of Pannonia (western Hungary and eastern Austria) from the time of Constantine into the first quarter of the fifth century, and well-preserved pieces are found in cemeteries in this area (Figure 11.9).[40] A great variety of traditional Roman shapes and many novelties were produced. In some cases (presumably relatively late pieces), pitchers are strikingly elongated, as in contemporary silverware. Glazed wares like those of Pannonia were found in lesser quantities in the upper Danube, middle Rhineland and northeastern Italy, where they were produced at various sites, including Carlino near Classe (Ravenna).[41] At Rome a few two-handled cups ("sessile canthari") take up glazing and are distinctive both for their shape and their high relief "pagan" figural decoration (deeds of Hercules, pagan sacrifice).[42] The Roman cups seem to be heavy-handed imitations of Early Imperial silverware. After a long interval, glazed ceramics were revived at Constantinople, Italy, and perhaps Crete in the late sixth and seventh centuries.[43]

Slip decoration: color-coated ware, marbleized ware, and painted ware

Slip was applied to clay vases either by dipping the vase or by painting it on with a brush or some other tool. The slip itself can be highly variable in color and luster. In *terra sigillata* the slip is a purified version of the body clay and is similar or identical in color to the body. In other kinds of pottery, the body clay is a different or, at any rate, not an identical color, and when the surface is not covered completely with slip, uncovered areas stand out (Figures 11.10–11.12). To distinguish high quality vessels with different colored body and slip from *terra sigillata*/red slip ware, the term "color-coated ware" is generally used. Much color-coated ware has a relatively matte surface and was used as a low-cost replacement for red slip ware. Some color-coated ware, however, was more ambitious.

In northwestern Europe beakers of color-coated ware were prestige items. They were usually dipped into a glossy black slip and fired in a reducing environment, and the coating often has a luster approaching that of *terra sigillata*, as on a beaker from Nijmegen on the lower Rhine (Figure 11.10).[44] The most notable producer of such dark-coated light-bodied drinking gear was the vast kiln district at Trier.[45] In the third century, dark-coated Trier ceramics were decorated with white and yellow barbotine (thick liquid clay). In the fourth century the thick

Figure 11.9 Glazed ceramics from tombs of the 4th and early 5th centuries, Aquincum. Aquincum Museum.

Figure 11.10 Color-coated "motto beaker" with barbotine decoration, inscribed REPLEME ("fill me!"), made in Trier, excavated in a tomb of 300–355. Museum Het Valkhof, Nijmegen.

Figure 11.11 Fragmentary Coptic painted ware bowl with a woman riding a camel, mid-7th century. Museum of Fine Arts, Boston, 1994.114, gift of Dr and Mrs Jerome M. Eisenberg.

Figure 11.12 Slip-painted jug (Crecchio Ware), 550–650. Crecchio (Chieti), Museo dell'Abruzzo Bizantino e Altomedievale. Photo: Giovanni Lattanzi. http://foto.inabruzzo.it/provincia%20Chieti/comuni%20A-E/Crecchio%20museo/index.html.

barbotine becomes thin paint, the use of yellow becomes rare, and the glossy, metallic effects tend to diminish. The Trier production ran from about 255 to 355 CE, and throughout this span it made extensive use of white-painted Latin inscriptions, which are primarily injunctions to enjoy life and to drink.[46] Commands on these "motto beakers," such as "drink everybody" (BIBITE), "give me something to drink" (DA BIBERE) and "mix for me" (MISCEMI), are similar to commands barked out in the contemporary banquet frescoes in the Catacomb of Saints Marcellinus and Peter in Rome.[47] The catacomb paintings, however, have benevolent serving women named Irene ("Peace") and Agape ("Love"), while the Trier beakers express an apparently unmitigated hedonism. In the case of the motto beaker in Nijmegen, the inscribed command is "fill me" (REPLEME) (Figure 11.10). The popularity of wine served hot probably explains the shape of such motto beakers; its globular belly and narrow neck would have tended to conserve the wine's heat.

In the fourth century vessels in northwest Gaul and Germany could also be thinly painted with slip to create a mottled effect that could suggest metal or veined marble. "Marbleized ware" of various kinds was produced in an area along the Moselle from Trier to the Rhine.[48] These vessels often have an extra embellishment of vine scrolls in white paint. In Greece color-coated ceramics were sporadically decorated with white vine scrolls or leaves throughout early Christian times.[49]

Coptic Egypt had a particularly colorful tradition of painted pottery stemming from much earlier times.[50] Various kinds of clay slip were applied to create polychrome effects. Jars and plates made of Nile silt were painted in red-brown, black, and occasionally yellow over a beige or white ground (Figure 11.11). During the fourth to sixth century, compositions were relatively restrained, and the subject matter is usually braids, stylized vegetation, and peaceful creatures: fish, birds, hares, and gazelles, which are arranged in bands around jars and on the interiors of plates. Arcs, dots, and hatching enliven the schemes. In contrast with most of the Mediterranean area, Coptic painted ceramics blossomed in the late sixth and seventh centuries.[51] Figures (usually busts) with huge eyes stare out. Compositions can be triglyph-and-metope arrangements, or even interlaced medallions. Painters often create an exuberant buzz by packing the backgrounds with dots, spirals, and scribbles. Occasionally novel figural subjects appear: in one especially surprising case, a woman has a rough ride on a camel (Figure 11.11). This image must allude to the Arabs, who could be referred to as "women who ride camels,"[52] and it probably dates after the conquest of Egypt in 641.

Some less spectacular Coptic painted ware was exported to Athens,[53] and it could have had an influence on some of the various slip-painted wares that appear sporadically elsewhere around the Mediterranean. Arched patterns and rows of dots are common in slip painted wares, whether in Egypt (Figure 11.11) or on the northern shores of the Mediterranean (Figure 11.12). An early manifestation of slip-painted pottery is in Sardinia, where jugs of the fourth century are painted in red and brown slip with a band of ornament, which usually includes hatched medallions or fish;[54] both recall common motifs of Coptic pottery. Central Greek ware, which was probably produced in Nea Anchialos during the sixth century, is rich in bowls and plates with precisely painted decoration, often based on a central cross or rosette.[55] Particularly exuberant is the slip-painted ware produced at Crecchio on the Adriatic coast of Italy *ca.* 550–700 (Figure 11.12).[56]

During the devastating wars of the sixth century, painted wares took a turn toward the chaotic in some hard-hit Mediterranean regions; in Naples and the surrounding region of Campania, the few surviving professional potters painted their wares with broad lines of red-brown slip scribbled erratically across the surface.[57] In a cave used as a refuge in the Peloponnesus, this kind of uninhibited, unstructured painting mixed spiraling bands and scribbled knots.[58]

Gouged and champlevé decoration on color-coated ware

Throughout the Mediterranean area color-coated jugs could be decorated with grooves gouged with a stylus, recalling chasing or fluting on bronze and silver pitchers.[59] In a small group of plates or bowls in Asia Minor, decoration is incised through the red slip and the background is cut away, a technique often referred to as "champlevé". The best-preserved piece is a plate with a large cross enclosed in an ovulo molding.[60]

Smooth and coarse wares: amphorae, cooking pots, and jugs

Most ancient pottery was made for entirely utilitarian purposes. Vessels of coarse ware were manufactured for cooking, storage, and transportation of agricultural products. The distribution of transport amphorae and other no-nonsense pots around the early Christian world provides important evidence for commercial exchange among different parts of Roman Empire and later the barbarian kingdoms.[61] Amphorae, whose primary contents were olive oil, wine, and fish sauce (*garum*), are a particularly vivid source of economic information, and their contrasting shapes may have served as identifiers for commercial purposes. Finds in Rome, for example, have shown that amphorae came from one end of the Mediterranean to the other (Figure 11.13).[62] The city's wide-ranging trade continued throughout Late Antiquity until it was sharply limited by the Arab conquest of the Maghreb at the end of the seventh century.[63]

Figure 11.13 Containers for food imports of late antique Rome: amphorae from (left to right) Spain, Tunisia, south Italy, Egypt, Cyprus, Syria, Aegean area/Asia Minor, Palestine. Display in Museo Nazionale Romano Crypta Balbi, Rome.

In the late sixth and seventh centuries, the custom of placing a jug in tombs seems to have taken on strength in the Mediterranean area. The jugs are normally without surface coating, but at times reflect a decorative impulse; in Athens pedestal feet and funnel mouths create a graceful profile, and the tall Classical oil bottle (*lekythos*) is revived, although without the traditional foot. In some places in Greece, tombs can contain poorly made jugs, which were probably used only for the burial ceremony.[64]

Lamps

Pottery producers in Tunisia came to dominate the market for lamps as they did the market for tableware in the Early Christian period. In the early fourth century some potters in Tunisia began to make lamps of the fine red clay used for *terra sigillata africana* (ARS), usually in kilns that also produced tableware, and this line of production went on to greater success in the fifth and sixth centuries (Figure 11.14). A popular variety of these red clay "African lamps" had a rather amorphous pear-shape; a channel connects the decorated disk to the relatively small spout, and the convex shoulder was usually decorated with a palm branch or striations (Figure 11.14, left). Such lamps, classified as Hayes 1972, type I or *Atlante I*, type VIII, could ride on the wave of North African exports of agricultural products and ARS dishes throughout the Mediterranean.[65] From about 420 CE, a newer, finer, and more influential type of lamp emerged, designated Hayes African lamp type IIA; *Atlante I*, type X (Figure 11.14, right). It had a flat shoulder, which was usually decorated with rosettes or jewel-like ornaments, and the central disc could be decorated with emblems, such as crosses or menorahs, or figural or ornamental designs. Usually the disc held a single figure, but some type IIA lamps produced at Sidi Marzouk Tounsi had multi-figural compositions with narrative biblical subjects. For example, Daniel in Oriental costume

Figure 11.14 Left: African lamp Hayes type I, with reaper, late 4th–early 5th century. Right: African lamp Hayes type IIA with Daniel in the lions' den, 460–530. Private collection.

prays in the lions' den, and the angel brings Habakkuk carrying food, as in Daniel 6:16–22 and 14:32–38.[66] Several different kiln sites in Tunisia produced lamps of Hayes type IIA, but the finest came from Sidi Marzouk Tounsi. Around the time of the Byzantine conquest of Tunisia in 530 and after a century of intense activity, production ceased at Sidi Marzouk. Lamps of the same general design but poorer in quality (Hayes type IIB) continued to be produced and exported from northern Tunisia until the end of the seventh century.

In general, early Christian and early Byzantine lamp-makers around the Mediterranean continued to produce ceramic lamps in their local tradition, or else they imitated imported African lamps.[67] A widely scattered group of more spectacular lamps, however, poses an authenticity problem. These lamps have the form of a fish with a Christian monogram on its side and come in two sizes, the larger of which is quite naturalistic. Examples of both types are on display in museums in Athens[68] and Zagreb.[69] An example of the large type in Seville lacks the Christian monogram.[70] Examples of the large type in the British Museum and the Catacomb of Ottavilla at Rome have been considered forgeries.[71] Suspicions seem justified since the fine technique used to produce these lamps is unusual, and no fragmentary examples seem to be known from excavations.

Smooth and coarse wares: architectural decoration

Terracotta plaques with relief decoration and normally without a decorative surface coating flourished in Spain and the Maghreb. The plaques presented Christian monograms, biblical scenes, or stylized floral ornaments and could be used in ceilings or as closure slabs for tombs.[72]

Smooth and coarse wares: tokens of pilgrimage

From the fifth century onwards mementos of pilgrimage (*eulogiae* or "blessings") were frequently made of plain ceramics. Often the *eulogiae* took the form of small flasks: two-handled bottles with a flattened cylindrical body (a "pilgrim's flask," *ampulla*, or costrel), which were intended to contain oil or water consecrated at the shrine of a saint. No color coating was applied to these *ampullae*. The most widespread are "Menas flasks," whose principal decoration is a roundel with St Menas of Alexandria praying in the *orans* position adored by two kneeling camels (Figure 11.15). An example in Paris presents Saint Menas in a relatively classical contrapposto pose and with relatively soft modeling (Figure 11.15).[73] His halo of hair, like that of Anastasius, consul of 517, probably indicates the approximate date of the flask. Later works are flatter and more symmetrical and enclose the saint's image within a circular frame embellished with an inscription, a wreath, or a string of pearls.

Small clay *ampullae* have been found in Asia Minor, and Ephesus seems to have been the main producer.[74] Some of the Ephesian *ampullae* show evangelists holding books; they may have been made to commemorate visits to the tomb of the Evangelist John at Ephesus (Figure 11.16).[75] Other Ephesian flasks show Christian scenes with no special connection to the city. *Ampullae* with evangelists or crosses also appear in significant numbers in Nea Anchialos in central Greece and could have been produced there.[76]

Ceramic "*eulogiae*" could be even simpler: small clay discs stamped with a holy image. Some show the column-sitting saints Simeon Stylites and Simeon the Wonderworker and must have been produced at their shrines near Antioch.[77] Others show images connected with the venerated sites in Palestine: the Annunciation, the Adoration of the Magi, and a symbolic image of Solomon.

Figure 11.15 Pilgrim's flask with St Menas adored by camels, Alexandria, *ca.* 520. Louvre, Legs Weill 1950, E 2445, AF 7035, © RMN-Grand Palais/Art Resource, NY.

Figure 11.16 Ampulla with St John the Evangelist, from Ephesus, 6th–7th century. Louvre, MNB 2066.

Statuettes

Figurines of soldiers, women, and animals, some brightly painted, rank as perhaps the most unexpected ceramic productions in these times of aversion to idols and idolatry. To some extent the ceramic statuettes of early Christian times could have been directed at a pagan clientele, but the ritual use of statuettes was clearly integrated into Christian religious culture. Sagalassos produced soldiers, who occasionally are marked with crosses.[78] In Coptic Egypt, female figures appear at a multitude of sites, including the pilgrimage shrine of St Menas.[79] The statuettes are usually emphatically maternal, ranging from nursing mothers and *orantes*, to fleshy nudes. David Frankfurter has conjectured that they were endowed with flexible identities, which could include Mary, Isis, ritual supplicants at shrines, saints on a domestic altar, or figures of communication in a family member's tomb.[80]

Further reading

Writing about early Christian ceramics as art tends to focus on iconographic issues and African Red Slip ware (ARS). The pioneering works of Jan Willem Salomonson are particularly rich and comprehensive from this point of view; he first anatomized the chronological development of ARS and extensively explored the iconography of its applied figural reliefs. Works by Jochen Garbsch and Bernhard Overbeck[81] and by us[82] explore issues of competition between religions and cultures. Meg Armstrong compiled a treasury of motives of all types while Sophie zu Löwenstein has done a vast and analytic study of the mythological subjects on ARS.[83] Peter Talloen writes on the evolution of iconography on early Christian ceramics at Sagalassos.[84] Paul Corby Finney contextualizes the early Good Shepherd lamps.[85]

The various Late Roman red-slip wares have been securely distinguished and classified by John Hayes.[86] He has established their chronologies and compiled and organized the vast array of stamped ornaments on ARS and other late red-slip wares. R.P. Symonds has described the life cycle of dark colored Rhenish wares, probably the most attractive aspect of late Roman pottery in northwestern Europe.[87] Refinements of chronology, distinction of workshops, and tracking of the distribution of these wares continues to the present and on into the foreseeable future.[88] Chris Wickham incorporates ceramic evidence into a major economic history.[89]

Notes

1 Irene Karra, in Anastasia Lazaridou, ed., *Transition to Christianity: Art of Late Antiquity, 3rd–7th century AD* (New York, NY: Onassis Foundation, 2011), cat. no. 3.

2 For Mediterranean sites with outstanding finds of pottery, see Paul Reynolds, Michel Bonifay and Miguel Ángel Cau, "Key contexts for the dating of late Roman Mediterranean fine wares: a preliminary review and 'seriation'," in Cau et al., *LRFW 1: Late Roman Fine Wares: Solving Problems of Typology and Chronology* (Oxford: Archaeopress, 2011), 15–32.

3 Jeffrey Spier, *Picturing the Bible: The Earliest Christian Art* (New Haven, CT: Yale University Press, 2007), 5, 171–172. On this and other shepherd lamps, see Paul Corby Finney, *The Invisible God: The Earliest Christians on Art* (Oxford: Oxford University Press, 1994), 116–145, figs 5.4–5.6.

4 Rachel Hachlili, *The Menorah, the Ancient Seven-Armed Candelabrum: Origin, Form and Significance* (Leiden: Brill, 2001).

5 Donatella Salvi, "Motivi cristiani ed ebraici nei corredi della necropolis di Pill'e Matta Quartucciu (CA). Materiali e contesti inediti," *XI Congrersso Nazionale di Archeologia Cristiana* (Cagliari: PFTS University Press, 2015) 588, figs 6, 9.

6 John W. Hayes, *Late Roman Pottery* (London: British School at Rome, 1972); John W. Hayes "The study of Roman pottery in the Mediterranean: 23 years after *Late Roman Pottery*," in Lucia Sagui, ed., *Ceramica in Italia: VI–VII secolo* (Florence: All'Insegna del Giglio, 1998), 9–21; and John W. Hayes, *Roman Pottery: Fine-Ware Imports, The Athenian Agora* 32 (Princeton, NJ: American School of Classical Studies at Athens, 2008).

7 Michael Mackensen, *Die spätantike Sigillata – und Lampentöpferein von El Mahrine (Nortunesien)* (Munich: Oscar Beck, 1993); Moncef Ben Moussa, *La production de sigillées africaines. Recherches d'histoire et d'archéologie en Tunisie septentrionale et central* (Barcelona: University of Barcelona, 2007).

8 Raymond Brulet in Raymond Brulet, Fabienne Vilvorder, Richard Delage and Dominique Laduron, *La céramique romaine en Gaule du Nord: Dictionnaire des céramiques. La vaisselle à large diffusion* (Turnhout: Brepols, 2010), 205; Michael Mackensen, "Terra Sigillata aus Nord-und Zentraltunesien," in Michael Mackensen and Florian Schimmer, eds, *Der römische Militärplatz Submuntorium/Burghöfe an der oberen Donau. Archäologische Untersuchungen im spätrömischen Kastell und Vicus 2001–2007* (Wiesbaden: Münchner Beitr. Provinzialröm. Archäologie, 2013), 347–360; Ferdinand Heimerl, *Nordafrikanische Sigillata, Küchenkeramik und Lampen aus Augusta Vindelicum/Augsburg* (Weisbaden: Münchner Beitr. Provinzialröm. Archäologie, 2014); Piroska Hárshegyi and Katalin Ottományi, "Imported and local pottery in late Roman Pannonia," *Late Antique Archaeology* 10 (2013): 474–483. For Athens, see Hayes, *Roman Pottery: Fine-Ware Imports*, 67–82, pls. 50–61.

9 Hayes, *Roman Pottery: Fine-Ware Imports*, 67–70; Michael Mackensen, "Technology and organization of ARS ware production-centres," in John H. Humphrey, ed., *Studies on Roman Pottery of the Provinces of Africa Proconsularis and Byzacena (Tunisia): Hommage à Michel Bonifay* (Providence: *Journal of Roman Archaeology*, 2009), 17–44.

10 *Atlante I* = Carandini, A., L. Saguì, S. Tortorella, E. Tortorici et al. 1981. "Atlante delle forme ceramiche, I: Ceramica fine romana nel bacino mediterraneo (medio e tardo impero)," *Enciclopedia dell'arte antica classica e orientale*, Roma, 167–76, pls. 82–88; Meg Anne Armstrong. *A Thesaurus of Applied Motives on African Red Slip Ware* (PhD dissertation, New York University, 1993); Jochen Garbsch and Bernhard Overbeck, *Spätantike zwischen Heidentum und Christentum* (Munich: Prähistorische Staatssammlung, 1989); Konrad Weidemann, *Spätantike Bilder des Heidentums und Christentums* (Mainz: Verlag des Römisch-Germanischen Zentralmuseums, 1990); Annewies van den Hoek and John Herrmann, *Pottery, Pavements, and Paradise: Iconographic and Textual Studies on Late Antiquity* (Leiden: Brill, 2013); Sophie Zu Löwenstein, Mythologische Darstellungen auf Gebrauchsgegenständen der Spätantike. Die appliken- und reliefverzierte Sigillat C3/C4", *Kölner Jahrbuch* 48 (2015): 397–823.

11 Salomonson, J.W., "Spätrömische rote Tonware mit Reliefverzierung aus nordafrikanischen Werkstätten, entwicklungsgeschichtliche Untersuchungen zur reliefgeschmückten Terra Sigillata Chiara 'C',"

BABesch 44 (1969): 4–109; Weidemann 1990, pls 1–11; Fathi Bejaoui, *Céramique et Religion Chrétienne: Les Thèmes Biblique sur la Sigillée Africaine* (Tunis: Institut National du Patrimoine, 1997); Annewies van den Hoek and John Herrmann, "Celsus' competing heroes: Jonah, Daniel, and their rivals," in *Poussières de christianisme et de judaïsme antiques. Études reunites en l'honneur de Jean-Daniel Kaestli et Éric Junod*, Albert Frey and Rémi Gounelle, eds (Lausanne: Éditions du Zèbre, 2007), 319–320, pls 2–4; reprinted in van den Hoek and Herrmann, *Pottery, Pavements, and Paradise*, 216–219, pl. 26–27.

12 Annewies van den Hoek and John Herrmann, "Thecla the Beast Fighter: A Female Emblem of Deliverance in Early Christian Popular Art," in David T. Runia and Gregory E. Sterling, eds, *In the Spirit of Faith: Studies in Philo and Early Christianity in Honor of David Hay* (Studia Philonica 13; Providence: Brown Judaic Studies, 2001), 212–49; reprinted in van den Hoek and Herrmann, *Pottery, Pavements, and Paradise*, 65–106, pls 6–10.

13 van den Hoek and Hermann, "Thecla the Beast Fighter"; reprinted in van den Hoek and Herrmann, *Pottery, Pavements, and Paradise*, 67–69, pl. 7.

14 Thomas Wiedemann, *Emperors and Gladiators* (London: Routledge, 1992), 156–159.

15 J.W. Salomonson, *Voluptatem spectandi non perdat sed mutet. Observations sur l'iconographie du martyre en Afrique Romaine* (Amsterdam: North Holland Publ., 1979), 42–50; Garbsch and Overbeck, *Spätantike zwischen Heidentum und Christentum*, 159–160.

16 Annewies van den Hoek, "Execution as Entertainment," in van den Hoek and Herrmann, *Pottery, Pavements, and Paradise*, 405–434.

17 Fabrizio Bisconti, "Il vinto nella *pietas* Cristiana," in Serena Ensoli and Eugenio La Rocca, eds, *Aurea Roma: Dalla città pagana alla città cristiana* (Rome: L'Erma di Bretschneider, 2000) 399–403, cat. no. 291.

18 For the iconography of *lances*, see J.W. Salomonson, "Late Roman Earthenware with Relief Decoration Found in Northern-Africa and Egypt," *Oudheidkundige Mededelingen uit het Rijksmuseum van Oudheden te Leiden* 43 (1962), 53–95; *Atlante I*, 163–165 (E. Tortorici), pls 78–80; Garbsch and Overbeck, *Spätantike zwischen Heidentum und Christentum*.

19 Anastasia Drandaki in Lazaridou, *Transition to Christianity*, 86–87, cat. no, 14.

20 Annewies van den Hoek, "Divine Twins or Saintly Twins: The Dioscuri in an Early Christian Context," in van den Hoek and Herrmann, *Pottery, Pavements, and Paradise*, 255–300.

21 Michael Mackensen, "Die spätrömische Pegasus-Platte Hayes 56 aus den sogenannten Heilthermen in den *canabae legionis* von Carnuntum," *Jahreshefte des Österreichischen Archäologischen Institutes in Wien* 84 (2015): 195–212, esp. 198, fig. 9.2.

22 Michael Mackensen, "Production centres of African red slip ware production (3rd–7th c.) in northern and central Tunisia," *Journal of Roman Archaeology* (Vol. 15), 121–158; Annewies van den Hoek, "Anicius Auchenius Bassus, African Red Slip Ware, and the Church," in van den Hoek and Herrmann, *Pottery, Pavements, and Paradise*, 133–147; Eadem, "Peter, Paul and a Consul: Recent Discoveries in African Red Slip Ware," *Zeitschrift für Antik und Christentum* 9/2 (2006): 197–246.

23 For comprehensive catalogues, see Hayes, *Late Roman Pottery*, 217–287; *Atlante I*, 122–130 (Tortorella), pls 56–64.

24 Michel Boixadera, Michel Bonifay, Jean-Pierre Pelletier, Jacqueline Rigoir, Yves Rigoir and Lucien Rivet, "L'habitat de hauteur de Sainte-Propice (Velaux, B.-du-Rh.): L'occupation de l'Antiquité tardive," *Documents d'Archéologie Méridionale* 10 (1987): 94–98, cat. no. 24.

25 Mackensen, "Production centres of African red slip ware," 131–134.

26 Hayes, *Late Roman Pottery*; *Atlante II* = John W. Hayes, María Ángeles Mezquíriz, Luisa Mazzeo Saracino, Andreina Ricci and Giuseppe Pucci, "Atlante delle forme ceramiche, II: Ceramica fine romana nel bacino mediterraneo (tardo ellenismo e primo impero)," *Enciclopedia Dell'arte Antica Classica e Orientale* (Roma: Istituto della Enciclopedia italiana, 1985), xxviii, 71–96 (Carrandini), pls 16–23.

27 *Atlante II*, 110–111 (Mezquíriz), pls. 25,11–14; 29,1–2; 47,1–5; 49, 3–5; 50,1.

28 *Atlante I*, 5 (Carandini), pl. 6; Claude Raynaud "Céramique Luisante", *Lattara* 6 (1993): 504–10.

29 Jereon Poblome, J., *Sagalassos Red Slip Ware: Typology and Chronology* (Turnhout: Brepols, 1999).

30 Hayes, *Late Roman Pottery*, 346–401.

31 British Museum 1882,0109.1: Peter Talloen, "From pagan to Christian: Religious iconography in material culture from Sagalassos," in Luke Lavan and Michael Mulryan, eds, *The Archaeology of Late Antique 'Paganism'* (Leiden: Brill, 2011), 575–607; Daniele Malfitana and Maria Louisa Scrofani, "La ceramica di Sagalassos decorata a matrice. Tipologia, cronologia, iconografia. Gli *oinophoroi*," in Daniele Malfitana and Giuseppe Cacciaguerra, eds, *Archeologia classica in Sicilia e nel Mediterraneano* (Catania: Richerche di Archaeologia Classica e Post Classica in Sicilia, 2014), 254–62.

32 Brulet in Brulet et al., 2010, 216–253.

33 Ensoli and La Rocca, *Aurea Roma*, cat. nos 323 (H. Hellenkemper), 324 (K. Göthert).
34 Jacquline Rigoir, "Les sigillées paléochrétiennes grises et oranges," *Gallia* 26 (1968): 177–244; *Atlante I*, 6 (Carandini), pls 7–12; Hayes, *Roman Pottery: Fine-Ware Imports*, 90, pl. 70.
35 Hayes, *Late Roman Pottery*, 405–407, figs 90–91; Hayes, *Roman Pottery: Fine-Ware Imports*, 90–91, pl. 70; Virginia Anderson-Stojanovic and James Wiseman, J., *Stobi: Results of the Joint American-Yugoslav Archaeological Investigations, 1970–1981: Volume 1: The Hellenistic and Roman Pottery* (Princeton, NJ: Princeton University Press, 2014), 61–72, pls. 48–55, note 105.
36 Anderson-Stojanovic and Wiseman, *Stobi*, 65, note 105.
37 Anderson-Stojanovic and Wiseman, *Stobi*, 65, note 105.
38 John Herrmann, "Nota archeological," in Piero Bargellini, Guido Morozzi and Giorgio Batini, eds, *Santa Reparata, la Cattedrale risorta* (Firenze: Bonechi, 1970), 108–115, esp. 115; John Herrmann, "L'antico ambiente intorno alla Cattedrale di Santa Reparata," in Guido Morozzi, Franklin Toker and John Herrmann, eds, *Santa Reparata, l'antica cattedrale fiorentina: I risultati dello sccavo condotto dal 1965 al 1974* (Firenze: Bonechi, 1974), 99, 106, fig. 64.
39 Renate Pirling and Margareta Siepen, *Die Funde aus den römischen Gräbern von Krefeld-Gellep: Katalog der Gräber 6348–6361* (Stuttgart: Franz Steiner, 2006), 174ff; D.C. Steures, *The Late Roman Cemeteries of Nijmegen: Stray Finds and Excavations 1947–1983* (Nymegen: Museum Het Valkhof, 2011) forms 113–125, 302–303, 736–737; Hárshegyi and Ottományi 2013, 499–509, figs 3–4.
40 Chiara Magrini and Francesca Sbarra, eds, *Late Roman Glazed Pottery in Carlino and in Central-East Europe: Production, Function and Distribution*, BAR International Series 2068 (Oxford: John and Erica Hedges Ltd., 2010); Brulet in Brulet et al. 2010, 296–299; Reuter, S., "glasierte Keramik," in Michael Mackensen and Florian Schimmer, eds, *Der römische Militärplatz Submuntorium/Burghöfe an der oberen Donau. Archäologische Untersuchungen im spätrömischen Kastell und Vicus 2001–2007*: *Münchner Beitr. Provinzialröm. Archäologie* (Wiesbaden: Reichert, 2013); Hárshegyi and Ottományi 2013, 489–499, figs 1–2.
41 Lidia Paroli, ed., *La ceramica invetriata tardoantica e altomedievale in Italia*. Atti del Seminario (Certosa di Pontignano) (Florence, 1990); Magrini and Sbarra, 2010; Brulet in Brulet et al., 2010, 296–299; Reuter, 2013.
42 Marco Ricci, "Su alcuni crateri invetriati tardo-antichi di Roma," in Lidia Paroli, ed., *La ceramic invetriata tardoantica e altomedievale in Italia* (Firenze: Edizioni All'insegna del Giglio, 1992), 346–350; Marco Ricci, in Maria Stella Arena, Paolo Delogu, Lidia Paroli, Marco Ricci, Lucia Saguì and Laura Venditelli, eds, *Roma dall'antichità al Medioevo, Archeologia e storia nel Museo Nazionale Romano Crypta Balbi* (Milano: Electa, 2001), 168.
43 John W. Hayes, "A Seventh-Century Pottery Group," in R. Martin Harrison and Nezih Firatli, eds, "Excavations at Saraçhane in Istanbul: Fifth Preliminary Report," *Dumbarton Oaks Papers* 22 (1968): 203–216; Hayes 1968; Andrea Staffa, "Le produzioni ceramiche in Abruzzo tra fine V e VII secolo," in *Sagui* 1998, 437–480, esp. 471, fig. 22; D. Romei, in *Arena, Roma dall'antichità al medioevo*, 306; Anastasia Yangaki, *La céramique des IVe–VIIIe siècles ap. J.-C. d'Eleutherna* (Athens: Université de Crète, 2002), 131–133.
44 Tomb B387.1: Steures 2011, 102, 648, 732.
45 Robin P. Symonds, *Rhenish Wares: Fine Dark Coloured Pottery from Gaul and Germany* (Oxford: Oxford University School of Archaeology, 1992); Brulet in Brulet et al., 2010, 359–366.
46 F. Vilvorder in Brulet et al., 2010, 355. For lists of the mottos: Symonds, *Rhenish Wares*, 112–121; Susanna Künzl, *Die Trierer Spruchbecherkeramik. Dekorierte Schwarzfirniskeramik des 3. Und 4. Jahrhunders n. Chr.* (Trier: Rheinischen Landesmuseums, 1997), 252–259; Steures 2011, 285–287.
47 For example, AGAPE MISC in the catacomb of Marcellinus and Peter: Hugo Brandenburg, "Frühchristliche Kunst in Italien und Rom," in Beat Brenk, ed., *Spätantike und frühes Christentum* (Frankfurt-am-Main: Propyläen, 1977), 107–141, esp. p. 134, pl. 53a.
48 Brulet in Brulet et al. 2010, 381–386; Steures 2011, 295.
49 *Atlante I*, 254–256; Hayes, *Late Roman Pottery*, 412–413; Yangaki 2002, 127–133, figs 15–18.
50 *Atlante I*, 245; John W. Hayes, *Roman Pottery in the Royal Ontario Museum* (Toronto: Royal Ontario Museum, 1976), 50–51, cat. nos 261–265; Michel Egloff, *Kellia-La poterie copte* (Geneva: Recherches Suisse d'Archéologie Copte III, 1978); Anna Wodzinska, *A Manual of Egyptian Pottery 4: Ptolemaic Period – Modern* (Boston, MA: Ancient Egypt Research Associates, 2010), 181–242.
51 Alexander Badawy, *Coptic Art and Archaeology* (Cambridge, MA: MIT Press, 1978), 305–314, figs 4.99–4.117; Tomasz Górecki, "Coptic painted amphora from Tell Atrib – introductory remarks on decoration," in Włodzimierz Godlewski, ed., *Coptic and Nubian Pottery Part I* (Warsaw: National Museum,

1990), 34–48; A. Effenberger et al., *Ägypten, Schätze aus dem Wüstensand: Kunst und Kultur der Christen am Nil* (Wiesbaden: Ludwig Reicher, 1996), cat. nos 147–162.

52 *Sahih Bukhari*, Book 4, Vol. 55, Hadith 643; *Sahih Muslim*, 6140.

53 Hayes, *Roman Pottery: Fine-Ware Imports*, 92–93, 253–254, pl. 71.

54 Donatella Salvi, "La campidanese. Ceramic commune da mensa dalla Sardegna meridionale nei contesti chiusi di età tardoantica nella necropolis di Pill' e Matta, Quartucciu (Cagliari – Sardegna – Italia)," in Simonetta Menchelli et al., eds, *LRCW3, Late Roman Coarse Wares, Cooking Wares and Amphorae in the Mediterranean* (BAR Int. Ser. 2185, 2010), 235–243, fig. 6; Donatalla Salvi, "La datazione dei materiali: conferme e smentite dai contesti chiusi tardo-romani e altomedievali," in Paola Corrias ed., *Forme e caratteri della presenza bizantina nel Mediterraneo occidentale: la Sardegna (secoli VI–XI)* (Cagliari: Condaghes, 2012), 174, fig. 15.

55 *Atlante I*, 254; Hayes, *Roman Pottery: Fine-Ware Imports*, 92, 252, pls 70; Ntina, A., "Early Christian Pottery from Thebes Phthiotides" (in Greek with English summary), in Demetra Papanikola-Bakirtzi and Ntina Kousoulakou, *ΚΕΡΑΜΙΚΗ ΤΗΣ ΥΣΤΕΡΗΣ ΑΡΧΑΙΟΤΗΤΑΣ ΑΠΟ ΤΟΝ ΕΛΛΑΔΙΚΟ ΧΟΡΟ* (3ο-7ο αι. μ.Χ.), Thessaloniki (Greek with English summaries), 2010, 563–79; Anastasia Chrisostomou, "Late Antique pottery from Edessa and Almopia in the prefecture of Pella" (in Greek with English summary), in Papanikola-Bakirtzi and Kousoulakou 2010, 505–19, esp. 509, 514, drawings 4, 6; 517, fig. 10. On Coptic influence, see Platon Petridis, "Roman and Early Byzantine pottery workshops in mainland Greece," in Papanikola-Bakirtzi and Kousoulakou 2010, 81, 96.

56 Staffa 1998, http://foto.inabruzzo.it/provincia%20Chieti/comuni%20A-E/Crecchio%20museo/index.html.

57 P. Arthur, "Local pottery in Naples and northern Campania in the sixth and seventh centuries," in Saguì 1998, 491–510.

58 Lina Kormazopoulou and Dimitris Hatzilazarou, "The pottery from the cave at Andritsa in the Argolid," (in Greek with English summary), in Papanikola-Bakirtzi and Kousoulakou 2010, 169–184.

59 Hayes, *Roman Pottery: Fine-Ware Imports*, 93, 254–255, pl. 72; Salvi 2010; Salvi 2012, 173, fig. 14.

60 Hayes, *Late Roman Pottery*, 409, pl. 23a; Cahill 2010, cat. no. 220.

61 For an effective use of ceramic evidence in a general history see Chris Wickham, *Framing the Early Middle Ages: Europe and the Mediterranean, 400–800* (Oxford: Oxford University Press, 2005), esp. "Methodological Issues," 7 ff. For bibliography and a synthetic approach to the issue, see Stefano Costa, "The Late Antique Economy: Ceramics and Trade", *Late Antique Archaeology*, 10 (2013): 91–130.

62 Pacetti, P., "I rifornimenti alimentari della città," and "Anfore," in Arena et al., *Roma dall'antichità al medioevo*, 209–218.

63 Saguì, Ricci and Romei in Arena et al., *Roma dall'antichità al medioevo*, 266–306.

64 Elli Tzavella, "Late Antique pottery from Athenian graves and its evidence for the 7th C. in Attica," (in Greek with English summary) in Papanikola-Bakirtzi and Kousoulakou 2010, 649–670; Chamilaki, "Late roman burials from a cemetery at Delion, Boeotia" (in Greek with English summary), in Papanikola-Bakirtzi and Kousoulakou 2010, 581–609.

65 For recent comprehensive studies, see Jean Bussière, J., *Lampes antiques d'Algérie II: Lampes tardives et lampes chrétiennes* (Montagnac: International Lychnological Association, 2007); Michel Bonifay, "Advances in the study of African Late Roman pottery (3rd–7th c.)" in Papanikola-Bakirtzi and Kousoulakou 2010, 37–64. For African lamps along the Danube, see Hárshegyi and Ottományi 2013, 480–481.

66 Van den Hoek and Herrmann, *Light from the Age of Augustine*, cat. no. 25; van den Hoek and Herrmann, *Pottery, Pavements, and Paradise*, 71–72, 221, 494, pl. 8b, 28b.

67 For Algerian imitations, see Bussière 2007. For Greece, see Antonis Tsakalos, in Lazaridou, *Transition to Christianity*, cat. nos 121–127.

68 Antonis Tsakalos, in Lazaridou, *Transition to Christianity*, cat. 123; www.byzantinemuseum.gr/en/search/?bxm=12; https://www.flickr.com/photos/johnsylee/3778255456/; https://c1.staticflickr.com/4/3519/3746372032_50471b235e.jpg.

69 Ivana Nikolic, *Rimske i ranokrscanske glinene svjetiljke iz Muzeja Mimara*, (Zagreb: International Lychnological Association, 1999); www.lychnology.org/rimske-i-ranokrscanske-glinene-svjetiljke-iz-muzeja-mimara/; www.pbase.com/bmcmorrow/image/139105911.

70 Archaeological Museum, Seville: www.arthurtaussig.com/photographs/travel/seville-spain-i/.

71 British Museum 1982,0302.40. Pontificia Commissione di Archeologia Sacra: www.archeologiasacra.net/pcas-web/scheda/fotografico/PCASST0217080/Catacomba-di-Ottavilla-e-basilica-di-S-Pancrazio/Lucerna-a-forma-di-pesce-falsificazione?page=3&query=storico_Catacomba-di-Ottavilla-e-basilica-di-S-Pancrazio&filter=catacomba&text=&jsonVal={}.

72 Pedro de Palol, *Arqueologia Cristiana de la España romana: siglos IV–VI*, (Madrid-Valladolid: Consejo Superior de Investigaciones Científicas, Instituto Enrique Flórez, 1967), 255–272, pls 67–63. See Metropolitan Museum of Art 1985, 147.

73 Catherine Metzger, *Les ampoules à eulogie du Musée du Louvre* (Paris: Ministère de la culture, Editions de la Réunion des musées nationaux, 1981); *Ägypten, Schätze aus dem Wüstensand* 1996, cat. no. 142a.

74 Metzger, *Les ampoules à eulogie du Musée du Louvre*; Sabine Ladstätter and Andreas Pülz, "Früchristliche Ampullen aus der archäologischen Sammlung des Instituts für klassische Archäologie in Wien," *Forum Archaeologiae, Zeitschrift für klassische Archäologie* 21 (2001).

75 Metzger, *Les ampoules à eulogie du Musée du Louvre*.

76 Ntina, "Early Christian Pottery from Thebes Phthiotides," 576, 578.

77 Gary Vikan, *Byzantine Pilgrimage Art*, Dumbarton Oaks Byzantine Collection 5 (Washington, DC: Dumbarton Oaks, 1982).

78 Elizabeth Murphy and Jereon Poblome, "Situating Coroplast and Moulded-Ware Productions in Late Antique Sagalassos (SW Turkey)," *Newsletter of the Coroplastic Studies Interest Group* 7 (2012), 2–3.

79 Cabrol and Leclercq, DACL, Vol. 11.2 (1933): s.v. "Ménas (Saint), cols. 374–375, figs 7962–7965; Effenberger et al., in *Ägypten, Schätze aus dem Wüstensand* (Berlin: Reichert 1996), cat. nos. 124–127, 130–135; David Frankfurter, "Female Figurines in Early Christian Egypt: Reconstructing Lost Practices and Meanings," *Material Religion*, 11.2 (2015): 191–223.

80 Frankfurter, "Female Figurines in Early Christian Egypt."

81 Garbsch and Overbeck, *Spätantike zwischen Heidentum und Christentum*.

82 John Herrmann and Annewies van den Hoek, *Light From the Age of Augustine: Late Antique Ceramics from North Africa (Tunisia)* (Cambridge, MA: Harvard Divinity School, 2002; 2nd ed., Austin: Institute for the Study of Antiquity and Christian Origins at the University of Texas at Austin, 2003).

83 Armstrong, *A Thesaurus of Applied Motives*; Sophie zu Löwenstein, "Mythologische Darstellungen auf Gebrauchsgegenständen der Spätantike: die appliken- und reliefverzierte Sigillata C3/C4," in *Kölner Jahrbuch / hrsg. vom Römisch-Germanischen Museum und der Archäologischen Gesellschaft Köln*, 48. Band (2015): 397–823.

84 Talloen, "From pagan to Christian," 575–607.

85 Finney, *The Invisible God*, 116–145.

86 Hayes, *Late Roman Pottery*.

87 Symonds, *Rhenish Wares*.

88 Cau, Reynolds and Bonifay, *LRFW 1: Late Roman Fine Wares*.

89 Wickham, *Framing the Early Middle Ages*, esp. pp. 72–108.

12
PANEL PAINTINGS AND EARLY CHRISTIAN ICONS

Katherine Marsengill

In the early fourth century, Bishop Eusebius of Caesarea (*ca.* 260–339/340) wrote a letter to Emperor Constantine's sister, Constantia, replying to her request to send her a portrait of Christ for her private devotion. The letter, which survives in fragments that were invoked by the Iconoclastic Horos in 754, though possibly manipulated by Iconoclasts in order to present how early church leaders argued against the use of icons, is generally accepted as authentic.[1] After a lengthy explanation of why Constantia's desire to know the face of Christ was both impossible and irresponsible, the bishop provides an anecdote from his own experience. He writes: "Once . . . a woman brought me in her hands a picture of two men in the guise of philosophers and let fall the statement that they were Paul and the Savior—I have no means of saying where she had this from or learned such a thing."[2] He goes on to state that he confiscated the image and kept it.

The anecdote is revealing for many reasons. The Christian woman had shown the image to Eusebius under the assumption that her possession was indeed what she had been told, suggesting that, despite Eusebius' rhetorical question to Constantia ("Have you ever heard anything of the kind [about portraits of Christ] either yourself in church or from another person?"), it was in fact not unheard of for Christians to believe that such portraits existed. Substantiating evidence can be found, strangely enough, in Eusebius's own *Ecclesiastical History*, written around 325, where Eusebius remarks upon painted portraits of Peter, Paul, and Christ that he himself had seen. Seemingly at odds with his earlier letter to Constantia, perhaps he had gained some experience in these matters, though he provides the caveat that such portraits were based in pagan practices.[3] Additionally, Eusebius' letter to Constantia describes the image as depicting two men guised as philosophers. That the woman may have confused philosophers with Christ and Paul is an interesting detail. Some scholarly conjecture proposes that this part of the letter might be Iconoclast invention. But the idea is actually consistent with Christian art of the time, given that some of the earliest surviving images of Christ among his disciples accord with contemporary imagery of philosophers. Misidentifying the philosophical men in the portrait was perhaps an honest mistake. Either the woman was understandably mistaken to think the philosophers represented Christ and Paul, or perhaps Eusebius was wrong to assume the painting was not, at the very least, *intended* to depict Christ and Paul. By contrast, Eusebius demonstrates no such concerns in his *Ecclesiastical History* about the identity of the figures portrayed, fully accepting the authenticity of Peter, Paul, and Christ. In both of these texts, Eusebius reveals that, most likely, portable paintings—icons—were already in the possession of Christians by the early fourth century. As will be presented here, it is likely that such images existed as early as the second century, even if perhaps few in number, and these painted images were a natural part of contemporary Greco-Roman culture that was adopted by Christians.

The origin of Christian icons in Greco-Roman panel painting

Unfortunately, no Christian icon firmly dated earlier than the sixth century survives. Nor does much survive to provide us with a clear picture of the very rich and complex tradition of Greco-Roman panel painting from whence icons developed. Painted wooden panels, the primary medium for ancient portable images as well as Christian icons, have proven too fragile for the most part to endure to the present, leaving us with a huge lacuna in our knowledge of this ancient art. But there is enough visual and textual evidence to piece together an overview of the Greco-Roman tradition in order to understand the conceptual reasons why the painted panel became so important in Christian worship.

Roman-era painted panels are known today mostly from textual descriptions, such as Pliny the Elder's first-century *Natural History* (Book 35), which offers us a glimpse of an ancient world covered with panel paintings by famous and celebrated artists, paintings that were hung in temples and put on display in public places; and from depictions of such paintings in more durable materials like mosaic and fresco. We see panel paintings mimicked in the wall paintings of Pompeii, for example, including illusory frames around their mural compositions, as if panel paintings were actually hung on the walls.[4]

A large part of ancient panel painting was dedicated to portraiture, the type of painting that is also the genre of Christian icons. Indeed, the definition of icon (*eikōn*) relates most directly to portraiture, and *eikon*, along with the Latin *imago*, is repeatedly found in antique sources when referring to real portraits, usually two-dimensional or in relief as opposed to portrait statues. Evidence for how portraits were produced can be seen on a first-century sarcophagus that was discovered in Kerch, which shows a portrait painter at work in his studio (Figure 12.1). The painter is depicted heating wax over a brazier for mixing with pigments—arranged in a compartmentalized box in front of him—according to the encaustic technique of painting. On the wall behind him are both rectangular panels with what are known as eight-point frames, and *clipeatae imagines*—portraits on round panels following a tradition of painting shields with commemorative portraiture.

Painted portraits served numerous important functions in antiquity. Portraits could be used in domestic settings, as were the painted portraits of ancestors and family members displayed in homes of the Roman elites, and about which Pliny provides information.[5] "Framed" portraits, too, are also found in surviving wall paintings from Pompeii, like the well-known double portrait of a bakery owner, Terentius Neo, and his educated wife, painted in their home's atrium.[6] Portraits in other media also provide information about the appearance of actual painted panels. For example, scholars have judged a floor mosaic in Pompeii showing a bust portrait of a woman so painterly in its execution that it must have been based on an original panel portrait.[7]

One important use for portraits was funerary, a tradition that transitioned smoothly into Christian practices. Roman tombs have been discovered that have framed portraits painted directly on walls, like the tomb of Aelia Arisuth in Tripoli from the fourth century (Figure 12.2). In this case, her portrait appears as a *clipeate*, rather than a rectangular panel. From tomb murals of framed portraits like this, one may reasonably assume that panel portraits were once placed in tombs, or that original panel portraits existed from which permanent mural portraits were copied in tombs; or possibly some tombs boasted both wall portraits and portable portraits.

Figure 12.1 Sarcophagus of a portrait painter. From Pantikapaion (Kerch), 1st century. State Hermitage Museum, St Petersburg. Photograph © The State Hermitage Museum, photo by Leonard Kheifets.

Figure 12.2 Aelia Arisuth in Tripoli from the 4th century Portrait of Aelia Arisuth, from the Tomb of Aelia Arisuth (fresco), Roman, 4th century CE, Gargaresh, Libya. Bridgeman Images.

A first-century inscription preserving the inventory of a tomb from Apateira near Epheson substantiates the use of portable portraits, describing how multiple panel portraits were part of the tomb furnishings. The list includes thirteen "painted portraits" (*eikones graptai*) of Nona and Paula, presumably the deceased occupants of the tomb.[8]

Another elucidating example concerning the integration of portable portraits in tomb murals is a ceiling painting from the fourth- or fifth-century cubiculum of Oceanus in the Christian Catacomb of San Callixtus, Rome. A portrait bust painted directly on the vault is missing its head, the intended area for which is outlined by a rectangle. Nail holes indicate that a separately executed portrait, perhaps painted on canvas or thin panel, had once been placed there (Figure 12.3). This may have been a portrait that was made earlier, before being placed in the tomb; or perhaps the tomb portrait was painted with care using another portrait as a model, before being set in the ceiling with its more formulaic bust already having been executed *in situ*. That Christians also relied upon such portraits to commemorate their dead is of even greater significance when one considers that such portraits served as devotional images in pagan ancestor cults. Early Christians, too, were known to celebrate with their dead, perhaps even venerating the portraits of the deceased at tombs, a practice that was chastised by Augustine of Hippo in the late 380s.[9]

Figure 12.3 Fresco with missing portrait, 4th or 5th century. Vault in the cubiculum of Oceanus, Catacomb of San Callixtus, Rome. Photo: Joseph Wilpert, *Die römischen Mosaiken und Malereien der kirchlichen Bauten vom IV. Bis XIII Jahrhundert* (Freiburg, 1916), IV, 182.I.

The bulk of what we know about ancient panel portraiture comes from mummy portraits that have survived from Egypt, mostly dating to the first through third centuries. Their preservation is a fortunate result of the desert climate, leaving many in near pristine condition. These strikingly naturalistic portraits in encaustic and others of lesser quality painted in tempera give us indication of the variety and appearances of portraits that would have been found all over the Mediterranean world. In Egypt, the painted portraits were adapted to fit over the faces of Egyptians' mummified bodies (Figure 12.4). In this way, painted portraits served as replacements for the older tradition of using sculptural masks on mummies to portray the deceased. Many scholars still consider these Egyptian portraits to be on the fringes of ancient funerary panel portraiture because they were essentially mummy masks (i.e., substitutes for the face in the afterlife), but it is important to note that some of the portraits show evidence that they were cut down to fit the respective mummies, suggesting a previous use for them. Others appear to have been stand-alone panels. Although their discovery in the nineteenth century was often poorly documented and thus their functions in tombs unclear, one description contemporary with the discovery of a tomb in Er-Rubayat reports that the walls, not the bodies, displayed numerous portraits on panel.[10] A portrait of a female now in the Getty Museum (Figure 12.5) may have come from Er-Rubayat. It is interesting to note the nail holes at the bottom of the panel and blank horizontal space at the top that may correspond to a now-missing frame. Perhaps it had hung in her tomb. Like other places in the Roman Empire, Egypt may have used funerary panels as tomb decoration rather than just mummy masks, lending the surviving panels even greater importance as objects intended for viewers' contemplation.

Figure 12.4 Mummy portrait of a woman. Attributed to the Isidora Master (Romano-Egyptian, active 100–125), *ca.* 100–110. From Er-Rubayat (?), Egypt. Digital image courtesy of the Getty's Open Content Program.

Figure 12.5 Mummy portrait of a woman, *ca.* 175–200. Digital image courtesy of the Getty's Open Content Program.

Very often these portraits were painted from life or copied from life portraits, and they went on to serve as commemorative images at tombs after death. Our best evidence for this comes from the only framed panel portrait that has survived from this early period. The portrait, dated to the second century, was found in a tomb near Hawara in Egypt (Figure 12.6). Though badly damaged, the panel clearly depicts a woman. It also preserves a rope attached to the corners of the frame that was used for hanging it on a wall. This, along with the size of the portrait—the painted face is much too small to have ever been intended for a mummy—makes it almost certainly an object that had originally been in a home. This practice was important to the development of the kinds of icons that were placed in saints' tomb-shrines, which relied upon many of the same conceptual aspects of the funerary portrait. Many accounts of icons follow similar patterns of being painted from life or copied from an original, and displayed in private contexts. In Late Antiquity, in the shrines of Christian saints and martyrs, portraits that claimed original likenesses would invariably adorn their tombs. However, it is important to note that funerary images could be typified, as well, relying not upon a portrait but upon an avatar-like idealized image as substitute for the deceased. For many early icons of saints there is no doubt that the legend of an accurate portrait icon arose well after an initial typified "holy" appearance had been accepted as the real image.

Figure 12.6 Portrait of a woman, 2nd century. From Hawara, Egypt. British Museum, London. Photo © Trustees of the British Museum.

Panel portraits set up in public or sacred spaces represent another antique tradition relevant to the origins of Christian icons. Analogous to the public statues set up in *fora* and temples throughout the Empire, portrait panels were frequently of ruling emperors. We know about these primarily from texts, as only one imperial panel survives from the second century (Figure 12.7). It features Emperor Septimius Severus, his wife, Julia Domna, and his sons Caracalla and Geta (the latter's image having been defaced on the order of his brother). Likewise, late antique Christian emperors had portrait panels, unsurprisingly referred to in texts as icons, which were copied and sent out to officials across the Empire, as well as displayed in public spaces and churches. This practice ran parallel to other kinds of Christian portraiture, where authoritative panel portraits of bishops occupied civic and ecclesiastical spaces. How and when holy icons became accepted parts of public display is not yet fully understood, though the sixth century presents itself in texts as a watershed moment for civic icons.

Panel portraits for spiritual access, veneration, and supplication

One of the most ubiquitous claims of portraiture for pagan and Christian alike was the ability to provide a means to see the features of someone who was not immediately available to sight. Thus, the psychological motivations for the production and acquiring of portraiture in the first few centuries CE were very much akin to our own. There was the desire to know the appearances of certain well-known people universally held in high regard. Pliny the Elder writes, "And indeed, it is my opinion, that nothing can be a greater proof of having achieved success in

Figure 12.7 Severan Imperial portrait, *ca.* 200. From Djemila (Algeria). Antikensammlung der Staatlichen Museen zu Berlin. Photo: Carol Raddato, Wikimedia Commons.

life, than a lasting desire on the part of one's fellow men, to know what one's features were."[11] Among the most common reasons was the desire to look intimately upon images of familiar loved ones and esteemed mentors, as is beautifully illustrated in the portrait painter's sarcophagus (Figure 12.1), which has, on the far right, a figure reverently carrying away a small portrait. In the life of Saint Pancratius, though written centuries after the martyr's death, a disciple emotes over a portrait of the saint: "When I see him in the image, I think that he is alive and that I am in his company."[12] The sentiment lets us know that the portrait bridged the separation of the disciple from his deceased mentor in a way that was likely perceived not merely metaphorically; it is quite reasonable to assume that the viewer believed Saint Pancratius to be spiritually accessible through his portrait and the perceived intimacy that it imparted.

Where such private portrait panels were kept is not entirely known: most likely in atria, perhaps in home libraries, workspaces, or bedrooms. In some cases, it appears that home shrines may have been set up for deceased family members or loved ones where painted portraits were displayed, like the tiny columned aedicule from Egypt with a child's portrait placed within (Figure 12.8). Objects like this may have joined images of gods on pagan domestic altars. Indeed, the portrait shrine from Egypt suggests a larger spectrum of representations were perceived as venerable than just the images of gods.

In the ancient world, loved ones who had passed on to the afterlife were believed to have sway over forces that were otherwise beyond the control of the living. Family members and ancestors would, theoretically, be invested in their own relatives, and therefore might be more responsive to evocations and placations by particular households. Portraits, whether in homes or in tombs, would have been useful to help focus prayers, but also would have been perceived as having a real and powerful connection to the portrayed.[13] Augustine of Hippo's chastisement

Figure 12.8 Columned aedicule with a child's portrait placed within, 3rd century. From the Fayum. Egyptian Museum, Cairo. Photo: C. C. Edgar, *Egyptian Coffins, Masks and Portraits* (Cairo, 1905), Plate XVIII.

mentioned above describes how his congregation gathered at the tombs to feast and drink and to adore the images there, which we can infer were most likely portraits of their deceased loved ones. However, if one's power had been strong in this world, and one's status had been high in the eyes of the gods, the potential to have influence in the supernatural realm was augmented and more widespread. Godly and spiritual men of great renown were considered especially efficacious. Indeed, it was believed that the venerable deceased offered better mediation on behalf of the living than the gods, a phenomenon that gained significant foothold in the religions of Late Antiquity, including Christianity.

The gods did not disappear from pagan religious life, though. A handful of panel paintings of pagan gods and goddesses has survived, mostly full length, but often rendered in bust, as if portraits, perhaps suggesting a merging of the intimacy offered by portraiture while retaining also the iconography of divine majesty. These kinds of panel paintings were almost certainly widely produced. Their precise function is debated. It is possible that they, too, were placed in homes for veneration, alongside or in place of statuettes that featured in private shrines called *lararia*. From texts we learn that *pinakes*, painted images of the gods, were also offered as votive gifts to temples and public shrines.[14] A few surviving "pagan icons" include smaller images of devotees that are presumed to be the donors of panels gifted to temples, though perhaps such portraits could be found in home shrines, too, as evidence for a supplicant's eternal devotion.

Christians donating images of Christ, saints, and angels hark back to this practice. Donor portraits only appear later in surviving Christian panel paintings, like the famous icon known as the Madonna della Clemenza in Santa Maria in Trastevere, Rome, which has been dated to either the late sixth or early seventh century. Yet texts provide more evidence for donor portraits on icons and suggest that the motivations for giving icons to churches were similar to the pagans who had in earlier times offered panels to temples. Thankful supplicants of Saint Daniel the Stylite, a pillar saint who lived in the fifth century and whose *vita* was likely written by a contemporary, donated a silver plaque with the saint's image (probably a relief panel rather than a painted icon) that included their own portraits on it.[15] Two epigrams from icons recorded in the sixth century by Agathias Scholasticus clearly denote paintings as thanks offerings.[16] One of the earliest icons of Christ, of which only the top half remains, preserves a votive inscription in Coptic identifying a supplicant named Timotheos (Figure 12.9). It is not impossible that Timotheos was once depicted on the now-missing lower half of icon.

Portraits of philosophers and early icons of holy men

While respect for the ancient gods remained, the early centuries CE saw another type of person added to the antique pantheon of venerable beings. Elites of the Roman Empire regarded important philosophers like Plato, Pythagoras, and Socrates, as spiritual masters and exemplars.[17] Textual sources reveal the existence of not only statues and statuettes of philosophers (of which there are numerous surviving examples, as well), but also painted panels (of which none survives). An epigram from one such panel, for example, addresses the painter of Socrates' encaustic portrait: "Painter, who has reproduced the form of Socrates, would that you could have put his soul into the wax!"[18]

Venerating these portraits appears to have occurred very early. According to Pliny, a group dedicated to Epicurus carried around his portrait, likely as a way to demonstrate their devotion.[19] In the following centuries, veneration of philosophers' portraits became more commonplace.

Figure 12.9 Part of an icon of Christ, 6th–7th century. From Egypt. Benaki Museum, Athens. Photo © Benaki Museum.

Bishop John Chrysostom's teacher, the pagan Sophist Libanius (313–394 CE), possessed two bust-length portraits of his favorite philosopher, the second-century Aristiedes.[20] Libanius further desired to acquire a full-length portrait of Aristiedes so that he could gaze upon the philosopher's hands and feet. These are clearly paintings, since Libanius describes having at first mistaken one of his portraits for a painting of a god, and so dedicated it to a temple of Zeus Olympius, where it was to be placed near a painting of Apollo with Asclepius and Hygea. In his mistake, we see how the appearance of philosophers' portraits was such that they came to occupy an ambiguous place between the portrait and cult image. The likenesses of ancient philosophers were frequently unknown and images had to be fabricated, circulated, and accepted as authentic portraits. More often than not, these "portraits" conformed to an expected and idealized type, usually an older bearded man with a high forehead or balding, while still maintaining certain traits or relying upon inscriptions to identify them. Viewers were ready to believe, even though Dio Chrysostom remarked upon this phenomenon, saying that the appearances of bearded, mature philosophers were actually based on Greco-Roman male divinities.[21] Libanius certainly invested in the belief that portraits of Aristiedes could accurately convey not just the appearance of his face, but also the particulars of his hands and feet, a sentiment echoed in John Chrysostom's devotion to the apostle Paul, including in his esteem the virtuous attributes of the saint's various body parts.[22]

One of the reasons for the popularity of philosopher cults was philosophy's gradual elision with theurgy and mysticism in the first few centuries CE. This led to greater veneration of ancient philosophers, who were attributed god-like qualities. It also produced new spiritual exemplars and purported miracle workers who became regarded as holy men.[23] Portraits were an important part of this phenomenon. In his *lararium*, Marcus Aurelius (r. 161–180 CE) venerated images of his own philosophy teachers alongside the images of gods, essentially deifying them.[24] According to Bishop Eusebius' letter to Constantia discussed at the beginning of this chapter, followers of Simon Magus possessed a painted portrait of the first-century mage, just as followers of the third-century Mani carried around a portrait of him. Apollonius of Tyana (*ca.* 15–100 CE), "a wise man of most celebrated fame, an ancient philosopher, the true friend of the gods, who himself deserves to be worshiped as a higher power,"[25] gained substantial status and had numerous images across the Empire. For example, the *lararium* of Alexander Severus (r. 222–235 CE) held a portrait of Apollonius. He also supposedly had images of Christ and Abraham.[26] The emperor Aurelian (r. 270–275 CE) beheld a vision of Apollonius, who was recognizable to the emperor because the emperor had seen images of Apollonius in temples. The emperor, now a believer, immediately promised to dedicate "an image, statues, and a temple" to the holy man.[27]

This widespread belief in holy men as capable of working miracles transitioned quite well into Christianity, as did the habit of keeping portraits of them. John Chrysostom describes how the congregation in Antioch had adorned all kinds of objects and places with the likeness of their bishop Meletius (d. 381 CE), including rings, bedroom walls, and cups.[28] This may have been for comfort while grieving, as Chrysostom claims. However, Gregory of Nyssa's funerary oration for Meletius, given at the time of Meletius' death five years before Chrysostom's oration, evinces the common belief that spiritual exemplars could help the living deployed within a purely Christian understanding of the cult of saints. On that day, Gregory told the congregation that Meletius, now residing in heaven, was able to intercede directly with God on behalf of the Antiochenes. It is reasonable to suggest that Meletius' images proliferated, in part, because of Gregory's reassurance of his intercession. Thus, the portraits described by Chrysostom could have functioned not only in the commemoration of Meletius, but also as visual foci for prayer to him and as objects made for his continued veneration. The incipience of Meletius' cult resembles how pagan men viewed spiritual teachers and also demonstrates aspects of the Roman ancestor cult, where deceased loved ones were believed to act on behalf of the living.

The earliest Christian icons and subsequent developments

Yet it was earlier than the late fourth century—indeed, as early as the second century—when the first portraits of Christian holy persons were made and venerated. Two texts provide evidence. The first was written by Irenaeus of Lyons, wherein he criticizes followers of Carpocrates—a heretical Christian sect—for keeping a portrait of Christ they believed was made by Pontius Pilate upon which they placed crowns.[29] It is interesting to note that Christ's portrait was venerated along with many images of philosophers, including Pythagoras, Plato, and Aristotle. The second text is found in the apocryphal *Acts of John*,[30] which has been dated to the early second century. It tells of a man named Lycomedes who was miraculously healed by Saint John. In his gratitude, Lycomedes hired an artist to paint John's portrait in secret so that he might have an image of the saint. The artist gave the portrait to Lycomedes, who took it into his bedroom where he set it up, hung garlands on it, and lit lamps on an altar before it.

Key points emerge from these texts. It is clear that the second century saw the use of Christian portraits—perhaps only a few—and that these could be venerated in the privacy of a bedroom, or in a more ritualized way in conjunction with other important figures, though these behaviors might not yet be within the bounds of official Christianity. Additionally, whether or not the portraits were authentic, the perception that life portraits of Christ and his apostles could exist was already in place well before Eusebius' time, an idea that became more prominent in later centuries with the advent of icon legends, especially of the Virgin and Christ. The textual evidence presented above also suggests that, at least in the beginning, it is possible that Christ's was not the most important portrait among Christian venerable images, that perhaps his image was one among a number of portraits of potential spiritual teachers that could be revered. This was certainly true for those outside of Christianity, like the Emperor Alexander Severus and his numerous images, including Christ, mentioned previously. Similarly, as stated above, Ireneaus describes Christ's image as one among many philosophers' images that the Carpocratians worshipped. Ireneaus also describes the heretical sect's view of Christ in such a way to suggest they believed Christ to have been, like the others whose images they venerated, a spiritual man who ascended to the highest realm of existence to become divinized.[31] Lycomedes, presumably a Christian convert, chose a portrait of John to keep as an image of his personal savior, saying, "but if, next to that God it be right that the men who have benefited us should be called gods, it is thou, father, whom I have had painted in that portrait, whom I crown and love and reverence as having become my good guide."[32] It was not Christ, but John, who was next to God in Lycomedes' esteem.

In a religious climate that aspired to direct knowledge of the divine realm and prized intimate contact with those spiritual men who had achieved such a state, so that personal saviors and teachers, venerated philosophers, and holy men were preferred to the ancient gods, Christ's vague status is perhaps not surprising, especially considering the debates about His human and divine natures that persisted for centuries. This may explain why the images of certain saints, such as Peter and Paul in Rome, and of martyrs and Christian holy men in their various churches across the Latin West and Greek East, proliferated and developed specific, recognizable portraits when compared with the various unspecified images of Christ. While there are no panel paintings of saints that have survived from the fourth and fifth centuries, there are images—often in bust—in other media where, even if abstracted, particular saints are yet recognizable either by inscriptions or characteristic traits. By contrast, Christ appears differently in his images from Late Antiquity: sometimes youthful, sometimes bearded; sometimes a philosopher and theurgic wonder-worker, sometimes a ruler, and sometimes a god. But, contrary to what one might expect, Christ rarely features in a "portrait."

To provide one example, a fifth-century text describes how portraits ("small icons") of Symeon Stylites the Elder (d. 459 CE) hung in every shop in Rome,[33] yet there is nothing similar in sources about Christ's image hanging throughout the private spaces of cities. Negative evidence certainly does not rule out the existence of large numbers of portable portraits of Christ. The first few icon-like portraits of Christ in wall paintings, floor mosaics, and gold glass appear in the late fourth century, and even if not always consistent in his appearance, the images demonstrate the spread of Christ's portrait in different media. An example such as the painted ceiling from the Catacomb of Commodilla, Rome (Figure 12.10), with its "framed" bust and recognizable (if not yet universally accepted) bearded face, makes it likely that there were portrait panels of Christ that looked like this in circulation and used as models for larger works.

Yet, as suggested above, it was perhaps the immediate contact with the divine offered by a particular saint, either via a living holy man or via the relics of a deceased saint in his tomb, that was more crucial to the precipitate growth and spread of icons in the fourth and fifth centuries than the exultation of images of Christ. Again, we hear about such icons only from

Figure 12.10 Cubiculum with image of Christ, 4th or 5th century. Catacomb of Commodilla, Rome. Photo: De Agostini Picture Library/Bridgeman Images.

texts. But within these texts, we may infer that the use of icons at martyria and shrines gave visibility to the present saint and allowed Christians greater intimacy in their experiences of the saint. And, just as the popular practice of burial *ad sanctos* augmented the cult of martyrs, a perceived closeness to local saints might have resulted in a greater investment in personal icons of them, which also boosted their cults and increased icon production. Local saints provided greater hagiographical possibilities about how their appearances were witnessed and documented in portraits, which let Christians more easily believe that they could actually view saints in their images, whether or not these images were clear and lifelike or sketched with the barest of lines. By means of portable icons, such as those of Saint Symeon described above, and *eulogia* (clay or lead impressed with the saint's image), visual contact with and perceived blessings from the saint were ongoing even after physical departure from the living holy person or his enshrined relics.

While Christians in the fourth and fifth centuries valued seeing holy persons in images, likely using them to channel their intercession in earthly matters and for veneration in preparation for their eternal life in heaven, at some point viewing icons also became spiritually charged and potentially transformative. Not just commemorative images, icons of virtuous, spiritual men and women, martyrs, and other godly persons were believed to convey their spiritual nature. The faces presented in icons were understood as the visible aspects of perfected souls. This perception was founded in antiquity, in the belief that virtue was apparent in one's face, and reinforced by the divinized philosophers who were said to radiate outwardly the beauty and serenity of their souls. The cultural phenomenon affected the development of Christian images. Icons were perceived to have *power.* Bishop Gregory of Nazianzus (*ca.* 329–390 CE), for example, tells of a portrait of a man named Polemon, who was a reformed profligate, though he was not a Christian saint. His portrait, however, inspired a prostitute who saw it hanging in the home of a man she was visiting. Though she did not recognize him, his portrait transformed her and she forswore her occupation and returned to a virtuous life.[34]

With powerful icons eventually came miraculous icons, which also provided definitive origin stories for what were believed to be authentic portraits of Christ. Of these, perhaps the most informative is the legend of the Mandylion. The early version of the story tells of the ill King Abgar of Edessa, who lived at the time of Christ and who sent a messenger to bring Christ to Edessa to heal him. Christ, unable to go in person, sent a letter to the king, which was kept as a relic. By the beginning of the fifth century, however, the story had grown to include a portrait of Christ by Abgar's court painter, Hannan, which was also sent back to Edessa. This already evinces the possible existence of an avowed, if jealously guarded, original court painting of Christ in the fifth century. Yet, by the next century, the painted portrait of Christ was no longer featured. The story instead told how Christ wiped his face with a cloth—the Mandylion—leaving a miraculous imprint of his face upon it, a perfect portrait without variation from the original that was sanctioned by Christ Himself. The account also saw the cloth re-imprinting itself on a ceramic tile. Later accretions to the story told how the Mandylion miraculously saved the city from invasion.[35]

In this way, icons of miraculous origins, called *acheiropoietic* icons (literally "not made by the hand [of man]"), and having miraculous powers, provided justification for all icons. Icons offered the opportunity to see what were believed to be true likenesses of the portrayed. For Christ, his true icon meant nothing less than the chance to see the face of God, an intimate engagement with the divine perhaps nowhere clearer than in the beautifully preserved, sixth-century encaustic icon of Christ from the Monastery of Saint Catherine, Mount Sinai (Figure 12.11).

Figure 12.11 Icon of Christ Pantokrator, 6th century. Monastery of St Catherine, Mt Sinai. Photo courtesy of the Michigan–Princeton–Alexandria Expedition to Mount Sinai.

Notes

1 C. Sode and P. Speck, "Ikonoklasmus vor der Zeit? Der Brief des Eusebius von Kaisareia an Kaiserin Konstantia," *Jahrbuch der Österreichischen Byzantinistik* 54 (2004): 113–134.
2 Eusebius, *Letter to Constantia*, trans. Cyril A. Mango, *Art of the Byzantine Empire, 312–1453, Sources and Documents* (Toronto: University of Toronto Press, 1997), 16–18.
3 Eusebius, *Ecclesiastical History*, 7.18.
4 Irene Bragantini and Valeria Sampaolo, *La pittura pompeiana* (Electa: Soprintendenza archeologica Napoli e Pompei, 2009); Umberto Pappalardo, *The Splendor of Roman Wall Painting* (Los Angeles, CA: J. Paul Getty Museum, 2009).
5 Pliny, *Natural History*, 35.4–6.
6 Bragatini and Sampaolo, *La pittura pompeiana*, 517, no.VI.2.
7 Bragatini and Sampaolo, *La pittura pompeiana*, 516, no.VI.1.
8 Maria Nowicka, *Le portrait dans la peinture antique* (Warsaw:Varsovie Institut d'archéologie et d'ethnologie, Académie polonaise des sciences, 1993), 141.
9 Augustine, *On the Morals of the Catholic Church and the Manicheans*, 1.34.75, CSEL 90:80.
10 Barbara Borg, *Mumienportrats: Chronologie und kultureller Kontext* (Mainz: Verlag Philipp von Zabern, 1996); Jane Fejfer, *Roman Portraits in Context* (Berlin: De Gruyter, 2008).

11 Pliny, *Natural History*, 35.15.
12 *Bibliotheca Hagiographica Graeca* 1410, trans. Mango, *Art of the Byzantine Empire*, 138.
13 Fejfer, *Roman Portraits in Context*.
14 Siri Sande, "Pagan Pinakes and Christian Icons, Continuity or Parallelism?" *Acta ad archaeologiam et artium historiam pertinentia* 18 (2005): 81–100.
15 *Life of St Daniel the Stylite*, 59, trans. Elizabeth A. S. Dawes and Norman Hepburn Baynes, *Three Byzantine Saints (St. Daniel the Stylite, St. Theodore of Sykeon, St. John the Almsgiver) Contemporary Biographies* (Oxford: Basil Blackwell, 1948), 42.
16 *The Greek Anthology*, Vol. 1, trans. W. R. Paton, Loeb Classical Library 67 (Cambridge, MA: Harvard University Press, 1916), 22–23, nos. 1.35–36.
17 Paul Zanker, *The Mask of Socrates: The Image of the Intellectual in Antiquity*, trans. A. Shapiro (Berkeley, CA: University of California Press, 1995).
18 *The Greek Anthology* Vol. 3, trans. W. R. Paton, Loeb Classical Library 84 (Cambridge, MA: Harvard University Press, 1917), 330–331, no. 9.594.
19 Pliny, *Natural History*, 35.3–8.
20 Libanius, *Epistle 143 to Theodorus*, trans. A. F. Norman, Loeb Classical Library 479 (Cambridge, MA: Harvard University Press, 1992), 294–297.
21 Dio Chrysostom, *On Personal Appearance* 72.2; 72.5; Bernard Frischer, *The Sculpted Word: Epicureanism and Philosophical Recruitment in Ancient Greece* (Berkeley, CA: University of California Press, 1982), 246.
22 John Chrysostom, *Homily* XIII; PG 61, 110.
23 Matthew W. Dickie, *Magic and Magicians in the Greco-Roman World* (London: Routledge, 2001), 195–206.
24 *Augustan History*, "Marcus Aurelius," 3.5.
25 *Augustan History*, "Aurelianus," 24.
26 *Augustan History*, "Alexander Severus," 29.2.
27 *Augustan History*, "Aurelianus," 24.
28 John Chrysostom, *On Saint Meletius*, 3.
29 Irenaeus, *Against Heresies*, 1.25.6.
30 *Acts of John* 26–29.
31 Irenaeus, *Against Heresies*, 1.25.1.
32 *Acts of John*, 27.
33 Theodoret of Cyrus, *Ecclesiastical History*, 26.11.
34 Gregory of Nazianzus, *Carmina*, 1.2.10, "On Virtue"; *PG* 37, 737–738.
35 Mark Guscin, *The Image of Edessa, The Medieval Mediterranean: Peoples, Economics and Cultures, 400–1500*, Vol. 82 (Leiden: Brill, 2009).

Further reading

Belting, Hans. *Likeness and Presence: A History of the Image before the Era of Art*. Chicago, IL: University of Chicago Press, 1994.

Gschwantler, Kurt. "Graeco-Roman Portraiture." In *Ancient Faces: Mummy Portraits from Roman Egypt*, edited by Susan Walker, 14–22. New York, NY: Routledge, 2000.

Jensen, Robin M. *Face to Face: Portraits of the Divine in Early Christianity*. Minneapolis, MN: Fortress Press, 2005.

Kitzinger, Ernst. "The Cult of Images in the Age before Iconoclasm." *Dumbarton Oaks Papers* 8 (1954): 83–150.

Marsengill, Katherine. *Portraits and Icons: Between Reality and Spirituality in Byzantine Art*. Turnhout: Brepols, 2013.

Marsengill, Katherine. "Portrait and Icons in Late Antiquity." In *Transition to Christianity: Art of Late Antiquity, 3rd–7th Century AD*, edited by Anastasia Lazaridou, 55–60. New York, NY: Alexander S. Onassis Public Benefit Foundation, 2011.

Mathews, Thomas. "Early Icons of the Holy Monastery of Saint Catherine at Sinai." In *Holy Image Hallowed Ground: Icons from Sinai*, edited by Robert S. Nelson and Kristen M. Collins, 39–55. Los Angeles, CA: J. Paul Getty Museum, 2006.

Sörries, Reiner. *Das Malibu-Triptychon: ein Totengedenkbild aus dem römischen Ägypten und verwandte Werke der spätantiken Tafelmalerei*. Dettelbach: Röll, 2003.

Walker, Susan. *Greek and Roman Portraits*. London: British Museum Press, 1995.

13

CHRISTIAN IVORIES

Containment, manipulation, and the creation of meaning

Niamh Bhalla

Ivory, or elephant dentine, was frequently used for the production of Early Christian objects on account of the same aesthetic and practical characteristics that made it desirable for pre-Christian art. Its density, durability, pearly off-white color, attractive grain and the high shine that it took when polished, due to its high collagen content, made ivory a popular material for exploitation since prehistoric times. Although Early Christian ivories were also likely painted, to a greater or lesser extent, in bright primary colors and often gilded, it seems that the appearance of the material was valued for its own sake and rarely covered up entirely.[1] The relatively large dimensions of elephant tusks also invited their exploitation since bigger objects could be made from them than from the tusks of the narwhal and walrus or from bone. The physiognomy of the elephant's tusk determined the appearance of the objects made from it in terms of scale, shape, technique, style and finish and it seems that the aesthetic that resulted from its inherent physical characteristics, along with its relative rarity, determined in large part the cultural desirability of ivory in Late Antiquity and the uses to which it was put.

The value and use of ivory

In 301 CE the emperor Diocletian issued his famous *Edict of Prices* with the intended aim of curbing rising inflation in an already volatile economy. The price of ivory, as recorded, was significantly lower than any previously documented price at 150 denarii per Roman pound.[2] Although the ostensible aim of the edict means that the prices found there cannot be considered precise indications of market value, the figures give us a comparative cost for the material: ivory was notably less expensive than precious metals and silk but cost considerably more than mundane materials such as bone and wood. Although ivory had been used since ancient times for its practical and decorative potential, its use and relative value fluctuated over time, mostly in relation to availability. Ivory, being an organic material—indeed the most dense and durable natural material available to ancient and medieval craftsmen—was subject to the vicissitudes of supply. It was above all a natural commodity that had to be sourced in either Africa or Asia and transported by means of trade before it could be wrought into functional, devotional and ornamental pieces. These broad categories of usage continued largely unchanged over time but the particularities of usage varied according to supply in different periods.

The form and function of ivories during the Early Christian period seem to have been informed by a relatively abundant supply of material, predominantly from North and East Africa, so that we find ivories being used for utilitarian objects such as pill boxes. Jerome, writing in 403 CE to the mother of a new daughter, recommends that she have a set of ivory or boxwood letters made for the child to learn the alphabet.[3] Despite this seeming abundance, the simultaneous preciousness of the material is revealed in its prevalent use for diplomatic gifts, holy icons, and containers for sacred objects. Cyril, Patriarch of Alexandria, for example, sent eight stools and fourteen chairs made from ivory to the emperor Theodosius II (r. 408–450 CE) in Constantinople suggesting both the profusion and prestige of the material.[4] Despite having no bullion value, one of its principal uses during the period lay in gift giving in this way. It was especially used in such a capacity in the fourth- to sixth-century phenomenon of issuing consular diptychs. The post of ordinary consul was the zenith of a life of public service. It was taken up at the beginning of each New Year and required a large outlay of capital for a week of games and festivities. The incentive was a permanent place in the Roman calendar because each year took its name from its ordinary consuls. At least some consuls commissioned a series of ivory diptychs to commemorate the occasion, which were distributed as gifts. Ivory seems to have been the perfect material with which to create a durable memorial for this post, mirroring the immortalizing of the consul's name in history.

In many ways, the use of ivory in a Christian context, primarily for diptychs, furniture revetment, book covers and boxes did not differ from its secular uses. Both Christian and secular ivories were inherently three-dimensional objects made with the purpose, or at least the pretense, of containing something, but very often they have not been approached with this in mind because of the attractive iconographies that they host on their surfaces. In this way, modern museums have turned what were once largely functional pieces made to be touched and handled into almost two-dimensional works of art, which are themselves contained in a vitrine and paralyzed under artificial lighting, frustrating any understanding of their original physical interaction with their viewers. Despite this, it was in fact subject matter, along with their now-lost contents, which separated Christian from profane ivories, though we will see that in some cases such modern taxonomies may be later categories that have been anachronistically imposed upon the material: the boundaries between sacred and secular were not so precise in the period.

Ivories remain one of the most important categories of artistic production for studying the Early Christian period. Large numbers survive due to their seeming profusion, relative durability and the general resistance of the material itself to recycling through re-carving. Despite this, as with other categories of late antique art, much has presumably perished. Ivory carving itself markedly declined around 600 CE. The decline seems to have resulted from the shifting geo-political, and thus economic, landscape of the Mediterranean at this time: the Byzantine–Sassanian wars of the late-sixth and early-seventh centuries and the Islamic conquests shortly thereafter disrupted established trade routes—and thus the supply of ivory—to the East and West. A liberal supply of ivory to the West would not be established again until around 1300 CE.

Diptychs

Ivory diptychs comprise two panels joined by hinges that allow them to be opened and closed in the manner of a book. Their outer surfaces host carved decoration, while their interiors have two slightly recessed planes surrounded by a narrow raised frame. These smooth depressed panels may have received wax for writing on: alternatively, these diptychs may merely have feigned such a function and could have been set up as display pieces in the manner of an inverted birthday card.[5] Although the forty or so surviving consular diptychs have received most attention, ivory diptychs were also commissioned in the West from the second half of the fourth century by other notables such as magistrates, patricians, senators, imperial personages and priests. Epistolary evidence makes clear that such diptychs were dispatched as diplomatic gifts accompanying silver items such as bowls, which by contrast held realizable profit for the receiver. The letters of the famous pagan orator Quintus Aurelius Symmachus (*c.* 345–402 CE) from Rome discuss those that were sent out to celebrate the quaestorial and praetorian games of his son Memmius Symmachus in 393 and 401 CE, respectively.[6] The ivory formed an enduring testimony to the gift and thus the relationship between the giver and the receiver, generating social rather than monetary capital for both parties.

A number of impressive ivory diptychs hosting Christian iconography survive from the period, along with single leaves that once belonged to diptychs. How these related to the practices surrounding other ivory diptychs remains unclear. Ivory diptychs have traditionally been categorized into consular, official and private types without any evidence of differentiated use.[7] Christian diptychs are presumed to fall into the third type, along with those hosting mythological subject matter, instead of imagery pertaining to a held office, and are thought to have been made for religious purposes rather than distribution. These boundaries have since been troubled by the discovery that some diptychs with mythological subject matter were in fact consular in nature. They were intended through their appearance and subject matter to display the erudition and social class of the consul, rather than the consul himself or his titles. Ivory diptychs hosting Christian subject matter remain obscure in scholarship because it is difficult to say what they were used for. Although it was once asserted that Christian diptychs were solely used as receptacles for wax to record the names of the living and the dead who were to be prayed for during the liturgy, no conclusive proof indicates that these ivories were used as such and not issued as diplomatic or commemorative gifts.[8] The appearance of the ivory diptychs used for such sociopolitical purposes is never articulated in the literature of the period so that it is perfectly plausible that those with Christian iconographies were part of the same tradition, expressing some of the social and religious status of the giver through their style and subject matter. The study of one of these surviving panels and its Christian iconography should suffice to elucidate the point.

Despite its inclusion in introductory volumes on Early Christian art, the ivory panel showing the visit of the holy women to the tomb of Christ, which was made in Rome and is now in the Civico Museo d'Arte in Milan, has received curiously little discussion in its own right (Figure 13.1). The panel, measuring 30.7 × 13.4 cm, and dated to around 400 CE on the basis of its classicizing appearance, once formed the left-hand leaf of an ivory diptych, the other side of which is now lost.[9] The subject matter of the ivory is one of the key biblical events on which the Christian faith was founded: the Resurrection. In the foreground, two holy women visit the tomb of Christ on the third day after his burial to find the door open and an angel seated outside. The angel has sometimes been identified as the risen Christ himself because of his halo, the attribute of a scroll in his left hand and the curious gestures of attempted touch by the two women. It may be deliberately ambiguous in merging the visit and a later appearance of Christ to the two Marys to thoroughly affirm the message of Christ's resurrection. Christ's resurrection is also affirmed by the inclusion of the Raising of Lazarus on the doors of the tomb, the miracle performed by Christ which prophetically foreshadowed his own death and resurrection. The tomb of Christ is represented as a two-story building surmounted by a domed drum. The two soldiers charged with guarding the tomb of Christ are unusually placed on the roof of the structure making gestures of fear and awe in the face of the event. Finally, in the upper corners of the panel the symbols of the evangelists Luke and Matthew emerge from the clouds.

Underscoring the story of the women visiting the tomb was the concept of witness: the account appears in all four gospels and the idea is that these women are the first to bear witness

Figure 13.1 Carved ivory leaf from a diptych featuring the visit of the holy women to the tomb of Christ. Civico Museo d'Arte, Milan, © Comune di Milano, tutti i diritti riservati.

to his resurrection after his death and entombment. The identities of these women shift in the various gospels so that it is difficult to name them with precision apart from Mary Magdalene who appears in all four. The number of women also differs in each account: there are often three in the iconography because there are three in Mark's gospel (Mary Magdalene, Mary the Mother of James and Mary Salome) and three in Luke, plus unnamed others. Only Mary Magdalene is included in John and there are two in Matthew. Based on the number of women, the astonished and dynamic appearance of the guards who seem unsteady and literally blown away by what has happened (note the dramatic upwards movement of the chlamys belonging to the guard on the left), it is quite likely that the representation was based on Matthew 28:1–6:

> After the Sabbath, at dawn on the first day of the week, Mary Magdalene and the other Mary went to look at the tomb. There was a violent earthquake, for an angel of the Lord came down from heaven and, going to the tomb, rolled back the stone and sat on it. His appearance was like lightning, and his clothes were white as snow. The guards were so afraid of him that they shook and became like dead men. The angel said to the women, "Do not be afraid, for I know that you are looking for Jesus, who was crucified. He is not here; he has risen, just as he said. Come and see the place where he lay."
>
> *NIV*

The economy of scale within the image also seems to confirm this: the importance of the angel is expressed through his exaggerated size and perhaps the halo was an attempt to denote the brilliance of his appearance as akin to lightning. In gesturing beneath to the scene as it unfolds, Matthew's symbol of the man in the top right corner of the ivory also seems to confirm the origins of the iconography.

Although the subject matter focuses on the historical event in this way, it also centers on the most sacred of contemporary pilgrimage sites. The tomb building has traditionally been interpreted as an intended representation of the Anastasis Rotunda of the Church of the Holy Sepulcher in Jerusalem, the structure built over the site of Christ's tomb. In this it is comparable with other Early Christian ivories such as the Ascension ivory, the leaf of a diptych now in Munich also dated to around 400 CE, which shows the three Marys visiting a similar structure, conflated with a depiction of the Ascension of Christ on the Mount of Olives.[10] These representations seem then to pose a connection to contemporary practices of pilgrimage on the part of these ivories.

Paulinus of Nola (354–431 CE) noted, "The foremost reason which draws people to Jerusalem is the longing to see and touch the places where Christ was present in the body."[11] The Resurrection, more than any other Christological belief, necessitated an emphasis on its actual physical occurrence and yet it was necessarily the most difficult event of all to source material traces for, given the whole body resurrection and ascension of Christ. All that remained was the empty space that needed to be witnessed nonetheless. The impetus to see, touch and experience the holy sites very often manifested in the arts connected to pilgrimage and this is palpably seen in the Milan panel. Based on contemporary pilgrimage accounts of visiting the site of the Resurrection in Jerusalem, clearly the pilgrim became caught up, not only in seeing and touching the places associated with Christ's burial and resurrection, but in ritually re-enacting the events themselves.[12] The ivory panel allowed viewers to become part of experiencing the historical event and the contemporary pilgrimage site, regardless of whether or not they had visited it. The panel diverges from the scriptural account in order to resonate with the experience of the pilgrim in the Holy Land: this is seen in the replacement of the rock cut tomb where Christ was actually buried with an architectural construction intended to represent the shrine erected over it by Constantine the Great (r. 306–337 CE). The resulting building on the ivory did not faithfully represent the building in Jerusalem but included its defining elements to allow for recognition.

The pictorial composition and gestures of the figures also allowed the viewer of the ivory to vicariously experience the holy site. Very often the frame of an ivory plays a role in separating the world of the image from the reality of the viewer but in the Milan panel it is used to the opposite effect. Here the frame of the composition is intentionally merged with the architectural structure so that the building projects into the space of the viewer, obliterating the framing device. The containment of the representation within its own parameters is further compromised through the manner in which the limbs of the protagonists overlap the frame and emerge into the temporal and spatial field of the viewer. The nature of the frame meant that the world of the viewer became merged with that of the historical event and the contemporary holy site. The women make a gesture of touching that is unnecessary to the biblical account. These women form the devotional model for the viewer who is encouraged to look, touch and believe in a similar manner. Everything in the image conspired so that viewers could take on the role of witness to this historical event and the contemporary pilgrimage site, simultaneously transporting them back to first-century and fifth-century Jerusalem.

The question remains then of who made and viewed this ivory. The general level of refinement and sumptuousness certainly reflects aristocratic patronage. This panel and the Munich panel are also considerably Hellenized in their appearance, on account of the poses of the figures and the classicizing folds of their draperies. A classicizing style at this date has often been connected to a perceived "pagan revival" in the 390s in Rome, whereby there was an increase in works of art espousing an intentionally pagan subject matter and associated classicizing style in response to the increasing Christianization of Roman society. An ironic transfer of this classicizing, "pagan" style into Christian ivories was posited to have occurred around 400 CE.[13] Such arguments depended, however, on these pagan ivories being earlier than surviving secular and Christian ivories which has since been invalidated, undoing any assumed link between paganism and classicism.[14]

The so-called *Consecratio* diptych, now in the British Museum (Figure 13.2), which likely commemorated the death of Quintus Aurelius Symmachus in 402 CE,[15] poses perhaps the greatest problem to making the case for elite families reviving classical art in the service of paganism. The notably unclassical tenor of this leaf, made for the Symmachi family who were connected to many of the surviving classicizing pagan pieces, is at odds with its subject matter of the apotheosis of Symmachus to meet his ancestors. The leaf lacks any convincing spatial representation: separate scenes showing Symmachus himself, his funeral pyre and elevation to the realm of his ancestors, are shown simultaneously and populated by simplified, stocky and rigid figures. Clearly, then, pieces for the same family were being commissioned according to different stylistic modes, so that the notion of a classical revival tied to a resurgence of defiant paganism in Rome at the end of the fourth century is untenable.

Figure 13.2 Carved ivory leaf from a diptych, *Consecratio*. © British Museum, London.

A potential workshop connection also exists between the Milan panel and other pagan and secular ivory diptychs, on the basis of a shared lotus and palmette border, demonstrating that the same ateliers were making both Christian and pagan ivories.[16] Overall, there seems to have been an attempt in these Christian panels to imbue Christian art with status through a classicizing style, keeping up with the best of pagan and secular offerings as the demographic of the church in Rome continued to shift towards an elite membership in the century after Constantine's *Edict of Tolerance* (313 CE). In this way, no real reason exists why such ivories might not have been commissioned as gifts, impacting the status of both giver and receiver, commemorating pilgrimage and providing for receivers an experience of the Holy Land from the comfort of their own home.

Pyxides

By far the most common type of Early Christian ivory is the elliptical storage box decorated with Christian scenes, which has subsequently been termed a pyxis. Around seventy ivory pyxides survive that can be dated between the fifth and seventh centuries and about forty of these host Christian imagery. These boxes suggest, more than any other type of ivory, the relationship between the tusk of the elephant and their finished form, implying very clearly their process of manufacture in the absence of any written treatise. The natural structure of the elephant's tusk suggested the shape of these boxes: transverse sections were taken from near the base where the pulp cavity is greatest in diameter, fixing the diameter of each box at around 11–12 cm. On account of the lesser limitations on height, pyxides vary from between 8 to 12 cm tall. Owing to a desire to exploit the tusk for a box of maximum dimensions, a second tusk was then used to provide longitudinal sections sufficient in width to be used as the base and lid, but not many boxes retain these original parts.[17] The *eborarius*—or ivory worker—necessarily worked alongside other craftsmen then, such as the metalworker for the hinges and locks of these boxes, and many of the pyxides seem to have been executed on a lathe, so that it appears that ivory workers operated in some form of fixed workshop. This is supported by the discovery of a late antique workshop on the northeast slope of the Palatine hill in Rome, which worked ivory and bone.[18]

The original purposes of these boxes remain tenuous. Some have been found in a context consistent with their use as a reliquary, such as a pyxis now in the Musée du Bardo in Tunis, which was found wrapped in canvas and integrated into a tomb in the crypt of a fifth-century basilica near the city of Yunca in southern Tunisia.[19] No evidence suggests that they were all used in this manner and the fact that they are found hosting both Christian and pagan subject matter indicates that they were likely multifunctional boxes made via serial production with a range of uses in mind. On the basis of their subject matter, however, some seem to have been more specifically suited to containing the eucharistic bread and may have been intended for such a purpose. A sixth-century ivory pyxis (10.8 × 12.7 × 12.1 cm) now in the Metropolitan Museum in New York (Figure 13.3) presents the same subject matter as the Milan panel but its treatment differs and this variance demonstrates how iconography can at times help to elucidate use.[20] This later and more symbolic treatment of the women at the tomb shows the possible purpose of the box as a container for the host but we cannot definitively rule out another role such as holding incense. Either way, the iconography points strongly to a liturgical use and its now-lost lock to the containment of a valuable sacred object.

The box unusually retains its original lid, although the current copper mountings are a later addition. The main subject is the visit of the holy women to the tomb. Most Early Christian pyxides host New Testament scenes, with only nine of the remaining forty displaying Old

Figure 13.3 Carved ivory pyxis, the visit of the holy women to the tomb of Christ. Metropolitan Museum of Art, New York.

Testament iconography. The context is clearly liturgical: two women arrive with swinging censers to an altar on a raised curved platform surmounted by three domed arches. The altar has a lamp hanging over it and a gospel book on it, while curtains hang in the other arched openings. The place where Christ's dead body was buried and resurrected is replaced by the altar where it was increasingly believed that his actual body was consumed.[21] The altar was also often considered a symbolic representation of the tomb of Christ in Christian literature, perhaps most famously in the *Historia ecclesiastica* (*Ecclesiastical History*) written by the seventh-century Byzantine patriarch Germanos.[22] No visual evidence relates this architectural structure to the Holy Sepulcher in Jerusalem; it merely intimates the general structure of a ciborium in the Syria/Palestine area.[23] Stylistically, the box has also been tied to this region. Again, Christ's tomb is not represented realistically or historically but according to the purposes of the object at hand and the message it wished to convey. The fact that the ivory conflates Christ's tomb with an altar betrays the eastern origins of the piece where it was commonly agreed at this date that the host was the actual body and blood of Christ.[24] The substitution of the altar for the tomb also suggests the probable use of this pyxis as a container for the consecrated bread for storage or for distribution to the incapacitated in their homes.

Early study of these boxes was largely confined to separating them into two stylistic schools based in Egypt or the Syria/Palestine area and they were predominantly seen as being an eastern, rather than western, phenomenon. Such stylistic studies of provenance have since reached an impasse compounded by a lack of securely placed and dated comparable material and the inherent portability of these pieces: the find-spots of these boxes range from as far afield as Gaul, Carthage, the Caucasus, Egypt, Syria/Palestine and Constantinople. What remains is that these Early Christian ivory boxes were originally and ostensibly meant to contain something. The relationship between their contents and iconographies is not now easily accessible, and may not have been prescriptive at the time, but it is worth thinking about the acts of handling that activated the relationship between the insides of these boxes and their decorated exteriors. A holistic approach is needed that goes beyond isolated stylistic or iconographical analysis.

Representations on ivory pyxides were not deployed as part of a coherent linear narrative around the box. Rather, they were constructed according to a meaningful program planned in connection with the manner in which the box was handled. Two scenes occupy both sides of the above pyxis to either side of the lock space (Figure 13.4). A simple cross is found beneath the original lock space and the viewer is encouraged to turn the box clockwise through the dynamic movement of the holy woman to the right of the lock to uncover the entire scene of the women at the tomb. The centralized motif of the altar seems to dominate this side of the box and prompts the viewer to arrest movement at this point with the altar in the middle so that, with the women at the tomb, it forms its own independent tableau on the box. If the viewer recommences turning the box in his or her hands three holy women with their hands elevated in prayer occupy the arcade that continues around the remainder of the box back to the lock space where the cross arrests movement once more. The original hinges encroached on the first of these praying figures so that their importance was undermined. This, in combination with the impressive tableau formed by the women at the altar and the amount of space that it occupies, underlines the first scene as the most important and the interpretative key for the entire box. Above all, this liturgical motif focuses on the liturgical body of Christ and its connection to the historical body of Christ at the tomb. This iconography would have resonated strongly with the purpose of carrying the host.

Figure 13.4 Carved ivory pyxis, praying female figures. Metropolitan Museum of Art, New York.

Book covers

Perhaps the only type of ivory object that was new to Early Christian art was the book cover. It is difficult to say with certainty when they originated but a number of impressive examples survive from the fifth and sixth centuries.[25] Four complete sets survive, with fragments of at least five others still extant. Each leaf of a book cover was usually a five-part composite piece and the various panels were likely carved from the same tusk to ensure consistency of color and grain. Where a humbler medium, such as leather, was not used it seems that ivory was a popular choice for the revetment of sacred scripture. It appears again that it was the inherent physical characteristics of ivory that made it a popular choice given its opulence and durability in the face of repeated handling. Perhaps an organic medium was also inherently suited to conveying themes of incarnation, both of Christ Incarnate, a theme that is often represented on the front cover, and the incarnation of the Word of God in the scriptures contained within. We cannot discount the fact that many covers in gold and silver may have been made and subsequently melted down. Those made of precious metals that do survive, however, were far less intricate in their detailing and less ambitious in their iconographic programs.[26]

An ivory panel of the Adoration of the Magi dating to the fifth to seventh century, originally from Syria and now in the John Rylands Museum in Manchester, has been identified as belonging to a book cover (Figure 13.5). Through its relatively flat abstracted style and the remains of a gilt star pattern that has not been removed through subsequent cleaning, it has been matched to several other fragments in museums around the world, so that its program has been reconstructed. It has also been paired with its back panel, now held in the Museo Nazionale, Ravenna (Figure 13.6). Collectively they are often termed the Murano diptych.[27] Composite ivory covers encasing sacred scripture usually comprised a large central panel surrounded by four narrower strips. This panel, measuring 23.3 × 12.3 cm, formed the central section of a front cover. The enthroned Virgin and Child dominate the largest section of the plaque attended by the three magi and an angel. The Virgin and Child greatly exceed in scale the three magi in Phrygian caps and eastern dress who approach the sacred pair, carrying their gifts in covered hands. Beneath the largest section is a narrow strip, found in the same position on the central panels of many book covers, showing the Nativity of Christ. Mary reclines on the left while the infant Christ is swaddled in a manger to the right and gazed upon by the donkey and a bull. The midwife Salome offers her shrunken hand to the child in accordance with the apocryphal story, recounted in the *Protoevangelium of James*, in which her hand withered because she had doubted and tested the virginity of Mary.[28]

A narrow strip, now in Berlin, that formed the upper panel of the front cover, displays a wreath-bound cross suspended by two angels, a scene commonly found in this position on book covers, while the panels from the right-hand side, now in St Petersburg, show scenes concerning the early life of the Virgin such as the Annunciation to St Anne from the *Protoevangelium of James* (3.2). The last surviving piece, now in the Louvre (Figure 13.7), formed the bottom panel of the cover and shows a series of scenes, also based on the *Protoevangelium of James*, concerning the life of the Virgin and the birth of Christ from the Annunciation to the Virgin while she spins the temple veil, and her trial by water in the temple, to her journey to Bethlehem (11.1; 16.1–2; 17.1–2). In this way, all of the scenes on the front cover deal with the conception and early life of Christ. Most surviving front covers similarly relate to the theme of the Incarnation, resonating with the story of Christ in the scriptures within. Back covers often dealt with the divine, rather than the human, nature of Christ: the back cover of the Murano diptych, for example, hosts the miracles of Christ that denoted the salvation that came through his divine nature such as the healings of the Gerasene demoniac and the paralytic and the Raising of Lazarus.[29] Taken

Figure 13.5 Carved ivory panel from a book cover (Murano Diptych), Adoration of the Magi and the nativity of Christ. John Rylands Museum, Manchester.

Figure 13.6 Carved ivory leaf from a book cover (Murano Diptych). Museo Nazionale, Ravenna.

Figure 13.7 Carved ivory panel from a book cover (Murano Diptych), scenes from the life of the Virgin. Louvre Museum, Paris. Photo © RMN-Grand Palais (Musée du Louvre)/Jean-Gilles Berizzi.

together then, the covers form not an illustration of what was found between them in the text, especially given that they very often hosted apocryphal stories, but a framework for its interpretation—the mystery of Christ, as fully God and man, made visible in the flesh for the salvation of humankind.

Ornately bound Early Christian books were likely displayed open with the covers, rather than the text, oriented towards the viewer.[30] This would explain the iconic nature of the central largest panel with the Virgin and Child gazing out at the viewer requiring devotion, while the smaller narrative strips surround and interpret it. When displayed as such the back panel became the left and thus the beginning of any program. What could have been read in a narrative biographical way when the book was closed—from the nativity and early life of Christ on the front to his later healing miracles on the back—is inverted when opened to form a theological affirmation of both the divine and human natures of Christ, with the former coming first.

Conclusion

Ivory was used in Early Christian art in the same manner as other mediums—such as precious metals and wood—for pyxides, reliquaries, diptychs and book covers. As a material it was desired for the same reasons that it was valued in classical antiquity: it was hard, durable, creamy-white in color, though painted and gilded to some extent, and it took a high shine. It was also relatively rare, which added to its cultural desirability. In Late Antiquity it was in good supply so that it was employed for a range of objects from utilitarian pieces to prestigious gifts. Most surviving Christian ivory objects were made to contain something, whether that was writing on wax, the eucharist or sacred scripture. Thinking about the way in which all of these ivory objects were handled, used, and displayed can transform any understanding of their iconography. In many cases their design appears to have been carefully planned so that the meanings of their Christian iconographies were constructed and activated through use.

Notes

1 Carolyn Connor, *The Colour of Ivory: Polychromy on Byzantine Ivories* (Princeton, NJ: Princeton University Press, 1998).
2 Siegfried Lauffer, ed., *Diocletian's Preisedikt* (Berlin: De Gruyter, 1971), 148–9.
3 Jerome, *Epistle* 107.
4 Pierre Batiffol, "Les Présents de Saint Cyrille à la Cour de Constantinople," *Bulletin D'ancienne Littérature et D'archéologie Chrétienne*, 6 (1911): 260–1.

5 Anthony Cutler, "Five Lessons in Late Roman Ivory," *Journal of Roman Archaeology*, 6 (1993): 175; Alan Cameron, "The Origin, Context and Function of Consular Diptychs," *Journal of Roman Archaeology*, 103 (2013): 190.
6 Symmachus, *Epistles*, 2.81; 5.56, 7.76, 9.119.
7 Wolfgang Fritz Volbach, *Elfenbeinarbeiten der Spätantike und des frühen Mittelalters*, 3rd ed. (Mainz: des römisch-germanischen Zencralmuseums, 1976).
8 Alice Christ, "The Importance of Being Stilicho: Diptychs as a Genre," in *Shifting Genres in Late Antiquity*, edited by Geoffrey Greatrex and Elton (Aldershot: Ashgate, 2015), 173–90.
9 Volbach, *Elfenbeinarbeiten der Spätantike*, no. 111; Kurt Weitzmann, *Age of Spirituality: Late Antique and Early Christian Art, Third to Seventh Century: Catalogue of the Exhibition at the Metropolitan Museum of Art* (New York, NY: Metropolitan Museum of Art, 1980), no. 453.
10 Volbach, *Elfenbeinarbeiten der Spätantike*, no. 110.
11 Paulinus of Nola, *Epistle* 49.402.
12 Gary Vikan, "Pilgrims in Magi's Clothing: The Impact of Mimesis on Early Byzantine Pilgrimage Art," in *The Blessings of Pilgrimage*, edited by Robert Ousterhout (Urbana and Chicago, IL: University of Illinois Press, 1990), 97–107.
13 Ernst Kitzinger, *Byzantine Art in the Making: Main Lines of Stylistic Development in Mediterranean Art 3rd–7th Century* (London: Faber & Faber, 1977), 34–40.
14 Alan Cameron, "Pagan Ivories," in *Symmaque: À L'occasion Du Mille Six Centième Anniversaire Du Conflit de L'autel de La Victoire*, edited by François Paschoud (Paris: Société d'Édition 'Les Belles Lettres', 1986), 41–64.
15 Volbach, *Elfenbeinarbeiten der Spätantike*, no. 56; Cameron, "Pagan Ivories," 45–52.
16 Volbach, *Elfenbeinarbeiten der Spätantike*, nos 55 and 62.
17 Gudrun Bühl, "The Making of Early Byzantine Pyxides," in *Spätantike Und Byzantinishe Elfenbeinbildwerke Im Diskurs*, edited by Arne Effenberger, Gudrun Bühl and Anthony Cutler (Wiesbaden: Reichert, 2008), 12.
18 Archer St. Clair, "Evidence for Late Antique Bone and Ivory Carving on the Northeast Slope of the Palatine: The Palatine East Excavation," *Dumbarton Oaks Papers*, 50 (1996): 369–74.
19 Bühl, "The Making of Early Byzantine Pyxides," 11.
20 Volbach, *Elfenbeinarbeiten der Spätantike*, no. 177; Weitzmann, *Age of Spirituality*, no. 520.
21 Robert Taft, *The Great Entrance: A History of the Transfer of Gifts and Other Preanaphoral Rites of the Liturgy of St. John Chrysostom* (Rome: Pont. Institutum Studiorum Orientalium, 1975), 35.
22 Germanus of Constantinople, *On the Divine Liturgy*, translated by Paul Meyendorff (New York, NY: St Vladimir's Seminary Press, 1984), 89–90.
23 Archer St. Clair, "The Visit to the Tomb: Narrative and Liturgy on Three Early Christian Pyxides," *Gesta*, 18.1 (1979): 130.
24 Taft, *The Great Entrance*, 37, 217.
25 Volbach, *Elfenbeinarbeiten der Spätantike*, nos 119, 125–9, 142, 145.
26 Weitzmann, *Age of Spirituality*, nos 554–5.
27 Volbach, *Elfenbeinarbeiten der Spätantike*, nos 127–9; Weitzmann, *Age of Spirituality*, nos 457–61.
28 *Protoevangelium of James*, 19–20.
29 Volbach, *Elfenbeinarbeiten der Spätantike*, no. 125.
30 John Lowden, "The Word Made Visible: The Exterior of the Early Christian Book as Visual Argument," in *The Early Christian Book*, edited by William E. Klingshirn and Linda Safran (Washington, DC: Catholic University of America Press, 2007), 45.

Further reading

Batiffol, Pierre. "Les Présents de Saint Cyrille à la Cour de Constantinople." *Bulletin D'ancienne Littérature et D'archéologie Chrétienne* 6 (1911): 251–61.

Bühl, Gudrun. "The Making of Early Byzantine Pyxides." In *Spätantike Und Byzantinishe Elfenbeinbildwerke Im Diskurs*, edited by Arne Effenberger, Gudrun Bühl and Anthony Cutler, 9–15. Wiesbaden: Reichert, 2008.

Cameron, Alan. "Pagan Ivories." In *Symmaque: À L'occasion Du Mille Six Centième Anniversaire Du Conflit de L'autel de La Victoire*, edited by François Paschoud, 41–64. Paris: Société d'Édition 'Les Belles Lettres', 1986.

———. "The Origin, Context and Function of Consular Diptychs." *Journal of Roman Archaeology* 103 (2013): 174–207.

Christ, Alice. "The Importance of Being Stilicho: Diptychs as a Genre." In *Shifting Genres in Late Antiquity*, edited by Geoffrey Greatrex and Hugh Elton, 173–90. Aldershot: Ashgate, 2015.

Connor, Carolyn. *The Colour of Ivory: Polychromy on Byzantine Ivories*. Princeton, NJ: Princeton University Press, 1998.

Cutler, Anthony. *The Craft of Ivory: Sources, Techniques, and Uses in the Mediterranean World, AD 200–1400*, Dumbarton Oaks Byzantine Collection Publications, 8. Washington DC: Dumbarton Oaks Research Library and Collection, 1985.

———. "Five Lessons in Late Roman Ivory." *Journal of Roman Archaeology* 6 (1993): 167–92.

Germanus of Constantinople, *On the Divine Liturgy*, translated by Paul Meyendorff. New York, NY: St Vladimir's Seminary Press, 1984.

Kitzinger, Ernst. *Byzantine Art in the Making: Main Lines of Stylistic Development in Mediterranean Art 3rd–7th Century*. London: Faber & Faber, 1977.

Lauffer, Siegfried, ed. *Diocletians Preisedikt.* Berlin: De Gruyter, 1971.

Lowden, John. "The Word Made Visible: The Exterior of the Early Christian Book as Visual Argument." In *The Early Christian Book*, edited by William E. Klingshirn and Linda Safran, 13–47. Washington, DC: Catholic University of America Press, 2007.

St. Clair, Archer. "Evidence for Late Antique Bone and Ivory Carving on the Northeast Slope of the Palatine: The Palatine East Excavation." *Dumbarton Oaks Papers*, 50 (1996): 369–74.

———. "The Visit to the Tomb: Narrative and Liturgy on Three Early Christian Pyxides." *Gesta*, 18.1 (1979): 127–35.

Taft, Robert. *The Great Entrance: A History of the Transfer of Gifts and Other Preanaphoral Rites of the Liturgy of St. John Chrysostom*. Rome, Pont. Institutum Studiorum Orientalium, 1975.

Vikan, Gary. "Pilgrims in Magi's Clothing: The Impact of Mimesis on Early Byzantine Pilgrimage Art," in *The Blessings of Pilgrimage*, edited by Robert Ousterhout (Urbana and Chicago, IL: University of Illinois Press, 1990), 97–107.

Volbach, Wolfgang Fritz. *Elfenbeinarbeiten der Spätantike und des frühen Mittelalters*, 3rd ed. Mainz: des römisch-germanischen Zencralmuseums, 1976.

Weitzmann, Kurt. *Age of Spirituality: Late Antique and Early Christian Art, Third to Seventh Century: Catalogue of the Exhibition at the Metropolitan Museum of Art*. New York, NY: Metropolitan Museum of Art, 1980.

14

TEXTILES

The emergence of a Christian identity in cloth

Jennifer L. Ball

Introduction: what is a Christian textile?

A sixth-century tunic fragment, today housed in The Brooklyn Museum, represents a paradox common in early Christian textiles, as it prominently features both Christian and Dionysiac imagery together (Figure 14.1). The panel, which originally would have covered the front of the torso from the neck to the knees, has ornamentation pretending to be two pendants, one a jeweled cross on a beaded string, the other a dancing Maenad (Figure 14.2). The panel front has *clavi*, stripes, that are joined by a horizontal band that would have fallen across the clavicle, all populated with a series of griffins and putti in flight. Whether the wearer of this tunic was a Christian or a follower of Dionysos, the god of wine, is not clear.[1] Maenads were often shown dancing before him with pinecones, which this Maenad may hold here. But the Dionysiac imagery, while certainly culturally important in Egypt where this textile was likely found, was not necessarily religious. Christians saw Dionysos as a precursor of Christ, with many aspects of his story parallel to Christ's. Griffins too were mythical, immortal beings in the Near Eastern pantheon who were coopted by Christians because they embodied Christ's dual nature by being half eagle, half lion.[2] What reads as an inconsistency to our modern mindset about religion is common during Late Antiquity in the lands of the Roman Empire between the third and seventh century, from Roman times to the early Medieval, Byzantine and Umayyad periods, a period characterized by many interwoven cultural and religious threads.

Vast numbers of late antique textiles, mostly in fragmentary condition, survive in museum collections around the world today.[3] Many, like the Brooklyn Museum tunic front, make it difficult to discern what might be deemed "Christian" in design or use. Because the textiles designated "Christian" were made using the same techniques and materials as any other Roman or secular textile it is principally important to explain what constitutes an "early Christian" textile.

Christian iconography on textiles made approximately between 200–600 CE determines an easily discernible group of early Christian textiles. However, many textiles used in churches or worn by monastics or clergy may have had no Christian symbolism whatsoever. Altar and other liturgical cloths, for example, were often donated by the faithful from their own household stores.[4] Monastic clothing could be culled from the clothing gathered from new monastics as they entered the life and donned the habit.[5] Thus, this chapter will discuss textiles in terms of their use in churches, as relics, on clothing, in homes and in burials rather than any clear

Figure 14.1 Coptic *Tunic Front with Marine Motifs*, 6th century CE. Wool, 13 × 44 1/2 in. (33 × 113 cm). Brooklyn Museum, Charles Edwin Wilbour Fund, 38.753. Creative Commons-BY.

Figure 14.2 Coptic *Tunic Front with Marine Motifs I* (detail of pendants), 6th century CE. Wool, 13 × 44 1/2 in. (33 × 113 cm). Brooklyn Museum, Charles Edwin Wilbour Fund, 38.753. Creative Commons-BY.

Christian symbolism to determine their status as Christian, while being fully cognizant that many textiles were not exclusively Christian.

Materials and techniques: continuity and innovation

Early Christian textiles, like all textiles of Late Antiquity, were made primarily from wool and linen, but silk and cotton were imported as well during this early period. Silk was particularly prized for the qualities of the fabric itself, which could be woven very tightly due to the strength of the fibers, took dye exceptionally well, and had natural sheen. Silk was also rare and had to be imported from China until the sixth century when the Byzantines learned to cultivate the "silk worm," really a larval moth (*bombyx mori*) from whose cocoon silk threads come. Silk was not made in the west until the twelfth century when the Normans of Sicily learned the secrets of sericulture. To get from the raw material to cloth, wool from sheep, linen fibers from the flax plant, silk, or cotton, first had to be spun into thread, which then was dyed with a myriad of vegetal, and sometimes animal, materials. Cloth was then woven (in most cases) on either vertical weighted looms, pit looms or foot-powered horizontal looms.[6] Weft threads were drawn through the supporting warp threads held taut by the loom. In a simple weave, weft threads were woven under alternating warp threads from one edge of the warp to the other. More complex weaves, such as tapestry, were woven with various colored wefts alternating with the ground warp, starting and stopping as the pattern demanded across the warp. Textiles could also be knitted or felted, rather than woven. In the final stages of production, textile goods such as clothing, household furnishings, or liturgical cloths, to name a few, might additionally be sewn or embroidered.

Weaving, the method by which the majority of early Christian textiles were made, was done by both professional workshops and in the home. Some monasteries, such as the Monastery of Epiphanius in Thebes, supported themselves in part through the production of cloth.[7] Thread could be spun from raw materials or purchased for use on a loom. The virtuous woman weaver shown in a domestic setting, exemplified by the Virgin Mary herself in a Christian context, was a common literary image.[8] The Virgin is depicted in fourth–sixth-century scenes of the Annunciation holding a distaff, spinning thread, such as on the fifth-century dyed linen fragment from the Victoria and Albert Museum.[9]

Archaeology of textiles: the complexities of interpretation

The majority of textiles survive merely in fragments when they survive at all. More often than most media, textiles have succumbed to the elements, been eaten by bugs, and been destroyed by fire. Thus, the archaeological record is spotty and skews toward dry climates, such as Egypt. Most surviving textiles made between 200 and 600, whether Christian or not, were excavated in Egypt, commonly found in burials. Burials are notably difficult to interpret from the perspective of a textile historian for several reasons.[10] The deceased was sometimes buried in clothing but the question of whether these clothes represent typical garments remains open; one could be wearing their most expensive clothes or specially made burial clothing. Bodies were then wrapped in most cases, with the wealthy being wrapped in finer textiles than less affluent persons. It was common to reuse a textile for a wrapping, however, no matter one's status, so the original purpose for the textile is often unclear. Burials sometimes had extra textiles inserted for padding around a body,[11] or were used to wrap objects inserted into the grave, which similarly are likely re-used textiles originally made to serve another purpose. People of all religions commonly used the same cemeteries and catacombs, making a secure identification of a grave and its accompanying textiles as belonging to a Christian difficult.[12] Many excavated corpses, however, rested their heads on small pillows, which often were decorated with clues, such as cross imagery, leading to an identification of the deceased as Christian.

The finds in these Egyptian sites can number in the tens of thousands. For example, the trash heap for a Roman quarry town used between the first–third centuries yielded an estimated 50,000 textiles![13] This should not mislead us into thinking that these were all made in Egypt, though Egypt was renowned for its linen and also known for its exceptional curtains.[14] A large number were also imported into Egypt, either as raw materials or as finished clothing and other textile goods.[15] Twentieth- and twenty-first-century excavations have turned up late antique textiles in Israel, the Caucasus, Syria, Jordan, Iran, and Ireland to name only some.[16] The origins of many textiles found in museum collections today are unknown. Some were kept safe in church and monastic treasuries in the West, sometimes finding their way on to the art market when the monastery or church fell out of use, particularly during the French revolution. Many were excavated, without proper care for the context, and scooped up by art dealers for their pretty designs, which has unfortunately left us with only the textile's material, technique, and iconography, that is, the images on the textiles, as clues as to their original use.

Textiles in the church: the range of uses

Churches employed a variety of textiles from curtains and cushions for clergy, to altar and other liturgical cloths. At the beginning of the early Christian period these textiles were not made with specifically Christian iconography, but were like any other cloth.

Curtains in the church

Like any building in Late Antiquity, churches had curtains for dividing spaces, such as aisle from nave, and for use in doorways to keep out the elements and pests. Curtains could also be used to cordon off the sanctuary from the laity, or separate catechumens in the aisles from the baptized in the nave, thus concretizing the hierarchical nature of access to the divine in Christianity.[17] A large, fifth-century linen and wool fragment featuring two peacocks facing a central, wreathed cross at the top, today housed in the Metropolitan Museum of Art, represents an early example of Christianizing decorative motifs (Figure 14.3).[18] Below the cross, surrounded by an undulating vine, are nine medallions containing fish, a typical early Christian symbol for Christ and for individual Christians,[19] and stylized flowers, with small floral patterns between each medallion. With the exception of the cross, the motifs on this curtain could have been found on any type of art in the late antique world, but in a Christian context took on Christian associations. For example, peacocks long symbolized immortality in the ancient world but came to be associated with Christ. The design is made in a weft loop, which creates a thick pile on top of the plain weave support, and may have added some warmth in addition to visual interest. We should imagine curtains such as these hanging at some threshold in a church, marking entrance into a sacred space, from outside to inside, narthex or aisle to nave, or perhaps into the sanctuary.

Epiphanius of Salamis, in a fourth-century passage famous for its stance against the use of holy images, describes a door curtain with a more pointedly Christian design. The passage also gives important clues about door curtains:

> I came to a villa called Anablatha and . . . I went in [to the church there] to pray, and found there a curtain hanging on the doors of the said church, dyed and embroidered. It bore an image either of Christ or of one of the saints; I do not rightly remember

Figure 14.3 Fragment, 5th century CE. Wool, linen; plain weave, weft loop weave, 64-15/16 × 50-9/16 in. (165 × 128.4 cm). Metropolitan Museum of Art, gift of George F. Baker, 1890, 90.5.808, metmuseum.org.

> whose the image was. Seeing this, and being loth that an image of a man should be hung up in Christ's church contrary to the teaching of the Scriptures, I tore it asunder and advised the custodians of the place to use it as a winding sheet for some poor person. They, however, murmured, and said that if I made up my mind to tear it, it was only fair that I should give them another curtain in its place . . . Since then there has been some little delay, due to the fact that I have been seeking a curtain of the best quality to give to them instead of the former one, and thought it right to send to Cyprus for one.[20]

First, the curtain is described as hanging *on the doors* of the church, suggesting that both doors, presumably made of wood, and a curtain were necessary. Locked doors were likely crucial for security, but the curtains could be used to keep out insects and birds, as well as to help regulate the temperature when the door was open. The passage also reveals that the curtain was dyed and embroidered with "an image of Christ or one of the saints." Epiphanius claims not to remember who was pictured, probably to illustrate his disdain for images rather than the image actually being unrecognizable. Yet, he readily identifies the technique of embroidery in the textile, an observation that may or may not be accurate. After tearing it down in an iconoclastic protest, he notes that the old curtain should be reused as a shroud, which is in keeping with the textiles commonly found in burials, as mentioned previously. Finally, he notes that he will "send to Cyprus" for a new curtain, as opposed to acquiring one in the environs of Jerusalem where the church being discussed was located. Cyprus must have been known for its fine textiles as he was trying to smooth over this scuffle with the bishop to whom he was writing.

For altar and sanctuary

A linen fragment in the Dumbarton Oaks Collection, nearly two feet long, with designs of geometric and floral motifs in dark and light reds and greens with touches of blue, woven into stripes and single buds in a floating diamond-shaped pattern on a plainly woven background, represents a typical late antique furnishing textile (Figure 14.4). It is not possible to tell if this undyed fabric covered an altar, a table, was used as a curtain, or had some other purpose. I propose, however, that the first furnishing textiles used in churches were ones like this fragment, largely functional and decorative, with the symbolic meanings of the motifs, and the expansion into Christian iconography, developing later in the early Christian period.

Egeria, a pilgrim who wrote a diary of her travels to the Holy Land and the eastern Mediterranean dated to the early fifth century,[21] describes the liturgy and decoration of the churches of Jerusalem she visits: the Church of the Nativity in Bethlehem, the Anastasis, and the Church of the Holy Cross on Golgotha. The textiles, of which no examples resembling Egeria's description survive, are resplendent: "You see nothing there but gold and gems and silk. If you look at the hangings, they are made of silk with gold stripes; if you look at the curtains, they are also made of silk with gold stripes."[22] It should not surprise us that these important churches, visited by masses of pilgrims annually, had luxurious silk textiles with gold, but notably they seem to be merely colorful and striped. No specific Christian symbols or figurative motifs are mentioned.

While we have no textile that we can definitively say was a liturgical textile or church furnishing belonging to a particular church, inventory and gift lists can give us a relatively clear idea of which textiles were common. Around twenty inventories of churches, in Greek and Coptic, written on papyrus between 400 and 800, are preserved.[23] The *Liber Pontificalis* (*Book of Pontiffs*) lists papal gifts of textiles and other items to churches of the west, mostly in Rome.

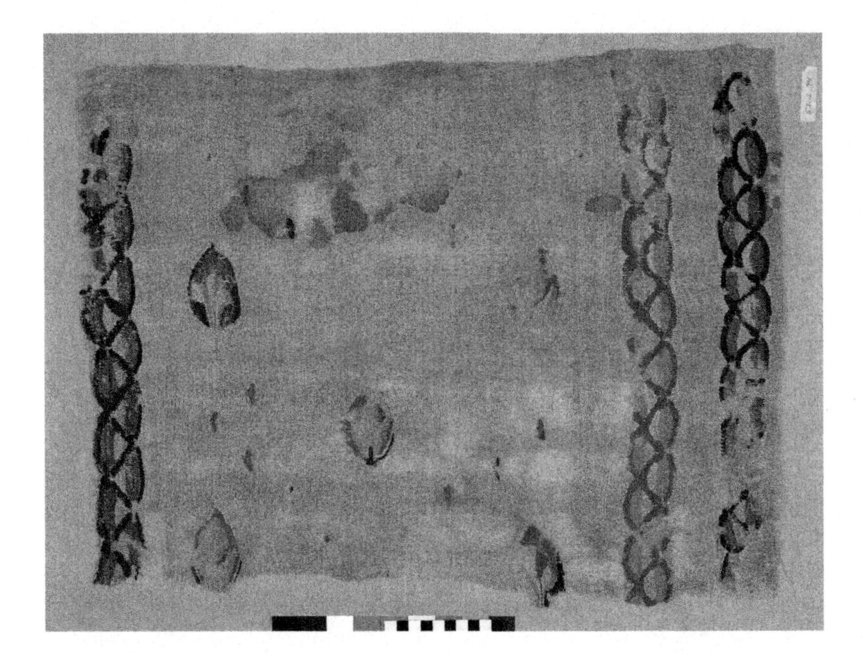

Figure 14.4 Fragment, late 5th century CE. Linen, wool, 58.1 × 44.6 cm. © Dumbarton Oaks, Byzantine Collection, Washington DC.

Some descriptions of actual churches found in *ekphrases*, like that of Paul the Silentiary, pilgrim accounts, or imagined ideal churches such as one described in the *Testamentum Domini* (The Testimony of the Lord) (below) provide still other descriptions of liturgical cloths and soft furnishings of churches.

In some areas, such as Egypt, covering the altar was of primary importance, in part to provide a clean surface on which to prepare the eucharist.[24] The fifth-century *Testamentum Domini* in its description of the ideal church calls for "the altar [to] have a veil of pure linen, because it is without spot."[25] While Constantine's gifts to the Lateran basilica in Rome do not list any textiles for an altar or otherwise, a small church in one Egyptian village had twenty-three linen cloths for its altar in addition to cloths of wool, several hangings, two curtains and cushions.[26] Any linen textile large enough to cover a table, such as the Dumbarton Oaks example, could have protected an altar (Figure 14.4). Altars are described as being covered by more than one cloth at once and finally topped by a white linen one, suggestive of a shroud covering the altar/tomb of Christ.[27]

In Greek, the altar cloths are typically called *mappa*, in Latin, *linteum*. But, it is notably difficult to find fixed terminology for altar cloths or indeed any liturgical or furnishing textile as there were many terms used for the same item. Available texts are in Greek, Latin, Coptic and Syriac, and terminology may have implied subtle differences that are no longer evident. The Latin word *linteum* is related to the term for flax, *linum*, from which linen is made, which begs the question whether altar cloths made from wool or silk would be called something else. The translator of the *Testamentum Domini*, from Syriac to Latin, chose to use the term *velum*, which can mean 'veil' or 'cover' even more generally.[28]

The *Testamentum Domini* also calls for the area where the priests stood as well as the baptistery to be "within a veil" (again *velum*).[29] Here we can imagine a curtain before the altar or sanctuary or baptismal font. The church of St Pshoi at the Red Monastery near Sohag, Egypt, may give us a picture of what the author intended (Figure 14.5). Tucked into a niche on the second registry, just below the image of Christ in the conch, are vibrant fifth-century paintings of curtains, hanging in imitation of real textiles, giving a sense of what was used in a church. The white curtain, with floriated wreaths in green and red in the center, top and bottom registers with red and green stripes, and a band containing a vine-like motif across the top, naturalistically folds as it dangles from rings on a rod, creating the illusion of three-dimensional space. The *trompe l'oeil* (literally 'trick of the eye,' an optical illusion) curtain gives an approximation of a church curtain where none survives and 'veils' the space, as the *Testamentum Domini* requires. While the central motif could be interpreted as cross imagery, importantly, it is not pointedly Christian.

The first mentions of altar cloths designed specifically as such are of the fifth century, but we know of textiles used for this purpose prior to that. Notably in the fourth century, the Byzantine Empress Pulcheria donated her robe to cover an altar that had been dedicated in honor of her virginity.[30] Presumably this textile had no Christian iconography, nor was it specifically white or linen. Later in our period, textiles designed with Christ and other holy persons were made for the altar and silk textiles come into use, as evidenced especially in the gifts listed in the *Liber Pontificalis*.[31] More than a century after Egeria described the textiles in churches of the Holy Land, Paul the Silentiary wrote about Hagia Sophia in Constantinople in 562, upon its re dedication after the dome was rebuilt. He describes the golden altar table of the great church being covered in a luxuriant purple silk with many colors, "the produce of the foreign worm."[32] Paul gives a very detailed description of the altar cloth stating that it was embroidered with colored, gold and silver threads and depicted Christ flanked by Peter and Paul. Around the hem there were scenes of the charitable deeds of the Byzantine Emperors interspersed with the miracle stories of Christ.

Figure 14.5 Painted niche with curtains, 5th century CE. Church of Pshoi, Red Monastery, near Sohag, Egypt. Photo by Arnaldo Vescovo, © American Research Center in Egypt.

Smaller *mapparia* are evident in the sources for use on the altar as well, sometimes in wool and often multi-colored.[33] These likely covered vessels. In Paul's description of Hagia Sophia's altar, he mentions other textiles in use with images of imperial couples being blessed by Mary and Christ, presumably figured in gold, which may have served as covers for various liturgical implements, "And upon other veils you may see monarchs joined together, here by the hand of Mary, the Mother of God, there by that of Christ, and all is adorned with the sheen of golden thread."[34]

It is not only the Great Church of the capital city where such resplendent textiles could be found. Andreas Angellus, writing in the early ninth century, describes the churches of Ravenna, Italy, in his *Liber Pontificalis Ecclesiae Ravennatis*. He tells of Bishop Theodore (seated 679–693) who had a purple cloth made to cover a casket that sat upon the altar (a reliquary?). This cloth had scenes from the Book of Genesis on it, which he remarks was unusual, "Who has ever seen anything like it?"[35]

Though it would become the norm in later Byzantine churches as well as those in the West to have figurative textiles adorning the altar and its implements, in the early Christian period it was still unusual enough to be remarkable. Purple and red are the most commonly mentioned colors, though we should always be cautious that the names of colors do not necessarily correspond to our understanding of them.[36] Some scholars wish to attribute symbolic meaning to colors but these meanings are so mutable as to be worthless; purple is not always imperial but rather only when it is the *murex* purple, made from mollusk shells, and used in an imperial context, for example.

Holy textiles: relics and icons

One of the reasons that many textiles, silks especially due to their special qualities discussed earlier, survive today is that they were used to protect relics and placed inside reliquaries. One fifth- or sixth-century example from the Sens Cathedral treasury depicts scenes from the story of Joseph (Genesis 37:13–18) in a yellow silk twill with a purple ground.[37] The story of Joseph was popular with both early Christians and Jews, especially on clothing, which this may indeed be.[38] Attesting to the specialness of this textile, it was wrapped around relics in the Holy Land and carried west. The initial impetus to wrap relics stemmed from the fact that most relics were body parts and therefore the relics were treated as the deceased.[39] In addition, wrapping a relic was thought to deter its theft (Figure 14.6).

Textiles were used to pad and secure relics inside their reliquaries and in addition it was commonly believed that the power of God worked through a textile. Numerous miracle stories found in various writings of the early Christian period have textiles figuring prominently, not because of any intrinsic power of the textile but rather because of their ubiquity in every

Figure 14.6 Open reliquary showing textiles wrapping relics, late 8th century. Copper gilt, glass, and probably amber on wood core with leather strap, 15.1 × 5.2 × 9.2 cm. Sens Cathedral treasury, F.63.70. Photo: © Genevra Kornbluth.

setting. For example, in John Moschos' *Pratum Spirituale* (*The Spiritual Meadow*) written *ca.* 600, a curtain hanging above an altar in a church "moved of its own volition and overshadowed the pope, the bishop, all the deacons who were in attendance and even the holy altar itself, for three hours."[40] The three-hour shrouding ended when the pope realized that he had imprisoned a bishop who had been falsely accused of eating from the consecrated eucharistic plate. In another story recounted by Moschos, a Christian man in Antioch was giving out clothing to the poor daily, garments that he bought in Egypt with his own money. One beggar, however, returned day after day to get a new garment until the fourth day when the almsgiver finally rebuked him for taking too much. The next night the almsgiver had a vision of Christ wearing all four tunics, ceremoniously removing them one by one, and he praised the almsgiver for his work for the poor.[41]

Indeed some of the most important and famous relics known in the early Christian and later medieval world were in fact textiles: the mantle of the Virgin, the shroud of Turin (believed to have been the burial wrapping of Christ due to the impression of a crucified figure on it), the Veil of Veronica (*sudarium*), and the Mandylion, to name just a few. The Mandylion was a towel on which Christ wiped his face, permanently imprinting his visage, not unlike Veronica's Veil, which she used to wipe blood and sweat from Christ's brow on the road to Calvary.

The story of the Mandylion is depicted in the upper right of a tenth-century icon from Mt Sinai (Figure 14.7). The sick King Abgar of Edessa (r. 4 BCE–between 13–50 CE) sent his messenger Ananias with a letter to Christ asking to be healed and Christ pressed his face into a towel, which Abgar holds here. The Mandylion was a true image of Christ and miraculously healed him. The other panels picture St Thaddeus, who converted the king to Christianity, in the upper left, and, below, Saints Paul of Thebes, Anthony, Basil and Ephrem. The textile relic was purchased in Edessa from local Muslims, processed into Constantinople by the Emperor Romanos I Lekapenos in 944,[42] a precious *archeiropoietos*, meaning an image made miraculously without hands. This icon was perhaps made in Constantinople to commemorate the anniversary of that event.[43]

While many people will be familiar with icons made on wood panels, less well known are icons woven in tapestry, perhaps due to their rarity, but maybe more likely due to their lack of survival. A notable example is the wool tapestry Icon of the Virgin and Child, flanked by the archangels Michael and Gabriel, with Christ seated above in a mandorla held aloft by angels, from the Cleveland Museum of Art (Figure 14.8). This enormous tapestry is nearly 6 1/2 feet tall and uses twenty different colors in the subtle shading found on the clothing, modeled faces of the figures, and dense flora of the frame, attesting to the complexity of the weave.[44] The Virgin sits on a jeweled throne while the archangels, donning blonde curls and blue and gold striated garments, stand at attention between columns befitting a royal throne room, set on a brilliant red background. An abundance of flowers, with medallion busts of apostles between, frame the entire icon, and creep into the fictive space where the Virgin is seated, perhaps symbolizing that she is in the earthly realm. Above, mounted on top of a starry firmament of heavenly space, a bearded, kingly Christ is enthroned in a full body halo. A tapestry icon such as this may have been hung in a church, and perhaps even treated as a miraculous icon, an *archeiropoietos*.[45] The many mentions of icons rarely describe the medium, so we should not assume that they were all panel paintings. The Cleveland textile is so luxurious that it could have also hung in a home of magnificent wealth, like the famous sixth-century hanging of Hestia Polyolbos, personifying a hearth of many blessings, today housed at Dumbarton Oaks (Figure 14.9).

Figure 14.7 Two icon panels with Saints Thaddeus, Paul of Thebes, and Antony, King Agbar and Messenger, and Saints Basil and Eprem, mid-10th century. Tempera on wood, 13 5/8 × 9 7/8 in. (34.5 × 25.2 cm). The Holy Monastery of Saint Catherine, Sinai, Egypt.

Christian textiles in the home: blessing and protecting the household

The Hestia hanging with its auspicious design intended to bless the home, seen in the attendants who bring her plaques inscribed with "wealth" and "abundance," for example, would have fit into an archway niche. An elite Christian home may have been decorated with a hanging like the Cleveland Virgin icon, discussed above, or like the Hestia hanging. As with the tunic front discussed at the opening of this chapter, a single home could be furnished with curtains, pillows, table covers, and hangings that signaled Christian identity alongside identifiers of other religions of the Roman world.

Figure 14.8 Icon of the Virgin and Child, 500s, slit- and dovetailed-tapestry weave in wool, 70 5/16 × 43 1/2 in. (78.7 × 110.5 cm). The Cleveland Museum of Art, Leonard C. Hanna, Jr. Fund, 1967.144.

Figure 14.9 Hanging with Hestia Polyolbos, sixth century. Tapestry weave in wool, 136.5 × 114 cm. Dumbarton Oaks, Byzantine Collection: BZ.1929.1, © Dumbarton Oaks, Byzantine Collection, Washington DC.

An individual textile could also be multivalent, as, for example, the fragment of hanging with a pomegranate tree from the Louvre Museum.[46] Such fruit trees were extremely popular subjects for hangings, curtains and other furnishing textiles as evidenced by over twenty extant examples of textiles with a similar motif. The pomegranate textile could have hung in a church or other public space, but garden imagery often appeared in the home, as the fifth-century poet Sidonius Apollinaris describes, "Let the round table be spread with linen purer than snow, and covered with laurel, with ivy and the green growths of the vine . . . Let the sideboard and couch be gay with garlands."[47] Enclosed, cultivated gardens were popular around the Mediterranean from Antiquity into the Middle Ages and these curtains have been seen by late antique viewers as an extension of those gardens, bringing the natural world indoors.[48]

This notion of natural imagery as pretty or ornamental suggests that a fruit tree was neutral, without meaning and there for aesthetic enjoyment. However, fruit trees connoted a heavenly Paradise in both Christianity and Islam, as seen, for example, in the famous mosaics of the Great Mosque of Damascus. Pomegranates in particular had been associated with immortality since Antiquity. I submit that in the home, the pomegranate tree conjured the promise of Paradise to the religious viewer and notions of immortality to all.

Parsing what is Christian and what is not in the home is difficult, in part because decorating decisions come down to taste, an elusive concept for an historian.[49] Furthermore, Christian art in the home, which included wall paintings, textiles, and mosaics, served many purposes, adding to the complexity of interpreting such material. Kim Bowes elucidates the many possible functions of Christian imagery:

> Christian images might be used in ritual contexts, as objects of veneration or as signposts to guide ritual activity. They might serve as protective agents to keep evil forces from penetrating the house and its occupants. And they might simultaneously be part of the elite house's status apparatus, deployed in the complex interactions between aristocratic peers, or woven into statements about individual identity.[50]

Despite all of these reasons for Christians to have specific Christian imagery in the home, the archaeological records indicate that narrative scenes in the home were rare.

In the home we also witness the melding of Christian ideas with long held cultural and religious practices from antiquity. For example, use of apotropaic (protective) or auspicious motifs was intertwined with the general belief in magic in Late Antiquity. A textile that was probably a pillow cover from Dumbarton Oaks serves as a case in point (Figure 14.10). The cross is represented here in a series of repeating crosses, radiating out from the central cross for greatest effect. The perimeter of the design is guarded with a series of concentric circles, recalling an eye or mirror, thought to deflect evil, a holdover from ancient belief going back at least to the story of Perseus defeating Medusa's stare that turned men to stone with a mirror.[51] The repetition of the cross motif and the mirror/eye symbol follow a practice common in spells that repeat phrases and actions for the desired effect, in this case protecting the head that rested on this textile.

Clothing: Christian tenets of modesty and self-identification

The beginning of the early Christian period witnesses a pattern of re-using secular textiles for a specifically Christian use, such as using donated textiles in churches. Clothing, and even vestments for clergy, follow a similar path, in that the wearer often did not don markers to identify him or her as Christian. Theodoret of Cyrrhus (*a.* 393–*a.* 460) mentions that the Emperor Constantine donated his own robe to the Bishop of Jerusalem specifically to wear during

Figure 14.10 Fragment of a garment or furnishing with cross in square panel, plain weave and embroidery of dyed wools and undyed linen, *ca.* 7th century CE. Dumbarton Oaks, Byzantine Collection: BZ.1953.2.66, © Dumbarton Oaks, Byzantine Collection, Washington DC.

baptisms, for example.[52] The archaeological record suggests that not until the sixth century was it common for garments to have Christian images on them, for example the tunic front with the cross pendant discussed earlier (Figures 14.1–2). However, at least one surviving garment fragment from the fourth to fifth century hints at the practice developing earlier.[53] The literary record though points to the wearing of Christian motifs already in the fourth century, as an oft-quoted passage from Bishop Asterius of Amasea attests. In it he complains about enthusiastic, and presumably wealthy, Christians wearing clothing with whole Christian stories on them,

> they devise for themselves, their wives and children gay-colored dresses decorated with thousands of figures . . . You may see the wedding of Galilee with the water jars, the paralytic carrying his bed on his shoulders, the blind man healed by means of clay,

> the woman with an issue of blood seizing [Christ's] hem, the sinful woman falling at the feet of Jesus, Lazarus coming back to life from his tomb. In doing this they consider themselves to be religious.[54]

A few textiles survive hinting at what such clothing may have looked like, such as the Joseph textile that was reused as a relic wrapping discussed previously.

Asterius' stern criticism is in line with Christian ideals about modesty, played out most prominently in the clothing of monastics who were encouraged to wear plain, coarse clothing, though in practice there is lots of evidence that monks and nuns ornamented their clothing.[55] Just as a range of taste explains how we find that a late antique home could be decorated with a rich array of cultural and religious identifiers, so too was the case with clothing, which may or may not have been used to mark a wearer as Christian.

Conclusion

Textiles were a highly valued and yet also a common element in the cultures of the Middle East, the Mediterranean, and Europe between 200 and 600. Early Christian textiles were, at first, those that were part of everyday life, marked as Christian because they were used by and for Christians in ritual, in sacred spaces, and on their bodies and in their homes. Beginning around the fourth century, Christians began to specially mark their textiles as Christian with iconography identifying them as such, though not exclusively, as many textiles survive with ambiguous iconography or iconography that points to multiple religious and cultural traditions at once. Some of the earliest mentions of Gospel stories and figurative images are on luxury clothing, where it is mentioned before use in churches. This may reflect a lack of comfort with figurative imagery in churches in the early Christian period or it may point to the ability and desire on the part of the wealthy to ornament themselves, and identify as Christian, which later trickled into the church proper. As textiles in Late Antiquity signaled status, it comes as no surprise that early Christians used gold thread, silk, a rich array of dyes, the finest linens and the softest wools in performing their rituals, securing relics, and decorating their homes, churches, and themselves.

Notes

1 Thelma K. Thomas, "Material Meaning in Late Antiquity," *Designing Identity: The Power of Textiles in Late Antiquity*, ed. Thelma K. Thomas (Princeton, NJ: Princeton University Press, 2016), 20–53.

2 For discussion of the griffin in the medieval west, see Juliette Wood, "Griffin," in *The Ashgate Encyclopedia of Literary and Cinematic Monsters* (London and New York: Routledge, 2014), 305–7. For discussion in Byzantine east, see Theocharis N. Pazaras, "Two Transenna Panels (cat. No. 2)," in *The Glory of Byzantium,* eds Helen C. Evans and William D. Wixom (New York: Metropolitan Museum of Art, 1997), 35–36.

3 To name a few examples: The Abbegg-Stiftung Foundation in Switzerland had 253 late antique textiles in its collection as of 2004, though they continue to collect, Sabine Schrenk *Textilien des Mittelmeerraumes aus spätantiker bis frühislamischer Zeit* (Riggisberg: Abegg-Stiftung, 2004), 11. The British Museum has over 300 examples of textiles catalogued online from this period, www.britishmuseum.org/collection, British Museum, 5/23/16. The Museum of Fine Arts, Boston, includes a single gift of over 700 textiles given between 1893–1928, though the MFA Boston began collecting in 1885 and still continues today. Christine Kondoleon, "Late Antique Textiles at the Museum of Fine Arts, Boston: Expanded Vistas," in *Designing Identity: The Power of Textiles in Late Antiquity*, ed. Thelma K. Thomas (Princeton and Oxford: Princeton University Press, 2016), 86–95. The Dumbarton Oaks Collection houses 258 late antique textiles, confirmed in correspondence with Dr Elizabeth Williams, Post-Doctoral Teaching Fellow in Byzantine Art History, Dumbarton Oaks/George Washington University and researcher for the Dumbarton Oaks Textile Catalogue Raisonne Project, 5/20/2106.

4 According to papyri evidence discussed in Willy Clarysee and Karolien Geens, "Textiles and Architecture in the Graeco-Roman and Byzantine Egypt," in *Clothing the House: Furnishing Textiles of the 1st Millennium AD from Egypt and Neighbouring Countries: Proceedings of the 5th Conference of the Research Group "Textiles from Nile Valley" Antwerp, 6–7 October 2007*, eds Antoine De Moor, Cäcilia Fluck and Susanne Martinssen-von Falck (Antwerp: Lannoo Publishers, 2009), 39–47. Additionally, the *Liber Pontificalis* (*Book of Pontiffs*) suggests that many of the precious textiles donated to churches by the earliest popes, prior to the ninth century, were originally Byzantine imperial gifts. Marielle Martianini-Reber, "Tentures et textiles des eglises romaines au haut moyen age d'apres le 'Liber Pontificalis,'" *Melanges de l'ecole francaises de Rome, moyen age 111.1* (1999): 289–305.

5 Jennifer Ball, "Decoding the Habit of the Byzantine Nun," *Journal of Modern Hellenism* 27 (2009–2010): 25–52.

6 For a history of looms see Eric Broudy, *The Book of Looms: A History of the Handloom from Ancient Times to the Present* (New York: Van Nostrand Reinhold Company, 1979). For looms of the eastern Mediterranean see Jennifer Ball, "The Missing Link: Filling the Gap in the Evolution of Medieval Domestic Looms," in *Anayemata Evrtika: Early Christian, Byzantine and Armenian Studies in Honor of Thomas F. Mathews* (Mainz: Philipp von Zabern GmBH, 2009), 38–44.

7 Herbert Winlock, W. E. Crum and Hugh G. Evelyn-White, *The Monastery of Epiphanius at Thebes* (New York: Metropolitan Museum of Art, 1926).

8 Nicholas Constas, "Weaving the Body of God: Proclus of Constantinople, the Theotokos, and the loom of the Flesh," *Journal of Early Christian Studies* 3 (1995): 169–194. See also Thelma K. Thomas, "Material Meaning in Late Antiquity," in *Designing Identities: Gender and Power in Late Antique Textiles*, ed. Thelma K. Thomas (New York: Institute for the Study of the Ancient World, NYU, February 2016).

9 For a full discussion of this image see Catherine C. Taylor, "Burial Threads: A Late Antique Textile and the Iconography of the Virgin Annunciate Spinning," *Greek and Roman Textiles and Dress: An Interdisciplinary Anthology*, eds Mary Harlow and Marie-Louise Nosch, Ancient Textiles Series 19 (Oxford: Oxbow Books, 2014), 20 and figure 20.1. Taylor discusses early images of the Virgin spinning thread, even proposing that the earliest image is in the catacomb of Priscilla in Rome, of the second century CE, in "Painted Veneration: The Priscilla Catacomb Annunciation and the *Protoevangelion of James* as Precedents for Late Antique Annunciation Iconography," *Studia Patristica* LIX 7 (2013), 21–38.

10 On this point see Yannick Lintz and Magali Coudert, *Antinoé: momies, textiles, céramiques et autres antiques: envois de l'État et dépôts du musée du Louvre de 1901 à nos jours* (Paris: Musee du Louvre, 2013).

11 See catalogue no. 112 for an example of this, Lintz and Coudert, *Antinoé: momies, textiles, céramiques et autres antiques: envois de l'État et dépôts du musée du Louvre de 1901 à nos jours*, 284.

12 For more on burials and Christianity, see Eric Rebillard, *The Care of the Dead in Late Antiquity* (Ithaca: Cornell University Press, 2009).

13 Jørgensen, Lise Bender and Ulla Mannering, "Mons Claudianus: Investigating Roman Textiles in the Desert," in *The Roman Textile Industry and its Influence*, eds Penelope Walton Rogers, Lise Bender Jørgensen and Antoinette Rast-Eicher (Oxford: Oxbow Books, 2014), 5.

14 See Jennifer L. Ball, "Rich Interiors: The Remnant of a Hanging from Late Antique Egypt in the Collection of Dumbarton Oaks" in *Liminal Fabric: Furnishing Textiles in Byzantium and Early Islam*, Conference proceedings, March 26–27, 2015, eds Gudrun Buhl and Elizabeth Williams (Washington DC: Dumbarton Oaks Research Library and Museum, expected 2018).

15 The importance of textile archaeology as a specialized field for processing and analyzing such finds cannot be overstated. For more on the field, see John Peter Wild, *Textiles in Archaeology* (Princes Risborough, Aylesbury, Bucks: Shire Publications, 1988), and Sabine Schrenk, ed., *Textiles in Situ: Their Find Spots in Egypt and Neighbouring Countries in the First Millennium CE* (Riggisberg: Abegg-Stiftung, 2006). For an understanding of scientific methods of textile archaeology and the state of the field through the massive finds of Antinoë, Egypt: Lintz and Coudert, *Antinoé: momies, textiles, céramiques et autres antiques: envois de l'État et dépôts du musée du Louvre de 1901 à nos jours.*

16 All finds outside of Egypt cannot be catalogued here, but the following will point the reader to some of the most well-known finds: Eliso Kvavadze and Iulon Gagoshidze, "Fibres of silk, cotton and flax in a weaving from the first century AD palace of Dedoplis Gora, Georgia," *Veget His Archaeobot* 17 (2008): S211–S215 (Republic of Georgia); Alisa Baginski and Amely Tidhar, "A Dated Silk Fragment from 'Avdat (Eboda)," *Israel Exploration Journal* 28.1/2 (1978): 113–115 (Israel); Anna A. Ierusalimskaja and Birgitt Borkopp, *Von China nach Byzanz: Fruhmittelalterliche Seiden auder Staatlichen Ermitage Sankt Petersburg* (Munich: Bayrisches Nationalmuseum und Staatliche Ermitage, 1996) (The Caucasus); Rodolphe

Pfister, *Textiles de Halabiyeh (Zenobia), découverts par le Service des Antiquités de la Syrie dans la Nécropole de Halabiyeh sur L'Euphrate* (Paris: Geuthner, 1951) (Syria); Andreas Schmidt-Colinet, Annemarie Stauffer and Khaled Al-As'ad, *Die Textilien aus Palmyra. Neue und alte Funde*, (Mainz amRhein:Von Zabern, 2000) (Palmyra, Jordan); Sabine Schrenk ed., *Textiles in situ: Their Find Spots in Egypt and Neighbouring Countries in the First Millenium* CE (Riggisberg: Abegg-Stiftung, 2006) (Ethiopia, Israel, Jordan, and Iran); Elizabeth Wincott Heckett, "Beyond the Empire: An Irish Mantle and Cloak," in *The Roman Textile Industry and its Influence. A Birthday tribute to John Peter Wild*, eds Penelope Walton Rogers, Lise Bender Jorgensen and Antoinette Rast-Eicher (Exeter: Oxbow Books, 2001), 91–97 (Ireland).

17 Canon 69 of the Council of Trullo (691–692) called for a division between laity and clergy inside the church, presumably already in practice, Pericles-Pierre Joannou, *Disciplina generale antiqua, I, Les Canons des conciles oecuméniques* (Rome: Tipografia Italo-Orientale S. Nilo, 1962), 207. Robert Taft, in his article concerning where women were allowed in churches of the Byzantine rite from the Levant to Italy, discusses the position of catechumens, laity, and clergy, in addition to women. See Robert F. Taft, "Women at Church in Byzantium: Where, When – and Why?" *Dumbarton Oaks Papers* 52 (1998): 27–87. Specific to churches in Constantinople, Vasileios Marinis discusses the use of church spaces by catechumens, women, laity and clergy noting the various ways that hierarchical divisions played out, see Vasileios Marinis, *Architecture and Ritual in The Churches of Constantinople* (New York: Cambridge University Press, 2014), 16 and 54–55.

18 This textile was sold in 1890 by Emil Brugsch-Bey, a German Egyptologist who was curator at the Bulaq Museum in Cairo, to George F. Baker, who then donated it to the Metropolitan Museum of Art in New York. See "Collection Records," *The Met*, accessed June 21, 2017, www.metmuseum.org/art/collection/search/444287. While we cannot say for sure that the textile was of Egyptian manufacture, it is highly likely that the cloth was excavated there.

19 The Greek word for fish, *ichthys*, is an acronym for "Jesus Christ, son of God, Saviour" (Ἰησοῦς Χριστός, Θεοῦ Υἱός, Σωτήρ). The fish symbolized Christians more generally as well: "But we, little fishes, after the example of our *Ichthys* Jesus Christ are born in water," Tertullian, *On Baptism*, 1. Thanks to Mark Ellison for pointing this reference out to me.

20 Jerome, *Epistle* IL1. For translation, see *The Principal Works of St. Jerome, Nicene and Post-Nicene Fathers of the Christian Church*, trans. W. H. Fremantle (Grand Rapids: Christian Classics Ethereal Library, 1892) www.ccel.org/ccel/schaff/npnf206.html.

21 For a discussion of dating, see *Egeria: Diary of a Pilgrimage*, Ancient Christian Writers 38, trans. George E. Gingras (New York and Ramsey: Newman Press, 1970), 12–15.

22 *Egeria*, 95.

23 These have been analyzed and compared with temple inventories of the same period by Willy Clarysse, "Textiles and Architecture," 44.

24 Sean Leatherbury, "Textiles as 'Gifts to God' in Late Antiquity: The Evidence of Christian Altar Cloths," in *Textiles and Cult in the Ancient Mediterranean*, eds. Cecilie Brøns and Marie-Louise Nosch (Oxford: Oxbow, 2017), 243–257. Thank you to the author for allowing me to see the paper in preparation.

25 Translation from Cyril Mango, *Art of the Byzantine Empire 312–1453: Sources and Documents* (Toronto: University of Toronto Press, 1986), 25. On dating and authorship, Simon Corcoran and Benet Salway, "A Newly Identified Greek Fragment of the *Testamentum Domini*," *The Journal of Theological Studies*, NS, 62.1 (2011): 133.

26 Constantine's gift to the Lateran: *Liber Pontificalis* (*Book of Pontiffs*) 34.9–34.12 and the inventory of the Egyptian church, *P.Grenf.* 2.111, in A. D. Lee, *Pagans and Christians in Late Antiquity: A Sourcebook*, 2nd ed. (London and New York: Routledge, 2016), 234–236, 239–240.

27 Clarysse and Geens, "Textiles and Architecture," 44.

28 Ignatius Ephraem II Rahmani, *Testamentum Domini Nostri Jesu Christi* I:19 (Moguntiae: Sumtibus Francisci Kircheim, 1899), 22 ff.

29 Mango, *Sources*, 25.

30 Nicholas Constas, "Weaving the Body of God: Proclus of Constantinople, the Theotokos, and the loom of the Flesh," *Journal of Early Christian Studies* 3.2 (1995): 189, n. 60.

31 Marielle Martianini-Reber, "Tentures et textiles des eglises romaines au haut moyen age d'apres le 'Liber Pontificalis,'" *Melanges de l'ecole francaises de Rome, moyen age 111.1* (1999): 289–305.

32 For Paul the Silentiary, see Mango, *Sources*, 88–89.

33 Clarysse and Geens, "Textiles and Architecture."

34 Mango, *Sources*, 89.

35 Mango, *Sources*, 131.
36 Clarysse and Geens, "Textiles and Architecture;" John Gage, *Colour and Culture: Practice and Meaning from Antiquity to Abstraction* (London: Thames and Hudson, 1995).
37 This textile, in three fragments, was removed from a reliquary casket of St Calais in 1947 and had remains of several saints inside; see André Bouton, "Le suaire de saint Calais," *Comptes rendus des séances de l'Académie des Inscriptions et Belles-Lettres* 91:3 (1947), 468–699. It has been variously dated between the fifth and sixth century and been attributed generally to the Near East, with a proposal of Antioch by Gary Vikan, *Age of Spirituality: Late Antique and Early Christian Art, Third to Seventh Century*, ed. Kurt Weitzmann (New York: The Metropolitan Museum of Art, 1977), cat. 413, 462.
38 Marielle Martiniani-Reber, ed., *Byzance En Suisse* (Paris: Bibliotheque Nationale, 1992), cat. 101, 152.
39 Martina Bagnoli, "Dressing the Relics: Some Thoughts on the Custom of Relic Wrapping in Medieval Christianity," in *Matter of Faith: An Interdisciplinary Study of Relics and Relic Veneration in the Medieval Period*, eds James Robinson, Lloyd de Beer and Anna Harnden (London: British Museum, 2015), 100–109.
40 John Moschos, *The Spiritual Meadow*, Cistercian Studies Series 39, trans. John Wortley (Kalamazoo: Cistercian Publications, 1992), 123–124.
41 Moschos, *The Spiritual Meadow*, 212–213.
42 Kathleen Corrigan, *Byzantium and Islam: Age of Transition*, eds Helen C. Evans with Brandie Ratliffe (New York: Metropolitan Museum of Art, 2012), cat. no. 30, 58.
43 Annie Labatt, *Holy Image, Hallowed Ground Icons from Sinai*, eds Robert S. Nelson and Kristen M. Collins (Los Angeles: The J. Paul Getty Museum, 2006), cat. no. 6.
44 For Cleveland Museum of Art documentation for *Icon of the Virgin and Child*, see Leonard C. Hanna, Jr. Fund (1967.144), *Cleveland Museum of Art*, accessed April 12, 2016, www.clevelandart.org/art/1967.144?sid=2162.
45 Abbot Adomnan of Iona (today in Scotland) (*ca.* 624–704) describes a woven icon, supposedly woven by the Virgin herself, depicting Christ and the apostles that was shown to pilgrims in Jerusalem. *Adomnan's 'De Locis Sanctis,'* D. Meehan ed., Scriptores Latini Hiberniae 3, Dublin: 1958, 1–34, cited in www.clevelandart.org/art/1967.144?sid=2162.
46 Jennifer Ball, "Textile Fragment with Tree" in *Byzantium and Islam: Age of Transition*, eds Helen C. Evans and Brandie Ratliff (New York: Metropolitan Museum of Art, 2012), cat. no. 2, 13.
47 Sidonius Apollinaris, *Letters* 3–9, trans. W. B. Anderson (Cambridge, MA: Harvard University Press, 1963), 9.13: 5.
48 For more on garden imagery in the home see Jennifer Ball, "Charms: Protective and Auspicious Motifs," in *Designing Identities: Gender and Power in Late Antique Textiles*, ed. Thelma K. Thomas (New York: Institute for the Study of the Ancient World, NYU, February 2016); and Jennifer Ball, *Byzantium and Islam: Age of Transition*, eds Helen C. Evans with Brandie Ratliffe (New York: Metropolitan Museum of Art, 2012), cat. no. 2 & 3, 13–14.
49 Kim Bowes, "Christian Images in the Home," *Antiquité tardive* 19 (2011): 171–190.
50 Ibid., 189.
51 Jennifer Ball, "Charms: Protective and Auspicious Motifs."
52 PG 82.1065 cited in Nicholas Constas, "Weaving the Body of God: Proclus of Constantinople, the Theotokos, and the Loom of the Flesh," *Journal of Early Christian Studies* 3:2 (1995): 184, n. 46.
53 The Abegg-Stiftung Collection has a fragment with scenes of the Virgin Mary on it that may have been part of a tunic, and is dated to the second half of the fourth to middle fifth century (Inv. 3100b) in Sabine Schrenk and Regina Knaller, eds, *Textilien des Mittelmeerraumes aus spätantiker bis frühislamischer Zeit*, (Riggisberg: Abegg-Stiftung, 2004), 185–189, cat. no. 62.
54 PG 40, 165–168. See Mango, *Sources* 50–51.
55 For a discussion of the differences in theory, practice and representation of monastic clothing see Thelma K. Thomas, "Mimetic Devotion and Dress in Some Monastic Portraits from the Monastery of Apa Apollo at Bawit" *Coptica* 11 (2012): 37–79. I discuss this in relation to nuns' dress specifically in "Decoding the Habit of the Byzantine Nun," *Journal of Modern Hellenism* 27 (2009–2010): 25–52.

Further reading

De Moor, Antoine, Cäcilia Fluck and Susanne Martinssen-von Falck, eds, *Clothing the House: Furnishing Textiles of the 1st Millennium AD from Egypt and Neighbouring Countries: Proceedings of the 5th Conference of the Research Group "Textiles from Nile Valley" Antwerp, 6–7 October 2007*. Antwerp: Lannoo Publishers, 2009.

Harlow, Mary and Marie-Louise Nosch, eds, *Greek and Roman Textiles and Dress: An Interdisciplinary Anthology*. Oxford: Oxbow Books, 2014.

Lintz, Yannick and Magali Coudert, eds, *Antinoé : momies, textiles, céramiques et autres antiques: envois de l'État et dépôts du musée du Louvre de 1901 à nos jours*. Paris: Musée du Louvre, 2013.

Maguire, Henry, "Garments Pleasing to God: The Significance of Domestic Textile Designs in the Early Byzantine Period." *Dumbarton Oaks Papers* 44 (1990): 217.

Schrenk, Sabine, *Textilien des Mittelmeerraumes aus spätantiker bis frühislamischer Zeit*. Riggisberg: Abegg-Stiftung, 2004.

Thomas, Thelma K., ed., *Designing Identity: The Power of Textiles in Late Antiquity*. Princeton and Oxford: Princeton University Press, 2016.

Upson-Saia, Kristi, *Early Christian Dress: Gender, Virtue and Authority*. New York: Routledge, 2011.

Wild, John Peter, *Textiles in Archaeology*. Princes Risborough: Shire Publications, 1988.

15

EARLY CHRISTIAN SILVER

Sacred and domestic

Ruth Leader-Newby

The craft of silver

Finely worked silver vessels were used in sacred and domestic contexts in the ancient world for hundreds of years before the advent of Christianity. The use of silver as an artistic medium by early Christians is both a continuation of and a departure from these long-established traditions. Individual Christians, especially those of elevated social rank, remained avid consumers of silver in their secular domestic life, despite the hostile attitude towards personal wealth displayed by many early Christian writers, while Christian communities put silver to new uses in the service of the Church, borrowing the material symbols of social rank to emphasise the Church's newly-acquired status as the dominant religion in the Roman world. However, before looking at how early Christians used silver in both sacred and secular settings, a short introduction to some of the key techniques and terminology of silverworking is necessary.

The techniques of Roman silverworking must be deduced from close examination of individual pieces, and comparison with more recent practice, since no ancient technical treatises for this art form exist. Although silver was mined in several locations in the Roman Empire, much of the silverware made in the late Roman period would have been recycled from old pieces, either provided by a client or acquired by the craftsman. Silver was collected in taxes during Late Antiquity but was not required for coinage, and so would often be released from the imperial treasuries in return for gold. This practice is thought to be behind the system of imperial control stamps, which are found on a significant proportion of silver vessels from the sixth and seventh centuries AD (including some liturgical silver), and allow these pieces to be dated closely.[1] Stamped silver would have originated in Constantinople, and possibly other eastern imperial centres such as Antioch and Alexandria. Vessels may have been roughly worked into basic shapes, stamped, and then sold on to private craftsmen, or they may have been fully finished in imperial workshops. In either case, the basic shape of a vessel could be created either by raising it from a sheet of silver by means of hammering, or by casting a blank in a mould. The former technique was used especially for closed forms, such as jugs, or the bowls of chalices, while the latter was frequently employed for plates, bowls and spoon handles. More complex vessels would be made in several pieces (for example the bowl and foot of a chalice, or a jug and its handle) and soldered together. Relief decoration was added subsequently, using the technique of chasing, whereby the metal is worked from the front with hammers and punches; or repoussé where the design is worked from the reverse. Two-dimensional surface decoration could be created with engraving and niello inlay. Niello is a soft mixture of silver sulphide that turns hard and black on heating, providing a contrast with the shiny surface of the silver. Relief decoration could also be further embellished with punched patterns, and details might be picked out with gilding. Both sacred and secular silver was made using various combinations of these different techniques; generally speaking, the more elaborate the object, the more different techniques are employed in its making.

Silver in churches

We do not know when silver vessels were first employed for administering Christian communion. The existing evidence suggests that by the time of the emperor Constantine's conversion in the fourth century AD, communion vessels made of precious metal were not a new phenomenon. An inventory of vessels confiscated in the persecution of 303 AD from a church in Cirta (later Constantine) in North Africa lists gold and silver chalices, and silver dishes and lamps.[2] However, the official sanctioning of Christianity with the Edict of Milan in 313 AD had the effect of substantially increasing the amount of wealth lavished upon church furnishings. Some of the key evidence can be found in the *Liber Pontificalis* ("Book of Pontiffs"), a series of biographies of the popes originally compiled in the sixth century in Rome. It incorporates detailed inventories of donations made by Constantine and his son to the churches he founded in Rome after his conversion, recording the gift of large numbers of both gold and silver patens, chalices, and other liturgical vessels, as well as light fittings, silver revetments and sculpture to the imperial foundations. The following extract, which describes the donation to the basilica of Saints Peter and Marcellinus, is typical:

> an altar of finest silver weighing 200 lb [a Roman pound = 327.45 g]; 2 patens of finest gold each weighing 15 lb; 2 silver patens each weighing 15 lb; a larger gold scyphus [chalice], with the imperial name represented on it, weighing 20 lb; a smaller gold scyphus weighing 10 lb, 5 silver scyphi each weighing 12 lb, 20 silver service chalices each weighing 3 lb, 4 silver amae [wine jars] each weighing 15 lb.[3]

Although these imperial donations were undoubtedly grander than anything used in churches up to that point—Constantine's ostentatious patronage signaling Christianity's new status as an imperially sanctioned religion—we can presume that they were inspired by more modest silver items already in use.

As well as being used to make portable liturgical objects to adorn churches, silver could also be fastened to the walls and furniture in the form of revetments: thin silver sheeting that was attached to a core of stone or wood. It has been calculated that the silver furniture donated to St Peter's and the Lateran, as listed in the *Liber Pontificalis*, outweighs silver objects by a ratio of about two and a half or two to one.[4] This is not surprising when one considers the scale of some of the structures that were covered in silver, such as the Lateran *fastigium* (a type of colonnaded screen or canopy) clad in silver and decorated with near life-size silver statues of Christ and the apostles.[5] Two centuries later when Procopius describes Justinian's church of Hagia Sophia in Istanbul, he tells his readers that they can gauge the amount of precious metal the emperor has lavished on his foundation from the fact that the sanctuary alone displayed forty thousand pounds of silver, most of which would have been in the form of revetments.[6] A silver *ciborium* (a type of domed canopy that enclosed an altar) was considered an essential part of a saint's shrine: that of St Demetrios in Thessalonike is perhaps the most famous from the early Byzantine period, and it features in several of the accounts of the saint's miracles that were compiled in the seventh century.[7] One miracle revolves around the means by which extra silver was acquired to repair St Demerios' *ciborium* (which unusually contained his tomb rather than an altar) after it had been damaged in a fire. In the story, the saint warns the archbishop against melting down his silver episcopal throne—yet another type of silver furnishing—and ensures that two donors appear with the necessary quantity of silver. Similarly, Severus of Antioch preached a homily in 516 exhorting his congregation to donate sufficient silver to cover the *ciborium* of local martyr St Drosis.[8]

The Constantinian liturgical vessels perished in the Gothic sack of Rome in 410 AD, nor does any trace remain of their replacements from the fifth and sixth centuries (although these are listed in the *Liber Pontificalis*). However, seven hoards of early Christian liturgical silver have been discovered in modern times, together with a handful of individual pieces, and it is from these that our knowledge of the forms of this medium, and its decoration, derives. Such a small sample means that our understanding of liturgical silver is necessarily limited. With the exception of the fourth-century hoard from Water Newton, all these hoards have been dated to the sixth century. Moreover, the geographical distribution of the hoards' find spots is uneven: two hoards were found in the west of the Roman empire (Water Newton in Britain and the Gallunianu Treasure from central Italy), and the remainder were discovered in the east, in Syria and Turkey. Indeed the Syrian hoards (the Kaper Koraon, Beth Misona, Phela, and Ma'aret en-Noman Treasures) are associated with a relatively small geographical area near the modern Syrian town of Idlib, and belonged to small village churches there, accounting for the very similar nature of much of their contents.[9]

The Sion or Kumluca Treasure (found in Lycia, south western Turkey) is the only one of the hoards that gives us some insight into the quality of vessels that might have adorned urban churches of this period.[10] Despite the limitations of the surviving body of material, a relatively large range of liturgical and paraliturgical objects are represented in the hoards. Almost all hoards contain the basic liturgical equipment of paten (Latin *patena*; Greek *diskos*) and chalice (Latin *calix*, *scyphos*; Greek *poterion*). Other objects relating to the preparation of the eucharist that are present in several hoards include ewers and jugs, spoons, strainers and ladles, while the broader adornment of the church is represented by a variety of different types of freestanding and hanging lamps, votive crosses, and embossed book covers for the gospels. There are even some unusual objects like the asterisk from the Sion Treasure (a star-shaped object used to support a cloth over the host), or the two silver fans (*rhipidia*) from the Kaper Koraon hoard, ceremonial versions of the peacock feather fans originally used to keep flies from the bread and wine during mass.

As with the liturgical and paraliturgical vessels, the surviving hoards offer evidence that silver revetments featured in church decoration outside the major metropolitan centres, which are the focus of our literary sources. The Kaper Koraon Treasure contains a wooden cross, sheathed in silver, which is held in place with 100 silver nails. The Sion Treasure has revetments from several objects: an altar table, one or more lampstands, and several pieces whose function is unknown, as well as 29 silver nails and 3 spirally fluted small columns. What is significant is that all these items seem to have been carefully removed from the cores to which they were fastened, in contrast to the cross from the Kaper Koraon hoard. Clearly silver revetments could, if the need arose, be removed for concealment together with the rest of a church's moveable wealth, lest they fall victim to looting and pillage. One theory suggests the Sion Treasure may have been hidden in the seventh century to escape Arab raids along the Lycian coast.[11] But it is also possible that the silver had been removed to fund a worthy cause: the sanctity of a church's holdings of silver did not prevent it from serving as a financial reserve if the need was deemed great enough. The foremost example of this is the "loan" made in 621 to the Byzantine emperor Heraclius of the silver from Hagia Sophia, in order to finance his campaign against the Persians.[12]

So far we have seen the range of ways in which silver vessels and sheeting could be used to adorn churches. What about the appearance of the pieces themselves and their decoration? The earliest of the seven surviving liturgical hoards is the Water Newton (or Durobrivae) Treasure, discovered in eastern England in 1975 and dated to the early fourth century AD (Figure 15.1).[13] This offers the earliest evidence of the shapes and decorative choices for liturgical vessels. It comprises nine silver vessels, as well as about 18 small votive plaques, and its total weight is about 12 Roman pounds—a tiny fraction of the huge weights listed in the *Liber Pontificalis* inventories.[14] Two things stand out about the Water Newton hoard. First, though modest, the objects it contains correspond closely to the types of vessel in the contemporary inventories: there is a paten and a chalice (an undecorated kantharos-type cup with handles), as well as jugs and strainers, and a bowl with suspension rings that could have served as a lamp. Second, their decoration is for the most part very simple, and inscriptions and symbols rather than images indicate their Christian liturgical character. One of the jugs and the bowl with suspension rings are decorated with mainly floral ornament; the chalice, another jug, and a bowl are undecorated. The paten—the largest piece in the hoard—has minimal decoration: a series of concentric rings, within the smallest of which is a lightly inscribed chi-rho, flanked by an alpha and omega (unfortunately hard to make out in photographs). Two small bowls each carry a votive inscription beneath the rim, and feature the chi-rho monogram flanked by an alpha and an omega as a device to mark the beginning/end of the inscription. Similarly, most of the votive plaques also feature the chi-rho/alpha-omega monogram, as does the handle of the silver strainer.

Simple decoration based upon Christian symbols and dedicatory inscriptions is a feature of the sixth-century liturgical hoards too, which are comparable in their relatively modest level of craftsmanship, fitting with the theory that the Syrian hoards belonged to small village churches, not

Figure 15.1 Water Newton Treasure. © The British Museum.

large urban establishments. Moreover, some vessel types changed little over the two centuries: the Water Newton paten is a large deep dish with a flat base, high sloping sides, and a flat horizontal rim, as are the patens in the Kaper Koraon, Phela and Beth Misona hoards (as well as that from the Italian Gallunianu hoard). If we compare the paten from Water Newton with the paten in the Beth Misona hoard (Figure 15.2), not only are they of a similar size (approximately 33 cm in diameter, though the Beth Misona paten weighs less), but the Beth Misona paten is also decorated with a series of concentric rings. Instead of the chi-rho, a cross with flaring arms is engraved in its centre, and enclosed by an inscription recording the donation of this paten by "Domnos son of Zacheos" to "(the church of) St Sergius of the village of Beth Misona."

The Kaper Koraon and Phela Treasures also contain multiple patens with the same simple decoration of cross and encircling dedicatory inscription. Although the Water Newton paten has no inscription, dedicatory inscriptions feature on the two small beaker-like bowls in the hoard, which conceivably could have served as chalices. Their shape (and that of the other chalice in the Water Newton hoard) is unlike that of surviving sixth-century chalices, which all have broad hemispherical bowls mounted on a flaring circular foot, often with a knop. However the mode of decoration, an engraved inscription around the rim naming the donor, remains the same.

Despite these important similarities, we can see a wider range of decorative options in use in the sixth century, even within the Syrian village treasures. In some cases, inscriptions are inlaid in niello, as in the chalice from the Kaper Koraon Treasure dedicated by Symeonius the magistrate, now in the Walters Art Museum (Figure 15.3). A further elaboration can be seen in the three

Figure 15.2 Three chalices and a paten, Beth Misona Treasure, *c.* 500–700. © The Cleveland Museum of Art, Purchase from the J.H. Wade Fund.

Figure 15.3 Chalice donated by Symeonios the Magistrate, Kaper Koraon Treasure. Walters Art Museum, Baltimore.

chalices that form the rest of the Beth Misona hoard, in the form of tondo busts of Christ and the evangelists worked in relief on the body of the chalice, and stylised leaves embossed on the knop (the round knob on the stem, Figure 15.2).

In two of these chalices, the inscription around the rim has been replaced by a pattern of concave discs alternating with palmettes: clearly the images of Christ and the evangelists, rather than word or symbols, are now being used to mark these chalices as liturgical vessels. Such tondo or clipeate busts are found on other types of liturgical vessel too, most notably the large silver ewer in the Louvre known as the "Homs Vase" (another Syrian find of the early 20th century) and a censer in the Sion Treasure. Figural imagery is used on patens too: possibly the most elaborate vessels in the Kaper Koraon hoard are the two "Communion of the Apostles" patens (now in Washington DC and Istanbul). These depict two similar (though not identical) versions of the same scene: Christ (shown twice) administering communion to the apostles at the altar of an early Byzantine church (Figure 15.4). Details of the scene are gilded (at least in the Washington paten) and both feature a dedicatory inscription in niello around the rim, but the two plates are clearly by different hands. This subject is highly appropriate for the patens' function since, rather than representing the Last Supper (the prototype of the eucharist), it represents the ritual itself, with Christ and the apostles taking the place of the sixth-century priest and his congregation. It is surprising, then, that these two patens are the only surviving representation of this subject on liturgical silver from the late antique period. Of course, we should remember that what survives is only a tiny fraction of the church silver that existed in that period, and we have no way of knowing how representative a sample has been preserved.

Figure 15.4 Communion of the Apostles paten, Kaper Koraon Treasure. © Dumbarton Oaks, Byzantine Collection, Washington DC.

The Communion of the Apostles patens are not the largest or heaviest that survive, or even the most skillfully crafted (despite their ambitious subject matter). The six patens in the Sion or Kumluca Treasure range in diameter from just under 60 cm to 77 cm, and weigh almost four and a half kilograms each, twice as large and more than four times as heavy as the Communion of the Apostles patens.[15] The Sion patens display superlative craftsmanship, but the basic concept of their design is relatively simple. Three have a cusped border worked in relief with alternating palmettes and acanthus leaves (picked out in gilding), enclosing a dedicatory inscription inlaid with niello, and a gilded christogram in the centre (Figure 15.5), while two others have a convex fluted rim, with the flutes alternately gilded to produce a striped effect, again enclosing a niello inscription and a large gilded cross in the centre. Despite differences in size, weight and workmanship, the basic formula is not so different from the simple patens in the Syrian hoards, or even the Water Newton paten.

In this context it is worth noting that we have little idea what the liturgical vessels mentioned in the *Liber Pontificalis* actually looked like. Descriptive details, such as "gold chalices . . . with [. . .] jewels", "a larger gold scyphus with the imperial name represented on it", or "a silver chalice decorated in relief" are rare.[16] An inventory is by its nature brief, and concerned primarily with the monetary value of the objects itemised (description simply serving to identify particular pieces), but the superlative quality yet simple design of the Sion patens suggests that not all "metropolitan" liturgical silver would have had elaborate figural decoration.

Christian silver in the domestic sphere

When Severus, the patriarch of Antioch, preached a sermon in the early sixth century, exhorting his congregation to donate silver to cover the ciborium of their local saint, Drosis, he argued

Figure 15.5 Paten with cusped border, Sion Treasure. © Dumbarton Oaks, Byzantine Collection, Washington DC.

that they could easily afford the expense. There were many in his congregation, he claimed, who ate their meals off silver dishes, while their wives visited the baths in silver-decorated chairs, pulled by mules with silver harnesses, taking with them silver vessels "weighing many pounds".[17] Despite the potential for rhetorical exaggeration, he nevertheless presents us with the image of a wealthy urban Christian community for whom silver was an essential sign of their status. While they might have enjoyed hearing about the ascetic renunciation practiced by St Drosis (described in the earlier part of the sermon), this was not a mode of life that many of them chose to emulate. This attitude to personal wealth was not restricted to the citizens of sixth-century Antioch; rather it is typical of Christianised elite Romans from the fourth century onwards. Severus' evocation of the types of silver objects used by the wealthy citizens of Antioch is believable, not least because it is closely mirrored by the contents of the Esquiline Treasure, a late fourth-century hoard from Rome that includes chair fittings, horse ornaments and women's toilet vessels, as well as items of tableware.[18] The Esquiline Treasure's most famous piece, the so-called "Projecta Casket" (Figure 15.6), is particularly relevant in this context, as it bears an inscription that identifies its owners as Christians, but at the same time is decorated with scenes from classical mythology and elite life. Overall it is a prime example of how the new Christian identity of the Roman elite was articulated in the medium of silver.

The Projecta Casket is a large silver box (approximately 55 cm × 43 cm × 28 cm), made in the form of two truncated rectangular pyramids, connected by hinges at their bases, and with flattened, rectangular tops that form the apex and the base of the casket respectively. The whole casket, with the exception of the base, is elaborately worked with figures in relief, and decorated further with engraved and punched details, as well as gilding. The apex of the lid shows the portrait of a bearded man and a richly dressed woman within a wreath supported by two cupids, a common way of portraying a husband and wife in fourth-century art, especially

Figure 15.6 Projecta Casket, Esquiline Treasure. London, British Museum. © The Trustees of the British Museum/Art Resource, New York.

on sarcophagi and gold glass medallions.[19] Beneath them, on the front panel of the lid, is the figure of the nude Venus, holding a mirror and a pin, supported on a shell by two tritons, each of whom has a cupid standing on his back bearing a box and a basket respectively. The two end panels of the lid continue the theme of the marine Venus, depicting nereids riding sea monsters, attended by more cupids. The back of the lid abandons this mythological iconography to show a woman accompanied by attendants, approaching a multi-domed bath building. This theme of "elite daily life" is continued on the front of the lower part of the casket, which depicts a rich woman seated in her dressing room, flanked by two female attendants holding a mirror and a casket. The remaining three sides of the casket body show a series of further male and female attendants (nine in total), framed by curtained arcading and holding a series of boxes, lights and cosmetic utensils.

Through close iconographic and thematic parallels the casket's decoration makes a clear equation between the goddess Venus and the Roman woman adorning herself: each is shown seated, placing a pin in her hair with an identical gesture, while her attendant (human or divine) holds the same round mirror so she can admire her reflection. Venus' attendants of tritons, nereids, cupids and sea-monsters are echoed in the Roman matron's retinue of male and female servants. The flattering comparison of the Roman wife of the casket's lid and sides with the goddess of love, Venus, might seem straightforward, but it is not. Engraved along the sill at the front of the casket—directly below the image of Venus—are the words: *Secunde et Proiecta vivatis in Christo* ("Secundus and Projecta, live in Christ"), preceded by a monogram cross with an alpha and omega. Thus the Projecta Casket combines the iconography of the toilet of Venus and scenes of elite life with an emphatically Christian inscription. An elaborate silver object whose purpose is purely secular (to transport its owner's possessions to the baths in ostentatious style, as in the scene on the back of the casket) at the same time exhorts its owners—by implication the husband and wife represented on the top of the casket—to pursue a Christian life. How are we supposed to interpret this juxtaposition?

As others have warned, it would be a mistake to claim that Venus was simply a meaningless decorative device, since the formal iconographic programme of the box is too carefully planned for this to be the case.[20] Nor can the inscription be reduced to a conventional expression of goodwill, given its emphatic evocation of the name of Christ, reinforced by the cross monogram that precedes it. Rather, through the inscription, the casket asserts that Christianity is an integral part of Projecta's identity as a wealthy Roman woman, standing alongside her familiarity with the classical culture that held up Venus as an archetype of feminine beauty and wifely love, and her use of jewellery, fine clothes, bathing and cosmetics to adorn herself for her husband.[21] Conflating these three facets of fourth-century Roman elite identity was not without its inherent contradictions, but it was a popular strategy and the Projecta Casket is not unique among fourth-century silver in doing this.

In fact, many of the major hoards of domestic silver surviving from the fourth century contain a variety of items that in one way or another advertise their owners' Christian allegiance, while at the same time other pieces in these hoards proclaim their affiliation to the mythological traditions of classical culture. The Mildenhall Treasure, found in eastern England like the Water Newton hoard, is best known for the "Great Dish", a huge circular plate decorated with an outer frieze of Dionysos and his followers, and an inner frieze of nereids riding sea monsters (very similar to the two short panels on the lid of the Projecta Casket). Two small companion plates depict maenads dancing with a satyr and Pan respectively. Yet this same hoard also contains a set of three spoons with the chi-rho monogram, flanked by an alpha and an omega engraved in the bowl (Figure 15.7).

Likewise the Kaiseraugst Treasure (discovered in Switzerland in the 1960s) is famed for its octagonal plate showing scenes from the childhood of Achilles, and also features a silver statuette of Venus and a rectangular plate depicting Ariadne and Dionysos. However, one of the smaller pieces in the hoard is a pointed utensil with a small spoon at one end, and at the other a pointed

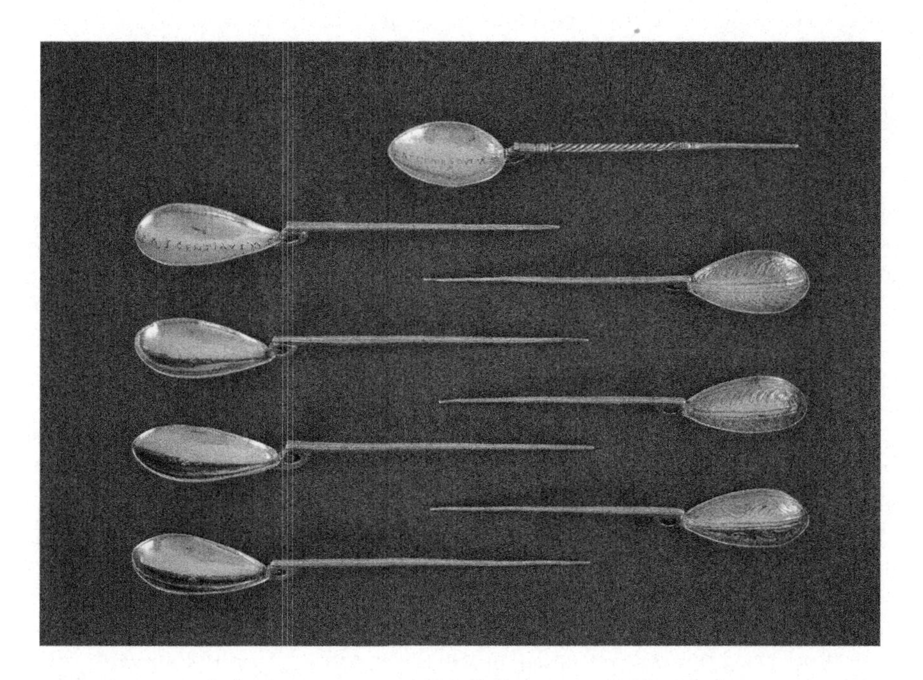

Figure 15.7 Spoons with chi-rho monogram, Mildenhall Treasure. © The British Museum.

comma-shaped finial, decorated with an openwork chi-rho monogram. It is conventionally described as a toothpick, but the function of such implements in a Roman dining service is not known for certain.

The Hoxne Treasure (from Suffolk, England) features a considerable number of Christian symbols on small dining utensils: there are two spoons with the chi-rho, one inscribed *Vivas in Deo* ("Live in God"), and a set of ten ladles decorated with the monogram cross on the handles. Unlike the Mildenhall and Kaiseraugst hoards, this hoard comprised only small bowls and other table implements (in addition to coins and gold jewellery) and we have no way of knowing whether the larger items, which its owners must have undoubtedly possessed, were decorated with the same type of mythological scenes as the pieces in the Mildenhall and Kaiseraugst hoards. The use of Christian symbols in the Hoxne Treasure even extended to the jewellery: one of the gold necklace clasps is decorated with a tiny filigree monogram cross.

The symbols of Christianity adorning spoons and ladles may seem insignificant in the wider context of their respective hoards. Unlike the Projecta Casket, Christian symbols and mythological imagery do not appear on the same objects, and one could argue that it would have been possible for an uninterested dinner guest to overlook the Christian references entirely. Nevertheless, the juxtapositions are significant, showing that for the owners of these hoards, adopting the imperially sanctioned religion did not entail a straightforward rejection of a long-established tradition of advertising one's classical culture at the dining table. Among those fourth-century Romans wealthy enough to afford a silver dinner service, a discreet advertisement of their religion was preferred. There is also the possibility that, for some individuals in the fourth-century, the use of the chi-rho or cross monogram may have been seen less as a profession of faith than a belief in the apotropaic, luck-bringing powers of this symbol (as proved by Constantine's successful deployment of it at the Battle of the Milvian Bridge).

Because we know next to nothing about the owners of these hoards, it is impossible to say exactly what meaning they would have ascribed to the Christian symbols on their possessions. Despite this caution, it is clear that the fourth-century domestic hoards provide important insights into the way in which Christianity came to be integrated into the self-image of the Roman elite. The most explicit manifestation of this (after the Projecta Casket) is the central medallion of the Great Hunting Plate from the Sevso Treasure (Figure 15.8). Using niello inlay upon an engraved silver surface, it combines scenes of hunting with an open-air banquet: both are idealised images of the male elite lifestyle, in the same way that the scenes of the procession to the baths and female adornment on the Projecta Casket represent an ideal of elite feminine activity. Like the casket, it features an inscription: a verse couplet expressing the hope that the ironically described "small vessels" should last a certain Sevso and his descendants for many years. The juncture between the beginning and end of the inscription, located conspicuously at the apex of the medallion, is marked by a tiny yet elegantly formed chi-rho in a wreath. The chi-rho symbol is an integral part of the design of the plate, but is simultaneously discreet. It only advertises Sevso's religious allegiance to those who look closely enough to read the inscription and study the miniature scene. But the very fact of its presence shows that Christianity was an integral part of Sevso's self-fashioning.

Our understanding of silver as a form of early Christian art is shaped by accidents of survival: while there are numerous hoards of domestic silver dating to the fourth century, there are far fewer comparable hoards from the fifth and sixth centuries. Similarly, liturgical hoards cluster around the sixth century, and there is very little later material surviving from either East or West with which we can compare it. Nevertheless, silver surviving from the sixth and seventh centuries casts an important light on the way that Christianity is evoked in a domestic context as it shifts from being one religion among many (as it was in the fourth century), to being the only recognised religion of the Roman empire.

Figure 15.8 Detail of central medallion of Great Hunting Plate, Sevso Treasure. Budapest, Hungarian National Museum.

One of these survivals is a type of silver dish from the eastern Empire known as a "cross monogram plate", of which there are many extant examples. A significant proportion of these can be dated through the imperial control stamps on them, revealing that while the earliest surviving example was made in the reign of Anastasius (491–518 AD), most were produced between 578 and 641.[22] They get their name from their decoration: a small niello cross, or a monogram of the owner's name arranged around a cross, enclosed in a wreath or scroll (Figure 15.9). Despite the presence of the cross (reminiscent of the decoration of some contemporary patens) these are not liturgical vessels and have been found as part of domestic dinner services, even as a set in a range of sizes.[23]

Unlike the discreet chi-rho symbols in the fourth century hoards, the crosses on these plates reflect a society where the image of the cross was ubiquitous, and the owner's Christian allegiance was expected. Their rate of survival suggests that they were produced in large numbers, and widely used. While domestic silver decorated with classical mythology (in the tradition of the Projecta Casket or the Mildenhall Great Dish) continued to be made into the seventh century, at the same time Christianised alternatives to these themes were developed, as shown by the set of nine plates depicting the early life of the biblical King David, dating from the early seventh century, which were discovered in Cyprus in the early twentieth century.[24] These represent David in classicising style as an equivalent to the heroes of Graeco-Roman mythology, and in doing so herald a new type of secular decoration for the Christianised domestic sphere. In the history of early Christian silver, both the David Plates and the cross monogram plates anticipate developments of later Christian art as much as they connect to their antecedents in this medium from the fourth century.

Figure 15.9 Plate with cross in ivy wreath, First Cyprus Treasure. London, British Museum. Werner Forman/Art Resource, New York.

Notes

1 Erica C. Dodd, *Byzantine Silver Stamps. With an Excursus on the Comes Sacrarum Largitionum by J.P.C. Kent* (Washington, DC: Dumbarton Oaks, 1961); Marlia Mundell Mango, "The purpose and places of Byzantine silver stamping", in *Ecclesiastical Silver Plate in Sixth Century Byzantium*, eds Susan Boyd and Marlia Mundell Mango (Washington DC: Dumbarton Oaks, 1961), 203–16.
2 Susan A. Boyd, "A bishop's gift: openwork lamps from the Sion Treasure", in *Argenterie romaine et byzantine: actes de la table ronde, Paris 11–13 octobre 1983*, ed. F. Baratte (Paris: de Boccard, 1988), 191–202.
3 Raymond Davis, ed. and trans., *The Book of Pontiffs (Liber Pontificalis)*. Translated Texts for Historians, Latin Series 5 (Liverpool: Liverpool University Press,1989), 23.
4 Marlia Mundell Mango, "The monetary value of silver revetments and objects belonging to churches, AD 300–700", in *Ecclesiastical Silver Plate in Sixth Century Byzantium*, eds Susan Boyd and Marlia Mundell Mango (Washington DC: Dumbarton Oaks, 1992), 124.
5 Davis, *Book of Pontiffs*, 16.
6 Procopius, *Buildings* 1.1.65.
7 Paul Lemerle, ed. and trans., *Les plus anciens recueils des miracles de S. Démétrius*, 2 vols (Paris: Éditions du Centre nationale de la recherche scientifique, 1979).
8 Ignazio Guidi, ed. and trans., *Severus of Antioch, Homiliae Cathedrales*, Patrologia Orientalis 22 (Paris: Firmin-Didot, 1930), 230–48.
9 Marlia Mundell Mango, *Silver From Early Byzantium: the Kaper Koraon and Related Treasures* (Baltimore, MD: Trustees of the Walters Art Gallery, 1986); *idem*, "The origins of the Syrian ecclesiastical silver treasures of the sixth-seventh centuries", in *Argenterie romaine et byzantine: actes de la table ronde, Paris 11–13 octobre 1983*, ed. F. Baratte (Paris: de Boccard, 1988), 163–78.
10 Susan A. Boyd, "A 'metropolitan' treasure from a church in the provinces: an introduction to the study of the Sion Treasure", in *Ecclesiastical Silver Plate in Sixth Century Byzantium*, eds Susan Boyd and Marlia Mundell Mango (Washington DC: Dumbarton Oaks, 1992), 5–38.
11 Boyd, "A bishop's gift", 191.
12 Theophanes, *Chronographia: Chronicle*, 1.302–3.
13 Kenneth S. Painter, *The Water Newton Early Christian Silver* (London: British Museum Publications, 1977).

14 Painter, *Water Newton Early Christian Silver*; Mango, "Monetary value of silver", 133.
15 Boyd, "A 'metropolitan' treasure", 19–20.
16 Davis, *Book of Pontiffs*, 23.
17 Guidi, *Severus of Antioch*, 247.
18 Kathleen Shelton, *The Esquiline Treasure* (London: British Museum Publications. 1981).
19 Jaś Elsner, "Visualising women in late antique Rome: the Projecta Casket", in *Through a Glass Brightly: Studies in Byzantine and Medieval Art and Archaeology presented to David Buckton*, ed. Christopher Entwistle (Oxford: Oxbow Books, 2003), 24.
20 Jaś Elsner, *Art and the Roman Viewer: the Transformation of Art from the Pagan World to Christianity* (Cambridge: Cambridge University Press, 1995), 254–55.
21 Eve D'Ambra, "The calculus of Venus: nude portraits of Roman matrons", in *Sexuality in Ancient Art*, ed. Natalie Boymel Kampen (Cambridge: Cambridge University Press, 1996), 219–32.
22 Dodd, *Byzantine Silver Stamps*; Ruth E. Leader-Newby, *Silver and Society in Late Antiquity: Functions and Meanings of Silver Plate in the Fourth to Seventh Centuries*, (Aldershot: Ashgate, 2004), 177.
23 David Buckton, ed., *Byzantium: Treasure of Byzantine Art and Culture from British Collections* (London: British Museum Press, 1994), 93.
24 Leader-Newby, *Silver and Society*, 173–216.

Further reading

Most research on silver is published in the form of catalogues, either of individual hoards or exhibitions. For liturgical silver, Mango *Silver From Early Byzantium* and Boyd and Mango *Ecclesiastical Silver Plate* are essential reading. The fourth-century hoards discussed in this chapter have been catalogued in detail (Cahn, Kaufmann-Heinimann et al. *Der spätrömische Silberschatz von Kaiseraugst*; Guggisberg and Kaufmann-Heinimann *Der spätrömische Silberschatz von Kaiseraugst, die neuen Funde*; Johns *The Hoxne Late Roman Treasure*; Mango and Bennett *The Sevso Treasure*; Painter *The Mildenhall Treasure*), while Painter *The Wealth of the Roman World* is still a useful reference source for a wide variety of objects. Leader-Newby *Silver and Society* offers a broader study of the key functions of silver in Late Antiquity, while Noga-Banai *The Trophies of the Martyrs* is an iconographical study of one type of object. On uses of silver (and other wealth) in sacred contexts, both pagan and Christian, Janes *God and Gold* and Lapatin *The Berthouville Silver Treasure* provide valuable insights.

Boyd, Susan A. and Marlia Mundell Mango, eds, *Ecclesiastical Silver Plate in Sixth- Century Byzantium*. Washington DC: Dumbarton Oaks, 1992.

Cahn, H.A., Annemarie Kaufmann-Heinimann and Elisabeth A. Rosenbaum, *Der spätrömische Silberschatz von Kaiseraugst*. Derendingen: Habegger, 1984.

Guggisberg, Martin and Annemarie Kaufmann-Heinimann, eds, *Der spätrömische Silberschatz von Kaiseraugst, die neuen Funde: Silber im Spannungsfeld von Geschichte, Politik und Gesellschaft der Spätantike*. Augst: Römerstadt Augusta Rarica, 2003.

Janes, Dominic, *God and Gold in Late Antiquity*. Cambridge: Cambridge University Press, 1998.

Johns, Catherine, *The Hoxne Late Roman Treasure: Gold Jewellery and Silver Plate*. London: British Museum Press, 2010.

Lapatin, Kenneth, ed., *The Berthouville Silver Treasure and Roman Luxury*. Los Angeles, CA: The J. Paul Getty Museum, 2014.

Leader-Newby, Ruth E., *Silver and Society in Late Antiquity: Functions and Meanings of Silver Plate in the Fourth to Seventh Centuries*. Aldershot: Ashgate, 2004.

Mango, Marlia Mundell, *Silver from Early Byzantium: The Kaper Koraon and Related Treasures*. Baltimore, MD: Trustees of the Walters Art Gallery, 1986.

Mango, Marlia Mundell and Anna Bennet, *The Sevso Treasure: Part I, Art Historical Description and Inscriptions, Methods of Manufacture and Scientific Analyses*. Ann Arbor, MI: Journal of Roman Archaeology, 1994.

Noga-Banai, Galit, *The Trophies of the Martyrs: An Art Historical Study of Early Christian Silver Reliquaries*. Oxford: Oxford University Press, 2008.

Painter, Kenneth S., *The Mildenhall Treasure: Roman Silver from East Anglia*. London: British Museum Publications, 1977.

_____________, *The Wealth of the Roman World: Gold and Silver AD 300–700*. London: British Museum, 1977.

16

EARLY CHRISTIAN ILLUMINATED MANUSCRIPTS

Dorothy Verkerk

Although early Christians did not invent the codex, it is widely accepted that they chose this form well before it became dominant in the Greco-Roman as well as Jewish cultures, and they did not waver from this choice whether as a persecuted minority or a favored majority. Unlike the scroll, the codex helped to unify a diversity of texts with multiple authors, multiple audiences, and multiple ethnicities and languages. The codex also had the advantage that it was not associated with any sacred texts, such as Torah scrolls, and was useful for study purposes. While the texts were gathered together early in Christianity, the surviving manuscripts indicate that the luxury of illuminations would take centuries to develop in any number. Illuminated manuscripts are rare, in part because they were not produced in the numbers of codices with only text and their expense was also prohibitive. It is not known how many illuminated manuscripts were made, but their appearance, and survival, begins in the early fifth century when Christianity was well established and enjoyed a wealthy patronage. Despite the small number of extant manuscripts, the variations in book design and the relationship of illustration to text indicate that between the years 400 and 700 was a period of experimentation. It can also be suggested that the earliest illuminated books were a relatively straightforward illustration of the text, while later illuminated books show a greater sophistication in how pictures might help to convey the Christian message. This chapter is organized by the type of book being illustrated moving from the Old Testament to the New Testament and then to more secular books. What is noticeable in this survey is that there are no surviving illustrated pandects, or a complete Bible as is used today. Single books, or gatherings of books such as the Pentateuch or the four Gospels, were the norm. Missing from this survey is an illustrated Psalter, since no illustrated book of Psalms has been discovered in the early Christian period; perhaps because poetry is more challenging to illustrate than narrative stories. In this early Christian period, however, there is a notable attempt to align Church teaching with the challenges of illustrating a sacred text. Although the illuminated codex was not the norm in the Roman Empire, the books created for an elite Christian audience would be firmly rooted in the aesthetics of the old religions.

Old Testament

The earliest Old Testament book with illustrations is the so-called *Quedlinburg Itala* (Berlin, Dt. Staatsbib., Cod. theol. lat., fol. 485) that is believed to have been produced in Rome in the second quarter of the fifth century (Figure 16.1). The five surviving pages, four with illustrations, were in poor condition when they were glued into the bindings of Quedlinburg's parish accounts in 1618. Two fragments of a sixth page also survive. Discovered between 1865 and 1887, the leaves contain parts of the four books of Kings (1–2 Samuel, 1–2 Kings). The text is one of many Latin texts in circulation before Jerome's canonical translation, the Vulgate, was fully accepted. Each page is filled with two or more illustrations in rectangular dark red frames and interspersed within the text. Multi-figural narrative scenes are set against backgrounds painted in an illusionistic style, suggesting that the reader is looking through a window into the distance.

Figure 16.1 Scenes from 1 Samuel 15, *Quedlinburg Itala*. Rome, early 5th century. Wikimedia Commons.

A fascinating aspect of the manuscript is the lengthy instructions in a cursive hand, which have become visible due to the flaking of the top layer of paint. They are formulated as guides to the artist: for example, "Make where the prophet withdraws and when King Saul tries to hold him by the end of his mantle, cuts it off, and withdraws running (fol. 2)." The kingly figures such as Saul, David, Solomon, and Agag are dressed in the garb of a Roman emperor, implying that contemporary patrons had a taste for linking the imperial Roman with the Old Testament past. When new subjects were needed for Christian art, artists often relied on stock motifs, such as a representation of the emperor sacrificing, which could be the model for an Old Testament king. Although reproductions of the illustrations do not show this feature, golden highlights were used throughout the illustration on items such as robes. The fourteen surviving miniatures that illustrate even minor scenes and the instructions to the artist(s) indicate that a complex, lengthy and expensive pictorial cycle was specially created for this book. Based on stylistic evidence and the choice of Latin, there is general agreement that the book was created in Rome.

There are two surviving illustrated Genesis manuscripts, the *Cotton Genesis* (London, BL, Cotton MS. Otho B. VI) and the *Vienna Genesis* (Vienna, Österreich. Nbib., Cod. theol. gr. 31). Both contain the text of Genesis alone and were originally profusely illustrated: the *Cotton Genesis* with an estimated 339 miniatures, and the *Vienna Genesis* with an estimated 400 separate scenes on 96 pages, of which only 24 have survived. Both manuscripts, which were produced in the late fifth century, or more probably the sixth, might be considered picture books; but the approach varies dramatically in both format and the relation of text to image. In the *Cotton Genesis*, the more numerous illustrations are interspersed within the Greek text, which was written above and below the framed scenes. Here the illustrations complement the text, while in the *Vienna Genesis* the pictures are the primary focus. Also, in the *Vienna Genesis*, the scenes are often left unframed so that they cohabitate with the abbreviated text. Some have argued for an Egyptian patron for the *Cotton Genesis*, though this has not been universally accepted.[1] Because the *Vienna Genesis*' parchment pages were stained purple and written in silver, some others have argued for an eastern Byzantine origin since purple is the color associated with royalty and the royal court.[2] In many further ways the manuscripts differ in their treatment of iconographic subjects and their style.

The *Cotton Genesis* was severely burned when, on 23 October 1731, a fire broke out at Ashburnham House, Westminster, where the manuscript was temporarily being housed. In the fierce heat of the fire, the parchment leaves shrank and were partly burned or charred. The fragments of the miniatures show that the artists adhered closely to the biblical narrative; for example, the scene of Lot and the Sodomites shows Lot gesticulating toward the crowd while an angel tries to pull him into the protection of his house. The painters of the creation scenes deviated from an exact rendering of the Genesis text by giving the Creator a cruciform halo, confirming that the Christ Logos was active in the beginning. By this simple means, the opening words of Genesis are linked to the opening words of the Gospel of John. The lively rendering of figures, the use of personifications for the six days of creation, and the framing of the scene in an atmospheric perspective places the *Cotton Genesis* in the world of late Roman painting. The *Cotton Genesis*, before entering the British Library, was in Venice where it served as the model for the early thirteenth-century creation mosaic in the Basilica of San Marco.[3]

The *Vienna Genesis* was written in silver on purple-dyed parchment with the lower half of each page dedicated to illustration. The Genesis text, written in Greek, is better described as a paraphrase, suggesting that the goal of the patron was to commission a Genesis in pictures for an audience already well versed in the stories. Like the *Cotton Genesis*, it uses personifications, and there is lots of attention given to architectural elements and scenery details such as trees. Unlike the *Cotton Genesis*, the scenes are arranged in three formats: a single scene, several scenes arranged in registers or several scenes that rotate around as if a continuous frieze turns back on itself and down. The artists of the manuscript were well attuned to the drama of the biblical stories, and the emphasis on the pictures may have encouraged a heightened emotional approach to the illustrations. For example, in the scene where Joseph rejects the advances of Potiphar's wife, Joseph dramatically bolts toward an open door while the woman desperately clings to the robes of the fleeing man. The majority of scholarship has focused on the place of origin, the date, or the influence of possible Jewish sources, so there remains much to be done in understanding the relationship of text and the programmatic illustration of the Genesis text. The damage to the surviving illustrations in both manuscripts may limit our understanding, but what does survive suggests that artists and patrons could vary widely in how they wanted a Genesis codex illustrated and how it would have been used.

The *Ashburnham Pentateuch* (late sixth–early seventh century; Paris, Bib. N., MS. nuov. acq. lat. 2334) is different again, with a liveliness and complexity not found in contemporary manuscripts. In addition to a frontispiece, it contains eighteen miniatures out of an estimated original total of sixty-nine, which are distributed irregularly through the first four books of the Old Testament. No part of Deuteronomy has survived, but it was presumably also illustrated. Most of the illustrations occupy a full page and are complex compositions, often subdivided into separate scenes in roughly horizontal registers. Unlike the *Quedlinburg Itala* or the Genesis manuscripts, the *Ashburnham Pentateuch* lacks the luxury trappings of gold highlights or stained purple pages. There are numerous lengthy inscriptions within the images, and there is a distinctive use of tertiary colors such as salmon pink or light green. The manuscript has been described as a teaching codex since the illustrations often deviate from the text to speak to a Christian, rather than a Jewish, audience.

In the scene of Moses offering holocausts, for example, a chalice, two pots, and loaves of bread have been substituted for the burnt offerings of the Exodus text (Figure 16.2). The substitution suggests a typological interpretation where Christians are the new Israelites and the priests are the new Levites. The illustrations, or rather interpretations, of the text go even further to explain what St Augustine described as stories that were "wont to cause anxiety." In the scene of the slaying of the Egyptian firstborn, the slain children are shown, not as infants as the text implies, but as older and black, an ominous attempt to represent their sinful nature and thus their deserving of death by the destroyer. The manuscript is from the Latin West, rather than Greek East, and it has been argued that it is Italian in origin. The style varies considerably from the eastern ones in the amount of detail given over to architecture, fauna, furniture and clothing. The manuscript was at the monastery of Saint-Martin of Tours in the middle ages, and it was consulted for the frontispiece cycles of Carolingian Bibles and in the late eleventh century for the decoration of the local church of St Julien.[4]

New Testament

The surviving New Testament books also show a remarkable variation in style, format and the relation of text to image. The wealth and desires of the patron no doubt played a large part in their production, but it also indicates that there was no one notion about what a New Testament book should look like in terms of its design. The approach to New Testament books was similar to that of the Old Testament: books were gathered together thematically rather than containing all the Gospels, the Acts, Letters, and the Apocalypse.

Figure 16.2 Scenes with Moses, *Ashburnham Pentateuch*. Latin West, late 6th/early 7th century. Wikimedia Commons.

The restoration and rebinding of the two Ethiopian Abba Garima Gospels have brought these ancient gospel books to the attention of students of early Christianity.[5] The oldest is Abba Garima III and dated to 390–650, while Abba Garima I is dated to 530–660.[6] Originally bound with Abba Garima III was a third gospel book, Abba Garima II, of a later date. Abba

Garima III has 322 pages, including a portrait of Eusebius, elaborately decorated canon table pages, an architectural structure that perhaps references the Temple in Jerusalem and four Evangelist portraits before each of their books. Matthew, Luke, and John are standing iconic figures holding a codex. Mark is given special treatment (Figure 16.3). He is seated on a leopard skin chair in front of a lectern that takes the form of a spotted dolphin, perhaps a reference to Christ's disciples as "fishers of men" (Matt. 4:19). Mark may have been given distinct treatment since he is credited with bringing Christianity to Egypt where he was martyred in Alexandria. The gospel texts are written in Ge'ez, the Ethiopic language of the Kingdom of Axum, which is the language of the Ethiopian Church. Also written in Ge'ez, Abba Garima I consists of 348 pages, beginning with 11 illuminated pages, including canon tables set in arcades. Inserted in the middle of the canon tables and the letter to Eusebius is a four-columned tholos, or small round temple. The Abba Garima I cover is believed to have been made at the same time as the manuscript, making it one of the earliest surviving book covers. Although it is missing its precious stones, the cover is made from gilt-copper backed with wood and decorated with a large foliated cross. According to tradition, Saint Abba Garima, one of the Nine Saints credited with establishing Christianity in Ethiopia by founding monasteries, wrote and illustrated the gospel books. If the carbon dating is correct, Abba Garima III, the older of the two gospels, would have been produced before the revered Abba resided at the monastery.

The *Glazier Codex* (New York, PML, Glazier Coll. G.67) contains the text of Acts 1:1–15:3, written in an archaic Coptic known as Middle Egyptian Proper. The wooden binding is thought to be original to the codex, suggesting that there would have been a companion volume containing the second half of the Book of Acts. Carbon dating of the leather on the binding, done in 1994, suggests a date between 420 and 598, pushing back the date of 400 assigned to the codex on paleographic evidence. The codex contains a decorated cross at the end of the text (Figure 16.4). Interlace fills the arms of the cross while peacocks flank the trunk and birds perch on the arms. The cross, with vegetation sprouting from it, takes the shape of an ankh, the hieroglyph for life that would have been understood by Egyptian Christians as a reference to the resurrection. The *Codex Usserianus Primus* (Dublin, Trinity Coll. Lib. 55), an early seventh-century gospel made in Ireland, also preserves a decorated cross between the end of Luke and the beginning of Mark, suggesting that the insertion of a cross at the end of a sacred book was widely practiced. Like the *Glazier* cross, the *Usserianus* cross contains an end times connotation with the inclusion of the alpha and the omega hanging from the arms of the cross.

In the Greek East, the period known as Iconoclasm may have had a dampening effect on book illumination. Only the *Rossano Gospels* (Rossano, Mus. Dioc.) and the Sinope fragment (Paris, Bib. N., MS. suppl. gr. 1286; both probably sixth-century) survive from before the iconoclastic controversy. The Syriac *Rabbula Gospels* (586; Florence, Bib. Medicea-Laurenziana, MS. Plut.I.56) can be added to this list; however, none of these is complete, and each adopts a radically different scheme for its format, style, and the relation between text and image.

The *Sinope Gospels* survive in fragmentary shape; however, what remains indicates that this was a luxury gospel book with purple-dyed pages and a large uncial script written in gold and silver. Only the text of Matthew survives in forty-four pages. The large font, the single column of text per page, and the Matthew text alone suggest that it may have been a single volume with the other gospels bound separately and that money was no object in

Figure 16.3 Evangelist Mark, Abba Garima Monastery, MS III. Ethiopia, c. 390–650. © Michael Gervers, 2004.

Figure 16.4 Decorated cross from the end of the text of Acts of the Apostles, *Glazier* codex (New York, Pierpont Morgan Library, MS G.67, p. 215). Middle Egypt, 5th century. Gift of the Trustees of the William F. Glazier Collection in 1984.

the creation of this book. Five small illustrations are found in the lower margins of the text pages: the feast of Herod and death of John the Baptist; feeding the five thousand; feeding the four thousand; the healing of the blind man from Jericho; the cursing of the fig tree. All are unframed and interlock with the text. The narrative scenes are flanked by two Old Testament figures who present texts that show that the scenes are a fulfillment of Old Testament prophecies. In the feast of Herod and the death of John, for example, Moses stands to the left holding a large scroll with the text of Exodus 16:15, "It is the bread that the Lord has given you to eat." To the right, next to the scene of John's followers finding his decapitated body, David's scroll reads from Psalm 116:15, "Precious in the sight of the Lord is the death of his faithful one."

The *Rossano Gospels* (*Codex purpureus Rossanensis*) are similar in many ways to the *Sinope Gospel*. Only the books of Matthew and Mark are included, suggesting there may have been a companion volume of Luke and John. It too features purple dyed parchment, silver and gold ink, and a typological approach to text and image. Unlike the *Sinope Gospel*, the *Rossano* makes several additions to the *Sinope* codex and reworks the relationship on the page between prophesy and narrative. In the *Rossano* much space was given over to Old Testament figures holding scrolls with inscriptions relevant to the scenes from the life of Christ, which are placed above, creating the visual link that the old covenant anticipates the new covenant. The single surviving full-page evangelist portrait, that of Mark, is thought to be a later addition, but one of the prefatory pages arranges all four evangelists together in medallion busts within a circular configuration. This is one of the earliest attempts to visually indicate the harmony of the four gospels, which often contain discrepancies in the story of Christ's life and ministry. The narrative scenes are gathered together in the front of the gospels with selections from the liturgical readings for passion week.

The scene of the wise and foolish virgins, a parable of the last judgment, contains elaborations of the allegorical story that direct the viewer to the correct understanding of the story (Figure 16.5). The women are aligned in a row: the five wise carrying flaming torches are

Figure 16.5 The wise and foolish virgins, *Rossano Gospels*. Constantinople or Syria, 6th century. Wikimedia Commons.

dressed in white robes signifying their purity; the five foolish, locked outside the golden gate of the marriage chamber, are attired in colorful robes indicating their more worldly behavior. The bridegroom's house is depicted as a lush orchard recalling the Garden of Eden, with the four rivers of Paradise flowing from the base of the trees. The bridegroom, with a cruciform halo, indicates that he is Christ who gathers his faithful into Paradise. The *Rossano Gospels* adds an unusual scene as a full-page illustration. It depicts the high priests Annas and Caiaphas bringing Christ before Pilate (Figure 16.6). The monumentally conceived composition with Pilate seated on a throne complete with flanking standards bearing the portraits of Roman emperors has prompted scholars to suggest that the departure from the book's design is the influence of a wall painting that was well known and depicted this scene.[7] The relationship between wall painting and book illustration has been discussed for decades, but there is no consensus on the topic to date. Like the *Sinope Gospels*, there is also no consensus on the place of origin for the *Rossano Gospels*, though there is general agreement that they are both from the Christian East, perhaps Syria or Constantinople.

Figure 16.6 Christ before Pilate, *Rossano Gospels*. Constantinople or Syria, 6th century. Wikimedia Commons.

The provenance and date of the *Rabbula Gospels* are not contested since it contains a colophon that states that the monk Rabbula, in the year 586, wrote the manuscript at the monastery of Saint John of Beth Zagba, which was located somewhere between Antioch and Damascus. The text is written from right to left in a Syriac Peshitta version of the gospels. The illustrations thus are also in a sequence that is the reverse of those in Latin or Greek. In the *Rabbula Gospels*, particular attention was paid to the Eusebian Canon tables, which are diagrams drawn up to assist the reader in cross-referencing between numbered passages in the text. Eusebius was a scholar and bishop who lived in Caesarea around 300 (260/265–339/340), who recognized that each gospel writer told the story through his unique perspective; thus, there were some small discrepancies in the gospel accounts. By emphasizing the harmony of the gospels, he compared the same story from different gospels to obtain a greater understanding of its significance. The canon tables are depicted as an arcaded arch, with vegetation sprouting from the arches and birds perched along the roofline (Figure 16.7). In the margins are figures of Old Testament prophets

Figure 16.7 Canon tables, *Rabbula Gospels*. Syria, 6th century. Wikimedia Commons.

and scenes from the New Testament that start with the annunciation to Zacharias and culminate in the scene of Christ before Pilate. Again, this arrangement is another strategy to stress the unity of the Old and the New Testaments.

The series of canon tables ends in the double opening of the four gospel writers seated under two arches, similar in style to the previous canon tables. Other "portraits" include Eusebius and Ammonius, who created the canon table and verse numbering system. In addition to the smaller vignettes, there is a full-page illustration of Crucifixion and the three Marys at the empty tomb that gives prominence to the Crucifixion and Resurrection. The story continues with three full-page miniatures depicting scenes from the Book of Acts: the Ascension, Pentecost, and the choosing of Matthias, who replaced Judas as the twelfth apostle. Non-narrative scenes include the Virgin Mary holding the Christ Child, and a scene of Christ Enthroned surrounded by monks who offer him the manuscript. The curious choice of the Matthias scene, which is a relatively obscure text, and the inclusion of the monks giving Christ the manuscript is one of the earliest examples of contemporary patrons linking themselves as the successors of the Apostles. The Syriac Peshitta text, which means simple or plain, and the canon tables for cross-referencing, suggest that the book was meant for accessible and serious study of the gospels. The lavish illustrations, some of which show later alterations, indicate the wealth of talent in the monastery of Beth Zagba.

The two folios of the *Golden Canon Tables* (late sixth or early seventh century; London, Brit. Lib., Add. MS 5111) are all that remains of what must have been a truly luxurious gospel book (Figure 16.8). Written in Greek, the first fragment includes the letter of Eusebius to Carpianus

Figure 16.8 Golden Canon Tables from a gospel book, late 6th/early 7th century. Wikimedia Commons.

that explains his work and the first canon table; the second fragment continues with the eighth and tenth canons. The pages are permeated with gold dust, making them even more rare and sumptuous than the purple-dyed books. As with the *Rabbula Gospels*, the cross-references are framed by elaborate architectural columns ornamented with stylized vegetation and birds. Within the arch of the canon table are bust-length portraits, no doubt depicting the gospel writers. The original pages were larger than what survives since they were cut down and bound up into a twelfth-century Latin gospel book.

The *Corpus Christi Gospels* (late sixth-century; Cambridge, Corpus Christi Coll. Lib., MS. 286) is one of the earliest surviving gospels known to have been used in the British Isles. It is believed to have been made in Italy since scholars generally agree on a sixth-century Italian script.[8] This Vulgate Latin book was arranged in a completely different format from the other extant gospels, though a lot has to be reconstructed since only two illuminated pages survive. Before St Luke's Gospel, there is a single page with twelve small framed scenes illustrating the life of Christ from the entry into Jerusalem up to Christ carrying the cross (see Figure 18.11). On the reverse of this page, facing the start of the Gospel, St Luke is seated like a philosopher, holding an open codex, with his symbol of the ox above (Figure 16.9). On either side of St Luke, within the columns of

Figure 16.9 Evangelist Luke and scenes from the life of Christ (Oxford, Corpus Christi College, MS 286, f. 125r). Italy, 6th century. Master and Fellows of Corpus Christi College, Cambridge.

the architectural frame, are an additional 12 scenes from the life of Christ from the annunciation to the Virgin Mary to Zacchaeus in the sycamore tree.

Unlike the style of illustration found in manuscripts such as the *Rabbula Gospels*, which are still tethered to the classical style, the *Corpus Christi* artist relied on a more linear technique with thin washes of color. The scenes emphasize the human figure with limited references to landscape features. Trees, for example, are stylized as to resemble the charming drawings of childhood. The scenes are simplified and abridged, relying on the viewer's knowledge of the biblical stories to identify the scenes. This may not have been as strategic an approach since a later scribe has penned in captions to identify the scenes. It is assumed that the full-page scenes followed by an evangelist portrait would have also prefaced the other three gospels.

Legend has it that St Augustine of Canterbury, by order of Pope Gregory the Great, brought the gospel book with him from Rome in 597 to aid in his mission to the British Isles. The connection to St Augustine was an early one since the codex was initially kept at St Augustine's abbey in Canterbury and venerated as a relic of the saint. The manuscript remained at Canterbury until the Dissolution of the Monasteries (1535–1540) and seemed to have been consulted by Insular and Romanesque artists. In January of 2016 the *Corpus Christi Gospels* once again revisited Canterbury to preside over the enthronement of the new Archbishop of Canterbury. This is a venerable tradition since it is well known that gospel books were placed on an altar or a throne during early Christian synods to remind the participants of Christ's presence.

Extra-biblical manuscripts

A small number of disparate codices raise the question of the range of manuscript types that were illustrated in the fourth to the seventh century. The most intriguing is the handsomely illustrated Calendar of the year 354 (*Calendar of Filocalus*), known principally through a 17th-century copy (Rome, Vatican, Bib. Apostolica, MS. Barb. lat. 2154). The dedication asks the patron, Valentinus, to flourish in God and names the scribe/illustrator as Filocalus. The full-page illustrations were portraits of emperors, zodiac signs, and personifications of months and cities, making it more of an almanac than a calendar. To some degree, all medieval calendar illustrations with their interest in Labors of the Months, zodiac signs, and personifications, can be seen to have developed from books such as the Calendar.

Another type of manuscript, the *Notitia dignitatum*, is a register of late Roman military and civil officials, with about 100 full-page illustrations of their insignia. Its existence is also known only through medieval copies (Codex Spirensis; Speyer Cathedral) and post-medieval copies (Munich, Bayer. Staatsbib., Clm. 10291; Oxford, Bodleian Lib., Canonici Miscell. 378). Its images were remarkably varied in compositional terms, including ships, chariots, townscapes and landscapes, and figures in a medallion, bust, or full-length formats. It is thought to be based on an original made around 400. The *Notitia Dignitatum* has preserved for us, as no other document has done, a complete outline view of the Roman administrative system in the early fifth century.

If the *Notitia Dignitatum* gives a picture of Roman organization, the *Corpus agrimensorum* gives a glimpse into the more pedestrian life of the countryside. A land-surveying treatise, it survives in an early sixth-century manuscript from northern Italy (Wolfenbüttel, Herzog August Bib., Cod. Guelf. 36. 23A, 'Codex Arcerianus A'). In addition to geometric diagrams and schematic views of town and countryside, the codex contains a fine full-page drawing of a seated author. The text is written in an uncial script, with red letters indicating the beginnings of paragraphs. Breaks in the single column of text allowed unframed illustrations to be inserted. The book gives instructions on how to divide a land properly for taxation, or how to find the best access route into a city for the design of a new road. The condition of the manuscript and the handsomeness of the illustrations suggest that this was a manuscript an affluent patron may have used to consult on judicial matters concerning land or property rights and not a handbook that would have been used in the field.

Early Christian patrons were also interested in herbals, which are directories of plants, their properties, and their medicinal uses. Herbals most likely were at first not illustrated, but in Late Antiquity they acquired illustrations. The *Johnson Papyrus* (London, Well. Lib. MS.5753), dated to 400, is thought to be the earliest surviving example of an illustrated herbal, though a mere five fragments currently exist. One of these fragments of a page from the illustrated herbal from Egypt shows a plant that is possibly *Symphytum officinale*, or comfrey.[9] The herbal was made of papyrus, a plant that flourished in the valley of the Nile, and the text is in Greek, the language of science throughout the eastern Mediterranean at this time. The fragment is probably from a copy of the herbal of Dioscorides of Anazarbus, a first-century Greek physician born in Asia Minor whose work became the foundation text of medieval botany. The date of the fragment suggests that most likely it was from a codex, as does the fact that it is written and illuminated on both sides, which would have made it difficult to consult in roll form.

Dioscorides' *De materia medica* (the Vienna Dioskurides, *c.* 512; Vienna, Österreich. Nbib., Cod. med. gr. 1), is justifiably one of the most famous herbals. It is an extensive compendium of almost 1,000 pages dealing with medicinal plants, drugs of animal origin (e.g., birds, earthworms, fish, and jellyfish), paraphrases of treatises on birds, and antidotes to venomous bites and other types of poisoning, attributed to Euteknios after Nicander's *Theriaka* and *Alexipharmaka* of the second century. Its predominant illustration consists of 383 full-page illustrations of plants, painted with an extraordinary naturalism and botanical accuracy. There are also full-page frontispieces of a peacock; a group of doctors around the centaur Cheiron, who was noted for educating youth, medicine, music, archery, hunting, and prophecy; and a second group around Galen (129–*c.* 200), the Greek physician, surgeon and philosopher. Personifications are used throughout such as Discovery displaying a mandrake to Dioscorides, and Thought holding a mandrake while an artist paints it on a sheet pinned to an easel and Dioscorides writes about it in a book on his knee. Anicia Juliana, the owner of the manuscript, is shown enthroned between Magnanimity and Prudence, and receiving the book from Gratitude of the Arts.

The inscription around the dedication portrait (f. 6v) of Anicia Juliana states that the book was a gift from the people of Constantinople for her gift, in 512/13, of a church dedicated to the Virgin. An extremely wealthy member of the imperial family, Anicia Juliana's use of ancient Greek knowledge and mythology, coupled with her patronage of church building, shows how the Hellenistic world and the Christian world were blended. The *Vienna Dioskurides* is thus an early example of how the knowledge and learning of the classical world would be preserved and passed on through Christian patrons and their books.

The advent of Christianity did not mean the cessation of interest in the classics. The principal direct evidence for the illustration of the Latin literary classics is provided by two manuscripts of Vergil. Other texts, such as an illustrated selection of *Comedies* of Terence, or the *Psychomachia* of Prudentius (d. 410), both well known through Carolingian (e.g., 9th century; Rome, Vatican, Bib. Apostolica, MS. lat. 3868) and later copies, may also be derived from books that are now lost. The *Vatican Vergil* and the *Roman Vergil* (Rome, Vatican, Bib. Apostolica, MSS lat. 3225 and 3867 respectively) provide a sharp contrast in the format and style of the illustrations. The *Vatican Vergil* is dated, like the *Quedlinburg Itala*, within a couple of decades of the year 400 and is thought to have been made in Rome.[10] The original codex may have had as many as 280 illustrations, of which some 50 have survived. The remaining pictures illustrate passages of the

Aeneid (41) and the *Georgics* (9). The illustrations are framed by a thin black line and then again in a thicker red line, a technique that enhances the illusion of looking into a window to a seascape or a landscape.

The capital script is written in one column in a manner that was typical of fine books; the scribe left two-thirds or sometimes an entire page for the insertion of illustrations, making the original a picture book rivaling the *Quedlinburg Itala* or the *Vienna Genesis*. The *Vatican Vergil* is painted in a convincing illusionistic style, with figures carefully modelled and placed within interiors, or in landscapes that recede into the distance. Like the biblical manuscripts, later centuries collected and studied the *Vatican Vergil*; for example, it was known to have been in the monastery of Saint-Martin in Tours by the ninth century where two of its figures were copied for a Bible illustration. The book then traveled to Rome where it was studied by artists and antiquarians in the sixteenth century before finally finding its way to the Vatican Library.

The *Roman Vergil* is dated toward the end of the fifth century and is also thought to have been made in Rome for a wealthy patron.[11] Originally, this exceptionally large book would have been composed of 410 pages of all Vergil's known writings and was intended to be placed on a stand as a display copy to impress visitors with the owner's taste and wealth. Today, about a quarter of the text is lost, and the prefatory illustrations have also been lost: three of the ten illustrations to the *Ecologues*; six of the eight *Georgics* illustrations, and fourteen of the original twenty-four *Aeneid* illustrations. The style of the figures, unlike the *Vatican Vergil*, anticipates the medieval aesthetic that will often exaggerate gestures and scale to bring out the expressive features of the narrative. A notable difference between the two Vergil manuscripts is how the frames around the pictures are used: in the Vatican example, the frame serves to increase the illusion of depth; in the *Roman Vergil*, the frame is often used as a ground line or is even ignored as objects and figures transgress its borders. These two Vergil codices and their illustrations are indicative of the trend away from the Classical style of the Roman Empire and the move toward the more expressive style of the early Medieval period.

Final thoughts

In this brief survey of illuminated manuscripts from the early Christian period, some general observations can be made. The challenge for artists illustrating the biblical text was twofold: how to fill in the visual information lacking in the text to make a reasonable representation of the narrative and, secondly, how to make the illustration theologically aligned with Church teaching. In the *Cotton Genesis*, for example, there is an attempt to insert the concept of the Trinity lacking in the Genesis text. By the sixth century, there is a growing boldness with how images could be manipulated to bring out the correct Christian understanding of the biblical stories from Jewish history, as in the *Ashburnham Pentateuch*. And finally, there was experimentation with emphasizing the unity not only of the Old and New Testaments, but also the unity of the four Gospels. What is remarkable is how these books were studied, collected, and copied in the following centuries, no doubt because they were understood to be "ancient" and a tangible link to the early Christians.

Notes

1 Kurt Weitzmann and Herbert Kessler, *The Cotton Genesis: British Library Codex Cotton Otho B. VI, Illustrations in the Manuscripts of the Septuagint*, Vol. 1 (Princeton, NJ: Princeton University Press, 1986), 30–34; and Anthony Cutler, "The End of Antiquity in Two Illuminated Manuscripts," *Journal of Roman Archaeology* 11 (1989): 401–409, argue for an Egyptian origin.

2 John Lowden, "Concerning the Cotton Genesis and Other Illustrated Manuscripts of Genesis," *Gesta* 31 (1992): 40–53.
3 Weitzmann and Kessler, *Cotton Genesis*, 18–20; Penny Howell Jolly, *Made in God's Image? Eve and Adam in the Genesis Mosaics of San Marco* (Berkeley, CA: University of California Press, 1997).
4 Herbert Kessler, *The Illustrated Bibles from Tours*, Studies in Manuscript Illumination no. 7 (Princeton, NJ: Princeton University Press, 1977), 139–143; Annabelle S. Cahn, "A Note: The Missing Model of the Saint-Julien de Tours Frescoes and the 'Ashburnham Pentateuch' Miniatures," *Cahiers archéologiques* 16 (1966): 203–207.
5 Mark Winstanley, "Tsbook – (Tigrinya for Good). An Ethiopian Odyssey – and the repair of the illuminated pages of the 6th-century Gospel of Abba Garima," *Skin Deep* 23 (2007): 2–10; Lester Capon, "Extreme bookbinding – a fascinating preservation project in Ethiopia," *Skin Deep* 26 (2008): 2–11.
6 The numbering of the manuscripts follows historical usage rather than the numbers used by Mercier and the Ethiopian Heritage Fund: Jacques Mercier, "La peinture éthiopienneà l'époque axoumite et au XVIIIe siècle," *Académie des Inscriptions & Belles Lettres. Comptes Rendus* (2000): 35–71. Mercier Garima 1 = Abba Garima I, Mercier Garima 2 = Abba Garima III and Mercier Garima 3 = Abba Garima II.
7 William C. Loerke, "The Miniatures of the Trial in the Rossano Gospels," *The Art Bulletin* 43 (1961): 171–195.
8 Patrick P. McGurk, *Latin Gospel Books from AD 400 to AD 800* (Paris: Éditions "Érasme," 1961).
9 David Leith, "The Antinoopolis Illustrated Herbal (PJohnson + PAntin. 3.214 = MP3 2095)," *Zeitschrift für Papyrologie und Epigraphik* 156 (2006): 141–156.
10 David H. Wright, *The Vatican Vergil: A Masterpiece of Late Antique Art* (Berkeley, CA: University of California Press, 1993), 84–90.
11 David H. Wright, *The Roman Vergil and the Origins of Medieval Book Design* (Toronto: University of Toronto Press, 2002), 7.

Further reading

Bober, Harry. "On the Illumination of the Glazier Codex: A Contribution to Early Coptic Art and its Relation to Hiberno-Saxon Interlace." In *Homage to a Bookman*, edited by Hellmut Lehmann-Haupt, 31–49. Berlin: Mann, 1967.

Brown, Michelle P., ed. *In the Beginning: Bibles Before the Year 1000*. Washington, DC: Freer Gallery of Art and Arthur M. Sackler Gallery, 2006.

Gamble, Harry Y. *Books and Readers in the Early Church: A History of Early Christian Texts*. New Haven, CT: Yale University Press, 1995.

Hoffman, Eva R. *Late Antique and Medieval Art of the Mediterranean World*. Malden, MA: Blackwell, 2007.

Levin, Isabelle I. *The Quedlinburg Itala: The Oldest Illustrated Biblical Manuscript*. Leiden: E.J. Brill, 1985.

Lowden, John. "Concerning the Cotton Genesis and Other Illustrated Manuscripts of Genesis." *Gesta* 31 (1992); 40–53.

____________. "The Beginnings of Biblical Illustration." In *Late Antique and Medieval Art of the Mediterranean World*, edited by Eva R. Hoffman, 117–34. Malden, MA: Blackwell, 2007.

McKenzie, Judith S. and Francis Watson. *The Garima Gospels: Early Illuminated Gospel Books from Ethiopia*. Oxford: Manar al-Athar, 2016.

Sharpe, John Lawerence and Kimberly van Kampen, eds. *The Bible as Book: The Manuscript Tradition*. New Castle, DE: Oak Knoll Press & British Library, 1998.

Sörries, Reinner. *Christlich-antike Buchmalerei im Überblick*. Wiesbaden: Dr. Ludwig Reichert Verlag, 1993.

Stanley, Timothy. "The Early Codex: Recovering Its Cosmopolitan Consequences." *Biblical Interpretation* 23 (2015): 369–98.

Stevenson, Thomas B. *Miniature Decoration in the Vatican Vergil: A Study in Late Antique Iconography*. Tübingen: Verlag E. Wasmuth, 1983.

Verkerk, Dorothy. "Black Servant, Black Demon: Color Ideology in the Ashburnham Pentateuch," *Journal for Medieval and Early Modern History* 31 (2001): 57–78.

_____________. *Early Medieval Bible Illumination and the Ashburnham Pentateuch*. Cambridge: Cambridge University Press, 2004.

Weitzmann, Kurt, ed. *Age of Spirituality: Late Antique and Early Christian Art, Third to Seventh Century*. New York, NY: The Metropolitan Museum of Art, 1979.

Weitzmann, Kurt. *Late Antique and Early Christian Book Illumination*. New York, NY: George Braziller, 1977.

Weitzman, Kurt and Herbert Kessler. *The Cotton Genesis: British Library Codex Cotton Otho B. VI, Illustrations in the Manuscripts of the Septuagint*, Vol. 1. Princeton, NJ: Princeton University Press, 1986.

Williams, John, ed. *Imaging the Early Medieval Bible*. University Park, PA: The Pennsylvania University Press, 1999.

Wormald, Francis. *The Miniatures in the Gospels of St Augustine*. Cambridge: Cambridge University Press, 1954.

Wright, David H. *The Roman Vergil and the Origins of Medieval Book Design*. Toronto: University of Toronto Press, 2002.

_____________. *The Vatican Vergil: A Masterpiece of Late Antique Art*. Berkeley, CA: University of California Press, 1993.

PART II

Themes

17
EARLY CHRISTIAN ART AND RITUAL

Michael Peppard

On the northwest shore of the Sea of Galilee, in an area now called Tabgha, the modern-day Church of the Multiplication stands guard over one of the most well-known examples of early Christian art in the Holy Land: a fifth-century mosaic of loaves and fishes (Figure 17.1). This early Byzantine mosaic floor commemorates Jesus's miraculous multiplication of his followers' meager victuals in order to feed thousands of people, a wonder narrated in all four of the canonical gospels. The fifth-century foundation covers an even earlier church on the site, which was visited by the pilgrim Egeria in 383. She notes, "the stone on which the Lord placed the bread has now been made into an altar. People who go there take away small pieces of the stone to

Figure 17.1 Floor mosaic with loaves and fishes. Church of the Multiplication, Tabgha, Galilee. Berthold Werner/Wikimedia Commons.

bring them prosperity, and they are very effective."[1] Today's pilgrims are not allowed such mementos, but the gift shop has plenty of other options. Hardly anyone leaves there without taking an image of that mosaic home in some form—on a postcard, a ceramic tile, or a coffee mug.

But there's a problem with the mosaic, or so it seems. Astute readers of the Bible know that Jesus begins with five loaves of bread; the mosaic here shows only four. Would the mosaicist have made such a glaring error, here at the very pilgrimage site for this event? One might conjecture that the fifth loaf needs to be imagined within the picture, as if buried down in the basket, behind or under the other four. However, when we examine other examples of the multiplication in early Christian art, a scene relatively common among depictions of Jesus's miracles, we do often see either five loaves or five baskets (Figures 17.2, 19.7). By comparison, this famous version at Tabgha seems unfulfilled, incomplete, in tension with its corresponding biblical narrative.

The resolution of the tension, the completion of the artistic program, and the fulfillment of the story only occur when one realizes the ritual context of the art. Early Christians consistently interpreted this miracle as foreshadowing the ritual meal called the eucharist or the Lord's supper. Egeria herself described how that rock, near which the mosaic was laid, was used as an altar for consecrated bread, a loaf multiplied through its fracture and distribution to pilgrims. The artistic form thus evokes an expectation in its viewers; in order to represent its biblical text faithfully, the art requires them to enact the text ritually, to break bread physically and share it graciously. In other words, the fifth loaf is not hiding there in the imagined basket; it is really there on the altar above. The mosaic, in its ritual context, invites present viewers to experience the eucharist as an extension of the past miracle. In this particular space, art and ritual work together to collapse time and fulfill the image. When the ritual context is taken into account, the supposed problem of this mosaic dissolves.

Most scholarship on early Christian art treats the interaction between visual form and biblical text. How does one do visual exegesis of art that was usually influenced by textual or narrative traditions but was not bound by correspondence to them? To that vital question, this chapter

Figure 17.2 Grave slab incised with five loaves and two fish. Museo Nazionale, Rome.

adds a third dimension. How can we interpret early Christian art at the nexus of text, image, and ritual? After an introductory summary of how two leading scholars have theorized the ritual contexts of ancient images, this chapter builds upon the opening example from Tabgha to explore ritual participation in artistic programs. It next moves beyond two-dimensional art to consider types of ritual objects from the period, particularly the special case of pilgrimage artifacts.

Bible, art, ritual

To deepen comprehension of early Christian art by incorporating the ritual dimension, one must broaden the set of correspondences and associations beyond the biblical. While the Bible does allude to the primary rituals of initiation and eucharist, sometimes only noncanonical narratives or liturgical sources—such as hagiographies, homilies, baptismal catecheses, church orders, and pilgrimage evidence—can provide the details to color in the guidelines of our understanding. Accessing actual rituals through these sources presents a challenge, of course, since the rituals are not witnessed as such, but only as mediated through texts and images, thereby creating a hermeneutic circle for the historian. But an example such as the mosaic from Tabgha shows that the benefits of an approach sensitive to ritual sometimes compensate for this challenge.

Among scholars successfully incorporating the ritual dimension of early Christian art, Robin Jensen's work stands out as the most fully developed, attending to the "ritual, visual, and theological dimensions" of artistic programs.[2] She is well aware of the potential pitfalls of such interdisciplinarity, since art historians, liturgical scholars, and textually trained interpreters of religion often begin from different premises. While Jensen inveighs against treating biblical narratives as a kind of "lode of definitive, preferential, or even validating data," she presses on with a rigorous interdisciplinarity that emphasizes the role of memory and imagination for interpreting both verbal and visual events.[3] Because so much extant early Christian art can be associated with a ritual context (baptism, anointing, pilgrimage, burial, funerary meal, etc.), an "effective visual exegesis requires the viewer to make certain connections that were experienced in liturgical performances (sermons, prayers, catecheses, and so forth) or developed in written treatises and commentaries. After all, an image generally, or at least initially, will mean what one has been taught that it means."[4]

Moreover, the ritual context of early Christian art already influences our interpretation of it, even if we do not always acknowledge that fact. For instance, the simple image of Noah coming out of a box-like ark (which Jensen calls the "Jack-in-the-box" style) has been found almost exclusively in funerary settings, and thus our interpretation of Noah as the individual "Christian rescued from death" is corroborated by a ritual context.[5] One could imagine, though, how the prevalent water imagery in the biblical narrative might engender different interpretations if the same Noah were to be found mainly in baptisteries (cf. 1 Pet 3:20) and the story's dove associated with that of Jesus's baptism (cf. patristic homilies). Or consider how the imagery of Jonah's ocean adventure is also found mainly in funerary contexts, indicating its symbolism of Christian hope for salvation from the belly of death (Figure 17.3; see also Figure 3.2, Figures 5.1–4). If other parts of the Jonah story were found mainly depicted on pulpits or book covers instead, we might rather interpret their connection to his preaching to Nineveh as a prophetic call to Christian evangelism—a reminder to preach God's word to those who had not yet heard it. Even the ubiquitous image of the shepherd with sheep depends for its meaning in part on ritual context: in a funerary context, it evokes the "good shepherd" who lays down his life for the sheep and opens the gate to life (John 10), but in a baptismal context, the more operative association may be Psalm 23, the shepherd who leads beside the waters, refreshes the soul (baptism), and also prepares a meal for an anointed guest (anointing and eucharist).

Figure 17.3 Marble table base carved with Jonah swallowed and cast up by the big fish. Metropolitan Museum of Art, gift of John Todd Edgar, 1877 (77.7).

Other art historians have also signaled ways forward in the interpretation of ritual spaces in antiquity. Jaś Elsner has encouraged a theorization of ancient visuality—ways of seeing—in specific ritualized moments from Greek, Roman, Jewish, and Christian materials. On the whole, he champions "a ritual-centered attitude to images in antiquity, which influenced both ways of seeing and ways of thinking about art."[6] What he calls ritual-centered visuality "may be defined in many ways—as the putting aside of normal identity and the acquisition of a temporary cult-generated identity, or as the surrendering of individuality to a more collective form of subjectivity constructed and controlled by the sacred site," among other possibilities.[7] Specific experiences conjured different modes of seeing, just as certain occasions call for one kind of rhetoric or another, one kind of dress or another. Thus religious participants' collective form of subjectivity may be considered constructed in part by their visuality, whether one sees oneself as an indistinguishable member of a flock of sheep or as an indistinguishably costumed and adorned member of a procession. "In effect, ritual-centered visuality denies the appropriateness of . . . interpreting images through the rules and desires of everyday life. It constructs a ritual barrier to the identifications and objectifications of the screen of discourse and posits a sacred possibility for vision, which is by definition more significant since it opens the viewer to confronting his or her god."[8] Ritual processes, in other words, prepare viewers to enact visual exegesis in typological, allegorical, and other distinctly theological modes. The everyday rules of visuality for encountering an image of a shepherd, a fish, a dove, a mother and child, a procession, a man reclining under a vine, or a battle scene are temporarily suspended. The viewer draws instead from the narrative and symbolic worlds specifically appropriate for a ritual context—and for which he or she has been both consciously and subconsciously prepared.

By this turn to subjectivities in understanding the ritual viewing of ancient art, Elsner must employ an imaginative process alongside other forms of analysis. In a series of case studies, he focuses on

> the pattern of cultural constructs and social discourses that stand between the retina and the world, a screen through which the subjects of this inquiry (that is, Greek and Roman people) had no choice but to look and through which they acquired (at least in part) their sense of subjectivity. Just as that screen—what I am calling "visuality"—was itself made up of subjective investments while being limited by the material and ideological constraints of the ancient cultural context, so our examination of it must depend upon a certain amount of empathetic imagination as well as critical analysis.[9]

In addition to this "empathetic imagination," he also gives credence to the precious few ancient testimonies about what it meant to see art. Coupling these testimonies with examples of the real presence of deities in statues and other figural objects, Elsner collapses the supposed dichotomy between the real and the imagined, the form and its instantiation, the god and its representation. "The represented is not just *in* the image," he writes, "the represented *is* the image."[10]

Elsner uses the first-person descriptions of art and ritual in authors such as Pausanias and Lucian as ways into the ritual-centeredness of Greco-Roman visuality. As a result, he questions the art historian's usual focus on naturalism and aesthetics instead of iconicism and ritual: "Art history has tended to assume that classical art—the art of naturalism and ekphrasis—was much more like Renaissance art and art writing than it was like the arts of the Middle Ages."[11] However, ancient evidence about people's experiences of statues, busts, and portraits indicates that the objects were highly charged with divine power and were encountered primarily through ritualized actions, e.g., at the culmination of pilgrimage, fasting, procession, or prayer.

Ritual participation in artistic programs

Early Christianity was a religion of conversion. In most cases, the life changes required of initiates were significant in terms of belief, ritual practice, and ethics. It is not surprising, then, that Christian leaders put considerable care into the design and execution of the artistic spaces that hosted the rites of initiation. We call these spaces "baptisteries" as a shorthand, since the immersion or affusion with water was usually central to the rites, and the fonts were often adorned with artistic programs. But we should not forget that many of the ancient baptisteries' painted walls did not survive, so we do not often know how other rituals of initiation (anointing, exorcism, eucharist) might have been portrayed visually. In addition, some regions of eastern Christianity seem to have emphasized anointing more than baptism and do not often prefer the term "baptistery" for their ritual spaces, as evidenced by inscriptions.

The artistic programs of baptisteries have been extensively documented and analyzed by Robin Jensen.[12] While there is no uniformity among extant baptisteries, nor can we discern clear chronological trends, they often include a cluster of popular visual motifs that relate to the ritual context. First, the shape of some fonts and the initiate's direction of passage through them required an embodiment of beliefs about baptism. Jensen notes several fonts whose shapes suggest a woman's vulva or womb, which "may have been specifically intended to emphasize the motif of rebirth from the womb of a spiritual mother."[13] Baptism as new birth was among the most widespread motifs in early Christianity, propagated in text, art, and ritual. Some baptisteries were also designed to move the initiate through a font from west to east, moving from darkness to light, even as the nighttime rituals—frequently called by the term *phōtismos* (illumination) rather than baptism—were accompanied by the illumination of candles, tapers, or torches by neophytes.

Another way the baptismal setting connected to its ritual was through artistic representation of the ritual or its attendant objects. The two Ravenna baptisteries, for example, show the baptism of Christ by affusion, an anachronistic portrayal that likely bore more resemblance in form to the contemporaneous ritual than to the one practiced centuries earlier in the Jordan River. Some baptistery mosaics show ritual objects such as candles or tapers, analogous to how sacrificial temples from antiquity might represent in two dimensions the very objects that existed as part of the ritual in the room (e.g., the altar in the Temple of the Palmyrene Gods, Dura-Europos). Even the common Christogram (the "chi-rho") has a ritual function in baptistery art, since its cruciform lettering shows the sign of the cross by which initiates are sealed on the forehead. Beyond these ritual markers, baptisteries evoke many intersections of Bible, art, and ritual through natural symbols—fish, sheep, and deer drinking from running water—that draw from contemporaneous art, Biblical psalms, or Gospel narratives and also mimic some of the chief metaphors for initiatory rites.

Perhaps the most prevalent artistic form that invited ritual participation was that of the procession, which was among the most ubiquitous forms of religious activity and religious visualization in antiquity. Around the Mediterranean region, the sheer number and variety of ancient, processional cultic activities encouraged a ritual-centered, processional visuality on the part of viewers. Art historian Thomas Mathews highlights depictions of processions from Greek and Roman antiquity, including the early third-century "Aventine Mithraeum" in Rome and fourth-century processions to temples of Apollo and Diana in Carthage or Bacchus/Dionysus in Spain.[14] Processions cover Christian sarcophagi and adorn Christian arcosolia in the catacombs. The Christian procession's primary mode—"convergence," according to Mathews—would hit its peak in the mosaics of fifth- and sixth-century Christianity, as in those of the two grand basilicas of Ravenna.[15] The wall mosaics of the Basilica of Sant' Apollinare Nuovo line the nave and feature, for example, a procession of virgin martyrs and the three magi on one side (Figure 17.4). Processional activity culminated in these basilica-style churches, but Christians

Figure 17.4 Mosaic with procession of virgin martyrs and Magi, north nave wall, Basilica of Sant'Apollinare Nuovo, Ravenna. Tango7174/Wikimedia Commons.

also celebrated "stational liturgies" that used various parts of cities, especially Jerusalem, Rome, and Constantinople.[16] The processional art that captured the spirit of these liturgies encouraged, in the words of Annabel Jane Wharton, a "haptic" mode of engagement with the images on the walls.[17] Processional art was meant to be not only viewed with one's eyes, but experienced by one's body in motion—a precursor of the most common stational liturgy of later centuries, the "stations of the cross."

The Dura-Europos house-church, the lone excavated site of Christian initiation from before the fourth century, had several features that suggest an exchange between artistic form and ritual practice.[18] The southern wall of its baptistery had a painting of David and Goliath underneath a wall niche likely used for oil of anointing. While anointing was common in antiquity overall, it held a particular significance for early Christian rituals in Syria.[19] The prebaptismal anointing of initiates was understood as a mimesis of the anointing of priests and kings in the Bible (Psalm 2). Just as the anointed David was a model for Jesus Christ ("anointed"), so was Christ the model for Christians. The anointed initiate was to gaze on the power of the anointed David and be empowered for battles with temptation and evil (1 Sam 16–17). The oil that sat over the head of David on the wall's art thus became the oil that anointed the head of each initiate in the ritual.

The painting of the shepherd and flock over the baptismal font also engages with the ritual movement in its location. The shepherd here carries a sheep aloft on his shoulders, while a flock of other sheep grazes or drinks water on the right side of the painting. The image is reminiscent of Psalm 23, a popular catechetical text across early Christianity, or parables of the lost sheep (Luke 15:3–7). When placed directly above a font, the image offers a striking interdependence between text, art, and ritual movement: the shepherd descends from above to lift a newly-branded sheep from the pit of the font and add it to the number of the flock already congregated nearby. While it is not definitively clear whether the painted sheep are only grazing or are also drinking water, the combination of the two seems more likely. If so, an art-ritual transitive exchange occurs also between the depicted water of the painting and the physical water of the font. The "refreshment" or "restoration" of the "soul," which Psalm 23 portrays as the result of the shepherd's care, offered a biblical backdrop for the ritualized encounter with the art.

The procession of women along the baptistery's eastern and northern walls offers a third way in which art and ritual interact to produce meaning for the Christian initiates of Dura. Processional art is also known from the other excavated sites there: the Temple of the Palmyrene Gods, the synagogue's "Purim panel," and the side walls of the Mithraeum, which show a hunt that converges on the central tauroctony, Mithras's slaying of the bull. Here in the baptistery, the procession begins on the eastern wall, where all that remain are five pairs of feet. On the northern wall is a partially preserved painting of a door, followed by a broken part of the wall (which probably showed two more female figures), until the procession resumes with portions of three female figures approaching a large structure (Figure 17.5). The women are dressed in white, veiled, and each carries two items: a torch in the right hand and a vessel in the left. The scene has often been interpreted as a representation of the women going to the empty tomb of Jesus to anoint his corpse.[20] According to this interpretation, the vessel in the left hand carries the anointing unguents, and the structure they approach is a sarcophagus. Other scholars argue for an entirely different identification: the scene may better represent marriage rituals, such as we find in textual or artistic depictions of ancient weddings and Jesus's own parable of the wise and foolish virgins (also called the parable of the ten virgins; Matt 25:1–13). These female figures may be the virgin bridesmaids, in torch-lit procession, approaching a bridal chamber of a wedding night.[21]

Figure 17.5 Fresco, procession of women, Dura-Europos baptistery. Yale University Art Gallery, Dura-Europos Collection.

This second interpretation accords better with eastern textual traditions about rites of initiation. Sources such as the *Acts of Thomas*, Cyril of Jerusalem, John Chrysostom, and Gregory of Nazianzus each emphasize the motif of marriage in Christian initiation. The opening of Cyril's catecheses for those about to be "illuminated," for example, describes how candidates "have carried the torches of a wedding procession" and the "door" has been "left open" for them to enter the "wedding feast" of their baptism.[22] This is likely how initiates entered Dura's baptistery too, each carrying a light for the night of "illumination." If they entered the room from the courtyard, as most scholars presume, the very first image they would have seen, directly ahead of them on the northern wall, bears noting: through the real open door, what they saw was another open door—the one painted on the wall, the door that separates exclusion from inclusion and death from life in the imagined world of the artistic program. From the first instant, art and ritual are fused across the threshold: the processional artistic program draws them forward into ritual action and demarcates the boundary of initiation. Whether the painted door is open or closed thus does not determine the image's correspondence to a text (or not), but rather its primary function is to influence the ritual experience of the viewer.

This mode of interpreting the art emphasizes the ritual experience and the processional visuality constructed for the participant: the female figures on the wall are "self-reflective embodiments of the initiates."[23] Rites of initiation frequently attempt to deemphasize individuality and draw participants into an undifferentiated communal experience, as a member of a flock or a procession. This type of visuality might even have temporarily muted one's own sense of gender identity, enabling a man to imagine himself as a virgin bride, just as the opposite wall enabled a woman to imagine herself as David, an unexpectedly mighty warrior. And while the effect of contemporary ritual theory on such interpretations is evident, we may note that just a few years after the discovery of the baptistery, ritual-centered interpretations of its art had already been offered. The Byzantinist Henri Grégoire argued that the processing women at Dura-Europos were not primarily painted as illustrations of a text: "Above all, the procession symbolizes the illumination of baptism."[24] The writing from ancient texts will aid our understanding, but so too will attempts to read the "riting" on the walls.

In addition to these ideas of ritual participation in artistic programs, through which the viewer completes a kind of transitive exchange between art and ritual, there are also occasional examples from early Christianity when an artistic program is left incomplete—to be completed by a ritual action or ritual celebration of an imagined action. The example of the four-loaved basket at Tabgha was described at the beginning of this chapter. In addition to this, one of the much less heralded (and, unfortunately, poorly preserved) examples of processing virgins from the Roman catacombs implies the same mode of interaction.

In the late 1800s, Joseph Wilpert had identified two catacomb paintings as representations of the parable of the wise and foolish virgins. The first of these paintings (not pictured) shows a complete rendering of the narrative's characters: five women with lit torches held upright and five others with torches, apparently extinguished, held downwards.[25] Coming from different sides of the painting, the two groups approach Christ, who stands in front of an archway at the center and greets the wise group. This painting conveys the parable's common allegorical interpretation, in which the foolish virgins lack the oil and thus the light (perseverance, good works, etc.) required for entry to the wedding (heaven). Christ was figured himself as both bridegroom and doorway (just as he is both good shepherd and sheep gate in John 10:1–18). Here the art performs and invites a visual exegesis of the biblical narrative, but it does not necessarily invite further participation by the viewer.

Wilpert's second example, which he photographed in Coemeterium Maius along the Via Nomentana (Figure 17.6, from the room now called Maius 19), shows a different and seemingly incomplete rendition of the parable in a lunette of an arcosolium. On the right side one sees five virgins processing with torches, in the middle an *orant* figure, and on the left a group of just four figures seated at a table. (Wilpert did not make a watercolor of this lunette, and so we rely on his autoptic observation and the single photograph, since the painting is no longer available for viewing.) The question is, why depict only four figures at the banquet? Wilpert

Figure 17.6 Fresco, Coemeterium Maius, Mag, D, 56 and 57, Rome. Pontificia Commissione di Archeologia Sacra.

emphasizes that this peculiarity was not caused by a lack of space but was quite intentional. He argues that the deceased person buried in that very arcosolium should be regarded "as one of the wise virgins; she was to have completed the number, and thus [Christ] had designated a seat at the meal for her."[26] The incomplete picture is thus completed by the transposition of the corpse; the faith in this particular body's resurrection was inscribed into the very painting by a conspicuous absence at the table. Instead of Christ pictured at the center, this artist shows the deceased in between the five and the four as an *orant*, probably to symbolize her liminal status between death and resurrection. Her place is being held, and she prays that she might be worthy of entry to take her seat.

At the same time, when her friends and relatives gathered at her tomb to commemorate her death—to celebrate a *refrigerium* and by that graveside meal invoke the hope for her eternal life—the nexus of meaning for this painting was triangulated from Bible–art to Bible–art–ritual. Some extant tabletops from Late Antiquity which may have been designed for graveside meals, were themselves adorned with figural imagery. One well-preserved example with circular lobes around the perimeter, presumably for cups of commemorative wine, shows four sheep converging in procession on a central Christogram (Figure 17.7). According to abundant early sources, a deceased Christian is compared with a sheep marked with the "seal" of membership in the flock of the good shepherd. A separate table base shows part of the Jonah cycle—very popular in early Christian art—to encourage the hope of resurrection from the belly of death for the deceased soul being celebrated at the meal (Figure 17.3). Returning now to the catacomb example, we can better imagine how, through the rituals of prayer and the *refrigerium*, the visitors to these graves joined with the body before them in order to move the *orant* on the wall one step closer to her banquet. The incomplete picture of the incomplete narrative was intended as such because the rituals performed in this space helped to complete it.

Figure 17.7 Marble tabletop. Metropolitan Museum of Art, Fletcher Fund, 1947 (47.100.50).

Art and ritual objects

Ritualized actions were undertaken by Christians daily (prayer), weekly (eucharist), or seasonally (processions, holy days), and many of these were accompanied by symbolic or figural art. In the home, Christians adorned oil lamps with biblical scenes or images of saints and connected the light of the flame with the light of salvation. They chose particularly religious scenes for use on their personal signet rings. Some used biblical amulets, such as a hematite intaglio with Christ healing the woman with the flow of blood (Figure 17.8), in order to ward off disease or unwelcome bodily fluctuations. Eucharistic liturgies featured items such as processional crosses, statuettes of doves suspended over the altar, and narrative or figural scenes on patens, ladles, chalices, strainers, candleholders, fans, and book covers, to name only the most common examples. Consecrated eucharist could be carried from a church to the homes of the sick or elderly in a pyxis, usually a cylindrical container with scenes carved around it that may call to mind the eucharist. A clear instance of such art-ritual congruence appears on a pyxis that shows the multiplication of the loaves and fishes—a story of the distribution of salvific food retold on the very vessel that carried such nourishment to the infirm (Figure 17.9).

The ritual of pilgrimage was rarer and thus worthy of unique memorialization. Pilgrims to the Holy Land or other sacred sites marked their experiences with ritual objects, many of which have been well preserved. Through decades of leadership, Byzantinist Gary Vikan has curated interpretation of the genre of early Christian pilgrimage art from the fourth to the seventh century, from the refounding of Jerusalem by Constantine to its conquest by Muslims. Following on the heels of Constantine's mother Helena's alleged discovery of the "true cross," a sense of Christian holiness

Figure 17.8 Amulet carved in intaglio (incised). Metropolitan Museum of Art, gift of J. Pierpont Morgan, 1917 (17.190.491).

Figure 17.9 Ivory pyxis with the miracle of Christ's multiplication of the loaves. Metropolitan Museum of Art, gift of J. Pierpont Morgan, 1917 (17.190.34a, b).

radiated outward from Golgotha and permeated Judea and Galilee. Soon ascetics from all over were emigrating to set up hermitages and monasteries in this holiest of lands. Growing flocks of pilgrims were not far behind. The most famous of these are known through their travel diaries passed down through history: the "Bordeaux pilgrim," the "Piacenza pilgrim," "Peter the Deacon," and the preeminent example, "Egeria," who offers detailed accounts of Holy Week in Jerusalem. Most do not give reason for their journeys, but they were likely drawn by the allure of religious blessing from both holy places and holy people. "For the early Byzantine pilgrim, the word *eulogia* (Latin, *benedictio*) held special meaning, referring to the blessing received by contact with a holy person, holy place, or holy object, sometimes realized through the reenactment of the event that had initially sanctified the *locus sanctus* [holy site]."[27] On their way to the culminating experience of reverence for the cross in Jerusalem, pilgrims visited a number of holy sites, and their mementos from this journey feature a *locus sanctus* cycle ranging from four to twelve scenes. The events commemorated by the locations were inscribed on metal flasks, terra cotta tokens, armbands, censers, reliquaries, and more.

Pilgrims used all their senses and "sometimes sought blessing through mimesis—action imitative of the sacred heroes and events along his or her route."[28] A typical example would be the tradition of throwing stones at the tomb of Goliath.[29] But in addition to throwing something at the tomb of an archetypal enemy, they could also gather something from the tomb of their Lord, once they finally arrived there. As the Piacenza pilgrim notes, dirt was brought into Jesus's tomb from outside, so that "those who enter it bear away a blessing with them from it when they depart."[30] Pilgrims brought back iconography of and reverence for the cross and empty tomb, which were featured prominently in the ritual encounter orchestrated by the Church of the Holy Sepulcher.[31] Several pilgrimage *ampullae* feature these scenes with an upper register that commemorates the cross and a lower register that portrays the empty tomb (Figure 17.10). The scene at the tomb perfectly demonstrates how, as is often the case in early Christian art, the image's correspondence to a biblical text was not as meaningful as its reminiscence of a ritual—in this case, the pilgrimage to the contemporaneous holy site of the Anastasis in Jerusalem. When the two registers are viewed together, the overall visual effect suggests that the women at the tomb are venerating not only the empty tomb, but also the cross that dominates the scene. Considering how uncommon crucifixion imagery was before the fourth century, it seems probable that the popularity of the cross itself was the greatest artistic legacy of the increase in religious pilgrimages to Jerusalem.

The Sancta Sanctorum Blessings Box (Figure 10.7), a rare example of a pilgrim's collection combined with early Christian painting from the Holy Land, captures well the interface of art and ritual on the pilgrim's path—and serves as a fitting conclusion to this essay. The box is packed with rocks, earth, and wood from various sites, and some of the mementos' labels are still legible. A piece here from the Mount of Olives, a piece there from the tomb of Jesus. The underside of the lid has five painted scenes from the *locus sanctus* cycle: nativity, baptism, crucifixion, women at the tomb, and ascension. As with the *ampulla*, the depiction of the empty tomb

> shows an architectural ensemble modeled on the tomb aedicula itself and the Anastasis rotunda as they existed at the time of the painting. . . . In the eyes of the pilgrim, the tomb aedicula was not a building but a large contact relic, on a par with the True Cross, both sanctified and empowered by having been touched by the body of Christ. In emphasizing the real, historical structure of the tomb at the expense of the biblical narrative, the painter of the Sancta Sanctorum reliquary lid was sharpening the focus of this documentation to show less the ultimate, biblical origin of sanctification and more the proximate, relic origin.[32]

Concerning the art's correspondence to the story of the empty tomb, the required "text" is not only the Bible, but also the pilgrim's ritual encounter. Just as in the case of the Tabgha mosaic or the Dura-Europos baptistery, this artifact demonstrates the benefits of artistic interpretations open to not only the relevance of ritual, but even its centrality.

Figure 17.10 Lead pilgrim ampullae, Treasury, Duomo, Monza, Italy. Photo: Foto Marburg / Art Resource, NY.

Notes

1 John Wilkinson, *Egeria's Travels*, 3rd ed. (Oxford: Aris & Philipps, 1999), 98.
2 Robin Margaret Jensen, *Baptismal Imagery in Early Christianity: Ritual, Visual, and Theological Dimensions* (Grand Rapids: Baker Academic, 2012).
3 Robin Margaret Jensen, "Early Christian Images and Exegesis," in *Picturing the Bible: The Earliest Christian Art*, ed. Jeffrey Spier (New Haven: Yale University Press, 2007), 69.
4 Jensen, "Early Christian Images and Exegesis," 77.
5 Jensen, "Early Christian Images and Exegesis," 77.
6 Jaś Elsner, *Roman Eyes: Visuality and Subjectivity in Art and Text* (Princeton: Princeton University Press, 2007), 48.
7 Elsner, *Roman Eyes*, 25.
8 Elsner, *Roman Eyes*, 25.
9 Elsner, *Roman Eyes*, xvii.
10 Elsner, *Roman Eyes*, 45.
11 Elsner, *Roman Eyes*, 48.
12 Jensen, *Baptismal Imagery in Early Christianity*; Robin Margaret Jensen, *Living Water: Images, Symbols, and Settings of Early Christian Baptism* (Leiden: Brill, 2011).
13 Jensen, *Living Water*, 247.
14 Thomas F. Mathews, *The Clash of the Gods: A Reinterpretation of Early Christian Art* (Princeton: Princeton University Press, 1993), 151–160.
15 Mathews, *The Clash of the Gods*, 153–166.
16 John F. Baldovin, *The Urban Character of Christian Worship: The Origins, Development, and Meaning of Stational Liturgy*, Orientalia Christiana Analecta 228 (Rome: Pontificum Institutum Studiorum Orientalium, 1987).
17 Annabel Jane Wharton, *Refiguring the Post Classical City: Dura Europos, Jerash, Jerusalem, and Ravenna* (Cambridge: Cambridge University Press, 1995).
18 Wharton, *Refiguring the Post Classical City*; Dominic E. Serra, "The Baptistery at Dura-Europos: The Wall Paintings in the Context of Syrian Baptismal Theology," *Ephemerides Liturgicae* 120 (2006): 67–78; Michael Peppard, *The World's Oldest Church: Bible, Art, and Ritual at Dura-Europos, Syria* (New Haven: Yale University Press, 2016).
19 Maxwell E. Johnson, *The Rites of Christian Initiation: Their Evolution and Interpretation*, rev. ed. (Collegeville: Liturgical Press, 2007).
20 Carl H. Kraeling, *The Christian Building, The Excavations at Dura-Europos, Final Report VIII, Part II* (New Haven: Dura Europos Publications, 1967).
21 Serra, "The Baptistery at Dura-Europos"; Peppard, *The World's Oldest Church*.
22 *Procat.* 1, 3–4.
23 Wharton, *Refiguring the Post Classical City*, 60.
24 Henri Grégoire, "Les Baptistères de Cuicul et de Doura," *Byzantion* 13 (1938): 593.
25 Joseph Wilpert, *Die gottgeweihten Jungfrauen in den ersten Jahrhunderten der Kirche* (Freiburg im Breisgau: Herder, 1892), 65–76.
26 Wilpert, *Die gottgeweihten Jungfrauen*, 69, trans. mine.
27 Gary Vikan, *Early Byzantine Pilgrimage Art*, rev. ed., Dumbarton Oaks Byzantine Collection Publications 5 (Washington: Dumbarton Oaks Research Library and Collection, 2010), 13.
28 Vikan, *Early Byzantine Pilgrimage Art*, 27.
29 *It. Plac.* "Piacenza pilgrim," 31.
30 *It. Plac.* "Piacenza pilgrim," 18; *Of the Holy Places Visited by Antoninus Martyr*, trans. Aubrey Stewart (London, 1884), 15.
31 Egeria, *Itin.* 36–37.
32 Vikan, *Early Byzantine Pilgrimage Art*, 20.

Further reading

Elsner, Jaś. *Roman Eyes: Visuality and Subjectivity in Art and Text.* Princeton: Princeton University Press, 2007.

Jefferson, Lee M. and Robin M. Jensen, eds. *The Art of Empire: Christian Art in its Imperial Context.* Minneapolis: Fortress Press, 2015.

Jensen, Robin Margaret. *Baptismal Imagery in Early Christianity: Ritual, Visual, and Theological Dimensions*. Grand Rapids: Baker Academic, 2012.

———. *Living Water: Images, Symbols, and Settings of Early Christian Baptism*. Supplement to *Vigiliae Christianae* 105. Leiden; Boston: Brill, 2011.

Mathews, Thomas F. *The Clash of the Gods: A Reinterpretation of Early Christian Art*. Princeton: Princeton University Press, 1993.

Peppard, Michael. *The World's Oldest Church: Bible, Art, and Ritual at Dura-Europos, Syria*. New Haven: Yale University Press, 2016.

Vikan, Gary. *Early Byzantine Pilgrimage Art*, rev. ed. Dumbarton Oaks Byzantine Collection Publications 5. Washington: Dumbarton Oaks Research Library and Collection, 2010.

Weitzmann, Kurt, ed. *Age of Spirituality: Late Antique and Early Christian Art, Third to Seventh Century*. New York: Metropolitan Museum of Art, 1979.

Wharton, Jane Annabel. *Refiguring the Post Classical City: Dura Europos, Jerash, Jerusalem, and Ravenna*. Cambridge: Cambridge University Press, 1995.

18
PICTURING THE PASSION

Felicity Harley-McGowan

The word "Passion" (from the Greek *pascho* and its Latin derivative, the noun *passio*, related to the verb meaning "to suffer") refers to the redemptive sufferings of Jesus and to the narrative of events leading up to and including his death, particularly as recorded in the four canonical gospels. These Greek texts, which had probably all appeared by the turn of the second century, laid out the "sufferings" of Jesus vividly and explicitly as a continuum, beginning with his agony and arrest in the Garden of Gethsemane and going through to his entombment (Mark 14.26–15.47, Matt 26.30–27.66, Luke 22.39–23.56, John 18.1–19.42). In the history of art, the term "Passion" has come to function as a label for images that illustrate some or all of these events.

The story of the Passion seems perfectly suited to illustration in view of the narrative structure of the gospel accounts, along with the broader theological significance attributed to the death of Jesus in the early church; and certainly this is the case from the eighth century on, when illustrated passion narratives came to form the bedrock of Christian visual culture. However, seeking the roots of this prominent pictorial tradition in early Christianity, it seems that the literary narratives did not furnish a blueprint for the visual narrative in the way that might be expected. Among early Christians, the priority was not to represent the historical events as described in the texts, but to interpret them, to express understandings of the death and resurrection of Jesus as they were evolving in the generations after the crucifixion. The following study considers the various attempts at pictorial expression of the Passion across the third to the fifth centuries, a highly innovative period of iconographic development fundamentally concerned with the representation of God's power through Jesus's victory on the cross.

Second and third centuries

The crucifixion (Matt 27.32–56, Mark 15.1–47, Luke 23.26–43, John 19.17–37) was central to early Christian discourse from the outset. Writers and preachers did not shirk from discussing the violence of the event; nonetheless its significance was fixed in its salvific import as a revelation of Jesus's power, which was also God's power. Just decades after Jesus died, the apostle Paul looked beyond the historical context of the crucifixion to interpret it as the final step in a divine plan for salvation (1 Cor 2.6–8); referring collectively to Jesus's "sufferings," he called attention to their redemptive significance (2 Cor 1.5). Highlighting the ramifications of the death for the broader future of the Church, the author of Acts noted that after his suffering Jesus appeared alive to the disciples, speaking about the kingdom of God (Acts 1.3). The accounts of the disciples who saw, spoke with and touched the risen Jesus prior to his ascension were events that confirmed the resurrection; and for early Christians, they enabled the story of "suffering" to be interpreted as one of glory, framed by the entry into Jerusalem (Matt 21.1–11, Mark 11.1–11, Luke 19.28–39) and the ascension (Mark 16.19, Luke 24.50–51, Acts 1.1–11). This extended narrative enabled a path to glory to be set out more explicitly, a path that subsequent writers across the first, second and third centuries (including Ignatius of Antioch, Melito of Sardis, Clement of Alexandria, Tertullian of Carthage, and Origen of Alexandria) were eager to articulate as they developed a theology of the cross in Christian apologetics and literature. The saving power of the crucified Jesus thus became the central, though paradoxical, reality of Christianity. Expressions of curiosity about it are manifest visually at an early date in different parts of the Mediterranean in various ways, by ordinary believers, by elite Christians, as well as by those who were not followers of Jesus.

The earliest pictorial references to the power of the crucified Jesus appear in the visual culture of late Roman antiquity *c.* 200 CE, almost two centuries after the crucifixion in 36 CE. Images of crucifixion are entirely absent from the public art of imperial Rome, and while depictions of Jesus on his cross are extremely rare before the fifth century, a handful of surviving images collectively attest that a set of iconographic conventions for the depiction of the crucified figure of Jesus had been formulated by the early third century and was circulated widely across the Mediterranean basin. The figure was shown upright, tied to a T-shaped cross, the head represented in profile. Appearing in various media in the third and fourth centuries, these key iconographic details were widely accessible within late Roman visual culture, being known to ordinary Romans and producers of Christian imagery alike.

In the eastern Mediterranean, sometime in the late second or early third century, the maker of an amulet used the model for an explicit depiction of Jesus crucified naked, which is preserved at the center of a large bloodstone (Figure 18.1). The iconography is modestly but confidently carved: a bearded Jesus is tied to the cross beam of the T cross, his legs hanging apart. Inscribed around this design is a long invocation that begins: "Son, Father, Jesus Christ."[1] Close analysis of the invocational language has suggested that the inscription and the image functioned closely together for the wearer of the gemstone as means of seeking redemption: in word, and in detailed iconography, the object explicitly exults in the death of Jesus as the Son of God, the image of the crucifixion already an integral part of the celebration of the soteriological power of the cross for Christians.[2]

Around the same time, the model was adopted in Rome for a satirical drawing, scratched onto a wall within the slave quarters of the Imperial palace on the Palatine Hill (Figure 18.2). In this case the Christian God is represented as a donkey-headed man, crucified and hailed by an onlooker; a Greek caption reads "Alexamenos worships his God."[3] The drawing may refer to the accusation that Christians worshipped a donkey-headed deity. It may also participate in contemporary humor wherein animal features were applied to a person in order to make fun of them. Graffiti practice was highly social and popular among all ages and classes as a means of direct communication in the Roman world. For this satirical image to succeed, for the joke to work, the concept of the crucified Jesus as a figure of power for Christians needed to be both widely understood and the picture recognizable to the viewer. While the drawing is rudimentary, the composition is complex and unlikely to have been imagined on the spur of the moment by this graffitist.[4] The iconographic similarities with the amulet point to the likelihood that a basic formula for picturing a crucifixion existed and was used by different individuals for different purposes.

Another drawing of a crucified figure, this time scratched in plaster on a wall of a Roman *taberna* in Pozzuoli (ancient Puteoli) perhaps only decades before, confirms this in deploying the same constituent elements: a T cross, the body rigidly upright and frontal, head in profile, arms stretched out beneath the cross-beam, and ties rather than nails attaching the body.[5] That the iconography was

Figure 18.1 Bloodstone amulet engraved with the Crucifixion, Christian invocation, and magical words. London, The British Museum. Photo: Jeffrey Spier.

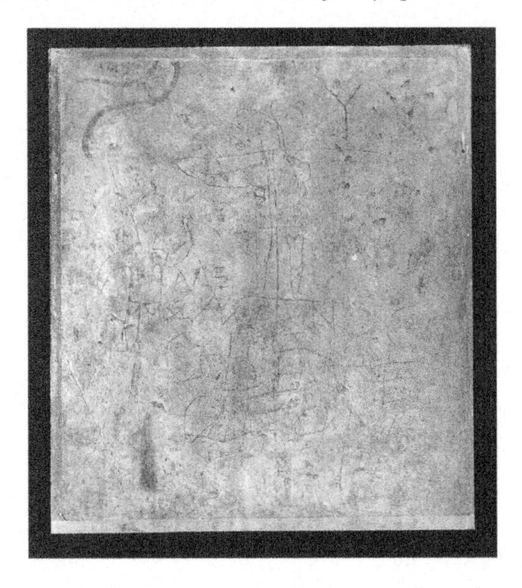

Figure 18.2 Roman graffito parodying the Crucifixion, late second–early third century. Scratched in plaster on an internal wall of the *Paedagogium*, a building that formed part of the Imperial Palace complex on the Palatine Hill, Rome, and possibly used as a training school for slaves and freedmen in the Imperial household. Rome, Museo Palatino. Photo: © The British School at Rome Photographic Archive, John Henry Parker Collection, jhp-0107.

reasonably well known, came to be understood as a way of depicting Jesus, and persisted in later art, is attested on a fourth-century Christian gemstone probably manufactured in a Syrian workshop for wearing in a finger ring (Figure 18.3).[6] In that context, an invocation of Jesus's name again accompanies the image—though Jesus is now flanked by the twelve apostles in a composition designed to emphasise his authority. The Palatine graffito has been used to support the argument that because Christian worship of a crucified messiah was open to misinterpretation or ridicule (as Paul attests, 1 Cor 1.23) Christians avoided depicting Jesus's cross or Passion. Yet Paul further noted that to those who are called, both Jews and Greeks, Christ crucified is also "the power of God and the wisdom of God." This is clearly understood by the amulet maker (perhaps a Christian) who deploys the image to invoke the soteriological power of the cross, by the slave who publicly parodies that image, and by fourth-century Christians who were wearing the image in public on finger rings.[7]

The power of Jesus on the cross was expressed symbolically and celebrated in other ways by Christians. In several early Gospel manuscripts, scribes make visual reference to the crucifixion by inserting the *staurogram* (a literary monogram comprising the Greek letters tau-rho) into the middle of the noun "cross" and the verb "crucify" (Figure 18.4). Often such ligatures functioned simply as abbreviations. In these papyrological contexts however, it also functions as a sacred image either of the cross or the crucified Jesus himself, having the appearance of a miniature crucifix. The deliberate and prominent placement constitutes another striking pictorial acknowledgement of the crucified Jesus, and highlights the salvific importance of the death.[8] Paleographic and codicological analyses agree that these papyri are probably similar in date; whether produced *c.* 200 or as late as *c.* 325, they constitute vital evidence for experimentation by elite, literate Christians with visual mechanisms by which to express the significance of the crucified Jesus.[9]

In light of this material, it is curious that in other aspects of Christian visual culture as it was emerging *c.* 200, there is no surviving evidence to suggest an interest in representing the crucifixion and other episodes from the Passion narrative. Yet at this period, with attention fixed on paradigmatic representations of Jesus, as teacher or healer for instance, there was little interest in portraying Jesus in historical settings. In the loose cycles of text-based images that were emerging at this time, episodes from Hebrew scripture were used to express the broad

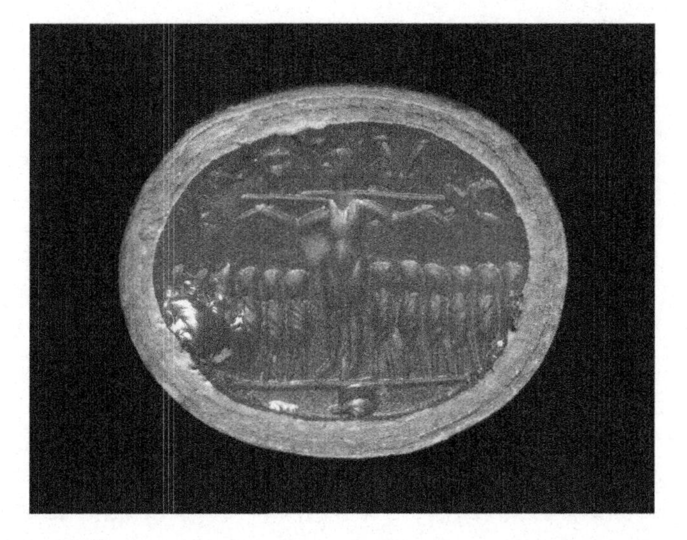

Figure 18.3 The Constanza gemstone, engraved with a representation of Jesus crucified among the twelve apostles. Carnelian, Syria (?), mid-4th century CE. London, The British Museum. Photo: © Trustees of the British Museum.

Figure 18.4 Papyrus Bodmer XIV–XV (75): manuscript of the Gospel of Luke. At the end of the fourth line, the Greek letters *tau* and *rho* are combined to form a monogram (the staurogram) in the word *stauron* (cross), at Luke 14.27. The staurogram, which resembles a miniature crucifixion image, also functions here as a pictogram, a visual reference to the cross or to Jesus crucified as a sacred sign of salvation. Rome, Biblioteca Apostolica Vaticana. Photo: V. Martin and R. Kasser, *Papyrus Bodmer XIV: Évangiles de Luc, ch. 3–24* (Geneva: Bibliotheca Bodmeriana, 1961) pl. 41, with permission Fondation Martin Bodmer.

concept of salvation begun in the Old Testament and completed in the New. Stories about deliverance from death were recalled joyfully, and these provided a framework for understanding and celebrating divine power that offered no place for stories about suffering, death or mourning.[10] Instead, the resuscitated bodies of Jonah (disgorged from the mouth of the ketos after three days in its belly, Jonah 1.17–2.10) and Lazarus (raised after four days in the grave, still in his burial wrappings, John 11.17) were popular across all media—examples of death being "swallowed up in victory" (1 Cor 15.54). The resuscitated body of Jesus was not. It had not been described in the Gospels; and art, like those texts, instead focused on testimony to Jesus's resurrection—the empty tomb indicating his resuscitation and his appearances to the women and the disciples confirming it. An early version of what became a strong pictorial interest in the tomb may be the painting datable to *c.* 240 CE on the walls of the baptistery-room in the Christian Building at Dura-Europos depicting women holding lamps and bowls and approaching a tomb-like structure. Although the identification is not certain,[11] it has long been considered as an early depiction of the women coming to the tomb (Mark 16.1–2, the other narratives being Matt 28.1, Luke 24.1, John 20.1), serving to articulate the promise of resurrection given in baptism and underscoring the idea of that sacrament as a rebirth.[12] The iconography has parity with later representations of that subject on sixth-century ivory pyxides where liturgy is likely to have influenced the composition, and later Syrian manuscript illumination.[13]

It is apparent that as part of this broad focus on divine victory over death, events related to the Passion were inserted into soteriologically focused pictorial cycles in funerary contexts as early as the first half of the third century. A fresco in the "Crypt of the Passion" (Catacomb of Praetextatus, Rome) depicting a man wearing a wreath and being hailed by two bystanders, one of whom extends a foliate branch, may be an early depiction of Jesus's crowning with thorns (Matt 27.27–30, Mark 15.16–19, John 19.2–3). Iconographically it seems to anticipate later versions of that scene, with the crown of thorns, rather than being a cruel act of humiliation, depicted as a Roman victory wreath to express the idea that Jesus will transform suffering into triumph.[14] Nonetheless, a firm identification remains difficult.

Fourth century

A growing interest in the varied interpretations of the death and resurrection of Jesus is apparent in private and public art following the conversion of the Roman emperor Constantine and the subsequent legitimization of the religion in the fourth century. The expansion of the church had a direct impact on the development both of literature (homiletic and commentary) and art in educating new converts in the content of scripture. Letters and poetic works document vigorous discussion among church leaders and aristocratic patrons about the merits of art in the service of faith. Just as exegetical writings between the fourth and fifth centuries probed correspondences between the Hebrew Scriptures and New Testament literature, some believed that art could pictorially explicate the meaning of stories to new converts.[15] As a result of this vibrant exegetical activity and growing interest in the pictorial arts a wider range of biblical subjects was illustrated, including events from the Passion narrative. Yet even as the setting for the image of Jesus more closely followed biblical text, these new subjects, and the pictorial cycles in which they appeared, remained faithful to the focus on deliverance and the triumph over death established in the previous century, and disinterested in suffering and death. For the illustration of the Passion, there were three general trends: increasing allusions were made to the Passion-theme within loose text-based cycles; an increasing number of events from the narrative were now illustrated; and Passion cycles emerged.

Typology: alluding to the Passion

Early in the fourth century a sophisticated system of referring to the theme of the Passion had emerged. Within cycles of text-based images, stories from the Hebrew Bible were interspersed among stories from the New Testament in order to allude to, but not illustrate, individual events from the Passion narrative. The Sacrifice of Isaac (Gen 22) is one example, discussed by the Church Fathers as a parallel to the Passion of Jesus and symbolizing Christian triumph over death.[16] Such visual allusions could express three principal theological interpretations of the crucifixion and death of Jesus in the early Church: the fulfilment of the Messianic prophecy of suffering and the culmination of Old Testament sacrifices; a victory over death and evil and so a passage to Jesus's Sovereignty; and events into which the faithful were baptised, and in which they could thus participate (according to Pauline teaching, as in Rom 6.3–4; 2 Tim 2.10–12). The last understanding was aided by the complicated memories of persecution and martyrdom, and particularly the martyrdoms of Peter and Paul, which appear in the catacomb paintings and on sarcophagi in the fourth century.[17] One monument could articulate several of these beliefs simultaneously. Within the complex typological arrangement of Old and New Testament scenes on the sarcophagus carved in Rome for the urban prefect of 359, Junius Bassus (Figure 18.5),[18] the figure of Jesus as law-giver at the center expresses his universal and eternal authority while biblical stories of suffering, dispersed across the sarcophagus, foreshadow the Passion (the sacrifice of Isaac; Daniel in the lion's den); original sin articulates the need for that suffering (Adam and Eve); and additional Passion scenes underscore Jesus's Passion victory and ongoing authority (the individual arrests of Peter and Paul; Jesus's triumphal entry into Jerusalem; Pilate's judgment).

Figure 18.5 Sarcophagus of Junius Bassus, marble, carved in Rome and dated by inscription to 359 CE. Rome, Museo Petriano. Photo: De Agostini Picture Library, G. Cigolini, Bridgeman Images.

In striving to express these understandings, some episodes from the Passion directly allude to the death and resurrection of Jesus but reflect interests that extend beyond the narrative from which they are taken. The episode of Jesus washing Peter's feet (John 13.1–5), which appeared on sarcophagi after 350, carried several layers of significance, illustrating Jesus's command to serve others and also his specific relationship with Peter, who became head of the church. When paired with the episode of Pilate washing his hands,[19] unique to Matthew's narrative (Matt 27.24), it made a typological reference to baptism and the cleansing of sin.[20]

Individual Passion episodes

By *c.* 350, explicit episodes from the Passion narrative began to appear within loose cycles of images and were illustrated more regularly across the century. The prophecy of Peter's denial (Matt 26.33–5, Mark 14.29–31, Luke 22.31–34, John 13.37–38) may have emerged *c.* 315,[21] and Jesus's entry into Jerusalem was known by *c.* 330.[22] The former story originally belonged to a sequence of Petrine scenes; nonetheless, as an individual moment in which Peter vows to lay down his life, it could allude to Christ's own death and be understood as an event in which all Christians, like the apostles, could participate. The latter scene, as the prelude to the Passion, was enormously popular in fourth-century Roman funerary art. In some contexts, surrounded by miracle scenes and Hebrew Bible stories foretelling mankind's salvation by Christ, it could be emblematic of Jesus's entry into the heavenly Jerusalem, thereby symbolizing his defeat of death and the redemption from sin won for all the faithful.[23]

The richest source of evidence for the development of Passion iconography in the fourth century is the group of sarcophagi produced around 340–370 in workshops in North Italy and Gaul, which focused specifically on events surrounding the crucifixion and resurrection.

The growing interest in depicting such scenes in funerary art must also have existed in other media, although there are few surviving examples. In the late fourth and early fifth centuries for example, from Milan to Constantinople, ivory had become an important medium in the luxury arts, preserving, for instance, highly sophisticated depictions of post-resurrection episodes[24] and complex narrative cycles.

One of the earliest and finest examples of the "Passion" sarcophagi, the so-called sarcophagus of Domitilla, illustrates four episodes from the narrative (Figure 18.6): Simon of Cyrene carrying the cross of Jesus (Matt 27.32, Mark 15.21, Luke 23.26); the crowning with thorns; and two episodes from the trial—Jesus led towards Pilate and Pilate preparing to wash his hands.[25] In the gospels, these events present extreme moments in Jesus's humiliation and challenge his authority and, for these reasons, the trial, presented as a kind of mini-narrative, was chosen. However, the specter of suffering, prominent in the text, is altered. The crowning episode, noted above, is transformed from a moment of shame to one of glory. The *crux invicta*, or triumphant cross, which drew on traditional Roman symbols of victory, now celebrates the eternal authority of Jesus. Evoking the structure of the Roman victory standard, the cross is shown as trophy, crowned by an eagle with a jeweled laurel wreath (traditional Roman symbols of victory and immortality). The wreath frames the monogram of Jesus, the *chi-rho* (the first letters of the name *Christ* in Greek) and the sun and moon sit above the eagle's wings denoting the cosmic significance of this victory. These symbols become fixtures in Byzantine art of the sixth century, including manuscript illumination as well as mass-produced items for private devotion, and throughout the Medieval and Renaissance periods when they are traditionally interpreted as giving pictorial expression to narrative: the darkness that descended during the crucifixion (Mark 15.33, Matt 27.45, Luke 23.44–45). In a further allusion to the story of the resurrection, the figures of two Roman soldiers guarding the tomb sit on either side of the cross (Matt 27.64, 28.4, 28.23).

This composite symbol, at once representing Christ's crucifixion and resurrection, remained popular as the central motif on Passion sarcophagi into the 390s. Other visual strategies were

Figure 18.6 Sarcophagus of Domitilla, marble, Rome, *c.* 350. Rome, The Vatican Museums. Photo: Alinari, Bridgeman Images.

attempted, however. Two engraved gems dating from the late fourth century (one from Constanza, Figure 18.3, the other now lost) indicate that experimentation with the theme took place in which the victorious, resurrected body of Jesus was placed onto the cross itself: in this image, Jesus had entered the heavenly Jerusalem as the crucified and resurrected savior, symbolically acclaimed by the smaller figures of the twelve apostles who assemble either side of him.[26] We have seen a different method of expressing this victory on the Junius Bassus sarcophagus, where the exalted Christ is flanked by just two apostles as the new ruler of the cosmos—usurping Caelus, the god of the sky, depicted beneath the throne and literally trodden underfoot (Figure 18.5). This celestial scene of glory has no basis in scripture, but was devised to emphasize the primacy of Peter and Paul as princes of the apostles and martyrs, having further, eschatological, meaning signifying Christ of the second coming. Similarly, the composition on the gems has no basis in scripture and is suggestive of the eschatological meaning of the cross. For the depiction of Jesus, it draws on the earlier model for crucified figures (T cross, wrist ties, head in profile), but foreshadows literal unions of the body and the cross in the fifth century where, in a narrative context, Christ's authority, and the connection between the crucifixion and resurrection, was maintained in new ways.

Passion cycles

The third broad implication of the increased attention on biblical imagery was that around 340 CE, along with a growing repertoire of Passion scenes and the establishment of conventional compositions for their depiction (for example, for the betrayal or kiss of Judas, denial, women at the tomb, incredulity of Thomas, and ascension), the Passion began to be depicted as a sequence of events following the gospel narratives. This interest emerged gradually. The treatment of the trial scenes on the Domitilla sarcophagus of *c.* 350 clearly illustrates a concern for sequence (Figure 18.6), but especially important is the Servanne sarcophagus, *c.* 370–380 CE (Figure 18.7), which preserves (in fragments) the earliest surviving Passion cycle.[27] Eight episodes were originally illustrated in sequence from left to right, beginning with the agony in the garden (Matt 26.36–46, Mark 14:32–42, Luke 22.39–46), through the betrayal (Matt 26.47–56, Mark 14.43–52, Luke 22.47–53, John 18.1–12), Christ taken to Pilate (Matt 27.2, Mark 15.1, Luke 23.1, John 18.28), Christ before Pilate (Matt 27.11–14, Mark 15.2–5, Luke 23.3–5, John 18.28), the women and soldiers at the tomb (Matt 28.29, Mark 16.1–6, John 20.14–17), Christ appearing to the disciples (Matt 28.16–20, Mark 16.14–16, Luke 24.48–49), suicide of Judas (Matt 27.3–5), and ending with the ascension.

Figure 18.7 The Servanne sarcophagus, marble, Rome, *c.* 370–380. Arles, Musée de l'Arles et de la Provence antiques. Photo: © DAI, Rome.

Significantly, it is the encounter between Jesus and Pilate that forms the central, pivotal moment in the narrative and dictates the overarching theme: victory. As one of the most popular Passion episodes in the later fourth century, often used to represent the entire narrative story,[28] the trial stands here for the death itself, and as such is the turning point in this narrative sequence: Roman judicial authority will be overcome by a greater authority, a fact declared in the post-resurrection scenes and underscored by the remorse of Judas (whose suicide according to Matthew (27.5) effects a powerful statement about Jesus's own defeat of death) and affirmed in the ascension. In the final order of scenes, the cycle refers to Acts (1:3–12) where, after his suffering, Jesus appeared to the disciples before being taken up to heaven from the Mount of Olives. In that text the future second coming is also implied; hence the cycle opens with the disciples sleeping in one garden and closes with an active farewell in another, anticipating his return. The frieze exhibits a new interest in unfolding the Passion narrative, yet, in presenting it as a victory, there is the same concern for the ongoing significance of those events now and in the eschatological future as was observed on the gems (Figure 18.3).

The sequence of events in the Passion cycle of the Servanne sarcophagus does not follow a single gospel narrative, but presents a synthesis of textual accounts, a tradition that would continue in Christian art to demonstrate the unity of the texts in their structure and detail. Individual episodes can also combine versions of the same story. The tomb composition recalls Matthew (28.9) where three women leave the empty tomb, encounter a man they recognize to be Jesus and subsequently worship him, but Jesus appears to be in motion, at once walking away from the women, while turning back to look at them. In this, and the subtle twist of the body as he gestures back towards them, the artist evokes the intimate exchange between Jesus and Mary Magdalene (Jn 20.17, known as the *Noli me tangere* episode), a composition that will persist in Medieval and Renaissance art. By the fifth century, an image in which the angel meets the women (Matt 28.1–7, Mark 16.1, Luke 24.1–8) had become standardized. Other Passion scenes also are first attested on this sarcophagus (Judas's suicide), the earliest preserved depictions of what will become traditional compositions in western Christian art (Judas's kiss).

The Servanne sarcophagus is part of a more extensive pictorial tradition illustrating the Passion that emerges by the close of the fourth century. Further evidence is furnished by an iconographically sophisticated ivory reliquary casket produced in a Northern Italian workshop (possibly Milan) and now in Brescia (Figure 18.8).[29] This object represents an important innovation: the use of a wide range of biblical subjects, drawn from both the Old and New Testaments, placed in a complex arrangement that serve as typologies proclaiming the unity of the Hebrew and Christian scriptures, specifically predicting the Passion and articulating its significance for the faithful. This format is abandoned for the lid however, where the Passion is prominently illustrated, envisaged as a coherent cycle of episodes laid out in sequence across two registers. The artist focuses on the first half of the Servanne cycle and so does not include the crucifixion; those biblical stories of salvation that had appeared alongside Passion scenes on sarcophagi to prefigure Jesus's death and resurrection and interpret it are now dispersed across the casket. The cycle begins with an entirely new composition of Jesus alone in the garden and includes a fuller arrest scene and an abbreviated version of the highly popular subject of Peter's denial, which was now preferred to the scene of Jesus's prophecy and routinely included in Passion cycles after 400 CE. On the second register, the trial is expanded to include the arraignment of Jesus before Annas and Caiaphas (Matt 26.57, Mark 14.53, Luke 22.54), as well as Pilate. Judas's suicide is displaced onto the back of the casket.[30]

Figure 18.8 The Brescia Casket (detail: lid), ivory, Northern Italy (Milan?), *c.* 380s. Brescia, Museo Civico dell'Eta Cristiana. Photo: De Agostini Picture Library, Bridgeman Images.

While explicit scenes of the crucifixion did not feature in Passion cycles up to this point, there can be little doubt that church decoration at this time provided the impetus for the further development of Christian imagery and narrative cycles specifically. While few monumental cycles survive, literary sources record that church leaders and aristocratic patrons, from Ambrose in Milan to Nilus in Sinai, promoted and experimented with large-scale pictorial programmes on the walls of churches for evangelisation, education, and spiritual nourishment. As part of this activity there was an increasing desire to draw out specific correspondences between the Jewish and Christian Scriptures (the "Old" and "New" Testaments) with the result that new contexts emerged for pictorial reflection on Passion episodes. An early model for the practice of decorating churches with cycles of images is documented by one of the most influential Latin Christian poets, Prudentius (348–405), in his poem of *c.* 400 *Tituli historiarum* ("Scenes from History," also known as *Dittochaeon*, "Double Nourishment"). The poem's verses describe biblical stories, and they likely functioned as captions for a sequence of images, whether imagined or written as a commission for a cycle that no longer survives. Six verses describe episodes from the Passion. Three of these are familiar from other contemporary monuments: Judas's suicide, the tomb, and Christ appearing to the disciples.[31] Three are new, and by introducing elements of violence into the pictorial narrative for the first time they document a significant shift of attention onto the process of Christ's death: the buffeting of Jesus (Matt 26.67, Mark 14.65, Luke 22.64), his scourging (Matt 27.26, Mark 15.15, John 19.1) and crucifixion. The buffeting is not known from surviving pictorial evidence until the sixth century (Figure 18.11), and the scourging is otherwise unknown before the ninth century.[32] The Brescia casket and Servanne sarcophagus demonstrate that the crucifixion was not regularly included in Passion cycles by the end of the fourth century; and conspicuous instances of omission can still be found in the early sixth century (notably the mosaic cycle illustrating the life of Christ in the nave of the basilica of Sant'Apollinare Nuovo, Ravenna).[33] Nevertheless, the absence would become exceptional; and as extant engraved gems attest, images of Jesus crucified had begun to circulate among Christians by the fourth century. Hence, even if Prudentius's poem was composed for a cycle of images that was not fulfilled, his inclusion of the crucifixion is important, further attesting that although the evidence is scant, designers and theologians were already considering public contexts for its representation in the fourth and early fifth century.

Beyond a growing interest in the gospel narrative, the influence of liturgy in the formulation of church cycles and the expansion of the pictorial repertoire must also be considered. Liturgies recalled and celebrated events that were historically and theologically important to Christianity. As liturgies enacted within churches might provoke particular interest in the celebration of the death of Jesus as the central feature of the Easter liturgy, so it might be seen to influence the development of literal representations of the last supper (Mark 14.22; Luke 22.19–20, Matt 26.26). A set of captions written by Bishop Ambrose (337–397) to accompany a cycle of biblical frescoes in the large basilica he erected and lavishly decorated in Milan *c.* 379 includes the supper, indicating that it was known in Milan by the fourth century, although it remained rare before the sixth.[34] The iconography was probably similar to the earliest surviving representation of the subject, preserved on the extraordinarily detailed ivory book-covers made in the same city in the following century and that, in their selection of episodes from the lives of Jesus and Mary, recall contemporary church decoration extant in Ravenna.[35] Following long-standing pictorial conventions for the depiction of formal dining, Jesus occupies the position of honor at the far right corner of a sigma-table, reclining with disciples on a circular couch, an iconographic composition that persists into the sixth century in the West and East. An alternative version that emerged by the sixth century in Italy shows liturgical influence in the interpretation of what was a narrative event: Jesus, seated behind and at the center of the table, now holds the bread while a cup stands prominently before him (Figure 18.11). The ancient gesture of speech or instruction, as given to the arrested Christ on the Domitilla sarcophagus (Figure 18.6), has here become one of blessing, seeming to consecrate the bread and wine as the priest would do at the altar; the story of the last supper is retold pictorially to recall the institution of the eucharist.

Fifth century

The Passion narrative was gradually expanded and depicted in various cycles both in monumental art and in miniature. The most notable fifth-century addition is the crucifixion itself. Where the unvanquished cross was the visual and thematic focus on the sarcophagi, literal representations of Jesus crucified were now set alongside images of post-resurrection episodes that had been developed in the previous century. Jesus continues, however, to be shown victorious, for he is not represented as dead and hanging from the cross, but alive: he looks directly at the viewer, before whom he stands with compelling vigor, just as the figure on the gemstone was (Figure 18.3). Only two examples of these developments survive: the four relief panels known as the Maskell Passion Ivories (*c.* 420–430, Figure 18.9), and the near-contemporary wooden doors from the church of Santa Sabina in Rome (Figure 18.10). Other evidence may be gleaned from now-lost mosaic cycles, documented in literature.

Figure 18.9 Plaques with Passion cycle (the "Maskell Passion Ivories"), ivory, Northern Italy or Rome (?), *c.* 420–430. London, The British Museum. Photo: © Trustees of the British Museum.

Figure 18.10 Panel with the Crucifixion, from the carved wooden doors of the church of Santa Sabina, Rome, *c.* 432 (in situ). © DeA Picture Library/Art Resource, New York.

The four ivories originally formed the sides of a small box (the lid and base now missing), likely made in a Northern Italian workshop for the purpose of storing or transporting a portion of the consecrated host, or perhaps a relic. They are exquisitely carved in high relief with a sequential cycle of seven episodes from the Passion: Pilate's judgment, the way to Calvary (Jesus now carrying his cross), Peter's denial, Judas's suicide, the crucifixion, women and soldiers at the empty tomb, and the appearance of Christ to the disciples, incorporating the incredulity of Thomas. Although the crucifixion is included, the earliest surviving example in a narrative cycle, the emphasis of the cycle as a whole continues to rest confidently on the resurrection.[36] The muscular body of Jesus stands boldly against the cross, impervious to the nails or spear that pierce his flesh. His heroic strength is emphasized through a remarkable visual and theological contrast with the limp body of Judas hanging dead alongside him, the noose having snapped the betrayer's neck. This affirmation of Jesus's dominion and divine power on the cross is further used to assert the triumph of the church: in the final panel, the risen Jesus appears among his disciples, announcing their mission as teachers in the church. Jesus extends his left arm as though in a gesture of speech; yet he simultaneously reveals to Thomas the wound in his side, which the artist shows being made by the soldier energetically thrusting his lance into the crucified Jesus. Thomas inserts the index finger of his right hand into the wound. This action had previously been depicted (on the sarcophagus of San Celso in Milan, second half of the fourth century),[37] but the composition set forth here establishes the pictorial tradition that would prove most influential in western Medieval and Byzantine art.

On the doors of Santa Sabina, still *in situ*, an even larger number of Passion episodes are recalled, not in sequence, but integrated within a complex cycle of Old and New Testament scenes: the prophesy of Peter's denial; the trial (Christ before Caiaphas and Pilate washing his hands), with Christ carrying his cross; the crucifixion; the women at the tomb; Christ appearing to two women; Christ appearing to the disciples; and, as on the Servanne sarcophagus, the ascension concludes the cycle.[38] Some scenes offer a full visualization of previously seen episodes, continuing the significant role played by Passion narratives of the fourth century, such as those on sarcophagi and the Brescia casket. The trial occupies two panels: Pilate washes his hands while Christ is led away, and Jesus appears before Caiaphas in a densely populated scene. Despite this fulsome treatment, the trial is rarely found in other media before the sixth century. Other scenes are sparing in their narrative detail. Just three figures evoke the entire crucifixion scene (Figure 18.10): the large naked figure of Jesus stands (and does not hang) between the two crucified thieves, who are shown on a much reduced scale. As in the Maskell crucifixion, nails are visible: but in the pictorial strategies of differentiation in scale and the highly symmetrical arrangement of the composition around Jesus as the axial figure, and his standing posture, the scene directly recalls the design of the Constanza gem. This very symmetry, with Jesus as the central dominant figure in the scene—which also emulates the *crux invicta* in its strict division of iconographic elements either side of the cross—would emerge as the standard template upon which crucifixion iconography is henceforth developed.

Thus, by the end of the fifth century, the repertoire of Passion episodes was well-developed and the inclusion of the crucifixion more frequent, and it is likely that longer narrative cycles were already known to both Eastern and Western Christians. In Gaza, the sixth-century rhetorician Choricius writes that the church of Saint Sergius was decorated with a cycle of images that began with the annunciation, included numerous Passion episodes that had become standard during the early Christian period (the crucifixion, the women and soldiers at the tomb, the post-resurrection appearance to Mary and the women), and concluded with the ascension.[39]

The manuscript known as the Gospels of St Augustine, written and illuminated in Italy in the late sixth century and taken to Canterbury before the end of the seventh century, attests to the continued iconographic connection to early Christian models and to the practice of conflating different gospel narratives versions to establish a single account of Christ's Passion (Figure 18.11). On the recto of folio 125, twelve small scenes illustrate a cycle that begins with the entry and concludes with Jesus carrying his own cross, a choice that has been taken to indicate the existence of a second page on which the Passion, including the crucifixion and resurrection, was completed.[40] The Passion story was familiar to the viewer, yet the choice and sequential arrangement of events in art reflected not the gospel narratives but the cycle of the Christian year, the liturgical celebration of feasts impacting on the way events were read together. This sort of reading is certainly true for the depiction of Passion episodes in Syria and Palestine in the sixth century, where celebration of the life of Jesus as a continuous liturgical cycle proved influential in the cyclical organization of images as well as in their depiction.[41] The cycle of the annunciation, nativity, baptism, crucifixion, and the women at the tomb is subsequently found repeated across personal objects (such as marriage rings or bracelets), liturgical objects (such as censers), and items produced for the pilgrim trade (small flasks or *ampullae* for collecting oil or water blessed at the holy sites; clay tokens). At the same time, the iconography of individual narrative scenes could be inflected with liturgical symbolism. In depictions of the women at the tomb on sixth-century ivory pyxides produced in the eastern Mediterranean for example, the women swing censers as they approach the "tomb," represented symbolically as an altar.[42]

Figure 18.11 Passion cycle containing twelve episodes: page from the Gospels of St Augustine (MS 286, fol. 125r), written and illuminated in Italy in the late sixth century. Cambridge, Corpus Christi College. Photo: By permission of the Master and Fellows of Corpus Christi College, Cambridge.

Conclusion

While evidence for the representation of the Passion is scarce, the various images of Jesus crucified produced before the fourth century and the distribution of that material across the western and eastern Roman Empires permits several observations. By the third century, the interest in Jesus as a crucified yet divine savior, as documented in literary sources, was beginning to find visual expression. The image of Jesus crucified was known across the ancient Mediterranean to be a powerful and efficacious symbol both to people who were and people who were not his followers; images were known to artisans, were familiar to the general populace, and remained influential as Christian art evolved in the fourth and fifth centuries. Parallels in iconography and the compositional arrangement of scenes across media also raise the possibility that models were developed and transmitted among artisans and designers as sketches, perhaps in manuscripts, pattern books, or other methods of direct copying within the workshop.

Finally, although depictions of Passion events were slow to appear, sarcophagi, which furnish the richest source of evidence for their representation in early Christianity, indicate that a repertoire of imagery was known by workshops in Gaul and Rome by the mid-fourth century. The iconographic developments seen in funerary sculpture establish patterns that would be influential in the luxury arts of the fifth and sixth centuries, from manuscript illumination and ivory carving to monumental cycles in mosaic and fresco. As narrative cycles evolved in this process, post-resurrection scenes played a pivotal role in the presentation of a triumphant route to ascension: they effectively place understandings of the crucifixion in the concept of victory, a victory secured by Jesus over death in the resurrection. This anchoring speaks not to an active avoidance or downplaying of Christ's sufferings, but powerful expression to contemporary theological priorities and early Christian preaching about the cross as a revelation of divine power.

These very priorities may be glimpsed in the use of the staurogram in specific literary contexts where the cross, and the figure of Jesus crucified, is understood as a sacred sign, and one of salvation. In the fifth century this focus on resurrection began to give way as curiosity about the events in Jerusalem arose, leading to the investigation of the historical remains of Passion events (notably the exposure of the rock of Golgotha and the discovery and veneration of the wood of the cross) and increased theological attention on the nature of Jesus's suffering on the cross. These developments, including the liturgical celebration of the eucharist as the blood and body of the crucified Christ, allowed new avenues for engagement with the death and triumph of Jesus in public ritual, private devotion, and pilgrimage. In the sixth century, this focus was displaced by an intensified concern and emotional engagement with the sufferings of Jesus. This signals a new era in the art of the Passion, where Christ's dominion is anchored in the historical crucifixion, and only then does pictorial interest come to focus on chronicling a more violent course to crucifixion.

Notes

1 Felicity Harley and Jeffrey Spier, "Magical Amulet with the Crucifixion," in Jeffrey Spier, ed., *Picturing the Bible: The Earliest Christian Art* (New Haven: Yale University Press, 2007), no. 55, 228–229.

2 Roy Kotansky, "The Magic Crucifixion Gem," *Greek, Roman and Byzantine Studies* 57 (2017): 631–659.

3 Heikki Solin and Marja Itkonen-Kaila, *Paedagogium* (Graffiti del Palatino, I, ed. Veikko Väänänen; Acta Institutum Romanum Finlandiae 3; Helsinki: 1966), 209–211; Martin Langner, *Antike Graffitizeichnungen: Motive, Gestaltung und Bedeutung* (Wiesbaden: L. Reichert, 2001), no. 1242, 60 and taf. 80.

4 Felicity Harley-McGowan, "The Alexamenos Graffito," in C. Keith, ed., *The Reception of Jesus in the First Three Centuries III* (London: Bloomsbury T&T Clark, forthcoming).

5 Langner, *Antike Graffitizeichnungen*, no. 1366, taf. 90; John G. Cook, "Crucifixion as Spectacle in Roman Campagnia," *Novum Testamentum* 54 (2012): 68–100.

6 Spier, *Picturing the Bible*, no. 56, 229.

7 Felicity Harley-McGowan, "The Constanza carnelian and the development of crucifixion iconography in Late Antiquity," in Christopher Entwistle and Noel Adams, eds, *"Gems of Heaven": Recent Research on Engraved Gemstones in Late Antiquity, AD 200–600* (London: British Museum, 2011), 214–220.
8 Erich Dinkler, *Signum Crucis* (Tübingen: J.C.B. Mohr, Paul Siebeck, 1967), 178.
9 Larry Hurtado, *The Earliest Christian Artifacts: Manuscripts and Christian Origins* (Grand Rapids: Eerdmans, 2006), 135–154; Brent Nongbri, "The Limits of Palaeographic Dating of Literary Papyri: Some Observations on the Date and Provenance of P. Bodmer II (P66)," *Museum Helveticum* 71 (June 2014): 1–35.
10 Felicity Harley-McGowan, "Death is Swallowed up in Victory: Scenes of Death in Early Christian Art and the Emergence of Crucifixion Iconography," *Cultural Studies Review* 17.1 (2011): 101–124.
11 Michael Peppard, *The World's Oldest Church* (New Haven: Yale University Press, 2016), Chapter 4.
12 André Grabar, *Christian Iconography: A Study of its Origins* (London: Routledge, 1969), 123–124.
13 Archer St. Clair, "The Visit to the Tomb: Narrative and Liturgy on Three Early Christian Pyxides," *Gesta* 18.1 (1979): 127–135 and figs 1, 4, 7.
14 Fabrizio Bisconti, *Le Pitture delle catacomb Romane: Restauri e interpretazioni* (Todi: Tau, 2011), fig. 20, 85–105.
15 Roald Dijkstra, *The Apostles in Early Christian Art and Poetry* (Leiden and Boston: Brill 2016), 232; Spier, *Picturing the Bible*, 15–20.
16 Robin M. Jensen, "Early Christian Images and Exegesis," in Spier, *Picturing the Bible*, 78–83.
17 Gertrud Schiller, *Iconography of Christian Art: Vol. 2, The Passion of Jesus Christ* (Greenwich: New York Graphic Society, 1972), 1–3.
18 Friedrich Wilhelm Deichmann, Giuseppe Bovini and Hugo Brandenburg, *Repertorium der christlich-antiken Sarkophage I. Rom und Ostia*, 2 vols (Wiesbaden: F. Steiner, 1967), no. 680, 279–283.
19 For example, Deichmann, *Repertorium*, nos 58, 56.
20 Schiller, *Iconography*, 42–43.
21 For example, Deichmann, *Repertorium*, no. 770, 316–317.
22 For example, ibid., nos 40 and 41, 35–37.
23 For example, ibid., no. 946, 394–395.
24 Bente Kiilerich, *Late Fourth Century Classicism in the Plastic Arts* (Odense: Odense University Press, 1993), 154–157 and figs 85, 86.
25 Deichmann, *Repertorium*, nr. 49; Spier, *Picturing the Bible*, no. 46, 219–220.
26 Harley-McGowan, "Constanza Carnelian," with the lost gem illustrated at 215, plate 2.
27 Brigitte Christern-Briesenick, *Repertorium der Christlich-Antiken Sarkophage, bd III: Frankreich, Algerien, Tunesien* (Mainz am Rhein: Verlag Philipp von Zanbern, 2003), no. 42, 29–31.
28 Schiller, *Iconography*, 64.
29 Catherine Brown Tkacz, *The Key to the Brescia Casket* (Notre Dame: University of Notre Dame Press; Paris: Institut d'Etudes Augustiennes, 2002).
30 Ibid., 241–242.
31 Dijkstra, *Apostles in Early Christian Art and Poetry*, 52–55.
32 Schiller, *Iconography*, 66.
33 Deborah Mauskopf Deliyannis, *Ravenna in Late Antiquity* (Cambridge: Cambridge University Press, 2010), 152–158.
34 Dijkstra, *Apostles in Early Christian Art and Poetry*, 52.
35 Spier, *Picturing the Bible*, no. 76, 256–258.
36 Felicity Harley-McGowan, "The Maskell Passion Ivories and Greco-Roman Art," in *Envisioning Christ on the Cross*, eds Juliet Mullins, Jenifer Ní Ghrádaigh and Richard Hawtree (Dublin: Four Courts Press, 2013), 13–33.
37 Jutta Dresken-Weiland, *Repertorium der christlich-antiken Sarkophage*, II: Italien mit einem Nachtrag Rom und Ostia, Dalmatien, Museen der Welt (Mainz: von Zabern, 1998), no. 250, 87–88.
38 Jean-Michel Spieser, "Le Programme Iconographique des Portes de Sainte-Sabine," *Journal des Savants* 21 (1991): 47–81.
39 Cyril Mango, *The Art of the Byzantine Empire 312–1453* (Toronto and London: University of Toronto Press in association with the Medieval Academy of America, 1986), 60–68.
40 Francis Wormald, *The Miniatures in the Gospels of St Augustine, Corpus Christi College ms. 286* (Cambridge: Cambridge University Press, 1954), 11–12.

41 Derek Krueger, *Liturgical Subjects: Christian Ritual, Biblical Narrative, and the Formation of the Self in Byzantium* (Philadelphia: University of Pennsylvania Press, 2014).
42 St Clair, "Visit to the Tomb."

Further reading

Jaś Elsner, "Image and Rhetoric in Early Christian Sarcophagi: Reflections on Jesus' Trial," in *Life, Death and Representation: Some New Work on Roman Sarcophagi*, eds Elsner and Huskinson (Berlin: de Gruyter, 2011), 359–386. The trial often served to refer to the entire Passion story; this analysis of the pictorial evidence for its depiction sheds light not only on the methods of treating the scene, but more broadly illuminates ways by which Christians used imagery on sarcophagi, and specifically the broader function of the Passion theme in that pictorial context.

Friedrich Gerke, *Die Zeitbestimmung der Passionssarkophage* (Berlin: De Gruyter, 1940). Still one of the most helpful examinations of the rich body of evidence that is the Passion sarcophagi.

Robin Jensen, "The Passion in Early Christian Art", in C. Joynes, ed., *Perspectives on the Passion: Encountering the Bible through the Arts* (London: T & T Clark International, 2007), 53–84. For a comprehensive overview of the representation of the Passion in early Christian art this should be the starting point, read in conjunction with Schiller.

Gertrud Schiller, *Iconography of Christian Art*, Vol. II, "The Passion of Jesus Christ," trans. J. Seligman (London: Lund Humphries, 1972). The most thorough survey of the iconographic evidence available, treating each episode individually while deftly addressing broader theological, liturgical, literary and historical issues. It remains essential.

Alexander Soper, "The Italo-Gallic School of Early Christian Art," *Art Bulletin* 20.2 (1938): 145–192. Excursus (no. III) furnishes an invaluable list of Western monuments documenting the emergence of the Passion cycle, even though it is no longer completely accurate. This should be read in conjunction with Schiller's more detailed treatment of the episodes and theme as a whole, and Jensen's overview.

19

MIRACLES AND ART

Lee M. Jefferson

Miracles—particularly miracles involving healing—elicited sincere devotion and faith in early Christianity. Miracles additionally addressed the maladies of human existence that afflict the general population. An argument for rationality simply could not quell the intense desire to believe in miraculous cures. In Late Antiquity, this desire manifested itself in art and material culture. In the early fifth century, the theologian and bishop Augustine notably adapted his negative stance on miracles due to the arrival of the relics of St Stephen in his bishopric of Hippo.[1] Laity flocked to the relics, some by desire of receiving a healing miracle. After witnessing the frenzy of belief by the laity, Augustine eventually recognized the value in miraculous healings procured by the relics of Stephen.[2] The healing miracles not only educed faith, they provided comfort; and comfort in fifth-century Hippo was likely difficult to come by.

This brief allegory involving Augustine reveals the power and importance the laity placed in miracles in Late Antiquity. Miracles were in fact the currency of the faithful in Late Antiquity, so powerful that it forced an early church author and notable theologian to soften his well-entrenched rational position on the subject. One vehicle for this nascent devotion to miracles was art and material culture. The subject of miracles was omnipresent in early Christian art and imagery. Augustine's Hippo provides just one example of their relevance and importance, as material culture and miracles converge, illustrating the desire to obtain relief, comfort, and proximity to God.

This chapter will discuss the prevalence of miracles in early Christian art by focusing on the mediums in which they appeared, and the specific categories of miracles that were depicted. Early Christians created their art in a funerary environment that included catacomb wall paintings and relief sculpture on sarcophagi. Art and imagery were also featured in the private sphere that included gold/glass objects, many of which depict miracles. These included healing miracles from the gospels such as the healing of the paralytic, the healing of the blind man, and the woman with the hemorrhage. Other miracles depicted could be classified as nature miracles such as the Cana miracle and the multiplication of loaves. Finally, an often-depicted miracle that defies classification is the raising of the dead. When Christ is depicted in the act of performing miracles, he bears a stylistic implement that appears to be a staff. This chapter will be structured to discuss each of these categories of miracles in due turn.

General observers typically wonder why miracles were so important and popular in early Christian art and why early Christians preferred to depict the miracles of Christ rather than Christ crucified. This chapter, by examining some of the evidence and explaining the historical context in which these images appeared, will offer an answer: miracles promoted the power of Jesus in a pluralistic religious environment, and provided comfort to a people that desired such support.

The historical context of miracle imagery in early Christian art

Early Christians were very visually oriented, cultivating an artistic language during their development. This point challenges the well-entrenched maxim of prior scholarship that early Christians refrained from creating art. Scholars such as Ernst Kitzinger in the twentieth century maintained that early Christians were hostile towards visual art, holding the position that it is tantamount to idolatry, and thus stunting its growth.[3] However, not only have discoveries from the third century at Dura-Europos revealed that early Christians (and Jews) were very invested in creating their visual culture, but also textual examples survive that support the notion that early Christians were interested in art. Notably, the third-century bishop Clement of Alexandria instructed his flock to avoid certain images and symbols such as swords and rather choose "a dove, or a fish, or a ship scudding in the wind, or a musical lyre" to use as decoration.[4] Clement's edict reveals that the laity were so interested in creating imagery that it had to be vetted.

Thus, both text and material evidence suggests that early Christians were not against creating a visual language, but were perhaps influenced by their religious neighbors and their Roman context. The image of Jesus performing miracles was a primary motif in early Christian art through the fifth century.[5] Viewers may be surprised that early Christians chose not to visualize the death of Jesus on a cross. Images of the crucifixion are stark in early Christianity, and do not appear readily in the visual record until the fifth and sixth centuries (see Felicity Harley-McGowan's chapter on the subject in this volume). Rather than show Jesus suffering on a cross, early Christians preferred to show a powerful Jesus performing wonders. When Christian supremacy was far from secured, early Christians deemed it important to show their savior god vibrant rather than dying a thief's death.

This choice also reflects the context of miracle-working imagery in Late Antiquity. The images of a miracle-working Christ did not appear *ex nihilo*. The images of Christ healing and performing miracles were similar to images of heroes and Olympian gods. The images of a healing Christ emphasize the efficacy of Jesus's miracles over against those touted by non-Christian cults. Moreover, these images largely occurred in a funerary environment, reminding observers of the future resurrection and life through Christ. Images of Jesus provided a sense of understanding and identity to early Christians. Viewers could witness their chosen healer and miracle worker as greater than any rival, efficacious both in performing earthly healings and providing for the future life.

By the late fourth century, the image of Christ healing and performing miracles had not only persisted but increased. In a post-Constantinian age, when Christians were more or less secure from persecution, the image of Jesus performing healings and miracles was more popular than in the earlier age of Christian persecution.[6] Miracle imagery likely proliferated in post-Constantinian Christianity partially because church leaders did not desire their congregations to be fractured in their observance, and it speaks to a continued rivalry with competing Greco-Roman religions.

Healing miracles

The baptistery in the Christian house church of Dura-Europos and the catacomb of Callistus in Rome both feature some of the earliest wall paintings in the Christian visual lexicon.

The catacomb of Callistus dates from the beginning of the third century CE while the Dura house church dates from the early to mid-third century CE. Both environments feature a similar portrayal of Jesus healing the paralytic, which also serves as one of the earliest images of Jesus. At Dura, Jesus stands at the top of the healing scene, stretching forth his right hand as if directing the action that takes place below, featuring the paralytic lying on his bed and, moments later, standing and holding his woven bed frame on his back (Figure 19.1). Immediately adjacent to the scene of Christ's baptism in the catacomb of Callistus is an image of the healed paralytic. This scene does not include an image of Jesus. Rather, the solitary figure of the healed paralytic is shown holding his bed frame above his head in a manner that becomes emblematic of Christ's healing act (Figure 19.2). The position of this scene next to the portrayal of Jesus's baptism is appropriate at Callistus, and its baptismal significance is also emphasized at the site of Dura where the earliest Christian baptistery was uncovered. Narratively, the healing of the paralytic is not the first miracle of Christ's ministry in the synoptic gospels.[7] Mark begins with Jesus's baptism, and immediately follows with several of Christ's healings and miracles. Matthew, Mark, and Luke include the healing of Peter's mother-in-law as well as the cleansing of a leper directly after Jesus's baptism and before the healing of the paralytic. The Gospel of John uses the episode in the healing scene at the pool of Bethesda in John 5:2–9. Christ encounters an invalid near the healing pool and orders him to take up his mat and walk.

Figure 19.1 Fresco of the healing of the paralytic, Dura-Europos baptistery, Syria, *ca.* 232 CE. Yale-French excavations at Dura-Europos 1932.1202. Yale University Art Gallery.

Figure 19.2 Fresco of the healing of the paralytic and the baptism of Jesus, Catacomb of Callistus, Rome, early 3rd century. Joseph Wilpert, *Roma sotterranea: le pitture delle catacomb romane* (Rome: Desclée, Lefebvre, 1903).

Why the Christians at Dura and the catacomb of Callistus chose to depict the paralytic rather than the earlier scenes of Jesus's healing is curious. Particularly at Callistus, following Jesus's baptism, a scene in which he heals the leper or casts out demons would follow narratively in the order of Jesus's ministry.[8] However, few catacomb painting depictions of such exorcisms survive in the corpus of early Christian art. Similarly, the cleansing of the leper was not a depiction included in the catacombs. The healing of the paralytic was a popular story due to its dramatic assertion that Jesus was unique with formidable authority to perform such miracles on the Sabbath. Jesus orders the paralytic to "Get up" (ἐγείρω), which the King James Version translates as "Arise." Such language serves as a metaphor for resurrection. Just as the paralytic rises up, so do the Christian dead. Mark and Luke ended the miracle narrative with the crowd exclaiming, "We have never seen anything like this" (Mark 2:12; Luke 5:26). Such a reading informs the paralytic's appearance at both Callistus and Dura. The funerary environment of Callistus obviously informs such an interpretation of "rising," and the baptismal environment of Dura contributes to a similar interpretation as the liturgical action of baptism is partly read through Romans 6: dying and rising with Christ as one is immersed and emerges from the font.[9]

Around fifteen catacomb examples of the healing of the paralytic have been recovered.[10] Along with the representation at the catacomb of Callistus, one more exists at the catacomb under the Vigna Massimo and another in the catacomb of Peter and Marcellinus. In the catacombs, the paralytic scene conveys the nature of narrative imagery in early Christian art and correlates to the cognate images in its immediate environment. While the paralytic scene is not the most duplicated of all the scenes depicting Christ as a miracle worker, it does portray a successful healing; the paralytic is walking proof of Christ's powers. While restoring sight to the blind, healing the woman with the issue of blood, or even raising Lazarus emphasizes the dramatic moment of the miracle itself, the healing of the paralytic more deeply captures the end result of the healing—the restored life of the man who was healed.

The iconography of the paralytic story in Christian relief sculpture is very similar to the scene's representation in the catacombs.[11] The standard portrayal of the young man as little more than a boy, carrying his mat after the act of healing, continues on sarcophagi in the Museo Pio Cristiano of the Vatican Museums (Figures 19.3–4). These relief sculptures include more surrounding figures (Figure 19.3). The disproportionate size of the figures in the art is significant.

Figure 19.3 Sarcophagus with miracle scenes, Museo Pio Cristiano, mid-4th century. Vanni Archive/ Art Resource, New York.

Christ is depicted on a larger scale than the recipients of his healing power; the paralytic is portrayed as much smaller than his healer and miracle worker. Other scenes of miracles often flank images of Christ performing his healing. Occasionally, sculpted columns or barriers frame each scene. With few significant narrative details, the identification of each scene usually relies upon repeated symbols such as the paralytic's mat. In the example immediately to the left of the paralytic scene, the cock at the feet of the bearded apostle indicates the figure as Peter and symbolizes his betrayal from the gospels (Figure 19.3).

While the boy carrying his bed frame clearly signifies the paralytic account in the synoptic gospels, reliefs on fourteen sarcophagi recall the Johannine account of the pool at Bethesda (Figure 19.4).[12] On a typical Bethesda sarcophagus, such as one featured in the Museo Pio Cristiano, a pool represents the setting of the miracle in John 5. In the central scene separating the upper and lower zones, a carved barrier with wavy striated lines suggests water. Since this central scene involves a ritual at a pool, the typical interpretation is that it alludes to baptism.[13] The association between water and a healing signals the restorative washing that takes place during this event. What makes this sarcophagus distinctive is the illustration in the central panel. In the lower register, the paralytic lies on his bed in the posture of Jonah/Endmyion (the mythic figure lured into eternal sleep by the moon goddess Selene), although the paralytic is not nude. The figure represents one of the disabled people whom John describes lying near the pool.[14] Above the depiction of the paralytic lying in repose, Christ orders him to walk, gestures toward the paralytic with his hand and almost appears to touch the top of his mat.

Figure 19.4 Bethesda sarcophagus, Museo Pio Cristiano, Vatican Museums, late 4th century. Vanni Archive/Art Resource, New York.

In these and other examples, the focus is the moment when Christ delivers his instruction and the paralytic takes up his mat and walks, highlighting Christ's authority and power. Jesus holds a scroll in his other hand as in cognate representations, emphasizing his authority, just as the biblical scene affirms his ability to forgive sins on earth. With few exceptions, in Christian relief sculpture the healing of the paralytic reminds its audience of the power associated with Jesus, also indicated by the scroll. And the healing act is signaled ambiguously by Jesus's gesture of speech or more blatantly through the touch of his hand. By contrast, depictions such as the healing of the blind more clearly underscore the power of touch in the execution of Jesus's miracles.

In the recovered evidence there are more instances of the healing of the blind man in relief sculpture than in catacomb wall painting, however it seems early Christians were interested in depicting the miracle.[15] Paintings in the catacomb of Peter and Marcellinus portray Christ touching the eyes of his patient, whose arms are raised in the position of prayer (Figure 19.5). Other scenes render Christ touching the patient with his entire hand. The healing of the blind exhibits Christ physically encountering and healing his supplicants. While few examples can be found in the catacombs, this healing image was popular in fourth- and fifth-century examples of Christian relief sculpture and is the most frequently represented healing image in extant Christian relief sculpture.

In the surviving Roman examples, the healing of the blind man appears more often than any other healing story.[16] The scene portrays Christ physically touching the patient with his hand or fingers. Unlike the healing of the paralytic represented in relief sculpture, which includes several divergent representations, those that portray Christ healing the blind man are fairly consistent. The representation describes the comparatively large figure of Christ touching the eyes or face of the patient, who is depicted on Jesus's left or right. All of the gospels include the story of Christ healing blind persons. Some accounts describe the events as predicated by the patients'

Figure 19.5 Wall painting of Christ healing a blind man, Catacomb of Peter and Marcellinus, Rome, late 3rd century. Image from Joseph Wilpert, *Die Malereien der Katakomben Roms* (Freiburg: Herder, 1903).

faith, as Christ affirms that their faith has healed them. Other accounts in the gospels (Mark 10:51; Matt. 9:27–30; 20:29–34; Luke 18:35–43; John 9:1–41) detail Christ's healing touch as the catalyst of the event. In Christian relief sculpture, the representations of Christ healing the blind man follow the accounts that describe the power of Christ's touch. That is, instead of emphasizing the gesture of Christ's hand, implying the healing action that is taking place, the healing power of Christ's touch is on display in the healing of the blind man.

Representative examples of the scene in relief sculpture from Rome offer insight into its significance. Certain Roman examples include the healing of the blind man along with a representation of the seated paralytic on his bed. The blind man is usually depicted as much smaller than the figure of Christ, and he is shown holding a staff similar to the one the Jesus occasionally wields. Christ places his hand or fingers on the blind man's face or touches the top of his head. The scene stresses Christ's touch; his fingers upon the face of the afflicted are shown in detail, and occasionally in other examples the blind man's sightless eyes are given definition.[17]

Images that feature the healing touch of Christ have an underlying message. His touch demonstrates his curative power, since his healings were a result of real physical interaction between physician and patient. By contrast, the healing god Asclepius's remedies were provided through the power of dreams. Temple priests would supply a prescription after the patient had slept in the Asclepieion. An image of Christ healing through touch spread the message of his superiority, since his healing power was depicted as a tangible action taking place between healer and patient. The power of the healer is promoted in these images. In other words, Jesus healed his patients immediately in the physical world, not through the power of dreams.

While miracle images promote the power of Jesus, they also reveal the importance of the faith of the patient. For example, the faith of the woman with the hemorrhage is indicated by Jesus as part of the healing process ("your faith has made you well"), and the viewing audience would be reminded of the text by witnessing the image in a funerary context (Luke 8:48). The woman in the image is depicted as reaching out to touch Jesus's clothes. She touches Jesus rather than Jesus touching her. This is a possible visual reinforcement of the gospel message where the main actor in the scene is the "patient" rather than the healer. In a funerary context, such images visually realized the connection between faith "making one well" in this world and faith in the resurrection.

While the narrative of the woman with the blood issue asserts that the woman's faith made her well, the story nevertheless emphasizes healing touch, although the normal direction is reversed. The woman touches Jesus out of her desire to be healed. The episode appears in all three synoptic gospels, while it is absent from the gospel of John.[18] The scene of the woman with the issue of blood appears in catacomb art that emphasizes physical contact in a healing context. At the catacomb of Peter and Marcellinus, the woman kneels below the figure of Christ, clutching the hem of his tunic. The woman touches him, recalling the moment when Christ realizes the healing power "goes out from him." Christ gestures toward the woman with his hand, possibly in recognition of the event or in blessing.[19] Christian relief sculpture depicts the scene of the woman with the issue of blood in a way similar to the catacomb painting of Peter and Marcellinus. Christ touches the woman while she touches him; it is a scene centered upon physical contact. Some examples include only the woman touching Jesus's robe, while others show Christ withholding his touch while motioning toward her in the gesture of address.

Nature miracles

Along with healing miracles, early Christian art includes multiple instances of the wedding at Cana and the division of loaves, miracles that can be classified as "nature miracles" since they deal with the natural world rather than a human patient.[20] Although these instances do not appear in the earliest catacomb art, the nature miracles are more apparent in Christian relief sculpture. Both stories imply sacramental and liturgical application. Both Jerome and Prudentius reveal in early Christian writings the practice of worshipping in the catacombs that possibly could have included meal rituals.[21] Jerome writes of the funerary environment of the catacombs as an aid in guiding his prayer, leading scholars like Margaret Miles to argue that the catacomb paintings were visual mnemonic devices to remind viewers of the liturgical action.[22] Paulinus, Ambrose, and Augustine all recall the habit of the laity of "dining with the dead," ritual observances that reflect Roman influence that, more often than not, became quite rowdy.[23] Thus, it seems quite unsurprising that Jesus's transformative miracles of turning water into wine and dividing loaves were depicted in early Christian art that was largely funerary.

The Cana miracle appears only in the gospel of John, inaugurates his miracles, and points towards the cross. The miracle itself, taking place at a wedding banquet, seems to overtly foreshadow the Last Supper and the establishment of the eucharist. Its appearance in art supports such a conclusion. At the catacomb of Peter and Marcellinus from the late third century, Christ is portrayed standing above the large jars, gesturing to them with a staff while a banquet scene takes place behind him (Figure 19.6). The scene recalls other banquet scenes at the same catacomb, in which captions indicate that the dinner guests are issuing orders for more wine to the servants Irene and Agape. Similarly, in artistic representations of the division of loaves, Jesus either points a staff towards baskets at his feet, or he holds bread in two outstretched hands indicating the miraculous action occurring. The eucharistic overtones in the Cana miracle and the division of the loaves are apparent. In a funerary environment where people either dined with the dead or celebrated the eucharist, the nature miracles of Christ mirrored the sacramental

Figure 19.6 Wall painting of the Cana miracle, Catacomb of Peter and Marcellinus, Rome, late 3rd century. Image from Joseph Wilpert, *Die Malereien der Katakomben Roms* (Freiburg: Herder, 1903).

action occurring within the sacred space. Recalling John 6 where Jesus feeds the five thousand, he proclaims "unless you eat the flesh of the Son of Man and drink his blood, you have no life in you" (John 6:53). In a funerary context, the nature miracle images reinforce and point towards a time where there will be no earthly life in the participant, but eternal life. In this environment, image, text and ritual point towards resurrection.

Nature miracles, chiefly the Cana miracle and the division of loaves, are also popular subjects in Christian relief sculpture (Figure 19.7).[24] Typically, on a sarcophagus example, Jesus holds two outstretched hands with baskets at his feet, revealing the subject of the miracle that is depicted. However, on the Sarcophagus of Marcus Claudianus that also resides in Rome, Christ's wonder-working staff is featured in both nature miracles, which flank a central orant figure (Figure 19.7). In the scene of the Cana miracle, Christ points the staff toward several small jars at his feet, indicating the miraculous transformative action that is occurring. In the representation of the multiplication of the loaves, Jesus also points his staff towards diminutive baskets of bread at his feet. Notably, many of the extant sarcophagi were discovered within the catacombs. As in the catacombs, representations of the Cana miracle and the multiplication of the loaves on funerary relief sculpture likely reflect the sacramental action proceeding in the immediate space, be it a catacomb or another environment. The representations of these miracles reflect dining practices, and point towards sacramental action that family members of the dead may have been enacting in the sacred space itself, exhibiting the function of miracle images in early Christian art.

Raising the dead

Four major scenes of raising the dead appear in early Christian art: Jesus raising the widow's son at Nain, Jesus raising Jairus's daughter, Jesus appearing as a type of Ezekiel in the Valley of the Dry Bones, and Jesus raising Lazarus.[25] Typically, each scene features Jesus gesturing toward a

Figure 19.7 Sarcophagus of Marcus Claudianus with Cana miracle and multiplication of the loaves, Rome, 330–340 CE. Museo Nazionale Romano.

body with his miracle-working implement, beckoning the figure to awake and rise. The raising of Lazarus is the most easily identifiable, since it normally features a mummified body within an *aediculum* (burial house). The other three scenes are slightly more challenging to identify, since they do not bear the iconographic hallmarks of the Lazarus scene. In the other three scenes, Christ uses his staff to touch either the bed of Jairus's daughter, a burial box containing a rising figure, or a figure lying inert at his feet. The viewer must make some interpretive decisions in order to discern which resurrection narrative is being depicted.

The scene of the raising of Lazarus is distinct in its popularity in Late Antiquity and its mode of depiction. Lazarus is another prominent miracle of Christ that is depicted first at the catacomb of Callistus and then at several other catacomb locations; it is also represented frequently on Christian funerary relief sculpture such as sarcophagi (Figure 19.8).[26] The resurrection scenes are slightly more varied in Christian relief sculpture than in catacomb wall paintings. However, the raising of Lazarus is still a primary motif, along with the healings of the widow's son at Nain and of Jairus's daughter. The raising of Lazarus occurs in sixty-five extant examples of Roman sarcophagi, and the image appears over twenty-three times in examples from Gaul and North Africa.[27] Considerably more recovered evidence featuring Lazarus survives than any other miracle depiction of raising the dead.

The catacomb of Priscilla image of Lazarus, like the paralytic scene, includes several typical elements (Figure 19.8). Christ stands to the side of a small *aediculum* that houses the wrapped figure of Lazarus. In this image Jesus is captured in the act of touching his staff to the burial house. Lazarus is small and diminutive, bearing no distinctive features other than the noticeable burial wrappings. The wrapped figure became the standard for portraying Lazarus. Arguably, the clear emphasis on the wrapped body could reveal a close reading of the Johannine text, where Lazarus's linen wrappings foreshadow the empty tomb scene with only Jesus's burial wrappings left behind on the floor (John 20:6). Thus, Lazarus's wrapped body is a sign that points towards the glory of the resurrection.[28]

On Christian sarcophagi, a larger-than-life Christ touches the *aediculum* with a wand or staff-like instrument, sometimes with Mary or Martha at his feet in the position remarkably similar to the woman with the blood issue (Figure 19.7). Christ wears a tunic with a *pallium*, and his staff emphasizes the miraculous action occurring. On the Marcus Claudianus sarcophagus, the scene appears on the far right side, bookending all of the miracles that appear on this front panel. On other Roman versions, the face of Lazarus is more distinctive while the linen wrappings are emphasized. Lazarus's sister is at Jesus's feet and flanking Jesus is what appears to be

Figure 19.8 Wall painting of the raising of Lazarus, Catacomb of Priscilla, Rome, early to mid-3rd century. Image from Wilpert.

a nude youth. This iconographic feature is rare, appearing in one other example at the Museo Pio Cristiano.

One question lingers: why was Lazarus featured more prominently than any other miracle of Jesus raising the dead? Arguably, it could reveal a fourth-century emphasis on the gospel of John. For example, all of the miracles involving Jesus on the Marcus Claudianus sarcophagus could be representative of a solitary reading of John, as Cana and Lazarus are unique to John's gospel (Figure 19.7). However, the canonical gospels portray Jesus's miracles differently than those of Moses or any Greco-Roman god in that he requires no intermediary (such as the God of Israel). In scripture and in Christian art, Jesus heals by virtue of his personal power. With his voice or his touch, Christ heals and performs miracles directly. In the miracles that include the use of a staff, such as the resurrection images, touch is still involved. This emphasis on the physicality of Jesus's miracles could intentionally contrast the mode of healing of Asclepius.[29] The prominence of the raising of Lazarus exhibited Christ performing a successful resurrection. In his myth, Asclepius performed the same action, but it brought about his death. Zeus killed him for raising the dead as he did not have the authority to restore life to the dead. The scene established the divine authority of Jesus as compared with Asclepius or any other god. In the imagery, Jesus accomplished his miracle through the power of physical touch. Jesus encountered and touched his patient Lazarus, and the art includes a witness with Lazarus's sister, vouching for his physical presence and the resulting miraculous act. Indeed, Origen argued against Celsus along these lines, claiming that Christ's miracles were real, since he had eyewitnesses.[30]

Lazarus's prominence seems more akin to a devoted interest in the Johannine narrative, and its usefulness in exhibiting the divine ability of Jesus over and against any rival or critic. Images of Jesus raising the dead were intended to remind viewers of the eternal life that was secured for Christians. The raising of the dead scenes also reiterated Jesus's power in a very clever way, in that they depicted Jesus as evocative of other gods and then as performing greater feats than those gods. The images conveyed the distinct abilities that set Christ above any other rival and his divine authority, proved by his work as a miraculous healer.

Early Christian art served many purposes in Late Antiquity. Images illustrated scenes from Scripture, exhibited theological understandings of Jesus, and served as propaganda. Images of Christ performing miracles like raising the dead fulfilled all of these functions marvelously. Featured in these particular miracles quite prominently is the curious inclusion of the miracle-working implement Jesus wields. It is to this tool that we now turn.

Wand or staff?

The curious tool (*virga* or *rabdos*) Jesus wields in the miracle images demands an explanation. In many of these miracle images, Jesus holds either a thin reed-like instrument or a thicker, ruddier tool. Upon initial examination, Jesus holds what appears to be a wand, thus suggesting that Jesus was a magician. Such a conclusion is based upon centuries of visual conditioning, and clichés concerning magicians wielding wands to enact their spell or feat of wonder. Through this lens, audiences may suggest that if a figure is performing a feat of wonder and bears a pointed tool, then it must be a wand. This identification of a "wand" is flawed, and the miracle-working tool should be identified as a "staff" rather than a "wand."

The staff in Christ's hand is not an empty symbol, the mark of a magician, or an example of the influence of non-Christian artists and workshops. And the staff of Jesus is more than just a symbol of power; it indicates his miracle-working and restorative ability. The staff shows Jesus as a powerful miracle worker, just as other iconographical features serve as symbols (Adam's nudity as recalling the ritual nudity at baptism, for example).

The term "staff" is a better identification for the implement, since it intentionally recalls not magic but the tool of another miracle worker that appears in early Christian art: Moses. The stylistic connection with Moses illustrates that early Christians utilized the visual medium to express the portrait of Christ as the superior wonder worker. The staff defines the consistent desire to portray Christ with a familiar stylistic accessory that places Moses in the minds of their viewers, so Jesus will be viewed not only as the fulfillment of prophecy but also as greater than Moses. Moses's miracles appear in the canon of early Christian art, particularly the separation of the waters of the Red Sea and the striking of the rock; both feature Moses using a staff as Jesus does (Figure 19.7; see also Figure 3.6). One other figure appears bearing a staff in early Christian art: the apostle Peter. Peter wields the staff in multiple scenes on early Christian relief sculpture.[31] On the sarcophagus of Marcus Claudianus as well as certain Vatican examples, Peter is depicted releasing water from the rock (far left side, Figure 19.7). These scenes recall a legend of Peter baptizing his Roman jailers before his martyrdom.[32] The legend is not from the canonical gospels but from the apocryphal *Acts of Peter*. The story describes Peter striking the "rock" of his cell walls, which released water he used to baptize the Roman converts, Processus and Martinianus.[33] The staff is meant to connect Jesus and Peter to Moses, and with the miracle of striking the rock, Peter is highlighted as a "new Moses" to a Christian audience.

The staff of Jesus has been explained as a relic of non-Christian influence or as evidence that early Christians considered Jesus to be a type of magician.[34] Viewers still may find it irresistible to quickly assume that Christ wielding a wand-like staff is an intentional evocation of Jesus as a magician.[35] The chief reason any portrait of Jesus as a magician fails is that magic was greatly maligned by Christians in Late Antiquity. Magic, like the Asclepius cult, offered a viable alternative for convalescence in a world where there were few options. People used magical incantations in Late Antiquity, much to the consternation of ecclesial leaders. The church fathers attacked the use of magic and any characterization of Jesus as a magician. Origen's rebuttal against Celsus, pointing out that Jesus did not use magical incantations, could work just as well against Smith.[36] Origen, Augustine, and Chrysostom all advocated for magic's banishment but found it persistent in Christian communities despite their vociferous attacks.[37]

From the comments of the church fathers, it appears that the hatred of magic and refusal to distinguish among levels of magic comes from the top down, not the ground up.[38] Publicly, Christian leaders denounced magic, but privately, magic was likely practiced by individuals who felt it was their only alternative to meet certain ends. "Magic" and "magician" were terms of slander and ridicule in Late Antiquity, and early Christians would not likely associate their savior with such a negative designation.[39] Moreover, Paul Corby Finney points out that no artistic renderings exist of magicians from Late Antiquity.[40] Images of purported magicians possibly existed; however, there were no known images of a magician in the act of exercising his trade.[41] There was no precedent for such an image in late antique art.

Depictions of the miracles of Jesus that also feature the staff appear in different media besides wall paintings or relief sculpture. Some fourth-century gold-glasses depict Jesus performing miracles. One fourth-century gold-glass bowl base in the Metropolitan Museum of Art includes three instances of Jesus bearing the staff in a miracle-working context (Figure 19.9; see also Figure 8.7). Jesus is depicted healing the paralytic, adjacent to the three youths in the fiery furnace, and on the lower left touches his staff to jars indicating the Cana miracle.

On another smaller example also at the Metropolitan Museum, Jesus is featured bearing the staff, touching it to the side, although the specific miracle is unclear (Figure 19.10). These two examples reiterate the popularity of the theme of Jesus performing miracles. Notably, instead of a funerary communal environment, these two art objects more likely come from the private sphere.

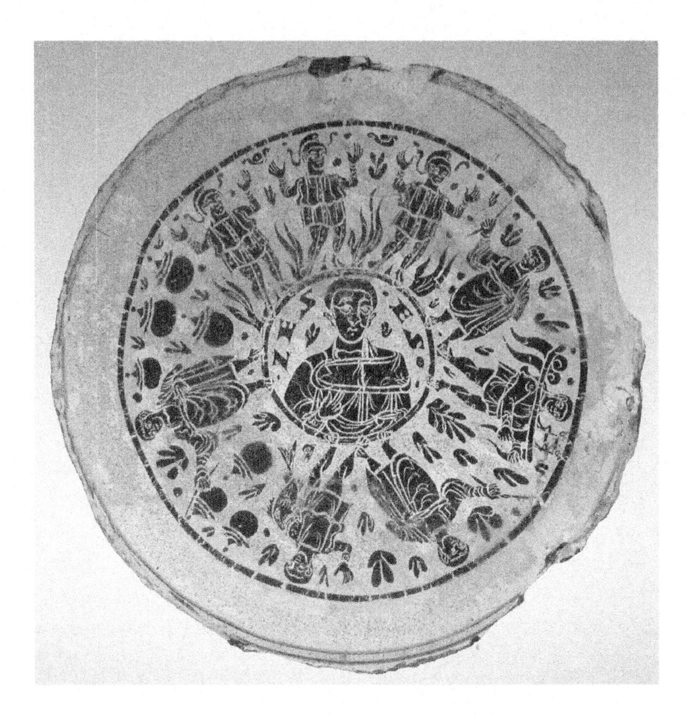

Figure 19.9 Gold-glass bowl base with miracle scenes surrounding central portrait, 350–400 CE. The Metropolitan Museum of Art, metmuseum.org, accession no. 16.174.2, Rogers Fund, 1916.

Figure 19.10 Gold-glass medallion with Jesus holding miracle-working staff, 300–500 CE. The Metropolitan Museum of Art, metmuseum.org, accession no. 18.145.8, Rogers Fund 1918.

The bowl indicates early Christians may have desired such themed art in a domestic setting, while the medallion shows that early Christians may have desired to "wear" the miracles of Jesus deriving some apotropaic value, and projecting the miracle in the public and private sphere. The broad dating of the medallion could indicate that this object was from post-Constantinian Christianity. In an age of Christian acceptance, viewers wanted to visually see and physically "wear" the miracles of Jesus.

Conclusion

Rather than declining after Constantine and the edict of Milan, appearances of the miracles of Jesus continued consistently for a period of time in the fourth and fifth centuries. Post-Constantinian Christian material culture illustrates that early Christian piety largely consisted of sincere devotion to the miracles of Christ. Early Christians surrounded themselves with this emphasis on miracles in their visual language, especially in funerary art. The images themselves provide a platform and an opportunity to examine how early Christians conceived this person called Christ. Combined with a study of textual evidence of the church fathers, the priority of miracles for a Christian audience seems apparent. The rise of pilgrimage and the cult of relics serves as a further testimony of their importance into the Middle Ages.

In their visual representation, the miracles and healings of Christ are portrayed with less frequency after the fifth century, with only the requisite miracles such as the raising of Lazarus remaining the most depicted in circulation.[42] More images involving a crucified Jesus or a Jesus enthroned begin to proliferate. Miracle images played an important role in establishing Christianity as a powerful religion in early Christianity and, when that position appeared secure, their appearances began to wane. The belief in miracles did not, as material relics of the saints became more dominant. However, the image of Jesus the miracle worker was less omnipresent after the fifth century, including representations of Jesus's staff. When Jesus performs healings and miracles in post fifth-century iconography, he emphatically demonstrates his divine power without paraphernalia. The staff of Christ is left to the era when Christ's miracles and healings were given more visual emphasis. After the fifth century, the staff of Jesus is not depicted as consistently. Perhaps the explanation for this is that the staff's depiction is not necessary. To repeatedly assert Jesus or Peter as the "new Moses" in art and imagery was inessential when that connection was already well established. For the nascent church the staff was an unnecessary accouterment, written out of the art and replaced with a cross, a hand, or nothing at all.

When early Christians began making and owning visual art in the third century, they favored scenes of the miracles of Jesus. The miracles touted Jesus visually as a superior miracle worker without rival, they asserted Christian dominance in a pluralistic landscape, they adapted existing Greco-Roman and Jewish visual themes making them "Christian," and they endowed the paragon of the Christian church in Rome, Peter, with unquestioned authority by exhibiting him as a miracle worker like Moses. Moreover, the miracles of Jesus served as visual "signs" of the Christian belief of the resurrection, particularly as the images appeared in a funerary context. Miracles that recalled the gospel of John such as the nature miracles or the raising of Lazarus certainly evoke a Christ that secures the ultimate miracle of eternal life. Miracles were undoubtedly valuable and powerful tools in early Christian visual culture, and their ubiquity serves as strident testimony that must be considered alongside textual evidence of the early Christian period.

Notes

1 See Augustine's position in his treatises *Of True Religion* and *On the Usefulness of Belief*. Augustine, *True Religion* 25.47 (CSEL 77.33; Burleigh): "nec miracula illa in nostra tempora durare permissa sunt;" Augustine, *The Usefulness of Belief* 15.33 (CSEL 25.41; Burleigh). In 415, a priest named Lucian discovered the remains of Stephen through revelation in a dream. It usually is cited that Orosius is responsible for returning with the relics of Stephen in 416. This is clouded slightly by *City of God* 22.8 (CSEL 40.604) where Augustine refers to Bishop Praejectus bringing the relics of Stephen. It is more likely that Augustine was referring to a specific establishment at Aquae Tibilitanae, rather than the general advent of the relics of Stephen into North Africa. See Augustine's contrasting position to his earlier treatises in *Serm.* 323.4 (PL 38, 1440). Augustine's situation is not out of the ordinary, note the discovery of the relics of Gervase and Protase in Milan.

2 See Peter Brown, *Augustine of Hippo: A Biography*, rev. ed. (Berkeley, CA: University of California Press, 2000), 418–22. I treat this subject more extensively in my *Christ the Miracle Worker in Early Christian Art* (Minneapolis, MN: Fortress, 2015).

3 Ernst Kitzinger, *Byzantine Art in the Making* (Cambridge, MA: Harvard University Press, 1977), 14–21.

4 Clement, *Paedagogus: Christ the Educator*, 3.11 (ANF 2.286).

5 For example, in Friedrich Wilhelm Deichmann, Giuseppe Bovini and Hugo Brandenburg, *Repertorium der christlich-antiken Sarkophage, Bd 1 Rom und Ostia* (Wiesbaden: F. Steiner, 1967), a catalog of Christian sarcophagi in Rome and Ostia, miracles and healings outnumber images of Christ enthroned in majesty or the *traditio legis* by a considerable margin. The enthroned images of Christ make up a little more than half of the number of occurrences of Christ healing the blind. There are over 40 examples of the *traditio legis* compared with 71 occurrences of the Healing of the Blind, see Deichmann, *Ikonographisches Register*, Band I, 122–24. As will be discussed later, the number of scenes of Christ's miracles in catacomb art and relief sculpture make it the predominant theme in early Christian art of the third and fourth centuries.

6 André Grabar, *The Beginnings of Christian Art, 200–395* (London: Thames and Hudson, 1966); also see Ernst Kitzinger, "The Cult of Images before Iconoclasm," in *Dumbarton Oaks Papers*, no. 8 (1954): 89; Hans Belting, *Likeness and Presence: A History of the Image before the Era of Art* (Chicago, IL: University of Chicago Press, 1994), 106; see also Lee M. Jefferson and Robin M. Jensen, eds, *The Art of Empire: Christian Art in Its Imperial Context* (Minneapolis, MN: Fortress, 2015).

7 Mark 2:1–12; Matt. 9:2; Luke 5:17. For Peter's mother-in-law, see Mark 1:29–31; Matt. 4:1–11; and Luke 4:1–13.

8 It is extremely difficult to depict an exorcism, and there was no direct precedent in pagan or Jewish art for such a scene. Consider Bosio's drawing, where the interpretation remains unclear; cf. Paul Corby Finney's figures 41.3 and 40.2 in "Do You Think God is a Magician?" in *Akten Des Symposiums Früchristliche Sarkophage*, ed. Guntram Koch (Marburg: Deutches Archäologisches Institut, 1999), fig. 40. 2 and fig. 41.3.

9 Early church authors such as Augustine found the paralytic story useful in preaching of the curative power of Christ. Augustine demanded that his listeners lower Christ the physician through the roof of their homes by expounding on Scripture, thereby binding up any fractures or maladies caused by greed or pride. Augustine, *Serm.* 46.13.

10 Joseph Wilpert, *Die Malereien der Katakomben Roms* (Freiburg im Breisgau: Herdersche Verlagshandlung, 1903), 218–24. Some themes are more prominent than others, as Wilpert noted fifteen instances of the healing of the paralytic and seven instances of the healing of the blind man.

11 See Robin M. Jensen, *Understanding Early Christian Art* (New York, NY: Routledge, 2000), 95.

12 See Antonella Nicoletti, *I sarcofagi di Bethesda* (Edizioni Stendhal: Milan, 1981), 3; and Guntram Koch, *Frühchristliche Sarkophage* (Beck: Munich, 2000), 314–15; see also Dennis Trout, "Borrowed Verse and Broken Narrative: Agency, Identity, and the (Bethesda) Sarcophagus of Bassa," in *Life, Death, and Representation: Some New Work on Roman Sarcophagi*, eds Jaś Elsner and Janet Huskinson (Berlin and New York, NY: DeGruyter, 2010), 337–58.

13 David Knipp, *"Christus Medicus" in der frühchristlichen Sarkophagskulptur: Ikonographische Studien der Sepulkralkunst des späten vierten Jahrhunderts* (Leiden: Brill, 1998), 154–6. However, he points out that it also reflects a competition with the Asclepius cult, arguing that this scene is a representation of a successful healing similar to the incubation treatment in a temple of Asclepius.

14 This before-and-after portrayal of the scene is distinctive to this particular sarcophagus, dating from 375 CE. Also note the similarity with the Dura fresco.

15 Wilpert, *Die Malereien der Katakomben Roms*, 218–24. Some themes are more prominent than others. Wilpert noted in the catacomb of Praetextus and the catacomb of Peter and Marcellinus fifteen instances of the healing of the paralytic and seven instances of the healing of the blind man compared with sporadic instances of the healing of the woman with the issue of blood.
16 There were seventy-one occurrences as recorded by Ulrike Lange, *Ikonographisches Register für das Repertorium der christlich-antiken Sarkophage Bd. 1 (Rom und Ostia)* (Dettelbach: Röll, 1996), 123, and forty-four in examples from Gaul and North Africa; see ibid., *Bd.* 3, 299.
17 See the ivory Andrews diptych (450–460 CE), now at the Victoria and Albert Museum, London, and in Jensen, *Understanding Early Christian Art*, fig. 48.
18 For the woman with the issue of blood, Mark 5:21–34; Matt. 9:18–26; Luke 8:40–48.
19 See Wilpert, *Die Malereien der Katakomben Roms* 218–24. The woman with the issue of blood appears rarely in the catacomb evidence that has been uncovered. Only one other instance has been discovered in addition to the image at Peter and Marcellinus, and that is at the catacomb of Praetextus. Roman catacomb art includes fifteen examples of the paralytic but only two examples of the woman with the issue of blood.
20 Jesus walking on water constitutes a nature miracle. This appears early at Dura, but is not depicted as consistently as Cana or the Division miracle.
21 Jerome, *Commentary on Ezekiel*, 12.40.5 (CSEL 75.549–556). See Prudentius, *Peristephanon: Crowns of Martyrdom*, 11.175–190.
22 Margaret Miles, *The Word Made Flesh: A History of Christian Thought* (Oxford: Blackwell, 2005), 58.
23 See Paulinus, *carm.* 27; and Augustine, *Confessions* 6.2.2. For further reading, see Andrew McGowan, *Ascetic Eucharists: Food and Drink in Early Christian Ritual Meals* (New York, NY: Oxford University Press, 1998); and Robin M. Jensen, "Dining with the Dead: From the Mensa to the Altar in Christian Late Antiquity," in *Commemorating the Dead: Texts and Artifacts in Context* eds Laurie Brink and Deborah Green (Berlin: Walter De Gruyter, 2008).
24 In the Roman body of evidence, the Cana miracle appears over forty-four times; in the Gallic and North African evidence, it appears over twenty-one times. See Deichmann, Bovini and Brandenburg, *Reportorium der Christlich-Antiken Sarkophage*, Band 1, pt. 3, 122; and see Brigitte Christern-Briesenick, *Repertorium der christlich-antiken Sarkophage. Dritter Band: Frankreich, Algerien, Tunesien*, ed. Thilo Ulbert (Wiesbaden: F. Steiner, 2003), 303. For the division of loaves, the miracle appears in the Roman evidence over eight-four times; in the Gallic and North African evidence, over twelve times. Band 1, 122; Band 3, 299.
25 The Lazarus account is in John 11; the widow's son in Luke 7:11–17; and Jairus' daughter in Mark 5:35–43; Matt. 9:18–26; and Luke 8:40–56. Ezekiel and the Valley of the Dry Bones appears in Ezek. 37:1–14.
26 Found in Level 2, Area I, Cubiculum A6. Paul Corby Finney, *The Invisible God* (New York, NY: Oxford University Press, 1994), 218.
27 Deichmann, Bovini and Brandenburg, *Reportorium der Christlich-Antiken Sarkophage*, Band 1, pts. 1, 123; Brigitte Christern-Briesenick, *Reportorium der Christlich-Antiken Sarkophage*, Band 3, 302. The widow's son and Jairus' daughter occur in sixteen examples in the Roman material, and in eight examples from Gaul and North Africa. See 1:123; 3:301–302.
28 To borrow Raymond Brown SS's influential terminology regarding the Johannine gospel, *The Gospel According to John* (New York, NY: Doubleday, 1966).
29 Aristides, *Sacred Tales*, 48.21.
30 Origen, *Against Celsus*, 3.24.
31 The scene of Moses striking the rock appears in twenty-two examples on Roman sarcophagi; Peter in cognate scenes occurs fifty-six times. See Deichmann, Bovini and Brandenburg, *Reportorium*, Band 1, pt. 3, 124. The Gallic and North African material is similarly conflated; see Christern-Briesenick, *Reportorium*, Band 3, 302. The problem is how to identify true Moses scenes and true Peter scenes. The evidence of the jailers and other symbols on the relief sculpture points towards a larger number of Peter scenes than Moses scenes.
32 Pseudo-Linus, *Martyrdom of the Blessed Apostle Peter* 5. For further reading, see Robin M. Jensen, "Moses Imagery in Jewish and Christian Art," *Society of Biblical Literature Seminar Papers* (*SBLSP*) (1992): 395–98. The *Acts of Peter* is difficult to date as it incorporates several strains. The text that includes the water miracle was narrated by Pseudo-Linus and dates from the mid-fourth century. For the Latin text, see Lipsius, *Acta Apostolorum Apocrypha* (Hildesheim: G. Olms, 1959), 1:1–22; for the text and transmission, see Wilhelm Schneemelcher, *New Testament Apocrypha* (London: SCM, 1975), 2:285.

33 *Acts of Peter* 5 (Linus text). The text certainly depicts Peter as a wonder worker. Processus and Martinianus are so grateful that they help Peter escape from jail. Upon his escape, Peter meets Christ on the road outside Rome and becomes aware of his destiny.
34 See Jaś Elsner, *Imperial Rome and Christian Triumph: The Art of the Roman Empire, AD 100–450* (New York, NY: Oxford University Press, 1998), 153; and Thomas Mathews, *The Clash of Gods: A Reinterpretation of Early Christian Art* (Princeton, NJ: Princeton University Press, 1993), 54–89.
35 A leap that Thomas Mathews takes. See Mathews, *Clash of Gods*, 54–89.
36 Origen, *Cels.* 68.
37 Chrysostom among other things ridiculed the wearing of amulets to little avail; see *Homily on Colossians* 8.5. See N. Brox, "Magie und Aberglaube an den Anfängen des Christentums," *Trierer theologische Zeitschrift*, 83 (1974): 157–80; A. A. Barb, "The Survival of Magical Arts," in *The Conflict between Paganism and Christianity in the Fourth Century*, ed. A. Momigliano (Oxford: Clarendon, 1963), 100–25.
38 There likely is a class element to the message expressed in the art. Patrons who could afford sarcophagi were likely middle- to upper-middle-class citizens, while adherents to magic were among the lower, uneducated classes. See Paul Corby Finney, "Do You Think God is a Magician?" 107. It seems logical that magical use would be associated with the poor. The relative accessibility of spells made magic a viable alternative. Pliny noted the use of herbal remedies by the magi, claiming Pythagoras and Democritus borrowed from their treatments, *Natural History* 24.99–10; and in Christian Late Antiquity, see Jerome, *Life of Hilarion* 21, for the use of a love spell. Sarcophagus art is also a genre that allows the patron to express outwardly noble qualities and beliefs, religious and self-serving, and magic would not fit into that sphere.
39 The early church evidence ridiculing magic is fairly considerable. See Justin Martyr, *1 Apol.* 26; Irenaeus, *Against Heresies* 1.13, 2.31.2; Origen, *Cels.* 1.68. For magic as the work of demons, see Tertullian, *The Soul* 57.7; Eusebius, *Against Hierocles* 26. Chrysostom ridiculed the wearing of amulets to little avail in *Homily on Colossians* 8.5. Also see Harold Remus, *Pagan–Christian Conflict over Miracle in the Second Century* (Cambridge, MA: Philadelphia Patristic Foundation, 1983), 56; N. Brox, "Magie und Aberglaube an den Anfängen des Christentums," 157–80.
40 Paul Corby Finney rebuts Mathews in "Do You Think God is a Magician?," 106. Finney simply answers that late antique art does not include a tradition of depicting a magician doing his job.
41 One possible image of a magician is Alexander Severus's bust of Apollonius in his domestic shrine, although the *Augustan History* is a widely criticized source. However, even this mention warrants some consideration, since it treats the existence of imagery. See *Life of Severus Alexander* 29.
42 In later depictions, the staff of Jesus evolves into a cross. On the fifth-century Andrews diptych, the staff is still present; however, on an ivory diptych in Ravenna from just a century later, the staff has visibly transitioned into a cross, as Christ gesticulates with his hand toward the *aediculum* with a newly discernible Lazarus. See W. F. Volbach, *Early Christian Art* (London: Thames and Hudson, 1961), pl. 223.

Further reading

Belting, Hans. *Likeness and Presence: A History of the Image before the Era of Art*. Chicago, IL: University of Chicago Press, 1994.

Betz, Hans Dieter, ed. *The Greek Magical Papyri in Translation, Including the Demotic Spells*. Chicago, IL: University of Chicago Press, 1986.

Brandenburg, Hugo. *Ancient Churches of Rome from the Fourth to the Seventh Century*. Turnhout: Brepols, 2005.

Brown, Peter. *Augustine of Hippo*. Berkeley: University of California Press, 1967.

————. *The Cult of the Saints: Its Rise and Function in Latin Christianity*. Chicago, IL: University of Chicago Press, 1981.

Elsner, Jaś. *Imperial Rome and Christian Triumph: The Art of the Roman Empire AD 100–450*. Oxford: Oxford University Press, 1998.

Finney, Paul Corby. *The Invisible God: The Earliest Christians on Art*. New York, NY: Oxford University Press, 1994.

Jefferson, Lee M. *Christ the Miracle Worker in Early Christian Art*. Minneapolis, MN: Fortress Press, 2015.

Jensen, Robin M. *Baptismal Imagery in Early Christianity: Ritual, Visual and Theological Dimensions*. Grand Rapids, MI: Baker Academic, 2012.

————. *Understanding Early Christian Art*. New York, NY: Routledge, 2000.

Lowden, John. *Early Christian and Byzantine Art*. New York, NY: Phaidon, 1997.
Mathews, Thomas. *The Clash of Gods: A Reinterpretation of Early Christian Art*. Princeton, NJ: Princeton University Press, 1993.
Nutton, Vivian. *Ancient Medicine*. New York, NY: Routledge, 2004.
Peppard, Michael. *The World's Oldest Church: Bible, Art, and Ritual at Dura-Europos, Syria*. New Haven, CT: Yale University Press, 2016.
Snyder, Graydon F. *Ante Pacem: Archaeological Evidence of Church Life before Constantine*. Macon, GA: Mercer University Press, 2003.
Spier, Jeffrey, ed. *Picturing the Bible: The Earliest Christian Art*. New Haven, CT: Yale University Press, 2007.

20

"SECULAR" PORTRAITS, IDENTITY, AND THE CHRISTIANIZATION OF THE ROMAN HOUSEHOLD

Mark D. Ellison

Gazing at the figured panels of early Christian sarcophagi, the viewer's eye is drawn to the imposing double-portraits framed at the center of many reliefs, representations of the married couples for whom the monuments were made (Figure 20.1).[1] Elsewhere one encounters similar portraits on much humbler, less expensive objects. A small silver seal bears the confronted busts of a man and woman, their daughter depicted between them, doves and a wreath-crown above, all encircled by an inscription addressing the man: "Maxentius, may you live happily with your loved ones" (Figure 20.2).[2] Incised gold foil at the base of a glass vessel depicts a family group—wife, husband, son, and daughter—a christogram placed at the center, an inscription above toasting the married couple: "Pompeianus and Theodora, may you live!" (Figure 20.3).[3]

Figure 20.1 Double portrait, sarcophagus of Catervius and Severina. Late fourth century (mid-380s–390 CE). Cathedral of San Catervo, Tolentino. Photo: Mark D. Ellison.

Figure 20.2 Silver seal (left) and impression (right) with busts of a husband and wife with their daughter. Photo: Th. Zühmer, © GDKE/Rheinisches Landesmuseum Trier.

Figure 20.3 Drawing of a gold-glass portrait of a family group, after Raffaele Garrucci, *Vetri ornati di figure in oro trovanti nei cimiteri dei cristiani primitivi di Roma* (Roma: Tipografia Salviucci, 1858), Tav. 29.4.

The emergent Christian art of the third and fourth centuries includes many such works containing portraits of individuals, couples, and family groups (e.g., Figures 2.7, 2.11, 3.8, 8.7, 15.6, 19.7, 19.9, 22.1–3, 23.3). These depictions of relatively ordinary Christians comprise a major category of early Christian portraiture in addition to images of Christ, apostles, Mary, and other saints and martyrs.[4] They are sometimes classed as "secular" portraits to distinguish them from representations of religious figures.[5] The term *secular* echoes the use of the word *saeculares* ("people of the world") by clergy and ascetics in Late Antiquity to refer to the majority of lay believers whose lives were characterized by such "worldly" pursuits as marriage, childrearing, wealth, working in a profession, and civic service.[6] However, the term masks the religious imagery that often appears with the portraits to express religious commitment and claim piety and blessedness on behalf of the individuals portrayed.

Images of Christ and saints have traditionally received more academic attention, but secular portraits (also called "private" portraits) have been of increasing interest in recent years.[7] This rising awareness follows in the wake of social historical work that has widened focus from the great men, deeds, and events of political or ecclesiastical history to encompass the experience of ordinary people, including women, children, slaves, and the middling and poorer strata of society.[8] Of course, many individuals represented in secular portraits were not "ordinary" in a socio-economic sense—they were wealthy enough to purchase and own works of art, sometimes at considerable expense. Sarcophagi, for example, were extremely costly and available only to the elite, upper strata of Roman society, while gold-glass vessels and metal seals would have been affordable to a greater proportion of the population, though still not the poorest.[9] Nevertheless, the portraits on these objects do represent people who were not religious elites; they comprised a segment of the early Christian population beyond those who authored Christian texts, oversaw congregations, or met in church councils. Their representations broaden the reconstruction historians can produce of the early Christian world, casting light on such subjects as the Christianization of the Roman populace, the perspectives of lay believers, and the late antique reconceptualizing of the Roman household.

The work of portraits

The term *portrait* may be defined as a manufactured image (*eikōn*, *imago*, *simulacrum*) representing an individual or group of persons.[10] Ancient and late antique portraits usually took the form of busts (showing the head and shoulders) posed frontally or in profile, or depicted persons standing either frontally, turned three-quarters, or in profile. The general intention of a portrait was to designate a person or persons in order to evoke thoughts or memories of them, suggest certain ideas about them, and create a sense of their presence; more specific purposes of portraits related to their various forms, uses, and physical contexts as they appeared in such media as sarcophagus reliefs, wall paintings in family tombs, free-standing sculpture, panel paintings, gold-glass vessel bases, finger rings, gems, seals, belt ornaments, and domestic silver.[11] Portraits of living persons served to honor them, enhance their reputation and status, and create a public persona if displayed for view, or foster a more intimate connection if carried on a small object. Funerary portraits, made either after death or during life, preserved the memory of deceased persons and facilitated "interaction" between the living and dead in funerary ceremonies.[12]

These purposes could be accomplished without necessarily replicating an exact likeness of individuals. Roman portraits at various times gravitated toward either realism or idealization, often employing degrees of each.[13] Late antique and early Christian portraiture reveals an even greater willingness to forego detailed and accurate individualizing, and a growing preference for generic or even stylized representation. On many sarcophagi the heads of figures intended to represent the deceased or a patron were left unfinished.[14] Evidently a symbolic depiction was often felt sufficient to designate an individual. Consequently some historians have preferred to speak in terms of "portrait-style," "an image of a portrait," or "self-representation" rather than "portraits" in a strict sense.[15]

Portraits were highly idealized, making use of stock types, poses, and attributes that signaled key characteristics or encoded certain social and gender roles. Though such images may be a means of identifying the discourses and social negotiations in which patrons and viewers participated, they are less likely to represent the complex realities of their actual lived experience. Nevertheless, idealized images spoke to certain values and a desire to be perceived and remembered in association with those values. Thus, portraits may be approached as visual rhetoric.

In their rhetorical function secular portraits have been of growing interest in the study of identity—the conception and expression of individuality (self-identity) or group affiliation (social, religious, or ethnic identity).[16] Portraits and the images placed around them were means of constructing and maintaining a sense of identity in the changing social landscape of Late Antiquity. Recent studies have explored the ways portraits of early Christians served to articulate degrees of assimilation and differentiation in relation to broader Roman society.[17] Studies have also highlighted the ways these portraits, especially in funerary contexts, connected persons with biblical images of salvation and expressed hope for a blessed afterlife, marking a shift in emphasis from commemorating individuals to making religious statements.[18]

A case study: reading identity on the sarcophagus of Catervius and Severina

The late fourth-century sarcophagus of Catervius and Severina at Tolentino illustrates many of the functions of portraits described above.[19] Commissioned by Septimia Severina for the burial of her deceased husband, Flavius Julius Catervius, the large monument later served as her own burial place alongside her husband. Severina had the sarcophagus and lid carved on all four sides and paid for the construction of a mausoleum where it could be seen in the round. (Its current display in a chapel within the cathedral of San Catervo preserves this viewing experience.) The couple's son and heir, Bassus, died unexpectedly at age eighteen and was also buried in the sarcophagus, while an inscription lamenting his death and the end of the family line was crowded into unused space on the front. Before that tragedy, however, Severina evidently intended the sarcophagus and its mausoleum to perpetuate the memory and example of her husband and herself in her son's family and among future generations of descendants and local residents.

Portraits of Catervius and Severina appear on both the front and back of the sarcophagus. On the front, acroteria on the lid contain individual busts of Catervius (left) and Severina (right) turned slightly towards each other (Figure 20.4). Between them an inscription announces the pair's full names, their senatorial rank, the length of their marriage (16 years less 13 days), Catervius's service as praetorian prefect, his age at death (56 years 18 days), the dates of his death and interment, and Severina's commissioning of the sarcophagus and mausoleum.[20] Catervius is shown wearing a toga and tunic, bearded (in his older years of civic office), and clutching a scroll; Severina also holds a scroll and is attired as an aristocratic Roman *matrona*.

The inscriptions and portraits are fairly conventional. They eulogize the pair and locate them as Roman elites who prize learning (symbolized by scrolls), the husband's activity in the public sphere, and the wife's familial piety, evident in her fulfillment of the duties of commemoration.[21] Though nothing in these portraits or the inscription identifies the pair as Christian, the strigillated casket below depicts a sheep-carrying shepherd in the center panel and scroll-bearing apostles, who stand with bundles of scrolls at their feet, in the panels at the left and right corners. Christian visitors to the tomb would have recognized these figures as Christ the Good Shepherd, Peter (left, beneath Catervius), and Paul. Viewers could have discerned a message that Catervius's departed soul, like the carried sheep, was in Christ's care. The alignment of the spousal portraits with the apostles, all holding scrolls, presents Catervius and Severina as not just educated, but more specifically as possessors of the faith and knowledge taught by the church—a claim for the couple's orthodoxy and religious harmony.[22]

Figure 20.4 Front, sarcophagus of Catervius and Severina, late fourth century, Tolentino. Photo: Mark D. Ellison.

Processing around the sarcophagus to its back side, the viewer encounters a more intimate representation (Figure 20.1). At the center of the panel Catervius and Severina appear together in a large *clipeus* (circular frame) set within a square that fills the casket's vertical height. They are posed frontally, their eyes staring straight ahead at the viewer, their right hands joined in the *dextrarum iunctio*, a traditional gesture that here symbolizes marital harmony. In addition to this gesture, Severina's veiled head and Catervius's more youthful appearance (with only hints of beard stubble) invite the viewer to think of the couple on their wedding day. Here their likenesses appear with key religious symbols. Above their heads a hand (the hand of God or Christ) extends a jeweled, ribboned wreath-crown, an iconic symbol of spiritual victory (see Figure 18.6) that could simultaneously allude to the couple's wedding (wreaths of flowers or laurels were customarily placed on the heads of the bride and groom in wedding celebrations). The spandrels above contain the *chi-rho* with *alpha* and *omega*, symbols of Christ suggesting divine protection and blessing upon the couple's life, marriage, tomb, and afterlife. The spandrels beneath feature inward-facing doves clutching olive branches, symbols that might have led the viewer to think of peace, divine assurance (as with Noah's dove), the Holy Spirit, the couple's own departed souls, and their marital devotion even beyond death.[23]

The symbolism in this portrait resonates with an inscription directly above it, evidently carved on the occasion of Severina's burial alongside her husband (likely according to her instructions and overseen by their bishop Probianus, who seems to have left his signature):

> [The two] whom the all-powerful Lord joined in sweet marriage with equal merits,
> The grave guards for eternity.
> Catervius, Severina rejoices that she has been joined to you.
> May you two rise together among the blessed with the help of Christ,
> Whom Probianus, the priest of God, baptized and anointed.[24]

The programs on the front and back present the pair in their public and private life, typical of elite commemoration in the period.[25] They serve to locate Catervius and Severina within society as citizens worthy of honor for their civic service and domestic harmony, yet distinguished from traditional Romans in terms of religious identity. This differentiation is reinforced by the reliefs on the small sides. The scene on the right side has been interpreted as the magi turning away from Herod, who is depicted as a Roman ruler flanked by two soldiers; a bust of the ruler behind him recalls the biblical story of the three Hebrew youths who refused to worship the image of Nebuchadnezzar (Figure 20.5).[26] On the left side, the magi bring their gifts to the seated Virgin and Christ child. Together the scenes suggest a rejection of Rome's past religious policy (both its emperor worship and its persecution of Christianity, embodied by Herod), and turning to worship the divine King.[27] The background of city gates and walls on these panels might evoke for the viewer the earthly or heavenly city, and the tensions between them. Severina distanced herself and her husband from aspects of Rome's past even as she claimed a place of honor for them in its transforming present.

She and Christian aristocrats like her felt a need to articulate continuities and exclusions in a climate where competing visions of society vied for preeminence. In Rome, Severina's non-Christian contemporary, Anconia Fabia Paulina, erected a monument for her deceased husband, the senator Vettius Agorius Praetextatus, that similarly proclaimed their merits, their patron deities (Cybele, Attis, Ceres, and Hecate), and Paulina's anticipation of a happy reunion with her husband after death.[28] Her defense of traditional Roman religions drew the ire of Jerome.[29] The late fourth century was a time of "competitive commemoration" in which couples like

Figure 20.5 Right side, sarcophagus of Catervius and Severina, showing the magi before Herod/three Hebrew youths. Photo: Mark D. Ellison.

Severina and Catervius, Paulina and Praetextatus, were visualizing alternate conceptions of Roman society, the ideal Roman household, and the God or gods who watch over it.[30]

Christianizing the Roman household: married couples and family groups

In addition to expressing social and religious identity, secular portraits of couples and family groups give visual evidence of the development of Christian discourses and practices regarding marriage and family life, and reflect the participation of lay believers in the Christianization of the Roman household. Interpreting portraits in this way entails recognizing their forms and then identifying what may be particularly "Christian" in their appearance—the modifications or additions they made to prior Roman iconography.[31] It also requires comparing this imagery with the evidence of Christian texts.

Roman precedents

Prior to the emergence of Christian art, depictions of married couples and family groups in Roman art appeared in several forms. Portrait busts, often set within a circular frame, were popular in funerary and domestic display (see Figures 12.1–2). An example of high quality in the Metropolitan Museum of Art is an Antonine relief that once topped a funerary pillar: a man and woman appear side by side, looking forward, the smaller figures of their two sons in front of them (Figure 20.6). The woman's veil alludes to her motherhood.[32] The same portrait form was used for the famous panel painting of emperor Septimius Severus with his wife Julia Domna and their sons Caracalla and Geta (whose face was removed in an act of *damnatio memoriae*) (see Figure 12.7).[33]

Figure 20.6 Marble funerary relief with tondo portrait of a family group, 2nd–3rd century CE. Photo: The Metropolitan Museum of Art, metmuseum.org, Fletcher Fund, 1949. Accession no. 49.69.5.

Figure 20.7 Dextrarum iunctio relief of a Roman marriage ceremony from the front of a marble sarcophagus, 2nd century CE. Photo © The Trustees of the British Museum/Art Resource, New York.

The circular tondo or more elaborate shell frame was also popular for portraits of married couples without their children (see Figure 22.6; 23.3). Typically the wife appeared on the viewer's left, partially behind the husband at right. The husband clutches a scroll and makes a speaking gesture, while the wife rests her right hand upon her husband's right arm or chest, and may drape her left arm over his shoulders. The pose emphasized the gendered social expectations of an authoritative male head of household, supportive wife, and domestic *concordia*.

Another popular form of spousal portraiture was the depiction of husband and wife standing, turned towards each other and clasping right hands in the *dextrarum iunctio*. (The gesture could also be incorporated into portrait busts, if awkwardly.) In earlier Greek and Etruscan art the handclasp signified close relationship, and in Roman art it was used in military and familial contexts to signify a bond of loyalty.[34] It became especially popular in depictions of married couples as a symbol of conjugal harmony, and might have alluded to a ritual joining of hands during marriage ceremonies.[35]

Beginning in the mid-second century CE a female figure (sometimes wearing a diadem) was added to the image, standing between the spouses and resting her hands on their shoulders as she joined them in marriage (Figure 20.7). Historians in the nineteenth and early twentieth centuries interpreted her as Juno *pronuba*, patron goddess of marriage, but more recent interpretation has favored identifying her as a personification of Concordia.[36] Viewers might have seen her as a goddess, a symbol of harmony, an allusion to an actual *matrona* who as *pronuba* oversaw the joining of spouses in the wedding ceremony, or a combination of these. This "wedding scene" originated in public statues and coins made during the reigns of emperors Antoninus Pius and his successor Marcus Aurelius, in which the emperor and his wife appeared as models of domestic harmony.[37] The image fostered a public valorization of the marital *concordia* that was held to stabilize the household, city, and empire. In the late second century it began appearing in Roman private art where individuals could portray themselves as upholders of the social order in both the domestic and public sphere.

Sometimes additional deities associated with weddings such as Venus, Cupid, or Hymenaeus stood in the scenes as attendants to the bride and groom. Images of still other gods—Sol, Hercules, Cupid—sometimes appeared instead of Concordia in the space between husband and wife as a patron deity of the married couple.[38] The presence of these deities in spousal portraits corresponds to the practice of propitiating various gods in Roman wedding celebrations, and to wedding poems (*epithalamia*) that described a mythological retinue of divine figures who attended the festivities as the newlyweds' unseen benefactors.

Patterns of Christian reception

A few early fourth-century Christian sarcophagi feature *dextrarum iunctio* portraits of the grave owners with a central Concordia figure, surrounded by biblical images placing the commemorands in a Christian context.[39] By the mid-fourth century, however, images were appearing on gold glasses, and later on sarcophagi and jewelry, in which Concordia was replaced by the figure of Christ between the spouses, reaching out his hands to each to place crowns upon their heads (Figure 20.8).[40] Variations of this "Christ between spouses" image multiplied. Couples were represented in portrait busts, facing forward or in profile, or standing turned three quarters toward each other. Between them the full-length figure of Christ might stand, a hand might extend a crown (Figure 20.1), or a crown might appear by itself as a symbol, as in a gold glass depicting a couple joining right hands beneath a floating crown and the inscription *VIVATIS IN DEO* ("May you [two] live in God") (Figure 20.9).[41] Instead of a figure of Christ or a crown, a symbol such as a christogram, cross, or staurogram might occupy the central position (Figure 20.3).[42] The reception pattern is one in which a visual reference to Christ served as a central, defining element, either in figural representation or by a symbol of Christ's spiritual victory and benefaction.

Alternatively, some portraits contain no religious elements but appear with inscriptions that present the couple or family group as Christian. Examples include the wreathed double-portrait on the lid of the Projecta Casket (see Figure 15.6) with the inscription, ⳨ *SECVNDE ET PROIECTA VIVATIS IN CHRISTO* (staurogram, followed by "Secundus and Projecta, may you [two] live in Christ"), and a gold glass in the Hungarian National Museum with busts of a married pair encircled by the inscription *SEMPER GAUDEAT[IS] IN NOMINE DEI* ("May you [two] rejoice always in the name of God").[43]

Some historians have interpreted these Christian adaptations as mere markers of Christian identity, examples of "continuity by transference" that simply substitute a reference to a new patron deity in space formerly occupied by Juno, Concordia, Hercules, or Cupid.[44] However, comparison with textual sources also makes it possible to consider these portraits as visualizations of distinctively Christian notions of marriage and familial life that were then developing.[45]

Figure 20.8 Gold-glass medallion with portrait busts of a husband and wife, Christ placing crowns on their heads, and the legend DVLCIS ANIMA VIVAS ("Sweet soul, may you live"), *ca.* 360–390 CE. Photo © The Trustees of the British Museum/Art Resource, New York (photo flipped horizontally).

Figure 20.9 Gold-glass vessel base with woman and man *dextrarum iunctio*, floating crown, pillar, and legend VIVATIS IN DEO, *ca.* 360–390 CE. Photo: The Metropolitan Museum of Art, metmuseum.org, Rogers Fund, 1915.

References to Christ

Centrally placed references to Christ in spousal portraits, particularly the figure of Christ extending his arms to the pair, express the concept of a divine role in the couple's relationship.[46] In the image of *Christus pronubus* Christian viewers might have seen a connection to the biblical tradition that a husband and wife are "what God has joined together" (Matt 19:6; Mark 10:9)—a notion that grew in the consciousness of Christians at Rome over the course of the fourth century as they developed the practice of a nuptial blessing. The earliest unambiguous evidence for blessings pronounced by a bishop or presbyter upon a marrying couple comes from fourth-century Rome. The author known as Ambrosiaster, a presbyter writing at Rome between 366–384, alludes in several places to these blessings, indicating that the practice had become common by his time.[47] Ambrosiaster refers to the divine formation of marriage when he states that the purpose of the blessing is "so that the creature of God may be joined under the blessing of God."[48]

The forming of marriage, traditionally a private matter that took place in the home, began to come under the authority of the church, whose clergy could speak to the role of deity in effecting the union. The bishop Ambrose, addressing his married parishioners, referred to "God, who is the author of your marriage," and wrote, "Where there is harmony, God joins them together."[49] The reference to Catervius and Severina as "the two whom the all powerful Lord joined in sweet marriage" (possibly the statement of their bishop Probianus) likewise reflects this notion of marriage as a divinely-formed bond. Paulinus of Nola, too, expressed this concept in his wedding poem for Julian of Eclanum and Titia. Paulinus prays for the bride and groom, "Christ God, draw these paired doves towards Your reins, and govern their necks beneath Your light yoke [*iugo*, used figuratively of marriage]." The central role of Christ in the married relationship arises repeatedly throughout the poem. "Young people, you belong to Christ," Paulinus reminds the newlyweds; "Christ as all in all must be our common Head." Alluding to the wedding at Cana in the Gospel of John as one of the biblical examples of proper marriage, Paulinus states, "When Jesus' friends were married like this, He attended as a groomsman [*pronubus*], and changed water into wine like nectar."[50]

The Verona Sacramentary, a collection of prayers compiled in the early sixth century, includes prayers for the nuptial veiling of a bride, and constitutes "the best claim to approximate the form of the blessing that would have been used in the late fourth-century church at Rome."[51] Three times the rite refers to the concept that the marriage is formed by God: "She is joined by your gift in the companionship of marriage"; "We beseech you, almighty God, . . . to keep in lasting peace those whom you will join in lawful union"; "Listen favorably, O Lord, to our prayers and graciously grant your help . . . so that what is joined by your authority might be preserved by your help."[52]

These liturgical and literary traditions suggest that a factor in the development away from Concordia wedding scenes was that *Christus pronubus* images could visually symbolize how Christians were conceptualizing the marriage of two believers as a divinely formed, blessed, and protected relationship. Though the role of an actual *pronuba* or *pronubus* at weddings might have been filled by a parent, family member, or priest pronouncing a blessing, Christians nevertheless imagined their unions created in an ultimate sense by deity, and developed visual and ritual ways to express this concept. It was an ideal Tertullian had extolled a century earlier:

> What a bond is this: two believers who share one hope, one desire, one discipline, the same service! . . . Together they pray, together they prostrate themselves, together they fast, teaching each other, exhorting each other, supporting each other. Side by

> side in the church of God and at the banquet of God, side by side in difficulties, in times of persecution, and in times of consolation. . . . Seeing and hearing this, Christ rejoices. He gives them his peace. Where there are two, he also is present; and where he is, there is no evil.[53]

In portraits of a married pair with their children (Figures 20.2–3), centrally placed Christian symbols resonate with New Testament passages that re-described traditional household relationships between wife and husband, children and parents, and slaves and masters in terms of each member's relation to Christ.[54] The guiding hands of parents resting upon the shoulders of their children (Figure 20.3), a gesture often present in teaching scenes, visually suggests the role of parents in bringing up children "in the discipline and instruction of the Lord" (Eph 6:4). Fourth-century homilies on these New Testament "household codes" urged the application of their ideals in Christian homes. John Chrysostom, for example, preached: "From the beginning God in His providence has planned this union of man and woman. . . . The love of husband and wife is the force that welds society together. . . . When harmony prevails, the children are raised well, the household is kept in order, and neighbors, friends and relatives praise the result. Great benefits, both for families and states, are thus produced."[55]

Crowns

The iconographic element of the crown bestowed simultaneously on bride and groom (Figure 20.8) was a Christian innovation; as Ernst Kantorowicz remarked, it had not previously been a custom in Roman art to depict "the *pronubus* . . . acting at the same time as the *stephanophorus*, holding the bridal crowns over the heads of the couple."[56] The crown by itself also appeared above portraits of family groups.[57] The form of crown in these Christian images is not the festive type seen in depictions of Dionysiac revelries, but the *stephanos* awarded to victorious emperors, military leaders, and athletes in prior Roman art.[58] The iconography of the Christian coronation images seen especially in gold glasses was used not only for portraits of married couples, but also for pairs of saints such as Peter and Paul.[59] Its form derived from imperial images; for example, a cameo of Marcus Aurelius and Lucius Verus depicts the two emperors clasping right hands in mutual loyalty as a diminutive Victory between them places a wreath upon Marcus's head.[60]

In fourth-century Christian art the crown became a symbol of spiritual victory, including the victory of Christ over death (see Figure 18.6), and the victory of martyrs. It evoked New Testament references to the crown of righteousness, the crown of life, and the crown of glory that would be the eternal reward of the faithful.[61] When used in wedding scenes the crown could allude simultaneously to the practice of placing garlands on the bride and groom's heads at wedding celebrations, and to a sense of religious merit in marriage, elevating the wedded pair to the status of spiritual victor. Some decades after these images began to appear in Rome, John Chrysostom remarked, "Crowns (*stephanoi*) are placed upon the heads of marrying couples as a symbol of victory, betokening that they approach the marriage bed unconquered by pleasure."[62]

These spousal coronation images seem quite bold when one bears in mind that crowns in early Christian art were typically reserved for exceptional heroes of the faith like apostles, saints, martyrs, and Christ himself. In addition to symbolizing the "crown of life" promised to the faithful, images of crowns over couples and family groups participate rhetorically in a long Christian conversation regarding the relative merits of marriage and celibacy. Christian teaching on this subject was complex from its origins. Some New Testament passages subverted traditional familial loyalties or at least subordinated them to the new "family" of Christ's followers, praised the unmarried for their undivided dedication to God, and referred to an angelic afterlife in which the faithful would not marry.[63] Other passages advanced an ideal permanence of marriage and reinforced traditional, hierarchical family structures within the Christian community.[64] In the fourth century, a tradition that virgins and celibate widows would receive a greater heavenly reward than married believers came into conflict with both Roman values (which prioritized marriage, childrearing, and familial stability as crucial to society) and strands of biblical tradition (which emphasized the goodness of creation and saw the blessing "be fruitful and multiply" spoken to Adam and Eve as a sign of divine approbation of marriage and procreation).[65] Episodes during the fourth century give evidence of efforts by both church teachers and married laypersons to resist extremes of the ascetic ideal and construct a position of honor for the great majority of believers who did not choose to practice lifelong celibacy.[66] The images Christians commissioned of married couples and family groups with crowns of eternal reward added a visual component to this fourth-century endeavor.

Christograms and crosses

The *chi-rho*, by definition an abbreviation of *Christ*, provided a visual alternative to a figure of Christ better suited for placement within small spaces on objects like gold glass medallions, gems, seals, and jewelry, or within pediments and spandrels on sarcophagi (Figures 20.1, 20.5). It could also signify "in Christ" and impart that status to portrayed individuals, couples, or family groups.[67] From the time of Constantine it was a symbol of victory, the defeat of enemies, and divine protection and patronage. In the decades after Constantine's accession the christogram gradually became a religious symbol representing victory over death.[68] Its use in portraits of couples and family groups could express their hopes of Christian salvation, as well as the patronage and protection of the Christian God on behalf of their household. The adoption of this symbol from the imperial sphere into the domestic sphere came naturally to Romans, who had long regarded the household as a microcosm of the city and the empire. As Constantine and his successors had employed the christogram as a symbol of the divine *oikonomia* in safeguarding the empire, Christian families now adopted it to signify the divine care of the individual *oikos*.[69]

In the late fourth century the cross began appearing between portraits of spouses on seals and the bezels of finger rings.[70] It too invoked divine protection upon the married pair, an amuletic function that seems to have been amplified in later Byzantine jewelry.[71] It also alluded to the conception of marriage as divinely formed, as described above. When Paulinus of Nola told the newlyweds Julian and Titia, "Let the holy cross be the yoke that pairs you together," it may be that he had in mind not only the notion of a Christian marriage but also an increasingly popular image.[72] Christians were seeking visual ways to express the concept that their marriages were "in Christ."

A new form of representation

In addition to the foregoing adaptations made to received forms of portraiture, fourth-century Christians innovated the new strategy of representing spouses on sarcophagi as diminutive figures kneeling or bowing at the feet of Christ (Figure 20.10; see also Figure 22.3).[73] Typically Christ was depicted at the center of the scene as a teacher or deliverer of the law, seated or standing, often upon the mount of Paradise, accompanied by two or more apostles. The husband and wife were placed at Christ's feet to the viewer's left and right, respectively. This form of representation, like earlier ones, located Christ at the center between spouses, but unlike

Figure 20.10 Detail, front panel of sarcophagus with Christ, apostles, and representations of the married grave owners kneeling at Christ's feet. Late fourth century. Cathédrale Saint-Sauveur, Aix-en-Provence. Photo: Mark D. Ellison.

earlier portraiture it emphasized the figure of Christ, and represented spouses generically, with little to no individualizing features, suggesting rather their humility and piety in "permanent acts of worship" with strong allusions to the afterlife.[74]

Some scholars detect in this new iconography a declining interest in personal commemoration and a waning of the earlier panegyrical functions of sarcophagi.[75] However, sarcophagi with small worshiping spouses sometimes contain additional, larger portraits of the pair, along with identifying inscriptions.[76] Representations of couples at Christ's feet may constitute a new, different type of visual panegyric, a redefining of honor in the late empire.

The iconography of worshiping spouses drew in part upon strategies used in imperial art to depict relationships of hierarchy and benefaction. In *liberalitas* and *congiarium* scenes, the seated emperor is depicted larger in scale than the recipients of his largesse at his feet, as can be seen on both Antonine and Constantinian reliefs on the Arch of Constantine. Images of a ruler's display of *clementia* portrayed defeated barbarians as war captives throwing themselves at the feet of a seated general, weeping or kissing the general's hand. A more proximate source for this new portrait-type was the kneeling figures in earlier sarcophagus reliefs illustrating Jesus's miracles such as the raising of Lazarus, the healing of the Canaanite woman's daughter, and the healing of the hemorrhagic woman (see Figures 19.4, 19.7). These scenes evoke biblical narratives in which supplicants plead at Jesus's feet, or recipients of his teaching and miracles express gratitude and adoration by bowing down at his feet, kneeling at his feet, taking hold of his feet, or bathing his feet with their tears.[77]

For fourth-century viewers, there was potential to discern multiple nuances in portrayals of married sarcophagus owners at Christ's feet. The representation of Christ as a teacher rather than an emperor or military conqueror would seem to subvert Roman imperial notions of power. The small figures portrayed at Christ's feet would have been seen not as subjugated enemies, but as supplicants, hearers, and worshipers in the tradition of biblical figures whose lives were affected by Jesus. Posing married grave owners as kneeling figures cast them in the role of individuals who, like their biblical forebears, were recipients of divine, saving power (compare Figure 8.7). (Paulinus of Nola urged Pneumatius and his wife Fidelis to such imitation: "Both of you must lick the holy feet of Christ the Lord, wipe them with your hair, and wash them with your tears."[78]) Yet they might also be seen as subjects and beneficiaries of a benevolent heavenly sovereign, with ultimate allegiance to the kingdom of God even as they participated in the culture of the Roman Empire on earth.

In the visual hierarchy created by the relative size and locations of Christ, apostles, and spouses, the married grave owners claimed a place simultaneously humble and honored, close to Christ and his most revered followers. The couple's larger portraits elsewhere on a number of the sarcophagi, sometimes accompanied by inscriptions, announce that they are worthy of remembrance and admiration as ones devoted to the Son of God and the church's apostolic tradition.

Conclusion

In the Christian art of the third and fourth centuries, portraits of "secular" subjects such as couples and family groups adapted prior forms of Roman portraiture by incorporating figures or symbols of Christ. In addition to communicating the memory, identity, and presence of those depicted, these images can inform questions of religious history, including the question of how lay believers contributed, by visual means, to the Christianization of the Roman household during the faith's formative period.

Notes

1 Figure 20.1: Sarcophagus of Catervius and Severina; Jutta Dresken-Weiland, *Repertorium der christlich-antiken Sarkophage, zweiter Band: Italien mit einem Nachtrag Rom und Ostia, Dalmatien, Museen der Welt* (Mainz am Rhein: Verlag Philipp von Zabern, 1998), no. 148; for others, see, e.g., Friedrich Wilhelm Deichmann, Giuseppe Bovini and Hugo Brandenburg, *Repertorium der christlich-antiken Sarkophage, Bd 1 Rom und Ostia* (Wiesbaden: Franz Steiner, 1967), nos 34, 39, 40, 42, 43, 44, 87, 112, 187, 188, 239, 244, 385, 435, 625, 650, 681, 689, 778, 782, 812, 896, 962, 1010. Parts of this chapter draw upon Mark D. Ellison, "Visualizing Christian Marriage in the Roman World" (PhD diss., Vanderbilt University, 2017).

2 Jeffrey Spier, *Late Antique and Early Christian Gems* (Wiesbaden: Reichert Verlag, 2007), 22, no. 37; *MAXSENTI V/IVAS TVIS F*, or *Maxenti vivas [cum] tuis f[eliciter]* ("Maxentius, may you live h[appily with] your [loved ones]") (my trans.). NB: Spier, 22, omits the final *F* in the inscription; cf. William Smith and Samuel Cheetham, *A Dictionary of Christian Antiquities*, Vol. 1 (Hartford: J. B. Burr, 1880), 722, who include the final *F*, "for *cum tuis feliciter*"; Antje Krug, *Römische Gemmen im Rheinischen Landesmuseum Trier* (Trier: Rheinisches Landesmuseum Trier, 1995), 65, no. 63.

3 Raffaele Garrucci, *Vetri ornati di figure in oro trovanti nei cimiteri dei cristiani primitivi di Roma* (Rome: Tipografia Salviucci, 1858), Tav. 29.4; Daniel Thomas Howells, *A Catalogue of the Late Antique Gold Glass in the British Museum* (London: British Museum, 2015), 129–131, cat. no. 39, Pl. 108; inscription: *POMPEIA/NE TEOD/ORA VIBA/TIS.*

4 Literary evidence suggests that as early as the third or perhaps even the mid-second century CE, Christians were creating visual representations of revered figures such as Christ, apostles, Mary, and various saints, and images with these subjects grew increasingly popular from the late fourth century forward; see *Acts of John* 26–29; Irenaeus, *Against Heresies* 1.25.6; Eusebius, *Ecclesiastical History* 7.18; see also Katherine Marsengill's chapter in this volume. On gold glass, over half the surviving pieces contain images of Christ and saints, while the second largest group is of secular portraits; see Lucy Grig, "Portraits, Pontiffs, and the Christianization of Fourth-Century Rome," *Papers of the British School at Rome* 72 (2004): 205.

5 E.g., Grig, "Portraits, Pontiffs, and the Christianization of Fourth-Century Rome," 203–230 (esp. 207); Howells, *Gold Glass in the British Museum*, 114–131.

6 See Lisa Kaaren Bailey, *The Religious Worlds of the Laity in Late Antique Gaul* (London and New York, NY: Bloomsbury, 2016), 2, 22, 42; for an example, see Jerome, *Epistle* 48.2.

7 For examples of greater attention to portraits of religious figures than ordinary believers, see Josef Wilpert, *Die Malereien der Katakomben Roms* (Freiburg: Herder, 1903), 106–114; André Grabar, *Christian Iconography: A Study of its Origins* (Princeton, NJ: Princeton University Press, 1968), 60–82; Grig, "Portraits, Pontiffs, and the Christianization of Fourth-Century Rome." Use of "private": e.g., Guntram Koch, "Portrait," in *The Eerdmans Encyclopedia of Early Christian Art and Archaeology*, ed. P.C. Finney (Grand Rapids, MI: Eerdmans, 2017), 350–352. Recent studies of "secular"/private portraiture: e.g., Janet Huskinson, "Degrees of Differentiation: Role Models on Early Christian Sarcophagi," in *Memoirs of the American Academy in Rome, Supplementary Volumes, Volume 7, Role Models in the Roman World: Identity and Assimilation* (2008): 287–299; Janet Huskinson, "Reading Identity on Roman Strigilated Sarcophagi," *Res: Anthropology and Aesthetics* 61/62 (2012): 80–97; Manuela Studer-Karlen, *Verstorbenendarstellungen auf frühchristlichen Sarkophagen* (Turnhout: Brepols, 2012); Jaś Elsner, "Rational, Passionate, and Appetitive: The Psychology of Rhetoric and the Transformation of Visual Culture from non-Christian to Christian Sarcophagi in the Roman World," in *Art and Rhetoric in Roman Culture*, eds Jaś Elsner and Michel Meyer (New York, NY: Cambridge University Press, 2014), 316–349; Stine Birk, "The Christian Muse: Continuity and Change in the Representations of Women on Late Roman Sarcophagi," *Marburger Beiträge zur Archäologie* Band 3 (Marburg: Eigenverlag des Archäologischen Seminars der Philipps-Universität, 2016), 63–72, 205–206, Taf. 20–21; Norbert Zimmermann, "Am Ende einer Gattung: Spätantike Verstorbenen-Porträts in christlichen Grabkontext," in *Privatporträt: Das Bildnis privater Personen zwischen Antike und Mittelalter*, Akten der Tagung 14.–16.02.2013 Wien, ÖAW (forthcoming).

8 See, e.g., Denis R. Janz, ed., *A People's History of Christianity*, 7 vols. (Minneapolis, MN: Fortress Press, 2005–2008).

9 See Robert Couzin, "The Christian Sarcophagus Population of Rome," *Journal of Roman Archaeology* 27 (2014): 284, 287–290; Andrew Meek, "Gold Glass in Late Antiquity: Scientific Analysis of the British Museum Collection," in *New Light on Old Glass: Recent Research on Byzantine Mosaics and Glass*, eds Chris Entwistle and Liz James (London: The British Museum, 2013), 128; Howells, *Gold Glass in the British Museum*, 61, 64. The fine attire of individuals depicted in some gold glass portraits might allude to their wealth or class, but might have a panegyrical function, and so cannot be taken as conclusive evidence of the owners' wealth, much as the attribute of the scroll was used somewhat gratuitously and might not necessarily signal the bearer's literacy. The cost of metal disc seals was likely the weight of the silver, perhaps 1–2 *siliquae*, plus a modest work fee (with thanks to Jeffrey Spier, personal correspondence).

10 Cf. Koch, "Portrait," 350. For an introduction to portraits in Roman art, see Jane Fejfer, *Roman Portraits in Context* (Berlin and New York, NY: Walter de Gruyter, 2008); Jane Fejfer, "Roman Portraits," in *A Companion to Roman Art*, ed. Barbara E. Borg (Malden, MA: Wiley-Blackwell, 2015), 233–251; Robin M. Jensen, *Face to Face: Portraits of the Divine in Early Christianity* (Minneapolis, MN: Fortress Press, 2005), 35–51; for introductions to portraits in Christian art, see Grabar, *Christian Iconography*, 60–82; Katherine Marsengill, "Portraits and Icons in Late Antiquity," in *Transition to Christianity: Art of Late Antiquity, 3rd–7th Century AD*, ed. Anastasia Lazaridou (New York, NY: Alexander S. Onassis Public Benefit Foundation; Athens: Byzantine & Christian Museum, 2011), 61–66.

11 For examples of "secular" portraits of Christian couples and family groups in sarcophagus reliefs: see Deichmann *Repertorium* I, nos 34, 39, 40, 42, 43, 44, 66, 86, 87, 112, 187, 188, 239, 241, 244, 385, 435, 625, 650, 678, 681, 688, 689, 778, 782, 788, 812, 853, 918, 922, 962, 1010; wall paintings: see Jensen, *Face to Face*, 48–49, fig. 31; Norbert Zimmermann's chapter in this volume; Umberto M. Fasola, *Le catacombe di S. Gennaro a Capodimonte* (Rome: Editalia, 1975), 73–74, 96; freestanding sculpture: see William D. Wixom, "Early Christian Sculptures at Cleveland," *The Bulletin of the Cleveland Museum of Art* 54.3 (1967): 67–88 (esp. 67–75), cf. Lazaridou, *Transition to Christianity*, 98–99, nos 37–38; panel paintings: see Katherine Marsengill in this volume, and "Portraits and Icons in Late Antiquity"; gold glass vessel bases: see Charles R. Morey, *The Gold-Glass Collection of the Vatican Library with Additional Catalogues of Other Gold-Glass Collections*, ed. Guy Ferrari (Vatican City: Biblioteca Apostolica Vaticana, 1959), nos 1, 5, 7, 9, 29, 39, 43, 59, 89, 91, 92, 93, 94, 97, 98, 99, 109, 113, 225, 237, 240, 244, 259, 289, 296, 308, 309, 310, 315, 316, 337, 366, 379?, 397, 399, 406?, 418, 420, 440, 441, 447, 451, 452; finger rings: Marvin C. Ross, *Catalogue of the Byzantine and Early Mediaeval Antiquities in the Dumbarton Oaks Collection*, Vols 1–2 (Washington, DC: Dumbarton Oaks, 1962, 1965), 50, nos 1–2; Gary Vikan, "Early Christian and Byzantine Rings in the Zucker Family Collection," *The Journal of the Walters Art Gallery* 45 (1987):

32–43; Gary Vikan, "Art and Marriage in Early Byzantium," *Dumbarton Oaks Papers* 44 (1990): 145–163; gems and seals: see Jeffrey Spier, *Late Antique and Early Christian Gems* (Wiesbaden: Reichert Verlag, 2007), 18–25; belt ornaments: see Metropolitan Museum of Art, accession no. 1993.166; domestic silver: see Kurt Weitzmann, ed., *Age of Spirituality: Late Antique and Early Christian Art, Third to Seventh Century* (New York, NY: Metropolitan Museum of Art, 1979), 330–332, no. 310.

12 For discussion of these practices, see Jocelyn M. C. Toynbee, *Death and Burial in the Roman World* (Baltimore, MD: John Hopkins University Press, 1996); Robin M. Jensen, "Dining with the Dead: From the Mensa to the Altar in Christian Late Antiquity," in *Commemorating the Dead: Texts and Artifacts in Context. Studies of Roman, Jewish, and Christian Burials*, eds Laurie Brink and Deborah Green (Berlin: De Gruyter, 2008), 107–143; Jensen, *Face to Face*, 44–51; Valerie M. Warrior, *Roman Religion* (New York, NY: Cambridge University Press, 2006), 27–40; see also the chapter by Zimmermann in this volume.

13 See discussion in Jensen, *Face to Face*, 37–42.

14 For a discussion of these unfinished portraits, see Stine Birk, *Depicting the Dead: Self-Representation and Commemoration on Roman Sarcophagi with Portraits*, Aarhus Studies in Mediterranean Antiquity, no. 11 (Aarhus: Aarhus University Press, 2013), 55–58. Additionally, many portrait heads on sarcophagi have been reworked in modern times; see Cristina Gennaccari, "Museo Pio Cristiano: Documenti inediti di rilavorazioni e restauri settecenteschi sui sarcofagi paleocristiani," *Bollettino: Monumenti, Musei e gallerie pontificie* 16 (1996): 153–284.

15 E.g., Howells, *Gold Glass in the British Museum*, 114; Birk, "The Christian Muse," 65; Robert Couzin, "Manuela Studer-Karlen, *Verstorbenendarstellungen auf frühchristlichen Sarkophagen*, Turnhout (Brepols) 2012 [review]," *Klio* 98 (2016): 389–392. But see an argument for using the term "portraits" in Grabar, *Christian Iconography*, 62–63.

16 For an introduction to the subject of identity, see Kimberly B. Stratton, "Identity," in *The Cambridge Companion to Ancient Mediterranean Religions*, ed. Barbette Stanley Spaeth (Cambridge: Cambridge University Press, 2013), 220–251. For recent studies on identity in early Christian portraiture, see works cited in note 7 above.

17 See Huskinson, "Degrees of Differentiation"; Elsner, "Rational, Passionate, and Appetitive."

18 See Studer-Karlen, *Verstorbenendarstellungen auf frühchristlichen Sarkophagen*; Robin M. Jensen, "Compiling Narratives: The Visual Strategies of Early Christian Visual Art," *Journal of Early Christian Studies* 23.1 (2015): 1–26; Birk, "The Christian Muse"; Elsner, "Rational, Passionate, and Appetitive"; Jutta Dresken-Weiland, *Bild, Grab, und Wort: Untersuchungen zu Jenseitsvorstellungen von Christen des 3. und 4. Jahrhunderts* (Regensburg: Schnell and Steiner, 2010); see also Zimmermann in this volume.

19 Aldo Nestori, *Il Mausoleo e il Sarcofago di Flavivs Ivlivs Catervivs a Tolentino* (Citta del Vaticano: Pontificio Instituto di Archeoogia Cristiana, 1996); Dresken-Weiland, *Repertorium* II, 52–54, no. 148.

20 CIL IX, 5566; for an English translation see John Osborne and Amanda Claridge, *Early Christian and Medieval Antiquities, Volume Two: Other Mosaics, Paintings, Sarcophagi and Small Objects* (London: Harvey Miller Publishers, 1998), 165.

21 For further discussion of how double portraits served commemoration and patronage of married sarcophagus owners, see Birk, *Depicting the Dead*, 23–31, esp. 25.

22 To a "pagan" viewer, the shepherd might have seemed to be the traditional Hermes *criophorus*, the bearer of departed souls safely into the afterlife; the bearded, togate men holding scrolls at left and right might have appeared to be philosopher-types alluding to the spouses' learnedness.

23 Doves as symbols of departed souls: see Ambrose, *On Isaac and the Soul*, 7.59; Erwin R. Goodenough, *Jewish Symbols in the Greco-Roman Period*, 13 vols (New York, NY: Pantheon Books, 1953–1968), 8:37–41; as symbols of conjugal devotion: Song of Songs 2:14; 5:2; 6:9; Paulinus of Nola, *Carmen* 25.3, CSEL 30, 238, "Christe deus, pariles duc ad tua frena columbas"; *Physiologus* 28.2–5; Bernhard Jussen, "Posthumous Love as Culture: Outline of a Medieval Moral Pattern," in *Love after Death: Concepts of Posthumous Love in Medieval and Early Modern Europe*, eds Bernhard Jussen and Ramie Targoff (Berlin: DeGruyter, 2015), 39; but cf. Elsner, "Rational, Passionate, and Appetitive," 336, who sees the doves in the portrait of Severina and Catervius as symbols of "the Holy Ghost." For paired doves on other tombs, see, e.g., Dresken-Weiland, *Repertorium* II, 32, Taf. 33–34, no. 102; 56–58, Taf. 59.3–8, 60.1–2, no. 150; cf. Brigitte Christern-Briesenick, *Repertorium der christlich-antiken Sarkophage, dritter Band: Frankreich, Algerien, Tunesien* (Mainz am Rhein: Verlag Philipp von Zabern, 2003), 35, no. 49, Taf. 17 (two doves, now broken off and lost, originally appeared on the *crux invicta* beneath portraits of spouses on the lid).

24 CIL IX, 5566: *QVOS PARIBVS MERITIS VINXIT MATRIMONIO DVLCI / OMNIPOTENS DOMINVS TVMVLVS CVSTODIT IN AEVVM / CATERVI SEVERINA TIBI CONIVNCTA LAETATVR / SVRGATIS PARITER CRISTO PRAESTANTE BEATI / QVOS DEI SACERDVS*

PROBIANVS LAVIT ET VNXIT; my trans., with assistance from Dr Max Goldman, and with thanks to Jutta Dresken-Weiland and Robin M. Jensen for discussing details of the inscription with me. To my knowledge, this is the first publication of an English translation of this inscription.

25 E.g., compare the verse epitaphs of Petronius Probus, ICUR 2, 347/8; see Dennis Trout, "The Verse Epitaph(s) of Petronius Probus: Competitive Commemoration in Late-Fourth-Century Rome," *New England Classical Journal* 28.3 (2001): 157–176.

26 Several sources identify this image only as the magi before Herod: Dresken-Weiland, *Repertorium* II, 53; Jutta Dresken-Weiland, Andreas Angerstorfer and Andreas Merkt, *Himmel, Paradies, Schalom: Tod und Jenseits in christlichen und jüdischen Grabinschriften der Antike* (Regensburg: Schnell & Steiner, 2012), 163; Nestori, *Il Mausoleo e il Sarcofago di Flavivs Ivlivs Catervivs*, 82; however, the king's bust atop a column, as well as the Persian-style caps worn by the three youths, allude to the story in Daniel. For more discussion of the Hebrew Youths/Magi image as anti-pagan visual rhetoric, see Elsner, "Rational, Passionate, and Appetitive," 342–346.

27 See Robin M. Jensen, "The Three Hebrew Youths and the Problem of the Emperor's Portrait in Early Christianity," in *Jewish Art in its Late Antique Context*, eds Uzi Leibner and Catherine Hezser (Tübingen: Mohr Siebeck, 2016), 303–320. Note: pediments on the lid with two lambs at wreathed christogram (right side), two lambs at staurogram (left), could be seen as allusions to the faith of the grave owners. If viewers processed counter-clockwise around the sarcophagus (favoring the right) they would have seen the images in this sequence of rejection and adoration.

28 CIL 6.1779; Maijastina Kahlos, "Fabia Aconia Paulina and the Death of Praetextatus—Rhetoric and Ideals in Late Antiquity (CIL VI 1779)," *Arctos: Acta Philologica Fennica* 28 (1994): 13–26.

29 Jerome, *Epistle* 23.

30 See Trout, "The Verse Epitaph(s) of Petronius Probus: Competitive Commemoration in Late-Fourth-Century Rome"; John F. Matthews, "Four Funerals and a Wedding: This World and the Next in Fourth-Century Rome," in *Roman Perspectives: Studies in the Social, Political and Cultural History of the First to Fifth Centuries* (Swansea: Classical Press of Wales, 2010), 255–274.

31 As proposed by Grabar, *Christian Iconography*, 62.

32 Paul Zanker, *Roman Portraits: Sculptures in Stone and Bronze in the Collection of the Metropolitan Museum of Art* (New York, NY: The Metropolitan Museum of Art, 2016), 242, 256–257, no. 100.

33 Staatliche Museum, Berlin, inv. no. 31329.

34 Glenys Davies, "The Significance of the Handshake Motif in Classical Funerary Art," *American Journal of Archaeology* 89:4 (October 1, 1985): 627–640.

35 See Karen K. Hersch, *The Roman Wedding: Ritual and Meaning in Antiquity* (New York, NY: Cambridge University Press, 2010).

36 August Rossbach, *Römischen Hochzeits- und Ehedenkmäler* (Leipzig: B. G. Teubner, 1871), 12–13; S. Weinstock, "Pronuba," *Real-Encyclopädie der klassischen Altertumswissenschaft* 23.1 (1957): 750–756; Louis Reekmans, "La 'dextrarum iunctio' dans l'iconographie romaine et paléochrétienne," *Bulletin de l'Institut historique belge de Rome* 31 (1958): 23–95; Carola Reinsberg, "Concordia: Die Darstellung von Hochzeit und ehelicher Eintracht in Spätantike," in *Spätantike und frühes Christentum: Ausstellung im Liebieghaus, Museum alter Plastik, Frankfurt am Main. 16. Dezember bis 11. März 1984*, eds Herbert Beck and Peter Bol (Frankfurt am Main: Das Liebieghaus, 1983), 312–317; Carola Reinsberg, *Die Sarkophage mit Darstellungen aus dem Menschenleben: Vita Romana*, Die antiken Sarkophagreliefs I, 3 (Berlin: Mann Verlag, 2006), 78, 81; Hersch, *The Roman Wedding*, 15, 190–212.

37 See Reekmans, "La 'dextrarum iunctio'," 31–37; Reinsberg, "Concordia."

38 Ernst H. Kantorowicz, "On the Golden Marriage Belt and the Marriage Rings of the Dumbarton Oaks Collection," *Dumbarton Oaks Papers* 14 (1960): 1–16; Howells, *Gold Glass in the British Museum*, 121–124, nos 35–36.

39 E.g., Deichmann, *Repertorium* I, nos 86, 853, 952.

40 Morey, *The Gold-Glass Collection of the Vatican Library*, nos 29, 109, 240, 310, 397; cf. 50, 278; for an example of this image on a sarcophagus, see Deichmann, *Repertorium* I, no. 922, cf. Joseph Wilpert, *I Sarcofagi Cristiani Antichi*, Vol. 1 (Roma: Pontifico Isstituto di Archeologia Cristiana, 1929), Tav. 74.3; for an example on jewelry, see the gold marriage medallion, Metropolitan Museum of Art accession no. 58.12, also Weitzmann, *Age of Spirituality*, 307–308, no. 281. For a couple portrait in which the figure of Christ is identified by the inscription *CRISTVS*, see Garrucci, *Vetri ornati di figure in oro*, 29.3.

41 For examples of these varieties on sarcophagi, see Deichmann, *Repertorium* I, no. 922; Dresken-Weiland, *Repertorium* II, no. 148; for gold-glass examples, see Morey, *The Gold-Glass Collection of the Vatican Library*, nos 29, 98, 109, 240, 259, 310, 315, 397, 420, 440, 441, 447.

42 See, e.g., Morey, *The Gold-Glass Collection of the Vatican Library*, nos 308–309, 315, 379; Osborne and Claridge, *Early Christian and Medieval Antiquities*, 2.244–245, no. 274; Garrucci, *Vetri ornati di figure in oro*, Tav. 26.12; Spier, *Late Antique and Early Christian Gems*, nos 25, 26, 40, 42, 45, 47, 48, 63, 64, 65, 66, 79. In framed portrait busts children sometimes appear with their parents, while *dextrarum iunctio* portraits typically do not include children.

43 See Kathleen J. Shelton, *The Esquiline Treasure* (London: British Museum Press, 1981); Ferenc Fülep, "Early Christian Gold Glasses in the Hungarian National Museum," *Acta Antiqua Adademiae Scientiarum Hungaricae* 16 (1968): 401–412.

44 See, e.g., Kantorowicz, "On the Golden Marriage Belt and the Marriage Rings of the Dumbarton Oaks Collection," 1–16, esp. 8.

45 For a discussion of such distinctively Christian notions as an indissoluble and sexually exclusive marriage, see Kyle Harper, "Marriage and Family," in *The Oxford Handbook of Late Antiquity*, ed. Scott Fitzgerald Johnson (Oxford: Oxford University Press, 2012), 667–714.

46 Huskinson, "Reading Identity on Roman Strigilated Sarcophagi," 90.

47 Ambrosiaster, *Quaestiones veteris et novi testamenti* 127, *De peccato Adae et Evae* 2–3, CSEL 50, 399–400; *Comm. in 1 Cor 7:40*, CSEL 81/2, 90; *Comm. in 1 Tim 3:12*, CSEL 81/3, 268. See also David G. Hunter, "'On the Sin of Adam and Eve': A Little-Known Defense of Marriage and Childbearing by Ambrosiaster," *Harvard Theological Review* 82.3 (1989): 283–299; David G. Hunter, "Sexuality, Marriage, and the Family," in *The Cambridge History of Christianity: Vol. 2 Constantine to c. 600*, eds Augustine Casiday and Frederick W. Norris (Cambridge: Cambridge University Press, 2008), 590–592.

48 Ambrosiaster: *Questions on the Old and New Testament* 127, *On the Sin of Adam and Eve* 2–3, CSEL 50, 399–400: "ut dei creatura sub dei benedictione iungatur."

49 Ambrose, *Expositio evangelii Lucae* 8.4, 3; CSEL 32.3.393.11, 8–10: "ubi armonia, Deus iungit"; trans. William Joseph Dooley, *Marriage According to St. Ambrose* (Washington, DC: Catholic University of America Press, 1948), 16–17.

50 Paulinus of Nola, *Carmen* 25, 3–4, 69, 151–152, 187; CSEL 30, 238, 240, 243, 244; trans. Searle and Stevenson, *Documents of the Marriage Liturgy*, 31, 34, 36, 37.

51 David G. Hunter, "Nuptial Metaphor and Nuptial Reality: Early Christian Marriage Liturgy and the Formation of a Scriptural Imagination" (paper given at the Patristic, Medieval, and Renaissance Conference, Villanova University, October 17, 2015), 5. With thanks to Dr Hunter for calling my attention to this text and sharing his paper with me.

52 *Sacramentarium Veronese* 31.1107–1109; Leo. C. Mohlberg, Leo Eisenhöfer and Petrus Siffrin, eds, *Sacramentarium Veronense* (Rome: Herder, 1956), 139–140; "sic consortio maritali tuo munere copulata<m> . . . Quaesumus, omnipotens deus, . . . quos legitima societate connectes, longeua pace custodi . . . Adesto, domine, supplicationi[bu]s nostris, et . . . benignus adsiste: ut quod te auctore iungitur, te auxiliante seruetur"; trans. Searle and Stevenson, *Documents of the Marriage Liturgy*, 42.

53 Tertullian, *Ad uxorem* 2.8.7–8; SC 273, 148, 150; trans. David G. Hunter, *Marriage in the Early Church* (Minneapolis, MN: Fortress Press, 1992), 38–39.

54 Eph 5:21–6:8; Col 3:18–4:1; 1 Tim 2:8–15; 5:11–16; 6:1–2; Titus 2:2–10; 1 Pet 2:18–3:7; for a discussion see Carolyn Osiek, "Family Matters," in *Christian Origins*, A People's History of Christianity, Vol. 1, ed. Richard A. Horsley (Minneapolis, MN: Fortress Press, 2005), 216–217.

55 John Chrysostom, *Homilia* 20 on Ephesians 5:22–33, PG 62; trans. Catharine P. Roth and David Anderson, *St John Chrysostom: On Marriage and Family Life* (Crestwood, NY: St Vladimir's Seminary Press, 1986), 44.

56 Kantorowicz, "On the Golden Marriage Belt and the Marriage Rings of the Dumbarton Oaks Collection," 8; cf. Reinsberg, "Concordia," 315.

57 E.g., Morey, *The Gold-Glass Collection of the Vatican Library*, no. 315; Fasola, *Le catacombe di S. Gennaro a Capodimonte*, 73–74, 96; Spier, *Late Antique and Early Christian Gems*, no. 37.

58 Christopher Walter, "Marriage Crowns in Byzantine Iconography," *Zograf* 10 (1979): 91.

59 E.g., Morey, *The Gold-Glass Collection of the Vatican Library*, nos 37, 50, 51, 58, 66, 241.

60 Cleveland Museum of Art, loan no. 7.2013, evidently made *ca.* 166 CE to celebrate Lucius's victory over the Parthians.

61 E.g., 2 Tim 4:8; Jas 1:2; Rev 2:10; 4:4; 1 Pet 5:4.

62 John Chrysostom, *Homilia* 9 on 1 Tim 2, PG 62, 546; trans. Philip Schaff, *Nicene and Post-Nicene Fathers* Series I, 13:437, with modifications.

63 For example, see Mark 3:31–35 (par. Matt 12:46–50; Luke 8:19–21); Luke 9:59–60 (par. Matt 8:21–22); Luke 11:27–28; Matt 19:29 (par. Mark 10:29–30; Luke 18:29–30); Luke 14:26; 1 Cor 7; Mark 12:25 (Matt 22:30; Luke 20:34–36)—but on this last saying see the discussion in Ben Witherington, *The Gospel of Mark: A Socio-Rhetorical Commentary* (Grand Rapids, MI: William B. Eerdmans, 2001), 328–329.

64 For example, see Matt 19:4–6 (par. Mark 10: 6–9); Eph 5:21–6:8; Col 3:18–4:1; 1 Tim 2:8–15; 5:11–16; 6:1–2; Titus 2:2–10; 1 Pet 2:18–3:7; for a discussion of these disparate teachings, see Osiek, "Family Matters," 216–220; and Luke Timothy Johnson, "The Complex Witness of the New Testament Concerning Marriage, Family, and Sexuality," in *Contested Issues in Christian Origins and the New Testament: Collected Essays* (Leiden: Brill, 2013), 659–678.

65 See Philip Sellew, "The Hundredfold Reward for Martyrs and Ascetics: Ps.-Cyprian, *De centesima, sexagesima, tricesima*," *Studia Patristica* 36 (2001): 94–98; David G. Hunter, *Marriage, Celibacy, and Heresy in Ancient Christianity: The Jovinianist Controversy* (New York, NY: Oxford University Press, 2007), 114–115; Peter Brown, *The Body and Society: Men, Women, and Sexual Renunciation in Early Christianity*, 20th anniversary edition (New York, NY: Columbia University Press, 2008).

66 See, e.g., Eusebius, *Demonstratio Evangelica*, 1.8, PG 22, 76–77; W. J. Ferrar, trans., *The Proof of the Gospel, Being the Demonstratio evangelica of Eusebius of Cæsarea* (London: Society for Promoting Christian Knowledge, 1920), 1.48–50; *Concilium Gangrense*, canons 1, 4, 9, 10, 14, 15, 16, and epilogue, *Ecclesiae Occidentalis Monumenta Iuris Antiquissima* II.145–214; the teachings of Ambrosiaster, Helvidius, and Jovinian and their reception; see Hunter, *Marriage, Celibacy, and Heresy*.

67 E.g., Spier, *Late Antique and Early Christian Gems*, 22, no. 40, Pl. 7; cf. the *chi-rho* in the first line of the epitaph of Bassa: Dennis Trout, "Borrowed Verse and Broken Narrative: Agency, Identity, and the (Bethesda) Sarcophagus of Bassa," in *Life, Death, and Representation: Some New Work on Roman Sarcophagi*, eds Jaś Elsner and Janet Huskinson (Berlin: DeGruyter, 2010), 337–358.

68 See Robin M. Jensen, "The Emperor Cult and Christian Iconography," in *Rome and Religion: A Cross-Disciplinary Dialogue on the Imperial Cult*, eds Jeffrey Brodd and Jonathan L. Reed (Atlanta, GA: Society of Biblical Literature, 2011), 153–171.

69 With thanks to Dr David A. Michelson for this insight.

70 See, e.g., Marvin C. Ross, *Catalogue of the Byzantine and Early Mediaeval Antiquities in the Dumbarton Oaks Collection*, Vols 1–2 (Washington, DC: Dumbarton Oaks, 1962, 1965), no. 50; Spier, *Late Antique and Early Christian Gems*, nos 45, 47, 63, 64, 79.

71 See Gary Vikan, "Art, Medicine, and Magic in Early Byzantium," *Dumbarton Oaks Papers* 38 (1984): 65–86; Gary Vikan, "Early Christian and Byzantine Rings in the Zucker Family Collection," *The Journal of the Walters Art Gallery* 45 (1987): 32–43; Gary Vikan, "Art and Marriage in Early Byzantium," *Dumbarton Oaks Papers* 44 (1990): 145–163; Alicia Walker, "A Reconsideration of Early Byzantine Marriage Rings," in *Between Magic and Religion: Interdisciplinary Studies in Ancient Mediterranean Religion and Society*, eds Sulochana Asirvatham, Corinne Ondine Pache and John Watrous (Lanham, MD: Rowman & Littlefield, 2001), 149–164; Alicia Walker, "Early Byzantine Marriage Rings," in *Sacred Art, Secular Context*, eds Asen Kirin, James Nelson Carder and Robert S. Nelson (Athens, GA: Georgia Museum of Art, 2005), 78–81.

72 Paulinus of Nola, *Carmen* 25, 192; CSEL 30, 244; trans. Searle and Stevenson, *Documents of the Marriage Liturgy*, 38.

73 Deichmann, *Repertorium* I, nos 217 (uncertain because fragmented and damaged), 241, 675, 679; Dresken-Weiland, *Repertorium* II, nos 149, 150; Christern-Briesenick, *Repertorium* III, nos 25, 80, 81, 291, 428; in two instances the kneeling figures at Jesus's feet are both men, so the scene was not always intended for the representation of a husband and wife: Dresken-Weiland, *Repertorium* II, no. 10 (uncertain, left figure damaged); Christern-Briesenick, *Repertorium* III, no. 32; cf. Peter and Paul as diminutive figures at Jesus's feet: Deichmann, *Repertorium* I, no. 58; a lone woman at Jesus's feet: Dresken-Weiland, *Repertorium* II, no. 151; Christern-Briesenick, *Repertorium* III, no. 160.

74 Elsner, "Rational, Passionate, and Appetitive," 336, with reference to the sarcophagus of Catervius and Severina; Studer-Karlen, *Verstorbenendarstellungen auf frühchristlichen Sarkophagen*, 209.

75 Janet Huskinson, *Roman Strigillated Sarcophagi: Art and Social History* (Oxford: Oxford University Press, 2015), 236; Elsner, "Rational, Passionate, and Appetitive," 341.

76 E.g., Dresken-Weiland, *Repertorium* II, nos 149–150; other sarcophagi with kneeling figures are missing their lids, which might similarly have contained additional portraits and inscriptions. Elsner, "Rational,

Passionate, and Appetitive," 335–336, includes the sarcophagus of Catervius and Severina (*Repertorium* II, no. 148), seeing the acroteria busts of Catervius and Severina as genuflecting toward the Good Shepherd below in a variation on the motif of small figures at Jesus's feet. Alternatively, they could be seen as turning toward each other and borne aloft on the lid above the Good Shepherd, like the sheep on his shoulders, lifted up by Christ to a place of honor and remembrance.

77 Supplication: Matt 5:22–23; 15:30; Mark 7:25–26; Luke 8:41; gratitude and adoration: Matt 28:9; Luke 7:38; 17:15–16; John 11:32; 12:3; Phil 2:10–11; Rev 19:10; 22:8; listening to teaching: Luke 8:35; 10:39.

78 Paulinus, *Carmen* 31.535, trans. P. G. Walsh, *The Poems of St. Paulinus of Nola*, Ancient Christian Writers, no. 40 (New York, NY: Newman Press, 1975), 326.

Further reading

Birk, Stine. *Depicting the Dead: Self-Representation and Commemoration on Roman Sarcophagi with Portraits*. Aarhus Studies in Mediterranean Antiquity, no. 11. Aarhus: Aarhus University Press, 2013.

__________. "The Christian Muse: Continuity and Change in the Representations of Women on Late Roman Sarcophagi." *Marburger Beiträge zur Archäologie* Band 3, 63–72, 205–206, Taf. 20–21. Marburg: Eigenverlag des Archäologischen Seminars der Philipps-Universität, 2016.

Elsner, Jaś. "Rational, Passionate, and Appetitive: The Psychology of Rhetoric and the Transformation of Visual Culture from non-Christian to Christian Sarcophagi in the Roman World." In *Art and Rhetoric in Roman Culture*, edited by Jaś Elsner and Michel Meyer, 316–349. New York, NY: Cambridge University Press, 2014.

Elsner, Jaś and Janet Huskinson, eds. *Life, Death and Representation: Some New Work on Roman Sarcophagi*. New York, NY: De Gruyter, 2010.

Ewald, Björn Christian. "Sarcophagi and Senators: The Social History of Roman Funerary Art and Its Limits." *Journal of Roman Archaeology* 16 (2003): 561–571.

__________. "Paradigms of Personhood and Regimes of Representation: Some Notes on the Transformation of Roman Sarcophagi." *Res: Anthropology and Aesthetics* 61/62 (2012): 41–64.

Fejfer, Jane. *Roman Portraits in Context*. Berlin and New York, NY: Walter de Gruyter, 2008.

Grig, Lucy. "Portraits, Pontiffs, and the Christianization of Fourth-Century Rome." *Papers of the British School at Rome* 72 (2004): 203–230.

Howells, Daniel Thomas. *A Catalogue of the Late Antique Gold Glass in the British Museum*. London: British Museum, 2015 (especially pages 114–131).

Huskinson, Janet. "Degrees of Differentiation: Role Models on Early Christian Sarcophagi." *Memoirs of the American Academy in Rome, Supplementary Volumes, Volume 7, Role Models in the Roman World: Identity and Assimilation* (2008): 287–299.

__________. "Reading Identity on Roman Strigilated Sarcophagi." *Res: Anthropology and Aesthetics* 61/62 (2012): 80–97.

Jensen, Robin Margaret. *Face to Face: Portraits of the Divine in Early Christianity*. Minneapolis, MN: Fortress Press, 2005 (especially pages 35–51).

Marsengill, Katherine. "Portraits and Icons in Late Antiquity." In *Transition to Christianity: Art of Late Antiquity, 3rd–7th Century AD*, edited by Anastasia Lazaridou, 61–66. New York, NY: Alexander S. Onassis Public Benefit Foundation; Athens: Byzantine & Christian Museum, 2011.

Spier, Jeffrey. *Late Antique and Early Christian Gems*. Wiesbaden: Reichert Verlag, 2007 (especially pages 18–25).

Studer-Karlen, Manuela. *Verstorbenendarstellungen auf frühchristlichen Sarkophagen*. Turnhout: Brepols, 2012. See also the review by Robert Couzin in *Klio* 98 (2016): 389–392.

21
THE MOSAICS OF RAVENNA

Deborah Mauskopf Deliyannis

The city of Ravenna in northeastern Italy contains some of the most spectacular works of art and architecture to have survived from Late Antiquity. These monuments were set up between 400 and 600 CE, at a time when Ravenna was one of the most important cities in the Mediterranean world. After 600 Ravenna experienced both economic and political downturns, but the artistic and architectural monuments remained as a testament to the splendor of the Christian Roman Empire in its early centuries, an inspiration both to later generations of the city's inhabitants and to visitors. Thus, Ravenna and its monuments are of critical importance to historians and art historians of the late antique world.

Ravenna's mosaics have always been fundamental to studies of early Christian art because Ravenna's surviving mosaics from the fifth and sixth centuries outnumber those of any other city, while Ravenna's political and cultural links with Constantinople and the East meant that her artists and architects were influenced by a very wide range of styles. Ravenna thus occupies an important place in every chronological narrative of medieval and/or Byzantine art, and Ravenna's monuments are cited in analyses of style, technique, iconography, viewer reception, color theory, and many other subjects of art historical interest.

By the ninth century, Ravenna and its suburbs (including the port city of Classe) had almost 60 church buildings, ranging from small chapels to large basilicas. Of the buildings that survive, eight contain some of their original mosaics. We know something about the decoration of the ones that are not extant from descriptions written by local historians, particularly the history of its bishops written by Agnellus in the early ninth century, and the history of Ravenna published by Girolamo Rossi in 1572. In addition, in some cases mosaic tesserae have been found in archaeological excavations of destroyed churches. Altogether, it is clear that most churches built in Ravenna from the early fourth to the late seventh centuries were decorated with mosaics, which implies an aesthetic that demanded this kind of decoration, and a persistence of mosaic workshops in the city throughout the period.

The surviving mosaic programs are briefly described in Table 21.1. The buildings include three basilicas and five centrally planned structures. Only two retain their full mosaic programs; all the rest underwent loss and/or modification at some point in their history. The remains include two apses, one set of nave wall mosaics, four domes or groin-vaults, and three triumphal arches.

Table 21.1 The mosaics of Ravenna.

Building	*Date*	*Location of mosaics*	*Iconography*
"Mausoleum of Galla Placidia"[1]	430s–440s	Cross-shaped chapel: barrel vaults, upper wall surfaces, central groin vault, lunettes	Christ the Good Shepherd, St Lawrence (?), eight apostles, stars and cross on the sky, vine-scrolls, urns and birds, four evangelist symbols
Orthodox Baptistery[2]	450s–460s	Octagonal baptistery: dome, lower zone of walls	Baptism of Christ with John the Baptist and the River Jordan, twelve apostles (labeled), books on thrones, architectural niches, inscriptions, male figures holding books/scrolls
Sant'Apollinare Nuovo[3]	*c.* 500 and 560s	Basilica: nave walls above arcade, to roofline	Early phase: Bearded Christ enthroned with angels, Virgin Mary enthroned with angels, "palatium" of Ravenna, port and city of Classe, male figures holding books and scrolls, 28 scenes from the miracles and passion of Christ (beardless and bearded). Later phase: male and female saints (labeled) in procession offering crowns, redecoration of palatium and Classe
Arian Baptistery[4]	*c.* 500	Octagonal baptistery: dome	Baptism of beardless Christ with John the Baptist and the River Jordan, twelve apostles, cross on throne
Capella arcivescovile[5]	*c.* 500	Narthex and cross-shaped chapel: narthex: barrel vault and tympanum; chapel: central groin vault, arches/barrel vaults	Narthex: Beardless Christ holding book and trampling lion and serpent, inscription. Chapel: medallions with apostles (labeled), male and female saints (labeled), chi-rho, angels, four evangelist symbols
San Michele in Africisco[6]	*c.* 545 (19th-century reconstruction)	Basilica: apse semi-dome, triumphal arch	Beardless Christ enthroned flanked by archangels, holding book and cross; Saints Cosmas and Damian; bearded Christ enthroned holding book, flanked by archangels, seven angels blowing trumpets
San Vitale[7]	*c.* 540s	Octagon with ambulatory: presbytery upper walls, lunettes, and groin vault; apse upper walls, semi-dome, and triumphal arch	Beardless seated Christ holding scroll, angels, St Vitalis and Bishop Ecclesius, Justinian and Theodora and their courts, medallions with twelve apostles (labeled), bearded Christ, Sts Gervase and Protase, Abel and Melchisedek, life of Abraham, life of Moses, four evangelist portraits, Isaiah and Jeremiah, Jerusalem and Bethlehem, vine scrolls, urns and birds, Lamb of God, angels.
Sant'Apollinare in Classe[8]	*c.* 540s, 670s	Basilica: apse walls, semi-dome, and triumphal arch	Early phase: Transfiguration, St Apollinaris with sheep/flock, landscape, four bishops of Ravenna (labeled), archangels Michael and Gabriel. Later phase: emperors give privileges to bishop, Abraham/Abel/Melchisedek, bearded Christ in medallion, four evangelist symbols, sheep, Jerusalem and Bethlehem.

Ravenna's mosaics span a century and a half. Only Rome has a similar sequence of surviving mosaics, and it is at Ravenna that we can best trace developments in mosaic art by seeing the ways in which patrons and mosaic artists adopted and adapted both techniques and iconographic motifs in response to each other. Moreover, we know a considerable amount about political, ethnic, and religious changes in Ravenna during this period, which has led scholars to identify stylistic changes with political, cultural, or theological programs. Some of these ideas are speculative; even at Ravenna the surviving mosaics are not sufficient in number to allow for overly broad generalizations about style or iconography. However, taken together, we can trace patterns of taste, artistic practice, and belief across two centuries of dramatic change.

Style and workshop practice

Mosaic workshops existed in Ravenna from the second century BCE, as attested by floor mosaics found in Ravenna's Roman houses. The oldest surviving wall mosaics date to the early fifth century, which is when the western Roman emperors moved their residence to Ravenna. The sudden change in the city's political status led to the construction of large churches sponsored by emperors, prominent laymen, and the city's bishops, and these were decorated in the most up-to-date styles with wall mosaics. These mosaics were made of glass and stone tesserae, using techniques and styles whose influence can be traced throughout the Mediterranean. Ravenna's mosaic workshops were very long-lived, producing both floor and wall mosaics as late as the twelfth century. Each of the buildings in which wall mosaics survive show evidence of replacement and repair, and, as we will see, the mosaic artists were very aware of the existing tradition and imitated or modified it.

Most of Ravenna's mosaics have been subject to detailed scientific analysis over the past seventy years. Examination of the chemical composition of tesserae can help to explain the origins of materials: while some of the earlier glass tesserae were made in southern Italy, most of the glass was probably imported from the eastern Mediterranean.[9] Furthermore, close examination of the materials in the mosaics shows that, starting in the early sixth century, glass tesserae were supplemented with tesserae of marble and limestone, perhaps because the supply of opaque glass had been interrupted; moreover, there was a shift in the makeup of gold tesserae between the early and middle sixth centuries.[10] Likewise, studies of the composition of the mortar beds into which the tesserae were set have allowed a precise recognition of repairs and replacements. For example, at Sant'Apollinare Nuovo, we can visually see, in the mosaic of the *palatium*, that some parts of the original mosaic had been erased (most notably by the presence of hands in front of the columns, indicating that human figures had once stood in the intercolumniations where now we see curtains) (Figure 21.1).[11] Detailed study of the mortar beneath all the mosaics show that in addition to these figures, the complete processions of saints on both sides of the church were additions made at the same time as the modifications to the *palatium*.[12] Similarly at San Vitale, we now know that in the mosaic of Justinian's procession, the original head of the bishop was replaced and an additional head and the name Maximian were inserted at a second phase of work.[13] We cannot know in either case what was originally there, but that has not stopped scholars from speculating on whether the changes were religiously or politically motivated.

In some cases, examination of the mortar has revealed interesting things about the design of the mosaic program. At Sant'Apollinare in Classe, restorations of the mosaics in 1948–1949 and 1970–1972 revealed the *sinopie*, or underdrawings that represent the original design of these mosaics, painted directly on the bricks (today on display at the Museo Nazionale in Ravenna).[14] Presumably this is how most mosaic programs were originally sketched out. Interestingly, these drawings differ from the mosaics that now exist; the original design of birds and fountains was

Figure 21.1 Mosaic of Palatium with hands. Sant'Apollinare Nuovo, Ravenna. Photo: Arthur Urbano.

changed to a procession of twelve sheep with Ravenna's founding bishop, St Apollinaris, at the center. Obviously the plan was changed, perhaps by Bishop Victor or Maximian, both of whom recognized the potential for visually enhancing the episcopal ideology of this church.[15]

It has been shown that in many of the surviving buildings, different groups of craftsmen executed the mosaic work, or the same craftsmen used different techniques, even though they did not necessarily alter the program. For example, in the Arian Baptistery, the color of the haloes and the shade of green used for the groundline differs between Sts Peter, Paul, and the apostle behind Paul and the rest, and there is a preference for marble tesserae and checkerboard shading in the central medallion and St Peter, while glass was primarily used for the other apostles (Figure 21.2). Thus, it seems that different craftsmen did the work in two or three different phases.[16] Similar conclusions are reached for individual craftsmen or workshops in the "mausoleum of Galla Placidia," Sant'Apollinare Nuovo, and San Vitale, based on the types of tesserae used and the style of the imagery.[17] Some have tried to argue that these differences are related to the origin of the artists (from Italy or from the East),[18] or that stylistic differences represent different modes of representation for the Old and New Testament subjects,[19] but they may also have to do with the availability of supplies, or with interruptions (perhaps of significant amounts of time) during the creation of the program.[20]

Indeed, there must have been many mosaic workshops operating in Ravenna at any one time between the fifth and the seventh century, given how many churches (far more than the ones that survive) were being decorated simultaneously. With outbreaks of war and plague, it is likely that from time to time work ceased, craftsmen died, or supplies were limited; and new workers and new materials must have been continually arriving at the city. With each new

Figure 21.2 Dome mosaic. Arian Baptistery, Ravenna. Photo: © Scott McDonough.

composition, the artists—designers and craftsmen—were familiar with the existing works, and could use motifs, techniques, and aesthetic effects borrowed from those earlier works. The result is a fascinating interplay between Ravenna's mosaic monuments.

Iconography

All of Ravenna's surviving wall mosaics are found in Christian religious buildings, although we have hints that there were also secular mosaics in the palace of Ravenna's rulers. We know enough about political and religious history in this period to be able to understand the meaning of certain motifs, but some interpretations must necessarily remain speculative. Notably, many of the same motifs, symbols, and themes appear in stone and plaster sculpture designed for the same spaces as the mosaic.

By far the most commonly depicted figure is Christ, who appears in all of the buildings. However, Christ is not depicted in the same way each time. There are two different ways to depict Christ as a man, and often they are both found in the same building, implying that each depiction served a different theological or spiritual meaning.[21] Sometimes, Christ is depicted as a beardless young man: in the "mausoleum of Galla Placidia," Sant'Apollinare Nuovo, the Arian Baptistery, the Cappella Arcivescovile, San Michele in Africisco, and San Vitale. At other times, Christ is a mature man with long dark hair and a beard: in Sant'Apollinare Nuovo, San Michele in Africisco, San Vitale, and Sant'Apollinare in Classe.[22] Because both versions are found in both fifth- and sixth-century mosaics in Ravenna, it does not seem as though the distinction was chronological. Indeed, in Sant'Apollinare Nuovo, the north side of the nave contains 14 narrative scenes illustrating Christ's miracles with a beardless youth, whereas the south side has 14 scenes of the Passion and Resurrection with a bearded Christ (Figure 21.3). Moreover, beneath

(a)

(b)

Figure 21.3 Mosaics of (a) Christ calling disciples, and (b) Christ being led to the cross. Sant'Apollinare Nuovo, Ravenna. Photos: Robin Jensen.

these scenes, the north wall features a depiction of the Virgin with infant Christ, while the south wall has a bearded, enthroned Christ in imperial robes. Thus, here, at least, the two versions serve to illustrate different facets of Christ's story.

In addition to their physiognomy, Christ's pose differs from church to church; indeed, none of the surviving examples is the same as any other. The closest are in the two baptisteries, where Christ is shown naked in the River Jordan, being baptized (Figure 21.2). In the "mausoleum of Galla Placidia," he is the Good Shepherd, dressed in imperial robes but seated in a landscape amid a flock of sheep (Figure 21.4). In the Cappella Arcivescovile, Christ is a young man dressed as standing warrior-emperor (the lower part of the image is almost entirely restored). In San Vitale, the apse contains Christ seated on a globe, holding a scroll with seven seals in one hand, and offering a crown (of martyrdom) to St Vitalis with the other (Figure 21.5). At the summit of the arch leading into the presbytery, however, a bust of a bearded Christ (mostly restored) appears in a medallion. In San Michele in Africisco, a beardless Christ in the apse stands, holding a processional cross in one hand and a book in the other, whereas on the triumphal arch just above, a bearded Christ sits on a throne holding a closed book (again mostly restored) (Figure 21.6). Finally, in Sant'Apollinare in Classe, the apse contains a version of the Transfiguration, but where we would expect a depiction of Christ, there is only a jeweled cross with a tiny medallion with a bust of bearded Christ in the center. On the triumphal arch of this church is a bearded Christ in a medallion, made in the seventh century or later (Figure 21.7).

Saints are frequently depicted in Ravenna's churches. Often they are labeled by name, although occasionally they are not. The twelve Apostles are depicted the most frequently, in the Orthodox Baptistery, the Cappella Arcivescovile, the Arian Baptistery, and San Vitale (Figure 21.8).[23] In all cases but the Arian Baptistery, they are labeled by name, but, interestingly, the lists differ slightly from one to the other: the Orthodox Baptistry includes Judah Zelotes, and the Cappella Arcivescovile and San Vitale instead have Thaddaeus. In all of the examples Sts Peter and Paul have face-types corresponding to the portrait types for these apostles already established by the fifth century—Peter with white hair and a beard, Paul balding with a brown beard—and in most cases St Andrew is beardless with wild gray hair, but the rest of the apostles have no consistent type. Indeed, both in the groups of apostles and the group of male martyrs in Sant'Apollinare Nuovo, there seems to be a deliberate attempt to render their appearance as different from one to the next.

Figure 21.4 Christ as the Good Shepherd. "Mausoleum of Galla Placidia," Ravenna. Photo: © Petar Milošević.

Figure 21.5 Apse mosaic with Justinian mosaic. San Vitale, Ravenna. Photo: © Scott McDonough.

Figure 21.6 Mosaics of the apse and triumphal arch. San Michele in Africisco, Ravenna. Photo: Juergen Liepe, Art Resource.

Figure 21.7 Apse and triumphal arch. Sant'Apollinare in Classe. Photo: Deborah Mauskopf Deliyannis.

Figure 21.8 View of apostles and the central vault. Capella arcivescovile, Ravenna. Photo: © Urs Peschlow.

Other saints also appear on Ravenna's walls. In churches dedicated to particular saints, the saint is depicted in the apse or other prominent place—probably St Lawrence in the "mausoleum of Galla Placidia,"[24] St Vitalis in San Vitale, and St Apollinaris in Sant'Apollinare Nuovo.

Sts Cosmas and Damian, doctor-saints, were placed on the walls of San Michele in Africisco, probably because it was a church dedicated in the wake of the plague.[25] But other groups of saints were also placed on the walls of churches, and we do not know the reason for the choices of these saints. In particular, the Cappella Arcivescovile has medallions with the busts of twelve named saints, six male and six female, and in Sant'Apollinare Nuovo, the walls were redecorated in the 560s with striking processions of saints, all labeled, 26 men on the south side and 22 women on the north. During a church service men stood on the south side of a church, and women on the north, thus the congregation mimicked the saints of the mosaic. The men's procession was headed by St Martin, to whom the church was rededicated; the women's procession was headed by the three Magi (Figure 21.9). All the richly dressed saints hold crowns, which they either offer to the enthroned Christ and the Virgin, or have just received from them. All the men and the women are dressed almost identically, with minor variations of details, and the women have the same hairstyle (albeit with different color hair). Scholars have speculated that both men and women were saints whose relics were found in the church, or whose names were mentioned in the litany read during the mass, but, in the absence of the relevant texts, this is only speculation.[26]

Other figures also appear in Ravenna's mosaic programs. Several include images of tunic-clad men holding scrolls or codices, but not identified by name: the "mausoleum of Galla Placidia," the Orthodox Baptistery, and Sant'Apollinare Nuovo. They are usually assumed to represent prophets, evangelists, and/or patriarchs, or simply as biblical authors in a generic sort of way, reinforcing the primacy of the written Word of God. Angels appear prominently in the five buildings decorated after the year 500—the Cappella Arcivescovile, Sant'Apollinare Nuovo, San Vitale, San Michele in Africisco, and Sant'Apollinare in Classe—flanking an enthroned Christ or flying in the vault. Emperors and empresses were depicted in San Giovanni Evangelista (now lost), and memorably appear in the apse of San Vitale (Figure 21.5). And finally, Ravenna's bishops were depicted in the churches that they founded or dedicated, often identified by name. In San Vitale, Bishop Ecclesius appears in the apse presenting a model of his church to Christ, one of the earliest such depictions of this motif,[27] while Archbishop Maximian stands next to the emperor Justinian (Figure 21.5). In Sant'Apollinare in Classe, the burial place of Ravenna's founding bishop Apollinaris, four of Ravenna's most notable bishops appear between the windows of the apse. We also have descriptions of now-lost churches—San Giovanni Evangelista, Sant'Agata, and St Stephen—stating that the founding bishop appeared in the apse, often described as "as though performing the mass."[28] All of these images reflect the intersection of the earthly world with the divine, immortalized forever in glass.[29]

Figure 21.9 Female saints and three magi. Sant'Apollinare Nuovo, Ravenna. Photo: Robin Jensen.

Finally, other Christian symbols and images are found in several of Ravenna's churches. The four beasts from Revelation 4:7—the lion, the ox, the man, and the eagle—were interpreted in early Christian exegesis as symbolizing the four Gospels, and they are shown in the "mausoleum of Galla Placidia," in the Cappella Arcivescovile, San Vitale (together with the four evangelists depicted as men holding books) and in Sant'Apollinare in Classe (in its 7th-century mosaics) (Figures 21.7–8). Scenes from the life of Christ decorate the nave walls of Sant'Apollinare Nuovo; scenes from the lives of Abraham and Moses are found in San Vitale.

Originality and imitation

The rich collection of images just described presents a coherent, evolving system of Christian representation and symbolism, but at the same time displays innovation in the way that these images and symbols were combined in each building. We have to assume that the many lost mosaics of Ravenna might have had similar iconography to those that survive, but it is quite striking that originality of depiction seems to have been prized.

We can see that in some cases mosaic designers were looking at earlier examples for ways to do things. For example, in three depictions, Christ holds a book with words written on the pages, and the words must have been chosen to convey particular messages. In the lost apse mosaic from San Giovanni Evangelista, there was a large image of an enthroned Christ holding a book that contained, "Blessed are the merciful, for God will show mercy to them" (Matt. 5:7). In the Cappella Arcivescovile's narthex, the book says, "I am the way, the truth, the life" (John 14:6). In San Michele in Africisco (restored), the book bears the inscription, "Whoever has seen me has seen the Father: I and the Father are one" (a conflation of John 14:9 and 10:30).

The later we go in time, the more derivative, in some ways, the mosaic programs appear. For example, many aspects of the mosaics from San Michele in Africisco are similar to other examples from Ravenna. A triumphal Christ holding a book and processional cross also appears in the narthex of the Cappella Arcivescovile. The angels flanking Christ are similar to those found in Sant'Apollinare Nuovo from the Ostrogothic period, and also to those in the apse of San Vitale. The archangels Gabriel and Michael are also found in Sant'Apollinare in Classe. The presence of a beardless Christ, a lamb, and a bearded Christ likewise reflects imagery in San Vitale. The landscape in the apse, representing paradise, is very similar to that of the apses of San Vitale and Sant'Apollinare in Classe. Sts Cosmas and Damian, whose cult was introduced into Italy in the early sixth century, are also found in the mosaics of the Cappella Arcivescovile. Most of these models are contemporary with San Michele, or nearly so, and imply a visual repertoire that could be used to create a desired effect.

Even more striking are the seventh-century (and later) mosaics from Sant'Apollinare in Classe.[30] We do not know what happened to the mosaics of the triumphal arch and the outer apse walls in Sant'Apollinare, whether they were damaged or deliberately replaced, nor, of course, do we know what was originally there. However, what we see today directly imitates, and even conflates, the program of mosaics in earlier churches, especially San Vitale. On Sant'Apollinare's triumphal arch, in the top zone, a bearded Christ, in a medallion, is flanked by the four beasts of the apocalypse, holding books (Cappella Arcivescovile), amid red and blue clouds (San Michele and San Vitale). Beneath them, six sheep on each side process out of the cities of Bethlehem and Jerusalem, with palm trees beneath (San Vitale). In the apse at the window level, the leftmost panel depicts two archbishops and three emperors, the latter giving a scroll labeled "privileges" to one of the archbishops, flanked by soldiers and clergy. The scene is laid out very similarly to the Justinian panel in San Vitale (Figure 21.10), although the act taking place is quite different. Facing this scene we see (very heavily restored) Abel, Melchisedek, and

Figure 21.10 Abel and Melchisedek at the altar, Moses and Isaiah above, side wall of presbytery. San Vitale, Ravenna. Photo: © Scott McDonough.

Abraham presenting their offerings at an altar, which is a conflation of the lunette mosaics from San Vitale. Possibly scenes like this were part of Sant'Apollinare's original decoration, which was contemporary with the mosaics in San Vitale, but it is also likely that later mosaicists were looking back to notable monuments from Ravenna's past for inspiration.

In addition to looking at Ravenna's mosaics for inspiration, there has been much speculation about external influences, usually identified as non-local origins for the artists who created the mosaics and their programs. Stylistic affinities with mosaics in Milan ("mausoleum of Galla Placidia," Orthodox Baptistery) and Rome (San Vitale) have been noted.[31] Iconographical motifs are also known from elsewhere; for example, the Transfiguration appears in other contemporary apse mosaics, such as the one at the monastery of St Catherine at Sinai in Egypt (where it is represented very differently from the one at Classe). Busts of saints and apostles in medallions are found at Sinai, and also at the church of Panagia Kanakaria in Lythrankomi, Cyprus (sixth century). A bishop offering a model of the church to Christ and a parade of sheep are found at Sts Cosmas and Damian in Rome (*c.* 520s) (see Figure 6.4).

Especially in the sixth century, however, it seems that Ravenna itself was exporting mosaic craftsmen; there are so many similarities between Ravenna's mosaics and the ones set up across the Adriatic Sea at Poreč that we assume that the latter had imported workers (and also marble decorative elements) from Ravenna (see Figure 6.6). The similarities include a bishop offering a model of a church, angels presenting the saints, saints in medallions, Christ seated on a blue globe, red and blue clouds, and more.[32] Costume and landscape details are also extremely similar. And yet, as usual, they are arranged differently from the Ravennate examples, thus preserving the uniqueness of Poreč's east end while linking it with common themes.

Arianism and Ravenna's mosaics

The proposition that Christ was a creation of God the Father, and hence a subordinate being, is attributed to Arius, a priest of Alexandria (d. 336). While many church leaders accepted

Arius's formulation, others vehemently opposed it, and Arianism was condemned at the ecumenical Council of Nicaea in 325. However, many important people, including emperors and church patriarchs, continued to profess Arian Christianity, and one result was that several of the "barbarian" tribes who took over the western Roman empire in the fifth century were led by Arian kings. This included the Ostrogoths, who conquered Italy in 489–492, led by their king, Theoderic (r. 489–526). As the capital of Theoderic's kingdom, Ravenna became a center of Arian Christianity in the sixth century, and Ravenna contains the only two Arian churches with surviving decoration, namely Sant'Apollinare Nuovo and the Arian Baptistery. Moreover, Theoderic famously had a policy of tolerance toward all branches of Christianity (and also Judaism!), and the orthodox bishops of Ravenna were allowed to keep their cathedral and to build new churches. One of these is the Cappella Arcivescovile, and San Vitale and Sant'Apollinare in Classe were founded under Ostrogothic rule, although probably decorated after the Byzantine empire had reconquered Ravenna.

Because we know that Arian Christians professed some beliefs that were anathema to the orthodox, and that debates about the nature of Christ were going on, albeit at a low level, in Theoderic's kingdom, many scholars have attempted to read Ravenna's Arian and orthodox mosaics from this period for evidence of belief and even propaganda against the other side.[33] Such evidence is particularly important because almost no texts written by Arians survive, so, in some ways, Ravenna's Arian mosaics are our only source for what Ostrogothic Arians were thinking. At the same time, the very fact that the surviving mosaics were allowed to remain in place indicates that they could be read as depicting perfectly orthodox Christian belief.[34]

On the Arian side, the mosaics in question are those in the Arian Baptistery and in Sant'Apollinare Nuovo. The baptistery's dome mosaics are clearly a copy of those in the Orthodox Baptistery, but with several twists.[35] For example, unlike in the Orthodox Baptistery, in the Arian, John the Baptist is on the right side of the mosaic, and the personification of the River Jordan is the same size as Christ and John (Figure 21.2; compare Figure 6.10). In the Arian Baptistery the apostles are not labeled by name. And, whereas in the Orthodox Baptistery the apostles' procession meets beneath the feet of Christ, to whom they offer their crowns, in the Arian Baptistery the medallion with the baptism has the opposite orientation to the procession, so that the apostles offer their crowns to an empty throne at the opposite side from the feet of Christ. Do these differences reflect theology? It has been suggested that the Arians did not want the apostles to offer their crowns to Jesus at the moment when he was being pronounced the Son of God, and thus the different orientation becomes an anti-Trinitarian statement.[36] There is no particular evidence for this, however, and whether any of the differences has theological meaning, as opposed to reflecting the skill of the artists or the desire to copy while making something fresh and different as an aesthetic choice, is unknown.

Likewise, in Sant'Apollinare Nuovo, some scholars have read elements of Arian theology or liturgy into the choice of scenes from the life of Christ, and the way that they are depicted.[37] For example, the beardless Christ in the miracles and the bearded Christ of the Passion scenes may indicate the transformation of Christ from miracle-working Son of Man to a glorified Son of God, possibly an Arian theological belief.[38] There is also the question of what was originally in the mosaics that were replaced with the processions of male and female martyrs. The very fact that some parts of the mosaic had to be replaced indicates that there was something objectionable about the content; while some propose that it was Theoderic's court, it is equally possible that it was a series of Arian saints.[39] One problem with these interpretations is that we do not really know enough to be able to reconstruct sixth-century Arian theology or liturgy.[40] Moreover, all of the scenes of the Life of Christ come from the Gospels, which were accepted by all theological factions; and as such, all were subject to interpretation by every faction.

When it comes to anti-Arian imagery in orthodox churches, we are on slightly firmer ground. In the first place, the mosaics in Sant'Apollinare Nuovo that were inserted in the 560s, at the time the church was converted from Arian to orthodox worship, have good reason to express orthodox ideas, and so do the images in other churches erected during or after the Byzantine reconquest of Ravenna, namely the Cappella Arcivescovile, San Vitale, and San Michele in Africisco. So, for example, the Three Magi are depicted in both Sant'Apollinare Nuovo and San Vitale, and can represent the concept of the Trinity. Indeed, in Sant'Apollinare Nuovo the Magi are prominently placed at the head of the procession of virgins, followed by St Euphemia of Chalcedon, a symbol of anti-Arian orthodoxy as expressed at the Council of Chalcedon. St Euphemia is also one of six women saints depicted in the Cappella Arcivescovile, and the quote "I am the way, the truth, the life," one of the key biblical passages used by Orthodox theologians against Arianism, was depicted on the book held by Christ in the narthex of that chapel.[41] Likewise, the inscription on the book in San Michele conflates two passages from John that were used by Orthodox theologians to argue for the consubstantiality of the Son and the Father.[42] Many elements of the decoration of San Vitale seem to reflect an anti-Arian agenda, including the fact that the mosaics in the presbytery can all be connected to the Epistle to the Hebrews, a text that was rejected by some Arians because it says that the Son is "the expression of the substance" of the Father.[43] And, as with the other churches, some motifs in Sant'Apollinare in Classe's mosaics may represent a specifically anti-Arian theology, although here this theme seems more muted than in some of the other churches.

Aesthetics and meaning

Mosaics began to be used to decorate churches at the same time as large candelabra with oil lamps were invented, and a theological aesthetic developed in which light and brilliance were seen as metaphors for religious truth and meaning.[44] Ravenna's mosaics provide evidence of this, because in Ravenna, as elsewhere (see the chapter by Sean Leatherbury in this volume), poems were written to accompany the mosaics and to celebrate the donors, and many survive because they were recorded by Agnellus in the ninth century. For example, the inscription commemorating the redecoration of the Orthodox Baptistery (*c.* 450s) says, "Behold the glory of the renewed font shines more beautifully."[45] And more famous is the beginning of the inscription in the Cappella Arcivescovile:[46]

> Either light was born here, or captured here it reigns free; it is the law, from whence the current glory of heaven excels. The roofs, deprived [of light], have produced gleaming day, and the enclosed radiance gleams forth as if from secluded Olympus.

Given the brilliance of the gold mosaics in the chapel, this poem offers a remarkable insight into its meaning as intended by the patron, Bishop Peter.

The color scheme for Ravenna's mosaics changes from the fifth to the sixth century, in line with similar changes elsewhere in the Mediterranean. In the fifth-century mosaics, namely the Orthodox Baptistery and the "mausoleum of Galla Placidia," the predominant background color is dark blue, with brighter blue for highlights. In the sixth century, there is a dramatic change to gold backgrounds, seen in the Arian baptistery, Sant'Apollinare Nuovo, the Cappella Arcivescovile, and the later monuments. This shift in taste may correspond to improvements in the manufacture of gold tesserae, or to a desire for greater brilliance. Dark colors were still used, for example in the presbytery vault at San Vitale and probably in the apse of the Cappella Arcivescovile (although what is there now is a modern reconstruction). Indeed, the motif of stars against a blue sky, seen first at the "mausoleum of Galla Placidia," is repeated in smaller areas in San Vitale and Sant'Apollinare in Classe.

An interesting aspect of the spaces in which mosaics were set up in Ravenna is the difference in the amount of natural light that would have illuminated them. The "mausoleum of Galla Placidia" has only fourteen very small windows, which would have allowed in little light, so any effects on the interior must have come from candles or lamps; the night-time effect of the dark blue backgrounds was thus enhanced by the actual darkness. The Cappella Arcivescovile likewise has a window only on one side. However, most of the other structures have much larger windows. The surviving apses have three or five large windows beneath the semidome, the basilicas have large windows all along the upper part of their length, and the baptisteries also have large windows below the dome. Of course, baptism was a ritual performed at night so, again, the rich mosaics in those locations must have been designed to look good by lamplight also. It should be noted that in many of Ravenna's churches today the windows are filled with alabaster, but this is a nineteenth-century restoration; evidence indicates that originally they would have been glass.

The mosaic aesthetic also prioritizes richness of abstract decoration, which is in full view in all of Ravenna's mosaics. Indeed, although they usually gain less attention than the figural and symbolic representations, the borders and abstract decorative fields show perhaps the most virtuosity, creativity, and brilliant use of color, and, like the figural motifs, are repeated in building after building. Birds facing urns, scallop-shell cupolas, vine-scrolls populated by birds and animals, lush foliage, jeweled thrones, rocky landscapes with flowers, palm trees, and *trompe l'œil* architectural elements with jewel-inset columns, all testify to the skill and creativity of Ravenna's mosaic artists, and the desire to produce beauty in the service of God.

Notes

1 D.M. Deliyannis, *Ravenna in Late Antiquity* (Cambridge: Cambridge University Press, 2010), 74–84.
2 Ibid., 88–100.
3 Ibid., 146–74.
4 Ibid., 177–87.
5 Ibid., 188–96.
6 Ibid., 250–54.
7 Ibid., 223–50.
8 Ibid., 259–74.
9 L. Sotira, "Materiali e techniche dei mosaici parietali (V–XII secolo)," in *Il mosaico a Ravenna: ideologia e arte*, ed. C. Rizzardi (Bologna: Ante Quem, 2011), 199–212.
10 C. Fiori, "Mosaic Tesserae from the Basilica of San Severo and Glass Production in Classe, Ravenna, Italy," in *New Light on Old Glass: Recent Research on Byzantine Mosaics and Glass*, eds C. Entwistle and L. James (London: The British Museum 2013), 33–41; C. Tedeschi, "Mosaics and Materials: Mosaics from the 5th and 6th centuries in Ravenna and Porec," in *New Light on Old Glass: Recent Research on Byzantine Mosaics and Glass*, eds C. Entwistle and L. James (London: The British Museum 2013), 60–9.
11 A. Urbano, "Donation, Dedication, and Damnatio Memoriae: The Catholic Reconciliation of Ravenna and the Church of Sant'Apollinare Nuovo," *Journal of Early Christian Studies* 13.1 (2005): 71–110.
12 G. Bovini, "Una prova di carattere tecnico dell'appartenenza al ciclo iconografico teodoriciano della madonna in trono, figurata sui mosaici di S. Apollinare Nuovo e Ravenna," *Studi Romagnoli* 3 (1952): 17–29; *idem*, "Antichi rifacimenti nei mosaici di S. Apollinare Nuovo a Ravenna," *Corso di Cultura sull'Arte Ravennate e Bizantina* 13 (1966): 51–81.
13 Andreescu-Treadgold, I. and W. Treadgold, "Procopius and the Imperial Panels of S. Vitale," *Art Bulletin* 79 (1997): 716–17.
14 G. Bovini, "Les 'Sinopie' récemment découvertes sous les mosaïques de l'abside de Saint-Apollinaire-in-Classe, à Ravenne," *Académie des inscriptions et belles-lettres. Comptes-rendus des séances* 1 (1974): 97–110; *idem*, "Qualche nota sulle sinopie recentemente rinvenute sotto il mosaico absidale di S. Apollinare in Classe di Ravenna," *Atti dell'Accademia delle scienze dell'Istituto di Bologna – Classe di scienze morali* 62.2 (1974): 95–107.

15 L. Abramowski, "Die Mosaiken von S. Vitale und S. Apollinare in Classe und die Kirchenpolitik Kaiser Justinians," *Zeitschrift für Antikes Christentum* 5 (2001): 304–5.
16 C.O. Nördstrom, *Ravennastudien: ideengeschichtliche und ikonographische Untersuchungen über die Mosaiken von Ravenna* (Stockholm: Almqvist & Wiksell, 1953), 34; F.W. Deichmann, *Hauptstadt des spätantiken Abendlandes*, Vol. II.1, *Die Bauten bis zum Tode Theoderichs des Großen* (Wiesbaden: F. Steiner, 1974), 255; S. Cummins, *The Arian Baptistery of Ravenna* (PhD Dissertation, Indiana University, 1994), 145.
17 "Mausoleum": Deichmann, *Hauptstadt des spätantiken Abendlandes*, Vol. II.1, *Die Bauten bis zum Tode Theoderichs des Großen*, 89–90; San Vitale: Andreescu-Treadgold and Treadgold, "Procopius and the Imperial Panels of S. Vitale, 715–6, and S. Pasi, *Ravenna, San Vitale: il corteo di Giustiniano e Teodora e i mosaici del presbiterio e dell'abside* (Modena: Franco Cosimo Panini, 2005), 63–4; Sant'Apollinare Nuovo: Deichmann, *Hauptstadt des spätantiken Abendlandes*, Vol. II.1, *Die Bauten bis zum Tode Theoderichs des Großen*, 140 and 189, and P.G. Nordhagen, "The Penetration of Byzantine Mosaic Technique into Italy in the Sixth Century," in *III Colloquio internazionale sul mosaico antico, Ravenna, 6–10 settembre, 1980*, ed. R. Farioli Campanati (Ravenna: Edizioni del Girasole, 1983), 75–9.
18 E.g., Nordhagen, "The Penetration of Byzantine Mosaic Technique into Italy in the Sixth Century," 75–9 and Pasi, *Ravenna, San Vitale: il corteo di Giustiniano e Teodora e i mosaici del presbiterio e dell'abside*, 63–4; *contra* see R.M. Jensen, *Face to Face: Portraits of the Divine in Early Christianity* (Minneapolis, MN: Fortress Press, 2005), 161.
19 C. Rizzardi, "Paradigmi ideologici ed estetici nei mosaici ravennati di età giustinianea," *Felix Ravenna*, 135–136 (1988): 59–60; *idem*, "I mosaici parietali di Ravenna da Galla Placidia a Giustiniano," in *Venezia e Bisanzio. Aspetti della cultura artistica bizantina da Ravenna a venezia (V–XIV secolo)*, ed. C. Rizzardi (Venice: Istituto veneto di scienze, lettere ed arti, 2005), 231–73.
20 I. Andreescu-Treadgold, "The Mosaic Workshop at San Vitale," in *Mosaici a S. Vitale e altri restauri: il restauro in situ di mosaici parietali. Atti del Convegno nazionale sul restauro in situ di mosaici parietali, Ravenna 1–3 ottobre 1990*, ed. A.M. Iannucci (Ravenna: Longo, 1992), 31–41.
21 Jensen, *Face to Face: Portraits of the Divine in Early Christianity*, 131–72; T.F. Mathews, *The Clash of Gods: A Reinterpretation of Early Christian Art* (Princeton, NJ: Princeton University Press 1993).
22 Today also in the Orthodox Baptistery, but that head is a 19th-century reconstruction, and we do not know what was originally there; Deichmann, 1974, *Hauptstadt des spätantiken Abendlandes*, Vol. II.1, *Die Bauten bis zum Tode Theoderichs des Großen*, 38, and C. Rizzardi, "La decorazione musiva del battistero degli ortodossi e degli ariani a Ravenna: Alcune considerazioni," in *L'Edificio Battesimale in Italia, aspetti e problemi. Atti del'VII Congresso Nazionale di Archeologia Cristiana Genova, Sarzana, Albegna, Rinale Ligure, Vetimiglia, 21–28 Settembre 1998*, Vol. 2. (Bordighera: Istituto internazionale di studi liguri, 2001), 915–30, agree that originally the Christ in the baptism was beardless.
23 Eight apostles, not labelled but, based on their appearance, including Sts Peter and Paul, are found in the central tower of the "mausoleum of Galla Placidia."
24 G. Mackie, "New light on the so-called Saint Lawrence panel at the Mausoleum of Galla Placidia, Ravenna," *Gesta* 29 (1990): 54–60 proposes that it was St Vincent, and C. Rizzardi, *Il mosaico a Ravenna: ideologia e arte* (Bologna: Ante Quem, 2012), 52–4, dubiously suggests it is Christ himself; see Deliyannis, *Ravenna in Late Antiquity*, 78–9.
25 Deliyannis, *Ravenna in Late Antiquity*, 252–4.
26 O. Von Simson, *Sacred Fortress: Byzantine Art and Statecraft in Ravenna* (Princeton, NJ: Princeton University Press, 1948), 81–110; B. Brenk, "Mit was für Mitteln kann einem physisch Anonymen *Auctoritas* Verliehen werden?" in *East and West: Modes of Communication. Proceedings of the First Plenary Conference at Merida*, eds E. Chrysos and I Wood (Leiden: Brill, 1999), 143–72; Deliyannis, *Ravenna in Late Antiquity* , 170–1.
27 D.M. Deliyannis, "Ecclesius and San Vitale: the Episcopal Donor in Text and Image," in *Envisioning the Medieval Bishop*, eds E. Gatti and S. Danielson (Turnhout: Brepolis Publishing, 2014), 41–62.
28 Deliyannis, *Ravenna in Late Antiquity*, 66–7, 103, and 255.
29 J.-P. Caillet, "L'évêque et le saint en Italie: le témoignage de l'iconographie haut-médiévale et romane," *Les cahiers de Saint-Michel de Cuxa* 29 (1998): 29–44; *idem*, "Affirmation de l'autorité de l'évêque dans les sanctuaires paléochrétiens du Haut Adriatique: De l'inscription à l'image," *Deltion tes Christianikes Archaiologikes Hetaireias*, s. 4, 24 (2003): 24–7.
30 A.M. Iannucci, "I vescovi Ecclesius, Severus, Ursus, Ursicinus, le scene dei privilegi e dei sacrifici in S. Apollinare in Classe – Indagine sistematica," *Corso di Cultura sull'Arte Ravennate e Bizantina* 33 (1986): 176–80.
31 Rizzardi, *Il mosaico a Ravenna: ideologia e arte*, 177–98.

32 A. Terry and H. Maguire, *Dynamic Splendor: The Wall Mosaics in the Cathedral of Eufrasius at Porec* (University Park, PA: The Pennsylvania State University Press, 2007); Tedeschi, "Mosaics and Materials: Mosaics from the 5th and 6th centuries in Ravenna and Porec."
33 R. Sörries, *Die Bilder der Orthodoxen im Kampf gegen den Arianismus. eine Apologie der orthodoxen Christologie und Trinitätslehre gegenüber der arianischen Häresie, dargestellt an den ravennatischen Mosaiken und Bildern des 6. Jahrhunderts; zugleich ein Beitrag zum Verständnis des germanischen Homöertums* (Frankfurt: Peter Lang, 1983); Rizzardi, "Paradigmi ideologici ed estetici nei mosaici ravennati di età giustinianea"; A. Effenberger, *Das Mosaik aus der Kirche San Michele in Africisco zu Ravenna: ein Kunstwerk in der Frühchristlich-byzantinischen Sammlung* (Berlin: Staatliche Museen zu Berlin, 1989); Abramowski, "Die Mosaiken von S. Vitale und S. Apollinare in Classe und die Kirchenpolitik Kaiser Justinians"; Rizzardi, *Il mosaico a Ravenna: ideologia e arte*, 185–95.
34 Cummins, *The Arian Baptistery of Ravenna*, 142.
35 Deliyannis, *Ravenna in Late Antiquity*, 184. Note that the heads, dove, and hands of the Baptist in the Orthodox Baptistery are a modern reconstruction.
36 Sörries, *Die Bilder der Orthodoxen im Kampf gegen den Arianismus. eine Apologie der orthodoxen Christologie und Trinitätslehre gegenüber der arianischen Häresie, dargestellt an den ravennatischen Mosaiken und Bildern des 6. Jahrhunderts; zugleich ein Beitrag zum Verständnis des germanischen Homöertums*, 99–100; Rizzardi, *Il mosaico a Ravenna: ideologia e arte*, 85–6.
37 R Sorriës, *Die Bilder der Orthodoxen im Kampf gegen den Arianismus. eine Apologie der orthodoxen Christologie und Trinitätslehre gegenüber der arianischen Häresie, dargestellt an den ravennatischen Mosaiken und Bildern des 6. Jahrhunderts; zugleich ein Beitrag zum Verständnis des germanischen Homöertums*, 77–97; Rizzardi, *Il mosaico a Ravenna: ideologia e arte*, 102–3.
38 Jensen, *Face to Face: Portraits of the Divine in Early Christianity*, 162–70.
39 Von Simson, *Sacred Fortress: Byzantine Art and Statecraft in Ravenna*, 81; Deichmann, *Hauptstadt des spätantiken Abendlandes*, Vol. II.1, *Die Bauten bis zum Tode Theoderichs des Großen*, 144–5; Deliyannis, *Ravenna in Late Antiquity*, 171–2.
40 Jensen, *Face to Face: Portraits of the Divine In Early Christianity*, 164; Urbano, "Donation, Dedication, and Damnatio Memoriae: The Catholic Reconciliation of Ravenna and the Church of Sant'Apollinare Nuovo," 99–107.
41 Deichmann, *Hauptstadt des spätantiken Abendlandes*, Vol. II.1, *Die Bauten bis zum Tode Theoderichs des Großen*, 203.
42 Sorriës, *Die Bilder der Orthodoxen im Kampf gegen den Arianismus. eine Apologie der orthodoxen Christologie und Trinitätslehre gegenüber der arianischen Häresie, dargestellt an den ravennatischen Mosaiken und Bildern des 6. Jahrhunderts; zugleich ein Beitrag zum Verständnis des germanischen Homöertums*, 226–43; Effenberger, *Das Mosaik aus der Kirche San Michele in Africisco zu Ravenna: ein Kunstwerk in der Frühchristlich-byzantinischen Sammlung*, 43–8.
43 *Charaktēr tēs hypostaseōs autou / figura substantiae eius*; Deliyannis, *Ravenna in Late Antiquity*, 248–50.
44 Benjamin Graham, "Profile of a Plant: The Olive in Early Medieval Italy, 400–900 CE" (PhD diss., University of Michigan, 2014) 157–222; D. Janes, *God and Gold in Late Antiquity* (Cambridge: Cambridge University Press, 1998); M. Roberts, *The Jeweled Style: Poetry and Poetics in Late Antiquity* (Ithaca, NY: Cornell University Press, 2010).
45 Agnellus, *The Book of Pontiffs of the Church of Ravenna*, trans. D.M. Deliyannis (Washington, DC: The Catholic University of America Press, 2004), Ch. 28.
46 Ibid., Ch. 50.

Further reading

There are many recent studies of Ravenna and its mosaics; these include Deborah M. Deliyannis, *Ravenna in Late Antiquity* (Cambridge: Cambridge University Press, 2010); Clementina Rizzardi, *Il mosaico a Ravenna: ideologia e arte* (Bologna: Ante Quem, 2012); Carola Jäggi, *Ravenna: Kunst und Kultur einer spätantiken Residenzstadt* (Regensburg: Schnell & Steiner, 2013); Massimiliano David, *Eternal Ravenna: from the Etruscans to the Venetians*, trans. Christina Cawthra and Jo-Ann Titmarsh (Turnhout: Brepols, 2013); and Jutta Dresken-Weiland, *Die frühchristlichen Mosaiken von Ravenna: Bild und Bedeutung* (Regensburg: Schnell & Steiner, 2015).

22

EARLY CHRISTIAN ART AND ARCHAEOLOGY IN SIXTEENTH- AND SEVENTEENTH-CENTURY ROME

Janet Huskinson

Early Christian art and artifacts of the kinds discussed in earlier chapters had an influential "after-life" in following centuries: they were reused (often for new purposes and contexts), their styles and forms imitated, and their archaeology developed and deployed in various ways. In this general respect, they differed little from their counterparts in the secular art and architecture of ancient Rome, which were appropriated by later societies to serve as cultural or moral exemplars or for political authentication.[1] Some of these reuses implied a sense of continuity with the past, some a distancing from it, which allowed space for critical study and reflection.[2]

But the religious nature of early Christian art brought other values to these processes. Firstly, the later societies involved were themselves Christian, and might evaluate its monuments and artifacts rather differently from the classical antiquities, which they also appropriated. Sometimes they applied critical scholarly analysis.[3] But on many other occasions they treated them as devotional objects whose own histories were subsumed (if not re-created) by the particular cults that they served; thus, in medieval Marseilles, the Christian man portrayed in Figure 22.1 was apparently identified with the female St Eusebia, whose tomb his sarcophagus had become.[4] Secondly, although early Christian art and artifacts evoked a particular formative period in church history, their themes and subjects could be interpreted as representing timeless Christian truths and traditions: the Marseilles sarcophagus dates to the fourth century, while its biblical scenes represent God's eternal covenant with man (Figure 22.1).

Marble sarcophagi, such as this, will feature prominently in this chapter, which focuses on sixteenth- and seventeenth-century Rome. Sarcophagi carved with biblical or symbolic imagery were by far the largest type of early Christian sculptures in Rome, in antiquity and surviving into later centuries. Like their pagan counterparts they were widely reused, either as whole coffins or as dismembered panels,[5] and in Rome by this time they had long provided prestigious resting-places for popes and the remains of early saints (Figure 22.2).[6] In short, they provide prolific examples of both material and symbolic worth.

Figure 22.1 Fourth-century sarcophagus reused as tomb of St Eusebia. Marseilles, S Victor. Photo: DAIR 60.1588 (Böhringer).

Figure 22.2 Fourth-century Christian sarcophagus (with scene of Jonah) reused in the basilica of Sta Prassede, Rome, for relics. Photo: DAIR 59.425A (Böhringer).

As a meeting-place of classical and Christian culture, Rome is unsurpassed, both for its surviving monuments and for the diversity of their advocates and interpreters. Wealthy and sophisticated collectors, pilgrims, humanists, antiquarians, and local Christians all had stakes in its past and different ideological positions to negotiate. Its early Christian history had shaped the later development of the Catholic Church, doctrinally and also topographically, through sites in the city where Christian communities had worshipped or buried their martyrs. Over centuries pilgrims came to visit these holy places, and also to marvel at the city's ancient sights. Together these formed a landscape and culture that was exclusively "Roman."[7] How to relate imperial and early Christian Rome in a history that could take account of both and form a basis for the city's present and future was a matter that occupied many scholars (such as Flavio Biondo) in the mid-fifteenth century.[8]

By the sixteenth and seventeenth centuries the material remains of Rome's pagan and Christian past had acquired a new potency and significance. They were at the forefront of two great movements: the humanist re-discovery of classical antiquity in the Renaissance, and the Counter-Reformation when the Catholic Church made strategic use of historical material to confront Protestant challenges to its authority. At the same time, the city's own soil yielded a stream of new discoveries that could help meet these new demands.

Sarcophagi from St Peter's in the Vatican

One site that increased the availability of early Christian sarcophagi in Rome was St Peter's in the Vatican. The long running building works for the new basilica involved demolishing many early Christian burials in and around the old church and uncovered a large number of sarcophagi. It makes a good starting-point for this discussion, which will re-visit several of these sarcophagi later.

In the early seventeenth century some of these sarcophagi were used for the reburial of churchmen whose original tombs had been in the old basilica. Popes Gregory V[9] and Marcellus II[10] each received an early Christian sarcophagus decorated with a central—and papally appropriate—scene of Christ in majesty with Peter and Paul. Marcellus's sarcophagus was installed in the Vatican Grottoes in 1606, on a new marble base sculpted with classicizing garlands, and a dedication carved on its lid.[11]

Some idea of what happened next to many of the sarcophagi from the Vatican site comes from Antonio Bosio's *Roma Sotterranea*[12] where—in systematic detail typical of his scholarship—he records them individually, with illustrations and a note of their subsequent location. Some went to buildings associated with the Church,[13] or were re-used as tombs of leading clerics and popes (including the two mentioned above). But many others had secular destinations: one fragment graced a Roman street,[14] and another a private museum,[15] while others ended up in the houses and palazzi of cardinals and Roman nobility,[16] showing that their Christian subject matter did not restrict them to religious settings.

Early Christian reliefs in Roman collections

Exactly how these sarcophagi were deployed in palaces and houses would be interesting to know. Bosio mentions some used as fountains,[17] and others displayed on walls[18] or in courtyards.[19] There is scarcely any other evidence for the inclusion of early Christian sculptures in the great Roman collections from the mid-fifteenth century on,[20] but this lack is not surprising. Collectors preferred prestigious freestanding statuary for display, and any sarcophagi they acquired were usually reused as containers or as decorative reliefs set into walls. Early Christian sarcophagi had a further disadvantage in that their figural style was generally seen as aesthetically inferior.[21]

This focus on classical antiquity and finer works was also true for popes and cardinals who, from the early sixteenth century, were the main collectors. As Rome's temporal leaders, they also wished to assert control of its ancient art and monumental heritage "for moral edifying purposes, advertising the idea that their collecting was as pious and beneficial to Rome as was the safeguarding of relics or the restoration of churches."[22] Their collections were enriched by material found on land in ecclesiastical control, and by the acquisition of antiquities once located in Roman churches.[23] In 1467 pope Paul II had taken a step too far and was heavily criticized when he removed the sarcophagus of Sta Costanza from the basilica of Sta Agnese to the great collection of antiquities in his palace, allegedly intending it to be his future tomb.[24] (It would have been a special attraction as the sarcophagus of a saint, with imperial connections, and made of porphyry.)

In sum, early Christian material appears to have featured little in Roman sculpture collections of the sixteenth century, even those of leading churchmen. Yet there were some instances, and the following three cases illustrate different approaches to its display, across nearly two centuries.

The first is the later fifteenth-century collection assembled by the Millini family, which had a strong focus on inscriptions, especially from ancient Roman funerary monuments.[25] They housed it in various properties around Rome, but kept the Christian epitaphs separately in the small church of Santa Croce on Monte Mario, which they had restored in 1470. This was located near to their own villa and, more significantly in Christian terms, to the site of Constantine's decisive vision at Milvian Bridge.[26] Here then, the Christian material was given a separate devotional setting, although the collection as a whole belonged in the wider context of renaissance humanist learning and enthusiasm for antiquities.

The second case involves a late fourth-century "City Gate" sarcophagus that Bosio recorded as originally found near the Vatican (and then stored in a nearby garden).[27] But by the time it was reused in the decoration of the Villa Borghese in Rome during the early seventeenth century it had been dismantled to create four panels of decorative reliefs.

The Villa had been built for Cardinal Scipione Borghese (1576–1633) and his collection of antiquities, and between 1616 and 1624 its main exterior walls were decorated with arrangements of ancient figured reliefs, including the front and side panels of this sarcophagus.[28] These introduced—for the first time in such displays—Christian images alongside the usual conventional subjects that celebrated the culture and civilization of ancient Rome.[29] The front panel (Figure 22.3), showing Christ and the apostles, decorated the front façade of the Villa's southern belvedere. The two side panels (Figure 22.4), with various scenes of Old Testament leaders (Elijah, Moses, and Abraham), were juxtaposed in a corresponding position on the north.[30]

Also part of the sculptural displays at the front of the Villa was another sarcophagus bearing a "Good Shepherd" figure (identified in one near-contemporary guide-book as Christ).[31] As in the corresponding group on the other side, this sarcophagus was flanked by Roman statues of an emperor and a captive barbarian. The sarcophagus is now in Louvre.[32] The prominent settings of all these Christian images and their deliberate juxtaposition with traditional Roman representations of culture and power project messages about a new Rome built on a combination of its classical and Christian past.[33]

The back of the "Borghese sarcophagus" also contributed to the adornment of the Villa, but in a corner of the garden (Figure 22.5).[34] It was further dismantled to produce separate figured reliefs of a shepherd and two saints, which were then set into richly ornamented sections of

LIBRO II. CAP. VIII. 69

Molti anni ſono con l'occaſione della nuoua fabrica di S. Pietro ſi trouò queſto Pilo, il quale fù meſſo in vn'horto vicino à S. Marta: è alto cinque palmi; longo vndeci; e profondo ſei: & è ſcolpito di Figure da tutte trè le parti.

Facciata

Figure 22.3 The front panel of the "Borghese sarcophagus." Paris, Musée du Louvre. Photo: from A. Bosio (1632), 69. By kind permission of the Syndics of Cambridge University Library.

a precinct wall.[35] There seems less of an ideological charge than with the other panels, as the figures were less obviously religious (and the shepherd may have represented a rustic idyll). Immuring sarcophagus fragments to decorate walls in this way was a local tradition, and other early Christian examples occur at the Villa Albani[36] and Villa Doria Pamphili.[37]

The third case also involves immuring, as a means of display favored by the seventeenth-century collector Francesco Gualdi (1574–1657). Gualdi frequently donated items for display in various public places in Rome, usually with accompanying inscriptions.[38] Two such gifts involved the dismantled front panels of early Christian sarcophagi. He gave two to the basilica

LIBRO II. CAP. VIII. 73

SARCOPHAGI EIVSDEM PARTES LATERALES

Sponde del medeſimo Pilo longhe palmi ſei, e mezo; e profonde palmi cinque.

G Queſto

Figure 22.4 The side panels of the "Borghese sarcophagus." Paris, Musée du Louvre. Photo: from A. Bosio (1632), 73. By kind permission of the Syndics of Cambridge University Library.

of Santa Maria Maggiore where they were displayed together as a single piece.[39] The inscription stated that he had donated the sarcophagus, which had been "made by the piety of early Christians during the persecution of the Church," so that it should be more venerable in its setting.[40] The front of a third sarcophagus formed the central element in an elaborate arrangement installed in the portico of the Pantheon in 1646 (Figure 22.6).[41] This showed busts of a couple within a double register of biblical scenes. Along with the arms of Gualdi and of Cardinal Mazzarin (the sponsor), it was accompanied by another lengthy inscription identifying the sarcophagus's figured scenes as a testament from the early Church against the "*iconomachos*"—in other words, against Protestants who attacked images as having had no place in it.

Figure 22.5 The back panel of the "Borghese sarcophagus", Centrale Montemartini, Rome no. 829. Photo: from A. Bosio (1632), 71. By kind permission of the Syndics of Cambridge University Library.

Gualdi's installations deliberately re-configured the sarcophagi to display them as part of a visual argument, which was re-stated in the accompanying texts. This process also celebrated the religious images, as well as the antiquity of the sarcophagi themselves, and the piety of their early Christian patrons.

Figure 22.6 Engraving by Girolamo Petrignani of Francesco Gualdi's installation in the Pantheon, incorporating the front panel of an early Christian sarcophagus, and an explanatory inscription. By kind permission of the Bibliothèque nationale de France.

Impacts of the Counter Reformation

Gualdi's explicit use of sarcophagus reliefs for the purpose of contemporary religious debate shows just how far the Church's polemical use of early Christian antiquities had developed since the mid-sixteenth century. The main impetus had come from the church itself, as it faced pressure to reform from within and from Protestant challenges without. Art, artifacts, buildings, and archaeology all became strategically important in this Catholic Counter Reformation, which "With its emphasis on sacred spaces, devotional objects and holy bodies ... was driven by material culture."[42]

For centuries since Late Antiquity, classical and Christian monuments of Rome had been appreciated together as joint tokens of the city's great past. Witness the twelfth-century visitor's guide, the *Mirabilia Urbis Romae*, which presented highlights of each. This inclusive approach survived into sixteenth-century antiquarian scholarship: for instance, Andrea Fulvio's account of the city's antiquities[43] also contained a section on early Christian burial places,[44] while, as we have seen, the sculpture collections of wealthy churchmen reflected their interests in classical culture and learning.

From the mid-sixteenth century the Church's pressing needs gave a new direction to such interests. Some leading antiquarians were drawn into this: Onofrio Panvinio (1529–1568), for instance, was asked by the future pope Marcellus II to prepare a history of the Church and its monuments of which only a section on early Christian burial, including catacombs, *De ritu sepeliendi mortuous apud veteres christianos et eorundem coemeteriis liber*, was completed in 1568.[45] Ancient churches were restored in Rome, with up-to-date liturgical arrangements and programmatic artwork, and interest in the art and artifacts of Rome's earliest Christians burgeoned. For many early Christian sarcophagi this meant a new lease on life, reused as altars[46] or tombs, and valued for their significant imagery.

Scholars and Oratorians

This urgent exploration of early Christian art and monuments was less concerned "with the material culture of paleo-Christian Rome per se, but rather with the spiritual reality it symbolized and mediated."[47] Such a spiritual quest is evident in the life of St Philip Neri (1515–1595) and in the work of the Congregation of the Oratory that he founded. Although debate continues about the degree of the Oratorians' contribution to the later sixteenth-century development of "Christian archaeology" as a separate field for study,[48] there is little doubt that their desire to return to the roots of the Roman Church galvanized an interest already present in the work of contemporary antiquarians.

Neri himself identified closely with Rome's sacred sites, especially those linked with its early martyrs. As a young man in the 1530s he used to retreat to the catacomb of S Sebastiano for lengthy personal meditation,[49] and in 1559 instituted an annual pilgrimage around the "Seven Churches" of Rome.[50] At the Oratory, he was surrounded by a circle of clerics and scholars, many of whom were greatly interested in the art and buildings of early Christian Rome, and their relevance to the Church's contemporary needs.

Among them, Cardinal Cesare Baronio (1538–1607) is best known, particularly for his prolific writing that emphasized the continuity of the Roman Church, in doctrine, cult, and holy places. He had lectured on church history at the Oratory and was also in contact with non-clerical scholars such as Philips van Winghe and Antonio Bosio, whose work will be discussed shortly.[51] Baronio's great multi-volumed history, *Annales Ecclesiastici* (published between 1588 and 1607), gave a chronological account of the Church from its start to 1198. It was essentially a work of Catholic apologetic that showed the origins of the Church's position on such matters as images and the cult of saints, and so set ecclesiastical tradition against Protestant claims. He also published two editions of historical annotations to the *Martyrologium Romanum*, which similarly had a focus on the times, monuments, and places associated with Roman saints.[52]

Baronio frequently cited early Christian archaeological material to support his arguments[53] and also translated it into built form, in ancient churches in Rome that he renovated. This restoration work, at SS Nereo ed Achilleo (his titular church) and S Cesareo de Appio, included the creation of new liturgical spaces (based on early Christian prototypes, as Baronio interpreted them), the reuse of older materials from other Roman churches, and artwork that followed early Christian forms and iconography.[54] It was a tangible re-statement of Rome's earlier Christian history.

Baronio's work represents a considered use of archaeological sources in chronicling the early Church, but other writers were far more partisan or dramatic, especially in describing the catacombs and how Christians allegedly used them during the persecutions.[55] Some accounts of horrific deaths and sufferings were so graphic that they colored not only contemporary representations of martyrdom (in Jesuit art, for example), but also the interpretation of some actual biblical scenes in the catacombs as depicting martyrs' deaths.[56] From the standpoint of Protestants, who claimed that religious images were products of later Catholic idolatry, the discovery of these early catacomb paintings proved problematic.[57] For Catholics the paintings seem to have been less important than their location in the catacombs, which were sites of great symbolic value because of their associations with the early martyrs.[58]

Catacomb archaeology

In this context of heightened interest there was great excitement at the chance discovery by workmen on 31 May 1578 of what is now known as the "*catacomba anonimo*" of via Anapo in Rome.[59] But this was by no means the beginning of catacomb exploration. Even before Neri's devotional retreats, pilgrims had long visited martyrs' tombs in catacombs where they remained accessible; the catacomb of S Sebastiano, for instance, is mentioned in a guidebook of the second half of the fourteenth century.[60] But from the fifteenth century there is evidence of antiquarian interest in the catacombs. Not all were motivated by a pursuit of the Christian past: for instance, Pomponio Leto and members of his *Accademia Romana degli Antiquari*, who explored in the later fifteenth century, were primarily interested in classical antiquity. The sixteenth century saw a new wave of scholars particularly after the 1578 discovery: Alfonso Ciacconio, Jean L'Heureux,[61] and Philips Van Winghe[62] were among those who recorded the "new" catacomb and others, taking a secular (rather than apologetic) approach to describing and mapping what they found.[63]

This approach also characterized the most substantial and groundbreaking work on the catacombs by Antonio Bosio (1575–1629). He had extensive knowledge of them, gathered from years of personal exploration and occasional excavation.[64] His influential work, *Roma sotterranea*, was published posthumously in 1632, with the Oratorian Giovanni Severano responsible for the editing and for the last of the four books (on the iconography of catacomb images). Bosio himself had contact with Neri and the Oratorians and in his book he made many references to Baronio's work.[65]

One reference is particularly telling about how Bosio saw his own methodology and purpose. It concerns the "Borghese sarcophagus" which, as mentioned, ended up as separate panels decorating the Villa Borghese (Figures 22.3–5). It had been found in the mid-fifteenth century in the mausoleum near St Peter's, belonging to the distinguished Christian family of the Anicii: Sextus Claudius Petronius Probus (who had been consul in 371) was a famous senatorial convert to Christianity, and his wife Anicia Faltonia Proba was renowned for her practical piety.[66] This connection made the sarcophagus a highly valuable piece of evidence for the early Christian community in Rome, and it featured in various seventeenth-century publications.

Baronio included it in the *Annales* as a devotional example for contemporary viewers,[67] but with an inaccurate representation of some figures on its front panel.[68] Bosio picked up on this, and to show what he describes as his own accuracy, conscientious attention to detail, and faithful drawings, illustrated all four sides of the sarcophagus (Figures 22.3–5).[69]

Such careful recording is a characteristic feature of Bosio's great work, but even more significant (in terms of the development of scholarship) was his systematic approach to the design and topography of the catacombs. He published plans of catacombs,[70] copious frescoes,[71] epigraphy,[72] and objects found in the catacombs such as gold glass[73] and lamps.[74]

Severano's contribution (in Book 4) on images in the catacombs and their iconography has also been influential. He was more polemical than Bosio had been,[75] and in his desire to prove the continuity of Christian images and the veneration of saints,[76] prefaced his discussions with chapters demonstrating that the catacombs had been used exclusively by Christians. This was a strategic Counter Reformation argument. In the contemporary religious context, the discovery of Christian subjects painted in the catacombs was highly significant as it apparently disproved Protestant claims that religious imagery was a later Catholic aberration.[77]

Bosio's work was widely disseminated through Latin editions (1651 and 1659) prepared by Paolo Aringhi, with additions of his own. Yet Bosio's archaeological approach, with its systematic topographical analysis and careful descriptions, rather fell into abeyance. Instead, reference to early Christian material culture remained polemical: interest in catacombs focused on martyrs, and what could be retrieved of their bodily remains.[78] Given "a *de facto* acceptance that every bone found belonged to a martyr," the number of martyrs alleged to have died in Rome increased exponentially.[79]

Relics and archaeology

The hunt for martyrs' relics in the Roman catacombs was intense during the later sixteenth and seventeenth century, particularly in sites such as S Sebastiano that were fairly accessible.[80] They found a ready market across Catholic Europe as tokens of traditional piety for individuals, rulers, and churchmen. This trade generated intense activity in the catacombs, which largely operated within the framework of the Church despite a series of papal measures intended to address the situation.[81]

This was more like tomb robbing than archaeology. But the reception of corporeal relics into their new resting places, or the rediscovery and refurbishment of their old, could involve activity that was more deliberate and historically aware. This happened across the Catholic world as communities sought to authenticate the history of local cults by uncovering and celebrating the material remains of their early Christian past in "sacred archaeology."[82]

In Rome itself many churches were renovated in the late sixteenth century for the Jubilee Year of 1600. This, and the decree by Clement VIII in 1596 that church altars had to contain sacred relics for legitimacy, encouraged investigations and new, more appropriate arrangements for housing the remains. This might involve creating new liturgical spaces around the high altar, often in supposed imitation of early Christian architectural arrangements,[83] or providing new reliquaries (for which ancient sarcophagi were popular choice as at Sta Cecilia).[84]

What happened at two Roman basilicas illustrates this well. Baronio had redesigned and redecorated his titular church of SS Nereo ed Achilleo, incorporating early Christian stylistic references (as mentioned above), but the procession that he devised in 1597 for the saints' return there from their resting place in the church of S Adriano in the Forum also commandeered the archaeology of ancient Rome. Famous triumphal monuments along the route were equipped with inscriptions that, in various formulations, celebrated the greater triumphs of the

Christian martyrs.[85] Thus the Catholic Christian past and its material remains were shown to have triumphed even over the mighty Roman empire and its physical vestiges—"and implicitly over heresy."[86] Past, present, and future triumphs were drawn together.

The basilica of Sta Cecilia in Trastevere was already rich in the history and material survivals of earlier Roman Christianity. It was supposedly built over Cecilia's house, where she had been martyred along with various companions, and since the ninth century contained their relics (preserved in ancient sarcophagi), which pope Pascal I had brought back from the catacombs.[87] These relics were exhumed in 1599 by Cardinal Paolo Emilio Sfondrato (an Oratorian and close associate of Neri) in the course of restoring the basilica. Intent on stressing the history and traditions of the early Church, he investigated the relics buried below the high altar, planning to re-house them more appropriately. The miraculous discovery of the saint's remains—to which Bosio was an invited eye-witness[88]—was received with great excitement and, after a period on public display, the relics were re-interred below the newly redesigned high altar. There too, in the altar's sculpture, reference was made back to the materiality of early Roman Christianity: like an enduring "relic," Stefano Maderno's famous statue replicated Cecilia's body as in death, while the black marble "box" in which it was enclosed resembled a *loculus* (a shelf-like tomb) in the catacombs where it had originally rested.[89]

Conclusion

This brief overview has shown how and why the sixteenth and seventeenth centuries were particularly important in Rome for the use and study of early Christian material remains, in various cultural and religious contexts. Its legacy continues, most especially in the appreciation of their value in representing the long traditions of the Roman Church and its connections with the city. For instance, sarcophagi found in mid-twentieth century excavations in the Vatican were reused after their discovery for the burial of earlier popes.[90] Others have become altars: one decorated with Christian symbolic images (of the chi-rho symbol resting on an empty throne) was rescued from its secular reuse as a fountain in a villa to become the new high altar in the church of S Maria in Vivario at Frascati in April 1968.[91] These instances are interesting for the antiquarian record, but even more significant for their symbolic value: the ancient artifact gains a new life but also reasserts continuity with Christian tradition of the earliest local Christians.

Notes

1 There is a now large literature on this: e.g., recently Richard Brilliant and Dale Kinney, eds, *Reuse Value: Spolia and Appropriation in Art and Architecture from Constantine to Sherrie Levine* (Farnham and Burlington, VT: Ashgate, 2011). For early Christian appropriation of Roman material: e.g., Maria Fabricius Hansen, *The Eloquence of Appropriation: Prolegomena to an Understanding of Spolia in Early Christian Rome*, Analecta Romana Instituti Danici Supplementum 33 (Rome: L'Erma di Bretschneider, 2003); and Jaś Elsner, "The Christian Museum in the South of France: Antiquity, Display and Liturgy from the Counter-reformation to Aftermath," *Oxford Art Journal* 31 (2009): 183.

2 Salvatore Settis, "Continuità, distanza, conoscenza: Tre usi dell'antico," in *Memoria dell'antico nell'arte italiana, III Dalla tradizione all'archeologia*, ed. S. Settis (Turin: Giulio Einaudi, 1986), 375–486.

3 Irina Oryshkevich, "Cultural History in the Catacombs: Early Christian Art and Macarius' Hagioglypta," in *Sacred History: Uses of the Christian Past in the Renaissance World*, eds Katherine Elliott van Liere, Simon Ditchfield and Howard Louthan (Oxford: Oxford University Press, 2012), 250–66.

4 Romy Wyche, *An Archaeology of Memory: The "Reinvention" of Roman Sarcophagi in Provence during the Middle Ages* (DPhil thesis, University of Oxford, 2013), Chapter 3, n. 364; Brigitte Christern-Briesenick, *Repertorium der christlich-antiken Sarkophage, dritter Band: Frankreich, Algerien, Tunesien* (Mainz am Rhein: Verlag Philipp von Zabern, 2003), no. 305; see Elsner, "The Christian Museum in the South of France," for these different modes of historical discourse.

5 Salvatore Settis, "Collecting Ancient Sculpture: The Beginnings," in *Collecting Sculpture in Early Modern Europe*, eds Nicholas Penny and Eike Schmidt (New Haven, CT: Yale University Press, 2008), 13–31; Björn C. Ewald, "Sarcophagi," in *The Classical Tradition*, eds Anthony Grafton, Glenn W. Most and Salvatore Settis (Cambridge, MA: The Belknap Press of Harvard University Press, 2010), 859–62; Janet Huskinson, "*Habent sua fata*: Writing Life Histories of Roman Sarcophagi," in *Life, Death and Representation: Some New Work on Roman Sarcophagi*, eds Jaś Elsner and Janet Huskinson (Berlin: DeGruyter, 2010), 55–82.
6 Renzo U. Montini, *Le tombe dei Papi* (Rome: Angelo Belardetti, 1957); 197–9 and 217–19; Caroline Goodson, *The Rome of Pope Paschal I: Papal Power, Urban Renovation, Church Rebuilding and Relic Translation* (Cambridge: Cambridge University Press, 2010), 242 and 246; Friedrich Wilhelm Deichmann, Giuseppe Bovini and Hugo Brandenburg, *Repertorium der christlich-antiken Sarkophage, Bd 1 Rom und Ostia* (Wiesbaden: Franz Steiner, 1967), no. 756. In this chapter I use "pagan" as shorthand for "non-Christian," and define "early Christian sarcophagi" as only those decorated with biblical or symbolic Christian scenes.
7 Simon Ditchfield, "Reading Rome as a Sacred Landscape *c.* 1586–1635," in *Sacred Space in Early Modern Europe*, eds Will Coster and Andrew Spicer (Cambridge: Cambridge University Press, 2005), 167–92.
8 Leonard Barkan, *Unearthing the Past: Archaeology and Aesthetics in the Making of Renaissance Culture* (New Haven, CT: Yale University Press, 1999), 35.
9 Deichmann, *Repertorium* I, no. 676.
10 Deichmann, *Repertorium* I, no. 684.
11 Montini, *Le tombe dei Papi*, 325–7.
12 Antonio Bosio, *Roma* Sotterranea *Opera postuma di Antonio Bosio romano* (Rome: Appresso Guglielmo Facciotti, 1632), 44–109.
13 Bosio, *Roma* Sotterranea 85, 89, 95.
14 Bosio, *Roma* Sotterranea 83.
15 Bosio, *Roma* Sotterranea 97.
16 Bosio, *Roma* Sotterranea 65, 79, 81, 83, 93, 97, 99.
17 Bosio, *Roma* Sotterranea 93, 101, 103.
18 Bosio, *Roma* Sotterranea 91, his own house, 101.
19 Bosio, *Roma* Sotterranea 83, 93.
20 Kathleen Wren Christian, "*Instauratio* and *Pietas*: The Della Valle Collections of Ancient Sculpture," in *Collecting Sculpture in Early Modern Europe*, eds Nicholas Penny and Eike Schmidt (New Haven, CT: Yale University Press, 2008), 33–65; Kathleen Wren Christian, *Empire without End: Antiquities Collections in Renaissance Rome, c. 1350–1527* (New Haven, CT: Yale University Press, 2010).
21 Simon Ditchfield, *Liturgy, Sanctity, and History in Tridentine Italy: Pietro Maria Campi and the Preservation of the Particular* (Cambridge: Cambridge University Press, 1995), 89; cf. Christian, *Empire without End*, 167–78.
22 Christian, "*Instauratio* and *Pietas*," 34.
23 Christian, *Empire without End*, 211–12.
24 Deichmann, *Repertorium* I, no.174; Christian, *Empire without End*, 97–9.
25 Sandro Santolini, "Pietro e Mario Millini fondatori di una dinastia di collezionisti antiquari," in *Collezioni di antichità a Roma tra '400 e '500*, ed. Anna Cavallaro (Rome: De Luca, 2007), 42–7; Christian, *Empire without End*, 345–6.
26 Santolini, "Pietro e Mario Millini," 42–7.
27 Bosio, *Roma* Sotterranea 45–7, 6–73.
28 Kristina Herrmann Fiore, "The Exhibition of Sculpture on the Villa Borghese Facades in the Time of Cardinal Scipione Borghese," in *Collecting Sculpture in Early Modern Europe*, eds Nicholas Penny and Eike Schmidt (New Haven, CT: Yale University Press, 2008), 219.
29 Herrmann Fiore, "The Exhibition of Sculpture on the Villa Borghese Facades," 221–6.
30 Christern-Briesenick, *Repertorium* III, no. 428; Herrmann Fiore, "The Exhibition of Sculpture on the Villa Borghese Facades," 233, 235–7, figs 23–5.
31 Giacomo Manilli, *Villa Borghese fuori di Porta Pinciana* (Rome: Per Lodouico Grignani, 1650), 35.
32 François Baratte and Catherine Metzger, *Musée du Louvre. Sarcophages en Pierre d' époques romaine et paléo-chrétienne* (Paris: Ministère de la Culture, Éditions de la Reunion des musées nationaux, 1985), 223–4, no. 132.
33 Herrmann Fiore, "The Exhibition of Sculpture on the Villa Borghese Facades," 226, 239.
34 Deichmann, *Repertorium* I, no. 829.

35 Joseph Wilpert, "Appunti su alcuni sarcofagi cristiani," *Atti della pontificia accademia romana di archeologia. Rendiconti* 2 (1923–1924): 172–4 a, fig. 4; Huskinson, "*Habent sua fata*."
36 Deichmann, *Repertorium* I, nos 919–25.
37 Deichmann, *Repertorium* I, nos 950–60.
38 Claudio Franzoni and Alessandra Tempesta, "Il Museo di Francesco Gualdi nella Roma del seicento tra raccolta private ed esibizione pubblica," *Bollettino d'arte* 73 (1992): 12; Settis, "Collecting Ancient Sculpture," 27–8.
39 Deichmann, *Repertorium* I, nos 13, 145, both mentioned by Bosio, *Roma* Sotterranea 589.
40 Franzoni and Tempesta, "Il Museo di Francesco Gualdi," 14–15, Ded. 2, fig. 16.
41 Franzoni and Tempesta, "Il Museo di Francesco Gualdi," 14–17, Ded. 3, figs 17–18; Deichmann, *Repertorium* I, no. 40.
42 Silvia Evangelisti, "Material Culture," in *The Ashgate Research Companion to the Counter Reformation*, eds Alexandra Bamji, Geert H Janssen and Mary Laven (Farnham and Burlington, VT: Ashgate, 2013), 394.
43 Evangelisti, "Material Culture," 394.
44 Anna Maria Ramieri, "Storia degli studi di archeologia Cristiana I," in *Lezioni di archeologia cristiana*, eds Fabrizio Bisconti and Olof Brandt (Vatican City: Pontifico Isstituto di Archeologia Cristiana, 2014), 16–17.
45 Ramieri, "Storia degli studi di archeologia Cristiana," 17.
46 See Elsner, "The Christian Museum in the South of France," 185–6, n. 16.
47 Simon Ditchfield, "Text before Trowel: Antonio Bosio's *Roma sotterranea* Revisited," in *The Church Retrospective, Studies in Church History 33*, ed. Robert N. Swanson (Woodbridge: Boydell Press, 1997), 344.
48 See Martine Gosselin, "The Congregation of the Oratorians and the Origins of Christian Archaeology: A Reappraisal," *Revue d'histoire ecclesiastique* 104.2 (2009): 471–93.
49 Ditchfield, "Text before Trowel," 347–9.
50 Ditchfield, *Liturgy, Sanctity, and History*, 86; Vincenzo Fiocchi Nicolai, "S. Filippo Neri, le catacombe di San Sebastiano, e le origine dell' archeologia Cristiana," in *San Fillippo Neri nella realtà romana del XVI secolo: atti del convegno di studio in occasione del IV centenario della morte di San Filippo Neri (1595–1995): Roma 11–13 maggio 1995*, eds M. Bonadonna Russo and N. Del Re (Rome: Presso la Società alla Biblioteca Vallicelliana, 2000), 105–30.
51 Fiocchi Nicolai, "S. Filippo Neri, le catacombe di San Sebastiano, e le origine dell' archeologia Cristiana," 118, 128; Gosselin, "The Congregation of the Oratorians," 481–6.
52 Ditchfield, "Reading Rome as a Sacred Landscape," 173–7.
53 Fiocchi Nicolai, "S. Filippo Neri, le catacombe di San Sebastiano, e le origine dell' archeologia Cristiana," 117–19; Giuseppe Antonio Guazzelli, "Cesare Baronio and the Roman Catholic Vision of the Early Church," in *Sacred History: Uses of the Christian Past in the Renaissance World*, eds Katherine Elliott van Liere, Simon Ditchfield and Howard Louthan (Oxford: Oxford University Press, 2012), 52–71; Lucrezia Spera, "Cesare Baronio, 'peritissimus antiquitatis' e le origini dell'archeologia Cristiana," in *Cesare Baronio tra santità e scrittura storica*, eds Giuseppe Antonio Guazzelli, Raimondo Michetti, Francesco Scorza Barcellona and Andrea Ceccherelli (Rome: Viella, 2012).
54 Richard Krautheimer, "A Christian Triumph in 1597," in *Essays in the History of Art Presented to Rudolf Wittkower*, eds Douglas Fraser, Howard Hibbard and Milton J. Lewine (London: Phaidon, 1967), 174–8; Alexandra Herz, "Cardinal Cesare Baronio's Restoration of SS. Nereo ed Achilleo and S. Cesareo de Appia," *Art Bulletin* 70 (1988): 590–620; Ditchfield, "Reading Rome as a Sacred Landscape," 177–78; Herwarth Röttgen, "Modello storico, modus e stile: Il ritorno dell' età paleocristiana attorno al 1600," in *Arte e committenza nel Lazio nell' età di Cesare Baronio (Atti del convegno internazionale di studi Frosinone, Sora 16–18 maggio 2007)*, ed. Patrizia Tosini (Rome: Gangemi, 2009), 33–47; Guazzelli, "Cesare Baronio and the Roman Catholic Vision of the Early Church," 63.
55 Ditchfield, *Liturgy, Sanctity, and History*, 87.
56 Thomas Buser, "Jerome Nadal and Early Jesuit Art in Rome," *Art Bulletin* 58.3 (1976): 424–33; Francis Haskell, *History and its Images: Art and the Interpretation of the Past* (New Haven, CT: Yale University Press, 1993), 109, fig. 82.
57 Haskell, *History and its Images*, 106–7.
58 Oryshkevich, "Cultural History in the Catacombs: Early Christian Art and Macarius' *Hagioglypta*;" Ditchfield, "Text before Trowel," 352.
59 Vincenzo Fiocchi Nicolai, Fabrizio Bisconti and Danilo Mazzoleni, *The Christian Catacombs of Rome: History, Decoration, Inscriptions* (Regensburg: Schnell & Steiner, 2009), 11.

60 Anna Maria Nieddu, *La basilica apostolorum sulla Via Appia e l'area cimiteriale circostante (Monumenti di antichità II serie, XIX)* (Vatican City: Pontificio Istituto di Archeologia Cristiana, 2009), 25.
61 Oryshkevich, "Cultural History in the Catacombs."
62 Cornelius Schuddeboom, "Research in the Roman catacombs by the Louvain antiquarian Philips van Winghe," in *Archives and Excavations: Essays on the History of Archaeological Excavations in Rome and Southern Italy from the Renaissance to the Nineteenth Centuries*, ed. Ilaria Bignamini (London: British School at Rome, 2004), 23–32.
63 Gosselin, "The Congregation of the Oratorians," 472–3.
64 W.H.C. Frend, *The Archaeology of Early Christianity: A History* (London: Geoffrey Chapman, 1996), 16; Fiocchi Nicolai, Bisconti and Mazzoleni, *The Christian Catacombs of Rome*, 11.
65 Ditchfield, "Text before Trowel," 357–9.
66 Jutta Dresken-Weiland, *Sarkophagbestattungen des 4.–6. Jahrhunderts im Westen des römischen Reiches* (Rome: Herder, 2003), 118–19.
67 Cesare Baronio, *Annales ecclesiatici* IV (Antwerp, 1601), 724.
68 Spera, "Cesare Baronio, 'peritissimus antiquitatis' e le origini dell'archeologia Cristiana," 406–8.
69 Bosio, *Roma* Sotterranea 55, 69–73.
70 Bosio, *Roma* Sotterranea 591A–F.
71 Bosio, *Roma* Sotterranea e.g., 219–73.
72 Bosio, *Roma* Sotterranea e.g., 105–9.
73 Bosio, *Roma* Sotterranea e.g., 509.
74 Bosio, *Roma* Sotterranea e.g., 203–11.
75 Ditchfield, "Text before Trowel," 355.
76 Bosio, *Roma* Sotterranea 593.
77 Haskell, *History and its Images*, 106–7.
78 Fiocchi Nicolai, Bisconti and Mazzoleni, *The Christian Catacombs of Rome*, 12.
79 Trevor Johnson, "Holy Fabrications: The Catacomb Saints and the Counter-Reformation in Bavaria," *Journal of Ecclesiastical History* 47 (1996): 279.
80 Nieddu, *La basilica apostolorum*, 34.
81 Johnson, "Holy Fabrications," 281–2; Ramieri, "Storia degli studi di archeologia Cristiana," 22–3.
82 Cf. Elsner, "The Christian Museum in the South of France," for examples from southern France.
83 Steven F. Ostrow, "The 'Confessio' in post-Tridentine Rome," in *Arte e committenza nel Lazio nell' età di Cesare Baronio (Atti del convegno internazionale di studi Frosinone, Sora 16–18 maggio 2007)*, ed. Patrizia Tosini (Rome: Gangemi, 2009), 210–21.
84 Goodson, *The Rome of Pope Paschal I*, 242.
85 Krautheimer, "A Christian Triumph in 1597," 176–8.
86 Krautheimer, "A Christian Triumph in 1597," 178.
87 Goodson, *The Rome of Pope Paschal I.*
88 Antonio Bosio, *Historia passionis B. Caeciliae virginis, Valeriani, Tiburtii, et Maximi martyrum. Necnon Vrbani, et Lucii pontificum, et mart. vitae. Atque Paschalis papae I. literae de eorumdem sanctorum corporum inuentione, & in vrbem translatione* (Rome, 1600), 132–84; Tobias Kämpf, "Framing Cecilia's Sacred Body: Paolo Camillo Sfondrato and the Language of Revelation," *Sculpture Journal* 6 (2001): 10–20.
89 Bosio, *Historia passionis B. Caeciliae virginis*, 172–3; Kämpf, "Framing Cecilia's Sacred Body," 17.
90 Deichmann, *Repertorium* I, nos 686, 687.
91 Jutta Dresken-Weiland, *Repertorium der christlich-antiken Sarkophage, zweiter Band: Italien mit einem Nachtrag Rom und Ostia, Dalmatien, Museen der Welt* (Mainz am Rhein: Verlag Philipp von Zabern, 1998), no. 115.

Further reading

Bamji, Alexandra, Geert H. Janssen and Mary Laven. *The Ashgate Research Companion to the Counter Reformation*. Farnham and Burlington, VT: Ashgate, 2013.
Barkan, Leonard. *Unearthing the Past: Archaeology and Aesthetics in the Making of Renaissance Culture*. New Haven, CT: Yale University Press, 1999.
Christian, Kathleen Wren. *Empire without End: Antiquities Collections in Renaissance Rome, c. 1350–1527*. New Haven, CT: Yale University Press, 2010.
Frend, W.H.C. *The Archaeology of Early Christianity: A History*. Minneapolis, MN: Fortress Press, 1998.

Nicolai, Vincenzo Fiocchi, Fabrizio Bisconti and Danilo Mazzoleni. *The Christian Catacombs of Rome: History, Decoration, Inscriptions*. Translated by C. Carlo Stella and L.-A. Touchette. Regensburg: Schnell & Steiner, 2009.

Van Liere, Katherine Elliott, Simon Ditchfield and Howard Louthan, eds. *Sacred History: Uses of the Christian Past in the Renaissance World*. Oxford: Oxford University Press, 2012.

23
"EARLY" "CHRISTIAN" "ART"

Robert Couzin

What kind of a category is "early Christian art?" Which objects, images, monuments, or artifacts does it include? How might this nomenclature affect the study of visual and material culture in Late Antiquity? The purpose of this chapter is not to explode the category underlying this Handbook but to invite reflection on its content, contours, coherence, and historiography.

Art

> "If we step outside this millennium [Late Antiquity and the Middle Ages] into the modern period, we find art in our way, a new function that fundamentally transformed the old image" (Hans Belting[1]).

The study of early Christian monuments and artifacts used to be called "Christian antiquities" until that expression was supplanted by "early Christian art" in the first decades of the nineteenth century. Antiquities are old things; archaeology is a discipline occupied with their discovery and examination. The term "art" may import somewhat different connotations and associations.

The word has long been associated with aesthetic quality and intention. Early Christian art has been challenged on both counts. Vasari opined that sculpture, painting, and architecture after Constantine went from bad to worse (*di male in peggio*).[2] By the twentieth century, historians had become more willing to recognize the beauty of late antique and medieval images, at least in the eyes of their original beholders. This aesthetic quality is, however, often regarded as a means rather than an end, a technique for expressing and reinforcing Christian doctrine or polemic. Mary Carruthers questioned this "modern tendency to over-moralize the medieval arts," proposing that inspirational impact, didactic function, and theological messaging are not inconsistent with a sensual experience of beauty.[3] Her essentially text-based argument is corroborated by a luxury object like the ivory Resurrection plaque in Munich (Figure 23.1). While its production and reception may have been predominantly spiritual in intention and effect, the purely visual and tactile pleasure seems obvious.

But is it art? This quintessentially modern question could not have been asked in Late Antiquity, although Christian apologists and authorities did invoke both artistic agency and aesthetic autonomy to justify the preservation of the patrimony of pagan statuary. Prudentius (*c.* 402) called it "the work of great artists [*artificum*]"[4] (perhaps less tendentiously translated

Figure 23.1 Ivory plaque with the Ascension (Reidersche tafel), Munich. Photo: Andreas Praefcke, Wikimedia Commons.

as "craftsmen"); an imperial decree of 382 ordered a provincial temple to be kept open even though it contained statues "which must be measured by the value of their art [*artis*] rather than by their divinity."[5]

Christian images, on the other hand, could be prized and venerated for their cultic or spiritual function quite apart from any judgment concerning the excellence of their appearance. Yet, this does not mean that aesthetic pleasure was necessarily absent or suppressed. "Early Christian art" is neither an oxymoron nor even especially misleading. Referring in particular to the "high end" of the market, Anthony Cutler saw no reason to avoid the term: "Once the important point is made, as it was by Hans Belting . . . that these were not primarily gratuitous aesthetic gestures, it is not worth belaboring."[6] Belting's observation is nonetheless a prudent admonition against the perils and pitfalls of trans-historical generalization and anachronism.

At a more mundane and practical level, one accepted if unexpressed distinction between the art of Late Antiquity or the Middle Ages and later periods is the breadth of material included. Standard texts on Renaissance or Baroque art are generally restricted to painting, sculpture, and architecture, but a more liberal definition is considered appropriate for early Christian art. Part I of this Handbook is indicative: it canvasses works in a gamut of media, deployed in such diverse functional contexts as funerary, liturgical, personal adornment, magic, and home decoration. The objects may be aniconic in their decoration, bearing only a cross (see Figures 4.11, 15.9), a Christogram (Figures 4.7, 9.2, 15.5), or even just the words "Jesus Christ" (Figure 9.1). The envelope might be pushed still further. Is a Corinthian capital deployed in an early Christian church (whether reused or newly carved) Christian art? If not, is this because it is not Christian (discussed below), or not art (but compare non-figural Islamic art)? What about a staurogram (a superposed tau and rho: ⳨) appearing in a written text, which could represent not only as an abbreviation of the Greek word for "cross" but also a pictogram of the Crucifixion (see Figure 18.4)?[7]

Early

"Strictly speaking, there are no periods in history, only in historians" (E.R. Dodds).[8]

The two adjectives in "early Christian art" are best understood as a compound, "early-Christian," alluding to historical notions of early Christianity, early Christians, and the early Christian centuries. It is nonetheless convenient to give separate consideration to each modifier and its implications.

"Early" can connote a condescending judgment within a narrative of artistic progress. Ernst Kitzinger objected to "early Christian" because it suggested "hesitant, tentative, perhaps even furtive beginnings," arguably evocative of the earliest catacombs but surely not appropriate to such monuments as Hagia Sophia in Constantinople and San Vitale in Ravenna.[9] Although these are works of the sixth century, the concern is not limited to later Late Antiquity: there is nothing hesitant, tentative or furtive about many earlier examples, like the bejeweled silver fastigium purportedly donated by Constantine to the Lateran basilica with its five-foot tall statues of Christ, apostles, and spear-bearing angels.[10] Every object is early in relation to another produced later; this does not make it primitive or preliminary. The earliness of early Christian art is relevant to the study of its subsequent reception, influence, incorporation, emulation, and even rejection, but a poor indicator of its quality, function, or meaning.

The more usual and less value-laden sense of "early" is as shorthand for a span of years. This raises the thorny issue of periodization. Periods may have heuristic value, but rarely ontological status. The definition and denomination of a period is often used to support a position or promote an agenda, as in the invention of the "Middle Ages" to fill a supposedly blank space between the end of Antiquity and its rebirth.[11]

Historical scholarship uses boundary events as bookends for its periods: wars, royal accessions, political, economic, or social upheavals, scientific revolutions. Most of these are of doubtful relevance or ambiguous application in art history. Nor can the chronology of images be strictly deduced from texts. The chronological markers of early Christian art are especially imprecise, notwithstanding the position of the Association of Art Editors that the initial "e" should be capitalized because the term refers to a "sharply delimited period."[12]

In theory, this period might begin with the career of Jesus or the dissemination of his gospels. In practice, a delay is dictated by the archaeological record.[13] Taking Christian art to be art the content of which is explicitly and identifiably Christian (the subject of the next section), objects of this description cannot be reliably dated before the third century and they remain scarce until one approaches the fourth. This visual reticence is commonly attributed to either scriptural scruples or inferior status.

The first theory claims that the early Church, its clergy, and apologists were mainly iconoclasts, whether from strict observance of the biblical second commandment or a philosophical position that favored the spiritual, intangible, and ineffable over the merely corporeal. The coherence and consistency of the literary evidence invoked to support this interpretation has been convincingly challenged, although one does sense what Jaś Elsner called a "residual resistance."[14] Some patrons seemed to prefer aniconic decoration, while others were more relaxed in this regard. André Grabar called it an affair of individual conscience rather than ecclesiastical dictation.[15]

The second conventional hypothesis to account for the tardy emergence of early Christian art cites either or both socio-economic mediocrity and political insecurity. Christians of the first centuries, it is said, were poor and of inferior rank; art was a luxury of the better-off higher orders. The great majority of Christians in the Roman Empire did live only marginally above subsistence, but so did the rest of the population. If Christians were proportionately under-represented in the higher social and economic echelons, the disparity was moderate, temporary, and insufficient to explain the absence of earlier Christian art.[16] The other limb of this argument claims that second- and third-century Christians of means chose mainstream Roman imagery over a visual display that would reveal or parade their affiliation to a religion lacking legal recognition and exposed to periodic bouts of persecution. However, it is not easy to demonstrate a robust correlation between the production of Christian images and religious repression or emancipation. Altogether, these economic, social, legal, and political factors, like iconoclasm, may have contributed to the late arrival of early Christian art but they remain incomplete and conjectural explanations.

An alternative answer is demography (which, of course, is not a fully independent variable). Population estimates are uncertain but the basic arithmetic is clear: Christians were far more numerous in the fourth century than in the third, and their presence in the Roman Empire before then was hardly noticeable.[17] If Christians did produce (or, more correctly, consume) a distinct and recognizable (to us) visual culture before 300, or even much before 400, it cannot have been abundant. Scholars tend to discount the hazards of survival as an explanation for the dearth of earlier Christian art, but natural losses would have eroded an already meager record.

Turning from the beginning to the end of early Christian art, the problem is how to identify an inflection point at which this period yields to the next. The transition might rely on a variety of criteria—stylistic, technical, iconographic, or functional—with potentially conflicting results. Geography is another source of dissonant chronology; early Christian art does not simultaneously become Byzantine in the East and "early medieval" in the West.

Guidance in seeking the end-point of early Christian art might be sought in the burgeoning field of historical studies known as Late Antiquity (usually, and tellingly, rendered with initial capital letters). It posits a coherent period, particularly in the social and cultural dimensions, extending broadly across space (the Mediterranean world) and time (in the foundational publication by Peter Brown, from 150–750).[18] This notion of a long Late Antiquity contrasts with a traditionally more restricted conception of the "later Roman Empire" ending, at its most generous, in the sixth century, and usually far earlier.[19] The chapters of this Handbook generally adopt a middle ground, extending past the traditional later Roman Empire but ending before the broad claims of Late Antiquity studies.

A clue to the suitability of an art historical period is its resonance with the image-makers and original viewers. In this respect, there is an interesting counterpoint between "late antique" and "early Christian." The former emphasizes continuity with the past; the latter conjures stirrings of the future. Producers and consumers of Christian art during this period (however circumscribed) must have experienced it as simultaneously retrospective and prospective, although not as "late" or "early." On the one hand, they recognized a visual tradition stretching back to ancient Rome and Greece, underscored by, but not limited to, punctuated classical revivals like the so-called Theodosian renaissance.[20] At the same time, they confronted new and sometimes puzzling forms of Christian iconography, with heightened intensity in the church or at the tomb. It is impossible to pinpoint a moment—applicable across all regions, media, and functions—when the comfort of stability was abandoned and the stimulation of novelty faded. This uncertainty is reflected in the range of individual chapters in this Handbook: Roman sarcophagus production ends earlier than its diaspora in Ravenna or Gaul; almost all gold glasses were produced before most church mosaics.

Whatever decision is made regarding the temporal boundaries of early Christian art, artifacts can be included and placed in chronological sequence only if they are dated. The difficulty of this task should not be underestimated. A review by Cyril Mango of Ernst Kitzinger's *The Art of Byzantium and the Medieval West* in *The Times Literary Supplement* led to an illuminating (and entertaining) exchange regarding the dating of early Byzantine art.[21] The reviewer criticized the author's tendency "to draw sweeping conclusions from insufficient evidence," an accusation to which Kitzinger responded with a spirited defense of stylistic dating. In a final rebuttal, Mango conceded the legitimacy of this technique "when it is based on a sufficient body of accepted facts," that is to say, firmly dated monuments; however, the widely divergent opinions of recognized experts in many instances undermined, in Mango's view, the construction of such a base line.

A paucity of "accepted facts" presents at least as serious a challenge in the dating of early Christian art. The substantial and well-studied corpus of Roman Christian sarcophagi is emblematic. Standard texts ascribe dates with only modest concession to uncertainty, usually expressed as a quarter century, sometimes as short as a decade. Yet, at most two dozen of these monuments bear an inscription that provides more or less precise evidence of their date.[22] Scholars therefore expand their horizons to stylistic comparisons with public monuments, notably the Arch of Constantine, or other media, like coins,[23] at the risk of eliding significant and consequential distinctions in function and idiom. Major ecclesiastical commissions, such as church mosaics, may be better documented through inscriptions or literary sources, although even in these cases the evidence, when it exists, is rarely conclusive· Panegyrists were often more dutiful than scrupulous in asserting a connection between church buildings and a favorite emperor or bishop; even the dating of such an iconic monument as Old St Peter's, and *a fortiori* its late antique mosaic decoration, remains disputed.[24]

Historical events are uneasy guides. Alaric's sack of Rome in 410 has been accepted by some scholars as the likely cause for the end of metropolitan sarcophagi production but rejected by others.[25] Less resistance is encountered to the magnetic attraction of Constantine's accession, and more specifically the "Edict of Milan," as a dating fulcrum.[26] As a purely factual matter, it is questionable whether there was any such edict, or any necessity in 313 for a general law legalizing the practice of Christianity or the operations of its church, particularly in the West.[27] Improvement in the status of the minority religion was gradual and uneven, advances punctuated by setbacks; one might expect a corresponding progressive if irregular increase in the quantity of overtly Christian art, reflecting especially the growing number of Christians. Dating individual objects on the premise that particular iconographical choices point to production before or after the Edict of Milan is tendentious, overly precise, and risks circularity: one cannot demonstrate the quantitative or qualitative impact of an historical event on early Christian art by citing as evidence objects that have been dated on the basis of their hypothesized relationship to this same event.

There is no evident solution to the dating conundrum, although broader ranges can help and assigning a probability rather than estimating the date of individual objects may be more realistic. Imprecise and unreliable dates do not prevent the study of early Christian art but should instill prudence and humility in claims of chronological priority or identification of temporal turning points.[28]

Christian

"I humbly offer this book to Christ the Redeemer. May my work, blessed by Him, contribute to the spread of archaeological knowledge, defense of the Holy Church, and expansion of the cult of the martyrs!" (Orazio Marucchi).[29]

The invention of early Christian art as a historical category is not shrouded in a secret agenda. It was a conscious and explicit project to discover, interpret, and valorize material and visual evidence of Christianity in the early centuries of its era.[30] A foundational event was Antonio Bosio's seventeenth-century study of the Roman catacombs. After a period of consolidation in catalogs of Christian antiquities, the field blossomed in the second half of the nineteenth century and the first decades of the twentieth through the "scientific," but still church-friendly, investigations by such prominent figures as Giovanni Battista de Rossi, Edmond-Frédéric Le Blant and Joseph Wilpert. The Vatican hierarchy has always been, and still is, a key participant through funding, sponsorship, publications, curatorial activity, control of access, and contributions by clerical scholars. The range of backgrounds and intentions among practitioners of early Christian art history has broadened considerably but echoes of its origins can still be heard, not least in its name.

Artifacts of visual culture are usually grouped by time or place of production (Medieval art, African art), shared qualities (Impressionism, Neoclassicism), or a combination of the two approaches (German Expressionism). The nomenclature of categorization can be used to promote an intellectual, academic, political, colonial, historical, or religious position. National designations, for example, sometimes harbor dubious claims regarding the ethnicity of the producers.[31] Such specific concerns aside, it is important to consider the implications of the qualification "Christian" art, however apparently neutral or anodyne, on academic research.

This terminology differs both conceptually and practically from a national category. A painting or sculpture is English because of its production or provenance; "Englishness" is a postulation of common characteristics in a pre-established corpus.[32] In contrast, a late antique sarcophagus, or even a church mosaic, is not Christian because of the confession of the artisan or the religious demographic of the region where it was made. The Christianity of early Christian art is not a derivative inference from a generally agreed body of material but rather the very criterion for classification.

This criterion is not style. The earliest Christian art adopted and adapted prevailing visual conventions.[33] It has been argued that the theological, doctrinal, and spiritual requirements of Christianity confronted and eventually transformed the classical aesthetic through abstraction or "dematerialization;"[34] alternatively, this characteristic of Christian imagery may be situated within a trend already in Roman art.[35] In either case, style provides no basis for classification.

Instead, an object is conventionally called Christian by reason of its iconography. Early Christian art is art that depicts events recounted in the Gospels and popular Christian literature and legend, or images evocative of Christian dogma, teachings, or theology. Narratives from the Hebrew Bible are also accepted as signals of Christian art because of their appropriation through typological or other interpretive strategies. The Old Testament, called by that name, had been accepted into the Christian canon. The range of Christian source material may even extend to classical Greco-Roman figures or motifs through an iconographical metamorphosis somewhat inaptly called *interpretatio christiana*.[36] If Orpheus underwent what Mary Charles-Murray called a "Christian annexation,"[37] then his image, in the appropriate context, was no less Christian than Daniel or Jonah (See Figure 2.10).

A critical but generally unspoken assumption is that an early Christian artifact, as defined by its visual content, is also an artifact *of* (commissioned, owned, used and seen by) an early Christian. Indexation of the patron, consumer, or viewer is central to the project's goal of using art to elucidate the early Christian story. This assumption becomes progressively more robust with the demographic tide of Christianity, although the character of the relationship

Figure 23.2 Fresco of Christ as Orpheus, Domitilla catacomb, Rome. Image: Joseph Wilpert, *Die Malereien der Katakomben Roms* (Freiburg: Herder, 1903), Taf. 229.

between Christian subjects and objects remains a matter for study and reflection. In the early period, the situation is still more complex.

Echoing and reifying an old classification (e.g., Acts 18:4, Rom 3:9, 1 Cor 1:22), fourth-century legislators and Church Fathers divided the population into Jews, Christians, and pagans. The neat segmentation was polemical, apologetic, and less than completely accurate; indeed, these same sources repeatedly condemn, and thereby confirm, backsliding, "Judaizing," and idolatry among professed Christians. Historians have documented and analyzed the evidence for religious compromise, accommodation, and shared practices in the polyethnic and pluralist later Roman Empire.[38] An oft-cited anecdote from the *Historia Augusta* describes how the Emperor Alexander Severus (r. 222–235) celebrated his morning ritual sacrifice in the presence of statues or pictures of divinized emperors and "certain holy souls, among them Apollonius . . . Christ, Abraham, Orpheus and others of this same character."[39] The story is likely apocryphal and anachronistic but nonetheless suggestive of attitudes still popular in some quarters late in the fourth century when this collection was written.

In such a milieu, one might anticipate a degree of ambiguity or inconsistency in the visual expression of religious motifs. Is it self-evident that a gold glass medallion picturing Hercules must have been made for a pagan, another with the Menorah for a Jew, and a third with Peter (or Jonah) for a Christian?[40] Are sarcophagi with orants and shepherds Christian? One group may have had first claim to a motif, but the image could easily have been shared, and therefore an equivocal marker of religious affiliation. Yet, notwithstanding these valid and important objections, the practical impact of this source of uncertainty on the study of early Christian art, even in the third or fourth centuries, should not be exaggerated.

First, accepting the phenomenon of fuzzy religious boundaries, the size and significance of the group that modern pollsters would call "undecided" is probably not destabilizing. Most individuals must have regarded themselves (however we might regard them) as falling within one of the socially, legally, and clerically designated religious groupings. Second, the confidence with which one can ascribe a given object to a self-identified Christian user is directly proportional to the complexity of its iconography. Perhaps some pagans might have accepted the inclusion of such a popular figure as Jonah on their funerary monuments,[41] but sarcophagi with dense and sophisticated biblical programs—as on the "Trinity" sarcophagus in Arles (Figure 23.3) or the sarcophagus of Junius Bassus in St Peter's (see Figure 18.5)—were presumably commissioned by serious Christians, albeit not necessarily mindful of the intricate interpretations sometimes proposed by modern scholars.[42] It may also be noteworthy that the juxtaposition of Christian and non-Christian imagery on a single artifact or within a coherent pictorial space is quite rare.[43]

Of course attributing a visually Christian object to an ostensibly Christian subject is not the end of the matter. The sophistication and intensity of Christian expression displayed on the former may not be commensurate with the depth and consistency of religious commitment of the latter. According to an inscription on the aforementioned sarcophagus of Junius Bassus, the deceased "went to God newly baptised" (*neofitus iit ad deum*) at age 42 while still in office as urban prefect. This could indicate a deathbed conversion before his presumably unexpected demise; alternatively it might just be the wishful thinking of a devout widow concerned with the post mortem well-being of a husband whose commitment was unconsummated.

Figure 23.3 "Trinity" sarcophagus, Arles, France. Photo: Robert Couzin, with kind permission of Musée départemental Arles Antique.

Along with variations in individual religious engagement, late antique Christianity was also subject to serious collective divisions. A proliferation of sects, schisms, and heresies was met by anathemas, repressions, deportations, and contentious, even violent, synods and councils. According to Ammianus Marcellinus, the Emperor Julian (r. 361–363), the only pagan emperor after Constantine, relied on the inability of these supposed co-religionists to present a united front, "knowing as he did from experience that no wild beasts are such enemies to mankind as are most of the Christians in their deadly hatred of one another."[44] Over the succeeding centuries the theological conflicts were repeatedly redefined but not resolved. In other historical periods, such ruptures manifest themselves in the visual culture, like the contrasting artistic tendencies of the Reformation and Counter-Reformation. Might the deep, numerous, and persistent rifts in early Christendom permit or require subdivisions within early Christian art?

Some doctrinal positions seem to call for special constraints on imagery. Marcionites, who rejected the canonical status of the Hebrew Bible, should have shunned Old Testament scenes; Donatist rigor might suggest avoidance of even the most innocent of classical motifs. Unfortunately, predictions of an absence rather than a presence of iconography are effectively unverifiable. More promising, by reason of numbers, longevity, and iconographical implications, are the successive waves of opposing Trinitarian doctrines. The Arian controversy, in particular, has evoked art historical claims of identifiably partisan imagery. Thomas Mathews perceived a Nicene condemnation of this heresy in the depiction of Christ's golden garments and massive throne in the apse mosaic of Santa Pudenziana, elements underscoring his divinity (see Figure 6.5);[45] Clementina Rizzardi saw in the mosaic of the "Arian" baptistery in Ravenna a response to its Orthodox predecessor and model, through a new emphasis on Christ's humanity and subordination to the Father (see Figure 21.2).[46] Some forms of representation attract multiple sectarian explanations: Christ in a mandorla is anti-Arian (Mathews) and anti-Monophysite (Mango).[47] Many scholars are skeptical of such interpretation, seeing few, if any, secure instances of the visual expression of internecine competition in early Christian art.[48] The search is nonetheless tempting. Picayune and obscure as these theological distinctions may appear now, they were matters of existential and eschatological importance with significant socio-political—and potentially visual—implications to many patrons and viewers.

The foregoing discussion of boundaries, commitments, and internal conflicts does not directly address the phenomenon of Christian *objects*—things owned and used by Christians—that are not, applying a strictly iconographical criterion, Christian *art*. Beyond hypothetical occurrences, like a decontextualized Hercules gold glass, there are also reasonably secure examples. Often cited in this regard is the Projecta Casket (see Figure 15.6), a silver box bearing both the representation of Venus and an explicitly Christian hortatory inscription. It is usually discussed in a category separate from Christian art, as evidence for the Christian assimilation (appropriation, borrowing, revival) of pagan imagery. To similar effect, sarcophagi that couple mythological, or more often classical, motifs with Christian epitaphs or signs are commonly labeled as instances of "reuse."[49] That term is not always literally accurate—the Christian marking may or may not have been added to a pre-owned coffin; nor does it address the significance of what has occurred, an inquiry that could be advanced by a contextual application of the rich theoretical literature on *spolia*.[50]

The potential advantages of integrating such Christian objects as these into the study of Christian art may be illustrated by recalling the sharp debates about the role of imperial forms of representation in the construction of early Christian iconography; for some, they were adapted and absorbed, for others, rejected and contested. In a retrospective review article, Anne-Orange Poilpré proposed a synthetic approach, on the premise that the cleavage between political and

Figure 23.4 Missorium of Theodosius I. Photo: Real Academia de la Historia, Madrid.

religious imagery in this period has been overstated.[51] It is interesting from this perspective to reimagine the relationship between certain secular and religious images. The silver Missorium of Theodosius I (dated 388, Figure 23.4) depicts this emperor enthroned between his co-Augustus and predecessor Valentinian II and his son and successor Arcadius, all three Christians.[52] The formal similarity with images of Christ between Peter and Paul is apparent and not likely coincidental (as in the apse mosaic of Santa Pudenziana, see Figure 6.5). The interesting questions posed by this comparison extend beyond binaries of appropriation or repudiation to include reciprocity, hybridity, accommodation, and renegotiation.[53]

Notes

1 Hans Belting, *Likeness and Presence: A History of the Image Before the Era of Art*, trans. Edmund Jephcott (Chicago, IL: University of Chicago Press, 1994), 9.
2 Giorgio Vasari, *Lives of the Painters, Sculptors and Architects*, trans. Gaston du C. de Vere (New York, NY: Everyman's Library, 1996), 1.35.
3 Mary Carruthers, *The Experience of Beauty in the Middle Ages* (Oxford: Oxford University Press, 2013), 8.
4 *Contra Symmachum*, in *Prudentius*, Vol. 2, trans. H.J. Thomson (Cambridge, MA: Harvard University Press, 1949), 388 (1.503).
5 *The Theodosian Code and Novels, and the Sirmondian Constitutions*, trans. Clyde Pharr (Princeton, NJ: Princeton University Press, 1952), 473 (16.10.8).

6 Anthony Cutler, "The Right Hand's Cunning: Craftsmanship and the Demand for Art in Late Antiquity and the Early Middle Ages," *Speculum* 72 (1997): 974, n.14.
7 Staurogram as pictogram: Larry W. Hurtado, "The Staurogram in Early Christian Manuscripts: The Earliest Visual Reference to the Crucified Jesus?" in *New Testament Manuscripts: Their Texts and Their World*, eds Thomas J. Kraus and Tobias Nicklas (Brill: Leiden, 2006), 207–26; Robin M. Jensen, *Understanding Early Christian Art* (London: Routledge, 2000), 138. See also Harley-McGowan, Chapter 18 of this volume.
8 E.R. Dodds, *Pagan and Christian in An Age of Anxiety: Some Aspects of Religious Experience from Marcus Aurelius to Constantine* (Cambridge: Cambridge University Press, 1990), 3.
9 Ernst Kitzinger, *Byzantine Art in the Making* (Cambridge, MA: Harvard University Press, 1977), 1–3.
10 No longer extant but referred to in the life of Silvester in *The Book of Pontiffs (Liber Pontificalis): The Ancient Biographies of the First Ninety Roman Bishops to AD 715*, 2nd ed. (Liverpool: Liverpool University Press, 2000), 16. See Sible De Blaauw, "Imperial Connotations in Roman Church Interiors: The Significance and Effect of the Lateran *Fastigium*," in *Imperial Art as Christian Art: Christian Art as Imperial Art: Expression and Meaning in Art and Architecture from Constantine to Justinian*, eds J. Rasmus Brandt and Olaf Steen (Rome: Bardi Editore, 2001), 137–48.
11 Jacques Le Goff, *Must We Divide History Into Periods?*, trans. M.B. DeBevoise (New York, NY: Columbia University Press, 2015).
12 Association of Art Editors, *Style Guide* (2013), https://artedit.org/style-guide.php#artmove.
13 On the hypothesis of earlier devotional Christian art that has not survived: Thomas F. Mathews with Norman E. Muller, *The Dawn of Christian Art in Panel Paintings and Icons* (Los Angeles, CA: Getty Publications, 2016).
14 Jaś Elsner, "Inventing Christian Rome: The Role of Early Christian Art," in *Rome the Cosmopolis*, eds Catherine Edwards and Greg Woolf (Cambridge: Cambridge University Press 2003), 71, n.1. On claims of early iconoclasm, see Mary Charles-Murray, *Rebirth and Afterlife: A Study of the Transmutation of Some Pagan Imagery in Early Christian Funerary Art* (Oxford: British Archaeological Reports, 1981), 13–36; Jensen, *Understanding Christian Art*, 1–34.
15 André Grabar, *L'iconoclasme byzantin: le dossier archéologique* (Paris: Flammarion 1957/1984), 16.
16 Robert Couzin, "The Christian Sarcophagus Population of Rome," *Journal of Roman Archaeology* 27 (2014): 290–92.
17 Rodney Stark, *The Rise of Christianity: A Sociologist Reconsiders History* (Princeton, NJ: Princeton University Press, 1996); Keith Hopkins, "Christian Number and its Implications," *Journal of Early Christian Studies* 6 (1998): 185–226.
18 Peter Brown, *The World of Late Antiquity: From Marcus Aurelius to Muhammad* (London: Thames and Hudson, 1971).
19 Andrew Gillett, "Rome's Fall and Europe's Rise: A View from Late Antiquity," *The Medieval Review* 07.10.12 (2007).
20 Herbert L. Kessler, "On the State of Medieval Art History," *The Art Bulletin* 70 (1988): 167–8.
21 Cyril Mango, "Ernst Kitzinger: The Art of Byzantium and the Medieval West," *The Times Literary Supplement*, March 25, 1977, 381; response by Ernst Kitzinger, May 6, 1977, 561; reply by Mango, May 20, 1977, 621.
22 Guntram Koch, *Frühchristliche Sarkophage* (Munich: C.H. Beck, 2000), 355–61. See also Jutta Dresken-Weiland, Chapter 3 of this volume.
23 Dagmar Stutzinger, *Die frühchristlichen Sarkophagreliefs aus Rom: Untersuchungen zur Formveränderung im 4. Jahrhundert n. Chr.* (Bonn: Rudolph Habelt, 1982).
24 Glen W. Bowersock, "Peter and Constantine," in *St. Peter's in the Vatican*, ed. William Tronzo (Cambridge: Cambridge University Press, 2005), 5–15; Paolo Liverani, "Saint Peter's, Leo the Great and the Leprosy of Constantine," *Papers of the British School at Rome* 76 (2008): 155–72.
25 Accepted by Stutzinger, *Die frühchristlichen Sarkophagreliefs*, 178; also by Koch, *Frühchristliche Sarkophage*, albeit with varying degrees of probability, at 223, 335 and 339. Rejected by Hugo Brandenburg, "Das Ende der antiken Sarkophagkunst in Rom: Pagane und christliche Sarkophage in Rom," In *Akten des Symposiums "Frühchristliche Sarkophage": Marburg, 30.6.–4.7.1999*, ed. Guntram Koch (Mainz: von Zabern, 2002), 21–2; Dresken-Weiland, Chapter 3 of this volume.
26 See, e.g., Jensen, *Understanding Christian Art*, 16; Brandenburg, "Das Ende der antiken Sarkophagkunst," 19; Graydon F. Snyder, *Ante Pacem: Archaeological Evidence of Church Life Before Constantine* (Macon, GA: Mercer University Press, 2003); contra Arnold Provoost, "The Apostolic World of Thought in Early Christian Iconography," in *The Apostolic Age in Patristic Thought*, ed. A. Hilhorst (Leiden: Brill, 2004), 161, n. 9.

27 Timothy Barnes, *Constantine: Dynasty, Religion and Power in the Later Roman Empire* (Chichester: Wiley-Blackwell, 2014), 93–7.
28 Examples: competing views regarding the priority of city-gate sarcophagi in Milan and Paris are remarked by Koch, *Frühchristliche Sarkophage*, 362; uncertainty concerning when a new figural type for Christ was adopted in the fourth century is underscored by Jean-Michel Spieser, *Images du Christ: des catacombes aux lendemains de l'iconoclasme* (Geneva: Droz, 2015), 183–4.
29 Orazio Marucchi, *Éléments d'archéologie chrétienne*, Vol. 1, 2nd ed. (Paris/Rome: Désclée, Lefebvre & Co., 1905), ix, https://archive.org/details/lmentsdarch01maruuoft. My translation.
30 W.H.C. Frend, *The Archaeology of Early Christianity* (London: Geoffrey Chapman, 1996); Jamie Beth Erenstoft, "Controlling the Sacred Past: Rome, Pius IX, and Christian Archaeology," PhD diss. State University of New York at Buffalo, 2008, ProQuest 3320468.
31 Cf. Lawrence Nees, "Ethnic and Primitive Paradigms in the Study of Early Medieval Art," in *Paradigms and Methods in Early Medieval Studies*, eds Celia Chazelle and Felice Lifshitz (New York, NY: Palgrave Macmillan, 2007), 41–60.
32 Nicolas Pevsner, *The Englishness of English Art* (London: British Broadcasting Corporation, 1955). The original lectures can be heard at www.bbc.co.uk/programmes/p00h9llv.
33 Mary Charles-Murray, "The Emergence of Christian Art," in *Picturing the Bible: The Earliest Christian Art*, ed. Jeffrey Spier (Fort Worth, TX: Kimbell Art Museum, 2007), 51–4; Robin Margaret Jensen, "Compiling Narratives: The Visual Strategies of Early Christian Visual Art," *Journal of Early Christian Studies* 23 (2015): 1–26.
34 André Grabar, "The Message of Byzantine Art," in *Byzantine Art: An European Art*, ed. Manolis Chatzidakis (Athens: Department of Antiquities and Archaeological Restoration, 1964), 51–66.
35 See James Trilling, "Late Antique and Sub-Antique, or the 'Decline of Form' Reconsidered," *Dumbarton Oaks Papers* 41 (1987): 469–76; Richard Brilliant, " '*Late Antiquity*': A Protean Term," in *Recycling Rome*, eds Turid Karlsen Seim and Marina Prusac, Acta ad Archaeologiam et Artium Historiam Pertinentia, Vol. 25 (Rome: Scienze e Lettere, 2012), 29–56.
36 See Dale Kinney, "Interpretatio Christiana," in *Maxima Debetur Magistro Reverentia: Essays on Rome and the Roman Tradition in Honor of Russell T. Scott*, eds Paul B. Harvey Jr. and Catherine Conybeare (Como: New Press Edizioni, 2009), 117–25.
37 Charles-Murray, *Rebirth and Afterlife*, 46.
38 Peter Brown, "Christianization and Religious Conflict," in *The Late Empire AD 337–425*, eds Averil Cameron and Peter Garnsey (Cambridge: Cambridge University Press, 1997), 632–64; Éric Rebillard, *Christians and Their Many Identities in Late Antiquity, North Africa, 200–450 CE* (Ithaca, NY: Cornell University Press, 2012); Christopher P. Jones, *Between Pagan and Christian* (Cambridge, MA: Harvard University Press, 2014).
39 *Historia Augusta*, trans. D. Magie (Cambridge, MA: Harvard University Press, 1924), 235.
40 See Jaś Elsner, "Archaeologies and Agendas: Reflections on Late Ancient Jewish Art and Early Christian Art," *Journal of Roman Studies* 93 (2003): 114–28.
41 Compare Steven Hijmans, "Language, Metaphor, and the Semiotics of Roman Art: Some Thoughts on Reading the Mosaics of Mausoleum M in the Vatican Necropolis," *BABESCH* 75 (2000): 147–64.
42 See, for example, Elizabeth Struthers Malbon, *The Iconography of the Sarcophagus of Junius Bassus* (Princeton, NJ: Princeton University Press, 1990).
43 Robert Couzin, "Syncretism and Segregation in Early Christian Art," *Studies in Iconography* 38 (2017): 18–54.
44 Ammianus Marcellinus. *History, Vol. 2*, trans. J.C. Rolfe (Cambridge, MA: Harvard University Press, 1940), 203 (22.5.4).
45 Thomas F. Mathews, *The Clash of Gods: A Reinterpretation of Early Christian Art*, revised and expanded ed. (Princeton, NJ: Princeton University Press, 1999), 101–8.
46 Clementina Rizzardi, "La decorazione musiva del battistero degli Ortodossi e degli Ariani a Ravenna: alcune considerazioni," in *L'edificio battesimale in Italia: Aspetti e problemi: Atti dell'VIII Congresso nazionale di archeologia cristiana, 21–26 settembre 1998* (Florence: All'Insegna del Giglio, 2001), 927–30. On the two mosaics, see Deborah Mauskopf Deliyannis, Chapter 21 of this volume.
47 Mathews, *Clash of Gods*, 117–18; Cyril Mango, "Constantinople as Theotokopoulis," in *Mother of God: Representations of the Virgin in Byzantine Art*, ed. Maria Vassilaki (Milan: Skira, 2000), 21.
48 David M. Gwynn, "Archaeology and the 'Arian controversy' in the Fourth Century," in *Religious Diversity in Late Antiquity*, eds David M. Gwynn and Susanne Bangert (Boston, Brill, 2010), 229–63; Antonio Ferrua, *La polemica antiariana nei monumenti paleocristiani* (Vatican City: Pontificio Istituto di Archeologia Cristiana, 1991); Massey H. Shepherd, Jr., "Christology: A Central Problem of Early

Christian Theology and Art," in *Age of Spirituality: A Symposium*, ed. Kurt Weitzmann (New York, NY: Metropolitan Museum of Art, 1980), 101–20.

49 Examples in Koch, *Frühchristliche Sarkophage*, 7–14.

50 See the essays and references in Richard Brilliant and Dale Kinney, eds, *Reuse Value: Spolia and Appropriation in Art and Architecture from Constantine to Sherrie Levine* (Farnham: Ashgate, 2011).

51 Anne-Orange Poilpré, "Bilan d'une décennie de réactions à l'ouvrage de Thomas F. Mathews, *Clash of Gods, A Reinterpretation of Early Christian Art*, Princeton, 1993," *Antiquité Tardive* 13 (2005): 383–5.

52 On the Missorium, see José Maria Blázquez, "*El Missorium* de Teodosio," in *El Gabinete de Antigüedades de la Real Academia* de la Historia, ed. Martin Almagro Gorbea (Madrid: Real Academia de la Historia, 1999), 175-200. Both the date and the identifications are contested by some scholars.

53 Compare Robin M. Jensen, "Allusions to Imperial Rituals in Fourth-Century Christian Art," in *The Art of Empire: Christian Art in its Imperial Context*, eds Lee M. Jefferson and Robin M. Jensen (Minneapolis, MN: Fortress Press, 2015), 13–47.

Further reading

Belting, Hans. *Likeness and Presence: A History of the Image Before the Era of Art*. Translated by Edmund Jephcott. Chicago, IL: University of Chicago Press, 1994.

Brilliant, Richard. "'Late Antiquity': A Protean Term." In *Recycling Rome*, eds Turid Karlsen Seim and Marina Prusac. Acta ad Archaeologiam et Artium Historiam Pertinentia, Vol. 25, 29–56. Rome: Scienze e Lettere, 2012.

Elsner, Jaś. "Archaeologies and Agendas: Reflections on Late Ancient Jewish Art and Early Christian Art." *Journal of Roman Studies* 93 (2003): 114–28.

Gwynn, David M. "Archaeology and the 'Arian controversy' in the Fourth Century." In *Religious Diversity in Late Antiquity*, edited by David M. Gwynn and Susanne Bangert, 229–63. Boston: Brill, 2010.

Jensen, Robin M. *Understanding Early Christian Art*. London: Routledge, 2000.

Kinney, Dale. "Interpretatio Christiana." In *Maxima Debetur Magistro Reverentia: Essays on Rome and the Roman Tradition in Honor of Russell T. Scott*, eds Paul B. Harvey Jr. and Catherine Conybeare, 117–25. Como: New Press Edizioni, 2009.

Spier, Jeffrey, ed. *Picturing the Bible: The Earliest Christian Art*. Fort Worth, TX: Kimbell Art Museum, 2007.

INDEX

Page numbers in bold denote tables.

Printed in Great Britain
by Amazon